# Kazakstan, Kyrgyzstan, Tajikistan, Turkmenistan, and Uzbekistan
## country studies

Federal Research Division
Library of Congress
Edited by
Glenn E. Curtis
Research Completed
March 1996

On the cover: Cultural artifacts from Kazakstan, Kyrgyzstan, Tajikistan, Turkmenistan, and Uzbekistan

First Edition, First Printing, 1997.

## Library of Congress Cataloging-in-Publication Data

Kazakstan, Kyrgyzstan, Tajikistan, Turkmenistan, and Uzbekistan : country studies / Federal Research Division, Library
  of Congress ; edited by Glenn E. Curtis.—1st ed.
    p. cm. — (Area handbook series, ISSN 1057–5294)
  (DA Pam ; 550–114)
    "Research completed March 1996."
    Includes bibliographical references (pp. 491–519) and
  index.
    ISBN 0–8444-0938–3  (hard : alk. paper)
    1. Asia, Central. I. Curtis, Glenn E. (Glenn Eldon),
  1946– . II. Library of Congress. Federal Research Division. III. Series. IV. Series: DA Pam ; 550–114.
DK851.K34 1997                                          97–5110
958—dc21                                                    CIP

Headquarters, Department of the Army
DA Pam 550–114

---

For sale by the Superintendent of Documents, U.S. Government Printing Office
Washington, D.C.  20402

# Foreword

This volume is one in a continuing series of books prepared by the Federal Research Division of the Library of Congress under the Country Studies/Area Handbook Program sponsored by the Department of the Army. The last two pages of this book list the other published studies.

Most books in the series deal with a particular foreign country, describing and analyzing its political, economic, social, and national security systems and institutions, and examining the interrelationships of those systems and the ways they are shaped by historical and cultural factors. Each study is written by a multidisciplinary team of social scientists. The authors seek to provide a basic understanding of the observed society, striving for a dynamic rather than a static portrayal. Particular attention is devoted to the people who make up the society, their origins, dominant beliefs and values, their common interests and the issues on which they are divided, the nature and extent of their involvement with national institutions, and their attitudes toward each other and toward their social system and political order.

The books represent the analysis of the authors and should not be construed as an expression of an official United States government position, policy, or decision. The authors have sought to adhere to accepted standards of scholarly objectivity. Corrections, additions, and suggestions for changes from readers will be welcomed for use in future editions.

Louis R. Mortimer
Chief
Federal Research Division
Library of Congress
Washington, DC 20540–4840

# Acknowledgments

The authors are indebted to numerous individuals and organizations who gave their time, research materials, and expertise on the five republics of Central Asia to provide data, perspective, and material support for this volume.

Raymond Zickel organized the early stages of the book's compilation and identified its chapter authors. Helen Fedor collected, selected, and organized the book's photographs, which were contributed by numerous individuals. Those individuals are acknowledged in the photo captions.

Thanks also go to Ralph K. Benesch, former monitor of the Country Studies/Area Handbook Program for the Department of the Army, under whose guidance the plan for the six volumes on the post-Soviet states was formulated. In addition, the authors appreciate the advice and guidance of Sandra W. Meditz, Federal Research Division coordinator of the handbook series. Special thanks go to Marilyn L. Majeska, who supervised editing and managed production; and to David P. Cabitto, who designed the book cover and the illustrations on the title page of each chapter, provided graphics support, and, together with the firm of Maryland Mapping and Graphics, prepared the maps. The following individuals are gratefully acknowledged as well: Askar Tazhiyev of the Embassy of Kazakstan, who provided economic statistics; Raymond Milefsky of the Defense Mapping Agency, who provided invaluable guidance on geographic names; Vincent Ercolano, who edited the chapters; Beverly Wolpert, who performed the final prepublication editorial review; Joan C. Cook, who indexed the volume; Barbara Edgerton and Izella Watson, who did the word processing and initial typesetting; and Janie L. Gilchrist and David P. Cabitto, who prepared the camera-ready copy.

# Contents

List of Figures

# Preface

At the end of 1991, the collapse of the Soviet Union transformed the fifteen republics of that union into independent states with various capabilities for survival. Among them were the five republics of Central Asia: Kazakstan, Kyrgyzstan, Tajikistan, Turkmenistan, and Uzbekistan. Until that time, Central Asia had received less attention from the outside world than most of the other Soviet republics, simply because it was the most remote part of the Soviet Union. Aside from their incidental coverage in the 1991 *Soviet Union: A Country Study*, the Central Asian republics have received no treatment in this series. Since their independence, these republics have attracted considerable attention in the West, largely because of the improved opportunities for exploitation of their rich natural resources, notably oil and natural gas. As the fourth of the six-volume subseries covering all the post-Soviet states, this volume brings new information about a region of enhanced relevance in the world's economy and geopolitical structure.

The marked relaxation of information restrictions, which began in the late 1980s and has continued into the mid-1990s, allows the reporting of much more complete information on Central Asia than what was available one decade ago. Scholarly articles and periodical reports have been especially helpful in accounting for most aspects of the five republics' activities since they achieved independence. The authors have provided a context for their current evaluations with descriptions of the historical, political, and social backgrounds of the countries. In each case, the author's goal was to provide a compact, accessible, and objective treatment of five main topics: historical background, the society and its environment, the economy, government and politics, and national security. Brief comments on some of the more useful, readily accessible sources used in preparing this volume appear at the end of each chapter. Full references to these and other sources used by the authors are listed in the Bibliography.

In most cases, personal names have been transliterated from the vernacular according to the transliteration system of the United States Board on Geographic Names (BGN). Some names, such as Boris N. Yeltsin and Joseph V. Stalin, are rendered in the conventional form widely used in Western sources. The same distinction has been applied to geographic names: the BGN spelling is used for the vast majority, but a few, such as the largest cities, Tashkent and Moscow, are given in their widely used conventional forms. Some geographical names regrettably are missing diacritics because the typesetting software being used cannot produce all the necessary characters (although they do appear on the maps). Organizations commonly known by their acronyms (such as the IMF—International Monetary Fund) are introduced by their full names, in both vernacular and English forms where appropriate. Adjectives derived from the name of a republic ("Kazakstani" and "Uzbekistani," for example) are used in all cases except where such a term denotes persons or groups of a specific ethnic origin. In the latter cases, the adjective is in the form "Kazak" or "Uzbek." The same distinction applies to the proper nouns for citizens of a republic ("Kazakstanis," for example) as distinguished from individuals of an ethnic group ("Kazaks").

A chronology at the beginning of the book combines significant historical events of the five countries. To amplify points in the text and provide standards of comparison, tables in the Appendix offer statistics on aspects of the five societies and national economies. Measurements are given in the metric system; a conversion table is provided in the Appendix.

The body of the text reflects information available as of March 1996. Certain other portions of the text, however, have been updated beyond that point. The Introduction discusses significant events and trends that have occurred since the completion of research; the Country Profiles and the Chronology include updated information as available; and the Bibliography lists recently published sources thought to be particularly helpful to the reader.

## Table A.  Chronology of Important Events

| Period | Description |
| --- | --- |
| **EARLY HISTORY** | |
| Fifth century B.C. | Bactrian, Soghdian, and Tokharian states dominate area of present-day Uzbekistan, including cities of Bukhoro (Bukhara) and Samarqand (Samarkand) and begin profit from trade on Silk Route. Province of Mawarannahr begins long period of prosperity in eastern Uzbekistan. |
| Fourth–third centuries B.C. | Kyrgyz tribes invade northern China. |
| 329 B.C. | Alexander the Great captures Maracanda (Samarqand) in conquest of southern Central Asia from Persian Achamenid Empire. |
| First century A.D. | Han Dynasty of China trades with Soghdians and Bactrians of Central Asia. |
| First–fourth centuries A.D. | Present-day Tajikistan ruled by Buddhist Kushans, who spread their faith to Soghdians. |
| ca. A.D. 500 | Feudal society emerges in present-day Kyrgyzstan. |
| **EIGHTH–TENTH CENTURIES** | |
| 750 | Arabs complete conquest of Central Asia with victory over Chinese at Talas River, imposing Islam and new culture. |
| 766 | Turkic Qarluq confederation establishes state in present-day eastern Kazakstan. |
| Eighth–ninth centuries | Under Arab Abbasid Caliphate, golden age of Central Asia; Bukhoro becomes a cultural center of Muslim world. |
| Late eighth–tenth centuries | Turkic Oghuz tribes migrate into Central Asia from Mongolia and southern Siberia. |
| Ninth century | Islam becomes dominant religion of all Central Asia. |
| 840 | Kyrgyz Khanate reaches greatest extent, defeating Uygur Khanate in Mongolia. |
| Tenth century | Term *Turkmen* first applied to southern Islamic Oghuz tribes; Persian Samanid Dynasty replaces Abbasids, continues cultural activity of Mawarannahr. |
| Late tenth century | Seljuk Empire founded, based on Oghuz tribes, including Turkmen. |
| 999 | Turkic Qarakhanids overthrow Samanids, ending last major Persian state in Central Asia. |
| **ELEVENTH–SIXTEENTH CENTURIES** | |
| Eleventh century | Seljuks and Qarakhanids end dominance of Ghaznavid Empire in south Central Asia, dominating west and east, respectively. |
| ca. 1100 | Persian replaces Arabic as standard written language in most of Central Asia, remains in official use through fifteenth century. |
| 1130s | Turkic Karakitais conquer Qarakhanids; dominate region for 100 years. |
| Mid-twelfth century | Revolts by Turkmen hasten disintegration of Seljuk Empire; Turkmen begin settling present-day Turkmenistan, notably Merv on Silk Route. |

## Table A. (Continued) Chronology of Important Events

| Period | Description |
|---|---|
| 1200 | Khorazm (Khorezm, Khwarazm), split from Seljuk Empire, consolidates empire including Mawarannahr and most of Central Asia; cultural activity continues. |
| 1219–25 | Mongols conquer Central Asia, pushing Turkmen westward toward Caspian Sea, intensifying Turkification of Mawarannahr, reducing Iranian influence, and destroying cultural centers. |
| ca. 1250 | Son of Chinggis (Genghis) Khan conquers Yenisey Kyrgyz, beginning 200 years of Mongol domination. |
| 1380–1405 | Timur (Tamerlane) unifies Mongol holdings in Central Asia, fosters last cultural flowering of Mawarannahr; Turkish first rivals Persian as literary language. |
| Fourteenth–sixteenth centuries | Turkmen tribes reorganize and consolidate. |
| Sixteenth century | Uzbek empire fragmented by fighting among khanates; decline of Silk Route. |
| 1501–10 | Uzbek nomadic tribes conquer Central Asia, establish Khanate of Bukhoro. |
| 1511 | Khan Kasym unites Kazak tribes. |
| Sixteenth–nineteenth centuries | Migration east and southeast of large nomadic Turkmen tribal groups descending from Salor group. |
| SEVENTEENTH–EIGHTEENTH CENTURIES | |
| Seventeenth–eighteenth centuries | Kazak nomads and Mongols raid and weaken Uzbek khanates; conflict with Iran isolates Uzbeks in Muslim world; Kyrgyz tribes overrun by Kalmyks and Manchus. |
| ca. 1700 | Khanate of Bukhoro loses Fergana region; Quqon (Kokand) Khanate founded, based in Fergana Valley. |
| 1726 | Kazak Khan Abul Khair seeks Russian protection from Kalmyk invaders, beginning permanent Russian presence in Kazakstan. |
| Mid-eighteenth century | Turkmen Yomud tribes invade Khorazm. |
| 1758 | Kyrgyz tribes become Chinese subjects with substantial autonomy. |
| 1785 | Kyrgyz seek Russian protection from Quqon Khanate. |
| Eighteenth–early nineteenth centuries | Three Uzbek khanates revived by strong dynasties, centralized states; British and Russians begin rivalry for Central Asia. |
| NINETEENTH CENTURY | |
| 1820s | Kazak Great Horde is last of three hordes to come under Russian control. |
| 1836–47 | Under Khan Kene (Kenisary Kasimov), Kazaks rise up against Russian occupation. |
| 1855–67 | Yomud tribes rebel against Uzbek authority, which disperses the eastern Yomud. |
| 1860s | Jadidist reform movement founded. |
| 1861 | Abolition of serfdom in Russian Empire begins migration of Russian peasants to Kazakstan. |

## Table A. (Continued) Chronology of Important Events

| Period | Description |
|---|---|
| 1865–68 | Russian conquest of Tashkent, Bukhoro, and Samarqand; Khanate of Bukhoro becomes Russian protectorate. |
| 1867 | Guberniya (Governorate General) of Turkestan established as central Russian administration, eventually including (1899) present-day Kyrgyzstan, Tajikistan, Turkmenistan, Uzbekistan, and southeastern Kazakstan; remainder of Kazakstan becomes Steppe District. |
| 1869 | Russians establish foothold in Turkmen territory at Krasnovodsk. |
| 1870s | Russian cotton cultivation significantly expanded; Russians carry out punitive raids against Turkmen in Khorazm. |
| 1873 | Russians capture Khiva. |
| 1876 | Russians incorporate Ququon Khanate; all Uzbekistan and northern Kyrgyzstan in Russian Empire. |
| 1881 | Russians crush Turkmen resistance at Gokdepe fortress; Turkmen territory annexed into Guberniya of Turkestan. |
| 1890s | Uzbek revolts against Russian rule quelled easily; large-scale Russian settlement begins in northern Kazakstan and Kyrgyzstan, diminishing Kazak and Kyrgyz nomadism. |
| **TWENTIETH CENTURY** | |
| 1900 | Jadidism becomes first major movement of Central Asian political resistance. |
| 1906–07 | Central Asians have six seats in first and second Russian Dumas. |
| 1907–17 | Central Asians have no seats in third and fourth Russian Dumas. |
| 1916 | Kazaks, Kyrgyz, Turkmen, and Uzbeks rebel against Russian land confiscation, conscription; many Kazaks, Kyrgyz flee to China. |
| 1917     May | Russian provisional government abolishes Guberniya of Turkestan; power divided among various groups, including Tashkent Soviet. |
|        November | Bolshevik Revolution begins establishment of Soviet state. |
| 1918 | Bolsheviks declare Turkestan Autonomous Soviet Socialist Republic, including most of present-day Central Asia in Russia; Bolsheviks crush autonomous government in Ququon; Jadidists and others begin decade-long Basmachi revolt involving elements from all five republics and mercenaries; Alash Orda establishes independent Kazak state. |
| 1918–19 | Widespread famine. |
| 1920 | Soviet General Frunze captures Ashgabat, ending anticommunist government there, and Bukhoro, ending khanate; Faizulla Khojayev becomes president of newly established Soviet Bukhoran People's Republic; Kyrgyz Autonomous Soviet Socialist Republic established, including Kyrgyzstan and Kazakstan. |

## Table A. *(Continued) Chronology of Important Events*

| Period | Description |
|---|---|
| 1921 | Communists win in Russian Civil War, reduce power of Central Asian party branches. |
| 1921–27 | New Economic Policy (NEP) expands cotton cultivation in Central Asia. |
| 1924 | Soviet socialist republics of Turkmenistan and Uzbekistan formed, with Tajikistan an autonomous republic in latter. |
| 1925 | Most Basmachi resistance in Tajikistan overcome; large-scale refugee movement from eastern Bukhoro; Kazak Autonomous Soviet Socialist Republic (Kazak ASSR) separated from Kyrgyz ASSR. |
| 1927–34 | Waves of communist party purges in all republic branches; Central Asian autonomy drives intensify purges there. |
| 1929 | Soviet Socialist Republic of Tajikistan established, northern territory added. |
| 1929–34 | Soviet collectivization induces widespread famine in Central Asia. |
| 1930s | Khojayev, other Central Asian communist leaders executed in Stalin purges, replaced by Russians. |
| 1936 | Kazak and Kyrgyz ASSRs given full republic status in Soviet Union; Karakalpakstan transferred from Russia to Republic of Uzbekistan. |
| Late 1930s | Nomadic lifestyle ends for most Turkmen. |
| 1941–43 | Many European Soviet plants moved to Central Asia to avoid capture by invading Nazis. |
| 1956–64 | Rehabilitation of some Central Asian communist leaders purged by Stalin; Russification remains prerequisite for party advancement; Virgin Lands program restructures agriculture in Central Asian republics. |
| 1959–82 | Tenure of Sharaf Rashidov as first secretary of Communist Party of Uzbekistan. |
| 1985 | Election of Mikhail S. Gorbachev as first secretary of Communist Party of Soviet Union, heralding impact of Moscow reform programs in Central Asia. |
| 1986 | Widespread purge of Communist Party of Uzbekistan leadership begins after exposure of corruption in Rashidov regime; nationalism, anti-Russian feeling intensify. |
| December | Widespread demonstrations in Kazakstan after appointment of Gennadiy Kolbin as party leader in Kazakstan; Kazak opposition groups appear; unrest continues through 1989. |
| Late 1980s | Uzbekistani intellectuals begin forming opposition political groups. |
| 1989 | Uzbeks clash with Meskhetian Turks and Kyrgyz in Osh; Moscow names Islam Karimov first secretary of Communist Party of Uzbekistan. |
|  | Political opposition group Agzybirlik formed in Turkmenistan; refused credentials. |

## Table A. (Continued) Chronology of Important Events

| Period | | Description |
|---|---|---|
| | June | Nursultan Nazarbayev named communist party head in Kazakstan. |
| 1990 | February | Riots in Dushanbe protest communist housing policy in Tajikistan; state of emergency declared, opposition parties suppressed. |
| | June–August | Violent conflict between Kyrgyz and Uzbeks and anti-communist demonstrations in Kyrgyz cities; opposition group, Democratic Movement of Kyrgyzstan, emerges. |
| | August | Republic of Turkmenistan declares sovereignty within Soviet Union. |
| | October | Saparmyrat Niyazov elected president of Turkmenistan, running unopposed. |
| | November | Askar Akayev elected president of Republic of Kyrgyzstan, defeating communist incumbent. |
| 1991 | August | Coup against Gorbachev government fails in Moscow; Uzbekistan, Kyrgyzstan declare independence from Soviet Union. |
| | September | Tajikistan declares independence from Soviet Union; communist Rahmon Nabiyev named president after ban of Communist Party of Tajikistan fails. |
| | October | Turkmenistan declares independence from Soviet Union; Akayev elected president of independent Kyrgyzstan, running unopposed. |
| | November | Communist Party of Uzbekistan reorganized, renamed People's Democratic Party of Uzbekistan. |
| | December | Nazarbayev elected president of Kazakstan, which declares independence from Soviet Union; five Central Asian states sign Alma-Ata Declaration formally establishing Commonwealth of Independent States (CIS); Communist Party of Turkmenistan renamed Democratic Party of Turkmenistan, retains political domination; Uzbekistan elects new parliament and Karimov its first president. |
| 1992 | | Five Central Asian states join Economic Cooperation Organization (ECO). |
| | | Niyazov introduces "Ten Years of Prosperity" economic reform program for Turkmenistan. |
| | March | Antigovernment riots begin in Dushanbe, escalate into civil war in April. |
| | May | Turkmenistan adopts new constitution; Kazakstan and Uzbekistan sign treaties of friendship and cooperation with Russia. |
| | June | Niyazov reelected president of Turkmenistan, running unopposed; Kyrgyzstan signs treaty of friendship and cooperation with Russia. |
| | Mid-year | Five Central Asian states begin taking over former Soviet military installations on their respective territories. |
| | July | Tajikistan signs treaty of cooperation and assistance with Russia, allowing Russian forces to clear antigovernment forces from Tajikistan. |

## Table A. *(Continued) Chronology of Important Events*

| Period | | Description |
|---|---|---|
| | September | Tajikistan's president Nabiyev forced to resign; coalition government takes power. |
| | November | Tajikistan's coalition government resigns, communist Rahmonov named head of state; opposition forces continue civil war. |
| | December | Uzbekistan adopts new constitution; Birlik, main opposition party, banned in Uzbekistan; Dushanbe falls to Tajikistani government forces. |
| 1993 | | "Cult of personality" of Niyazov extended in Turkmenistan with renaming of streets, buildings, and city of Krasnovodsk (Turkmenbashy). |
| | | Repression of opposition and media increases in Uzbekistan; by December, only state organs can register. |
| | January | New Kazakstani constitution adopted, names Kazak official state language; Akayev requests government emergency measures to end Kyrgyzstan's drastic economic decline. Kazakstani government forms National Council for Economic Reform; government of Tajikistan makes criminal charges against opposition leader Hajji Akbar Turajonzoda. |
| | April | Chevron Oil finalizes joint venture to develop Tengiz offshore oil fields with Kazakstan. |
| | June | Tajikistan bans three major opposition parties; Gorno-Badakhshan Autonomous Province ends claims of independence from Tajikistan. |
| | July | Kyrgyzstan signs military cooperation agreements with Russia; Afghan and Tajik rebels kill twenty-eight Russians in capturing border post in Tajikistan. |
| | September | Agreement for new ruble zone signed by Kazakstan, Tajikistan, and Uzbekistan; four Central Asian states, excluding Turkmenistan, join five other CIS states, including Russia, in economic union. |
| | November | Tenge becomes official currency of Kazakstan; Tajik rebels resume fighting in Gorno-Badakhshan. |
| | December | Turkmenistan signs treaty of cooperation, mutual assistance, and joint border security with Russia; Akayev dismisses Kyrgyzstani government of Tursunbek Chyngyshev after vote of no confidence; Kazakstan approves Nuclear Nonproliferation Treaty as non-nuclear signatory; Kazakstan's parliament dissolves itself. |
| 1994 | January | Referendum approves extension of Niyazov's term as president of Turkmenistan to 2002. |
| | March | First multiparty elections in Kazakstan (for parliament), dominated by Nazarbayev supporters. |
| | May–July | Kazakstan, Kyrgyzstan, Turkmenistan, and Uzbekistan join North Atlantic Treaty Organization (NATO) Partnership for Peace. |
| | June | Kyrgyzstan eases language, citizenship restrictions to slow emigration of Russians. |
| | September | Kyrgyzstani government resigns; parliament dissolved. |
| | October | Cease-fire begins in Tajikistani civil war. |

## Table A. (Continued) Chronology of Important Events

| Period | | Description |
|---|---|---|
| | November | Rahmonov elected president of Tajikistan, without participation of major opposition parties; plebiscite approves new Tajikistani constitution. |
| | December | New Majlis (assembly) elected in Turkmenistan, dominated by Democratic Party. |
| | December–January 1995 | Uzbekistan's parliamentary elections dominated by People's Democratic Party. |
| 1995 | | Sporadic cease-fires, peace talks, and resumption of fighting in Tajikistan. |
| | February | Kazakstan and Kyrgyzstan sign ten-year partnership and cooperation agreement with European Union (EU); parliamentary elections in Tajikistan boycotted by opposition; first of three election rounds for new bicameral parliament of Kyrgyzstan. |
| | March | Referendum extends Karimov's term as president of Uzbekistan to 2000; Kazakstani parliament resigns, Nazarbayev begins rule by decree. |
| | April | Referendum extends Nazarbayev's term to 2000. |
| | May | Tajikistan introduces new currency, Tajikistani ruble. |
| | June | Two Turkmen opposition leaders sentenced to prison terms. |
| | August | Kazakstan's new constitution approved by popular referendum. |
| | December | Parliamentary elections held in Kazakstan under protest by opposition parties. |
| 1996 | February | Referendum extends presidential powers of Akayev; Kazakstan and Kyrgyzstan sign extended customs union agreement with Belarus and Russia; Turkmenistan signs major natural gas sales agreement with Turkey. |
| | March | After resignation of Kyrgyzstan's government, Akayev names new cabinet headed by Apas Jumagulov, prime minister of previous government. |
| | April | Directors of seventeen banks in Kyrgyzstan charged with illegal use of funds, triggering national bank scandal; Kyrgyzstan bans Ittipak, Uygur separatist organization; Kazakstan, Kyrgyzstan, and Tajikistan sign Shanghai border security treaty with China and Russia, pledging aid to China against separatists from Xinjiang Uygur Autonomous Region. |
| | May | Kazakstan bans Russian newspaper *Komsomol'skaya pravda* for article by Aleksandr Solzhenitsyn claiming parts of Kazakstan as Russian territory; to ease severe economic crisis, Kazakstani government cancels US$300 million of agriculture sector's debts; Uzbekistan's Karimov threatens withdrawal from Economic Cooperation Organization (ECO) for Iran's "politicization" of ECO by criticism of Israel and United States; Kazakstan, Kyrgyzstan, and Tajikistan support Karimov. |
| | June | Kazakstan opens widespread antinarcotics offensive and amnesties 20,000 prisoners to relieve prison overcrowding; Tajikistan signs plan for energy export to Russia; Karimov makes official visit to |

## Table A. (Continued) Chronology of Important Events

| Period | Description |
|---|---|
| | United States to improve bilateral and UN relations; Uygurs in Kazakstan continue protests against Shanghai treaty; Nazarbayev's threat to dissolve parliament gains passage of unpopular pension bill; chairman of Kazakstan's Supreme Court dismissed for corruption. |
| July | Rahmonov of Tajikistan consolidates power by organizing National Security Council under presidential control and by antinarcotics campaign in rebel stronghold Gorno-Badakhshan, using nominally neutral Russian border troops. |
| August | Presidents of Kazakstan, Kyrgyzstan, and Uzbekistan sign accord for creation of single economic market by 1998; UN-sponsored cease-fire of July is broken by heavy fighting in Tajikistan's central region, as rebels renew thrust toward Dushanbe. |
| October | Antigovernment United Tajikistan Opposition proposes National Reconciliation Council including 80 percent opposition and 20 percent government members; Tajikistan government rejects formula. Japan commits US$140 million to upgrade three airports in Uzbekistan and US$200 million for infrastructure and medical centers in Kazakstan; bilateral accords with Iran and Russia reaffirm Turkmenistan's "permanent neutrality." |
| | Turkmenistan's Nabiyev confers in Moscow with Prime Minister Chernomyrdin, reaching no agreement on natural gas deliveries to Russia or on ownership of Caspian Sea resources. |
| October–November | Rebel forces open corridors from Afghanistan into eastern Tajikistan, threatening to take full control of eastern and central regions; government forces offer weak resistance. |
| November | Acute energy shortage brings winter rationing of electric power and heat in Kazakstan, Kyrgyzstan, and Tajikistan. |
| December | Tajikistan's Rahmonov signs new cease-fire agreement with rebel coalition; ensuing peace agreement calls for reconciliation council to amend constitution; Kazakstan sells its first bond issue on the international bond market; Turkmenistan's 1996 inflation rate estimated at 140 percent, highest among Central Asian republics; Kazakstan and international consortium set terms for pipeline construction to export Kazakstan's Tengiz oil. |
| 1997 January | Kazakstan begins shipping oil from its Tengiz field by tanker across Caspian Sea for resale by Iran; 2 million tons to be shipped annually until new export pipeline completed; two Japanese firms agree to build $US138 million telephone network in Uzbekistan; at meeting of Central Asian Economic Union, Kazakstan, Kyrgyzstan, and Uzbekistan sign mutual defense treaty and discuss mutual convertibility of currencies; Topchubek Turgunaligev, head of opposition Erkin Party in Kyrgyzstan, sentenced to prison for embezzlement as political repression tightens. |

## Table A. (Continued) Chronology of Important Events

| Period | Description |
|---|---|
| January–March | Six rounds of peace talks between Tajikistan government and United Tajikistan Opposition yield significant agreements on reintegration of political and military organizations. |
| February | Japan signs US$580 million agreement to build polypropylene plant in Turkmenistan. |
| March | Kyrgyzstan extends Russian border troop presence through end of 1997. |
| | Nazarbayev restructures Kazakstan's government, reducing power of Prime Minister Akezhan Kazhegeldin. |
| May | Terms set for pipeline connecting Tengiz oil field in Kazakstan with Russia's Black Sea port of Novorossiysk, to open September 1999. |
| June | Peace accord between Rahmonov government and United Tajik Opposition formally ends civil war in Tajikistan. |
| July | New National Reconciliation Commission scheduled to begin work on procedures for parliamentary elections to be held in Tajikistan by the end of 1998. |
| | Andijan-Osh-Kashgar Highway opens, connecting points in Uzbekistan and Kyrgyzstan with China. |
| August | Kazakstan and Russia sign treaty easing conditions for Russians in Kazakstan, aimed at reducing emigration of Russian technical experts. |
| | Political negotiations in Tajikistan delayed by scattered fighting and disagreements over conditions. |
| September | United States forces join troops of Kazakstan, Kyrgyzstan, Russia, Turkey, and Uzbekistan in peacekeeping exercise in south-central Kazakstan, the first such combined exercise. |

# Introduction

IN 1991 THE FIVE SOVIET REPUBLICS of Central Asia—Kazakstan, Kyrgyzstan, Tajikistan, Turkmenistan, and Uzbekistan—were faced for the first time with the prospect of existence as independent states. In critical respects, they were unprepared for this event: their economies all had performed specific tasks in the Soviet system, mainly the supply of raw materials; only outdated Soviet-era political structures remained behind in the five republics, with no tradition of national political institutions; and the end of the union fragmented the armed forces units of the former Soviet Union that remained on the republics' territory. In the 1990s, the progress of the five republics toward resolving these problems has been quite uneven. The republics with the richest natural resources—Kazakstan, Turkmenistan, and Uzbekistan—have developed the strongest economies—albeit with serious defects in each case—and have attracted substantial Western investment. In all cases, movement away from the Soviet model of strong, one-party central government has been extremely slow. Some degree of military autonomy has appeared in all republics save Tajikistan, which still is bedeviled by rebel forces and a porous southern border. At the same time, the strategic doctrine of all Central Asian countries remains based on protection from Russia's military.

The total area of the five republics is approximately 3.9 million square kilometers, slightly more than 40 percent of the area of the United States and less than one-quarter of the area of Russia (see fig. 1). The region stretches from the Caspian Sea in the west to China in the east, and from central Siberia in the north to Afghanistan, Iran, and Pakistan in the south. The area of the republics varies greatly: Kazakstan, by far the largest, occupies about 2.7 million square kilometers, more than two-thirds of the region. The smallest republic, Kyrgyzstan, occupies only 198,500 square kilometers. The Central Asian republics also feature quite different topographies, varying from the wide expanses of desert in primarily flat Kazakstan and Turkmenistan to the steep slopes and river valleys of mountainous Tajikistan and Kyrgyzstan (see fig. 2).

The region contains enormous natural and agricultural resources. All five republics have favorable agricultural regions and some combination of attractive minerals and fuels. Their industrial bases include trained workers, and their populations have relatively high educational levels and literacy rates. Unfortunately, the moribund, highly inefficient system through which the Soviet Union exploited those resources has proved very difficult to disassemble. The Central Asians have suffered all the typical transitional ills of former communist states moving toward a market economy: erratic supply of critical industrial inputs, increased unemployment, sharply increased inflation, declining capacity utilization and output by industry, and acute shortages of goods. In response, all five governments have pledged meaningful reform, but obstacles such as unworkable government structure, ethnic rivalries, and a variety of social tensions have made all five move cautiously.

Central Asia has a rich history to which numerous tribes and nationalities have contributed over at least 2,500 years. A vital factor in the history of the southern part of the region was its location astride the most direct trade route between China and Europe, the so-called Silk Route, which began to develop in the heyday of the Roman Empire (see fig. 3). Cities such as Samarqand (Samarkand) and Bukhoro (Bukhara), founded by Iranians, became powerful cultural and commercial centers as East-West trade increased. That prosperity made part or all of the region the object of many conquests (including those by the Arabs in the eighth century A.D., several Turkic groups beginning in the ninth century, and the Mongols in the early thirteenth century). The Arabs and the Turks brought Islam to much of Central Asia. Meanwhile, the northern part of the region was inhabited by nomadic herding peoples, including the Turkic predecessors of the Kazaks and Kyrgyz, who also fell under the control of the Mongols.

In the sixteenth century, the Uzbeks established powerful khanates along the Silk Route. Those entities flourished until the nineteenth century, when they were overtaken gradually by the traders and settlers of the expanding Russian Empire. The Russians moved southward from the steppes of Kazakstan in search of trade and later of the cotton that could be grown in present-day Tajikistan, Turkmenistan, and Uzbekistan. In the ensuing decades, cotton became the vital economic magnet for increased Russian occupation, and large tracts of the region were devoted to that crop to supply Russia's domestic needs.

In 1917 the region passed from the Russian Empire to the Soviet Union, with little participation by its inhabitants. Full

Soviet control did not occur until the mid-1920s, as guerrilla bands continued to resist Soviet authority. In the 1920s, four of the five republics came into existence for the first time as Soviet authorities drew borders in anticipation of reordering all of Central Asian society. (Kyrgyzstan gained full republic status in 1936.) In the 1930s, the primarily agricultural region was traumatized by the forced collectivization campaign of Joseph V. Stalin's regime; episodes of widespread famine were common. (By 1900 the Kazak, Kyrgyz, and Turkmen nomads already had suffered massive disruption of their traditional lifestyles as a result of Russian settlers taking their grazing land for farms.)

Throughout the Soviet period, the Central Asian republics participated in the life of the union in a rather peripheral sense, and many phases of cultural life were unaffected by Soviet rule. Local communist parties suffered the same purges as those in other republics, but they exercised little political influence in Moscow. Regional economies were stunted by increased demands for production of cotton and other specifically assigned items. As was discovered in the 1980s, decades of Soviet intensive cultivation caused massive pollution, from which the region still suffers. Interrepublican animosities over access to scarce resources went largely ignored by Soviet authorities. The more liberal Soviet regime of Mikhail S. Gorbachev (in office 1985–91) saw increased airing of grievances that long had been withheld by the peoples of the Central Asian republics, but before 1991 no organized movement for independence had evolved from that discontent.

The five post-Soviet states of Central Asia still are defined by the arbitrary borders created in the early years of the Soviet era, and the demarcation among them still fails to correspond to the ethnic and linguistic situation of the region. Thus, Kyrgyzstan and Turkmenistan have substantial Uzbek minorities, and Tajikistan and Uzbekistan have large numbers of their respective neighbor's people. Kazakstan has few Central Asian people of other nationalities; its largest minorities are Russian, Ukrainian, and German.

Until the 1990s, the Soviet Central Asian states were viewed from the outside world largely as parts of a single, homogeneous region. Since 1991, however, the Western world has begun to discover substantial differences in almost all aspects of those new nations. The West also has discovered the possibility of commercial gain from oil, natural gas, gold, and other natural resources abundant in the region. The presence of these materials was known in the Soviet era, but they were accessible only by way of Moscow.

In responding to their neighbors in the new independence period, the policy makers of the five states have moved in two contrary directions: toward establishing common goals and greater unity in a regional grouping, and toward individual economic and political development and identification with countries outside the region. The philosophical ideal of Pan-Turkism, an ethnically based unity concept that originated among Central Asian intellectuals in the nineteenth century, still receives support, but relatively few concrete steps have been taken to realize the ideal. Furthermore, the people of Tajikistan are of predominantly Persian rather than Turkic origin. Meanwhile, Central Asians have placed special emphasis on ethnic self-differentiation as a belated reaction against the stereotyping of non-Slavs that was common practice in the Soviet Union. That ethnic generalization continues in the Russian Federation, which still exerts enormous influence in the Central Asian republics.

The most important single cultural commonality among the republics is the practice of Sunni Islam, which is the professed religion of a very large majority of the peoples of the five republics and which has experienced a significant revival throughout the region in the 1990s. Propaganda from Russia and from the ruling regimes in the republics identifies Islamic political activity as a vague, monolithic threat to political stability everywhere in the region. However, the role of Islam in the five cultures is far from uniform, and its role in politics has been minimal everywhere except in Tajikistan. For Kazaks, Kyrgyz, and Turkmen, whose society was based on a nomadic lifestyle that carried on many traditional tribal beliefs after their nominal conversion, Islam has had a less profound influence on culture than for the sedentary Tajik and Uzbek Muslims, who have a conventional religious hierarchy.

Regional economic cooperation, another type of unity that has received substantial lip service in the 1990s, has failed to materialize on a large scale. All five republics joined the Economic Cooperation Organization (ECO—see Glossary) shortly after independence, and Kazakstan, Kyrgyzstan, and Uzbekistan established a limited common market in 1994. But Uzbekistan vetoed the membership of unstable Tajikistan, and Turkmenistan refused to join. Existing arrangements within the free-trade zone have not significantly promoted large-scale commerce within the group of three. For all five republics, Russia remains the top trading partner because much of the emphasis in their agricultural and industrial infrastructures remains the same as when the republics had assigned roles in supplying Moscow. Those roles and dependence on Russian trade are changing slowly in the mid-1990s, however, as diversification occurs.

Several factors encourage economic rivalry rather than cooperation. Water, a crucial resource for agriculture and power generation, has been the object of bitter bilateral and multilateral disputes both before and after independence. In the 1990s, the republics at the headwaters of major rivers, Kyrgyzstan and Tajikistan, have chafed at apportionment of water consumption favoring downstream consumers Turkmenistan and Uzbekistan, and Turkmenistan has complained about excessive water consumption by the Uzbekistanis upstream. Kyrgyzstan and Uzbekistan have come close to conflict over water in the Fergana Valley, where vital agricultural reform and land privatization programs are endangered by unresolved water disputes.

The republics still offer a similar range of commodities for trade. Their common emphasis on cotton, natural gas, and oil limits the potential for advantageous commerce within the group and fosters rivalry in trade with outside customers. Some of the commercial relationships that have developed—such as the sale of fuels to Kyrgyzstan and Tajikistan by the other three fuel-rich republics—have been one-sided and subject to shutdown in response to nonpayment or in attempts to gain economic and political leverage.

The five republics have several major problems in common. All remain in the economic, military, and political shadow of their giant neighbor to the north. In the mid-1990s, Russian policy makers, encouraged by a very vocal nationalist faction in the federation, speak openly of recapturing influence in the "near abroad"; Central Asia usually is the first region cited as an example. In the first two years of independence, the five republics remained in the ruble zone (see Glossary), their monetary activities restricted by the nonconvertibility of the old Soviet ruble that remained the currency of that grouping. In 1993 all but Tajikistan introduced new currencies with limited convertibility. Russia had attempted to keep Kazakstan and Uzbekistan in a new Russian ruble zone, but ruble distribution problems and harsh conversion conditions forced those republics to follow the independent course of Kyrgyzstan and Turkmenistan. The Tajikistani ruble (for value of the Tajikistani ruble—see Glossary) introduced in 1995 remained closely connected with its Russian counterpart. In 1996 Kazakstan and Kyrgyzstan established a new customs union and other economic ties with Russia and Belarus, hoping to gain selected advantages while avoiding large-scale concessions that would increase Russian influence.

The Soviet legacy includes an economic infrastructure in which all republics depend heavily on other republics for vital inputs. A complex Soviet-designed system of pipelines and electric cables connects the five republics. Pending completion of Turkmenistan's new line to Iran, only one railroad line leading out of Central Asia connects the region with a destination other than Russia (the one line goes only to the Xinjiang Uygur Autonomous Region in China). Heavy industry in all five republics also has depended heavily on local Russian skilled labor.

The Central Asian republics also suffer common geographic disadvantages. All are landlocked and located far from potential markets outside the Commonwealth of Independent States (CIS—see Glossary) and the Middle East. Nations such as Azerbaijan and Afghanistan, through which goods must travel overland to reach Western markets, still are quite unstable, and others such as China and Russia are powerful neighbors with a history of taking advantage of weaker nations that need commercial favors. Kazakstan and Turkmenistan, both in need of a route to move oil and gas to Western customers, have been especially frustrated by Russia's failure to support new pipelines. The landlocked position also presents a national security obstacle.

Although the region is blessed with ample arable land, most of that land becomes useful only when irrigated. Large-scale irrigation, in turn, has taken a huge toll on the hydrological systems of the region—in the most obvious case, the system that feeds the fast-disappearing Aral Sea. Regional cooperation on the Aral Sea problem, recognized as one of the most serious environmental crises in the world, received much lip service and little action in the first half of the 1990s. By 1995 an estimated 36,000 square kilometers of the sea's bed had been exposed, and an estimated 3 million inhabitants of nearby Turkmenistan, Uzbekistan, and Kazakstan had developed chronic health problems associated with that process. In October 1995, a United Nations (UN)-sponsored regional conference produced the Nukus Declaration, which resulted in the promise of intensified joint efforts to stabilize the sea and a pledge of US$200 million from the UN and the World Bank (see Glossary) for regional development and aid.

When independence was declared in 1991, none of the five republics had experienced an independence movement or had a corps of leaders who had considered how such a change might be managed. Five years after independence, in four of the states political leadership remains in the hands of the same individual as in the last years of the Soviet Union: Nursultan Nazarbayev in Kazakstan, Askar Akayev in Kyrgyzstan, Saparmyrat Niyazov in Turkmenistan, and Islam Karimov in Uzbekistan. President Imomali Rahmonov of Tajikistan was not president in 1991, but, like his cohorts, his roots are in his republic's pre-1992 political world. Political power in all five republics is based on clan and regional groupings that make national coalitions risky and fragile. Clan rivalries have played a particular role in the civil war of Tajikistan and in Akayev's difficulties in unifying Kyrgyzstan behind a reform program.

Although all the republics had adopted new constitutions by 1995, the three government branches prescribed by those documents are severely imbalanced in favor of the executive. In all five cases, the political opposition of the early 1990s has been virtually extinguished in the name of preserving stability and preventing the putative onset of Islamic politicization. Although the new constitutions of the republics specify independent judicial branches, the concept of due process has not been established consistently anywhere.

All five republics have suffered increasing rates of crime in the liberalized atmosphere of the postindependence years. Drug trafficking, official corruption, and white-collar crime have increased most noticeably. All republics lack the resources to equip and train qualified police and specialized forces, and their judicial systems are not sufficiently removed from their Soviet antecedents to deal equitably with new generations of criminals. Evaluation and quantification of crime in post-Soviet Central Asia have been hampered by changes in responsible agencies, by irregularities in reporting procedures, and by lack of control and responsiveness in law enforcement agencies, particularly in Tajikistan. Statistics for the years 1990 and 1994 from Kazakstan and Kyrgyzstan show dramatic increases in every type of crime, although those from the other three republics, where record keeping is known to be substantially less comprehensive, show considerable drops in many categories. In 1995 and 1996, Kazakstan and Uzbekistan set up new, specialized police units to deal with economic and organized crime.

## Kazakstan

By far the largest of the Central Asian republics, Kazakstan extends almost 2,000 kilometers from the Caspian Sea in the west to the border of China in the east and nearly 1,300 kilometers from central Siberia in the north to eastern Uzbekistan in the south. Despite its size, in population Kazakstan is a distant second to Uzbekistan among the Central Asian republics. With the lowest birth rate and the highest emigration rate in the region, Kazakstan's population has remained virtually stable for the past ten years. Kazakstan has by far the largest non-Asian population (45 percent in 1994, equaling the Kazak population) and the smallest population of other Central Asian ethnic groups (for example, only 2 percent are Uzbek).

The largest minority in Kazakstan is its Russian population (36 percent in 1994), which until the 1990s was the plurality group. The status of the Russians, whose number includes many irreplaceable technical experts, has been one of Kazakstan's burning post-Soviet issues. The government has resisted making Russian an official second language, although Russian is understood by most Kazaks and used in most official communications. In May 1996, a treaty established the status of Kazak and Russian citizens in Russia and Kazakstan, respectively, ending a long disputed aspect of the nationality issue.

Of the five Central Asian republics, Kazakstan played the most important industrial role in the Soviet system because of the abundant coal and oil deposits in the northern sector of the republic, closest to Russia. Although the Soviet Union developed specific sectors of industry such as chemicals, metals, and military equipment, the republic also inherited an antiquated industrial infrastructure geared to feed materials into the Soviet economy. Energy industries, which also played a large part in the economy, have suffered from substantial reductions in Russia's post-Soviet demand, as have other industries that remain dependent on Russian markets.

In 1996 most of Kazakstan's economy was still state-owned and lacked fundamental restructuring, despite large-scale privatization of smaller enterprises in the preceding years. Some large firms have been sold to solid international companies (such as the Republic of Korea's (South Korea's) Samsung, which now manages the Zhezqazghan Nonferrous Metallurgy complex and refinery), but many were awarded to unknown companies whose contracts later were cancelled. In June 1996, the government sold the country's largest oil refinery at Shymkent, Yuzhneftegaz, one of its largest oil enterprises, and the Vasilevskoye gold mine, one of the largest in the world, by public tender to foreign companies. Those sales, together worth an estimated US$1 billion, were a major departure from previous policy and were aimed at improving the confidence of international investors.

In 1996 the healthiest parts of the economy were the oil, gas, and mineral extraction industries. However, infrastructural decay and slow structural reform have delayed the recovery of those sectors from post-Soviet lethargy. Many of the state enterprises concentrated in northern Kazakstan are far in debt and unable to pay wages to their workers. The transfer of the national capital from Almaty along the border of Uzbekistan to Aqmola in the industrial north, planned for 1998, is an attempt to revive that zone, as well as to retain the cadre of Russian technical experts who continue to leave the country.

Foreign investment in Kazakstan has been frustrated by complex bureaucratic rules, and the domestic consumer market is restricted by the very low average wage of US$96 per month. The Western oil companies Chevron and Mobil have invested heavily in the Tengiz oil fields offshore in the Caspian Sea, but they have been frustrated by a long dispute with the consortium of Kazakstan, Oman, and Russia over the structure of a new delivery pipeline. The common customs regime established with Russia in 1995 has accelerated trade, but conditions favored Russia in the first year.

The Central Bank of Kazakstan, President Nazarbayev, and the Council of Ministers play a strong role in economic policy making. The bank has advocated market reform and inflation control the most strongly of the three. Experts rate Nazarbayev's economic initiatives as erratic. Government goals for 1996 included reducing inflation to 28 percent (the 1995 rate was 60 percent), reducing the budget deficit to about 3.3 percent of the gross domestic product (GDP—see Glossary); and limiting devaluation of the tenge (for value of the tenge—see Glossary) to a 10 percent decline against the dollar.

The exchange rate of the tenge against the United States dollar has improved steadily, allowing upper-class Kazaks to expand foreign goods purchases. For 1997 the Economist Intelligence Unit forecasts significant stabilization and recovery, with overall GDP growth of 1 percent and consumer price inflation of 45 percent. Substantial aid was expected from the International Monetary Fund (IMF—see Glossary) in 1996. Full membership in the Islamic Development Bank, achieved in mid-1996, brought Kazakstan additional aid for trade operations, personnel training, and infrastructure improvements.

Despite the abundance of fuel in Kazakstan, in 1996 the republic continued to be plagued by its Soviet-era transportation system, which failed to connect population centers with distant hydrocarbon deposits within the country. As a result, in the winter of 1996–97 Almaty and others cities suffered severe shortages of electric power and heat.

In December 1996, Russia finally stopped blocking a multinational agreement to build an export pipeline that would allow Kazakstan to sell its abundant oil directly to Western customers. Because the pipeline will not be available until 1999 or later, in 1997 Kazakstan began shipping oil across the Caspian Sea for resale in Iran—a procedure that risked Western condemnation because of the ongoing economic embargo of Iran.

As the Soviet Union faced dissolution late in 1991, Nazarbayev was one of the last advocates of the union's preservation in some form. Since that time, he has pursued a careful foreign policy aimed at preserving both close relations with Russia and as much as possible of his nation's economic and political independence. In domestic politics, he nominally expanded some of the republic's democratic institutions, pushing through a new constitution and a popularly elected parliament. However, Nazarbayev also consolidated his executive power steadily in the mid-1990s. Parliaments were dissolved in 1993 and 1995, and Nazarbayev made numerous changes in the personnel and structure of his cabinets, all in an effort to obtain cooperation in his reform programs. In April 1995, a referendum overwhelmingly extended the president's term to 2000, canceling the 1995 presidential election. Decrees by Nazarbayev in December 1995 and April 1996 further extended the president's powers. Nazarbayev also dissolved the Constitutional Court in 1995 and replaced members of the Supreme Court in 1996.

Party politics in Kazakstan have not worked well, although a substantial opposition movement exists. Despite efforts by the ruling People's Unity Party (SNEK) to minimize opposition activity, the top three opposition parties gained twenty-two of sixty-seven seats in the lower house (Majilis) of parliament in the December 1995 elections, and another fourteen seats went to independent candidates. Indicating the inferior role of parliament in the Kazakstani government, however, was the lack of competition in those elections; only forty-nine candidates vied for the forty Senate (upper-house) seats being contested. In both houses, Kazaks outnumbered Russians, by forty-two to nineteen in the Majilis and by twenty-nine to fifteen in the Senate (the president appoints seven senators).

In the Soviet era, Semipalatinsk (now Semey) in northeastern Kazakstan was the world's largest and most frequently used test site for nuclear weapons. During the long Cold-War period of nuclear weapons testing, an estimated 1.5 to 2 million people were affected by radioactive pollution in northern Kazakstan. Demonstrations against nuclear testing began in 1989, and a major environmental movement sprang from that opposition.

When the Soviet Union dissolved, Kazakstan was one of four republics possessing nuclear weapons and materials. In November 1994, the United States completed Project Sapphire, which involved the purchase and removal of more than 600 kilograms of weapons-grade plutonium from Kazakstan, whose insecure storage facilities and possible nuclear sales to Libya and Iran had aroused international concern. In May 1995, the last of Kazakstan's nuclear weapons was destroyed, removing a major shadow from the Soviet past. The United States has promised aid in permanently sealing the Semey test site.

In the 1990s, Kazakstan's foreign policy has continued Nazarbayev's early support of a federation among the former Soviet states, now loosely united in the CIS. Because the country's industrial and energy bases are located close to Russia's southern border, experts have identified Kazakstan as the former Soviet republic most likely to experience Russian pressure toward reunification. Despite the strains caused by the uncertain status of the large Russian minority in his republic, Nazarbayev has maintained close relations with Russia; in early 1996, he brought Kazakstan into a new commercial confederation with Belarus, Russia, and Kyrgyzstan. In June 1996, Prime Minister Akezhan Kazhegeldin reiterated Kazakstan's full support for additional CIS integration (while preserving member-state sovereignty) and for the reelection of Boris N. Yeltsin as president of Russia. Meanwhile, Kazakstan worked with Kyrgyzstan and Uzbekistan to extend the activities of the Central Asian Economic Union, which was established in 1993. At the Bishkek summit of January 1997, a treaty of "eternal friendship" guaranteed mutual security assistance among the three member nations; the summit also discussed mutual convertibility of the three currencies.

## Kyrgyzstan

Kyrgyzstan, the second-smallest of the Central Asian republics in both area and population, is located between two giants: Kazakstan to its north and China to its south and east. The rural population, already the largest by percentage in Central Asia, is growing faster than the cities. Like Kazakstan, Kyrgyzstan has a minority population of Russians (22 percent in 1994) whose accelerated emigration threatens the country's technological base. The country's legal and political systems give clear priority to the Kyrgyz majority, alienating not only Russians but also the large Uzbek minority concentrated in the Osh region of southwestern Kyrgyzstan. Friction persists over control of the scarce land of the Fergana Valley, which overlaps the territory of three republics: Kyrgyzstan, Tajikistan, and Uzbekistan. The regime of President Askar Akayev (first elected in 1990) has attempted to balance sorely needed national reform programs with the demands of ethnic groups and clans that still exercise strong influence on the country's political and social structures.

Kyrgyzstan, ranked as the second-poorest republic in Central Asia, possesses a more limited range of natural resources than its neighbors. In the Soviet era, Kyrgyzstan contributed a specific group of minerals—antimony, gold, and mercury—to Moscow's economic plan. Of the three, only gold is a valuable asset in the post-Soviet world; it has attracted several Western investor companies. Kyrgyzstan has only limited amounts of coal and oil. The major energy resource is water power from the republic's fast-moving rivers. However, despite a government program of increased emphasis on hydroelectric power, Kyrgyzstan must import a large proportion of its energy supply. Kyrgyzstan's industry, which had been specialized to serve the Soviet military-industrial complex, suffered heavily when that demand disappeared; conversion has proven very difficult.

After independence, Kyrgyzstan suffered one of the worst economic declines among the CIS states (particularly in industrial output), despite a reform program that was deployed more rapidly than most others. Statistically, privatization was very effective, but because meaningful economic change did not occur after privatization, inefficient state enterprises continued to drag down the economy. Government and commercial corruption also diluted the effects of economic reform.

In the mid-1990s, official measurements of Kyrgyzstan's economic performance were very negative; they were, however, not completely accurate. By 1996 an estimated 30 percent of real GDP came from the "black economy"—independent, unregistered entrepreneurs selling their wares on the street or in private shops—while state-owned enterprises continued to go bankrupt or failed to pay their employees. However, even official GDP bottomed out in 1995; it dropped 6.2 percent after slumping by 26 percent in the previous year. The Economist Intelligence Unit forecast GDP rises of 1 percent in 1996 and 2.5 percent in 1997, the latter spurred by the opening of the Canadian joint-venture gold mine at Kumtor. In 1995 the volume of industrial production dropped 12.5 percent, and consumer goods production dropped 25.4 percent, but agriculture improved by 38.8 percent.

Other indicators are more positive, however. By early 1996, the inflation rate, which had reached 1,400 percent in 1993, was about 1 percent per month. The government's goal was to halve the end-of-1995 rate by the end of 1996. The exchange rate of the som (for value of the som—see Glossary) remained stable in 1996 at eleven to US$1. The budget deficit remained high at about 12 percent of GDP, with foreign loans applied to make up the shortfall.

Foreign investment remained very sparse in 1996. Many joint ventures with Turkey have failed, and the sale of Kyrgyzstani firms to foreign investors has provided embarrassingly little revenue for the government. International loans continue, but Kyrgyzstan already has fallen behind in repayments to Russia and Turkey. Repayment of pending international debts inevitably will raise the national debt. Debt and the failure of foreign investment have forced Kyrgyzstan to rely more heavily on Russia. The customs union that Kyrgystan joined with Belarus, Kazakstan, and Russia early in 1996 will add to Moscow's power over Kyrgyzstan's trade policy.

At the same time, Kyrgyzstan's parliament has resisted reform legislation that would modernize the tax code and privatization of large state enterprises in energy, telecommunications, mining, and aviation. According to a government estimate, as many as 70 percent of privatized enterprises were bankrupt in 1996 because, under existing economic conditions, they simply lacked customers. A limited capital market includes the Kyrgyzstan Stock Exchange, which opened in early 1995, and some independent brokerage houses, but because there is no legal framework or government regulation for capital exchange, cash transactions were few in 1996.

Although President Akayev began his regime with ideals of multiparty democracy, strong opposition stymied his reform programs and moved him gradually closer to the authoritarian positions of his four Central Asian colleagues. Power struggles between the legislative and executive branches of government promoted Akayev's expansion of executive power. In the mid-1990s, two elections—the first reelecting Akayev by a huge margin in December 1995 and the second giving 95 percent approval in a referendum on extending his power in February 1996—were approved by international observers as free and fair, although the opposition claimed otherwise. The referendum empowers the president to conduct domestic and foreign policy and to name and dismiss cabinet ministers and judges without consulting parliament. The parliament retains approval rights over the presidential appointment of the prime minister, Supreme Court judges, and other officials, but the president may dissolve parliament if it fails three times to approve a nominee. Akayev had argued that centralizing presidential power was necessary to speed economic, political, and legal reform and to reduce the influence of regional political centers. In March 1996, he exercised his new power by securing the resignation of the government, naming four new ministers, and redesignating the positions of five others. He also reorganized local government to reduce the power of provincial leaders and assign them direct responsibility for enactment of national reforms.

In May 1996, a new government document described social conditions and listed goals for social programs in the ensuing years. Kyrgyzstan, which has made earnest efforts to maintain social support programs in the lean years of the 1990s, is emphasizing job creation and prevention of unemployment, reorganization of social insurance and pension systems, and reforms in education and health care. The official unemployment figure in mid-1996 was 76,600; about 60 percent of the unemployed received unemployment benefits. The government goal is to keep unemployment below 100,000 while mounting a new, long-term job creation program. In 1996 a proposal was made for a government-controlled social fund to run a uniform state insurance and pension system that would remove the severe inequities of Kyrgyzstan's current system.

Meanwhile, nearly one-third of the population (1.257 million) are estimated to live below the poverty line, and the 14,000 refugees arriving annually from Tajikistan create additional social pressures. Kyrgyzstan became a preferred refugee destination when Kazakstan and Uzbekistan tightened their migration controls in 1993.

In the 1990s, Kyrgyzstan's foreign policy has been shaped by the small country's reliance on Russia for national security. In 1996 President Akayev reiterated that Kyrgyzstan always would view Russia as a natural ally and partner. At the same time, Kyrgyzstan has appealed to the North Atlantic Treaty Organization (NATO—see Glossary) and the Organization for Security and Cooperation in Europe (OSCE—see Glossary) to replace the CIS force in Tajikistan and, in fact, to guarantee the security of the entire region—a position at odds with Russia's strong opposition to NATO influence anywhere in the former Warsaw Pact regions. However, in early 1997 Akayev backed Russia's opposition to NATO expansion in Europe. In 1996–97 Kyrgyzstan diversified its national security policy somewhat by participating in the Central Asian peacekeeping battalion under the aegis of the Central Asian Economic Union.

Difficult relations with Central Asian neighbors increase the need for an outside source of security. Uzbekistan, which has a 13 percent minority population in western Kyrgyzstan, has flexed its muscles by shutting off fuel supplies. Kyrgyzstan depends heavily on the Kazakstani capital, Almaty, for air traffic in the absence of a first-class domestic airport. Unresolved border issues and a continuing flow of civil war refugees have inflamed relations with Tajikistan. Greatly expanded trade relations with China also have brought large numbers of Chinese merchants who threaten to stifle domestic commerce in some Kyrgyzstani cities. Kyrgyzstan has expressed the need to balance its policy between China and Russia, and has praised China for its relative restraint in exerting influence over Central Asia.

# Tajikistan

Located on the western slopes of the Pamir Mountains, Tajikistan occupies one of the most rugged and topographically divided regions in the world. Possessing extremely convoluted frontiers, it borders Uzbekistan to the west, China to the east, Afghanistan to the south, and Kyrgyzstan to the north. Tajikistan is the smallest in area and third-largest in population of the Central Asian republics. Unlike the ethnically dominant groups of the other four republics, the Tajiks have a culture and a language based on Iranian rather than Turkic roots. Despite their differing cultural backgrounds, the Tajiks and the Uzbeks did not consider themselves separate until the Soviet Union's artificial demarcation of the republics in the 1920s. (Until 1929 the Autonomous Republic of Tajikistan was part of the Soviet Socialist Republic of Uzbekistan.)

The Soviet Union brought Tajikistan significant advancement in education, industry, and infrastructure compared with the primitive conditions of 1917. In the mid-1990s, however, the country remained the most backward of the Central Asian republics, partly because of specifically focused Soviet development policies and partly because of topographical factors that enormously complicate exploitation of existing resources.

In the Soviet system, the Tajikistani economy was designed to produce cotton, aluminum, and a few other mineral products, including uranium and gold. Waged across a large portion of the republic, the civil war has caused great and lasting damage to the national economy. In 1994 damage to industry was estimated at about US$12 billion. Production levels in all industries had dropped an estimated 60 percent in 1994 compared with 1990. Many Germans and Russians, a high percentage of the country's key technical personnel, fled the civil war. The rate of inflation was steep in 1992–93.

In 1996 Tajikistan's economy still was in desperate condition. It remains the least attractive of the former Soviet republics for foreign investment. Only the export of cotton and aluminum has brought significant profits. A joint cotton venture with the United Arab Emirates was scheduled to begin in mid-1996. In 1995 the Regar (Tursunzoda) aluminum plant produced 230,000 tons of primary aluminum, about half its capacity but enough to make aluminum the second-largest export product. As it was earlier in the 1990s, aluminum production has been limited by continued reliance on imported raw materials and

1

energy. Tajikistani industry remains handicapped in general by the country's inability to pay foreign energy suppliers.

Some movement toward economic reform was seen in 1996, although the unreliability of performance statistics makes evaluation difficult. Prime minister Yahyo Azimov, who took office in February 1996, has stressed the need for quick privatization and assistance from the IMF and the World Bank. In early 1996, controls were lifted on bread prices, a move that led to riots in some cities but that was considered a sign of commitment to market reform. The Azimov government set a 1996 budget deficit cap of 6 percent of GDP. In mid-1996 the World Bank was considering a loan of US$50 million, but the IMF withheld aid pending improvement of foreign exchange and other conditions. The privatization target for the end of 1996 was 50 percent of total enterprises, after only 8 percent of the country's enterprises were privatized in the first four years of independence. The Economist Intelligence Unit forecast additional GDP reductions of 12.4 percent in 1996 and 10 percent in 1997.

In 1996 and 1997, Tajikistan attempted to join regional organizations that would improve its economic position. The customs union of Belarus, Kazakstan, Kyrgzstan, and Russia considered Tajikistan for membership, but the Central Asian Economic Union of Kazakstan, Kyrgyzstan, and Uzbekistan refused Tajikistan's overtures.

Some improvements were made in 1995–96 in Tajikistan's woefully shabby infrastructure. The Daewoo firm of South Korea modernized the telephone system, and United States, German, and Turkish firms were scheduled to add new features. The Dushanbe Airport still needs modernization, although in the mid-1990s regular flights were established to Moscow, India, and some other points.

Especially in comparison with the stable regimes that have dominated the other republics since 1991, the political scene in Tajikistan has been unsettled from the day of independence onward. Throughout the 1990s, an old guard with roots in the Soviet era parried the efforts of various opposition groups to share or monopolize power. In 1992 a short-lived coalition government broke down, sending the country into a civil war that was won nominally when the old guard forces captured Dushanbe and named Imomali Rahmonov chief executive. But conflict persisted, based partly on the geographical and clan divisions of the country and partly on the political question of reform versus reaction. Between 1993 and 1996, fighting flared, mostly in limited engagements, in several regions of Tajikistan and across the border in Afghanistan. In 1993 a multinational CIS force, dominated by Russian units, entered the country with the primary mission of enforcing the southern border, across which opposition forces had received substantial support. In early 1994, the UN arranged a first round of peace talks, and five more rounds followed over the next two years. None of the talks led to an agreement on peace terms, however.

In 1996 Tajikistan's political situation remained as unstable as it had been for the previous three years. The Rahmonov regime was unable to defeat rebel forces or to compromise enough to reach a satisfactory agreement with them. As it had in the previous three years, Russia failed to bring the government and the opposition to the peace table. Meanwhile, continued instability provided Russia the pretext for maintaining substantial "peacekeeping" forces in a key region of the former Soviet Union. The situation has led some outsiders to doubt the sincerity of Russia's efforts to bring peace to the area.

In early June 1996, the civil war in Tajikistan intensified once again, and observers saw similarities between Russia's military activity there and its occupation of Chechnya. Russian air attacks on opposition villages in south-central Tajikistan contravened the latest three-month extension of the UN-sponsored cease-fire (originally signed in 1994), which had been set in May. In a new campaign apparently coordinated with Moscow, Tajikistani troops moved with Russian air support eastward into the country's narrow central corridor toward opposition strongholds. Meanwhile, in May the Rahmonov regime refused to reconvene UN-sponsored talks as scheduled, and the UN Observer Mission in Tajikistan (UNMOT) was refused access to the combat zone. In August 1996, opposition troops moved close to Dushanbe amid intensified fighting that ended yet another cease-fire agreement.

In the fall of 1996, the government's military position was unfavorable as rebel forces drove from Afghanistan into central and eastern Tajikistan. In December Rahmonov signed a peace agreement with Sayed Abdullo Nuri, leader of the opposition Islamic Rebirth Party. The agreement called for a National Reconciliation Council that would be a forum to negotiate the terms of a permanent peace. In the months that followed, the Rahmonov government negotiated with the United Tajikistan

Opposition to reintegrate the political and military organizations of the two sides. Scattered fighting continued into the spring of 1997, however.

According to a Russian report in May 1996, the Tajikistani army was lacking 40 percent of its nominal officer cadre, and only 40 percent of those in service, many of them callups from the reserves, had a military education. The Tajikistani force was evaluated as inferior to its opposition in training and armament. Instances of troop mutiny reinforced that opinion, paralleling the situation in Afghanistan during the 1980s. In both Tajikistan and Afghanistan, Russian troops operated in a highly unstable civil war atmosphere, and the opposing sides were deeply divided within themselves.

As the civil war continued, the Rahmonov regime took steps to avoid internal sources of opposition. Although the new constitution approved in November 1994 contained substantial guarantees of human rights (also staples of all the Soviet-era constitutions), prescribed legislative and review functions for the legislature, and mandated an independent judiciary, in fact the country's governance amounted to one-man rule based on declarations of emergency executive powers extended from 1993 and 1994. The result has been imprisonment, exile, and assassination of opposition political figures and some foreign observers. Rahmonov won a decisive victory in the presidential election of 1994, with opposition only from a second hard-line politician of similar background, in what was generally labeled a rigged outcome. The unicameral legislature offers decisive majority support for Rahmonov's programs, and the judiciary is fully under the control of the president, who has the power to dismiss any judge. The Gorno-Badakhshan Autonomous Province, which accounts for nearly 45 percent of the republic's territory, has disputed status and is a main stronghold of separatist opposition forces.

Tajikistan's foreign policy increasingly has sought the economic and military security of close relations with Russia. In Tajikistan, the Russian minority enjoys a more liberal set of privileges than it finds in any other Central Asian republic. For example, Russians are allowed dual citizenship and Russian remains an official language. In April 1996, Rahmonov appointed the Russian mayor of Dushanbe, Yuriy Ponosov, as first deputy prime minister, continuing the policy of granting high government positions to ethnic Russians. Despite favorable treatment of the Russian minority, Russians have fled

Tajikistan steadily since 1992. In early 1996, only about 80,000 of the 500,000 Russians identified in the 1989 Soviet census remained. Most have complained that Russian government authorities did not afford them adequate aid or security in Tajikistan, leaving them no choice but to leave.

## Turkmenistan

Turkmenistan was known for most of its history as a loosely defined geographic region of independent tribes. Now it is a landlocked, mostly desert nation of only about 3.8 million people (the smallest population of the Central Asian republics in the second-largest land mass). The country remains quite isolated on the eastern shore of the Caspian Sea, largely occupied by the Qizilqum (Kyzyl Kum) Desert. Traditional tribal relationships still are a fundamental base of society, and telecommunications service from the outside world has only begun to have an impact. Like the Kazaks and the Kyrgyz, the Turkmen peoples were nomadic herders until the second half of the nineteenth century, when the arrival of Russian settlers began to deprive them of the vast expanses needed for livestock.

Agriculture contributes about half of Turkmenistan's GDP, whereas industry accounts for only about one-fifth. However, irrigation is necessary for nearly all the republic's arable land. In the early 1990s, government subsidies protected consumers from the shock of leaving the insulated Soviet system. Nevertheless, the standard of living protected by those subsidies had been among the lowest in the Soviet Union, and it deteriorated further in the 1990s. Although the Niyazov regime launched ambitious privatization programs in 1992 and 1993—with energy, transportation, agriculture, and communications to remain under state control—only minor progress had been made toward the programs' goals by the mid-1990s. Progress also has been quite slow in the reform of commercial and banking legislation.

Turkmenistan played a vital role in the Soviet system as a natural gas supplier. In the post-Soviet period, Russia remained the republic's top trade partner, with Turkey moving into second place in the mid-1990s. A crucial rail link with Iran also was an important commercial improvement.

The single most important mineral resource is natural gas; Turkmenistan's reserves may be among the largest in the world, with estimates as high as 15 trillion cubic meters. Nearly all the republic has been identified as potentially productive, and important offshore reserves exist in the Caspian Sea. The second major resource is petroleum, of which Turkmenistan has an estimated 63 billion tons. However, the range of the republic's mineral resources is small: sulfur, mineral salts, and clays complete the list.

In the mid-1990s, Turkmenistan's economic policy continued to rely heavily on the West's demand for natural gas. But, for a nation isolated along the east coast of the Caspian Sea, gas sales depend strictly on pipeline movement. Existing lines, built to serve the Turkmenistan-Russia north-south axis, cannot fill this need. New lines moving from east to west have been planned, but all plans encounter strong geopolitical opposition from a regional power or from the United States. Until the pipeline problem is solved, Turkmenistan can sell gas only to the same customers it served in the Soviet era, who now are its impoverished fellow members of the CIS. Armenia and Ukraine, major CIS customers, have been chronically late in paying. In February 1996, Turkmenistan made a long-term agreement to sell as much as 15 billion cubic meters of gas per year to Turkey between 1998 and 2020. Turkey also received development rights for a field in Turkmenistan believed to contain 20 million tons of oil.

Many recent economic indicators can only be approximated because Turkmenistan has not issued precise statistics. The national currency, the manat (for value of the manat—see Glossary), was devalued in late 1995 from a ratio of 500 to US$1 to 2,100 to US$1; it has remained non-convertible. It is believed that inflation in 1995 exceeded 1,000 percent; the 1996 annual rate, 140 percent, still was the highest in Central Asia. Exports for 1995 were about US$1.9 billion and imports about US$1.5 billion in official estimates. However, Turkmenistan conducts much barter trade, and payment failures of gas customers further undermine the application of cash trade figures. For 1996 the Economist Intelligence Unit forecast a 5 percent reduction of GDP following a drop of 15 percent in 1995. It also forecast a reduction in inflation in 1996 to 800 percent and a further drop in the value of the manat to a rate of 3,000 to US$1.

The state still strongly dominates the national economy. Little private enterprise occurs without some form of government approval or support, and about 90 percent of the work force is in state enterprises. In 1996 plans called for modernization of tax and business laws, including joint-venture conditions for the oil and gas industries. Pending those developments, foreign investors face a mass of state bureaucracy.

Foreign investment has been small, and experts predict no short-term improvement, partly because of the republic's insufficient legal and bureaucratic infrastructure, and partly because the very small and impoverished population provides little market opportunity. (The official average monthly wage was US$7 in early 1996.) The European Bank for Reconstruction and Development (EBRD) and other international banks are funding a textile complex, and Ashgabat Airport will be modernized with a loan of US$31 million from the British Export Credit Agency. However, for 1996 total direct investment was only US$32 million, with another US$61 million in joint ventures and US$161 million in foreign loans.

Turkmenistan has pursued the most independent and pragmatic foreign policy of the five Central Asian republics. The overall goal has been to form advantageous regional relationships without becoming involved in regional conflicts such as the Tajikistani civil war. In December 1996, Turkmenistan passed legislation declaring permanent neutrality and prohibiting membership in any military or political-military alliance entailing responsibilities for collective action by its members.

President Niyazov has run the country's foreign policy personally; he has faced little pressure at home to orient policy in a particular direction. Thus, he has been able to form ties with diverse foreign nations, maintaining economic advancement as the primary goal. Through the mid-1990s, Iran has been the top regional partner, although national security relations with Russia also have been a high priority during that period. In 1995 Turkmenistan signed a series of bilateral agreements with Russia, expanding economic and political cooperation and proclaiming the two nations "strategic partners" through 2000.

Turkmenistan has explicitly avoided multilateral arrangements, most of them sponsored by Uzbekistan, with the other Central Asian republics. It refused membership in the Central Asian customs union established by Kazakstan, Kyrgyzstan, and Uzbekistan in 1994, and in the Central Asian Economic Union that sprang from the initial agreement. Turkmenistan also contributed nothing to the CIS peacekeeping force sent to Tajikistan by those three nations and Russia in 1993. Substantial tension has arisen with Uzbekistan over water consumption, competition on the world cotton market, the Uzbek minority population's potential for unrest, and resentment of Uzbekistan's ambitions for regional leadership. By the end of 1995, tensions with Uzbekistan were so high that Turkmenistan boycotted all regional meetings. However, in January 1996 a meeting of the two nations' presidents produced a package of economic cooperation agreements, and new agreements on road and railroad transportation were discussed in the first half of 1996.

## Uzbekistan

Uzbekistan is the third-largest of the Central Asian republics in area and the first in population (estimated at 23 million in 1994 and growing at the fastest rate in Central Asia). Uzbekistan is completely landlocked between Kazakstan to the north, Turkmenistan to the south, and Kyrgyzstan and Tajikistan to the east. It shares the Aral Sea, and hence the environmental problems of that area, with Kazakstan. The territory of modern Uzbekistan was at the center of the rich cultural and commercial developments that occurred in Central Asia over a period of two millennia, especially along the axis defined by the Silk Route between Europe and China. Included in Uzbekistan are the three chief Silk Route outposts of Bukhoro (Bukhara), Khiva, and Samarqand (Samarkand).

Besides the agricultural base that yields cotton, vegetables, and grain, Uzbekistan's economy is blessed with gold, several other valuable minerals, and substantial reserves of energy resources, especially natural gas. In the mid-1990s, the economy still is based primarily on agriculture, following substantial increases in irrigation-dependent output in the 1970s and 1980s. Cotton remains the most valuable crop, and Uzbekistan is the fourth-largest cotton producer in the world.

Uzbekistan has suffered from high inflation, mainly because the state has continued Soviet-era social protection programs, bank credits for unprofitable enterprises, budget deficits, and price supports that require expanding the supply of money. As inflation has redistributed wealth, many Uzbekistanis have suffered substantial losses of real income. By 1994 annual inflation reached 1,300 percent, but government restrictions in 1995 lowered the year-end figure to 77 percent.

Throughout the post-Soviet period, a primary goal of Uzbekistan's economic reform policy has been to avoid the disruptions associated with rapid transition. While proclaiming the eventual goal of a market economy, economic planners have moved very slowly in privatization and in the creation of a

Western-style financial sector that would offer economic incentives and encourage private entrepreneurial initiative. This strategy has succeeded in reducing the transition shocks experienced by other post-Soviet societies. Since independence, Uzbekistan's GDP has fallen about 20 percent, compared with the Central Asian average of 50 percent. Part of that moderation results from Uzbekistan's initially more favorable situation in 1992. Because the cotton monoculture gave Uzbekistan a commodity with sales value worldwide (in 1995 some 75 percent of cotton exports went outside the CIS) and because Uzbekistan was less dependent on foreign trade and imported energy supplies than the other Central Asian countries, the end of the Soviet Union imposed fewer economic hardships. The 1995 cotton crop, expected to set a record, was significantly below forecast levels, however. Meanwhile, in 1996 the republics of the region continued nominal efforts to improve the Aral Sea environmental disaster, amid significant doubts that Uzbekistan would sacrifice cotton irrigation water from Aral tributaries to achieve that goal.

In late 1995, the IMF lent the regime US$260 million for economic reform, the first money accepted by Karimov from the IMF. In its evaluation at that time, the IMF noted that Uzbekistan's structural reform had been slow, notably in the banking sector, but that its tight monetary policy had slowed the economy's previous runaway inflation and liberalization of foreign exchange had been effective. Inflation for 1995 was 77 percent; the IMF year-end inflation target for 1996 was 21 to 25 percent; the exchange rate of the Uzbekistani som (for value of the som—see Glossary) fell from thirty to the United States dollar in 1995 to thirty-five to the dollar in 1996. The Economist Intelligence Unit forecast a 1996 drop in GDP of 1 percent, followed by growth of 1 percent in 1997. The projected budget deficit for 1996 was 3.5 percent of GDP, which conforms with IMF loan guidelines. An IMF credit of US$124 million was granted in December 1995.

Uzbekistan's economy is one of the most stable in the Central Asian region, and foreign investment activity there has been the highest in the region. In December 1995, the United States Overseas Private Investment Corporation agreed to provide US$500 million to convert the Soviet-era military industry, and United States oil companies committed US$1.3 billion of long-term investments in the oil and gas industry. Uzbekistan is the regional distribution center for electronic and domestic appliances from Dubai, based on a favorable tariff system that places no tax on most imports (a 15 percent tariff was levied on electronics in 1996). A large Daewoo (South Korean) television and videocassette plant in Tashkent is the most visible foreign electronics enterprise. The British Massey-Ferguson firm plans an agricultural machinery plant at some future date, and the British Quickstop supermarket chain opened outlets in Tashkent in 1996. Although some improvement has been made in Uzbekistan's tax and legal system, the dominance of the state bureaucracy continues to complicate foreign investment.

In 1996 the Karimov regime became noticeably less cautious in its approach to economic reform. Karimov criticized some bureaucrats for hindering execution of reform decrees, and the president began advocating private enterprise as the surest path to individual and national prosperity.

Overall foreign trade goals still include expanded commercial agreements with East Asia and the West, but by 1996 Uzbekistan had expressed willingness to join a customs union with Belarus, Kazakstan, and Russia, which already had reached a series of commercial accommodations early in 1996. Self-sufficiency in oil, gained for the first time in 1996, has freed Uzbekistan from dependence on Russia in a key area.

Uzbekistan's position as the only Central Asian state bordering all the other four has combined with other advantages (the largest population in the region and significant natural resources) to advance its claim as the leader and potential unifying force of the Central Asians. That putative role also has gained Uzbekistan considerable distrust among the other four republics, each of which has a significant Uzbek minority population and each of which has felt the impact of Uzbekistan's drive for supremacy in different ways. In 1992 Uzbekistani troops—the best-equipped in Central Asia—were instrumental in the triumph of Imomali Rahmonov's communist forces in Tajikistan, and since that time Uzbekistan has participated in the CIS force attempting to keep the peace in that country. In tandem with its drive for Western economic ties and privatization, in 1996 Uzbekistan intensified its promotion of regional economic and security agreements. Partly as a counterweight to Russia's influence in the region, Uzbekistan has encouraged broader activities by the Central Asian Economic Union, which it shares with Kazakstan and Kyrgyzstan. In 1996 the most notable departure from dependency on Russia was establishment of the Central Asian peacekeeping battalion, which held an initial exercise in the United States under the auspices of the NATO Partnership for Peace program. In January 1997, the economic union's members signed a treaty of "eternal friendship" that included mutual security guarantees.

The armed forces, which had inherited a substantial infrastructure from the Soviet period, were the best-equipped force in the region by 1996, after developing steadily in the interim years. In 1996, Uzbekistan's armed forces numbered 30,000 persons, including 25,000 ground and 4,000 air force troops. At that time, the government announced that ethnic Uzbeks constituted 80 percent of the country's armed forces, compared with 6 percent in the former Soviet force of 1992.

After independence, much of Uzbekistan's political structure remained essentially unchanged. Although some impetus had existed toward more democratic governance prior to independence, Karimov set the tone for political activity by winning a rigged presidential election in 1991. The new constitution approved in December 1992 prescribed a secular, multiparty democracy with full observance of human rights. However, the trial and harassment of opposition political figures and the restriction of the media began immediately; international protests in the next few years achieved scant results. Only two parties, Karimov's and a token opposition group, were permitted to participate in the parliamentary election of 1994. In March 1995, a rigged referendum extended the presidency of Karimov until 2000. Shortly thereafter, Karimov sentenced seven leaders of the political opposition to prison terms. Although the stable atmosphere fostered by Karimov's regime had tended to soften international criticism, Uzbekistan's human rights record still left much to be desired. In 1995 and 1996, however, a general improvement in government observation of human rights was noted; the government apparently has attempted to attract Western investors by responding to criticism of its handling of human rights cases. Two new political parties were formed and registered officially in mid-1995.

Uzbekistan's relations with Russia have been characterized by a combination of resentment and dependence, representing one of the few areas where the Karimov regime does not exercise full control. Although Karimov has strongly encouraged business activities by Western countries, especially Germany, he has been careful not to alienate Russia's commercial interests. In 1994 and 1995, Uzbekistan signed commercial treaties with a variety of CIS countries, but Russia always was the primary partner in such deals.

The issue of dual citizenship for the Russian minority in Uzbekistan, strongly pressed by Russia in the early 1990s, has caused serious irritation, as did Russia's unsuccessful pressure for Uzbekistan to remain in the ruble zone in 1993. Like the other Central Asian republics, Uzbekistan has suffered a rapid loss of its Russian technocrat population. Since independence, an estimated 500,000 Russians (out of the 1.65 million in 1989) have left, and the emigration of Germans, Jews, and Koreans further depleted the republic's base of technical know-how.

Just beyond the borders of Central Asia, Uzbekistan has established new relationships with Iran, Pakistan, and Turkey, based chiefly on economic exchanges. Stimulated by the economic stability of Uzbekistan, international lenders such as the EBRD and the IMF have offered fairly generous loans. The United States, conscious of human rights violations, has offered less generous assistance to Uzbekistan than to other Central Asian countries.

The republics of Central Asia emerged from the Soviet Union with a combination of assets and handicaps. Their geographic isolation has complicated establishment of commercial relationships, and even name recognition, in the West. The complete lack of democratic tradition has kept the republics from complying with Western legal and commercial standards, and the expression of political dissent has been erratic and sometimes costly to dissenters. Serious deterioration of the Soviet-era education systems in all five countries threatens to diminish the capabilities of the next generation to contribute to the national economies at a time when those economies may be ready to flourish. At the same time, ample natural resources hold out the prospect that at least the republics most blessed in this way—Kazakstan, Turkmenistan, and Uzbekistan—may ultimately enrich their economies and hence the standard of living of their people. The prospect of full regional cooperation remains only theoretical, in spite of numerous bilateral and trilateral agreements. And relations with Russia, traditionally the dominant outside force in Central Asia's geopolitical situation, remain close and vital, although fraught with misgivings. In early 1997, the future of the region remained nearly as unclear as it was in 1991, the year of independence.

March 31, 1997                                             Glenn E. Curtis

# Chapter 1. Kazakstan

*Kazak belt buckle depicting snow leopard on a mountain*

## Country

**Formal Name:** Republic of Kazakstan.

**Short Form:** Kazakstan.

**Term for Citizens:** Kazakstani(s).

**Capital:** Almaty, scheduled to move to Aqmola 1998.

**Date of Independence:** December 16, 1991.

## Geography

**Size:** Approximately 2,717,300 square kilometers.

**Topography:** Substantial variation according to region; Altay and Tian Shan ranges in east and northeast, about 12 percent of territory, reach elevation of nearly 7,000 meters; more than three-quarters of territory desert or semidesert, with elevations below sea level along Caspian Sea coast in far west.

**Climate:** Continental and very dry except in eastern mountains, where snowfall heavy; wide temperature variation between winter and summer.

## Society

**Population:** By 1994 estimate, 17,268,000; annual growth rate 1.1 percent in 1994; population density 6.2 persons per square kilometer in 1994.

**Ethnic Groups:** In 1994, Kazaks 45 percent, Russians 36 percent, Ukrainians 5 percent, Germans 4 percent, Tatars and Uzbeks 2 percent each.

**Languages:** Official state language a contentious issue; 1995 constitution stipulates Kazak and Russian as state languages. Russian primary language in business, science, and academia. Non-Kazak population exerts pressure against requirements for use of Kazak.

**Religion:** In 1994, some 47 percent Muslim (Sunni branch), 44 percent Russian Orthodox, 2 percent Protestant (mainly Baptist), with smaller numbers of Roman Catholic, Pentecostal, and Jewish believers.

**Education and Literacy:** Literacy in 1989 was 97.5 percent. Education, fully supported by state funds, hampered by shortage of facilities and materials and low pay for teachers; major program to restructure Soviet system in progress mid-1990s; primary language of instruction Russian at all levels.

**Health:** Soviet-era free health system declined drastically in early 1990s, mainly because of low funding. Drugs and materials in short supply, doctors underpaid and leaving medicine, child health care especially poor. Infant mortality and contagious diseases rising, mid-1990s.

## Economy

**Gross National Product (GNP):** Estimated 1993 at US$26.5 billion, or US$1,530 per capita. In 1994 estimated growth rate –25.4 percent. In early 1990s, growth hindered by Soviet-era specialization and centralization, slow privatization.

**Agriculture:** Large-scale misallocation of land in Soviet Virgin Lands program, emphasizing cultivation over livestock, continues to distort land use. Main crops wheat, cotton, and rice; main livestock products meat and milk. State farms continue to dominate, 1996; land privatization minimal.

**Industry and Mining:** Outmoded heavy industry infrastructure inherited from Soviet era, specializing in chemicals, machinery, oil refining, and metallurgy; coal, iron ore, manganese, phosphates, and various other minerals mined. Some light industry. Industrial productivity hampered by lost markets and enterprise debt.

**Energy:** Plentiful reserves of oil, coal, and natural gas make energy production dominant industrial sector. Offshore Caspian Sea fields, in early production stages, have huge capacity; extraction expanding with Western investment and new pipeline project. Natural gas fields, notably Karachaganak, will expand output in later 1990s. Thermoelectric power plants, main source of power, fueled by lignite mines. Kazakstan remains net importer of energy and fuel, 1995.

**Exports:** Mainly raw materials: metals, oil and petroleum products, chemicals, worth US$3.08 billion in 1994; share of bartered goods, substantial in early 1990s, smaller in 1995 and mainly with Commonwealth of Independent States (CIS) partners. Cash sales to CIS partners increased substantially in 1995, partially replacing barter. Export structure shifting steadily to non-CIS partners, mid-1990s, as Western oil sales increase; non-CIS expansion needed to balance imports for industrial restructuring.

**Imports:** In 1994, worth US$3.49 billion, mainly energy products, machinery, vehicles, chemicals, and food. Industrial machinery and technology imports will increase, energy products decrease, in late 1990s. Trade deficits with both CIS and non-CIS groups, 1994. Main trading partners Russia, Ukraine, Germany, Netherlands, Switzerland, Czech Republic, Italy, and China.

**Balance of Payments:** In 1994, deficit of US$2.5 billion.

**Exchange Rate:** Tenge introduced November 1993 when Kazakstan left ruble zone. Exchange rate sixty-four to US$1, January 1996.

**Inflation:** Hyperinflation, 1993 and 1994, brought under better control with tightened loan policy; estimated 1995 annual rate 190 percent.

**Fiscal Year:** Calendar year.

**Fiscal Policy:** Centralized system; fundamental streamlining of tax code, 1995, emphasizing taxation of individuals over taxation of enterprises. Targeted 1995 budget shortfall 3.5 percent of gross domestic product (GDP).

## Transportation and Telecommunications

**Highways:** In 1994, about 189,000 kilometers of roads, of which 108,000 kilometers gravel or paved. Road transport declining element of economic infrastructure; maintenance and truck fleet inadequate to expand service.

**Railroads:** Three railroad companies provide about 90 percent of national freight haulage, but infrastructure and equipment supply unreliable. In 1993, system had 14,148 kilometers of track, of which 3,050 kilometers electrified, concentrated in north, mainly connecting with Russian system.

**Civil Aviation:** Kazakstan Airlines and six private companies use twenty airports, one of which (Almaty) has international connections. Regular flights to some major cities in CIS countries, Western Europe, Asia, and Middle East.

**Inland Waterways:** Two rivers, Syrdariya and Ertis, total 4,000 kilometers of navigable water; nineteen river transport companies, under state control. In 1992, 1.6 million passengers, 7 million tons of freight moved.

**Ports:** On Caspian Sea, Aqtau, Atyrau, and Fort Shevchenko, with limited commercial value.

**Pipelines:** In 1992, some 3,480 kilometers for natural gas, 2,850 kilometers for crude oil, and 1,500 kilometers for refined products. Systems mainly connected with Russian lines to north; new lines in planning stage, 1996, with Western aid, to connect with Europe and other international destinations.

**Telecommunications:** Limited service, inadequate to planned economic expansion. In 1994, seventeen of 100 urban citizens had telephones, heavily concentrated in Almaty. Most equipment outmoded, overburdened. All international connections through Moscow. Radio and television broadcasting government controlled; satellite television broadcasts from other countries; sixty-one domestic radio stations, one domestic television network, 1996.

## Government and Politics

**Government:** Strong presidential system, prescribed in 1993 constitution and reinforced by dismissal of parliament and beginning of direct presidential rule by Nursultan Nazarbayev, 1995. Presidential election delayed by referendum until 2000. New constitution, approved in August 1995 referendum, mandates bicameral parliament and increases presidential power. Parliamentary election for both houses held December 1995. Nineteen provinces and city of Almaty run by executives appointed by national president.

**Politics:** Close government control of legal political parties has not prevented numerous groups from forming. Participation in 1994 and 1995 parliamentary elections limited to approved parties, but 1994 parliament strongly opposed many of

Nazarbayev's programs. Election of 1994 declared invalid, and parliament dissolved in early 1995. Nazarbayev's People's Unity Party retained plurality in 1995 elections. Several Kazak and Russian nationalist parties with small representation in government.

**Foreign Policy:** Post-Soviet broad search for international support, role as bridge between East and West, under personal direction of President Nazarbayev. Critical balance of Russian and Chinese influence, careful reserve toward Muslim world outside Central Asia; proposal of Euro-Asian Union to replace CIS, 1994. Active diplomatic role in CIS crises (Nagorno-Karabakh, Tajikistan).

**International Agreements and Memberships:** Member of United Nations (UN), North Atlantic Treaty Organization (NATO) Partnership for Peace, Organization for Security and Cooperation in Europe (OSCE), Economic Cooperation Organization (ECO), Asian Bank, International Monetary Fund (IMF), World Bank, CIS, International Criminal Police Organization (Interpol).

## National Security

**Armed Forces:** Planned strength 80,000 to 90,000; 1996 army strength about 25,000, air force about 15,000, border troops 5,000 to 6,000, naval force in planning stage.

**Major Military Units:** Army has two motorized rifle divisions, one tank division, one artillery regiment. National Guard operates 25 percent of boats in Caspian Sea Flotilla. Air force has one heavy bomber regiment; one division with three fighter-bomber regiments; and single, independent reconnaissance, fighter, and helicopter regiments.

**Military Budget:** In 1995, estimated at US$297 million.

**Internal Security:** System largely unchanged from Soviet period. National Security Committee, successor to Committee for State Security (KGB), performs intelligence and counter-intelligence operations. Ministry of Justice runs police (militia) and prison systems.

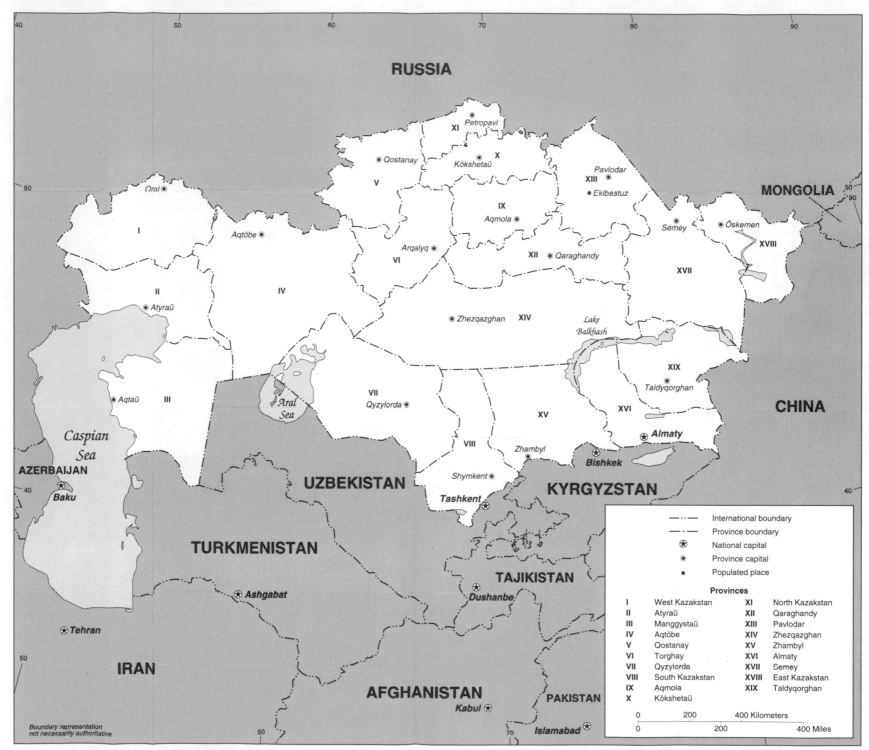

*Figure 4. Kazakstan: Administrative Divisions, 1996*

| | Provinces | | |
|---|---|---|---|
| I | West Kazakstan | XI | North Kazakstan |
| II | Atyraū | XII | Qaraghandy |
| III | Manggystaū | XIII | Pavlodar |
| IV | Aqtöbe | XIV | Zhezqazghan |
| V | Qostanay | XV | Zhambyl |
| VI | Torghay | XVI | Almaty |
| VII | Qyzylorda | XVII | Semey |
| VIII | South Kazakstan | XVIII | East Kazakstan |
| IX | Aqmola | XIX | Taldyqorghan |
| X | Kökshetaū | | |

International boundary
Province boundary
National capital
Province capital
Populated place

BY FAR THE LARGEST of the Central Asian republics of the former Soviet Union, independent Kazakstan is the world's ninth-largest nation in geographic area. The population density of Kazakstan is among the lowest in the world, partly because the country includes large areas of inhospitable terrain. Kazakstan is located deep within the Asian continent, with coastline only on the landlocked Caspian Sea. The proximity of unstable countries such as Afghanistan, Tajikistan, and Azerbaijan to the west and south further isolates Kazakstan (see fig. 4).

Within the centrally controlled structure of the Soviet system, Kazakstan played a vital industrial and agricultural role; the vast coal deposits discovered in Kazakstani territory in the twentieth century promised to replace the depleted fuel reserves in the European territories of the union. The vast distances between the European industrial centers and coal fields in Kazakstan presented a formidable problem that was only partially solved by Soviet efforts to industrialize Central Asia. That endeavor left the newly independent Republic of Kazakstan a mixed legacy: a population that includes nearly as many Russians as Kazaks; the presence of a dominating class of Russian technocrats, who are necessary to economic progress but ethnically unassimilated; and a well-developed energy industry, based mainly on coal and oil, whose efficiency is inhibited by major infrastructural deficiencies.

Kazakstan has followed the same general political pattern as the other four Central Asian states. After declaring independence from the Soviet political structure completely dominated by Moscow and the Communist Party of the Soviet Union (CPSU) until 1991, Kazakstan retained the basic governmental structure and, in fact, most of the same leadership that had occupied the top levels of power in 1990. Nursultan Nazarbayev, first secretary of the Communist Party of Kazakstan (CPK) beginning in 1989, was elected president of the republic in 1991 and remained in undisputed power five years later. Nazarbayev took several effective steps to ensure his position. The constitution of 1993 made the prime minister and the Council of Ministers responsible solely to the president, and in 1995 a new constitution reinforced that relationship. Furthermore, opposition parties were severely limited by legal restrictions on their activities. Within that rigid framework, Nazarbayev gained substantial popularity by limiting the economic shock of separation from the security of the Soviet Union and by maintaining ethnic harmony, despite some discontent among Kazak nationalists and the huge Russian minority.

In the mid-1990s, Russia remained the most important sponsor of Kazakstan in economic and national security matters, but in such matters Nazarbayev also backed the strengthening of the multinational structures of the Commonwealth of Independent States (CIS—see Glossary), the loose confederation that succeeded the Soviet Union. As sensitive ethnic, national security, and economic issues cooled relations with Russia in the 1990s, Nazarbayev cultivated relations with China, the other Central Asian nations, and the West. Nevertheless, Kazakstan remains principally dependent on Russia.

Kazakstan entered the 1990s with vast natural resources, an underdeveloped industrial infrastructure, a stable but rigid political structure, a small and ethnically divided population, and a commercially disadvantageous geographic position. In the mid-1990s, the balance of those qualities remained quite uncertain.

## Historical Setting

Until the arrival of Russians in the eighteenth century, the history of Kazakstan was determined by the movements, conflicts, and alliances of Turkic and Mongol tribes. The nomadic tribal society of what came to be the Kazak people then suffered increasingly frequent incursions by the Russian Empire, ultimately being included in that empire and the Soviet Union that followed it.

### Early Tribal Movements

Humans have inhabited present-day Kazakstan since the earliest Stone Age, generally pursuing the nomadic pastoralism for which the region's climate and terrain are best suited. The earliest well-documented state in the region was the Turkic Kaganate, which came into existence in the sixth century A.D. The Qarluqs, a confederation of Turkic tribes, established a state in what is now eastern Kazakstan in 766. In the eighth and ninth centuries, portions of southern Kazakstan were conquered by Arabs, who also introduced Islam. The Oghuz Turks controlled western Kazakstan from the ninth through the eleventh centuries; the Kimak and Kipchak peoples, also of Turkic origin, controlled the east at roughly the same time. The large central desert of Kazakstan is still called Dashti-Kipchak, or the Kipchak Steppe.

In the late ninth century, the Qarluq state was destroyed by invaders who established the large Qarakhanid state, which occupied a region known as Transoxania, the area north and east of the Oxus River (the present-day Syrdariya), extending into what is now China. Beginning in the early eleventh century, the Qarakhanids fought constantly among themselves and with the Seljuk Turks to the south. In the course of these conflicts, parts of present-day Kazakstan shifted back and forth between the combatants. The Qarakhanids, who accepted Islam and the authority of the Arab Abbasid caliphs of Baghdad during their dominant period, were conquered in the 1130s by the Karakitai, a Turkic confederation from northern China. In the mid-twelfth century, an independent state of Khorazm (also seen as Khorezm or Khwarazm) along the Oxus River broke away from the weakening Karakitai, but the bulk of the Karakitai state lasted until the invasion of Chinggis (Genghis) Khan in 1219–21.

After the Mongol capture of the Karakitai state, Kazakstan fell under the control of a succession of rulers of the Mongolian Golden Horde, the western branch of the Mongol Empire. (The horde, or *zhuz*, is the precursor of the present-day clan, which is still an important element of Kazak society—see Population and Society, this ch.) By the early fifteenth century, the ruling structure had split into several large groups known as khanates, including the Nogai Horde and the Uzbek Khanate.

## Forming the Modern Nation

The present-day Kazaks became a recognizable group in the mid-fifteenth century, when clan leaders broke away from Abul Khayr, leader of the Uzbeks, to seek their own territory in the lands of Semirech'ye, between the Chu and Talas rivers in present-day southeastern Kazakstan. The first Kazak leader was Khan Kasym (r. 1511–23), who united the Kazak tribes into one people. In the sixteenth century, when the Nogai Horde and Siberian khanates broke up, clans from each jurisdiction joined the Kazaks. The Kazaks subsequently separated into three new hordes: the Great Horde, which controlled Semirech'ye and southern Kazakstan; the Middle Horde, which

13

occupied north-central Kazakstan; and the Lesser Horde, which occupied western Kazakstan.

Russian traders and soldiers began to appear on the north-western edge of Kazak territory in the seventeenth century, when Cossacks established the forts that later became the cities of Oral (Ural'sk) and Atyrau (Gur'yev). Russians were able to seize Kazak territory because the khanates were preoccupied by Kalmyk invaders of Mongol origin, who in the late sixteenth century had begun to move into Kazak territory from the east. Forced westward in what they call their Great Retreat, the Kazaks were increasingly caught between the Kalmyks and the Russians. In 1730 Abul Khayr, one of the khans of the Lesser Horde, sought Russian assistance. Although Abul Khayr's intent had been to form a temporary alliance against the stronger Kalmyks, the Russians gained permanent control of the Lesser Horde as a result of his decision. The Russians conquered the Middle Horde by 1798, but the Great Horde managed to remain independent until the 1820s, when the expanding Quqon (Kokand) Khanate to the south forced the Great Horde khans to choose Russian protection, which seemed to them the lesser of two evils.

The Kazaks began to resist Russian control almost as soon as it became complete. The first mass uprising was led by Khan Kene (Kenisary Kasimov) of the Middle Horde, whose followers fought the Russians between 1836 and 1847. Khan Kene is now considered a Kazak national hero.

### Russian Control

In 1863 Russia elaborated a new imperial policy, announced in the Gorchakov Circular, asserting the right to annex "troublesome" areas on the empire's borders. This policy led immediately to the Russian conquest of the rest of Central Asia and the creation of two administrative districts, the Guberniya (Governorate General) of Turkestan and the Steppe District. Most of present-day Kazakstan was in the Steppe District, and parts of present-day southern Kazakstan were in the Governorate General.

In the early nineteenth century, the construction of Russian forts began to have a destructive effect on the Kazak traditional economy by limiting the once-vast territory over which the nomadic tribes could drive their herds and flocks. The final disruption of nomadism began in the 1890s, when many Russian settlers were introduced into the fertile lands of northern and eastern Kazakstan. Between 1906 and 1912, more than a half-million Russian farms were started as part of the reforms of Russian minister of the interior Petr Stolypin, shattering what remained of the traditional Kazak way of life.

Starving and displaced, many Kazaks joined in the general Central Asian resistance to conscription into the Russian imperial army, which the tsar ordered in July 1916 as part of the effort against Germany in World War I. In late 1916, Russian forces brutally suppressed the widespread armed resistance to the taking of land and conscription of Central Asians. Thousands of Kazaks were killed, and thousands of others fled to China and Mongolia.

## In the Soviet Union

In 1917 a group of secular nationalists called the Alash Orda (Horde of Alash), named for a legendary founder of the Kazak people, attempted to set up an independent national government. This state lasted less than two years (1918–20) before surrendering to the Bolshevik authorities, who then sought to preserve Russian control under a new political system. The Kyrgyz Autonomous Soviet Socialist Republic was set up in 1920 and was renamed the Kazak Autonomous Soviet Socialist Republic in 1925 when the Kazaks were differentiated officially from the Kyrgyz. (The Russian Empire recognized the ethnic difference between the two groups; it called them both "Kyrgyz" to avoid confusion between the terms "Kazak" and "Cossack.")

In 1925 the autonomous republic's original capital, Orenburg, was reincorporated into Russian territory. Almaty (called Alma-Ata during the Soviet period), a provincial city in the far southeast, became the new capital. In 1936 the territory was made a full Soviet republic. From 1929 to 1934, during the period when Soviet leader Joseph V. Stalin was trying to collectivize agriculture, Kazakstan endured repeated famines because peasants had slaughtered their livestock in protest against Soviet agricultural policy. In that period, at least 1.5 million Kazaks and 80 percent of the republic's livestock died. Thousands more Kazaks tried to escape to China, although most starved in the attempt.

Many European Soviet citizens and much of Russia's industry were relocated to Kazakstan during World War II, when Nazi armies threatened to capture all the European industrial centers of the Soviet Union. Groups of Crimean Tatars, Germans, and Muslims from the North Caucasus region were deported to Kazakstan during the war because it was feared that they would collaborate with the enemy. Many more non-Kazaks arrived in the years 1953–65, during the so-called Virgin Lands campaign of Soviet premier Nikita S. Khrushchev (in office 1956–64). Under that program, huge tracts of Kazak grazing land were put to the plow for the cultivation of wheat and other cereal grains. Still more settlers came in the late 1960s and 1970s, when the government paid handsome bonuses to workers participating in a program to relocate Soviet industry close to the extensive coal, gas, and oil deposits of Central Asia. One consequence of the decimation of the nomadic Kazak population and the in-migration of non-Kazaks was that by the 1970s Kazakstan was the only Soviet republic in which the eponymous nationality was a minority in its own republic (see Ethnic Groups, this ch.).

## Reform and Nationalist Conflict

The 1980s brought glimmers of political independence, as well as conflict, as the central government's hold progressively weakened. In this period, Kazakstan was ruled by a succession of three Communist Party officials; the third of those men, Nursultan Nazarbayev, continued as president of the Republic of Kazakstan when independence was proclaimed in 1991.

In December 1986, Soviet premier Mikhail S. Gorbachev (in office 1985–91) forced the resignation of Dinmukhamed Kunayev, an ethnic Kazak who had led the republic as first secretary of the CPK from 1959 to 1962, and again starting in 1964. During 1985, Kunayev had been under official attack for cronyism, mismanagement, and malfeasance; thus, his departure was not a surprise. However, his replacement, Gennadiy Kolbin, an ethnic Russian with no previous ties to Kazakstan, was unexpected. Kolbin was a typical administrator of the early Gorbachev era—enthusiastic about economic and administrative reforms but hardly mindful of their consequences or viability.

The announcement of Kolbin's appointment provoked spontaneous street demonstrations by Kazaks, to which Soviet authorities responded with force. Demonstrators, many of them students, rioted. Two days of disorder followed, and at least 200 people died or were summarily executed soon after. Some accounts estimate casualties at more than 1,000.

Kunayev had been ousted largely because the economy was failing. Although Kazakstan had the third-largest gross domestic product (GDP—see Glossary) in the Soviet Union, trailing only Russia and Ukraine, by 1987 labor productivity had decreased 12 percent, and per capita income had fallen by 24 percent of the national norm. By that time, Kazakstan was underproducing steel at an annual rate of more than a million tons. Agricultural output also was dropping precipitously.

While Kolbin was promoting a series of unrealistic, Moscow-directed campaigns of social reform, expressions of Kazak nationalism were prompting Gorbachev to address some of the non-Russians' complaints about cultural self-determination. One consequence was a new tolerance of bilingualism in the non-Russian regions. Kolbin made a strong commitment to promoting the local language and in 1987 suggested that Kazak become the republic's official language. However, none of his initiatives went beyond empty public-relations ploys. In fact, the campaign in favor of bilingualism was transformed into a campaign to improve the teaching of Russian.

While attempting to conciliate the Kazak population with promises, Kolbin also conducted a wholesale purge of pro-Kunayev members of the CPK, replacing hundreds of republic-level and local officials. Although officially "nationality-blind," Kolbin's policies seemed to be directed mostly against Kazaks. The downfall of Kolbin, however, was the continued deterioration of the republic's economy during his tenure. Agricultural output had fallen so low by 1989 that Kolbin proposed to fulfill meat quotas by slaughtering the millions of wild ducks that migrate through Kazakstan. The republic's industrial sector had begun to recover slightly in 1989, but credit for this progress was given largely to Nursultan Nazarbayev, an ethnic Kazak who had become chairman of Kazakstan's Council of Ministers in 1984.

As nationalist protests became more violent across the Soviet Union in 1989, Gorbachev began calling for the creation of popularly elected legislatures and for the loosening of central political controls to make such elections possible. These measures made it increasingly plain in Kazakstan that Kolbin and his associates soon would be replaced by a new generation of Kazak leaders.

Rather than reinvigorate the Soviet people to meet national tasks, Gorbachev's encouragement of voluntary local organizations only stimulated the formation of informal political groups, many of which had overtly nationalist agendas. For the Kazaks, such agendas were presented forcefully on national television at the first Congress of People's Deputies, which was convened in Moscow in June 1989. By that time, Kolbin was already scheduled for rotation back to Moscow, but his departure probably was hastened by riots in June 1989 in Novyy Uzen, an impoverished western Kazakstan town that produced natural gas. That rioting lasted nearly a week and claimed at least four lives.

## The Rise of Nazarbayev

In June 1989, Kolbin was replaced by Nazarbayev, a politician  trained as a metallurgist and engineer. Nazarbayev had become involved in party work in 1979, when he became a protégé of reform members of the CPSU. Having taken a major role in the attacks on Kunayev, Nazarbayev may have expected to replace him in 1986. When he was passed over, Nazarbayev submitted to Kolbin's authority and used his party position to support Gorbachev's new line, attributing economic stagnation in the Soviet republics to past subordination of local interests to the mandates of Moscow.

Soon proving himself a skilled negotiator, Nazarbayev bridged the gap between the republic's Kazaks and Russians at a time of increasing nationalism while also managing to remain personally loyal to the Gorbachev reform program. Nazarbayev's firm support of the major Gorbachev positions in turn helped him gain national and, after 1990, even international visibility. Many reports indicate that Gorbachev was planning to name Nazarbayev as his deputy in the new union planned to succeed the Soviet Union.

Even as he supported Gorbachev during the last two years of the Soviet Union, Nazarbayev fought Moscow to increase his republic's income from the resources it had long been supplying to the center. Although his appointment as party first secretary had originated in Moscow, Nazarbayev realized that for his administration to succeed under the new conditions of that time, he had to cultivate a popular mandate within the republic. This difficult task meant finding a way to make Kazakstan more Kazak without alienating the republic's large and economically significant Russian and European populations. Following the example of other Soviet republics, Nazarbayev sponsored legislation that made Kazak the official language and permitted examination of the negative role of collectivization and other Soviet policies on the republic's history. Nazarbayev also permitted a widened role for religion, which encouraged a resurgence of Islam. In late 1989, although he did not have the legal power to do so, Nazarbayev created an independent religious administration for Kazakstan, severing relations with the Muslim Board of Central Asia, the Soviet-approved oversight body in Tashkent.

In March 1990, elections were held for a new legislature in the republic's first multiple-candidate contests since 1925. The winners represented overwhelmingly the republic's existing elite, who were loyal to Nazarbayev and to the Communist Party apparatus. The legislature also was disproportionately ethnic Kazak: 54.2 percent to the Russians' 28.8 percent.

## Sovereignty and Independence

In June 1990, Moscow declared formally the sovereignty of the central government over Kazakstan, forcing Kazakstan to elaborate its own statement of sovereignty. This exchange greatly exacerbated tensions between the republic's two largest ethnic groups, who at that point were numerically about equal. Beginning in mid-August 1990, Kazak and Russian nationalists began to demonstrate frequently around Kazakstan's parliament building, attempting to influence the final statement of sovereignty being developed within. The statement was adopted in October 1990.

In keeping with practices in other republics at that time, the parliament had named Nazarbayev its chairman, and then, soon afterward, it had converted the chairmanship to the presidency of the republic. In contrast to the presidents of the other republics, especially those in the independence-minded Baltic states, Nazarbayev remained strongly committed to the perpetuation of the Soviet Union throughout the spring and summer of 1991. He took this position largely because he considered the republics too interdependent economically to survive separation. At the same time, however, Nazarbayev fought hard to secure republic control of Kazakstan's enormous mineral wealth and industrial potential. This objective  became particularly important after 1990, when it was learned that Gorbachev had negotiated an agreement with Chevron, a United States oil company, to develop Kazakstan's Tengiz oil fields. Gorbachev did not consult Nazarbayev until talks were nearly complete. At Nazarbayev's insistence, Moscow surrendered control of the republic's mineral resources in June 1991. Gorbachev's authority crumbled rapidly throughout 1991. Nazarbayev, however, continued to support him, persistently urging other republic leaders to sign the revised Union Treaty, which Gorbachev had put forward in a last attempt to hold the Soviet Union together.

Because of the coup attempted by Moscow hard-liners against the Gorbachev government in August 1991, the Union Treaty never was signed. Ambivalent about the removal of Gorbachev, Nazarbayev did not condemn the coup attempt until its second day. However, once the incompetence of the plotters became clear, Nazarbayev threw his weight solidly behind Gorbachev and continuation of some form of union, largely because of his conviction that independence would be economic suicide.

At the same time, however, Nazarbayev pragmatically began preparing his republic for much greater freedom, if not for actual independence. He appointed professional economists and managers to high posts, and he began to seek the advice of foreign development and business experts. The outlawing of the CPK, which followed the attempted coup, also permitted Nazarbayev to take virtually complete control of the republic's economy, more than 90 percent of which had been under the partial or complete direction of the central Soviet government until late 1991. Nazarbayev solidified his position by winning an uncontested election for president in December 1991.

A week after the election, Nazarbayev became the president of an independent state when the leaders of Russia, Ukraine, and Belarus signed documents dissolving the Soviet Union. Nazarbayev quickly convened a meeting of the leaders of the five Central Asian states, thus effectively raising the specter of a "Turkic" confederation of former republics as a counterweight to the "Slavic" states (Russia, Ukraine, and Belarus) in whatever federation might succeed the Soviet Union. This move persuaded the three Slavic presidents to include Kazakstan among the signatories to a recast document of dissolution. Thus, the capital of Kazakstan lent its name to the Alma-Ata Declaration, in which eleven of the fifteen Soviet republics announced the expansion of the thirteen-day-old CIS. On December 16, 1991, just five days before that declaration, Kazakstan had become the last of the republics to proclaim its independence.

## Physical Environment

With an area of about 2,717,300 square kilometers, Kazakstan is more than twice the combined size of the other four Central Asian states. The country borders Turkmenistan, Uzbekistan, and Kyrgyzstan to the south; Russia to the north; Russia and the Caspian Sea to the west; and China's Xinjiang Uygur Autonomous Region to the east.

## Topography and Drainage

There is considerable topographical variation within Kazakstan. The highest elevation, Khan Tengri Mountain, on the Kyrgyz border in the Tian Shan range, is 6,995 meters; the lowest point, at Karagiye, in the Caspian Depression in the west, is 132 meters below sea level (see fig. 2). Only 12.4 percent of Kazakstan is mountainous, with most of the mountains located in the Altay and Tian Shan ranges of the east and northeast, although the Ural Mountains extend southward from Russia into the northern part of west-central Kazakstan. Many of the peaks of the Altay and Tian Shan ranges are snow covered year-round, and their run-off is the source for most of Kazakstan's rivers and streams.

Except for the Tobol, Ishim, and Irtysh rivers (the Kazak names for which are, respectively, Tobyl, Esil, and Ertis), portions of which flow through Kazakstan, all of Kazakstan's rivers and streams are part of landlocked systems. They either flow into isolated bodies of water such as the Caspian Sea or simply disappear into the steppes and deserts of central and southern Kazakstan. Many rivers, streams, and lakes are seasonal, evaporating in summer. The three largest bodies of water are Lake Balkhash, a partially fresh, partially saline lake in the east, near Almaty, and the Caspian and Aral seas, both of which lie partially within Kazakstan.

Some 9.4 percent of Kazakstan's land is mixed prairie and forest or treeless prairie, primarily in the north or in the basin of the Ural River in the west. More than three-quarters of the country, including the entire west and most of the south, is either semidesert (33.2 percent) or desert (44 percent). The terrain in these regions is bare, eroded, broken uplands, with sand dunes in the Qizilqum (red sand; in the Russian form, Kyzylkum) and Moyunqum (in the Russian form, Moin Kum) deserts, which occupy south-central Kazakstan. Most of the country lies at between 200 and 300 meters above sea level, but Kazakstan's Caspian shore includes some of the lowest elevations on Earth.

## Climate

Because Kazakstan is so far from the oceans, the climate is sharply continental and very dry. Precipitation in the mountains of the east averages as much as 600 millimeters per year, mostly in the form of snow, but most of the republic receives only 100 to 200 millimeters per year. Precipitation totals less than 100 millimeters in the south-central regions around Qyzylorda. A lack of precipitation makes Kazakstan a sunny republic; the north averages 120 clear days a year, and the south averages 260. The lack of moderating bodies of water also means that temperatures can vary widely. Average winter temperatures are –3°C in the north and 18°C in the south; summer temperatures average 19°C in the north and 28°–30°C in the south. Within locations differences are extreme, and temperature can change very suddenly. The winter air temperature can fall to –50°C, and in summer the ground temperature can reach as high as 70°C.

## Environmental Problems

The environment of Kazakstan has been badly damaged by human activity. Most of the water in Kazakstan is polluted by industrial effluents, pesticide and fertilizer residue, and, in some places, radioactivity. The most visible damage has been to the Aral Sea, which as recently as the 1970s was larger than any of the Great Lakes of North America save Lake Superior. The sea began to shrink rapidly when sharply increased irrigation and other demands on the only significant tributaries, the Syrdariya and the Amu Darya (the latter reaching the Aral from neighboring Uzbekistan), all but eliminated inflow. By 1993 the Aral Sea had lost an estimated 60 percent of its volume, in the process breaking into three unconnected segments. Increasing salinity and reduced habitat have killed the Aral Sea's fish, hence destroying its once-active fishing industry, and the receding shoreline has left the former port of Aral'sk more than sixty kilometers from the water's edge. The depletion of this large body of water has increased temperature variations in the region, which in turn have had an impact on agriculture. A much greater agricultural impact, however, has come from the salt- and pesticide-laden soil that the wind is known to carry as far away as the Himalaya Mountains and the Pacific Ocean. Deposition of this heavily saline soil on nearby fields effectively sterilizes them. Evidence suggests that salts, pesticides, and residues of chemical fertilizers are also adversely affecting human life around the former Aral Sea; infant mortality in the region approaches 10 percent, compared with the 1991 national rate of 2.7 percent.

By contrast, the water level of the Caspian Sea has been rising steadily since 1978 for reasons that scientists have not been able to explain fully. At the northern end of the sea, more than a million hectares of land in Atyrau Province have been flooded. Experts estimate that if current rates of increase persist, the coastal city of Atyrau, eighty-eight other population centers, and many of Kazakstan's Caspian oil fields could be submerged by 2020.

Wind erosion has also had an impact in the northern and central parts of the republic because of the introduction of wide-scale dryland wheat farming. In the 1950s and 1960s, much soil was lost when vast tracts of Kazakstan's prairies were plowed under as part of Khrushchev's Virgin Lands agricultural project. By the mid-1990s, an estimated 60 percent of the republic's pastureland was in various stages of desertification.

Industrial pollution is a bigger concern in Kazakstan's manufacturing cities, where aging factories pump huge quantities of unfiltered pollutants into the air and groundwater. The capital, Almaty, is particularly threatened, in part because of the postindependence boom in private automobile ownership.

The gravest environmental threat to Kazakstan comes from radiation, especially in the Semey (Semipalatinsk) region of the northeast, where the Soviet Union tested almost 500 nuclear weapons, 116 of them above ground. Often, such tests were conducted without evacuating or even alerting the local population. Although nuclear testing was halted in 1990, radiation poisoning, birth defects, severe anemia, and leukemia are very common in the area (see Health Conditions, this ch.).

With some conspicuous exceptions, lip service has been the primary official response to Kazakstan's ecological problems. In February 1989, opposition to Soviet nuclear testing and its ill effects in Kazakstan led to the creation of one of the republic's largest and most influential grass-roots movements, Nevada-Semipalatinsk, which was founded by Kazak poet and public figure Olzhas Suleymenov. In the first week of the movement's existence, Nevada-Semipalatinsk gathered more than 2 million signatures from Kazakstanis of all ethnic groups on a petition to Gorbachev demanding the end of nuclear testing in Kazakstan. After a year of demonstrations and protests, the test ban took effect in 1990. It remained in force in 1996, although in 1995 at least one unexploded device reportedly was still in position near Semey.

Once its major ecological objective was achieved, Nevada-Semipalatinsk made various attempts to broaden into a more general political movement; it has not pursued a broad ecological or "green" agenda. A very small green party, Tagibat, made common cause with the political opposition in the parliament of 1994.

The government has established a Ministry of Ecology and Bioresources, with a separate administration for radioecology, but the ministry's programs are underfunded and given low priority. In 1994 only 23 percent of budgeted funds were actually allotted to environmental programs. Many official meetings and conferences are held (more than 300 have been devoted to the problem of the Aral Sea alone), but few practical programs have gone into operation. In 1994 the World Bank (see Glossary), the International Monetary Fund (IMF—see Glossary), and the United States Environmental Protection Agency agreed to give Kazakstan US$62 million to help the country overcome ecological problems.

## Population and Society

Total population was estimated in 1994 at 17,268,000, making Kazakstan the fourth most populous former Soviet republic. As of 1990, 57 percent of the country's residents lived in cities. Because much of the land is too dry to be more than marginally habitable, overall population density is a very low 6.2 persons per square kilometer. Large portions of the republic, especially in the south and west, have a population density of less than one person per square kilometer. In 1989 some 1.4 million Kazaks lived outside Kazakstan, nearly all in the Russian and Uzbek republics. At that time, an estimated 1 million Kazaks lived in China, and a sizeable but uncounted Kazak population resided in Mongolia.

### Demographic Factors

The birth rate, which is declining slowly, was estimated at 19.4 births per 1,000 population in 1994 (see table 2, Appendix). The death rate, which has been climbing slowly, was estimated at 7.9 per 1,000 population—leaving a rate of natural increase of 1.1 percent, by far the lowest among the five Cen-

*Panoramic view of the capital city, Almaty*
*Courtesy Lorraine Predham*
*The opera house in Almaty*
*Courtesy Stanley Bach*

tral Asian republics. In 1995 the total fertility rate—2.4 births per woman, a drop from the 1990 figure of 2.8—also was far below the rates for the other Central Asian republics. In the first six months of 1994, some 1.8 percent fewer babies were born than in the same period the previous year. In the same months, the number of deaths rose by 2.5 percent compared with those in the same period in 1993. In some provinces, death rates are much higher than the average, however. Shygys Qazaqstan (East Kazakstan) Province has a death rate of 12.9 per thousand; Soltustik Qazaqstan (North Kazakstan) Province, eleven per 1,000; and Almaty Province, 11.3 deaths per 1,000. The cause of nearly half of these deaths is cardiovascular disease.

Because of declining life expectancy and decreases in the size of the Russian population, which is demographically older and has a low birth rate, the republic's residents are a relatively young group; in 1991 there were only 149 pensioners per 1,000 population, as opposed to 212 per 1,000 in the former Soviet Union as a whole (see table 3, Appendix). The republic is experiencing a pronounced outflow of citizens, primarily non-Kazaks moving to other former Soviet republics. Although figures conflict, it seems likely that as many as 750,000 non-Kazaks left the republic between independence and the end of 1995. Official figures indicate that in the first half of 1994 some 220,400 people left, compared with 149,800 in the same period of 1993. In 1992 and 1993, the number of Russian emigrants was estimated at 100,000 to 300,000. Such out-migration is not uniform. Some regions, such as Qaraghandy, have lost as much as 10 percent of their total population, resulting in shortages of technicians and skilled specialists in that heavily industrial area.

To some extent, the outflow has been offset by in-migration, which has been of two types. Kazakstan's government has actively encouraged the return of Kazaks from elsewhere in the former Soviet Union and from China and Mongolia. Unlike other ethnic groups, ethnic Kazaks are granted automatic citizenship. More than 60,000 Kazaks emigrated from Mongolia in 1991–94, their settlement—or resettlement—eased by government assistance. Most were moved to the northern provinces, where the majority of Kazakstan's Russian population lives. Because these "Mongol Kazaks" generally do not know Russian and continue to pursue traditional nomadic lifestyles, the impact of their resettlement has been disproportionate to their actual numbers.

The other major source of in-migration has been non-Kazaks arriving from other parts of Central Asia to avoid inhospitable conditions; most of these people also have settled in northern Kazakstan. Although officially forbidden and actively discouraged, this in-migration has continued. In a further attempt to control in-migration, President Nazarbayev decreed that no more than 5,000 families would be permitted to take up residence in the republic in 1996.

## Ethnic Groups

Kazakstan is the only former Soviet republic where the indigenous ethnic group is not a majority of the population. In 1994 eight of the country's eleven provinces had Slavic (Russian and Ukrainian) population majorities. Only the three southernmost provinces were populated principally by Kazaks and other Turkic groups; the capital city, Almaty, had a European (German and Russian) majority. Overall, in 1994 the population was about 44 percent Kazak, 36 percent Russian, 5 percent Ukrainian, and 4 percent German. Tatars and Uzbeks each represented about 2 percent of the population; Azerbaijanis, Uygurs, and Belarusians each represented 1 percent; and the remaining 4 percent included approximately ninety other nationalities (see table 4, Appendix).

Kazakstan's ethnic composition is the driving force behind much of the country's political and cultural life. In most ways, the republic's two major ethnic groups, the Kazaks and the "Russian-speakers" (Russians, Ukrainians, Germans, and Belarusians), may as well live in different countries. To the Russians, most of whom live in northern Kazakstan within a day's drive of Russia proper, Kazakstan is an extension of the Siberian frontier and a product of Russian and Soviet development. To most Kazaks, these Russians are usurpers. Of Kazakstan's current Russian residents, 38 percent were born outside the republic, while most of the rest are second-generation Kazakstani citizens.

The Nazarbayev government has announced plans to move the capital from Almaty in the far southeast to Aqmola in the north-central region by 1998. That change would cause a shift of the Kazak population northward and accelerate the absorption of the Russian-dominated northern provinces into the Kazakstani state. Over the longer term, the role of Russians in the society of Kazakstan also is determined by a demographic factor—the average age of the Russian population is higher, and its birth rate much lower.

## The Role of Women

Like its 1993 predecessor, the constitution of 1995 defends women's rights implicitly, if not entirely explicitly. The document guarantees citizens the right to work and forbids discrimination based on geographic origin, gender, race, nationality, religious or political belief, and language.

In practice, social opinion tends to associate women in the workplace with the abuses of the Soviet past. The early 1990s saw the loss of more than 100,000 day-care spaces, and public opinion strongly favors returning primary responsibility for the rearing and educating of children to mothers. In April 1995, President Nazarbayev said that one of the republic's goals must be to create an economy in which a mother can work at home, raising her children. This general opinion has been reflected in governmental appointments and private enterprise; almost no women occupy senior positions in the country, either in government or in business.

The declining birth rate is another issue with the potential to become politicized because it affects the demographic "race" between Kazaks and Russians. With demographic statistics in mind, Kazak nationalist parties have attempted to ban abortions and birth control for Kazak women; they have also made efforts to reduce the number of Kazak women who have children outside marriage. In 1988, the last year for which there are figures, 11.24 percent of the births in the republic were to unmarried women. Such births were slightly more common in cities (12.72 percent) than in rural areas (9.67 percent), suggesting that such births may be more common among Russians than among Kazaks.

Women's health issues have not been addressed effectively in Kazakstan. Maternal mortality rates average 80 per 10,000 births for the entire country, but they are believed to be much higher in rural areas. Of the 4.2 million women of childbearing age, an estimated 15 percent have borne seven or more children. Nevertheless, in 1992 the number of abortions exceeded the number of births, although the high percentage of early-stage abortions performed in private clinics complicates data gathering. According to one expert estimate, the average per woman is five abortions. Rising abortion rates are attributable, at least in part, to the high price or unavailability of contraceptive devices, which became much less accessible after 1991. In 1992 an estimated 15 percent of women were using some form of contraception.

## Clans

One aspect of Kazak traditional culture, clan membership, is acquiring importance in the postindependence environment. Historically the Kazaks identified themselves as belonging to one of three groups of clans and tribes, called *zhuz*, or hordes, each of which had traditional territories. Because the Lesser Horde controlled western Kazakstan and the Middle Horde migrated across what today is northern and eastern Kazakstan, those groups came under Russian control first, when colonial policies were relatively benign. The traditional nobles of these hordes managed to retain many of their privileges and to educate their sons in Russian schools. These sons became the first Kazak nationalists, and in turn their sons were destroyed by Stalin, who tried to eradicate the Kazak intelligentsia during his purges of the 1930s.

The Large, or Great, Horde was dominant in the south, and hence did not fall under Russian control until colonialism was much harsher. Substantially fewer Great Horde Kazaks became involved in politics before the revolution, but those who did became socialists rather than nationalists. For that reason, the Great Horde members came to dominate once the Bolsheviks took power, especially after Kazakstan's capital was moved from the Lesser Horde town of Orenburg (now in Russia) to a Great Horde wintering spot, Almaty. Kunayev and Nazarbayev are said to have roots in clans of the Great Horde.

With the collapse of the CPK and its patronage networks, and in the absence of any other functional equivalent, clan and *zhuz* membership has come to play an increasingly important role in the economic and political life of the republic at both the national and the province level. The power of clan politics has been visible in the dispute over moving the national capital to Aqmola, which would bolster the prestige of the Middle Horde, on whose lands Aqmola is located. In general, members of the Lesser and Middle hordes are more Russified and, hence, more inclined to cooperate with Russian industrial and commercial interests than are the members of the Great Horde. Akezhan Kazhegeldin, prime minister in 1996, was a Middle Horder, as was the opposition leader Olzhas Suleymenov. Although mindful of Russia's strength, the Great Horders have less to lose to Russian separatism than do the Lesser and Middle horders, whose lands would be lost should the Russian-dominated provinces of northern Kazakstan become separated from the republic.

# Religion

By tradition the Kazaks are Sunni Muslims of the Hanafi school, and the Russians are Russian Orthodox. In 1994, some 47 percent of the population was Muslim, 44 percent was Russian Orthodox, and 2 percent was Protestant, mainly Baptist. Some Jews, Catholics, and Pentacostalists also live in Kazakstan; a Roman Catholic diocese was established in 1991. As elsewhere in the newly independent Central Asian states, the subject of Islam's role in everyday life, and especially in politics, is a delicate one in Kazakstan.

## Islam in the Past

As part of the Central Asian population and the Turkic world, Kazaks are conscious of the role Islam plays in their identity, and there is strong public pressure to increase the role that faith plays in society. At the same time, the roots of Islam in many segments of Kazak society are not as deep as they are in neighboring countries. Many of the Kazak nomads, for instance, did not become Muslims until the eighteenth or even the nineteenth century, and urban Russified Kazaks, who by some counts constitute as much as 40 percent of the indigenous population, profess discomfort with some aspects of the religion even as they recognize it as part of their national heritage.

Soviet authorities attempted to encourage a controlled form of Islam as a unifying force in the Central Asian societies while at the same time stifling the expression of religious beliefs. Since independence, religious activity has increased significantly. Construction of mosques and religious schools has accelerated in the 1990s, with financial help from Saudi Arabia, Turkey, and Egypt. Already in 1991, some 170 mosques were operating, more than half of them newly built; at that time, an estimated 230 Muslim communities were active in Kazakstan

## Islam and the State

In 1990 Nazarbayev, then party first secretary, created a state basis for Islam by removing Kazakstan from the authority of the Muslim Board of Central Asia, the Soviet-approved and politically oriented religious administration for all of Central Asia. Instead, Nazarbayev created a separate muftiate, or religious authority, for Kazak Muslims. However, Nazarbayev's choice of Ratbek hadji Nysanbayev to be the first Kazak mufti proved an unpopular one. Accusing him of financial irregularities, religious mispractice, and collaboration with the Soviet and Kazakstani state security apparatus, a group of believers from the nationalist Alash political party attempted unsuccessfully to replace the mufti in December 1991.

With an eye toward the Islamic governments of nearby Iran and Afghanistan, the writers of the 1993 constitution specifically forbade religious political parties. The 1995 constitution forbids organizations that seek to stimulate racial, political, or religious discord, and imposes strict governmental control on foreign religious organizations. As did its predecessor, the 1995 constitution stipulates that Kazakstan is a secular state; thus, Kazakstan is the only Central Asian state whose constitution does not assign a special status to Islam. This position was based on the Nazarbayev government's foreign policy as much as on domestic considerations. Aware of the potential for investment from the Muslim countries of the Middle East, Nazarbayev visited Iran, Turkey, and Saudia Arabia; at the same time, however, he preferred to cast Kazakstan as a bridge between the Muslim East and the Christian West. For example, he initially accepted only observer status in the Economic Cooperation Organization (ECO), all of whose member nations are predominantly Muslim. The president's first trip to the Muslim holy city of Mecca, which did not occur until 1994, was part of an itinerary that also included a visit to Pope John Paul II in the Vatican.

By the mid-1990s, Nazarbayev had begun occasionally to refer to Allah in his speeches, but he had not permitted any of the Islamic festivals to become public holidays, as they had elsewhere in Central Asia. However, certain pre-Islamic holidays such as the spring festival Navruz and the summer festival Kymyzuryndyk were reintroduced in 1995.

## National Identity

As in the other Central Asian republics, the preservation of indigenous cultural traditions and the local language was a difficult problem during the Soviet era. The years since 1991 have provided opportunities for greater cultural expression, but striking a balance between the Kazak and Russian languages has posed a political dilemma for Kazakstan's policy makers.

## Language

The two official languages in Kazakstan are Russian and Kazak. Kazak is part of the Nogai-Kipchak subgroup of northeastern Turkic languages, heavily influenced by both Tatar and Mongol. Kazak was first written only in the 1860s, using Arabic script. In 1929 Latin script was introduced. In 1940 Stalin decided to unify the written materials of the Central Asian republics with those of the Slavic rulers by introducing a modified form of Cyrillic. In 1992 the return of a Latin-based alphabet came under discussion, but the enormous costs involved appear to have stopped further consideration of the idea.

Kazak first became a state language in the late Soviet period, when few of the republic's Russians gave serious thought to the possibility that they might need Kazak to retain their employment, to serve in the armed forces, or to have their children enter a Kazakstani university. At that point, fewer than 5 percent of Russians could speak Kazak, although the majority of Kazaks could speak Russian. However, with the separation between Russia and Kazakstan that followed independence, Russian nationalist sentiment and objections to alleged discrimination in official language policies have increased, especially in the north, as Russians have felt the threat of Kazak becoming the sole legal state language. Meanwhile, Kazaks have strongly defended the preeminence of their tongue, although mastery of the language is far from universal even among Kazaks. According to some estimates, as much as 40 percent of the Kazak population is not fluent in Kazak. The standard language of business, for example, is Russian.

Even those who are fluent find Kazak a difficult language to work with in science, business, and some administrative settings because it remained largely a "kitchen" language in Soviet times, never developing a modern technical vocabulary. Nor has there been extensive translation of technical or popular literature into Kazak. Thus, for most Kazaks Russian remains the primary "world language." In fact, President Nazarbayev defended making Kazak the sole official language on the grounds that decades of Russification had endangered the survival of Kazak as a language. The practical primacy of Russian is reflected in the schools. Despite efforts to increase the number of schools where Kazak is the primary language of instruction, Russian appeared to continue its domination in the mid-1990s. In 1990 about twice as many schools taught in Russian as in Kazak. Although institutions of higher learning now show a strong selection bias in favor of Kazak students, Russian remains the language of instruction in most subjects.

The issue of languages is one of the most politicized and contentious in Kazakstan. The volatility of the language issue has been augmented by Russia's controversial proposals, beginning in 1993, that Kazakstan's Russians be granted dual citizenship. Although Nazarbayev rejected such a policy, the language controversy prompted him to postpone deadlines for implementation of laws making Kazak the sole official language. Thus, it is unlikely that most adult non-Kazaks will have to learn Kazak. Nevertheless, demographic trends make it probable that the next generation will have to learn Kazak, a prospect that generates considerable discomfort in the non-Kazak population. The 1995 constitution does not provide for dual citizenship, but it does alleviate Russian concerns by declaring Russian an official language. That status means that Russian would continue as the primary language of communication for many ethnic Kazaks, and it will remain acceptable for use in schools (a major concern of Russian citizens) and official documents.

## Culture

Before the Russian conquest, the Kazaks had a well-articulated culture based on their nomadic pastoral economy. Although Islam was introduced to most of the Kazaks in the seventeenth and eighteenth centuries, the religion was not fully assimilated until much later. As a result, it coexisted with earlier elements of shamanistic and animistic beliefs. Traditional Kazak belief held that separate spirits inhabited and animated the earth, sky, water, and fire, as well as domestic animals. To this day, particularly honored guests in rural settings are treated to a feast of freshly killed lamb. Such guests are sometimes asked to bless the lamb and to ask its spirit for permission to partake of its flesh. Besides lamb, many other traditional foods retain symbolic value in Kazak culture.

Because animal husbandry was central to the Kazaks' traditional lifestyle, most of their nomadic practices and customs relate in some way to livestock. Traditional curses and blessings invoked disease or fecundity among animals, and good manners required that a person ask first about the health of a man's livestock when greeting him and only afterward inquire about the human aspects of his life.

The traditional Kazak dwelling is the yurt, a tent consisting of a flexible framework of willow wood covered with varying thicknesses of felt. The open top permits smoke from the central hearth to escape; temperature and draft can be controlled by a flap that increases or decreases the size of the opening. A properly constructed yurt can be cooled in summer and warmed in winter, and it can be disassembled or set up in less than an hour. The interior of the yurt has ritual significance; the right side generally is reserved for men and the left for women.

Although yurts are less used for their original purpose than they once were, they remain a potent symbol of "Kazakness." During demonstrations against Nazarbayev in the spring of 1992, demonstrators and hunger strikers erected yurts in front of the government building in Almaty. Yurts are also frequently used as a decorative motif in restaurants and other public buildings.

Because of the Kazaks' nomadic lifestyle and their lack of a written language until the mid-nineteenth century, their literary tradition relies upon oral histories. These histories were memorized and recited by the *akyn*, the elder responsible for remembering the legends and histories, and by *jyrau*, lyric poets who traveled with the high-placed khans. Most of the legends concern the activities of a *batir*, or hero-warrior. Among the tales that have survived are *Koblandy-batir* (fifteenth or sixteenth century), *Er Sain* (sixteenth century), and *Er Targyn* (sixteenth century), all of which concern the struggle against the Kalmyks; *Kozy Korpesh* and *Bain sulu*, both epics; and the love lyric *Kiz-Jibek*. Usually these tales were recited in a song-like chant, frequently to the accompaniment of such traditional instruments as drums and the *dombra*, a mandolin-like string instrument. President Nazarbayev has appeared on television broadcasts in the republic, playing the *dombra* and singing.

The Russian conquest wreaked havoc on Kazak traditional culture by making impossible the nomadic pastoralism upon which the culture was based. However, many individual elements survived the loss of the lifestyle as a whole. Many practices that lost their original meanings are assuming value as symbols of post-Soviet national identity.

*Bust of Zhambyl Zhambayev,
poet of the nineteenth and
twentieth centuries, after whom
a city was named
Courtesy Stanley Bach*

For the most part, preindependence cultural life in Kazakstan was indistinguishable from that elsewhere in the Soviet Union. It featured the same plays, films, music, books, paintings, museums, and other cultural appurtenances common in every other corner of the Soviet empire. That Russified cultural establishment nevertheless produced many of the most important figures of the early stages of Kazak nationalist self-assertion, including novelist Anuar Alimzhanov, who became president of the last Soviet Congress of People's Deputies, and poets Mukhtar Shakhanov and Olzhas Suleymenov, who were copresidents of the political party Popular Congress of Kazakstan (see Structure of Government; Political Organizations, this ch.). Shakhanov also chaired the commission that investigated the events surrounding the riots of December 1986.

An even more powerful figure than Shakhanov, Suleymenov in 1975 became a pan-Central Asian hero by publishing a book, *Az i Ia,* examining the *Lay of Igor's Campaign,* a medieval tale vital to the Russian national culture, from the perspective of the Turkic Pechenegs whom Igor defeated. Soviet authorities subjected the book to a blistering attack. Later Suleymenov used his prestige to give authority to the Nevada-Semipalatinsk antinuclear movement, which performed the very real service of ending nuclear testing in Kazakstan. He and Shakhanov originally organized their People's Congress Party as a pro-Nazarbayev movement, but Suleymenov eventually steered the party into an opposition role. In the short-lived parliament of 1994–95, Suleymenov was leader of the Respublika opposition coalition, and he was frequently mentioned as a possible presidential candidate.

The collapse of the Soviet system with which so many of the Kazak cultural figures were identified left most of them in awkward positions. Even more damaging has been the total collapse of public interest in most forms of higher culture. Most of the books that Kazakstanis buy are about business, astrology, or sex; the movies they see are nearly all American, Chinese, or Turkish adventure and action films; most concerts feature rock music, not infrequently accompanied by erotic dancing; and television provides a diet of old Soviet films and dubbed Mexican soap operas. Kazakstan's cultural elite is suffering the same decline affecting the elites of all the former Soviet republics. Thus, cultural norms are determined predominantly by Kazakstan's increasing access to global mass culture.

## Education

The constitution of 1995 specifies that education through secondary school is mandatory and free, and that citizens have the further right to compete for free education in the republic's institutions of higher learning. Private, paid education is permitted but remains subject to state control and supervision.

In 1994 Kazakstan had 8,575 elementary and secondary schools (grades one through twelve) attended by approximately 3.2 million students, and 244 specialized secondary schools with about 222,000 students. In 1992 about 51 percent of eligible children were attending some 8,500 preschools in Kazakstan. In 1994 some 272,100 students were enrolled in the republic's sixty-one institutes of higher learning. Fifty-four percent of the students were Kazak, and 31 percent were Russian.

The educational situation since independence is somewhat difficult to judge because of incomplete information. The republic has attempted to overhaul both the structure of its education system and much of its substance, but the questions of what should be taught and in what manner continue to loom large. A particularly sensitive and unresolved issue is what the language of instruction should be, given the almost equal distribution of the population between ethnic Kazaks and ethnic Russians. In 1994 most instruction still was in Russian because Kazak-language textbooks and Kazak teachers were in short supply. Enrollment was estimated to be 92 percent of the total age-group in both primary and secondary grades, but only 8 percent in the postsecondary age-group.

Serious shortages in funding and resources have hindered efforts to revamp the education system inherited from the Soviet Union. Even in 1990, more than half the republic's schools were operating on two and even three shifts per day; since then, hundreds of schools, especially preschools, have been converted to offices or stores. Elementary- and secondary-school teachers remain badly underpaid; in 1993 more than 30,000 teachers (or about one-seventh of the 1990 teaching staff) left education, many of them to seek more lucrative employment.

Despite the obstacles, efforts have been made to upgrade the education system, especially at the highest level. Kazakstani citizens still can enroll in what once were the premier Soviet universities, all of which are now in foreign countries, in particular Russia and Ukraine. In the mid-1990s, however, such opportunities have become rare and much more expensive. This situation has forced the upgrading of existing universities in Kazakstan, as well as the creation of at least one new private university, Al-Farabi University, formerly the S.M. Kirov State University, in Almaty. The largest institution of higher learning in Kazakstan, Al-Farabi had 1,530 teachers and about 14,000 students in 1994. A second university, Qaraghandy State University, had about 8,300 students in 1994. In addition, technical secondary schools in five cities—Aqmola, Atyrau, Pavlodar, Petropavl (formerly Petropavlovsk), and Taldyqorghan (formerly Taldy-Kurgan)—have been reclassified as universities, increasing regional access to higher education. Altogether, in 1994 Kazakstan had thirty-two specialized institutes of higher learning, offering programs in agriculture, business and economics, medicine, music, theater, foreign languages, and a variety of engineering and technical fields. In the area of technical education, the republic has taken aggressive advantage of offers from foreign states to educate young Kazaks. In 1994 about 3,000 young people were studying in various foreign countries, including the United States.

One trend that particularly worries republic administrators is the pronounced "Kazakification" of higher education, as the republic's Russians either send their children to schools across the Russian border or find it impossible to enroll them in local institutions. Kazakstan's law forbids ethnic quotas, but there is evidence of prejudicial admittance patterns. The class that entered university in 1991, for example, was 73.1 percent Kazak and only 13.1 percent Russian.

# Health

The early years of independence have had a disastrous effect on public health. In the 1980s, Kazakstan had an extensively developed public health system that delivered at least basic care without charge even to very remote communities. By 1993, however, Kazakstan rated below average or lower among the former Soviet republics in medical system, sanitation, medical industry, medical research and development, and pharmaceutical supply.

## Health System

In 1994 the health system had twenty-nine doctors per 1,000 people and 86.7 other medical personnel per 1,000. There were 1,805 hospitals in the republic, with seventy-six beds per 1,000 people. There were 3,129 general health clinics and 1,826 gynecological and pediatric clinics. Conditions and services at these facilities varied widely; it was not uncommon, for example, for rural clinics and hospitals to be without running water.

The constitution of 1995 perpetuates the Soviet-era guarantee of free basic health care, but financing has been a consistent problem. In 1992 funding allotted to public health care was less than 1.6 percent of GDP, a level characterized by the World Bank as that of an underdeveloped nation.

Because doctors and other medical personnel receive very low pay, many medical professionals have moved to other republics—a large percentage of Kazakstan's doctors are Russian or other non-Kazak nationalities—or have gone into other professions. Nonpayment even of existing low wages is a common occurrence, as are strikes by doctors and nurses.

In the 1980s, Kazakstan had about 2,100 pharmaceutical-manufacturing facilities; drugs were also available from other Soviet republics or from East European trading partners within the framework of the Council for Mutual Economic Assistance (Comecon). Since independence most such supply connections have been terminated, and many domestic pharmaceutical plants have closed, making some types of drugs virtually unavailable. As a result, vaccination of infants and children, which reached between 85 and 93 percent of the relevant age-groups in 1990, decreased sharply in the early 1990s. Kazakstan ran out of measles and tuberculosis vaccine in late 1991, and the World Health Organization (WHO) estimated that more than 20 percent of children were not receiving basic vaccinations in 1992.

To some extent, the provision of drugs has been taken over by a government-owned company, Farmatsiya, which purchases about 95 percent of the medical equipment and supplies for the government. There have been persistent complaints that Farmatsiya pays far too much for foreign equipment and medicines in return for nonmedical considerations.

Private medical practice is permitted in general medicine and in some specialized fields; private surgical practice is forbidden, as is private treatment of cancer, tuberculosis, venereal disease, pregnancy, and infectious diseases. Some types of private practice have been introduced directly into the state clinics, creating a confusing situation in which identical procedures are performed by the same personnel, some for state fees and others for higher private fees. A substantial unofficial market has developed in the distribution of hospital supplies; patients often are expected to pay for the bandages, anesthesia, and other materials and services required for the "free" treatment received at medical facilities. Kazakstan has no system of medical insurance.

In the mid-1990s, the largest growth area in medicine was in services not requiring large capital outlays by the practitioner. This area, which includes acupuncturists, fertility consultants, substance-abuse therapists, physical therapists, and dentists, is only lightly regulated, and the incidence of charlatanism is high.

Kazakstan has negotiated some international agreements to improve health care. In 1992 an association of scientific organizations specializing in contagious diseases established its headquarters in Almaty. The group, which includes doctors and technicians from Kyrgyzstan, Tajikistan, Turkmenistan, and Uzbekistan, conducts joint research with scientists in China, Mongolia, and Vietnam. A 1995 medical cooperation agreement between the Kazakstani and Iranian ministries of health called for exchanges of medical students and experts, joint research projects, exchanges of information on the latest medical advances (with an emphasis on contagious diseases), and mutual natural-disaster assistance.

## Health Conditions

The deterioration of the public health system has hit Kazakstan's population hard. Rates of infant mortality and overall mortality have risen in the 1990s as the fertility rate has decreased, contributing to the first drop in the republic's population since World War II. Infant mortality was twenty-seven per 1,000 live births in 1991, the lowest rate among the five Central Asian republics but higher than that for any non-Central Asian republic. A lack of medicines and facilities, together with a general deterioration in physical environment and living standards, has promoted outbreaks of several potentially epidemic diseases, including diphtheria (its incidence increased from thirty-five cases in 1993 to 312 in the first ten months of 1994), poliomyelitis (two cases in 1994), viral hepatitis, and cholera (of which outbreaks occurred in 1992 and 1993). The incidence of tuberculosis has grown substantially, with as many as 11,000 new cases and 2,000 deaths reported annually (see table 5, Appendix). According to a 1995 report of the Contagious Disease Association in Almaty, a bubonic plague-carrying rat population was moving from the Balkhash region, where the plague is endemic, southward toward Almaty, whose municipal government had taken no measures to control rats.

The first death in Kazakstan attributed to acquired immune deficiency syndrome (AIDS) was reported in July 1993. At that time, nineteen carriers of the human immunodeficiency virus (HIV) reportedly were registered in Kazakstan. Of that number, three were identified as homosexuals, two were preschool children, and nine were foreign citizens, who were deported. In mid-1995, the WHO reported that twenty-seven people had been diagnosed with AIDS or as HIV-positive between 1993 and 1995. The Kazakstan AIDS Prevention and Control Dispensary was established in Almaty in 1991, with twenty-two branch offices and diagnostic laboratories elsewhere in the republic. However, in the early 1990s diagnosis and treatment relied on foreign funds and equipment because domestic health funds were barely sufficient to maintain clinic buildings. Fewer than 500 requests for screening were received in 1993. In mid-1995, the government set up the Coordinating Council for Combating AIDS under the direct administration of the prime minister.

The shortage of health care has put children at particular risk. Approximately 15 percent of newborns in 1994 were unhealthy, most often suffering from bronchiopulmonary and cardiovascular problems. Measles, diphtheria, brucellosis, and other childhood diseases became more prevalent during the early 1990s.

Extensive pollution and degradation of large segments of the natural environment have increased the strain on public health. Both the air and water of many of the large cities are badly polluted. Three regions have been identified as having particularly hazardous environments. Öskemen (formerly Ust-Kamenogorsk) in the far northeast has been rated the third most polluted city in the former Soviet Union, with ten times the maximum permitted levels of lead in the air and high concentrations of beryllium, thallium, mercury, cadmium, antimony, and arsenic in the municipal water supply. Just west of Öskemen, in Semey, a major site of Soviet nuclear testing from 1949 to 1991, radiation has contaminated the air and soil. Experts believe that the tests, which were conducted in the atmosphere until 1963, contaminated the environment of the entire country of Kazakstan. In one village, Kaynar, near the main proving ground, 140 of 3,400 children were found to have been disabled since birth; in a random sample of another 600 of the town's children, all were found to be suffering ill health of one form or another. Radiation is believed the cause of such statistics. The third major area of environmental degradation is the Aral Sea Basin along the southwestern border, where agricultural runoff and untreated sewage have caused advanced pollution of groundwater (see Environmental Problems, this ch.).

Water contamination is a serious environmental health hazard in Kazakstan because of poor management of drinking water and insufficient sewage treatment. About 30 percent of rural communities obtain water from shallow wells; the water is vulnerable to contamination by materials leached from the surface. As late as 1985, only 37 percent of homes had sewerage systems and running water, and even schools and hospitals had primitive sanitary systems that caused frequent outbreaks of intestinal illness.

The diet and lifestyle of many citizens, especially in the cities, contribute further to poor health. The average diet is high in meat and salt and low in vegetables and fruits. The hyperinflation of 1992–93 cut deeply into family budgets, limiting both the variety and quantity of food most ordinary people consume. Smoking is almost universal, especially among men, and alcoholism is common. Other forms of substance abuse such as the use of hemp, morphia products, and glue are common, especially among young people.

Occupational hazards constitute another major health problem. Especially during the economic hardships of the early 1990s, public health authorities refrained from measures such as closing polluting factories or restricting the use of fertilizers, pesticides, and irrigation water out of a fear of accelerating the general decline in production. Because of the dangers posed by exposure to toxic smoke and fumes, lead and phosphate plants limit workers to ten years of employment. With little restriction on how they are operated, factories in Kazakstan note high rates of morbidity, absenteeism, and permanent disability among their employees.

## Social Welfare

The Soviet system of social welfare, which remained in place in Kazakstan in the early 1990s, presupposed a very high level of public services. The 1993 constitution maintained most of the assumptions of the Soviet era without providing a clear mechanism for paying for "guaranteed" workers' benefits such as free education, medical care, pensions, and vacations. The constitution ratified in 1995 somewhat reduces the list and scale of guaranteed protections, but remaining guarantees include a minimum wage, pensions for the retired and the disabled, social benefits for orphans and for people who are elderly or infirm, legal assistance, housing, and what is called "social defense against unemployment."

In practice, social benefits have proven difficult to supply because of financial considerations and the lack of a firm organizational structure for service provision. For example, in the Soviet period housing was supplied by the state or by employers. In 1990 housing began to be privatized, a process almost completed by the mid-1990s. The result has been a healthy resale market for existing housing. In 1995 apartment costs in Almaty could exceed 15,000 tenge (for value of the tenge, see Glossary) per square meter, but there had been no corresponding boom in new housing construction, in part because privatization of the land on which such housing would stand remained a sensitive and unresolved issue. As a result, the republic's housing crisis, already acute in the Soviet period, has grown far worse. In the mid-1990s the housing shortage was especially serious in Almaty, where tens of thousands were on waiting lists. In 1995 housing construction decreased by about 25 percent.

Perhaps the biggest problems have emerged in the areas of pensions, aid to large families and other social assistance, and unemployment compensation. An independent pension fund was created in 1991 on the basis of a social insurance tax on enterprises (37 percent of wages in 1992) and contributions by employees (1 percent of wages in 1992). The national budget nominally covers remaining deficits in the pension fund. Pensions initially were set at 60 percent of average pay, with minimal pensions available even to elderly citizens such as housewives who never had drawn a salary. However, the high inflation of 1991–93 badly eroded existing pensions; the state has continually adjusted pensions upward in a futile struggle to keep pace (see Prices, Wages, and Currency, this ch.). In addition, the administration of pensions has been reconfigured several times, leading to lengthy delays in the payment even of the small sums pensioners are owed. Such delays have prompted numerous public demonstrations. Although the value of pensions has shrunk dramatically in real terms, by 1992 government expenditures on them were 4.7 percent of the GDP. In March 1995, the government had to divert 632 million tenge from the national budget to cover pension arrears.

Similar problems have occurred in other categories of allowances to citizens, especially lump-sum payments to newborns; child allowances to large families (those with four or more children) and abandoned children; assistance to single mothers; and assistance to the children of soldiers. In 1992 payments in these categories reached 5 percent of Kazakstan's GDP. Slow payment and the lag between inflation and cost-of-living adjustments have had a particularly severe effect on Kazakstan's poorer families, for some of whom government subsidies provide as much as one-quarter of total income. In 1994 about 2.1 million citizens received retirement pensions, and about 800,000 received other types of pension.

Unemployment is perhaps the most difficult category of social problem because it is a phenomenon that officially did not exist until 1991 and still carries a considerable social stigma. As of January 1, 1995, some 85,700 people officially were registered as unemployed, about 55 percent of them in rural areas. However, this figure is commonly assumed to be too low because many workers still are nominally employed, even though their salaries have been reduced or stopped altogether under a variety of cutback conditions. In January 1995, some 230 enterprises, with a normal work force of about 51,000 employees, were standing idle; by April 1995, the number had grown to 376 enterprises with more than 90,000 employees.

## The Economy

Although Kazakstan has the potential to be a wealthy nation, since independence it has suffered consistent and precipitous economic decline. Reporting problems and incompatibility of data make precise measurement of the republic's economic shrinkage difficult, but it is generally accepted that, by the mid-1990s, GDP had dropped to about half of what it was in 1990 (see table 6, Appendix). Despite the presence of rich deposits of natural resources, the republic's industrial sector was developed in the Soviet period only in specific areas such as metal processing, chemicals, textiles, and food processing. The semi-arid condition of much of Kazakstan's territory does not preclude the export of wheat, meat, and some vegetables.

### Natural Resources

Soviet geologists once boasted that Kazakstan was capable of exporting the entire Periodic Table of Elements. During the Soviet period, Kazakstan supplied about 7 percent of the union's gold, or about twenty-four tons per year. Since independence, the republic has attracted large foreign partners to develop existing or new mines. President Nazarbayev announced intentions to increase annual gold production to fifty or sixty tons by 1995 or 1996.

In 1989 the mines of Kazakstan yielded 23.8 million tons of iron ore and 151,900 tons of manganese. The republic also possesses deposits of uranium, chrome, titanium, nickel, wolfram, silver, molybdenum, bauxite, and copper. Major phosphate mines feed fertilizer plants in the southern city of Zhambyl. Three major coal fields—Torghay, Qaraghandy, and Ekibastuz—produced 140 million tons of hard coal in 1991, but by 1994 Kazakstan's national total had dropped to 104 million tons.

In the mid-1990s, all minerals in Kazakstan belonged to the republic. Authority for decisions concerning their development was delegated to the prime minister, provided that these decisions were consistent with laws on natural resource development. The fundamental law "On Natural Resources and the

*Karatau Mountains, reportedly containing huge reserves of lead and*
*zinc, southern Kazakstan*
*Courtesy Paul Hearn*

Development of Mineral Resources" was passed in May 1992,
but its treatment of foreign development of minerals is limited
to two brief paragraphs stipulating that foreign development
be conducted in accordance with international and national
law.

## Agriculture

In the early 1990s, agriculture was the second largest sector
of the economy, contributing about 36 percent of GDP and
employing about 18 percent of the workforce in 1993. The climate and soil of most of Kazakstan are best suited to the light
grazing by which the nomadic Kazaks had traditionally supported themselves, following herds of sheep, cattle, camels,
and horses about the open steppe. Despite such natural advantages, Soviet policy encouraged cultivation, especially in the
northern parts of the republic. The major transformation
occurred under premier Khrushchev during the Virgin Lands
program of the late 1950s and early 1960s. Its objectives were to
reduce Soviet grain imports to Central Asia and settle the
remaining nomadic herdsmen of Kazakstan and Kyrgyzstan.
Under that program, 60 percent of Kazakstan's pastureland

45

went under cultivation. An estimated 30 percent of that land was not suitable for cultivation, however, and Khrushchev was ousted in 1964 after a series of crop failures in Kazakstan. In 1992 the total area under cultivation was 36.5 million hectares, of which 2.3 million hectares were irrigated. Much of this land is dedicated to large-scale wheat farming, which requires intensive capitalization and does not lend itself to privatization. Even with the emphasis on grain production, about 84 percent of the republic's agricultural land, or about 187 million hectares, remains devoted to pasturage, mainly of cattle and sheep. Continuation of the Soviet system of intensive livestock management, dependent on fodder more than on natural grazing, has left much grazing land unused and has distorted cultivation in favor of fodder production.

The primary agricultural regions are the north-central and southern parts of the republic. Grain production is especially important in the north-central region, and cotton and rice predominate in the south (see table 7, Appendix). Kazakstan also is a major producer of meat and milk.

In 1993 only about 1.5 percent of agricultural land was in private hands. Although some privatization had occurred, the bulk of Kazakstan's agriculture remained organized in 7,000 to 8,000 state and collective farms that averaged 35,000 to 40,000 hectares each. Many of those farms had moved into a transitional stage of joint-stock ownership, private collectives, or farming associations (see Post-Soviet Economic Developments, this ch.). The state also has maintained control of agricultural inputs and equipment, as well as some processing and marketing policies and operations. In the wake of price liberalization, the mandated state share of agricultural sales has decreased annually from the 1991 level of 70 percent.

Until the early 1990s, western Kazakstan was an important fishing area, but sharply increased salination has made the Aral Sea sterile. Fishing output dropped from 105,300 tons in 1960 to 89,600 tons in 1989. The current figure is probably close to zero, judging by the decision of Soviet central planners in 1990 to fly Arctic fish to Kazakstan for processing as a means of maintaining local employment in that operation.

## Industry

Kazakstan inherited a decaying but still powerful manufacturing and processing capacity from the centrally managed Soviet system. In that system, among Kazakstan's designated products for the general all-union market were phosphate fertilizer, rolled metal, radio cables, aircraft wires, train bearings, tractors, and bulldozers. Kazakstan also had a well-developed network of factories producing military goods that supplied about 11 percent of the total military production of the Soviet Union. In some areas of military production, Kazakstan had a virtual monopoly. In the post-Soviet era, much of the defense industry has stopped or slowed production; some plants now produce nonmilitary electronic equipment and machines.

Most of the republic's manufacturing, refining, and metallurgy plants are concentrated in the north and northeast, in Semey, Aqmola, Petropavl, and Aqtöbe (see fig. 5). In south-central Kazakstan, the most important industrial centers are Shymkent (chemicals, light industry, metallurgy, and food processing), Almaty (light industry, machine building, and food processing), and Zhambyl (chemicals, machine building, and food processing).

### Structure of Industry

The energy sector is the most productive component of Kazakstan's industrial structure, accounting for about 42 percent of total output. Metallurgy generates about one-quarter of industrial output, divided equally between the processing of ferrous and nonferrous metals (see table 8, Appendix). Engineering and metalworking account for 6.2 percent of industrial output, chemicals and petrochemicals for 3.6 percent, and construction materials for 2.7 percent. Kazakstan's entire light industry sector accounts for only 4.8 percent of industrial output. In the Soviet era, the republic had more than fifty military-industrial enterprises, employing as many as 75,000 workers. Because Baykonur, one of the world's two largest spaceports, was located in Kazakstan, as were 1,350 nuclear warheads, the prosperity of this sector was assured during the Soviet period. Military-related enterprises produced or processed beryllium, nuclear reactor fuel, uranium ore, heavy machine guns, anti-ship missiles, torpedoes, chemical and biological weapons, support equipment for intercontinental ballistic missiles, tactical missile launcher equipment, artillery, and armored vehicles.

### Production Levels

In general, Kazakstan's industry suffered a disastrous year in 1994, when overall output dropped 28.5 percent. The metallurgy and energy industries were the main contributors to the

1994 decline, although by percentage light industry (down 56 percent) and engineering and metalworking (down 43 percent) suffered the sharpest reductions. However, in the last few months of 1994 and the first half of 1995, production decreased more slowly. Although monthly production continued to decline compared with 1994, the rate of decline between 1994 and 1995 was about half the rate shown between 1993 and 1994. By mid-1995, the chemical, oil-refining, natural gas, timber, ferrous metallurgy, and oil extraction industries were showing higher outputs than they had for the same periods of 1994. Reduced consumer purchasing power exacerbated declines in most processing and consumer goods industries, however; overall light industry output was 61.2 percent lower in the first five months of 1995 than in the same period of 1994. In the first five months of 1995, the republic's industries produced goods valued at 253.1 billion tenge, or about US$4 billion—a drop of 16.5 percent from the five-month output value for 1994.

Kazakstan has remained highly dependent on Russia as a customer for its manufactured products; this dependence has been the main cause of the shrinkage in the industrial base, as Russia has reduced its demand for most of Kazakstan's export products in the early and mid-1990s (see International Financial Relations, this ch.). Although more than 80 percent of Kazakstan's industrial production is still intended for sale in Russia, trade with Russia in 1995 was only about 20 percent of what it was in 1991. In January 1995, some 230 enterprises, with about 51,000 employees, were idle; by April the figures had grown to 376 enterprises and more than 90,000 employees. Also alarming is the growing debt load of the enterprises, which continue to support their unprofitable operations by unregulated borrowing among themselves. By March 1994, total agricultural and industrial indebtedness had reached 230.6 billion tenge. One consequence of falling production and growing indebtedness is that the republic's enterprises are increasingly unprofitable. As of March 1995, the government categorized 2,483 enterprises, or about one-third of the republic's total, as unprofitable. As of early 1996, however, very few had been forced into formal bankruptcy.

## Energy

Kazakstan is well endowed with energy resources, including abundant reserves of coal, oil, and natural gas, which made the

Figure 5. Kazakstan, Kyrgyzstan, Tajikistan, Turkmenistan, and Uzbekistan: Industrial Activity, 1996

republic one of the top energy-producing regions of the Soviet Union. In 1993 Kazakstan was the second largest oil producer, third largest coal producer, and sixth largest natural gas producer among the former Soviet republics. Industry in Kazakstan is dominated by the energy sector; in 1994 electric power generation accounted for 19 percent of GDP, and fuel extraction and processing accounted for nearly 23 percent. Thus, the national economy is strongly affected by changes in levels of fuel extraction and energy production (see fig. 6).

## Oil

Kazakstan's oil reserves have been estimated at as much as 2,100 million tons, most of which is in relatively new fields that have not yet been exploited. In addition, new offshore discoveries in the north Caspian more than replaced the annual drawdown of known reserves in the early 1990s. In 1993 Chevron Oil made an initial investment in a joint venture, Tengizchevroil, to exploit the Tengiz oil fields at the northern end of the Caspian Sea in what was envisioned as the leading project among foreign oil investments. Recoverable reserves at Tengiz are estimated at 25 billion barrels, or about twice the amount in the Alaskan North Slope, although Tengiz oil is extremely high in sulfur. The French firm Elf-Aquitaine has leased about 19,000 square kilometers of land in the Emba region northeast of the Caspian, where there are known to be large quantities of sulfur-free oil and natural gas. Other oil deposits, with paraffin, asphalt, or tar (all harder to process), have been found in the Caspian Sea near Novyy Uzen and Buzachiy.

Oil production, which increased by an average of 3 percent per year through 1991, reached a peak production of 26.6 million tons that year before output began to decline in 1992. The most productive region in the early 1990s was the Mangyshlak Peninsula on the east shore of the Caspian Sea. In the early 1990s, Mangyshlak yielded more than 50 percent of the republic's oil output before experiencing a decline of 11 percent in 1992. Kazakstan also is known to be rich in deposits of heavy oil, which currently are not commercially viable but which are potentially valuable.

The republic planned to increase its oil exports from the 7.8 million tons of 1992 (15 percent of total exports) to as much as 37 million tons in 1996 (50 percent of total exports), for which anticipated revenue was about US$2.9 billion. By 1993, however, domestic and CIS industry conditions made such goals unrealistic. The most important obstacles to increased oil production and export involve Russia. In 1994 Russian refineries in western Siberia, upon which Kazakstan's oil industry continues to rely heavily for processing, cut their operations drastically because paying customers could not be found; this cut resulted in the plants' lower demand for crude oil from Kazakstani suppliers. Thus, in the first nine months of 1994, Kazakstan's oil sales fell to 4.5 million tons from 8 million tons in the same period of 1993, and production for the year fell 11.7 percent. Because of the oil-exchange agreement with Russia, the cutback in Russian refinery production also reduced domestic refinery production nearly 25 percent in 1994.

The second obstacle to greater production and export of oil is pipeline access through Russia to Western customers, which Russia has curtailed because of capacity limits and political maneuvering. The lack of pipeline facilities caused Chevron to announce substantial capital investment cutbacks in the Tengiz oil fields for 1995. In the mid-1990s, the pipeline that connects Kazakstani oil fields with the Russian Black Sea port Novorossiysk provided the sole access to the oil of the Tengiz fields for Chevron and its Western customers (see Transportation and Telecommunications, this ch.). The uncertainties of relying on the existing Russian line or on a second line passing through the war-torn Caucasus region led to discussions of new pipeline projects passing through Iran or even eastward across China to the Pacific Ocean. In September 1995, a new agreement with Turkey laid plans for pipelines crossing Georgia to ports in Georgia and Turkey, providing a new outlet possibility for Kazakstan's Tengiz oil. Also, in October 1995 Kazakstan joined in a new consortium with Russian and United States companies to build a pipeline to the Black Sea. Chevron and Mobil Oil of the United States, British Gas, Agip of Italy, and Russia's LUKoil enterprise were to fund the entire pipeline project in return for a 50 percent share in the pipeline. The governments of Kazakstan and Russia were to receive the other 50 percent. However, pipeline construction was delayed amid further international negotiation over alternative routes.

In the first quarter of 1995, major accidents and power shortages at drilling sites reduced production by about 10 percent compared with output in the first quarter of 1994. Refinery output in that period was even lower; only about half the

## Region and Plants

I    Tokmak Hydroelectric Plant
II   Alamedin Hydroelectric Plant
III   Kürp-Say Hydroelectric Plant
IV   Roghun Hydroelectric Plant
V   Charvak Hydroelectric Plant

—··—··—   International boundary
●   Populated place
▓   Coal basin
▨   Oil and gas basin
⚡   Thermoelectric power plant
Ω   Hydroelectric power plant
🏭   Oil refinery

0   200   400 Kilometers
0   200   400 Miles

**RUSSIA**

**MONGOLIA**

Pavlodar 3
*Pavlodar*
Ekibastuz 1   Yermak
*Ekibastuz*
Öskemen

*Torghay*

*Qaraghandy*
Zhartas

**KAZAKSTAN**

*North Caspian*
Gur'yev

*Lake Balkhash*

*Tengiz and Korolev*

*Aral Sea*

*Caspian*

*Syrdariya*
Zhambyl
Shymkent   II   I

**AZERBAIJAN**
*Transcaucasus*

Nukus
**UZBEKISTAN**

**KYRGYZSTAN**

Khamza
V   III
Fergana

Turkmenbashy
**TURKMENISTAN**

*Caspian Sea*

Nawoiy
Chärjew

*Central Asia*

**TAJIKISTAN**

**CHINA**

IV

**IRAN**

**AFGHANISTAN**

Cease-Fire Line
Chinese line of control
Indian claim

**PAKISTAN**

**INDIA**

**NEPAL**

*Boundary representation not necessarily authoritative*

*Figure 6. Kazakstan, Kyrgyzstan, Tajikistan, Turkmenistan, and Uzbekistan: Fuel and Energy Centers, 1996*

first quarter's oil was refined, and the Pavlodar refinery closed entirely because it received no crude oil from Russia.

### Natural Gas

Kazakstan has enormous reserves of natural gas, most notably the giant Karachaganak field in the northwest near the Russian border, under codevelopment by a consortium of Agip of Italy, British Gas, and the Russian Natural Gas Company (Gazprom). In 1992 natural gas production was 8.5 million cubic meters, half of which came from Karachaganak. By 1994, however, production was only 4.1 million cubic meters because Russian consumption had dropped drastically in the early 1990s. A 1995 deal with Gazprom gave that organization part ownership of Karachaganak in exchange for a guaranteed purchase of natural gas from Kazakstan. Foreign investment projects at Tengiz and Karachaganak were expected to triple domestic gas output and enhance gas processing capabilities in the later 1990s. The usefulness of increased output depends on new pipeline agreements—still in the formative stage in 1996—with Russia and other countries in the region.

### Coal

In 1994 coal production decreased 6.7 percent to 104.4 million tons, after a production peak of 140 million tons was reached in 1991. About thirty major coalfields exist, most of them within 400 kilometers of Qaraghandy in north-central Kazakstan. This region offers some of the most accessible and cheaply extracted coal in the CIS; however, most of Kazakstan's coal is high in ash. The largest open-pit mines are located in the Ekibastuz Basin northeast of Qaraghandy. According to estimates, presently exploited mines contain 100 years of coal reserves at today's rate of consumption. Coal is a key input for industry; in the early 1990s, more than 75 percent of coal consumption in Kazakstan went to thermoelectric stations for power generation, and another 14 percent went to the steel industry. In the early 1990s, Kazakstan exported about 40 percent of its coal to CIS customers, mainly Russia.

The coal industry has been plagued by poor management and strikes that shut down major underground operations at Qaraghandy and surface operations at Ekibastuz in 1994 and 1995. The large metallurgical works of Qaraghandy, built under the Soviet concept of the territorial-industrial complex combining heavy industry with on-site fuel reserves, has been forced to curtail production when strikes are called.

### Current Fuel Supply and Consumption

Despite its fuel endowments, Kazakstan remains a net importer of energy, partly because of falling production in the early 1990s and partly because of remaining barter agreements from the Soviet era. Undeveloped east-to-west transportation infrastructure has prevented efficient supply of domestic fuels to industries, which are energy intensive. As a consequence, Kazakstan still must import oil, natural gas, lubricating oil, gasoline, and diesel fuel from Russia, which in the postindependence years has taken advantage of its neighbor's vulnerability to economic pressure. In the mid-1990s, the oil exchange system between Kazakstan and Russia meant that declining demand in Russia reduced availability of those Russian products to Kazakstan. In 1994 Russia sent only 40 percent of the crude oil and 48 percent of the refined products prescribed in the bilateral agreement for that year. Gas imports showed a similar drop.

The national electric power system is divided into three grids. The northern grid, which serves a large part of heavy industry, is connected to the adjacent Siberian grid in Russia, and the southern grid is connected to the Central Asian System. Kazakstan depends on Russia for electricity and fuel. Although the Siberian generating stations that supply the northern grid are located in Russia, they are fired largely by coal exported from Kazakstan. Some electric power also is received from Kyrgyzstan's hydroelectric stations to the south in exchange for coal (see Energy, ch. 2).

In 1991 Kazakstan consumed 101.6 billion kilowatt-hours of electricity (84.7 percent of which was produced domestically), making it a relatively heavy energy consumer among nations of its economic stature. About 85 percent of domestic generation occurs in coal-fired thermoelectric plants. A few thermoelectric plants use natural gas or oil; the remaining 15 percent of energy comes from those plants and from hydroelectric stations. The main sources of coal-generated electricity are the fields of Ekibastuz, Maykubin, Torghay, and Borlin. There are three large hydroelectric stations, at Bukhtarmin, Öskemen, and Kapchagay. The republic's one nuclear power station is located near the city of Aqtau.

## Work Force

In 1992 some 16 percent of Kazakstan's work force was employed in manufacturing 24 percent in agriculture and forestry, 9 percent in construction, 9 percent in transportation and communications, and 32 percent in trade and services (see table 9, Appendix). An estimated 28.3 percent of the work force had at least a secondary education at the time of independence. Russians generally were employed in higher-paying sectors such as industry, transportation, and science, and Kazaks predominated in lower-paying areas such as health care, culture, art, and education. Overall, about two-thirds of workers and about 80 percent of industrial workers were non-Kazaks. In state enterprises, which provided 95 percent of employment before independence, one-half of the work force was female in 1990. The high participation rate of women contributed to an overall participation rate of 79 percent of working-age citizens in some form of employment.

In 1990 the working population of the republic peaked at around 6.7 million people, in a command economy where the legal requirement of full employment of both men and women meant substantial underemployment not revealed by official statistics. By the end of 1994, the number of employed people had declined about 8.9 percent, to about 6.1 million. This drop was caused in part by the privatization of Kazakstan's economy (by 1993 about 7 percent of Kazakstanis were working outside the state sector), but it also reflected growing unemployment and underemployment. In January 1995, there were 85,700 officially registered unemployed people in the republic, up from 4,000 in 1992. That figure does not include an unknown but significant number of workers whose names remained on official payroll lists while they were on forced leave, reduced hours, and delayed wage-payment schedules.

## Post-Soviet Economic Developments

Until 1990, when the whole central planning system collapsed, Kazakstan was part of the Soviet command economy. Even at the time of the 1991 coup that led to independence, 43 percent of the republic's industrial capacity was under Moscow's direct control, 48 percent was under joint republic and union control, and only 8 percent was strictly under republic control.

Although economic production declined dramatically in the early 1990s, some indicators showed a slower rate of decline by early 1995. In 1994 GDP declined 25.4 percent compared with 1993, including drops of 28.5 percent in industry and 21.2 percent in agriculture. In January and February 1995, additional GDP declines of 18.8 percent and 15.8 percent occurred (against the same months in 1994); however, March 1995 showed an increase of 4 percent (against 1994), fueled mainly by an increase in industrial production. Agricultural production, however, continued to drop in early 1995; 1994 first-quarter production was 79 percent of the same period in 1993, and the first quarter of 1995 almost duplicated that decline.

Much of Kazakstan's economic future depends upon its ambitious three-stage privatization program, which began in 1992 and reached the end of its second stage in 1995. The Kazakstan State Property Committee has responsibility for all three phases. In the first stage, housing and small enterprises employing fewer than 200 people were privatized. Most conversions of small enterprises were accomplished by auction to groups of employees, often under the leadership of the incumbent manager. Housing, which by 1995 was nearly all in private ownership, was privatized either by giving the residence outright to its current occupant or by payment of government-issued vouchers. The second stage entailed the privatization of almost everything except the republic's mineral wealth and industrial plants employing more than 5,000 people (such plants accounted for most of Kazakstan's military-related industry).

Privatization of the largest state enterprises is the principal goal of stage three, which did not begin as scheduled in late 1995. Until that time, these enterprises were run as self-managing joint-stock companies in which the government of Kazakstan was the largest stockholder. This interim stage, which was considered beneficial, required preparation of profit-and-loss statements in anticipation of full commercial operation sometime in the future. Meanwhile, 3,500 medium-sized firms, including 70 percent of state-owned industries, were offered for sale in a mass privatization program beginning in April 1994. These firms could be purchased with government-licensed investment funds.

Under Kazakstan's privatization system, vouchers are issued to individual citizens. Vouchers then can be deposited in privatization investment funds, which in turn can buy up to 20 per-

*Typical apartment building,*
*Almaty*
*Courtesy Stanley Bach*

*Indoor marketplace, Almaty*
*Courtesy Lisa Batey*

cent of large companies being privatized. The initial voucher issue reached an estimated 95 percent of citizens. After four auctions, in mid-1994 about 85 percent of forty-five small-to-medium-sized enterprises, mainly in light industry, machinery manufacturing, and fuel distribution, had been sold.

By the end of 1994, about 60 percent of enterprises were owned by individuals or cooperatives. (In 1990 the figure already had reached 40 percent, however.) The success of the privatization of small enterprises, together with the formation of new private enterprises, meant that in 1994 some 61 percent of retail trade occurred in the private sector, an increase of 17 percent over the 1993 figure. Large-enterprise privatization has been less successful, however. Nominally privatized enterprises often maintain close contact with government officials who permit firms to maintain outdated production practices and supply relationships, and even to keep unpaid workers on their rolls.

Distribution of vouchers among the 170 government-licensed investment funds also has been problematic. In 1994 and early 1995, twenty companies collected nearly 60 percent of the vouchers, while another nineteen funds accumulated more than 20 percent; half the funds received a total of only 4 percent of the vouchers. One fund, Butia-Kapital, received nearly 10 percent of the vouchers, the largest single holding. This fund was widely rumored to be controlled by a nephew of President Nazarbayev. Although proceeds from privatization amounted to an income of 242 million tenge for the state treasury in the first quarter of 1995, complaints persisted that objects of privatization were priced too low and that favored funds received "sweetheart" deals.

Privatization of land has been handled differently than that of industry because the concept of individual land ownership does not exist in Kazakstan. Individuals and corporations can purchase only the right to use the land, and that right can be resold. Initial sale prices of state land are determined by the State Committee on Land Relations and Tenure. Government efforts to legalize a private land market have been stymied by both Russian and Kazak groups, each fearing that the other might gain control of the country's agriculture. By June 1995, some form of ownership or management change had occurred in 1,490 state farms, about three-quarters of the total remaining in operation. Many state farms, or portions of them, were converted into joint-stock companies that retained the same group of occupants and state-dominated arrangements for supply and marketing as under the previous nomenclature. The creation of small, individually managed farms was uncommon because capital, inputs, equipment, and credit were in very short supply for individuals attempting to start agricultural enterprises.

## Banking and Finance

Restructuring of the state-controlled banking and financial systems that Kazakstan inherited in 1991 has been a long, slow process. As in the Soviet era, the national bank continues to dominate the financial system, including currency management. Other commercial institutions have been established, but they play small roles in the country's financial life.

### Banks

Kazakstan's banking industry was created on the basis of a subsequently modified law enacted in April 1993. That law created a central institution, the National Bank of Kazakstan

(NBK), which has regulatory authority over a system of state, private, joint-stock, and joint banks. Licensed banks are authorized to perform all of the traditional banking functions.

The introduction of a modern banking system has not progressed smoothly. Scandals have involved swindles by bank employees, questionable loans, and the maintenance of heavy portfolios of nonproductive loans. Several bank failure scares also have occurred. Major modifications of banking regulations have been introduced several times. In June 1994, Kazakstan instituted a fifteen-month program of financial and economic reform, tightening banking and credit laws, liberalizing price policies, and ending the granting of credits to state-owned institutions. Another short-term reform was introduced in March 1995, in part to tighten regulation of capital requirements and to increase the professionalism of the existing bank's operations. To that end, a system of partnership with foreign banks was introduced, pairing domestic banks with experienced foreign partners. Guidance for this bank reform is being provided by the IMF, as well as by international auditing firms such as Ernst and Young and Price Waterhouse.

In 1994 the national bank system included a State Export and Import Bank and a State Bank for Development, both of which functioned under full government control rather than as market institutions. Four large, state-owned banks controlled 80 percent of financial assets. Of the 200 small commercial banks in operation in 1994, the majority were attached to enterprises. About thirty private banks were licensed to deal in foreign exchange.

The aim of the 1995 reform was to create a republic-wide banking system, including ten to fifteen large banks with total capital of at least US$10 million, headquartered in Almaty and with branches throughout Kazakstan; foreign branch banks, most of which would have single representative offices in Almaty; several dozen smaller banks, both in Almaty and in the provinces, with capital in the range of US$2–US$3 million; and savings banks, some with specialized purposes such as the Agricultural and Industrial Bank (Agroprombank).

In 1995 the NBK planned to release 80 percent of the credit funds it granted to an auction market, departing from the previous policy of rationing credit by directing it to designated enterprises. No stock exchange or capital markets existed as of 1995, although a law on securities and stock exchange had been adopted in 1991.

### Fiscal Management

State revenue is derived primarily from various taxes, the introduction of which has been somewhat problematic. A fundamental revision of the national tax code in 1995 reduced the number of taxes from forty-five to eleven and the volume of prospective revenue by 17 percent. Five national corporate taxes remained after the reform, which reduced the corporate tax rate to 30 percent. Prior to that revision, the largest contributions to state income were business-profit taxes (15 percent); a uniform, 20 percent value-added tax (see Glossary), a personal income tax (ranging from 12 to 40 percent and accounting for 16 percent of tax income); and special-purpose revenue funds (17 percent). However, the system has suffered from chronic undercollection. The primary long-term goal of the 1995 tax reform was to encourage fuller compliance with tax laws. The 1996 budget called for reducing the deficit to 3.3 percent of GDP.

## Prices, Wages, and Currency

The freeing of government price controls, followed by introduction of the tenge as Kazakstan's independent currency unit, set off hyperinflation, which badly eroded real wages, pensions, and savings (see table 10, Appendix). Introduced in November 1993 at approximately five to the United States dollar, the tenge fell to about fifty-six per dollar by late November 1994. Subsequently, the currency remained relatively stable, falling only to sixty-four per US$1 at the beginning of 1996. The tenge's stabilization was due in part to the government's determination to control the state budget, in part to the availability of an IMF stabilization fund, and in part to the backing of government reserves of US$1.02 billion in hard currency and gold. By 1995 inflation had decreased substantially from the levels of 1993 and 1994, when the rate was 1,880 percent, although the annualized rate for 1995 was estimated at midyear at 190 percent, well above the prime minister's target figure of 40 percent.

Inflation has strongly affected wages and family budgets. In July 1994, for example, nominal wages in the republic increased by an average of twenty times, but the costs of food, services, and goods increased by more than thirty-two times in the same month. As a result of such conditions, real wages in the republic declined by about one-third in the first half of 1994. The overall average monthly wage in the republic in February 1995 was 3,650 tenge, or about US$61 at the exchange rate of the time. In mid-1995, the overall average wage was 4,613 tenge, but the disparity between industrial and agricultural wages was growing steadily: the industrial average was 7,452 tenge, the agricultural average 2,309 tenge. Wages in service occupations such as education and health are quite low, and government employees in those occupations often are not paid on time. Chronic nonpayment of wages has caused strikes in industrial enterprises and coal mines.

Many enterprises have made wage payments in merchandise rather than money; this practice has led to a large volume of merchandise resale at bazaars, either by workers or by private wholesalers. The actual level of consumer welfare is unknown because prices and the availability of goods change rapidly. Because Kazakstan lacks a strong consumer-goods industry, imports have begun to replace CIS products, notably clothing, housewares, and electronics. In 1995 wage increases continued to lag behind the rising cost of living, causing spending power to decline by 2 to 3 percent per month. The greatest losses in real wages have been suffered in industrial (and mostly Russian) northern Kazakstan. One consequence of declining purchasing power is that families now devote as much as 10 percent of their budgets to the purchase of foreign currency, presumably as a hedge against inflation. In 1995 the purchase of food became the largest family expenditure, exceeding 50 percent of average budgets. Even so, purchases of all categories of foodstuffs have declined in the republic, while purchases of nonfoodstuffs have dropped 40 percent or more.

## International Financial Relations

Shortly after independence, Kazakstan began seeking diversification of its commercial activities, which had focused completely on the Soviet Union until 1992. Because the regime has been stable and abundant natural resources make investment potentially profitable, the search for new foreign partners has been successful in many cases, although substantial limitations remained in the mid-1990s.

### Foreign Investment

World Bank figures showed foreign direct investment in Kazakstan of US$400 million in 1993, projected to rise to an annual average of about US$775 million by 1997. By mid-1994, fourteen British firms, fifty American firms, and twenty-four

French firms were registered as investors. A March 1994 survey showed one foreign acquisition in the republic, twenty-five new economic projects, and seventy working joint ventures, with total foreign investment of $US10.44 billion. Average investment was computed at US$108.7 million, but that figure was distorted by Chevron's huge single investment in the Tengiz oil development project.

In the mid-1990s, Kazakstan's investment climate was considered liberal compared with that of the other non-Baltic former Soviet republics. In December 1994, existing trade legislation was consolidated into the Law on Foreign Investments, which, among other things, offered foreign investors 100 percent ownership of enterprises and full conversion of profits into hard currency. Liberal tax incentives, including a five-year initial forgiveness of all corporate taxes, also have been implemented. Regulations have been loosened on the export of precious metals and on terms for foreign participation in oil field development. For these reasons, international investor ratings place Kazakstan high among the former Soviet republics.

The international lending community also has been attracted to Kazakstan. In 1994 the Paris Club of Western creditor countries committed US$1.33 billion for use in reconstructing Kazakstan's industry and agriculture. The sum was the first large-scale foreign assistance received by the republic. Kazakstan also received US$296.9 million in trade credits in 1994, US$220 million of which came from Japan. Projections called for Kazakstan's external debt to peak at US$5.1 billion in 1996, then begin to decline. However, that figure was based on expectations of drastic increases in foreign oil sales by 1996, an eventuality made impossible by the intervening decline in output.

### Foreign Trade

Traditionally, most of the goods that Kazakstan produced for export went to markets in Russia and elsewhere in the Soviet Union. In 1990 some 88.7 percent of Kazakstan's exports followed this route, including more than 70 percent of its industrial production and mined products and 27 percent of its agricultural production. By 1992 the trade situation among the CIS countries was characterized by the World Bank as "verging on the chaotic," with the old Soviet payments system deteriorating and a common currency, the ruble (see Glossary), showing uncertain value. That situation prompted Kazakstan to undertake a vigorous search for diversified trade markets, and in fact its exports to the CIS declined by nearly 80 percent between 1990 and 1994. By 1994 Russia still accounted for 40 percent of Kazakstan's total trade and for 74 and 80 percent of the republic's total CIS exports and imports, respectively. Kazakstan's largest volume of non-Russian CIS trade is with Kyrgyzstan, Uzbekistan, Belarus, and Ukraine, all of which are net importers of Kazak goods. The most important West European trading partners are Germany, the Netherlands, Switzerland, the Czech Republic, and Italy (see table 11, Appendix). Non-CIS Asian countries account for 11 percent of trade, with China the major partner in this category.

The predominant pattern of trade has continued from the Soviet era: exports are mostly raw materials, and imports are mostly manufactured goods. Ferrous and nonferrous metals—mainly rolled steel, copper, ferroalloys, zinc, titanium, and aluminum—account for 40 percent of export earnings, followed by oil and petroleum products (33 percent) and chemicals (10 percent). Energy products are also the largest import category, mainly because of the ongoing geographically determined exchange agreement that sends Russian oil from western Siberia to refineries in eastern Kazakstan and oil from Kazakstan's western oil fields to refineries across the border in Russia. Thus, in 1994 some 31 percent of imports were energy products, followed by machinery, equipment, and vehicles (29 percent); chemicals; and food. By 1994 private traders also imported large amounts of consumer products that did not appear in official statistics.

In 1994 Kazakstan's total exports were worth US$3.076 billion, and its imports were worth US$3.488 billion. Comparison with 1993 is not meaningful because in that year unstable ruble values and heavy barter transactions skewed statistics. In fact, an estimated 70 percent of 1994 trade also was in the form of barter. Of the 1994 totals, US$1.266 billion, or 41 percent, of exports went to the "far abroad," beyond the CIS, and US$1.286 billion, or 37 percent, of imports came from the "far abroad." Experts forecast slightly lower overall export figures in 1995 because of restricted access to Russian pipelines. The trade deficit with non-CIS partners is financed by borrowing from international financial institutions. The deficit with CIS partners is financed simply by delaying payments to Russia.

## Transportation and Telecommunications

Kazakstan's transportation and telecommunications networks are poorly developed because of the distance between population centers (see fig. 7) and because of the inhospitable terrain that separates them. Only the largest cities are linked by roads and railroad. Railroad lines carry the overwhelming bulk of freight traffic, and more than half of the passenger traffic moves by road. In 1996, two ministries were responsible for transportation: the Ministry of Transport and Communications for transport operation of railways, roads, and airlines; and the Ministry of Construction and Housing, for construction of highways and airport and port facilities.

### Transportation

Overall transportation volume probably peaked in the late Soviet period, when enormous inefficiencies added time and distance to all types of movement. The postindependence correlation of prices to cost has meant abandonment of uneconomical transportation practices. The pipeline system, although crucial to the economic welfare of oil-rich Kazakstan, remains without direct connection to potential customers in the West and elsewhere. The national telephone system serves only a small percentage of the population; domestic radio and television remain limited and state owned.

#### *Roads*

In 1994 and 1995, annual freight movement by road, which already accounted for less than 10 percent of Kazakstan's freight haulage, declined more than 50 percent per year because of the shift to more efficient means of transport and the country's overall economic decline. In 1993 Kazakstan counted about 400,000 road vehicles for freight transport, many of which were pieces of farm equipment. Available tractors and trailers are mostly small and in poor condition; the shortage of spare parts and the lack of a domestic truck-manufacturing industry hinder long-distance haulage.

The passenger bus fleet, which numbered 25,500 vehicles in 1991, has declined in numbers and quality since the last new buses were added in 1988. Spare parts are also a problem in bus maintenance, and local bus service is impeded by government caps on fares.

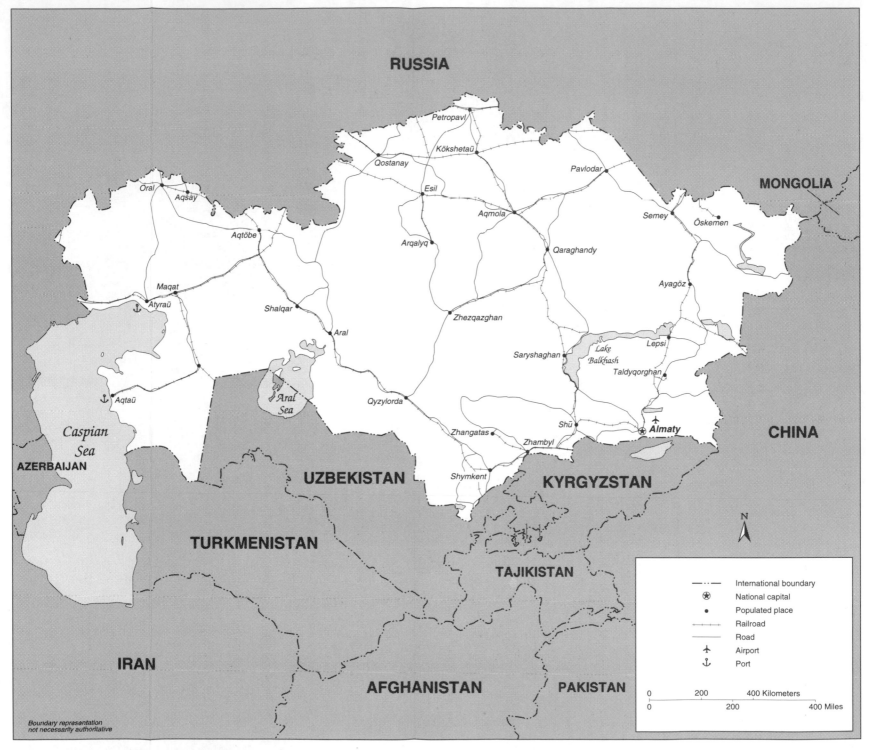

*Figure 7. Kazakstan: Transportation System, 1996*

The basic road infrastructure (about 88,000 kilometers, of which about 83,000 kilometers are paved or gravel) serves the widely dispersed population and economic centers adequately. However, there is a shortage of road maintenance equipment, and construction and repair contracts are allocated to as many as seventy different companies and plants owned by the Ministry of Construction and Housing and the Ministry of Transport and Communications. As a result, construction and repair operations are disorganized and uneconomical.

### Railroads

Kazakstan Railways is the third largest rail system in the former Soviet Union, smaller only than the systems of Russia and Ukraine. In 1991 railroads carried 90 percent of Kazakstan's freight and 30 percent of its passenger traffic. In 1993 the rail system included 14,148 kilometers of track, of which 3,050 kilometers were electrified. All track was 1,520-millimeter gauge. In 1993 the system carried about 39.7 million passengers and hauled about 517 million tons of freight, but haulage declined 42 percent in 1994, most notably in chemicals, cement, iron ore, and ferrous metals. Like the road system, Kazakstan Railways suffers from a shortage of spare parts; as much as 95 percent of spare parts, equipment, and rolling stock must be purchased from Russia, Ukraine, and other countries. Repair plants for rolling stock are in poor condition and use outmoded equipment.

### Pipelines

In 1992 Kazakstan had 2,850 kilometers of pipeline for crude oil, 3,480 kilometers for natural gas, and 1,500 kilometers for refined products. The oil pipeline system was designed to ship domestic oil, most of which is in the western part of the republic, and to bring Russia's Siberian oil to Kazak refineries. Construction of a pipeline that would bring Kazakstan's oil to world markets has proven a major obstacle in the development of the Tengiz field because of disagreements over routing, financing, and ownership. Russian control of Kazakstan's only pipelines to the outside world has restricted oil exports to the West and discouraged foreign investment in the oil and gas industries. In 1995 Kazakstan, Turkmenistan, and Azerbaijan, all of which have suffered export shutdowns in their cross-Russia pipelines, began discussing a massive pipeline project that would bring their products across China to the Pacific Ocean and into Japan (see Energy, this ch.).

### Air Transport

Kazakstan Airlines was founded in 1993 as a joint-stock company initially based on 100 aircraft that the republic received as its share when the Soviet Aeroflot fleet was divided among the former republics. Six private airline companies also operate within the republic. The republic airlines of Ukraine and Uzbekistan began service to Kazakstan's regional airports in 1992, and Lufthansa of Germany and Turkish Airlines have begun international flights into Almaty. Air traffic between Kazakstan and other CIS republics is handled mainly by Aeroflot. The airport at Almaty, Kazakstan's only international facility, underwent a gradual modernization of instrumentation, air control, and communications facilities in the early 1990s; beginning in 1993, international traffic to and from Kyrgyzstan also moved through Almaty. In 1994, besides connections with CIS destinations, regular flights went to Frankfurt, Hannover, Vienna, Zurich, Istanbul, Delhi, Karachi, Tel Aviv, and Sharjah. In 1991 some 7.9 million passengers and about 36.4 million tons of freight passed through Kazak airports. In 1994 the republic had twenty commercial airports and another 132 classified as usable, of which forty-nine had permanent-surface runways and eight had runways longer than 3,600 meters.

### Water Transport

The republic's two inland waterways, the Syrdariya in south-central Kazakstan and the Ertis River in the northeast, have a total of 4,000 kilometers of waterway navigable by commercial craft. A state agency, the Kazakstan River Fleet Industrial Association (Kazrechmorflot), administers river traffic. In 1992 the association's eleven water transport companies carried about 1.6 million passengers and about 7 million tons of freight.

## Telecommunications

Experts consider Kazakstan's telecommunications facilities inadequate to support the type of economic expansion sought in the mid-1990s. The Ministry of Transport and Communications is the only provider of telecommunications services; its responsibilities include management and regulation of all aspects of the republic's telephone, telex, telegraph, data communications, radio, television, and postal services.

In 1994 only seventeen of every 100 people in urban areas and 7.6 of every 100 people in rural areas had telephones. These figures were above average for Central Asia but lower than those for other CIS countries. Of the republic's total of about 2.2 million telephones, 184,000 were located in Almaty. Current equipment is utilized at a rate of 98 percent, leaving no room for expansion or new subscribers, although in 1992 the waiting list had about 1 million names.

Sixty breakdowns per 100 telephone lines occur annually, a very high rate. Because much of Kazakstan's telephone equipment, most of which came from the Soviet Union and Eastern Europe, is obsolete, spare parts are scarce. In 1992 only 8 percent of exchanges used fiber-optic and digital equipment. International connections go through Moscow and via satellite links to Australia and Israel. In 1992 a total of 100 channels connected with countries outside the CIS, and 3,000 channels connected with CIS countries.

In 1994 there were about 4.75 million televisions and 10.17 million radios in Kazakstan. Landlines and microwave carry radio broadcasts from other CIS republics and China; the International Telecommunications Satellite Organization (Intelsat) and the Russian Orbita satellite system provide satellite transmission of television broadcasts from other countries, and the Moscow gateway switch sends international radio broadcasts through eight telecommunications circuits. With Turkish aid, a new satellite ground station went into operation at Almaty in 1992.

Radio and television broadcasting is the exclusive domain of the Kazakstan State Radio and Television Company. In 1995 the broadcasting system included three national and thirteen regional radio programs broadcast over fifty-eight stations, an irregular Moscow relay of the Voice of Russia and Radio Netherlands, Radio Almaty (a foreign broadcast service offering English, German, Kazak, and Russian programming), one domestic television channel available through eight regional stations, and relays of two Russian channels and Kyrgyz and Turkish programming in Almaty.

## Government and Politics

In 1995 Kazakstan passed through a period of political turmoil that fundamentally changed the shape of the republic's government and political forces. The republic came under direct presidential rule in March 1995, and a new constitution adopted shortly thereafter strengthened the power of the executive. Presidential elections, originally scheduled for sometime in 1996, were postponed until December 2000 after a 1995 referendum provided the basis for such an extension.

## Constitution

In May 1995, Nazarbayev convened a council of experts to draw up a new constitution under his guidance. The resulting constitution was adopted in August 1995 by a popular referendum. The official participation figure, 90 percent, and the fairness of this vote were contested by opposition groups. The constitution guarantees equal rights to all nationalities and prescribes both Kazak and Russian as "official" state languages, suitable for use in government documents and education. The president and the legislature, the Supreme Kenges (Supreme Soviet), are to be elected by universal adult suffrage for five-year terms. The president is head of state. The second component of the executive branch is the Council of Ministers, key members of which are presidential appointees. The prime minister, as head of the Council of Ministers, appoints the other ministers.

## Structure of Government

The postindependence government was structured by the 1993 constitution with a strong executive branch, a parliament, and a judicial branch. In practice, the administration of Nursultan Nazarbayev dominated governance sufficiently to impel the writing of a new constitution providing justification for the one-man rule that developed in the early 1990s.

### Executive Branch

The constitution formalizes the increased power that President Nazarbayev assumed upon the invalidation of parliament in early 1995. It continues the previous constitutional definition of Kazakstan as a unitary state with a presidential form of government. The president is the highest state officer, responsible for naming the government—subject to parliamentary approval—and all other republic officials. The 1995 constitution expands the president's power in introducing and vetoing legislation. The government that the president appoints consists of the Council of Ministers, headed by a prime minister, and several state committees. In early 1996, after Nazarbayev had reshuffled the government in October 1995, the Council of Ministers included the heads of twenty-one ministries and nine state committees; the prime minister was Akezhan Kazhegeldin. In the October 1995 shift, Nazarbayev himself assumed the portfolio of the Ministry of National Security.

The new constitution does not provide for the position of vice president, although it permitted the incumbent vice president, Yerik Asanbayev, to remain in office until 1996. The president has the power to declare states of emergency during which the constitution can be suspended. The president is the sponsor of legislation and the guarantor of the constitution and of the proper functioning of government, with the power to override the decisions and actions of local authorities and councils. The only grounds on which a president can be removed are infirmity and treason, either of which must be confirmed by a majority of the joint upper and lower houses of the new parliament. In the event of such a removal from power, the prime minister would become the temporary president.

### Legislative Branch

The 1993 constitution created a unicameral parliament, which was to replace the 350-seat Supreme Soviet when the mandates of that body's deputies expired in 1995. Composed overwhelmingly of career communists, the 1990 parliament had been a balky and turgid partner for the task of economic and political reform. Although he probably lacked the legal authority to do so, Nazarbayev pressured this parliament into a "voluntary" early dissolution in December 1993 in order to allow the seating of a smaller and presumably more pliant "professional parliament." Under the 1995 constitution, the parliament consists of two houses, the Senate and the Majlis, both operating in continuous session. Each of Kazakstan's nineteen provinces and the city of Almaty, which has province status, have two senators. These are chosen for four-year terms by joint sessions of the provinces' legislative bodies. An additional seven senators are appointed directly by the president. In addition, ex-presidents automatically receive the status of senators-for-life. The Majlis has sixty-seven representatives, including one from each of fifty-five districts drawn to have roughly equal populations, and the Senate has forty seats. Direct elections for half the seats are held every two years. In the first election under the new parliamentary structure, all seats in both houses of parliament were contested in December 1995; runoff elections filled twenty-three seats in the Majlis for which the initial vote was inconclusive. International observers reported procedural violations in the Majlis voting. The new parliament, which was seated in January 1996, included sixty-eight Kazak and thirty-one Russian deputies; only ten deputies were women.

The initiative for most legislative actions originates with the president. If parliament passes a law that the president vetoes, a two-thirds vote of both houses is required to override the veto. A similar margin is needed to express no confidence in a prime minister, an action that requires the president to name a new prime minister and Council of Ministers.

### Judicial System

The judicial system is the least developed of Kazakstan's three branches of government. Although Minister of Justice Nagashibay Shaykenov objected strenuously, the constitution retains the practice of presidential appointment of all judges in the republic. The 1993 constitution specified terms of service for judges, but the 1995 document makes no mention of length of service, suggesting that judges will serve at the president's pleasure.

Under the 1993 constitution, lines of judicial authority were poorly defined, in part because the republic had three "highest courts"—the Supreme Court, the State Arbitrage Court, and the Constitutional Court—which among them employed a total of sixty-six senior judges. Many of these senior judges, as well as numerous judges in lower courts, had been retained from the Soviet era, when the judicial branch was entirely under the control of the central government. The 1995 constitution makes no provision for the State Abritrage Court, which had heard economic disputes among enterprises and between enterprises and government agencies. Provisions for the new judiciary clearly subordinate all other courts to the Supreme Court, which also has a consultative role in appointing senior judges.

### Local Government

Kazakstan is divided into nineteen provinces, and the city of Almaty has administrative status equal to that of a province. In turn, the provinces are divided into regions that consist of a number of settlement points. Each province and region and most settlements have their own elective councils, charged with

*Headquarters building of parliament, Almaty*
*Courtesy Stanley Bach*

drawing up a budget and supervising local taxation. Cities have their own local councils as well, and large cities are divided into regions, each of which has its own council.

The local legislatures lack the authority to choose the local executive, who is appointed directly by the president. The local executive has the job of ensuring that decisions of the national government are enforced and that the constitution is observed. Province and regional "heads of administration," known by the Russian term *glav* or the Kazak term *hakim*, are presidential appointees. The *hakim*, in turn, appoints the members of his staff, who are the department heads of the jurisdiction. The *hakim* also can reverse budgetary decisions of the local councils.

There has been considerable pressure, especially in the predominantly Russian north, to make the *hakim* posts elective rather than appointive. In 1994 Nazarbayev indicated that he would consider doing so, but the 1995 constitution provides only that the local councils can express no confidence in their *hakim* by a two-thirds vote. The president also has the power to override or revoke decisions taken by local councils; a *hakim* has the power to control budgetary decisions taken by the local council.

## The Election of 1994 and Its Aftermath

After the early dissolution in 1993 of Kazakstan's first parliament, an election for the 177 seats of the new, "professional" parliament was held in March 1994. The election was so closely managed and restricted by the government that observers from the Organization for Security and Cooperation in Europe (OSCE; before 1995, the Conference on Security and Cooperation in Europe—CSCE—see Glossary) initially were reluctant to certify the election as fair.

Despite his careful electoral management, Nazarbayev netted a reliable bloc of only about sixty of the 177 seats. The remaining deputies quickly organized themselves into a "constructive" opposition bloc, a center-left configuration calling itself Respublika. It included a number of disparate political groups. A subgroup of Respublika organized a shadow cabinet to provide alternative viewpoints and programs to those of the government.

At the end of May 1994, the parliament passed a vote of no confidence in the government of Prime Minister Sergey Tereshchenko, who had been in office since 1991. Nazarbayev put off dismissing Tereshchenko, citing the provision of the 1993 constitution giving the president the right to name the prime minister, subject only to parliamentary confirmation. By midyear, however, parliament was in rebellion against the president, and a new faction of Respublika, including a broad range of communist, nationalist, and special-issue parties, demanded the resignations of Nazarbayev and Tereshchenko.

In mid-October, following a month-long scandal over the private dealings of Tereshchenko's ministers of internal affairs and the economy (the second of whom was indicted), Nazarbayev was finally forced to dismiss the Tereshchenko government. Nazarbayev named industrialist Akezhan Kazhegeldin to replace Tereshchenko. As chief of a northern industrial conglomerate, Kazhegeldin, a Kazak, was closely associated with the Russian-controlled sector of Kazakstan prior to 1991.

Thus, by late 1994 parliament was emerging as a particular focus for anti-Nazarbayev sentiment. Although extremely unproductive itself, passing only seven laws during its year of existence, parliament severely impeded Nazarbayev's privatization programs, causing the complete cessation of privatization voucher distribution. At the end of 1994, the parliament issued its own alternative New Economic Policy, in competition with Nazarbayev's, and parliament also attempted to take over actual disbursement of funds for the state budget. At the same time, parliament was providing a forum for several skilled and well-financed men to position themselves for a challenge to Nazarbayev in the presidential election scheduled for 1996.

In March 1995, Kazakstan's Constitutional Court ruled the 1994 parliamentary election invalid because of procedural irregularities that, among other things, waived certain requirements for pro-Nazarbayev candidates. After filing a token objection, Nazarbayev announced the dissolution of parliament and new elections to be held in two or three months. The Council of Ministers that had been approved by that parliament then resigned en masse. Using emergency powers granted him upon the dissolution of the 1990–93 parliament, Nazarbayev reappointed Prime Minister Kazhegeldin, who installed a new Council of Ministers. Unlike its virtually all-Kazak predecessor, the new body put the key Ministry of Finance under a Russian, Aleksandr Pavlov, and gave the Ministry of the Economy portfolio to a Middle Horde Kazak from the Russified north. One of Kazhegeldin's two new first deputy prime ministers was Kazak; the other was Russian. The new head of the Privatization Commission, Sarybay Kalmurzayev, also apparently was a Middle Horder. He not only began to permit privatization auctioneers to accept cash in addition to vouchers, but also began to give Russian companies rights of first refusal in privatization of large industrial plants, especially military ones. In April 1995, Nazarbayev staged a referendum that ratified extension of his presidency until December 2000 by a 95 percent majority. In December 1995, Nazarbayev issued a decree enabling him to annul any existing law, demand the government's resignation, or order new parliamentary elections. This step furthered the authoritarian direction of Kazakstan's government.

## Political Organizations

Economic and ethnic differentiation in Kazakstan has led to the appearance of more than 2,000 social organizations, movements, political parties, and social action funds across a broad political spectrum. Although Nazarbayev prevented electoral participation by many opposition parties, the formation and reformation of parties and coalitions have occurred at a rapid pace in the postindependence years. In the parliamentary election of December 1995, thirty parties and other organizations registered candidates.

### The President's Party

Significantly, the one type of party that has failed to thrive in Kazakstan is a "presidential party" that would serve as a training ground for future officials, as well as a conduit for their advancement. Nazarbayev lost control of his first two attempts at forming parties, the Socialists and the People's Congress Party (NKK). The latter particularly, under the leadership of former Nazarbayev ally Olzhas Suleymenov, became a center of parliamentary opposition. Nazarbayev's third party, the People's Unity Party (SNEK), remained loyal to the president, although it was unable, even with considerable government help, to elect enough deputies to give Nazarbayev control of the 1994–95 parliament. SNEK formally incorporated itself as a political party in February 1995.

### Other Parties

With the exception of SNEK and some smaller entities, such as the Republican Party and an entrepreneurial association known as For Kazakstan's Future, most of Kazakstan's parties and organizations have little or no influence on presidential decision making. Because privatization and the deteriorating economy have left most citizens much worse off than they were in the early 1990s, most of the republic's organizations and parties have an oppositional or antipresidential character.

The Communist Party of Kazakstan, declared illegal in 1991, was allowed to re-register in 1993. Kazakstan also has a small Socialist Democratic Party. Both parties made poor showings in the 1994 election, but two former communist organizations, the State Labor Union (Profsoyuz) and the Peasants' Union, managed to take eleven and four seats, respectively.

### Nationalist Groups

At least four large Kazak nationalist movements were active in the mid-1990s. Three of them—Azat (Freedom), the Republican Party, and Zheltoksan (December)—attempted to form a single party under the name Azat, with the aim of removing "colonialist" foreign influences from Kazakstan. The fourth movement, Alash (named for the legendary founder of the Kazak nation, as well as for the pre-Soviet nationalist party of the same name), refused to join such a coalition because it advocated a more actively nationalist and pro-Muslim line than did the other three parties. In the March 1994 election, Azat and the Republicans were the only nationalist parties to run candidates. They elected just one deputy between them.

Four exclusively Russian political organizations in Kazakstan have nationalist or federative agendas. These are Yedinstvo (Unity), Civic Contract, Democratic Progress, and Lad (Harmony). Party registration procedures for the 1994 election made places on the ballot very difficult to obtain for the Russian nationalist groups. Although Lad was forced to run its candidates without party identification, four deputies were elected with ties to that party.

The Russian group most unsettling to the Nazarbayev government was the Cossacks, who were denied official registration, as well as recognition of their claimed status as a distinct ethnic group in the northeast and northwest. Not permitted to drill, carry weapons, or engage in their traditional military activities, Kazakstan's Cossacks have, in increasing numbers, crossed the border into Russia, where restrictions are not as tight.

### Opposition Coalitions

In 1994 parliament's success at countering presidential power encouraged the legislators, many of whom were connected with the former Soviet ruling elite, to use their training in the political infighting of Soviet bureaucracy to form effective antipresidential coalitions. Ironically, these coalitions were the only political groupings in the republic that transcended ethnic differences. The Respublika group was elastic enough to contain both Kazak and Russian nationalists, and the Otan-Otechestvo organization forged a coalition of Kazaks, Russians, and even Cossacks who desired a return to Soviet-style political and social structures.

## Nazarbayev and Political Prospects

Public opinion in Kazakstan appears to have accepted the imposition of presidential rule, at least partly because the parliament Nazarbayev dissolved had focused on its own wages and benefits rather than on solving the nation's problems. In the short run, the imposition of direct presidential rule seemed likely to reduce ethnic tensions within the republic. Indeed, one of Nazarbayev's primary justifications for assuming greater power was the possibility that bolstered presidential authority could stem the growing ethnic hostility in the republic, including a general rise in anti-Semitism.

The ethnic constituency whose appeasement is most important is, however, the Russians, both within the republic and in Russia proper. Stability in Kazakstan is overwhelmingly shaped by developments in Russia, especially as that country returns its attention to some measure of reintegration of the former Soviet empire. Because of Kazakstan's great vulnerability to Russian political, economic, and military intervention, experts assume that Russian national and ethnic interests play a considerable part in Nazarbayev's political calculations (see Foreign Policy; National Security Prospects, this ch.).

It also seems likely that Nazarbayev would use presidential rule to increase the linguistic and cultural rights of the republic's Russians. Although Nazarbayev had taken a firm stand on the issue of formal dual citizenship, a treaty he and Russia's president, Boris N. Yeltsin, signed in January 1995 all but obviated the language question by permitting citizens of the respective countries to own property in either republic, to move freely between them, to sign contracts (including contracts for military service) in either country, and to exchange one country's citizenship for the other's. When the Kazak parliament ratified that agreement, that body also voted to extend to the end of 1995 the deadline by which residents must declare either Kazakstani or Russian citizenship. After the dissolution of that parliament, Kazakstan considered extending the deadline until 2000, as Russia already had done.

In the mid-1990s, Nazarbayev seemed likely to face eventual opposition from Kazak nationalists if he continued making concessions to the republic's Russians. Such opposition would be conditioned, however, by the deep divisions of ethnic Kazaks along clan and family lines, which give some of them more interests in common with the Russians than with their ethnic fellows. The Kazaks also have no institutions that might serve as alternative focuses of political will. Despite a wave of mosque building since independence, Islam is not well established in much of the republic, and there is no national religious-political network through which disaffected Kazaks might be mobilized.

The lack of an obvious venue for expression of popular dissatisfaction does not mean, however, that none will materialize. Nazarbayev gambled that imposition of presidential rule would permit him to transform the republic's economy and thus placate the opposition through an indisputable and widespread improvement of living standards. Experts agree that the republic has the natural resources and industrial potential to make this a credible wager. But a number of conditions outside Nazarbayev's control, such as the political climate in Russia and the other Central Asian states, would influence that outcome. By dismissing parliament and taking upon himself the entire burden of government, Nazarbayev made himself the obvious target for the public discontent that radical transformations inevitably produce.

## The Media

Kazakstan has enjoyed the same flourishing of media as have most of the other former Soviet republics. To some extent, the republic also continues to be influenced by the Moscow media, although changes in currency and the simple passage of time are steadily reducing that influence. Also similar to the processes in other republics is a certain erosion of the freedom that the media enjoyed in the earlier days of independence. Although the government always has retained some control, there was a certain tendency to view the proper relationship between the media and government as adversarial. However, Nazarbayev steadily chipped away at Kazakstan's central press, which as a result became more noticeably pro-government in 1994 and 1995. The 1995 constitution guarantees freedom of ideas and expression and explicitly bans censorship. In practice, however, the government influences the press in several ways. Government presses (the only ones available) have refused to publish private newspapers for various "technical" reasons; financial pressure has been brought through court cases or investigations of a given newspaper's sponsors; and, in some cases, outright censorship has been exercised for "security reasons." Strictly enforced laws forbid personal criticism of the president or members of the president's family.

The major official newspapers are the Russian-language *Kazakstanskaya pravda* and *Sovety Kazakstana,* which are supported by the government. Nominally, the former is the organ of the Council of Ministers and the latter that of the parliament. The newspaper *Ekspress K* has taken some independent positions, although in the mid-1990s the editor in chief was a senior official in SNEK, the presidential political party. The small-edition papers *Respublika* and *NKK* are somewhat more oppositional. The first was the organ of the Socialist Party until it was sold to commercial interests, and the second is the organ of the People's Congress Party. *Respublika* is said to be underfinanced, but *NKK* enjoys the resources of Olzhas Suleymenov's large Nevada-Semipalatinsk commercial organization. *Panorama,* perhaps the largest independent newspaper in the republic, is owned by some of the largest business interests in the republic and is oriented toward political and economic issues (on which it generally takes an objective view). The Karavan commercial organization publishes two newspapers, *Karavan* and *ABV* (short for Almaty Business News). The former inclines toward tabloid-style muckraking, while the latter is entirely commercial in character.

The electronic media remain under state control. Many private production companies exist, but access to television and radio is still controlled by the State Television and Radio Broadcasting Corporation (see Transportation and Telecommunications, this ch.).

As it does most activities, ethnicity complicates media operations. Inevitably the nationality of the owners of a newspaper or television production company affects how its product is received. The most obvious example is that of the newspaper *Karavan.* Although its muckraking approach is similar to that taken by newspapers in Moscow and Bishkek, the fact that the paper is Russian-owned makes it seem, in the context of Kazakstan, to be more vividly partisan. In early 1995, a fire in the *Karavan* warehouse prompted rumors of sabotage, which never were substantiated.

## Human Rights

Considering the power available to the Nazarbayev regime, Kazakstan's observation of international human-rights standards in the mid-1990s was given a relatively high rating. In one celebrated case of attempted censorship, historian Karishal Asanov was tried three times before being acquitted on a charge of defaming the president for an article he published in a Moscow newspaper.

Although antigovernment activities of the nationalist-religious group Alash have been actively discouraged, there have been no recorded instances of extrajudicial killings or disappearances, or of unsubstantiated grounds for arrest. Prisons are generally overcrowded because of the eruption of crime in the republic, but international organizations record no instances of torture or of deliberately degrading treatment.

The state security organs continue some of their Soviet-era ways; there have been complaints that proper procedures for search warrants are not always followed, and some credible accusations have been made about tampering with or planting evidence in criminal proceedings. In general, however, the republic's investigative and security organs seem to be making an effort to follow the constitution's guidance on the inviolability of person, property, and dwelling.

Free movement about the country is permitted, although residence is still controlled by the Soviet-era registration system, which requires citizens to have official permission to live in a particular city. In practice, this system has made it almost impossible for outsiders to move into Almaty.

The exercise of political rights in Kazakstan is closely controlled, and the number of parties is limited by registration restrictions. Imposition of presidential rule and the general strengthening of the president's role have limited popular political participation. The Russian population has attempted to depict the imposition of language laws and the refusal to grant dual citizenship as violations of human rights, but these claims generally have not been accepted by the international community. Several Russian political groups and human rights alleged that irregularities in the August 1995 constitutional referendum invalidated the document's ratification on human rights grounds. The nine official foreign observers reported no major irregularities, however.

## Foreign Policy

From the onset of independence, President Nazarbayev sought international support to secure a place for Kazakstan in the world community, playing the role of bridge between East and West, between Europe and Asia.

Almost immediately upon its declaration of independence, the republic gained a seat in the United Nations, membership in the CSCE, and a seat on the coordinating council of the North Atlantic Treaty Organization (NATO—see Glossary). The United States and other nations also gave Kazakstan quick recognition, opening embassies in Almaty and receiving Kazakstani ambassadors in return. Its status as an apparent nuclear power got Kazakstan off to a fast start in international diplomacy. President Nazarbayev became a signatory to the Strategic Arms Reduction Treaty (START) and its so-called Lisbon Protocol by which Belarus, Kazakstan, and Ukraine pledged to eliminate nuclear weapons in the 1990s. In addition, Nazarbayev was able to negotiate US$1.2 billion in prepayment by the United States against sale of the enriched uranium contained in Kazakstan's warheads, as well as another US$311 million for maintenance and conversion of existing missile silos. Equally important was that the nuclear warheads prompted the United States to become a party to negotiations concerning the warheads between Kazakstan and Russia. The United States eventually became a guarantor of the agreement reached by the two countries. In May 1995, the last nuclear warhead in Kazakstan was destroyed at Semey, completing the program of removal and destruction of the entire former Soviet arsenal and achieving the republic's goal of being "nuclear free."

Under the leadership of Nazarbayev, who maintained personal control of foreign policy, Kazakstan eagerly courted Western investment. Although foreign aid, most of it from Western nations, began as a trickle, significant amounts were received by 1994. In practice, however, Nazarbayev was ambivalent about moving too fully into a Western orbit.

### Turkey

In the period shortly after independence, policy makers often discussed following the "Turkish model," emulating Turkey in incorporating a Muslim cultural heritage into a secular, Europeanized state. Turkey's president Turgut Özal made a state visit to Kazakstan in March 1991 and hosted a return visit by Nazarbayev later the same year. Soon afterward Nazarbayev began to echo Turkish talk of turning Kazakstan into a bridge between Muslim East and Christian West. In practice, however, the Turks proved to be more culturally dissimilar than the Kazakstanis had imagined; more important, Turkey's own economic problems meant that most promises of aid and investment remained mostly just statements of intentions.

### China

As Turkey proved itself a disappointment, President Nazarbayev began to speak with increasing enthusiasm about the Asian economic "tigers" such as Singapore, the Republic of Korea (South Korea), and Taiwan. Among the republic's first foreign economic advisers were Chan Young Bang, a Korean American with close ties to South Korea's major industrial families, and Singapore's former prime minister, Li Kwan Yew.

The most compelling model, however, was provided by China, which quickly had become Kazakstan's largest non-CIS trading partner. The Kazakstani leadership found the Chinese

*President Nursultan Nazarbayev with French President François*
*Mitterrand during the former's official*
*visit to France, September 1992*
*Courtesy Hermine Dreyfuss*

combination of rigid social control and private-sector prosperity an attractive one. China also represented a vast market and appeared quite able to supply the food, medicine, and consumer goods most desired by the Kazakstani market.

However, the relationship with China has been a prickly one. Kazakstan's fears of Chinese domination remain from the Soviet era and from the Kazaks' earlier nomadic history. A large number of Kazaks and other Muslims live in the Xinjiang Uygur Autonomous Region of China, just over the border. Direct rail and road links have been opened to Ürümqi in Xinjiang, and Chinese traders in Kazakstan are prominent in the thriving barter between the two nations. However, China is plainly nervous about any contact that would encourage separatist or nationalist sentiments among its own "captive peoples." For its part, Kazakstan has expressed unease about the large numbers of Chinese who began buying property and settling in the republic after the end of Soviet rule. Kazakstan also has reacted angrily but without effect to Chinese nuclear tests at Lob Nor, China's main testing site, located within 300 kilometers of the common border.

### The Middle East

Nazarbayev was hesitant to court investment from the Middle East, despite high levels of Turkish and Iranian commercial activity in Central Asia. Unlike the other Central Asian republics, Kazakstan initially accepted only observer status in the Muslim-dominated ECO, largely out of concern not to appear too "Muslim" itself. Over time, however, the president moved from being a professed atheist to proudly proclaiming his Muslim heritage. He has encouraged assistance from Iran in developing transportation links, from Oman in building oil pipelines, from Egypt in building mosques, and from Saudi Arabia in developing a national banking system.

### Russia and the CIS

Most of Kazakstan's foreign policy has, not unnaturally, focused on the other former Soviet republics and, particularly, on the potential territorial ambitions of Russia. Since Gorbachev's proposal for a modified continuation of the Soviet Union in late 1991, Kazakstan has supported arrangements with Russia that guarantee the republic's sovereignty and independence, including a stronger and institutionally complex CIS.

As the CIS failed to develop a strong institutional framework, Nazarbayev attempted to achieve the same end in another way, proposing the creation of a Euro-Asian Union that would subordinate the economic, defense, and foreign policies of individual member states to decisions made by a council of presidents, an elective joint parliament, and joint councils of defense and other ministries. Citizens of member nations would hold union citizenship, essentially reducing the independence of the individual member republics to something like their Soviet-era status. The proposal, however, met with little enthusiasm, especially from Russia, whose support was crucial to the plan's success.

Nazarbayev pursued bilateral trade and security agreements with each of the former republics and in September 1992 unsuccessfully attempted to have Kazakstan broker a cease-fire between Armenia and Azerbaijan that also would set a precedent for settling interrepublic and interregional strife in the former republics. Nazarbayev also participated in the fitful efforts of the five Central Asian leaders to create some sort of regional entity; the most promising of these was a free-trade zone established in 1994 among Uzbekistan, Kyrgyzstan, and Kazakstan (see Foreign Trade, ch. 2).

Kazakstan also has contributed to efforts by Russia and Uzbekistan to end the civil war in Tajikistan. Kazakstani troops were part of a joint CIS force dispatched to protect military objectives in and around the Tajikistan's capital, Dushanbe. Although Nazarbayev and Uzbekistan's President Islam Karimov warned in 1995 that their countries soon would consider withdrawal if peace talks made no progress, the multinational CIS force remained in place in early 1996.

## National Security

Kazakstan's national security policy remains closely associated with that of Russia, partly because the military forces of Kazakstan have developed more slowly than planned and partly because of long-standing habits of interdependence. The internal security organization of police, prisons, intelligence gathering, and criminal justice remains substantially as it was in the Soviet era.

### Military Establishment

At independence Kazakstan had no army because defense and security needs always had been met by the Soviet army. Initially Nazarbayev, unlike many of his fellow new presidents, argued that his country should function without an independent army, assuming that collective security needs would continue to be met by armies under CIS command. Even when the Russian military establishment changed its oath of service to refer solely to Russia rather than to the CIS, Nazarbayev continued the policy of drafting youth into the CIS forces rather than those of the republic. Even though the republic's strategic thinkers saw Kazakstan as the intersection of three potential military theaters—Europe, the Near East, and the Far East—in the first years of independence, the republic was thought to require only a national guard of no more than 2,500 men, whose duties were envisioned as primarily ceremonial.

When Russia transformed the troops on its soil into a Russian army in the spring of 1992, Kazakstan followed suit by nationalizing the former Soviet Fortieth Army, which remained in Kazakstan, creating the formal basis for a Kazakstani national defense force (see table 12, Appendix).

### Command Structure

The armed forces established in 1992 are subordinate to the Ministry of Defense and to the president in his capacities as commander in chief and chairman of the National Security Council. The second-ranking military office is chief of the General Staff. The General Staff consists of deputy defense ministers for personnel, ground forces, air defense, and airborne forces. The president's main advisory body for national defense is the National Security Council, which includes the prime minister, the first deputy prime minister, the minister of foreign affairs, the chairman of the Committee for Defense of the Constitution, the chairman of the State Committee for Emergency Situations, the minister of defense, the commander of the Border Troops, the commander of the ground forces, and the minister of internal affairs. When it is active, parliament has a four-member Committee for National Security and Defense for coordination of defense policy with the executive branch.

### Force Structure

In the mid-1990s, plans called for developing a military force of 80,000 to 90,000 personnel, including ground forces, air forces, and a navy (for deployment in the Caspian Sea). In 1996 the army included about 25,000 troops, organized into two motorized rifle divisions, one tank division, and one artillery brigade. Attached to that force were one multiple rocket launcher brigade, one motorized rifle regiment, and one air assault brigade. Overall army headquarters are at Semey, with division headquarters at Ayagöz, Sary Ozyk, Almaty, and Semey.

According to national defense doctrine, Kazakstan has a minimal requirement for naval forces. In late 1993, Kazakstan received about 25 percent of the patrol boats and cutters in Russia's Caspian Sea Flotilla, which subsequently constituted the entire naval force. In 1993 naval bases were planned for Fort Shevchenko on the Caspian Sea and at Aral, north of the Aral Sea, but a scarcity of funds delayed completion. Likewise, naval air bases were planned for Aqtau and the Buzachiy Peninsula on the Caspian Sea and at Saryshaghan on Lake Balkhash.

In 1995 the air force included an estimated 15,000 troops. After the withdrawal in 1994 of forty Tu–95MS nuclear-capable bombers, the Kazakstan Air Force was left with 133 combat aircraft, whose offensive capability relied on MiG–23, MiG–27, MiG–29, and Su–24 fighters with support from An–24 and An–

26 transport and MiG–25 surveillance aircraft. Thirty air bases are scattered throughout the republic. Since 1992 Kazak pilots have received little air training because units have been staffed at only 30 to 50 percent of operational levels.

### Officer Cadre

Creating the projected national armed forces has proved more difficult than expected. Since independence, the officer corps, which was overwhelmingly Slavic in the early 1990s, has suffered a severe loss of manpower. In 1992 nearly two-thirds of the company and battalion commanders in Kazakstan had to be replaced as Russian-speaking officers took advantage of CIS agreements permitting transfer to other republics. When these transfers occurred, almost no Kazak officers were available as replacements. In the entire Soviet period, only three Kazaks had graduated from the Military Academy of the General Staff, and only two had earned advanced degrees in military science.

Kazaks have dominated the top administrative positions in the post-Soviet military establishment. In addition to Minister of Defense Sagadat Nurmagambetov, President Nazarbayev appointed two Kazak colonels as deputy ministers of defense and a Kazak general to head the Republic National Guard (the guard unit responsible for protecting the president and other dignitaries as well as antiterrorist operations). Kazakstan's first National Security Council consisted of seven Kazaks, one Russian, and one Ukrainian. In October 1994, both Slavs left office and were replaced by ethnic Kazaks. Despite a secret call-up of officers in reserve, by the fall of 1993 Kazakstan was short at least 650 officers, while the Border Troops Command, 80 percent of whose officers were non-Kazak, was understaffed by 45 percent.

### Border Troops

Kazakstan's extensive land borders are highly vulnerable to penetration by international smugglers, illegal immigrants, and terrorists. In 1992 the Eastern Border Troops District of the former Soviet Union was dissolved; this action resulted in the formation of the Kazakstan Border Troops Command under a Kazak general. After this transition, overall control of border security remained with the National Security Committee, formerly the Kazakstan Committee for State Security (KGB). The border troops commander is a member of the National Security Committee and a member of the Council of

CIS Border Troops Commanders, which was established in 1993 to foster regional cooperation. Cooperation with Russia, with which Kazakstan shares roughly half its borders, is the primary goal of border policy, and several agreements provide for Russian aid. Cooperative agreements also are in effect with the other four Central Asian republics.

Kazakstan's border troops force is estimated at 5,000 to 6,000 personnel. Troops are trained at the Almaty Border Troops School (formerly run by the KGB) or under a cooperative agreement at four Russian facilities. Headquarters are at Almaty, with several subordinate commands, including a coastal patrol squadron headquartered at Atyrau on the north Caspian Sea coast.

### Training and Recruitment

Exacerbating the severe shortage of trained military personnel is the virtual absence of higher-level military training facilities. The only two such schools in existence, the general All Arms Command School and the Border Troops Academy, both in Almaty, are capable of graduating only about 200 junior officers a year, and in 1993 three-quarters of those left the republic. There were also three military secondary boarding schools—in Almaty, Shymkent, and Qaraghandy—and a civil aviation school in Aqtöbe, which is to be converted to a military flight school sometime after 2000.

There are indications of severe problems in filling the ranks of the armed services. Some accounts indicate that as many as 20,000 soldiers were absent without leave from the army in 1993, and desertion and low morale among conscripts continued to be a major problem in the mid-1990s. Another concern is the deteriorating physical condition of inductees, one-third of whom are said to be unfit for conscription. Discipline appears to be problematic as well. In 1993 more than 500 crimes by soldiers were reported in Almaty Province alone; members of the Kazakstani peacekeeping force in Tajikistan reportedly have robbed and raped villagers they were sent to protect. At the command level, in 1993 one general was dismissed for selling weapons and other military goods.

## Military Infrastructure

The quality of military support installations declined in the first years of the post-Soviet period. For instance, the chief planner of Kazakstan's Institute for Strategic Studies has estimated that only in the next century will the republic have the capability to use air-to-surface missiles for defensive purposes. In addition, sensitive facilities inherited by military authorities from the Soviet army all are said to be on the point of collapse. Facilities in bad repair include nuclear test and storage facilities at Kökshetau, the BN–350 breeder-reactor at Aqtau, and a tracking and monitoring station at Priozersk. Even the first Kazak cosmonaut, who was sent into space with great pomp in June 1994, was in fact a Russian citizen and career officer in the Russian air force, as were his two "Ukrainian" shipmates.

Before the dissolution of the Soviet Union, Kazakstan was the most significant site of military-industrial activity in Central Asia. The republic was home to roughly 3 percent of Soviet defense facilities, including more than fifty enterprises and 75,000 workers, located mostly in the predominantly Russian northern parts of the country.

A plant in Öskemen fabricated beryllium and nuclear reactor fuel, and another at Aqtau produced uranium ore. Plants in Oral manufactured heavy machine guns for tanks and antiship missiles. In Petropavl, one plant produced SS–21 short-range ballistic missiles, and other plants manufactured torpedoes and naval communications equipment, support equipment for intercontinental ballistic missiles (ICBMs), tactical missile launcher equipment, artillery, and armored vehicles. There was a torpedo-producing facility in Almaty as well. Chemical and biological weapons were produced in Aksu, and chemical weapons were manufactured in Pavlodar.

By 1994 most of Kazakstan's defense plants had ceased military production. All of them required component parts from inaccessible sources outside Kazakstan, principally in Russia. Even more important, the Russian military-industrial complex was itself in collapse, so that Kazakstan's military enterprises no longer could rely on Russian customers. In addition, the great majority of key workers at all these facilities were ethnic Slavs, the most employable of whom moved to Russia or other former Soviet republics.

Substantial elements of Kazakstan's military-production infrastructure nevertheless remain in the republic. In addition, in early 1992 the army nationalized all of the standard-issue Soviet military equipment remaining on the republic's soil. An unknown percentage of this equipment is still in use in Kazakstan, and another portion of it likely has been sold to other

91

countries. Since independence, at least one new ship, a cruiser named in honor of Nazarbayev, has been commissioned.

The weapons of greatest concern to the world, however, have been the 1,350 nuclear warheads that remained in Kazakstan when the Soviet Union disbanded. Although two other new states—Ukraine and Belarus—also possessed "stranded" nuclear weapons, the Kazakstani weapons attracted particular international suspicion, and unsubstantiated rumors reported the sale of warheads to Iran. Subsequent negotiations demonstrated convincingly, however, that operational control of these weapons always had remained with Russian strategic rocket forces (see Foreign Policy, this ch.). All of the warheads were out of Kazakstan by May 1995.

Kazakstan's other military significance was as a test range and missile launch site. The republic was the location of only about 1 percent of all Soviet test ranges, but these included some all Soviet Union's largest and most important, especially in the aerospace and nuclear programs. Test sites included a range at Vladimirovka used to integrate aircraft with their weapons systems; a range at Saryshaghan for flight testing of ballistic missiles and air defense systems; a similar facility at Emba; and the Semipalatinsk Nuclear Weapons Proving Grounds, which was the more important of the two major nuclear testing facilities in the Soviet Union. In the four decades of its existence, there were at least 466 nuclear explosions at Semipalatinsk.

The other major Soviet military facility on Kazakstani soil was the Baykonur space launch facility, the home of the Soviet space exploration program and, until 1994, Russia's premier launch site for military and intelligence satellites. Kazakstan and Russia debated ownership of the facility, while the facility itself suffered acute deterioration from the region's harsh climate and from uncontrolled pilfering. In 1994 Russia formally recognized Kazakstan's ownership of the facility, although a twenty-year lease ratified in 1995 guaranteed Russia continued use of Baykonur.

## Military Doctrine

In 1992 Kazakstan adopted a three-stage defense doctrine, calling for creation of administrative, command, and support organizations in 1992, restructuring of field forces between 1993 and 1996, and a modernization process leading to establishment of a fully professional military force by 2000. In 1992

Minister of Defense Sagadat Nurmagambetov abandoned the last goal as impractical, calling rather for a combination of conscripts and contract service personnel. In the summer of 1994, Kazakstan's Institute for Strategic Studies called for the complete abandonment of the official defense doctrine. The existing doctrine was criticized for being based on outmoded Soviet precepts that combined fear of hostile military encirclement with a commitment to peace that approached pacificism.

The institute argued that Kazakstan should instead base its defense policies on the assumption that the republic likely would find itself amid border confrontations involving CIS nations, an expansionist China, and Islamic neighbors with enhanced power and ambition. To prepare for such events, the institute recommended de-emphasizing military development and instead pursuing multinational defense agreements along the lines of Nazarbayev's proposed Euro-Asian Union or, absent that, a military alliance with Russia and active pursuit of NATO membership. Kazakstan became a member of NATO's Partnership for Peace in 1994.

Following the appearance of the institute's evaluation, the Ministry of Defense has acknowledged that the second of its original goals—restructuring of field forces by 1996—likely could not be achieved. This admission meant that Kazakstan's dependence upon Russia likely would become even greater. In January 1995, the two countries signed agreements committing them to creation of "unified armed forces." To deflect criticism that such an agreement was inimical to national sovereignty, Nazarbayev likened the new arrangement to the Warsaw Pact and NATO, as distinct from the formation of a single armed force. At the same time, Russia formally took up shared responsibility for patrol of Kazakstan's international borders (under a nominally joint command), which in practice meant the border with China.

## Law Enforcement Systems

Kazakstan's police, court, and prison systems are based, largely unchanged, on Soviet-era practices, as is the bulk of the republic's criminal code. Major legislative changes have concentrated on commercial law, with a view to improving the atmosphere for foreign investment. Formal responsibility for observation of the republic's laws and for protection of the state's interests is divided among the National Security Committee (successor to the Kazak branch of the KGB), the Ministry of Internal Affairs, and the Office of the Procurator General. Intelligence and counterintelligence are the responsibility of the National Security Committee. The police (still called the militia) and prisons are the responsibility of the Ministry of Internal Affairs. The Office of the Procurator General, formerly charged with investigation and prosecution of unlawful acts, was removed from its investigative capacity by the 1995 constitution. Investigation of crimes shifted to the Ministry of Internal Affairs, which also is responsible for fire protection, automotive inspection, and routine preservation of order. As of 1992, Kazakstan became a member of the International Criminal Police Organization (Interpol), and Kazakstani authorities have worked particularly closely with the law enforcement agencies of Russia, Belarus, Uzbekistan, Ukraine, and Kyrgyzstan.

### Courts

The present court system functions at three levels: local courts, which handle petty crimes such as pickpocketing and vandalism; province-level courts, which handle offenses such as murder, grand larceny, and organized crime; and the Supreme Court, to which decisions of the lower courts are appealed. Until mid-1995, the Constitutional Court ruled as final arbiter on the constitutionality of government laws and actions in cases of conflict.

The present constitution provides guarantees of legal representation for persons accused of a crime, including free representation if necessary, but this right appears to be little recognized by authorities or realized by the public. Pretrial detention is permissible, and a suspect may be held for three days before being charged. After being charged, an accused individual may be held for up to a year before being brought to trial. There is no system of bail; accused individuals remain incarcerated until tried.

Both the police and the National Security Committee have the right to violate guarantees of privacy (of the home, telephone, mail, and banks) with the sanction of the procurator general. The theoretical requirement for search warrants and judicial orders for wiretaps and other violations of privacy often is ignored in practice. When the 1995 constitution was approved, a United States official criticized its lack of protection of civil and human rights. Before the approval referendum, Nazarbayev had announced the dissolution of the

Constitutional Court, which he replaced in October with a Constitutional Council whose decisions the president could veto.

## Prisons

The Kazakstani prison system came under attack from human rights organizations in the mid-1990s. In the late Soviet period, eighty-nine labor camps, ten prisons, and three psychiatric hospitals (under the administration of the Ministry of Internal Affairs) were known to be operating in the republic. At least two of the prisons, at Öskemen and Semey, date from tsarist days. There also were at least four special prisons for women and children, at Pavlodar, Zhambyl, and Chamalghan. The facilities remaining from the Soviet period are badly overcrowded and understaffed. According to a 1996 report from the Ministry of Internal Affairs, government funding of prisons is less than half the amount required, and corruption and theft are common throughout the prison system. The total prison population in 1996 was 76,000, and about 1,300 died of tuberculosis in 1995. Health conditions are extremely poor. Overcrowding has been exacerbated by an explosion of crime among the country's youth and by President Nazarbayev's ongoing policy of harsh sentences for convicted criminals.

## Crime

In the early and mid-1990s, crime was increasing at an alarming rate. The police were badly understaffed, overworked, and underfinanced. In 1995 police in Almaty received no pay for three months. A significant drain of personnel has occurred since independence, as investigators and police officers either move to other republics or enter other lines of work offering higher pay. Even before independence, militia authorities complained that staffing was more than 2,000 below full force. In numerous instances, police officers themselves have been involved in crime, especially in such potentially lucrative branches of law enforcement as highway patrol and customs inspection. Under these circumstances, public respect for the police declined seriously.

Since independence Kazakstan has suffered an enormous increase in crime of almost all types. One indication of this explosion has been a series of measures ordered by President Nazarbayev in September 1995, aimed primarily at ending corruption in the police force. The incidence of reported crimes has grown by about 25 percent in every year since independence, although in the first months of 1995 the growth rate slowed to about 16 percent. The average crime rate for the republic is about 50 crimes per 10,000 population, but the rate is significantly higher in Qaraghandy, North Kazakstan, East Kazakstan, Aqmola, Pavlodar, and Almaty. Crime-solving rates have fallen to under 60 percent across the republic and to as low as 30 percent in cities such as Qaraghandy and Temirtau.

Particular increases have been noted in violent crimes and in crimes committed by teenagers and young men. Contract murders and armed clashes between criminal groups increased noticeably in 1995 and were cited by Nazarbayev as a reason for tightening police procedures. Although Soviet crime statistics were not especially reliable, it is still revealing that in 1988 only 5 percent of the republic's convicts were under thirty years of age, but by 1992 that figure had risen to 58 percent. In addition, there has been an enormous increase in official malfeasance and corruption, with bribe taking reported to be nearly ubiquitous.

### Narcotics

Kazakstan offers natural conditions favorable to accelerated narcotics use and trade. Many parts of the country offer excellent growing conditions for cannabis and opium poppies, and the country is located on the route to lucrative markets in the West. Until it ceased production in 1991, Kazakstan's Shymkent plant was the Soviet Union's only supplier of medicinal opiates. The Ministry of Internal Affairs estimated narcotics production and traffic to be 30 percent higher in 1993 than in the previous year. The focus of attention for that ministry, which coordinates the republic's antinarcotics program, is the Chu Valley in south central Kazakstan, where an estimated 138,000 hectares of cannabis and an unknown area of opium poppy fields are under cultivation, providing exports for international smugglers. Because of low funding, efforts to eradicate cannabis and poppy cultivation virtually ceased in 1995.

Almaty has become a crossroads for opiates and hashish from southwest Asia. This role has resulted in large part from lax customs controls and the city's position as a transportation hub. In 1994 an estimated 1.4 tons of morphine base from Afghanistan were stored in Almaty.

An active government narcotics control program began in 1993, although limited personnel and funding have handicapped its efforts. In 1994 only 400 police, 100 sniffer dogs, and twelve special investigators were active. Most Ministry of Internal Affairs interdiction occurs along the Chinese border. Cooperation has been sought with the narcotics programs of other Central Asian states and Russia. In 1993 and 1994, Russian forces made eradication sweeps through the Chu Valley, but Russian helicopter support ceased in 1994. Antinarcotics agreements have been signed with Turkey, Pakistan, China, and Iran. Kazakstan also has requested United States aid in drafting narcotics provisions in a new penal code.

Domestic use of narcotics has been confined largely to areas of production, notably around Shymkent. Although only 10,700 addicts were registered in 1991, experts believe the actual number to be much higher. The use of homemade opiates increased significantly in the early 1990s. The Ministry of Health runs a center offering treatment and prevention programs. However, by 1994 lack of resources had made treatment on demand impossible and stimulated reorganization of the program.

## National Security Prospects

Like the other four Central Asian republics (with the possible exception of Uzbekistan), Kazakstan lacks the resources to create an independent military establishment or an effective internal security force. By 1995 policy makers, headed by President Nazarbayev, had recognized the need to remain under the umbrella of Russian military protection, a status reinforced by a number of bilateral treaties and expected to become further institutionalized in future years. The poor state of internal security was a crisis that eluded control in the mid-1990s, despite authoritarian measures by Nazarbayev. But Kazakstan has committed itself to encouraging foreign investment in the effort to salvage the national economy. To provide an appropriate atmosphere for such commercial activity, improved internal security, perhaps with substantial Western assistance, is a necessary step.

\*     \*     \*

Relatively few monographs have been written on Kazakstan. For historical background in the modern era, *Central Asia: 120 Years of Russian Rule*, edited by Edward Allworth, offers a comprehensive treatment. Useful economic information on the post-Soviet period is available from the World Bank's *Kazakstan: The Transition to a Market Economy,* the PlanEcon *Review and Outlook for the Former Soviet Republics,* and the Central Intelligence Agency's *Kazakstan: An Economic Profile.* A more concise summary of Kazakstan's geopolitical position in the 1990s is found in Charles Undeland and Nicholas Platt's *The Central Asian Republics.*

Among the most complete historical and social analyses of the country is Martha Brill Olcott's *The Kazakhs,* the second edition of which was published in 1995. *Central Asia,* edited by Hafeez Malik, offers a collection of articles on the history and geopolitics of the region. Current information on political and economic events is found in the Foreign Broadcast Information Service's *Daily Report: Central Eurasia,* and current information on environmental issues is contained in that service's *FBIS Report: Environment and World Health,* which before August 1995 was titled *FBIS Report: Environment.* For further information and complete citations, see Bibliography.)

# Chapter 2. Kyrgyzstan

*Kyrgyz* kookor, *a jug for mare's milk*

# Country Profile

## Country

**Formal Name:** Kyrgyz Republic.

**Short Form:** Kyrgyzstan.

**Term for Citizens:** Kyrgyzstani(s).

**Capital:** Bishkek.

**Date of Independence:** August 31, 1991.

## Geography

**Size:** Approximately 198,500 square kilometers.

**Topography:** Dominated by Tian Shan, Pamir, and Alay mountain ranges; average elevation 2,750 meters. Mountains separated by deep valleys and glaciers. Flat expanses only in northern and eastern valleys. Many lakes and fast-flowing rivers draining from mountains.

**Climate:** Chiefly determined by mountains, continental with sharp local variations between mountain valleys and flatlands. Precipitation also varies greatly from western mountains (high) to north-central region (low).

## Society

**Population:** In 1994, estimated at 4.46 million; annual growth rate 1.9 percent; 1994 population density 22.6 people per square kilometer.

**Ethnic Groups:** In 1994, 52 percent Kyrgyz, 22 percent Russian, 13 percent Uzbek, 3 percent Ukrainian, 2 percent German.

**Languages:** Aggressive post-Soviet campaign to make Kyrgyz official national language in all commercial and government uses by 1997; Russian still used extensively, and non-Kyrgyz population, most not Kyrgyz speakers, hostile to forcible

Kyrgyzification.

**Religion:** Dominant religion Sunni Muslim (70 percent), with heavy influence of tribal religions. Russian population largely Russian Orthodox.

**Education and Literacy:** Literacy 97 percent in 1994. Strong tradition of educating all citizens; ambitious program to restructure Soviet system hampered by low funding and loss of teachers. School attendance mandatory through grade nine. Kyrgyz increasingly used for instruction; transition from Russian hampered by lack of textbooks. Twenty-six institutions of higher learning.

**Health:** Transition from Soviet national health system to public health insurance system slowed by low funding. In 1990s, health professionals not well-trained; supplies, facilities, and equipment insufficient, unsanitary. Contaminated water a major health hazard.

## Economy

**Gross National Product (GNP):** In 1993, estimated at US$2.77 billion, US$590 per capita, declining steadily in early and mid-1990s. In 1994 growth rate –26.2 percent. Economic growth stopped by insufficient privatization and restructuring, Soviet-era banking system, and rampant corruption.

**Agriculture:** Heavily state controlled, reducing profitability and encouraging subsistence farming; irrigation necessary for more than 70 percent of land. Main use of land livestock raising; main crops corn, wheat, barley, vegetables, potatoes, and sugar beets. Bank credits and input materials scarce for farmers; severe output decline 1991–95.

**Industry and Mining:** Production decline 58 percent, 1992–94, caused by energy shortage and loss of Russian skilled workers. Political pressure maintains unprofitable Soviet-era state enterprises. Main industries machine building, textiles, food processing, electronics, and metallurgy. Iron ore, copper, gold, lead, zinc, molybdenum, mercury, and antimony are mined.

**Energy:** Insignificant oil and natural gas deposits, and coal deposits not fully exploited. In 1994, some 39 percent of imports were fuels. Coal-powered thermoelectric power production replaced by hydroelectric power, early 1990s; emphasis on electric power based on abundant water power, providing exportable power bartered for coal from Kazakstan.

**Exports:** In 1994, value US$339 million. Main commodities wool, hides, cotton, electric power, electronics, metals, food products, and shoes. Main partners Russia, Ukraine, Uzbekistan, Kazakstan, and China. Export taxes and licensing substantially relaxed by 1995.

**Imports:** In 1994, mainly fuels, construction materials, ferrous metals, pharmaceuticals, chemicals, and machinery. Main suppliers Russia, Kazakstan, Uzbekistan, and China. Import licenses and tariffs liberalized, 1994. Value US$347 million, 1994.

**Balance of Payments:** In 1992, deficit US$147.5 million.

**Exchange Rate:** Som introduced as national currency, May 1993, with floating exchange rate. Early 1996, eleven som per US$1.

**Inflation:** Hyperinflation (1,400 percent per year), 1992 and 1993; rate about 180 percent 1994; 1995 government target 55 percent; value of som supported by international banks beginning in 1993, and price controls reintroduced 1993.

**Fiscal Year:** Calendar year.

**Fiscal Policy:** Drastic tax revenue shrinkage caused revenue crisis and reduced government spending, 1994; widespread tax reform program in place 1995, focusing on enforcement and new land and excise taxes.

## Transportation and Telecommunications

**Highways:** In 1990, 28,400 kilometers of roads, of which 22,400 hard-surfaced. Nearly all freight moves by road; plans to supplement connection with China-Pakistan highway, mid-1990s. Fuel shortage restricts vehicle use, mid-1990s.

**Railroads:** Little developed; 370 kilometers of track, one main line in north, 1994. Plans for north-south line begun 1995.

**Civil Aviation:** Two international airports, at Bishkek and Osh; about twenty-five smaller facilities. Beginning in 1991, fuel shortage diverts international traffic to Almaty in Kazakstan, with reduction in overall transport; regular service to Tashkent and Moscow.

**Inland Waterways:** None.

**Ports:** None.

**Pipelines:** In 1994, 220 kilometers for natural gas.

**Telecommunications:** Little developed; in 1994, about 7 percent of population with telephones. Equipment outmoded, operating at capacity, and difficult to replace. Three national radio stations, very limited domestic television.

## Government and Politics

**Government:** Constitution of 1993 prescribes three branches; executive strongest and reinforced with special powers assumed by President Askar Akayev, early 1990s. In election held December 1995, Akayev reelected by 71.6 percent of vote. Council of Ministers, nominally administering executive branch, subservient to president. Bicameral parliament of 105 (upper house 35, convened full-time; lower house 70 members, convening twice yearly) established 1994 at Akayev's request, elected to five-year terms; parliament has opposed Akayev on some issues. Judges appointed by president with parliamentary approval. Some local governments with strong power bases.

**Politics:** Numerous groups appeared early 1990s but no organized party system; government has denied registration to some parties; some neocommunist parties active.

**Foreign Relations:** Post-Soviet attempts at relations with wide variety of Western and Asian countries, based on neutrality, using Akayev's personal diplomacy. Careful cultivation of powerful neighbors Russia, Kazakstan, and Uzbekistan; border tensions with Tajikistan. Fast increasing Chinese economic role watched carefully by government; Western sources of aid endangered by antidemocratic tendencies.

**International Agreements and Memberships:** Member of United Nations (UN), Organization for Security and Cooperation in Europe (OSCE), Economic Cooperation Organization (ECO), Islamic Bank, Asian Development Bank, North Atlantic Treaty Organization (NATO) Partnership for Peace, World

Bank, International Monetary Fund (IMF), Commonwealth of Independent States (CIS).

## National Security

**Armed Forces:** Ground forces had 12,000 troops, 1996; air and air defense forces 4,000 troops, border guards about 2,000 troops. Manpower and weapon levels in development stage, 1995. Heavy reliance on Russian command and equipment expected to continue indefinitely.

**Major Military Units:** Ground forces with one motorized rifle division with armor and artillery, attached sapper, signals, and mountain infantry units. Air force with one fighter, one training, one helicopter regiment.

**Military Budget:** Estimated at US$13 million, 1995.

**Internal Security:** State Committee for National Security, replacing Soviet Committee for State Security (KGB), responsible for intelligence and runs National Guard (about 1,000 troops assigned as "palace guard") and border guards. Police (militia) system, unchanged from Soviet era, includes 25,000 personnel under centralized command.

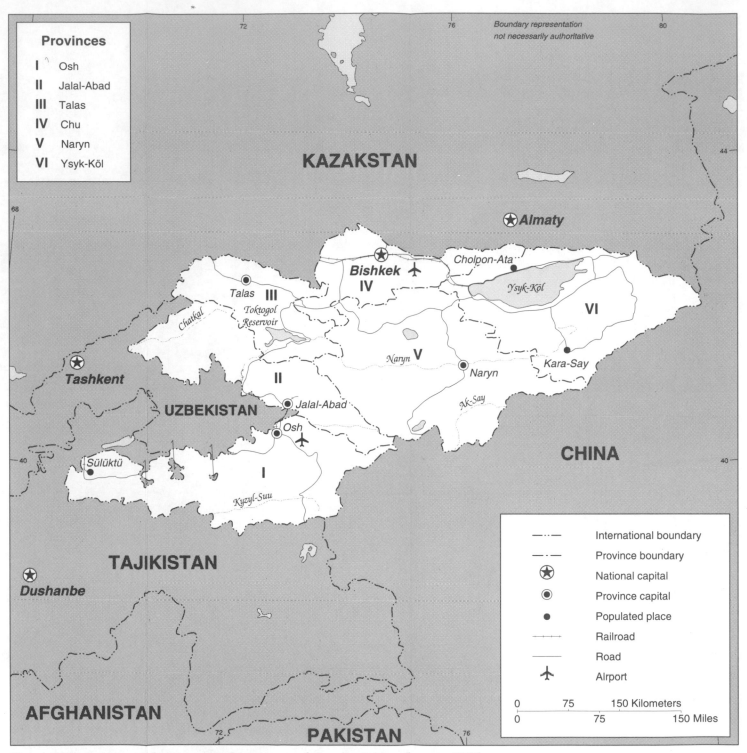

*Figure 8. Kyrgyzstan: Administrative Divisions and Transportation System, 1996*

ELEVATED TO THE STATUS of a union republic by Joseph V. Stalin in 1936, the Kyrgyz Soviet Socialist Republic was until 1990 one of the poorest, quietest, and most conservative of all the Soviet republics. It was the Kyrgyz Republic that celebrated the election of a sheepherder as president of its parliamentary executive committee, the Presidium, in 1987. Three years later, however, that quiescence ended, and Kyrgyzstan's history as a separate nation began.

Kyrgyzstan began the new phase of its existence by declaring independence in August 1991. At that point, it possessed a combination of useful resources and threatening deficiencies. Geographic location fits in both categories; landlocked deep inside the Asian continent, Kyrgyzstan has minimal natural transportation routes available to serve its economic development, and its isolation has been an obstacle in the campaign to gain international attention. On the other hand, Kyrgyzstan also is isolated from most of the Asian trouble spots (excepting Tajikistan), making national security a relatively low priority. The natural resources that Kyrgyzstan possesses—primarily gold, other minerals, and abundant hydroelectric power—have not been managed well enough to make them an asset in pulling the republic up from the severe economic shock of leaving the secure, if limiting, domain of the Soviet Union.

In the mid-1990s, the most ambitious economic and political reform program in Central Asia caused more frustration than satisfaction among Kyrgyzstan's citizens, largely because the republic inherited neither an economic infrastructure nor a political tradition upon which to base the rapid transitions envisioned by President Askar Akayev's first idealistic blueprints. Although some elements of reform (privatization, for example) went into place quickly, the absence of others (credit from a commercial banking system, for example) brought the overall system to a halt, causing high unemployment and frustration. By 1995, democratic reform seemed a victim of that frustration, as Akayev increasingly sought to use personal executive power in promoting his policies for economic growth, a pattern that became typical in the Central Asian countries' first years of independence.

Since independence Kyrgyzstan has made impressive strides in some regards such as creating genuinely free news media and fostering an active political opposition. At the same time, the grim realities of the country's economic position, which exacerbate the clan- and family-based political tensions that have always remained beneath the surface of national life, leave long-term political and economic prospects clouded at best. Kyrgyzstan has no desire to return to Russian control, yet economic necessity has forced the government to look to Moscow for needed financial support and trade.

## Historical Background

The modern nation of Kyrgyzstan is based on a civilization of nomadic tribes who moved across the eastern and northern sections of present-day Central Asia. In this process, they were dominated by, and intermixed with, a number of other tribes and peoples that have influenced the ultimate character of the Kyrgyz people.

### Early History

Stone implements found in the Tian Shan mountains indicate the presence of human society in what is now Kyrgyzstan as many as 200,000 to 300,000 years ago. The first written records of a Kyrgyz civilization appear in Chinese chronicles beginning about 2000 B.C. The Kyrgyz, a nomadic people, originally inhabited an area of present-day northwestern Mongolia. In the fourth and third centuries B.C., Kyrgyz bands were among the raiders who persistently invaded Chinese territory and stimulated the building of the original Great Wall of China in the third century B.C. The Kyrgyz achieved a reputation as great fighters and traders. In the centuries that followed, some Kyrgyz tribes freed themselves from domination by the Huns by moving northward into the Yenisey and Baikal regions of present-day south-central Siberia.

The first Kyrgyz state, the Kyrgyz Khanate, existed from the sixth until the thirteenth century A.D., expanding by the tenth century southwestward to the eastern and northern regions of present-day Kyrgyzstan and westward to the headwaters of the Ertis (Irtysh) River in present-day eastern Kazakstan. In this period, the khanate established intensive commercial contacts in China, Tibet, Central Asia, and Persia.

In the meantime, beginning about 1000 B.C., large tribes collectively known as the Scythians also lived in the area of present-day Kyrgyzstan. Excellent warriors, the Scythian tribes farther west had resisted an invasion by the troops of Alexander the Great in 328–27 B.C. The Kyrgyz tribes who entered the region around the sixth century played a major role in the development of feudalism.

The Kyrgyz reached their greatest expansion by conquering the Uygur Khanate and forcing it out of Mongolia in A.D. 840, then moving as far south as the Tian Shan range—a position the Kyrgyz maintained for about 200 years. By the twelfth century, however, Kyrgyz domination had shrunk to the region of the Sayan Mountains, northwest of present-day Mongolia, and the Altay Range on the present-day border of China and Mongolia. In the same period, other Kyrgyz tribes were moving across a wide area of Central Asia and mingling with other ethnic groups (see Ethnic Traditions, this ch.).

## Mongol Domination

The Mongols' invasion of Central Asia in the fourteenth century devastated the territory of Kyrgyzstan, costing its people their independence and their written language. The son of Chinggis (Genghis) Khan, Dzhuchi, conquered the Kyrgyz tribes of the Yenisey region, who by this time had become disunited. For the next 200 years, the Kyrgyz remained under the Golden Horde and the Oriot and Jumgar khanates that succeeded that regime. Freedom was regained in 1510, but Kyrgyz tribes were overrun in the seventeenth century by the Kalmyks, in the mid-eighteenth century by the Manchus, and in the early nineteenth century by the Uzbeks.

The Kyrgyz began efforts to gain protection from more powerful neighboring states in 1758, when some tribes sent emissaries to China. A similar mission went to the Russian Empire in 1785. Between 1710 and 1876, the Kyrgyz were ruled by the Uzbek Quqon (Kokand) Khanate, one of the three major principalities of Central Asia during that period (see fig. 3). Kyrgyz tribes fought and lost four wars against the Uzbeks of Quqon between 1845 and 1873. The defeats strengthened the Kyrgyz willingness to seek Russian protection. Even during this period, however, the Kyrgyz occupied important positions in the social and administrative structures of the khanate, and they maintained special military units that continued their earlier tradition of military organization; some Kyrgyz advanced to the position of khan.

111

## Russian Control

In 1876 Russian troops defeated the Quqon Khanate and occupied northern Kyrgyzstan. Within five years, all Kyrgyzstan had become part of the Russian Empire, and the Kyrgyz slowly began to integrate themselves into the economic and political life of Russia. In the last decades of the nineteenth century, increasing numbers of Russian and Ukrainian settlers moved into the northern part of present-day Kyrgyzstan. Russian specialists began large-scale housing, mining, and road construction projects and the construction of schools. In the first years of the twentieth century, the presence of the Russians made possible the publication of the first books in the Kyrgyz language; the first Kyrgyz reader was published in Russia in 1911. Nevertheless, Russian policy did not aim at educating the population; most Kyrgyz remained illiterate, and in most regions traditional life continued largely as it had before 1870.

By 1915, however, even many Central Asians outside the intelligentsia had recognized the negative effects of the Russian Empire's repressive policies. The Kyrgyz nomads suffered especially from confiscation of their land for Russian and Ukrainian settlements. Russian taxation, forced labor, and price policies all targeted the indigenous population and raised discontent and regional tension. The Kyrgyz in Semirech'ye Province suffered especially from land appropriation. The bloody rebellion of the summer of 1916 began in Uzbekistan, then spread into Kyrgyzstan and elsewhere. Kazaks, Turkmen, Uzbeks, and Kyrgyz participated. An estimated 2,000 Slavic settlers and even more local people were killed, and the harsh Russian reprisals drove one-third of the Kyrgyz population into China.

## Into the Soviet Union

Following a brief period of independence after the 1917 Bolshevik Revolution (see Glossary) toppled the empire, the territory of present-day Kyrgyzstan was designated the Kara-Kyrghyz Autonomous Region and a constituent part of the Union of Soviet Socialist Republics (Soviet Union) in 1924. In 1926 the official name changed to the Kyrgyz Autonomous Republic before the region achieved the status of a full republic of the Soviet Union in 1936.

## Recent History

In the late 1980s, the Kyrgyz were jolted into a state of national consciousness by the reforms of Soviet leader Mikhail S. Gorbachev and by ethnic conflict much closer to home. As democratic activism stirred in Kyrgyzstan's cities, events in Moscow pushed the republic toward unavoidable independence.

### Ethnic Conflict

The most important single event leading to independence grew from an outburst of ethnic friction. From the perspective of the Kyrgyz, the most acute nationality problem long had been posed by the Uzbeks living in and around the city of Osh, in the republic's southwest. Although Kyrgyzstan was only about 13 percent Uzbek according to the 1989 census, almost the entire Uzbek population was concentrated in Osh Province. Tensions very likely had existed between the Kyrgyz and the Uzbeks throughout the Soviet period, but Moscow was able to preserve the image of Soviet ethnic harmony until the reforms of Gorbachev in the mid-1980s. In the general atmosphere of *glasnost* (see Glossary), an Uzbek-rights group called Adalat began airing old grievances in 1989, demanding that Moscow grant local Uzbek autonomy in Osh and consider its annexation by nearby Uzbekistan.

The real issue behind Adalat's demand was land, which is in extremely short supply in the southernmost province of Osh. To protect their claims, some Osh Kyrgyz also had formed an opposing ethnic association, called Osh-aimagy (Osh-land). In early June 1990, the Kyrgyz-dominated Osh City Council announced plans to build a cotton processing plant on a parcel of land under the control of an Uzbek-dominated collective farm in Osh Province.

The confrontation that erupted over control of that land brought several days of bloody riots between crowds led by the respective associations, killing at least 320 Kyrgyz and Uzbeks in Osh. The precise cause and sequence of events in early June 1990 is disputed between Uzbek and Kyrgyz accounts. Scores of families were left homeless when their houses were burned out. The government finally stopped the rioting by imposing a military curfew.

Because the telephone lines remained open in the otherwise blockaded city, news of the violence spread immediately to Frunze. In the capital, a large group of students marched on the headquarters of the Communist Party of Kyrgyzia (CPK), which also served as the seat of government, in the center of the city. In the violent confrontation that ensued, personal injuries were minimized by effective crowd control, and the riotous crowd eventually was transformed into a mass meeting.

### Democratic Activism

The Osh riots and the subsequent events in Frunze quickly brought to the surface an undercurrent of political discontent that had been forming among both the intelligentsia and middle-level party officials. A loose affiliation of activists calling themselves the Democratic Movement of Kyrgyzstan (DDK) began to organize public opinion, calling among other things for the resignation of Absamat Masaliyev, who was president of the republic's parliament, the Supreme Soviet, as well as a member of the Soviet Union's Politburo and the head of the CPK. The DDK called for Masaliyev's resignation because he was widely viewed as having mishandled the Osh riots.

Democratic activists erected tents in front of the party headquarters, maintaining pressure with a series of hunger strikes and highly visible public demonstrations. The continuing atmosphere of crisis emboldened CPK members, who also wished to get rid of the reactionary Masaliyev. Four months later, in a presidential election prescribed by Gorbachev's reform policies, Masaliyev failed to win the majority of Supreme Soviet votes required to remain in power.

### The Rise of Akayev

With none of the three presidential candidates able to gain the necessary majority in the 1990 election, the Supreme Soviet unexpectedly selected Askar Akayev, a forty-six-year-old physicist, who had been serving as head of the republic's Academy of Sciences. Although he had served for a year in a science-related post on the Central Committee of the Communist Party of the Soviet Union (CPSU) and was a party member, Akayev was the first president of a Soviet republic who had not held a high party position.

At the same meeting of the Supreme Soviet, the deputies changed the name of the republic to Kyrgyzstan. They also began to speak seriously of seeking greater national sovereignty (which was formally declared on November 20, 1990) and of attaining political domination of the republic by the Kyrgyz, including the establishment of Kyrgyz as the official language.

By mid-summer 1991, the Kyrgyz were beginning to make serious moves to uncouple the government from the CPSU and its Kyrgyzstan branch. In early August, the Ministry of Internal Affairs of Kyrgyzstan, which governs the police and the internal security forces, announced a ban of all CPSU affiliation or activity within the ministry. Events elsewhere precluded a seemingly inevitable conflict with Moscow over that decision; in August 1991, the attention of the entire union moved to Moscow when reactionaries in Gorbachev's government attempted to remove him from power.

Unlike the leaders of the other four Central Asian republics, who temporized for a day about their course following the coup, Akayev condemned the plot almost immediately and began preparations to repel the airborne forces rumored to be on the way to Kyrgyzstan from Moscow. The quick collapse of the coup made the preparations unnecessary, but Akayev's declaration of support for Gorbachev and for the maintenance of legitimate authority gained the Kyrgyz leader enormous respect among the Kyrgyz people and among world leaders. On August 30, 1991, days after the coup began, Akayev and the republic's Supreme Soviet declared Kyrgyzstan an independent nation, and the president threw the CPSU and its Kyrgyzstan branch out of the government. However, he did not go as far as officials in most of the other former Soviet republics, where the party was banned totally.

At the same time independence was declared, the republic's Supreme Soviet scheduled direct presidential elections for October 1991. Running unopposed, Akayev received 95 percent of the popular vote, thus becoming the country's first popularly elected president. The so-called Silk Revolution drew much international sympathy and attention. In December 1991, when the Belarusian, Russian, and Ukrainian republics signed the Tashkent Agreement, forming a commonwealth that heralded the dissolution of the Soviet Union, Akayev demanded that another meeting be held so that Kyrgyzstan might become a founding member of the Commonwealth of Independent States (CIS—see Glossary), as the new union was to be called.

The sympathy that Akayev had won for Kyrgyzstan earlier in his presidency served the country well once the world generally acknowledged the passing of the Gorbachev regime and the Soviet Union. Kyrgyzstan was recognized almost immediately by most nations, including the United States, whose secretary of state, James Baker, made an official visit in January 1992. A United States embassy was opened in the capital (which had reassumed its pre-Soviet name of Bishkek in December 1990) in February 1992. By early 1993, the new country had been recognized by 120 nations and had diplomatic relations with sixty-one of them.

### Akayev's Early Years

Despite initial euphoria over the possibilities of independence and membership in the CIS, Akayev recognized that his country's economic position was extremely vulnerable and that the ethnic situation exacerbated that vulnerability. Thus, the Akayev administration devoted much attention to creating a legal basis of governance while struggling to keep the economy afloat.

In the first two years of his presidency, Akayev seemed to work effectively with the Supreme Soviet that had put him in office. By 1992, however, Akayev's good relations with the legislature had fallen victim to the rapidly declining economy, the failure of the CIS to become a functioning body, and the country's inability to attract substantial assistance or investment from any of the potential foreign partners whom he had courted so assiduously.

In advancing his reform programs, Akayev experienced particular difficulties in gaining the cooperation of entrenched local politicians remaining from the communist government apparatus. To gain control of local administration, Akayev imitated the 1992 strategy of Russia's president Boris N. Yeltsin by appointing individuals to leadership positions at the province, district, and city levels (see Structure of Government, this ch.). Akayev filled about seventy such positions, the occupants of which were supposed to combine direct loyalty and responsibility to the president with a zeal to improve conditions for their immediate locales. The system became a source of constant scandal and embarrassment for Akayev, however. The most flagrant abuses came in Jalal-Abad Province (which had been split from neighboring Osh in spring 1991 to dilute political power in the south), where the new *akim*, the provincial governor, appointed members of his own family to the majority of the positions under his control and used state funds to acquire personal property. The situation in Jalal-Abad aroused strong resentment and demonstrations that continued even after the governor had been forced to resign.

In 1992 and 1993, the public perception grew that Akayev himself had provided a model for the tendency of local leaders to put family and clan interests above those of the nation. Indeed, several prominent national government officials, including the head of the internal security agency, the heads of the national bank and the national radio administration, the minister of foreign affairs, and the ambassador to Russia, came from Akayev's home area and from Talas, the home district of his wife.

Akayev's loss of momentum was reflected in the debate over the national constitution, a first draft of which was passed by the Supreme Soviet in December 1992. Although draft versions had begun to circulate as early as the summer of 1992, the commission itself agreed on a definitive version only after prolonged debate. An umbrella group of opposition figures from the DDK also began drawing up constitutional proposals in 1992, two variations of which they put forward for public consideration.

Although broad agreement existed on the outlines of the constitution, several specific points were difficult to resolve. One concerned the status of religion. Although it was agreed that the state would be secular, there was strong pressure for some constitutional recognition of the primacy of Islam. Another much-debated issue was the role of the Russian language. Kyrgyz had been declared the official state language, but non-Kyrgyz citizens exerted pressure to have Russian assigned near-equal status, as was the case in neighboring Kazakstan, where Russian had been declared the "official language of interethnic communication." The issue of property ownership was warmly debated, with strong sentiment expressed against permitting land to be owned or sold. Another important question was the role of the president within the new state structure.

The proposed constitution was supposed to be debated by the full Supreme Soviet (as the new nation's parliament continued to call itself after independence) and by a specially convened body of prominent citizens before its acceptance as law. However, some members of the democratic opposition argued that a special assembly of Kyrgyz elders, called a *kuraltai*, should be convened to consider the document. A final draft of the constitution was passed by the Supreme Soviet in May 1993, apparently without involvement of a *kuraltai*.

In drafting a final document, the Supreme Soviet addressed some of the most controversial issues that had arisen in pre-draft discussions. Specific passages dealt with transfer and ownership of property, the role of religion in the government, the powers of the president, and the official language of the country (see Constitution, this ch.).

Akayev had spoken of the need to have a presidential system of government—and, indeed, the constitution sets the presidency outside the three branches of government, to act as a sort of overseer ensuring the smooth functioning of all three. However, by the mid-1990s dissatisfaction with the strong presidential model of government and with the president himself was growing. With economic resources diminished, political infighting became commonplace. Although the prime minister and others received blame for controversial or unsuccessful policy initiatives, President Akayev nonetheless found himself increasingly isolated politically amid growing opposition forces.

Although the "democratic" opposition that had helped bring Akayev to power had grown disenchanted, its constituent factions were unable to exert serious pressure on the president because they could not agree on ideology or strategy. In October 1992, the main democratic opposition party Erk (Freedom) fractured into two new parties, Erkin and Ata-Meken (Fatherland). More serious opposition originated within the ranks of the former communist elite. Some of this opposition came directly from the ranks of the reconstituted and still legal CPK (see Political Parties, this ch.).

In January 1993, Akayev made an unusually harsh statement to the effect that he had been misled by his economic advisers and that Kyrgyzstan's overtures to the outside world had only raised false hopes. The continuing outflow of ethnic Russians (who constitute the greater part of Kyrgyzstan's technicians), the war in Tajikistan (which has driven refugees and "freedom fighters" into Kyrgyzstan), the growing evidence of wide-scale official corruption and incompetence, rising crime, and—more than anything else—the spectacular collapse of the economy increasingly charged the country's political atmosphere in the first half of the 1990s.

## Physical Environment

The smallest of the newly independent Central Asian states, Kyrgyzstan is about the same size as the state of Nebraska, with a total area of about 198,500 square kilometers. The national territory extends about 900 kilometers from east to west and 410 kilometers from north to south. Kyrgyzstan is bordered on the southeast by China, on the north and west by Kazakstan, and on the south and west by Uzbekistan and Tajikistan. One consequence of the Stalinist division of Central Asia into five republics is that many ethnic Kyrgyz do not live in Kyrgyzstan. Three enclaves, legally part of the territory of Kyrgyzstan but geographically removed by several kilometers, have been established, two in Uzbekistan and one in Tajikistan (see fig. 8). The terrain of Kyrgyzstan is dominated by the Tian Shan and Pamir mountain systems, which together occupy about 65 percent of the national territory. The Alay range portion of the Tian Shan system dominates the southwestern crescent of the country, and, to the east, the main Tian Shan range runs along the boundary between southern Kyrgyzstan and China before extending farther east into China's Xinjiang Uygur Autonomous Region. Kyrgyzstan's average elevation is 2,750 meters, ranging from 7,439 meters at Pik Pobedy (Mount Victory) to 394 meters in the Fergana Valley near Osh. Almost 90 percent of the country lies more than 1,500 meters above sea level.

## Topography and Drainage

The mountains of Kyrgyzstan are geologically young, so that the physical terrain is marked by sharply uplifted peaks separated by deep valleys (see fig. 9). There is also considerable glaciation. Kyrgyzstan's 6,500 distinct glaciers are estimated to hold about 650 billion cubic meters of water. Only around the Chu, Talas, and Fergana valleys is there relatively flat land suitable for large-scale agriculture.

Because the high peaks function as moisture catchers, Kyrgyzstan is relatively well watered by the streams that descend from them. None of the rivers of Kyrgyzstan are navigable, however. The majority are small, rapid, runoff streams. Most of Kyrgyzstan's rivers are tributaries of the Syrdariya, which has its headwaters in the western Tian Shan along the Chinese border. Another large runoff system forms the Chu River, which arises in northern Kyrgyzstan, then flows northwest and disappears into the deserts of southern Kazakstan. Ysyk-Köl is the second largest body of water in Central Asia, after the Aral Sea, but the saline lake has been shrinking steadily, and its mineral content has been rising gradually. Kyrgyzstan has a total of about 2,000 lakes with a total surface area of 7,000 square kilometers, mostly located at altitudes of 3,000 to 4,000 meters. Only the largest three, however, occupy more than 500 square kilometers. The second- and third-largest lakes, Songköl and Chatyr-Köl (the latter of which also is saline), are located in the Naryn Basin.

Natural disasters have been frequent and varied. Overgrazing and deforestation of steep mountain slopes have increased the occurrence of mudslides and avalanches, which occasionally have swallowed entire villages. In August 1992, a severe earthquake left several thousand people homeless in the southwestern city of Jalal-Abad.

## Climate

The country's climate is influenced chiefly by the mountains, Kyrgyzstan's position near the middle of the Eurasian landmass, and the absence of any body of water large enough to influence weather patterns. Those factors create a distinctly continental climate that has significant local variations. Although the mountains tend to collect clouds and block sunlight (reducing some narrow valleys at certain times of year to no more than three or four hours of sunlight per day), the country is generally sunny, receiving as much as 2,900 hours of sunlight per year in some areas. The same conditions also affect temperatures, which can vary significantly from place to place. In January the warmest average temperature (–4°C) occurs around the southern city of Osh, and around Ysyk-Köl. The latter, which has a volume of 1,738 cubic kilometers, does not freeze in winter. Indeed, its name means "hot lake" in Kyrgyz. The coldest temperatures are in mountain valleys. There, readings can fall to –30°C or lower; the record is –53.6°C. The average temperature for July similarly varies from 27°C in the Fergana Valley, where the record high is 44°C, to a low of –10°C on the highest mountain peaks. Precipitation varies from 2,000 millimeters per year in the mountains above the Fergana Valley to less than 100 millimeters per year on the west bank of Ysyk-Köl.

## Environmental Problems

Kyrgyzstan has been spared many of the enormous environmental problems faced by its Central Asian neighbors, primarily because its designated roles in the Soviet system involved neither heavy industry nor large-scale cotton production. Also, the economic downturn of the early 1990s reduced some of the

KAZAKSTAN

N

VII

Bishkek

Ysyk-Köl

Toktogol Reservoir

VI

V

IV

UZBEKISTAN

III

I

CHINA

II

TAJIKISTAN

| | |
|---|---|
| —··—··— | International boundary |
| ⊛ | National capital |

| | |
|---|---|
| I | Tian Shan |
| II | Alay Mountains |
| III | Fergana Valley |
| IV | Kyrgyz Range |
| V | Terskey Alataū Range |
| VI | Chatkal Range |
| VII | Fergana Range |

0    50    100    150    Kilometers

0        50        100        150    Miles

AFGHANISTAN

*Figure 9. Kyrgyzstan: Topography*

122

more serious effects of industrial and agricultural policy. Nevertheless, Kyrgyzstan has serious problems because of inefficient use and pollution of water resources, land degradation, and improper agricultural practices.

### Water Resources

Although Kyrgyzstan has abundant water running through it, its water supply is determined by a post-Soviet sharing agreement among the five Central Asian republics. As in the Soviet era, Kyrgyzstan has the right to 25 percent of the water that originates in its territory, but the new agreement allows Turkmenistan and Uzbekistan unlimited use of the water that flows into them from Kyrgyzstan, with no compensation for the nation at the source. Kyrgyzstan uses the entire amount to which the agreement entitles it, but utilization is skewed heavily in favor of agricultural irrigation. In 1994 agriculture accounted for about 88 percent of total water consumption, compared with 8 percent by industry and 4 percent by municipal water distribution systems. According to World Bank (see Glossary) experts, Kyrgyzstan has an adequate supply of high-quality water for future use, provided the resource is prudently managed.

Irrigation is extremely wasteful of water because the distribution infrastructure is old and poorly maintained. In 1993 only an estimated 5 percent of required maintenance expenditures was allocated. Overall, an estimated 70 percent of the nation's water supply network is in need of repair or replacement. The quality of drinking water from this aging system is poorly monitored—the water management staff has been cut drastically because of inadequate funds. Further, there is no money to buy new water disinfection equipment when it is needed. Some aquifers near industrial and mining centers have been contaminated by heavy metals, oils, and sanitary wastes. In addition, many localities rely on surface sources, making users vulnerable to agricultural runoff and livestock waste, which seep gradually downward from the surface. The areas of lowest water quality are the heavily populated regions of the Chu Valley and Osh and Jalal-Abad provinces, and areas along the rivers flowing into Ysyk-Köl.

In towns, wastewater collection provides about 70 percent of the water supply. Although towns have biological treatment equipment, as much as 50 percent of such equipment is rated as ineffective. The major sources of toxic waste in the water supply are the mercury mining combine at Haidarkan; the antimony mine at Kadamzai; the Kadzyi Sai uranium mine, which ceased extraction in 1967 but which continues to leach toxic materials into nearby Ysyk Köl; the Kara-Balta Uranium Recovery Plant; the Min Kush deposit of mine tailings; and the Kyrgyz Mining and Metallurgy Plant at Orlovka.

## Land Management

The most important problems in land use are soil erosion and salinization in improperly irrigated farmland. An estimated 60 percent of Kyrgyzstan's land is affected by topsoil loss, and 6 percent by salinization, both problems with more serious long-term than short-term effects. In 1994 the size of livestock herds averaged twice the carrying capacity of pasturage land, continuing the serious overgrazing problem and consequent soil erosion that began when the herds were at their peak in the late 1980s (see Agriculture, this ch.). Uncertain land tenure and overall financial insecurity have caused many private farmers to concentrate their capital in the traditional form—livestock—thus subjecting new land to the overgrazing problem.

The inherent land shortage in Kyrgyzstan is exacerbated by the flooding of agricultural areas for hydroelectric projects. The creation of Toktogol Reservoir on the Naryn River, for example, involved the flooding of 13,000 hectares of fertile land. Such projects have the additional effect of constricting downstream water supply; Toktogol deprives the lower reaches of the Syrdariya in Uzbekistan and the Aral Sea Basin of substantial amounts of water. Because the Naryn Basin, where many hydroelectric projects are located, is very active seismically, flooding is also a danger should a dam be broken by an earthquake. Several plants are now in operation in zones where Richter Scale readings may reach eleven.

## The Aral Sea

In response to the internationally recognized environmental crisis of the rapid desiccation of the Aral Sea, the five states sharing the Aral Sea Basin (Kazakstan, Kyrgyzstan, Tajikistan, Turkmenistan, and Uzbekistan) are developing a strategy to end the crisis. The World Bank and agencies of the United Nations (UN) have developed an Aral Sea Program, the first stage of which is funded by the five countries and external donors. That stage has seven areas of focus, one of which—

land and water management in the upper watersheds—is of primary concern to Kyrgyzstan. Among the conditions detrimental to the Aral Sea's environment are erosion from deforestation and overgrazing, contamination from poorly managed irrigation systems, and uncontrolled waste from mining and municipal effluents. Kyrgyzstan's National Environmental Action Plan (NEAP) has addressed these problems as part of its first-phase priorities in cooperation with the Aral Sea Program.

### Environmental Policy Making

The NEAP, adopted in 1994, is the basic blueprint for environmental protection. The plan focuses on solving a small number of critical problems, collecting reliable information to aid in that process, and integrating environmental measures with economic and social development strategy. The initial planning period is to end in 1997. The main targets of that phase are inefficient water resource management, land degradation, overexploitation of forest reserves, loss of biodiversity, and pollution from inefficient mining and refining practices.

Because of severe budget constraints, most of the funds for NEAP operations come from international sources, including official institutions such as the World Bank and the Asian Development Bank and numerous international nongovernmental organizations. Implementation is guided by a committee of state ministers and by a NEAP Expert Working Group, both established in 1994 by executive order. A NEAP office in Bishkek was set up with funds from Switzerland.

The main environmental protection agency of the Kyrgyzstani government is the State Committee on Environmental Protection, still known by its Soviet-era acronym, Goskompriroda. Established by the old regime in 1988, the agency's post-Soviet responsibilities have been described in a series of decrees beginning in 1991. In 1994 the state committee had a central office in Bishkek, one branch in each of the seven provinces, and a total staff of about 150 persons. Because of poorly defined lines of responsibility, administrative conflicts often occur between local and national authorities of Goskompriroda and between Goskompriroda and a second national agency, the Hydrometeorological Administration (Gidromet), which is the main monitoring agency for air, water, and soil quality. In general, the vertical hierarchy structure, a relic of Soviet times, has led to poor coordination and duplication of effort among environmental protection agencies.

# Population

The population of Kyrgyzstan is divided among three main groups: the indigenous Kyrgyz, the Russians who remained after the end of the Soviet Union, and a large and concentrated Uzbek population. Topography divides the population into two main segments, the north and the south. Each has differing cultural and economic patterns and different predominant ethnic groups.

## Demographic Characteristics

The censuses of 1979 and 1989 indicated annual population growth of a little over 2 percent, with a birth rate of 30.4 per 1,000 in 1989. The estimated birth rate in 1994 was twenty-six per 1,000, the death rate seven per 1,000, with a rate of natural increase of 1.9 percent (see table 2, Appendix). In 1993 average life expectancy was estimated at sixty-two years for males, seventy years for females—the second lowest rate among the former Soviet republics. In 1993 the infant mortality rate was estimated at 47.8 deaths per 1,000 live births. Early marriage and large family size have combined to make Kyrgyzstan's population a relatively young one. In 1989, some 39.5 percent of the population was below working age, and only 10.1 percent was of pension age. The 1989 census indicated that only about 38 percent of the country's population was urbanized (see table 3, Appendix).

## Ethnic Groups

In 1993 the population of Kyrgyzstan was estimated at 4.46 million, of whom 56.5 percent were ethnic Kyrgyz, 18.8 percent were Russians, 12.9 percent were Uzbeks, 2.1 percent were Ukrainians, and 1.0 percent were Germans (see table 4, Appendix). The rest of the population was composed of about eighty other nationalities. Of some potential political significance are the Uygurs. That group numbers only about 36,000 in Kyrgyzstan, but about 185,000 live in neighboring Kazakstan. The Uygurs are also the majority population in the Xinjiang Uygur Autonomous Region of China, whose population is about 15 million, located to the northeast of Kyrgyzstan. In November 1992, the Uygurs in Kyrgyzstan attempted to form a party calling for establishment of an independent Uygurstan that also would include the Chinese-controlled Uygur territory. The Ministry of Justice denied the group legal registration.

Between 1989 and 1993, a significant number of non-Kyrgyz citizens left the republic, although no census was taken in the early 1990s to quantify the resulting balances among ethnic groups. A considerable portion of this exodus consisted of Germans repatriating to Germany, more than 8,000 of whom left in 1992 alone. According to reports, more than 30,000 Russians left the Bishkek area in the early 1990s, presumably for destinations outside Kyrgyzstan. In 1992 and 1993, refugees from the civil war in Tajikistan moved into southern Kyrgyzstan. In 1989 about 64,000 Kyrgyz were living in Tajikistan, and about 175,000 were living in Uzbekistan. Reliable estimates of how many of these people subsequently returned to Kyrgyzstan have not been available.

The Fergana Valley, which eastern Kyrgyzstan shares with Central Asian neighbors Uzbekistan and Tajikistan, is one of the most densely populated and agriculturally most heavily exploited regions in Central Asia. As such, it has been the point of bitter contention among the three adjoining states, both before and after the collapse of the Soviet Union. Members of the various ethnic groups who have inhabited the valley for centuries have managed to get along largely because they occupy slightly different economic niches. The sedentary Uzbeks and Tajiks traditionally have farmed lower-lying irrigated land while the nomadic Kyrgyz have herded in the mountains. However, the potential for ethnic conflict is ever present. Because the borders of the three countries zigzag without evident regard for the nationality of the people living in the valley, many residents harbor strong irredentist feelings, believing that they should more properly be citizens of a different country. Few Europeans live in the Fergana Valley, but about 552,000 Uzbeks, almost the entire population of that people in Kyrgyzstan, reside there in crowded proximity with about 1.2 million Kyrgyz.

## Geographic Factors

Population statistics depict only part of the demographic situation in Kyrgyzstan. Because of the country's mountainous terrain, population tends to be concentrated in relatively small areas in the north and south, each of which contains about two million people. About two-thirds of the total population live in the Fergana, Talas, and Chu valleys. As might be expected, imbalances in population distribution lead to extreme contrasts in how people live and work. In the north, the Chu Valley, site of Bishkek, the capital, is the major economic center, producing about 45 percent of the nation's gross national product (GNP—see Glossary). The Chu Valley also is where most of the country's Europeans live, mainly because of economic opportunities. The ancestors of today's Russian and German population began to move into the fertile valley to farm at the end of the nineteenth century. There was a subsequent influx of Russians during World War II, when industrial resources and personnel were moved en masse out of European Russia to prevent their capture by the invading Germans. In the era of Soviet First Secretary Leonid I. Brezhnev, a deliberate development policy brought another in-migration. Bishkek is slightly more than 50 percent Kyrgyz, and the rest of the valley retains approximately that ethnic ratio. In the mid-1990s, observers expected that balance to change quickly, however, as Europeans continued to move out while rural Kyrgyz moved in, settling in the numerous shantytowns springing up around Bishkek. The direct distance from Bishkek in the far north to Osh in the southwest is slightly more than 300 kilometers, but the mountain road connecting those cities requires a drive of more than ten hours in summer conditions; in winter the high mountain passes are often closed. In the Soviet period, most travel between north and south was by airplane, but fuel shortages that began after independence have greatly limited the number of flights, increasing a tendency toward separation of north and south (see Topography and Drainage; Transportation and Telecommunications, this ch.).

The separation of the north and the south is clearly visible in the cultural mores of the two regions, although both are dominated by ethnic Kyrgyz. Society in the Fergana Valley is much more traditional than in the Chu Valley, and the practice of Islam is more pervasive. The people of the Chu Valley are closely integrated with Kazakstan (Bishkek is but four hours by car from Almaty, the capital of Kazakstan). The people of the south are more oriented, by location and by culture, to Uzbekistan, Iran, Afghanistan, and the other Muslim countries to the south.

Geographical isolation also has meant that the northern and southern Kyrgyz have developed fairly distinct lifestyles. Those in the north tend to be nomadic herders; those in the south have acquired more of the sedentary agricultural ways of their Uygur, Uzbek, and Tajik neighbors. Both groups came to accept Islam late, but practice in the north tends to be much less influenced by Islamic doctrine and reflects considerable influence from pre-Islamic animist beliefs. The southerners have a more solid basis of religious knowledge and practice. It is they who pushed for a greater religious element in the 1993 constitution (see Religion, this ch.).

## Society and Culture

The ethnic identity of the Kyrgyz has been strongly linked to their language and to ethnic traditions, both of which have been guarded with particular zeal once independence provided an opportunity to make national policy on these matters. Less formally, the Kyrgyz people have maintained with unusual single-mindedness many elements of social structure and a sense of their common past. The name Kyrgyz derives from the Turkic *kyrk* plus *yz*, a combination meaning "forty clans."

### Language

In the period after A.D. 840, the Kyrgyz joined other Turkic groups in an overall Turkification pattern extending across the Tian Shan into the Tarim River basin, east of present-day Kyrgyzstan's border with China. In this process, which lasted for more than two centuries, the Kyrgyz tribes became mixed with other tribes, thoroughly absorbing Turkic cultural and linguistic characteristics.

The forebears of the present-day Kyrgyz are believed to have been either southern Samoyed or Yeniseyan tribes. Those tribes came into contact with Turkic culture after they conquered the Uygurs and settled the Orkhon area, site of the oldest recorded Turkic language, in the ninth century (see Early History, this ch.). If descended from the Samoyed tribes of Siberia, the Kyrgyz would have spoken a language in the Uralic linguistic subfamily when they arrived in Orkhon; if descended from Yeniseyan tribes, they would have descended from a people of the same name who began to move into the area of present-day Kyrgyzstan from the Yenisey River region of central Siberia in the tenth century, after the Kyrgyz conquest of the Uygurs to the east in the preceding century. Ethnographers dispute the Yeniseyan origin, however, because of the very close cultural and linguistic connections between the Kyrgyz and the Kazaks (see Early Tribal Movement; Ethnic Groups, ch. 1).

In the period of tsarist administration (1876–1917), the Kazaks and the Kyrgyz both were called Kyrgyz, with what are now the Kyrgyz subdenominated when necessary as Kara-Kyrgyz (black Kyrgyz). Although the Kyrgyz language has more Mongolian and Altaic elements than does Kazak, the modern forms of the two languages are very similar. As they exist today, both are part of the Nogai group of the Kipchak division of the Turkic languages, which belong to the Uralic-Altaic language family. The modern Kyrgyz language did not have a written form until 1923, at which time an Arabic-based alphabet was used. That was changed to a Latin-based alphabet in 1928 and to a Cyrillic-based one in 1940. In the years immediately following independence, another change of alphabet was discussed, but the issue does not seem to generate the same passions in Kyrgyzstan that it does in other former Soviet republics (see National Identity, ch. 1; Culture and the Arts, ch. 3; The Spoken Language, ch. 4; The Written Language, ch. 4; Language and Literature, ch. 5).

One important difference between Kyrgyzstan and Kazakstan is that the Kyrgyz people's mastery of their own language is almost universal, whereas the linguistic phase of national identity is not as clear in the much larger area and population of Kazakstan (see Language, ch. 1). As in Kazakstan, mastery of the "titular" language among the resident Europeans of Kyrgyzstan is very rare. In the early 1990s, the Akayev government pursued an aggressive policy of introducing Kyrgyz as the official language, forcing the remaining European population to use Kyrgyz in most public situations. Public pressure to enforce this change was sufficiently strong that a Russian member of President Akayev's staff created a public scandal in 1992 by threatening to resign to dramatize the pressure for "Kyrgyzification" of the non-native population. A 1992 law called for the conduct of all public business to be converted fully to Kyrgyz by 1997. But in March 1996, Kyrgyzstan's parliament adopted a resolution making Russian an official state language alongside Kyrgyz and marking a reversal of earlier sentiment. Substantial pressure from Russia was a strong factor in this change, which was part of a general rapprochement with Russia urged by Akayev.

## Ethnic Traditions

The Kyrgyz also have retained a strong sense of cultural tradition. Figures from the 1989 Soviet census show that Kyrgyz males were the least likely of the men of any Soviet nationality to marry outside their people (only 6.1 percent of their mar-

*Falconer wearing traditional* kalpak *(hat) and coat*
*Kalmyk woman baking little breads in traditional adobe oven*
*Courtesy Hermine Dreyfuss*

131

riages were "international") and that Kyrgyz women did so in only 5.8 percent of marriages. Moreover, although the degree of such changes is difficult to measure, Kyrgyz "mixed" marriages seem uncommonly likely to assimilate in the direction of a Kyrgyz identity, with the non-Kyrgyz spouse learning the Kyrgyz language and the children assuming the Kyrgyz nationality. Even ordinary citizens are thoroughly familiar with the Kyrgyz oral epic, *Manas,* a poem of several hundred thousand lines (many versions are recited) telling of the eponymous Kyrgyz hero's struggles against invaders from the east. Many places and things in Kyrgyzstan, including the main airport, bear the name of this ancient hero, the one-thousandth anniversary of whose mythical adventures were cause for great national celebration in 1995.

## Social Structure

The age-old geographic separation of pockets of the Kyrgyz population has tended to reinforce conservatism in all of the country's society. The modern Kyrgyz still apply great significance to family and clan origins. The majority of Kyrgyz continued a nomadic lifestyle until the Soviet campaigns of forcible collectivization forced them first into transitional settlements and then into cities and towns or state and collective farms in the 1930s. Within the centralized farm systems, however, many Kyrgyz continued to move seasonally with their herds. There has been strong resistance to industrial employment.

### Clans

Kyrgyz identity in public and private life is said to be determined primarily by membership in one of three clan groupings known as "wings" (right, or *ong;* left, or *sol;* and *ichkilik,* which is neither) and secondarily by membership in a particular clan within a wing. The history of this grouping is unknown, although several legends explain the phenomenon. The left wing now includes seven clans in the north and west. Each of the seven has a dominant characteristic, and all have fought each other for influence. The Buguu warrior clan provided the first administrators of the Kyrgyz Republic under the Soviet Union; when the purges of Stalin eradicated their leaders in the 1930s, their place was taken by a second northern warrior clan, the Sarybagysh, who have provided most Kyrgyz leaders since that time, including Akayev. The right wing contains only one clan, the Adygine. Located in the south, the Adygine are considered the most genuinely Kyrgyz clan because of their legendary heritage. The southern Ichkilik is a group of many clans, some of which are not of Kyrgyz origin, but all of which claim Kyrgyz identity in the present.

Acutely aware of the roles each of the clans traditionally has played, the Kyrgyz are still very conscious of clan membership in competing for social and economic advantage. Support for fellow clan members is especially strong in the northern provinces. Kyrgyz men frequently wear traditional black-on-white felt headgear, which informs others of their clan status and the degree of respect to be accorded them. Larger clans are subdivided by origin and by the nobility of their ancestors; although there is no prohibition of advancement for those of non-noble descent, descent from a high-born extended family still is considered a social advantage.

Like other Central Asian groups, the Kyrgyz venerate history and see themselves as part of a long flow of events. A traditional requirement is the ability to name all the people in the previous seven generations of one's family. Clan identity extends this tradition even further, to the legendary origins of the Kyrgyz people. Kyrgyz clans are said to spring from "first fathers," most of whom appear in both oral legends and in history. Clan history and genealogy are entrusted to tribal elders, whose ongoing knowledge of those subjects makes falsification of lineage difficult. Because clan identity remains an important element of social status, however, Kyrgyz do sometimes claim to have descended from a higher branch of their clan than is actually the case.

### Domestic Life

The Kyrgyz are classified as nomadic pastoralists, meaning that they traditionally have herded sheep, horses, or yaks, following the animals up and down the mountains as the seasons change. The basic dwelling is the yurt, a cylindrical felt tent easily disassembled and mounted on a camel or horse. The image of a yurt's circular smoke opening is the central design of Kyrgyzstan's flag. Various parts of the yurt have ritual significance. Because the herding economy continues in many parts of the country, the yurt remains a strong symbol of national identity. Families living in Western-style dwellings erect yurts to celebrate weddings and funerals.

Traditional domestic life centers on the flocks. The diet of the nomads is limited to mutton and noodles; fruit and vegetables are rare even in today's Kyrgyz cuisine. The most traditional dishes are *besh barmak*, a mutton stew, and roast lamb. For ceremonial meals, the lamb is killed without spilling its blood, and the head is served to the guest of honor, who slices portions of the eyes and ears and presents them to other guests to improve their sight and hearing. Horsemeat is eaten fresh and in sausages. Traditional beverages are *kumys*, fermented mare's milk, and two varieties of beer.

Family traditions continue to demonstrate the patriarchal and feudal character of a nomadic people. Family relations are characterized by great respect for older family members and the dominance of male heads of households. Traditional celebrations of special events retain the markings of religious and magical rites. For example, the cutting of a child's umbilical cord is celebrated with elaborate consumption of food and humorous games. The naming of a child and the cutting of the child's hair are conducted in such a way as to appease supernatural forces. The full observance of the most important family event, the wedding celebration, requires considerable expense that relatively few Kyrgyz can afford: payment for a bride, dowry, animal sacrifice, and an exchange of clothing between the relatives of the bride and the groom.

### The Role of Women

In traditional Kyrgyz society, women had assigned roles, although only the religious elite sequestered women as was done in other Muslim societies. Because of the demands of the nomadic economy, women worked as virtual equals with men, having responsibility for chores such as milking as well as child-rearing and the preparation and storage of food. In the ordinary family, women enjoyed approximately equal status with their husbands. Kyrgyz oral literature includes the story of Janyl-myrza, a young woman who led her tribe to liberation from the enemy when no man in the tribe could do so. In the nineteenth century, the wife of Khan Almyn-bek led a group of Kyrgyz tribes at the time of the Russian conquest of Ququn.

In modern times, especially in the first years of independence, women have played more prominent roles in Kyrgyzstan than elsewhere in Central Asia. Since 1991 women have occupied the positions of state procurator (the top law enforcement official in the national government), minister of education, ambassador to the United States and Canada, and minister of foreign affairs. Women have also excelled in banking and business, and the editor of Central Asia's most independent newspaper, *Respublika*, is a woman. Roza Otunbayeva, who was minister of foreign affairs in 1996, has been mentioned frequently as a successor to Akayev.

## Contemporary Culture

As the capital of a Soviet republic, Bishkek (which until 1990 had been named Frunze after the Soviet general who led the military conquest of the Basmachi rebels in the mid-1920s) was endowed with the standard cultural facilities, including an opera, ballet, several theater companies, and an orchestra, as well as a Lenin museum, national art and craft museums, and an open-air sculpture museum. Since independence, funding for those institutions has decreased dramatically, and the cultural facilities have also been hard hit by the departure of local Russians. It also is unclear whether younger Kyrgyz will continue their parents' substantial interest in classical music, which in the Soviet era led several generations to support the national orchestra.

In the Soviet-directed propagation of "all-union culture," Kyrgyz actors, directors, and dancers achieved fame throughout the Soviet Union. Chingiz Aitmatov, the republic's most prominent writer, became one of the best-known and most independent artists in the Soviet Union in the 1980s. The Kyrgyz film industry, which had been very productive while supported by Soviet government funds, essentially vanished after 1991. Film projects that survive, such as a large-scale production on the life of Chinggis Khan directed by noted Kyrgyz director T. Okeyev, do so through foreign financing (an Italian film company has supported production of the Okeyev film).

Perhaps the best indicator of the condition of the fine arts in postcommunist Kyrgyzstan is the fate of the open-air sculpture museum in Bishkek, which began suffering a series of thefts in early 1993. Because the targets were all bronze, presumably the sculptures were stolen for their value as metal, not as art. When a large statuary group commemorating Aitmatov's Ysyk-Köl Forum (a notable product of the early *glasnost* period) disappeared, the museum's remaining statues were removed to a more secure location.

## Religion

The vast majority of today's Kyrgyz are Muslims of the Sunni

135

(see Glossary) branch, but Islam came late and fairly superficially to the area. Kyrgyz Muslims generally practice their religion in a specific way influenced by earlier tribal customs. The practice of Islam also differs in the northern and southern regions of the country. Kyrgyzstan remained a secular state after the fall of communism, which had only superficial influence on religious practice when Kyrgyzstan was a Soviet republic. Most of the Russian population of Kyrgyzstan is atheist or Russian Orthodox. The Uzbeks, who make up 12.9 percent of the population, are generally Sunni Muslims.

## The Introduction of Islam

Islam was introduced to the Kyrgyz tribes between the ninth and twelfth centuries. The most intense exposure to Islam occurred in the seventeenth century, when the Jungars drove the Kyrgyz of the Tian Shan region into the Fergana Valley, whose population was totally Islamic. However, as the danger from the Jungars subsided and Kyrgyz groups returned to their previous region, the influence of Islam became weaker. When the Ququon Khanate conquered the territory of the Kyrgyz in the eighteenth century, the nomadic Kyrgyz remained aloof from the official Islamic practices of that regime. By the end of the nineteenth century, however, most of the Kyrgyz population had been converted to at least a superficial recognition of Islamic practice.

## Tribal Religion

Alongside Islam the Kyrgyz tribes also practiced totemism, the recognition of spiritual kinship with a particular type of animal. Under this belief system, which predated their contact with Islam, Kyrgyz tribes adopted reindeer, camels, snakes, owls, and bears as objects of worship. The sun, moon, and stars also played an important religious role. The strong dependence of the nomads on the forces of nature reinforced such connections and fostered belief in shamanism (the power of tribal healers and magicians with mystical connections to the spirit world) and black magic as well. Traces of such beliefs remain in the religious practice of many of today's Kyrgyz.

Knowledge of and interest in Islam are said to be much stronger in the south, especially around Osh, than farther north. Religious practice in the north is more heavily mixed with animism (belief that every animate and inanimate object

*Gate leading to prayer house on
Suleyman's Mountain, Osh
Courtesy Lisa Batey*

*New mosque under
construction, Naryn
Courtesy Rurie E. Miller*

contains a spirit) and shamanist practices, giving worship there
a resemblance to Siberian religious practice.

## Islam and the State

Religion has not played an especially large role in the politics of Kyrgyzstan, although more traditional elements of society urged that the Muslim heritage of the country be
acknowledged in the preamble to the 1993 constitution. That
document mandates a secular state, forbidding the intrusion of
any ideology or religion in the conduct of state business. As in
other parts of Central Asia, non-Central Asians have been concerned about the potential of a fundamentalist Islamic revolution that would emulate Iran and Afghanistan by bringing
Islam directly into the making of state policy, to the detriment
of the non-Islamic population. Because of sensitivity about the
economic consequences of a continued outflow of Russians,
President Akayev has taken particular pains to reassure the
non-Kyrgyz that no Islamic revolution threatens (see Ethnic
Groups, this ch.). Akayev has paid public visits to Bishkek's

main Russian Orthodox church and directed 1 million rubles from the state treasury toward that faith's church-building fund. He has also appropriated funds and other support for a German cultural center. The state officially recognizes Orthodox Christmas (but not Easter) as a holiday, while also noting two Muslim feast days, Oroz ait (which ends Ramadan) and Kurban ait (June 13, the Day of Remembrance), and Muslim New Year, which falls on the vernal equinox.

# Education

In the mid-1990s, much of the Soviet-era education system remained in Kyrgyzstan, which had made a conscientious effort to educate all of its citizens before 1991 and continued to do so after that date. Substantial structural and curriculum changes were underway by 1995, however. The 1993 constitution continues the Soviet guarantee of free basic education at state institutions to all citizens; education is compulsory through grade nine. Free education at the vocational, secondary specialized, and higher levels also continues to be offered by the state to qualified individuals. The fundamentals of post-Soviet education policy were enumerated in the 1992 law on education, which established the Ministry of Education as the central administrative body of the national system. Although Soviet-era statistics indicated that 100 percent of the people between the ages of nine and forty-nine were literate, the actual literacy rate probably is somewhat less.

## Education System

Once independence was achieved, the Ministry of Education began working energetically to revamp the old Soviet course of study. The ministry is responsible for developing curriculum, setting national standards and educational policy, developing certification examinations, and awarding degrees. The ministry is divided into departments for general education, higher education, and material support. Below the ministry level, the education hierarchy includes the six provinces and the separate city of Bishkek, representatives from each of which provide input to the ministry on local conditions. The level of basic local administration is the district (*rayon*), where the district education officer hires faculty and appoints school inspectors and methodology specialists.

*Kindergarten for children of government officials, Bishkek*
*Courtesy Hermine Dreyfuss*

General education is financed from district budgets, and the college preparatory and higher education programs are financed by the national budget. For the former category of expenditures, school principals negotiate their requirements with district officials, but the central government sets norms based on previous expenditures and on the relative resources of the provinces. In the last years of the Soviet period, Kyrgyzstani schools had a surplus of money, but available funds declined sharply beginning in 1992. Since that time, insufficient funds in local budgets have forced the Ministry of Education to make special requests for support from the Ministry of Economics and Finance.

## Instruction

General education traditionally has been accessible to nearly all children in Kyrgyzstan. In primary and secondary grades, about 51 percent of students are female; that number increases to 55 percent in higher education, with a converse majority of males in vocational programs. There is little difference in school attendance between urban and rural areas or among the provinces. Higher education, however, has been much more available to the urban and more wealthy segments of the population. Because of a shortage of schools, 37 percent of general education students attend schools operating in two or three shifts. Construction of new facilities has lagged behind enrollment growth, the rate of which has been nearly 3 percent per year.

In line with the reform of 1992, children start school at age six and are required to complete grade nine. The general education program has three stages: grades one through four, grades five through nine, and grades ten and eleven. Students completing grade nine may continue into advanced or specialized (college preparatory) secondary curricula or into a technical and vocational program. The school year is thirty-four weeks long, extending from the beginning of September until the end of May. The instruction week is twenty-five hours long for grades one through four and thirty-two hours for grades five through eleven. In 1992 about 960,000 students were enrolled in general education courses, 42,000 in specialized secondary programs, 49,000 in vocational programs, and 58,000 in institutions of higher education. About 1,800 schools were in operation in 1992. That year Kyrgyzstan's state system had about 65,000 teachers, but an estimated 8,000 teachers resigned in 1992 alone because of poor salaries and a heavy work load that included double shifts for many. Emigration also has depleted the teaching staff. In 1993 the national pupil-teacher ratio for grades one through eleven was 14.4 to 1, slightly higher in rural areas, and considerably higher in the primary grades. The city of Bishkek, however, had a ratio of almost 19 to 1.

## Curriculum

Post-Soviet curriculum reform has aroused much controversy in Kyrgyzstan. A fundamental question is the language of instruction, which has become increasingly Kyrgyz as non-indigenous citizens leave the country and textbooks in Kyrgyz slowly become available. The Ministry of Education has held competitions, supported by foreign donations, for the design of new textbooks in Kyrgyz. Until 1992 textbook production and distribution were inefficient and costly aspects of the education system. By the mid-1990s, the single, state-supported publisher of textbooks had gradually improved the quality and availability of its products. In 1992 the first major curriculum reform provided for mandatory foreign language study (English, French, or German) beginning in grade one; computer science courses in grades eight through eleven (a program hampered by lack of funds); and the replacement of Soviet ideology with concepts of market economy and ethnic studies. The reformed curriculum requirements also leave room for elective courses, and instructional innovation is encouraged.

### Higher Education

In 1994 Kyrgyzstan had twenty-six institutions of higher learning, all but seven of which were located in Bishkek. Seven of the institutions were private and the remainder state-funded. Approximately 4,700 faculty were employed there, of which only 150 had doctoral degrees and 1,715 were candidates, the step below the doctorate in the Soviet system. The language of instruction remained predominantly Russian in the mid-1990s, although the use of Kyrgyz increased yearly. Long-term plans call for a more Western style of university study, so that, for example, the universities would begin to offer a baccalaureate degree. In 1992 President Akayev created a Slavic University in Bishkek to help Kyrgyzstan retain its population of educated Russians, for whom the increased "Kyrgyzification" of education was a reason to emigrate. Because Russian students from outside the Russian Federation had lost their Soviet-era right to free education in Russian universities, Akayev hoped to provide a Russian-language institution for Russian-speaking students from all the Central Asian states. The shortage of education funds in Kyrgyzstan brought strong objections to a project that did not promote the education of ethnic Kyrgyz students, however.

## Health and Welfare

In 1993 the World Bank reported that the population of Kyrgyzstan enjoyed better health care than most other countries with similar per capita income, which averaged US$3,410 per year for Kyrgyzstan's category in 1992. The current health conditions and health prospects of Kyrgyzstan's population are difficult to calculate, however, because of the sudden change that independence visited upon the medical community. Until 1991 Kyrgyzstan's medical system was financed through the Soviet Union's Ministry of Health, which guaranteed a health establishment equal to that of other Soviet republics. With the dissolution of the Soviet Union and the slow collapse of fiscal ties between Kyrgyzstan and Moscow, the medical community has inherited an aging but generally adequate physical plant. However, the system often lacks the vaccines, medicines, and other resources needed to maintain the health of the population.

## Health Care System

Kyrgyzstan inherited the Soviet system of free universal health care, which in Kyrgyzstan's case generally provided sufficient numbers of doctors, nurses, and doctor's assistants, as well as medical clinics and hospitals. However, since 1991 citizens often have received inadequate care because medical personnel are not well trained; pharmaceuticals, medical supplies, and equipment are insufficient; and facilities are generally inadequate and unsanitary.

In 1991 Kyrgyzstan had 15,354 doctors, or 34.2 per 10,000 people. Paramedical workers totaled 42,448, or 94.6 per 10,000 people. Some 588 outpatient clinics were in operation, averaging 139 hours of patient visits per eight-hour shift. In addition, 246 general and twenty specialized hospitals were in operation; nearly one-third of all hospitals were located in Osh Province (which also had about one-third of the country's total population). By contrast, the capital city, Bishkek, had the fewest hospital facilities per capita of all regions, providing 1.55 general hospitals per 100,000 population. Like other Central Asian countries, Kyrgyzstan has continued the Soviet practice of state enterprises having their own clinics and sanatoriums. With the dissolution of the Soviet Union, Kyrgyzstan's residents lost the right to free treatment in the hospitals of other former republics, making unavailable many types of specialized treatment that the Soviet system had apportioned among adjacent republics.

Very few truly private health facilities have developed in the early post-Soviet period, and those that exist face very high licensing fees. Although it is illegal for state employees in the health field to diversify their activity into private practice, by 1993 many health workers were accepting unreported payments for providing additional treatment. In 1992 the maxi-

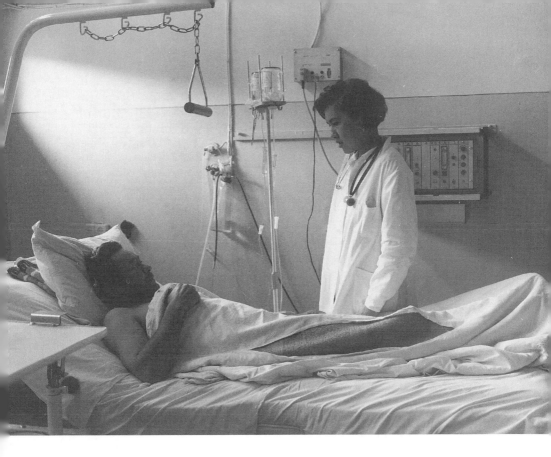

*Patient in specialized cardiac hospital, Bishkek*
*Courtesy Hermine Dreyfuss*

mum salary of a medical specialist such as a surgeon was only about 18 percent higher than the maximum salary of a technician or laboratory worker. Under such conditions, the rising cost of living in 1992 and 1993 forced many doctors to leave medicine for higher salaries in other professions.

Kyrgyzstan produces no vaccines of its own and almost no medicines or other pharmaceuticals. Drug availability is substantially higher at regional facilities than at smaller ones, but items such as antihistamines, insulin, antiseptics, vaccines, and some narcotics are either extremely scarce or extremely expensive. The other former Soviet republics now demand payment in United States dollars, which Kyrgyzstan does not have, for medical supplies. Because of the scarcity of vaccines, there is a greatly increased likelihood of epidemics of diseases such as diphtheria and measles. An outbreak of measles in Bishkek in early 1993 was said to be just below epidemic level. It has become common practice in hospitals and clinics to require patients to provide their own medicines for operations and other medical procedures. Because virtually the only available medicines are those for sale in the public bazaars, quality is questionable, and accidental poisonings caused by misuse and spoilage have been reported.

Kyrgyzstan's post-Soviet financial crisis has reduced government support of the Soviet-era health system, forcing government planners to formulate an ambitious health care delivery reform program. The center of the program is a transformation of the national health system into a system of public health insurance, in which compulsory employer fees and a health insurance tax on employees would support care for employees, and state contributions would support care for unemployed citizens. All employed citizens would be required to carry health insurance. All care providers would switch from the salary basis of the old system to a fee-for-service payment system. Because the banking, record-keeping, and tax systems of the country are not ready to support such a nationwide program, however, installation has lagged far behind the original timetable, which called for a pilot program in Bishkek in 1993.

## Health Conditions

The main causes of adult deaths in Kyrgyzstan are, in order of occurrence, cardiovascular conditions, respiratory infections, and accidents (see table 5, Appendix). Sexually transmitted diseases reportedly are very low in incidence; only five cases of acquired immune deficiency syndrome (AIDS) were recorded in 1992. In the early 1990s, major health hazards have been posed by growing shortages of chlorine to purify water supplies and the increasing danger of typhus outbreaks resulting from the closure of most of the country's public baths. In 1993 Kyrgyzstan suffered increasing cases of hepatitis and gastrointestinal infections, especially in the southern provinces of Osh and Jalal-Abad. The cause of such infections is believed to be the use of open water supplies contaminated by livestock and improper disposal of waste (see Environmental Problems, this ch.). Although adults traditionally consume most of their water in the form of boiled tea, children have greater access to untreated water and foods.

Additional stress is placed on the population by the rising cost of food, which has reduced the quality and quantity of most people's diets. In 1993 meat consumption was reported to have dropped by 20 percent since 1990, intake of milk products by 30 percent, and consumption of fish (which was imported in the Soviet period) by 70 percent. The average caloric intake was reported to have decreased by about 12 percent since 1990. There are also frequent reports of deaths or injuries caused by tainted or falsely labeled food and drink, particularly alcoholic beverages, which are widely sold by extralegal private concerns. The rising cost of energy has meant insufficient heat for many apartments and public buildings. Naryn Province, the coldest and most remote part of the country, has been particularly affected. In that region, many buildings lack central heating, and residents have been forced to devise homemade stoves vented directly out the windows. In addition, the availability and range of ambulance services have been restricted severely by fuel shortages.

## Social Welfare

Like the other former Soviet republics, Kyrgyzstan inherited a social welfare system that allocated benefits very broadly without targeting needy groups in society. In this system, nearly half of society received some sort of benefit, and many benefit payments were excessive. By necessity, the post-Soviet government has sought to make substantial reductions in state social protection payments, emphasizing identification of the most vulnerable members of society.

### The Soviet Heritage

In 1991, the last year of the Soviet Union, the payment of pensions, child allowances, and other forms of support amounted to 18 percent of the Kyrgyz Republic's gross domestic product (GDP—see Glossary). At that point, about 600,000 pensioners and 1.6 million children received some form of payment. Eligibility requirements were extremely liberal, defined mainly by age and work history rather than by social position or contributions to a pension fund. This generous system failed to eliminate poverty, however; according to a 1989 Soviet survey, 35 percent of the population fell below the official income line for "poorly supplied" members of society. Thus poverty, which became an increasingly urgent problem during the economic decline of the transition period of the early 1990s, already was rooted firmly in Kyrgyzstan when independence was achieved.

### Reforming Social Welfare

The Akayev government addressed the overpayment problem by reducing categorical subsidies and government price controls; by indexing benefits only partially as inflation raised the cost of living; and by targeting benefits to the most needy parts of society. Under the new program, child allowances went only to people with incomes below a fixed level, and bread price compensation went only to groups such as pensioners who lacked earning power. By 1993 such measures had cut government welfare expenses by more than half, from 57 percent of the state budget to 25 percent.

Nevertheless, the percentage of citizens below the poverty line grew rapidly in the early 1990s as the population felt the impact of the government's economic stabilization program (see Economic Reform, this ch.). In addition, the Soviet system delegated delivery of many social services, including health, to state enterprises, which in the post-Soviet era no longer had the means to guarantee services to employees (or, in many cases, even to continue employing them). The state's Pension Fund (a government agency with the relatively independent status of a state committee) went into debt in 1994 because workers who retired early or worked only for a short period remained eligible for pensions and the poor financial state of enterprises made revenue collection difficult. The pension system is supported by payroll taxes of 33 percent on industries and 26 percent on collective and state farms. Besides retirement pensions, disability and survivors' benefits also are paid. Of the amount collected, 14 percent goes to the labor unions' Social Insurance Fund and the remainder to the Pension Fund. The standard pension eligibility age is sixty for men and fifty-five for women, but in 1992 an estimated 156,000 people were receiving benefits at earlier ages. In 1994 the minimum pension amount was raised to forty-five som (for value of the som—see Glossary) per month, the latest in a long series of adjustments that did not nearly keep pace with inflation's impact on the real value of the pension.

New pension legislation prepared in 1994 made enterprises responsible for the costs of early retirement; established a five-year minimum for pension eligibility; clearly separated the categories of work pensions from social assistance payments; abolished supplementary pension payments for recipients needing additional support; eliminated the possibility of receiving a pension while continuing to work (the position of an estimated 49,000 workers in 1992); and provided for long-term linkage of contributions made to pensions later received.

Child allowances are paid for children up to the age of eighteen, and a lump sum payment is made on the birth of a child. In 1991 child allowances consumed 6.7 percent of GDP; since that time, targeting of benefits has been a major concern in this category to reduce spending but cover vulnerable groups. The first alteration of eligibility standards occurred in 1993. Cash for this category is provided by direct transfers from the state budget combined with Pension Fund contributions.

Besides pensions and family allowances, Kyrgyzstani citizens also receive maternity benefits and sick pay covered by the Social Insurance Fund, which is managed by the Federation of Independent Labor Unions and the individual unions; it receives money only from its 14 percent share of payroll taxes, not from the state budget or individual contributions. All public and private employees are eligible for sick leave, with payments depending on length of service. The maternity allowance is a single payment equal to two months' minimum wage. World Bank experts consider the sick and maternity benefits excessive in relation to the state of the economy and the state budget.

In assessing the future of social assistance in Kyrgyzstan, experts predict that economic restructuring through the 1990s will increase the number of citizens requiring assistance from the state system. To meet such needs, thorough reform of the system—aimed mainly at tightening eligibility standards—will be necessary. It is also expected that Kyrgyzstan will require other methods of social assistance to provide for individuals who do not fall into existing categories, or for whom inflation erodes excessively the value of payments now received. The officially and unofficially unemployed (together estimated at 300,000 at the end of 1994) are an especially vulnerable group because of the unlikelihood of workers being reabsorbed rapidly into the country's faltering economy. (Unemployment benefits are paid for twenty-six weeks to those who register, but the number of "non-participants" is much greater than the number of registered unemployed.)

## The Economy

In the first five years of independence, Kyrgyzstan's economy made more progress in market-oriented reform legislation but less progress in economic growth than the other four Central Asian states. This disparity was largely because Kyrgyzstan lacked the diversified natural resources and processing infrastructure that enable a national economy to survive the shutdown of some sectors by shifting labor and other inputs to new areas of production.

The economic system of Kyrgyzstan is undergoing a slow, painful, and uncertain transition. Once a highly integrated provider of raw materials for the centrally controlled economy of the Soviet Union, the republic's economy is reorienting itself toward processing its own raw materials and producing its own industrial products. During the late 1980s and early 1990s, however, industry accounted for only about one-third of the country's net material product (NMP—see Glossary) while employing less than one-fifth of the labor force. The primary emphasis of the economy remained agriculture, which accounted for about 40 percent of NMP and officially employed about one-third of the labor force. The transportation and communications sector employed only about 3.2 percent of the labor force in 1991. As in other Soviet republics, the vast majority of workers were employed by the state, while most of the remainder worked on private agricultural plots.

## Role in the Soviet Economy

As part of the Soviet Union, Kyrgyzstan played a small but highly integrated role in the centrally controlled economy. Figures for 1990 show that agriculturally the republic contributed 1 percent or less of the total Soviet output of preserved vegetables, animal fats, plant oils, and meat, and 3 percent of the total Soviet output of beet sugar. Kyrgyzstan also produced small proportions of Soviet wine products and tobacco. Industrially, the republic supplied 1 to 2 percent of the Soviet Union's total output of cotton cloth, silk cloth, linen, and woolen cloth, and an equal proportion of ready-made clothing and shoes. Machine-assembly plants, steel plants, motor-assembly plants, and miscellaneous light industry contributed another 1 percent or less of the Soviet total. The only energy resources that Kyrgyzstan contributed in any volume were coal (0.5 percent of the Soviet total) and hydroelectric power (0.8 percent). Kyrgyzstan's radio-assembly and other electronic plants accounted for a small portion of the defense industry. A torpedo-assembly plant was located on the shores of Ysyk-Köl. One of the Soviet Union's two military airbases for the training of foreign pilots was located outside Bishkek.

Kyrgyzstan's largest role in the Soviet economy was as a supplier of minerals, especially antimony (in which the republic had a near monopoly), mercury, lead, and zinc. Of greatest significance economically, however, was gold, of which Kyrgyzstan was the Soviet Union's third-largest supplier.

## Natural Resources

Soviet geologists have estimated Kyrgyzstan's coal reserves at about 27 billion tons, of which the majority remained entirely unexploited in the mid-1990s. About 3 billion tons of that amount are judged to be of highest quality. This coal has proven difficult to exploit, however, because most of it is in small deposits deep in the mountains. Kyrgyzstan also has oil resources; small deposits of oil-bearing shale have been located in southern Kyrgyzstan, and part of the Fergana oil and natural gas complex lies in Kyrgyzstani territory. In the Osh region, four pools of oil, four of natural gas, and four mixed pools have been exploited since the 1950s; however, the yield of all of them is falling in the 1990s. In 1992 their combined output was 112,000 tons of oil and 65 million cubic meters of natural gas, compared with the republic's annual consumption of 2.5 million tons of oil and 3 billion cubic meters of natural gas.

Kyrgyzstan's iron ore deposits are estimated at 5 billion tons, most containing about 30 percent iron. Copper deposits in the mountains are located in extremely complex mineral deposits, making extraction costly. The northern mountains also contain lead, zinc, molybdenum, vanadium, and bismuth. The south has deposits of bauxite and mercury; Kyrgyzstan was the Soviet Union's main supplier of mercury, but in the 1990s plummeting mercury prices have damaged the international market. A tin and tungsten mine was 80 percent complete in 1995. Kyrgyzstan had a virtual monopoly on supplying antimony to the Soviet Union, but post-Soviet international markets are small and highly specialized. Uranium, which was in high demand for the Soviet Union's military and atomic energy programs, no longer is mined in Kyrgyzstan.

The Soviet Union's largest gold mine was located at Makmal in Kyrgyzstan, and in the Soviet period Kyrgyzstan's 170 proven deposits put it in third place behind only Russia and Uzbekistan in gold production in the union. Two more promising deposits, at Kumtor and Jerui, have been discovered. Kumtor, said to be the seventh-largest gold deposit in the world with an estimated value of US$5.5 billion, is being explored by the Canadian Metals Company (Cameco), a uranium company, in a joint-venture operation. Gold deposits are concentrated in

Talas Province in north-central Kyrgyzstan, where as much as 200 tons may exist; deposits in Makmal are estimated at sixty tons. Deposits adjacent to the Chatkal River in the northwest amount to an estimated 150 tons.

The terms of the agreement for Kumtor exploitation with Cameco, which gains one-third of profits from gold extraction, caused public concern in 1992. To improve control of the mineral-extraction and refining processes, and to address the uncontrolled movement of precious metals out of the country, President Akayev created a new administrative agency, Kyrgyzaltyn (Kyrgyzstan Gold), to replace Yuzhpolmetal, the Soviet-era body responsible for precious metals. In January 1993, Akayev also brought the country's antimony and mercury mines into Kyrgyzaltyn. The latter are especially important because mercury is used to refine gold. Control of the mercury mines makes more likely the realization of Akayev's hope that Kyrgyzstan will become more than just a supplier of raw materials.

Although Kyrgyzstan has one of the largest proven gold reserves in the world, in the early 1990s fuel and spare parts shortages combined with political disputes to hamper output (see Government and Politics, this ch.). Production in 1994 was 3.5 tons, but the output goal for 1996 was ten tons.

Kyrgyzstan's major energy source, water, has also been discussed as a commercial product. The export of bottled mineral and fresh water was the object of several unrealized plans in the mid-1990s.

## Agriculture

The condition of agriculture in Kyrgyzstan is determined by the state's continuing control of production, marketing, and prices, as well as by the republic-wide specialization mandated by the former Soviet Union to promote interdependence among the republics. Most agricultural production continues to occur in the state farm and collective farm systems, which are slowly being privatized. In the early post-Soviet years, government policy encouraged self-sufficiency in cereal grains to provide food security. Maintaining such self-sufficiency, however, has entailed continued government regulation such as compulsory marketing, which in turn has discouraged the development of diversified farm enterprise. The main agricultural regions are in the Fergana Valley (Osh and Jalal-Abad provinces), in the northern Chu and Talas valleys, and in the

Ysyk-Köl basin in the northeast. In the early 1990s, income declined steadily in both state-run and privatized agricultural enterprises.

### Agricultural Land

Kyrgyzstan has about 1.4 million hectares of arable land, which is only about 7 percent of the nation's total area. More than 70 percent of the arable area depends on irrigation for its productivity. In the Soviet period, only about 4 percent of agricultural land was owned privately, although private plots contributed a much higher percentage of overall output, especially in fruits and vegetables. In 1994 only an additional 6 percent of agricultural land had passed to some form of private ownership. The privatization of land was a difficult issue that was contested between President Akayev and more conservative government officials. The latter reflected the Soviet-era view that land should be common property protected and disposed of only by the state. More immediately, these officials represented the interests of state farm administrators, whose enterprises suffered greatly from post-Soviet economic shocks and redistribution of resources.

In 1992 and 1993, the land redistribution program also was hindered by poor cooperation between the national and local governments and by lack of clarity in the program outline. Nevertheless, by early 1993 some 165 of the 470 existing state and collective farms had been reorganized or privatized into about 17,000 peasant enterprises, cooperatives, or peasant associations. However, the state retained control over vital agricultural inputs and market distribution channels, meaning that private land users often lacked material support and that price controls limited the profitability of private farms. The privatization program was halted in early 1993, and a more comprehensive reform program was developed. In early 1995, the government offered debt relief to state and collective farms that expedited the availability of land to private farmers.

According to privatization law, state agricultural assets are distributed according to a share system in which all citizens have the right to a garden plot, but only individuals in the rural population have the right to occupy land and other agricultural assets formerly owned by state and collective farms. Recipients of shares can maintain the property as part of the collective, transfer it to a cooperative, or establish an individual farm. In the early 1990s, the former alternative was much more

151

popular because of the perception that larger units offered greater security in a time of financial uncertainty. Private ownership of land remained illegal in 1995, but use rights are guaranteed for forty-nine years, and use rights can be bought, sold, and used as collateral for loans. In 1994 a new decree on land reform expanded and clarified the legal basis for the use and exchange of land and improved the administration of land privatization, which is the responsibility of the Ministry of Agriculture and Food.

### Agricultural Production

In the post-Soviet years, Kyrgyzstan has continued to emphasize production of raw materials for industrial processing, a role assigned to the republic in the Soviet system. An estimated 62 percent of the population is rural (see Population, this ch.). The chief crops are fodder crops, wheat, barley, and cotton. Other agricultural products are sugar beets, tobacco, fruit, vegetables, and silk (see table 13, Appendix). In 1994 the largest crop harvests were of wheat (611,000 tons), barley (300,000 tons), potatoes (288,000 tons), and tomatoes (160,000 tons).

The chief agricultural use of land is pasturage for livestock, mainly sheep, goats, and cattle, the tending of which is the traditional vocation of the Kyrgyz people. An estimated 83 percent of land in agricultural use is mountainous pastureland. In the 1980s, livestock production accounted for about 60 percent of the value of the country's agricultural output; such production included mutton, beef, eggs, milk, wool, and thoroughbred horses. In 1987, when herds reached their largest numbers, about twice as much grain was used for animal feed as for human consumption. However, the prices of and demand for livestock products have dropped significantly in the 1990s relative to those of crops. For this reason and because Soviet-era herds had been supported largely by cheap imported grain, in 1994 livestock contributed less than half the total value of Kyrgyzstan's agricultural earnings. In 1994 the most important livestock products were cow's milk (750,000 tons), beef and veal (70,000 tons), mutton and lamb (50,000 tons), eggs (30,600 tons), wool (56,300 tons), pork products (30,000 tons), and poultry meat (25,000 tons). All of those figures were below the totals for the previous two years.

### Agricultural Trends and Problems

The early 1990s saw many farmers turn from commercial

production to subsistence crops, a trend that hurt the country's export activities (roughly half of its exports were agricultural in 1990) as well as the availability of foods within Kyrgyzstan. Experts believe that Kyrgyzstan's main agricultural problems are inappropriate and slow-moving reforms (especially land redistribution), intrusive bureaucratic regulations, poor availability of credit, and delayed payments to farmers for their crops. More immediately, both water and fertilizers have been in short supply since the end of the Soviet Union. In addition, Kyrgyzstan's agriculture uses an average of less than 50 percent of the amount of pesticides used by agriculture in the Western nations.

In 1994 the agriculture sector was in the fourth and most difficult year of a major decline that included reduced output, isolation from commercial markets, decreased earnings, and a deteriorating natural resource base (see table 6, Appendix). In 1994 total agricultural output dropped by 17 percent, and the decline in marketed and processed output was substantially greater because of the trend toward subsistence farming. Production ceased to increase at about the time of the collapse of the Soviet system, an event that initiated the loss of markets and trading partners, the loss of transfer payments from Moscow, and a condition of general monetary instability. The national government did not address these problems effectively in the first years of independence; in fact, government marketing quotas, price controls, and trade restrictions exacerbated the decline. By restricting farmers' marketing and pricing practices, the government in effect levied a tax on agriculture that redistributed income to other sectors of society. National reforms in land tenure, farm organization, and the financial system, together with privatization of services, were eroded by the continued authority of local officials to interfere in administration of those reforms.

A key agricultural resource, pastureland, was degraded severely by the Soviet-era practice of mandating livestock populations too large for available pasturage on state farms and by post-Soviet transfer of livestock from inefficient collective and state farms to private ownership without limiting grazing rights on common pastures. By 1994 over-grazing had led to serious erosion of much pasture land (see Environmental Problems, this ch.).

In 1994 a continuing controversy over granting central bank credits to support farmers during the growing season again made financial support a dubious proposition. Without such support, planting and fertilization would be severely limited because farmers in many rural areas lack financial resources to buy seed and fertilizer. On the other hand, such credits have always been a threat to the government's overall economic program. For several reasons, including the state's failure to pay farmers on time for their crops, the agricultural sector's bank debts increased rapidly in the early 1990s. This situation was the basis of arguments that the government could not afford to pay agricultural credits.

## Industry

Industrial production in Kyrgyzstan declined significantly in 1992 and 1993, especially in comparison to the average annual growth rate from 1985 to 1990, which was 3.3 percent. Important factors in this decline were the energy crisis caused by the loss of Soviet-era fuel supply agreements and the outflow of skilled Russian industrial and management personnel. By 1994, when output had fallen by another 25 percent, Kyrgyzstan's production was only 42 percent of its 1990 level. Only four of the country's 200 most important industrial products—oil, electrical power, household electric appliances, and alcoholic beverages—showed an increased output in 1994. By the first quarter of 1995, some 120 enterprises, more than one-third of the national total, were idle. The decline was caused by problems in obtaining raw materials, components, and other inputs; a drop in effective demand; the economic weakness of trading partners; and problems in arranging for payments. An important additional problem, however, is the nature of Kyrgyzstan's Soviet-era industrial structure, which was specialized for defense-related manufacturing. Many defense-related industries closed in the early 1990s because they could not find alternative types of production once Soviet defense contracts ended. The government's initial policy was to avoid supporting unprofitable state enterprises, but intense political pressure has kept many such firms open.

Including mining, the electric power industries, and construction, industry contributed about 45 percent of GDP in 1991, but that percentage dropped significantly in the following years, even with a parallel agricultural decline. For example, between 1991 and 1993 production of crude steel decreased 45 percent, cement production decreased by 49 percent, and production of metal cutting machines dropped by 77 percent. Gross capital formation decreased an estimated 55 percent in 1994, and investment for that year was below 25 percent of the rate at the end of the Soviet period. Private investment, however, rose slightly to nearly half of total investment for 1994.

None of the major industrial projects planned for 1993–94 was completed on time. Included in major construction postponements was a cigarette factory in Osh, which could have taken advantage of southern Kyrgyzstan's favorable tobacco-growing conditions. Many other projects were completed on a much smaller scale than originally planned. As conversion to useful new lines of manufacture was delayed, the national economy shrank. In addition, unemployment grew rapidly as state-owned enterprises were phased out but not replaced.

In the mid-1990s, the most valuable industrial components of Kyrgyzstan's economy were machine building, textiles, and food processing, which are centered in Bishkek, Osh, and Jalal-Abad (see fig. 5; table 14, Appendix). Some electronics and instruments are produced in former defense plants, and a limited metallurgical industry also exists. The most productive"industry" is electric power, which is produced in the country's numerous hydroelectric plants.

### Energy

Unlike its neighbors Kazakstan and Uzbekistan, Kyrgyzstan has no significant exploited reserves of oil or natural gas; in 1994 petroleum production was 88,000 tons, and natural gas production was 39 million cubic meters. Although substantial coal deposits are present, in the mid-1990s experts described Kyrgyzstan's coal industry as in a state of collapse. In the early 1990s, only four of the fourteen state-owned coal mines were considered economically viable, and little coal came from privately owned mines. Between 1991 and 1993, brown coal production decreased by 50 percent (to 959,000 tons), and black coal production decreased by 53 percent (to 712,000 tons). The domestic price of conventional fuels rose slightly above world levels after the much cheaper energy-sharing arrangements of the Soviet era ended. (In 1992 oil and gas import costs were 50 percent of the total state budget, compared with 10 percent in 1991.) In 1994 some 39 percent of Kyrgyzstan's total import expenditures went for the purchase of conventional fuels, contributing an estimated US$100 million to the country's trade imbalance (see Foreign Trade, this ch.). Energy consumption, meanwhile, has declined sharply since 1991, and experts do not expect it to return to its 1990 level.

Management of national energy and fuel policy is distributed among several ministries and other state agencies—an arrangement that has hindered efficient acquisition and distribution. Distribution of heat and electricity is the responsibility of the state-run Kyrgyzstan National Energy Holding Company, and natural gas purchases are managed by the Kyrgyzstan Natural Gas Administration (Kyrgyzgas). Oil, gas, and coal exploration is the responsibility of the State Geological Commission (Goskomgeologiya). Natural gas, provided by the Republic of Turkmenistan in the Soviet era, now comes mainly from neighboring Uzbekistan. Coal, used to heat households and to fuel some thermoelectric plants, is mainly received from Kazakstan in a barter arrangement for electrical power. Kazakstan's coal is preferred because the heaviest demand in Kyrgyzstan is concentrated in the north, and Kyrgyzstan's remaining coal mines are in the south, from which transportation is problematic.

For these reasons, existing thermoelectric stations have been deemphasized in the 1990s in favor of expanded hydroelectric production. Thus, in 1994 thermoelectric power production dropped by 46 percent while hydroelectric production rose by 30 percent. These statistics enabled the national energy sector to show a modest drop of 4 percent in total power generation in 1994, but district heating, which comes from coal- and gas-powered combined heat and power plants, suffered heavily from the transition. Meanwhile, government promotion of electricity brought an increase of 117 percent in household power use between 1991 and 1994, although overall household energy consumption declined by 36 percent during that period. Some aspects of the promotion plan have been criticized, including the large-scale promotion of electric heat in a country with poorly insulated houses.

Emphasis on electricity is backed by abundant water power, mainly from the country's location at the mountain headwaters of the Syrdariya, one of the two largest rivers in Central Asia. On the Naryn River, chief tributary of the Syrdariya, a series of hydroelectric stations has been built, the largest of which is the Kürp-Say Hydroelectric Plant, fed by the Toktogol Reservoir in central Kyrgyzstan. Other major hydroelectric plants are located at Atabashin, Alamedin, and Uchkorgon. Such stations have made possible the net export of electric power, worth an estimated US$100 million in 1994. That figure was only about

*Construction work at Tash-Kumyr hydroelectric station*
*Courtesy Hermine Dreyfuss*

half the value of Kyrgyzstan's 1990 export, however, because demand in neighboring republics dropped considerably in the early 1990s. The main customer is Kazakstan, with which power is exchanged through the Central Asian Integrated System.

Only about 10 percent of Kyrgyzstan's hydroelectric power potential and only about 3 percent of the potential of its smaller streams are currently being exploited; the Naryn River is estimated to afford an additional 2,200 megawatts of easily accessible rated capacity. Meanwhile, the Fergana Valley, the only working oil field in the country, has remaining reserves of 14 million tons of oil that require expensive recovery technolgy. No serious oil exploration has been done elsewhere, although the Chu and Ak-Say valleys are believed to be promising.

## Economic Reform

Since independence, Kyrgyzstan has undertaken significant structural reforms of its economy; in 1994 the International Monetary Fund (IMF—see Glossary) ranked Kyrgyzstan fourth among former Soviet republics (behind the three Baltic states) in the pace of economic reform, but positive results have not been forthcoming. As elsewhere in the former Soviet Union, one of the most significant reforms is privatization. The goal of privatization, a high priority in the early 1990s, has been to create new productive enterprises with efficient management systems while involving the population in the reform program at a fundamental level. The process began in December 1991 with the adoption of the Privatization and Denationalization Law and the creation of the State Property Fund as the agency to design and implement the program. In late 1992, a new parliamentary "Concept Note" reoriented the program toward rapid sale of small enterprises and ownership transition in larger enterprises by vouchers and other special payments. By the end of 1993, about 4,450 state enterprises, including 33 percent of total fixed enterprise assets, were fully or partially privatized. By mid-1994, nearly all services and 82 percent of assets in trade enterprises, 40 percent of assets in industry, and 68 percent of construction assets were in private hands.

However, the practical results of those statistics have not been nearly so positive. Most privatization (and almost all privatization in industry) was accomplished by creation of joint-stock companies, transferring enterprise shares to labor groups within them. Almost no public bidding for enterprise shares occurred, and the state maintained significant shares in enterprises after their conversion to joint-stock companies. Also, because the sale of shares was prohibited, shareholders wishing to leave the company had to return their holdings to the labor collective. The 1994 Law on Privatization remedied this situation by providing for competitive bidding for shares in small enterprises (with fewer than 100 employees) as well as long-term privatization of medium-sized (with 100 to 1,000 employees) and large enterprises by competitive cash bidding among individuals. The new law also provided for the auctioning of all enterprise shares remaining in state hands, over an undetermined period of time. In 1994 and early 1995, voucher privatization moved toward its goals quickly; by the end of 1994, an estimated 65 percent of industrial output came from non-state enterprises.

Privatization was not the final step in economic success, however. After that step, many firms needed drastic restructuring—most notably in management and technology—to function in a market environment. Because the commercial banking system had not been reformed substantially, enterprises found little financial or technical support for such upgrading (see Financial System, this ch.). On the other hand, enterprises (especially state enterprises) have not been discouraged from defaulting on loans because they often are closely associated with banks, whose pliable loan policy is backed by the National Bank of Kyrgyzstan. Plans called for establishment of an intermediary agency to distribute foreign and international funds to privatized enterprises until the banking system is able to take over lending activities. A stock exchange opened in Bishkek in May 1995 and was considered an important step in expediting this process.

In the early years of independence, a major cause of Kyrgyzstan's economic distress has been corruption and malfeasance. In a January 1993 speech, President Akayev reported that as much as 70 percent of the money that the country had invested in its economy had been diverted into private hands. Meanwhile, a poll of the country's few entrepreneurs found that 85 percent of them reported having to offer bribes to stay in business. The truth of Akayev's statement was difficult to verify, but reports in newspapers and elsewhere suggest that it could be correct. Official data indicated that since independence at least 100,000 tons of cast iron, steel, aluminum, and zinc had been sold abroad without legal permission, and that a credit for 1.7 billion rubles for the purchase of grain had vanished. Other anecdotal evidence of corruption, often connected with local centers of political power, was plentiful (see Structure of Government, this ch.).

## Financial System

In mid-1995, the banking system continued to be dominated by the central savings bank (the National Bank of Kyrgyzstan, created in 1991) and by the three major commercial banks that succeeded the sectoral banks of the Soviet era and remained under state control. Those banks—the Agricultural and Industrial Bank (Agroprombank), the Industrial and Construction Bank (Promstroybank), and the Commercial Bank of Kyrgyzstan—owned 85 percent of banking assets in 1994. New commercial banks, of which fifteen were established in 1993 and 1994, were owned by individuals or enterprises and had much less financial power than the state-owned banks. The new commercial banks have the right to buy and sell foreign currency and open deposit accounts. The National Bank is the official center of currency exchange, but in the mid-1990s it did not adhere to official exchange rates. In mid-1994, the government established the Bank for Reconstruction and Development, which uses state funds, foreign currency assets, and loans from abroad to aid small and medium-sized enterprises and to invest in targeted spheres of the economy, especially housing, construction, power generation, and agriculture.

The banking system has remained concentrated in the same areas as in the Soviet period. Although some diversification has occurred, loans tend to go to traditional clients. Because new commercial banks are small and initially were owned by state ministries and state-owned enterprises, competition has developed slowly. Through 1994 Soviet-style accounting and reporting systems remained in use, and banking services such as domestic and international payments have remained at the same noncompetitive level as they were prior to 1991. Capabilities vital to a market-type economy, such as credit risk assessment and project appraisal, are lacking. Post-Soviet regulations on capital funds, exposure limits, and lending practices have not been enforced. The technical infrastructure of the banks also requires substantial overhaul. In addition, the National Bank has been plagued by scandal; the first director, an Akayev protégé, was linked to several illegal financial operations in 1993 and 1994.

The limitations of the banking system have made it unable to efficiently mobilize and allocate financial resources into the national economy. This failure has hindered privatization and other types of economic reform that require substantial amounts of risk capital upon which borrowers can rely. Especially critical are the bad loans held by the three state-owned banks (influenced by government interference in loan decisions, together with poor financial discipline on the part of major enterprises) and eroded capital base. In 1995 the National Bank's outstanding loans to agricultural and industrial enterprises totaled 1 billion som each.

### Prices, Monetary Policy, and Debt

Kyrgyzstan paid dearly for its designated role as an exporter of raw materials when the Soviet Union unraveled and retail prices began to be freed: the prices paid for raw materials rose much more slowly than did prices of finished goods. Thus, in 1992, for example, the cost of what Kyrgyzstan imported rose by fifty to 100 times, while the amounts received for exports rose by fifteen to twenty times. This explains in part why the GNP for 1992 was valued at 250 billion rubles (for value of the ruble—see Glossary), while the cost of Kyrgyzstan's imports was put at 400 billion rubles. In 1992 Russia began discounting the paper value of the Kyrgyzstan ruble, effectively devaluing the goods that Kyrgyzstan was supplying. Moscow then required that the country assume the imposed "difference" as a loan, which had the effect of increasing Kyrgyzstan's debt burden.

To escape the disparities inherent in dependence on the ruble, in May 1993 Kyrgyzstan was the first former Soviet republic to leave the ruble zone (see Glossary) and introduce its own currency, the som. This new policy earned Kyrgyzstan the hostility of neighboring Kazakstan and Uzbekistan, which had declared loyalty to the ruble and feared an avalanche of devalued Kyrgyzstani rubles entering their countries. The som, which is fully convertible to foreign currency and has a floating exchange rate, has been underwritten largely by the IMF, which has provided a large measure of stability. After introduction at a rate of two som to the United States dollar, the som traded at eleven to the dollar at the end of 1995. According to President Akayev, about half the som in circulation are backed by gold or by international loans. Although the som has received strong international backing, experts questioned the likelihood that such support would continue once other new national currencies emerged in former Soviet republics, eliminating the som's status as a unique experiment. Such doubt grew clear as Kyrgyzstan's first international loans came due in 1995, with scheduled payments of approximately US$58 million that year, rising to nearly US$100 million the next year. The republic's collapsed economy made it possible that Kyrgyzstan would become a permanent international client state.

Especially in the first year of independence, hyperinflation seriously eroded buying power (see table 10, Appendix). At the end of 1992, wholesale prices were more than eighteen times higher than in 1991. Retail prices rose 40 percent in December 1992 alone, explaining in part why retail sales declined by 64 percent from 1991, the greatest decline in all of Central Asia. Between 1990 and 1992, meat consumption dropped 20 percent, milk product consumption by 30 percent, and fats consumption by 40 percent. Beginning in 1993, however, international support for the som and for Kyrgyzstan's economy in general has kept inflation much lower than it is elsewhere in the CIS. From a high of about 1,400 percent annually in 1992 and 1993 (caused mainly by large increases in fuel costs), inflation dropped to about 180 percent for 1994 (mainly because of tighter credit and the government's reduced expenditures); the government's inflation target for

1995, set in cooperation with the IMF, was 55 percent, with monthly declines throughout the year. Prices rose by 16 percent in the first quarter of 1995, slightly above target, but budgetary expenditures for the first half of the year were far above the IMF target of 5 percent of GDP.

In the spring of 1995, average monthly pay in Kyrgyzstan was 508 som, compared with a government-estimated minimum family budget of 487 som. Earning statistics are not considered totally reliable, however. In 1995 food required an average of 61 percent of the family budget. To eliminate price distortions inherited from price support policies of the Soviet regime, the Akayev government decontrolled most prices in 1992, which had the immediate result of fueling inflation and reducing individual purchasing power. The economic decline of 1993 caused reintroduction of price controls, notably on agricultural products, and ceilings of 10 to 25 percent were placed on price increases for a wide range of retail commodities. The state Anti-Monopoly and Pricing Committee restricted pricing decisions in most of Kyrgyzstan's large enterprises. Although such institutional mechanisms did not work consistently, they encouraged development of unofficial economic arrangements and barter arrangements, which further undermined the national economy. In 1994 the government again reversed its policy, ending obligatory sale and price controls on agricultural goods that had depressed the agricultural market. The reform would nominally free farmers to negotiate commodity prices with government agencies and other buyers. However, because the government remained the only large-scale purchaser of many products, liberalizing the procurement process was not expected to have immediate effects.

### Foreign Investment

Domestic economic investment declined precipitously in the early 1990s, with government investment falling 55 percent in 1994 alone. In the first quarter of 1995, total public and private investment was reported to be 391 million som, of which about 75 percent went to the Kumtor joint-venture gold field. To stimulate foreign investment, the Kyrgyz government has adopted a series of measures to improve the republic's deteriorating economic environment. In the late 1980s, the republic already had begun creating a legal infrastructure to support private investment. The Basic Foreign Investment Law, adopted in June 1991, has been amended several times since that time. In general, this law allows foreign investors full use of their profits, including unlimited export of profits in the form of foreign currency or merchandise.

Foreign firms also enjoy considerable tax advantages, which extend to Kyrgyzstani partners in joint ventures. Investors are granted relief from import duties on materials needed to establish a business, and they continue receiving tax relief for up to five years, depending on their type of business. After that time, several other types of tax relief are available, including various forms of reinvestment in Kyrgyzstan's economy.

As of April 1995, some 328 joint ventures were registered, but only 128 were actually in operation, the vast majority in trade. Only thirty-eight joint ventures were active in manufacturing or mining. At that time, sixty-eight foreign firms (outside the CIS) were registered, the majority of which were Chinese, Afghan, and Turkish. Some fifty-two Russian and thirty-six United States firms were present in some capacity. Kyrgyzstan was among the first of the former Soviet republics to create free economic zones, on the Chinese model, where taxes would be abated and duties waived. The government initially created two such zones, in Naryn and Osh, with another under consideration in Bishkek. The zones became the object of heated debate, however, and by 1995 only the Naryn zone had taken form as planned. The only large-scale foreign investment has been in the gold industry, where the Cameco and the United States Morrison-Knudson Corporation are participating in joint ventures.

## Foreign Trade

Kyrgyzstan's principal exports include wool, hides, and cotton (which combined to provide nearly 80 percent of total exports in 1994), together with electric power, electronic products, ferrous and nonferrous metals, food products, and shoes. Besides fuels, the largest volume of imports is in construction materials, ferrous metals, pharmaceuticals, chemicals, and machinery. The largest CIS trading partners are Russia, Kazakstan, and Uzbekistan, and the largest non-CIS partner is China (see table 15, Appendix). The predominance of barter agreements makes quantification of the latter relationship approximate, however. Of the estimated US$44 million of trade with China in 1994, less than one-quarter was in cash. During the late 1980s and early 1990s, Kyrgyzstan's economy was highly dependent on external trade. Total exports and imports in

1991 amounted to nearly 80 percent of the country's GDP, but by 1993 that total had shrunk to 52.5 percent. External trade, which in the early 1990s was conducted principally with the other republics of the former Soviet Union, resulted in a large trade deficit, mainly because of the need to obtain petroleum products and natural gas at the much higher prices of post-Soviet markets. During the first years of independence, the deficit from interrepublic and hard-currency (see Glossary) trade was about 20 percent of GDP.

In 1994 Kyrgyzstan substantially liberalized state regulation of trade. All export and import license requirements, the issuance of which was the center of recurring corruption rumors in the early 1990s, were eliminated excepting some hazardous materials. Export taxes, which had been levied mainly in retaliation for Russian export taxes, were reduced or eliminated, and plans called for their complete elimination by the end of 1995. Import duties on goods from non-CIS countries were fixed at 5 to 15 percent; there are no duties on goods from within the CIS.

The Ministry for Industry, Trade, and Material Resources is the chief agency for obtaining goods for export and distributing imports. Until the liberalization of 1994, a number of government-signed clearing agreements with former Soviet republics set terms for barter agreements that often avoided the problems caused by late payments. In 1993 such an agreement with Russia exchanged raw cotton, wool, and tobacco and scrap metal for petroleum products, wood, and metal products. Another agreement with Uzbekistan brought natural gas and fertilizers in exchange for nonferrous metals, electrical products, and butter. A third example is the coal-for-electricity arrangement with Kazakstan (see Energy, this ch.). Commodity values for such agreements usually were close to world levels, but the rigid procurement methods required for such bilateral trades have distorted the rest of the national economy.

In 1994 Kyrgyzstan's foreign trade decreased by 16.6 percent (to US$93.4 million, after a drop of 65 percent in the 1992–93 period) for exports and by more than 50 percent (to US$52.6 million) for imports. Trade with non-CIS partners showed a surplus, but more than 85 percent of trade still was transacted with CIS nations. Although the condition of the domestic economy did not seem to favor an upturn in foreign trade for 1995, Kyrgyz policy makers expected that increased foreign assistance would improve the trade situation somewhat.

In February 1994, Kyrgyzstan joined with Kazakstan and Uzbekistan in creating the Central Asian Free Trade Zone in reaction to the collapse of the new ruble zone proposed by Russia in late 1993. Although not the full organization of Central Asian nations that had been envisioned by intellectuals since before independence, this exclusively economic agreement was able to abolish trade barriers among the partners immediately, and trade between Kyrgyzstan and Kazakstan increased in 1994. But further conditions on credit, prices, taxes, customs, currency convertibility, and creation of a common economic zone in the Fergana Valley, the vital economic region shared by the three partners and Tajikistan, were delayed throughout 1994 and the first half of 1995. Kyrgyzstan has announced its intention to join the World Trade Organization (WTO—see Glossary), successor to the General Agreement on Tariffs and Trade (GATT).

## Transportation and Telecommunications

For reasons of commerce and national unity, Kyrgyzstan urgently needs improved systems of transportation and telecommunications, neither of which has received adequate attention since the 1980s. Some projects did, however, benefit from substantial foreign investment in the early and mid-1990s.

### Transportation

The failure to develop Kyrgyzstan's internal communications has exacerbated the republic's tendencies toward regional division between the north (dominated by the population center of Bishkek) and the south (dominated by the population center of Osh). The two regions are separated by sparsely populated, mountainous terrain (see fig. 2; Topography and Drainage, this ch.). Transportation problems have been exacerbated by the country's energy dependence, which includes the import of 100 percent of its gasoline supply. The republic's road and railroad systems are divided into two parts. The northern part is integrated with the transportation networks of Kazakstan, and the southern part is integrated with the networks of Uzbekistan. Three government agencies are responsible for transportation: the Ministry of Transportation, the State Civil Aviation Agency, and the Bishkek Railway Department. Kyrgyzstan is part of a large-scale project to coordinate development of the transportation infrastructure in the heartland of

Asia, sponsored by the UN Economic and Social Commission for Asia and the Pacific. The agency plans to spend as much as US$1.5 trillion between 1993 and 2000 to facilitate trans-Asian railroad and highway connections.

In 1990 Kyrgyzstan had 28,400 kilometers of roads, of which 22,400 were hard-surfaced. Some 371 million passengers and 43.9 million tons of freight traveled by road in 1992, accounting for 95 percent and 72 percent of total passengers and freight, respectively. The Karakorum Highway, a Chinese-built road from Ürümqi, at the eastern end of the Tian Shan in China's Xinjiang Uygur Autonomous Region, to Islamabad in northern Pakistan, has a connector to Bishkek, which is 1,900 kilometers from Islamabad (and 3,500 kilometers from Karachi on the Arabian Sea) by that route. A planned connector from Osh via Sary-Tash would cut 200 kilometers from those distances. In 1994 the condition of the country's roads was made a state secret.

Although Kyrgyzstan imports 100 percent of the gasoline it uses, government subsidies have kept gasoline prices relatively low because of the economic role of the nation's roads; in early 1995, tariff increases pushed the average price to roughly US$.30 per liter. The subsidy system has meant that supply is quite erratic and unpredictable; an acute shortage occurred in April 1995, raising the black-market gasoline price above US$.50 per liter.

In a country where 95 percent of freight moves by truck, the gasoline shortage has largely isolated the more remote provinces, and it has made ambulance, fire, and police services difficult to maintain. In at least one town in Osh Province, officials responded to the fuel shortage simply by shutting off all services, leaving the people without light, heat, or power. Public transportation has been doubly burdened because the gasoline shortage has restricted use of private cars and crowded an increased number of riders onto a reduced number of buses. In some cities, such as Kant and Naryn, the city bus services simply stopped running, making it almost impossible for people to get to work. Naryn's solution was to replace the municipal buses with horse-drawn omnibuses.

Rail transport plays a minor role, with a total of 370 kilometers of track, mostly in the north, providing links to Russia via Kazakstan. In the Soviet system, all rail freight moved along this corridor. Short lines in the south connect towns with the Ursatevskaya-Andijon Line in Uzbekistan. In 1992 some 1.7 million passengers and 5.5 million tons of freight were transported by rail. A rail link from Ürümqi to Ashgabat, Turkmenistan, was opened in 1994, widening Kyrgyzstan's export possibilities. In 1995 a spur of that line opened from Ashgabat to Bandar-Abbas on the Strait of Hormuz in southern Iran. Although a proposal has been made to build a north-south rail link connecting Balychki with Kara-Keche, the money for such a project is not expected to be available in the foreseeable future.

In the early 1990s, available air transport facilities were inadequate. The national airline was formed from a share of the aircraft and personnel allocated from the Soviet airline Aeroflot. Manas, the international airport at Bishkek (named after the mythical national hero), was modernized in 1988 to make it the most modern commercial airport in Central Asia. A second international facility is located at Osh, and about twenty-five usable local fields supplement air service. Manas Airport originally offered flights to fifty cities in the CIS, including regular service to Moscow and Tashkent, and charter flights to China, Turkey, and Saudi Arabia. However, that facility has been almost unused since 1991. The shortage of jet fuel has forced Kyrgyzstan to rely almost completely on the Almaty international airport, four hours by road from Bishkek, for international connections, and the availability of air transport greatly decreased in the early 1990s. The loss of air services has exacerbated the country's tendency toward a north-south split.

## Telecommunications

Telecommunications in Kyrgyzstan, generally inadequate, suffer from the historically low priority accorded by Soviet authorities to development of that type of infrastructure. In 1994 only 364,000 main telephone lines, or one per twelve Kyrgyzstanis, were in service. Since independence a thriving black market has developed in cable stolen from existing telephone installations, removing many portions of the telephone system from operation. The average age of system components is about fifteen years. Because much existing equipment is operating at capacity, heavier service loads (which experts judge an absolutely necessary element of economic expansion) require large-scale equipment replacement. In 1991 about 600 lines connected Kyrgyzstan to the rest of the Soviet Union; sixty channels connected the republic to international lines via Moscow. In 1995 international calls still were connected through Moscow, allowing Kyrgyzstan to benefit indirectly from the general upgrading of services that has occurred in Russia in the early 1990s. In 1994 Kyrgyzstan received a loan of US$8 million and US$1.5 million in technical assistance from the European Bank for Recovery and Development (EBRD) to upgrade its telecommunications services, especially in the mountainous regions. The Ministry of Communications is responsible for local, national, and international telephone, telex, telegraph, and data communications. The ministry also is charged with postal services, radio and television broadcasting, and manage ment of subscriptions and deliveries of news publications. Tele- communications, despite low tariffs, have been profitable enough to operate independently of the state budget since 1986. But without a revision of the tariff structure and institu- tional and regulatory restructuring, the state of telecommuni- cations places a major constraint on the development of a market-oriented economy.

Kyrgyzstan Radio and Kyrgyzstan Television are state broad- casting companies. The two state-run national radio stations broadcast some English and German programming. One com- mercial radio station is in operation. In 1993 three hours of television programming were available per day; Kyrgyzstan Television receives its color broadcasts from the Secam net- work.

## Government and Politics

As independence has progressed, politics have grown increasingly tangled in Kyrgyzstan. President Akayev, who took office amid a chain of events that lent credence to an idealistic promise of democratic reform and stability, has proven more able to formulate goals than to carry them out. Although a constitution was ratified in 1993, many terms of that document have not yet gone into force.

### Background

In March 1990, while still part of the Soviet Union, the republic elected a 350-member Jogorku Kenesh (parliament), which remained in power until it dissolved itself in September 1994. This body was elected under the rules prescribed by the *perestroika* (see Glossary) policy of Soviet President Mikhail S. Gorbachev, which mandated that at least 80 percent of legisla- tive seats be contested even though communists likely would win most seats. In the case of Kyrgyzstan, five seats went to the initial opposition movement, the Democratic Movement of Kyrgyzstan (DDK).

Over time it has become apparent that President Akayev prefers dealing with administrators subordinate to him rather than with legislators. The initial harmony between Akayev and the parliament began to sour in 1993. A number of specific points of contention arose, most of them related to growing legislative resistance to what was widely viewed to be government corruption and mismanagement. Throughout 1993 the parliament sought aggressively to extend control over the executive branch. The allotment of development concessions for two of the republic's largest gold deposits was a particular rallying point (see Natural Resources, this ch.). The chief representative of Cameco, Boris Birshtein, was a Swiss citizen who had been named in a number of financial scandals in Russia and elsewhere in the CIS. When it was discovered that the Kyrgyzstani negotiating team that had sealed the Cameco transaction had financial interests in the deal, the agreement nearly was cancelled entirely. In December 1993, public protest about this gold concession brought down the government of Prime Minister Tursunbek Chyngyshev and badly damaged Akayev's popularity and credibility.

Chyngyshev was replaced by Apas Jumagulov, who had been prime minister during the late Soviet period. Jumagulov was reappointed in March 1995 and again in March 1996. Akayev was not publicly accused of being involved in the gold scandals, but numerous rumors have mentioned corruption and influence-peddling in the Akayev family, especially in the entourage of his wife. As these rumors circulated more widely, President Akayev held a public referendum of approval for his presidency in January 1994. Most impartial observers regarded the 96 percent approval that Akayev claimed after the referendum as a political fiction.

## Constitution

Besides electing Akayev, the 1990 parliament fashioned the legislative foundation for the political transformation of the republic, in concert with the president. Perhaps the biggest accomplishment in this phase was the drafting and passage, in May 1993, of the country's constitution. The constitution mandates three branches of government: a unicameral parliament; an executive branch, consisting of government and local officials appointed by the president; and a judiciary, with a presidentially appointed Supreme Court and lower courts.

In many ways, however, the constitution has not been put into force. Akayev is still president under a popular mandate gained in an uncontested election in 1991, and most of the judicial system has not been appointed. The existing bicameral parliament, which was elected early in 1995, does not match the unicameral body prescribed by the constitution. This structural change was attained through popular referendum, for which the constitution does not provide, although the same referendum simultaneously gave popular (and retroactive) permission for this abrogation of the constitution. In February 1996, Akayev's proposed constitutional amendments strengthening the office of president were approved by 94 percent of voters in a national referendum.

## Structure of Government

Although the constitution calls for a government of three branches, in practice the presidency has been the strongest government office. As economic and social conditions deteriorated in the early 1990s, President Akayev sought extraconstitutional authority in dealing with a series of crises. Under these conditions, Akayev faced occasional opposition from parliament, and pockets of local resistance grew stronger in the southern provinces.

### *President and Council of Ministers*

Akayev is able to act as he does because under the constitution the president stands outside the three-branch system in the capacity of guarantor of the constitutional functioning of all three branches. The president names the prime minister and the Council of Ministers, subject to legislative confirmation.

According to the constitution, the president is to be elected once every five years, for no more than two terms, from among citizens who are between thirty-five and sixty-five years of age, who have lived at least fifteen years in the republic, and who are fluent in the state language, which is Kyrgyz. There is no vice president. Akayev defied predictions that he would seek referendum approval of an extension of his term rather than stand for reelection in 1996 as mandated in the constitution. (The presidents of Kazakstan, Turkmenistan, and Uzbekistan had followed the former course in 1994 and 1995.) In the presidential election of December 1995, Akayev gained 71.6 percent of the vote against two communist challengers. Several other political figures protested that they had been prevented illegally from participating. International observers found the election free and fair. Earlier, newly elected deputies of the 1995 parliament had proposed that presidential elections be postponed until at least the year 2000, with Akayev to remain president in the interim. According to rumors, Akayev favored using a referendum to extend his own term of office, but he found acceptance of parliament's proposal unwise. Kyrgyzstan depends heavily on the loans of Western banks and governments, who objected strenuously to the cancellation of elections as a "step back from democracy."

The Council of Ministers nominally is entrusted with day-to-day administration of the government. In general, however, the office of the presidency has dominated policy making; in most cases, Akayev's prerogative of appointing the prime minister and all cabinet positions has not been effectively balanced by the nominal veto power of parliament over such appointments. The new parliament of 1995 showed considerably more independence by vetoing several key Akayev administrative appointments. In February 1996, the government resigned following the approval of Akayev's constitutional amendments. The new government that Akayev appointed in March 1996 included fifteen ministries: agriculture, communications, culture, defense, economy, education and science, finance, foreign affairs, health, industry and trade, internal affairs, justice, labor and social welfare, transportation, and water resources, plus deputy prime ministers for agrarian policy, sociocultural policy, and industrial policy and the chairmen of nine committees and agencies. Many individuals retained their positions from the preceding government; changes occurred mainly in agencies dealing with social affairs and the economy.

### Legislature

In October 1994, Akayev took the legally questionable step of holding a referendum to ask public approval for bypassing legal requirements to amend the constitution. The referendum asked permission to amend the constitution to establish a bicameral legislature that would include an upper chamber, called the Legislative House, which would have only thirty-five members. Those deputies would receive government salaries and would sit in permanent session. A lower chamber, the

171

House of National Representatives, would have seventy members and would convene more irregularly. Akayev's plan also provided that deputies in this new parliament would not be able to hold other government positions, a clause that caused most of the republic's prominent politicians to drop out of consideration for election to parliament.

In the elections to the new parliament that began in February 1995, only sixteen deputies managed to get clear mandates on the first round of balloting. Second-round voting also proved indecisive. When the parliament was convened for the first time, in March 1995, fifteen seats remained unfilled; two important provinces (Naryn and Talas) had no deputies in the upper house at all, prompting angry cries that regional interests were not being properly represented when the two houses elected their respective speakers. A later round of elections, which extended into May, was marked by widespread accusations of fraud, ballot-stuffing, and government manipulation.

Such circumstances aroused strong doubts about the legislative competency of the parliament. Only six of the deputies have previous parliamentary experience, and a number of prominent political figures, including Medetkan Sherymkulov, speaker of the 1990–94 parliament, failed to win what had been assumed were "safe" seats. Even more serious were concerns about the incomplete mandate of the new legislative system. The constitutional modifications voted on by referendum did not specify what the duties and limitations of the two houses would be. Thus, the early sessions of 1995 were preoccupied by procedural wranglings over the respective rights and responsibilities of the legislative, executive, and judicial branches. Because little business of substance was conducted in that session, several deputies threatened that this parliament, like the previous one, might "self-dissolve." However, the body remained intact as of mid-1996.

### Judiciary

According to the constitution, judges are to be chosen by the president, subject to parliamentary confirmation. Potential judges must be Kyrgyzstani citizens between thirty-five and sixty-five years of age who have legal training and at least ten years of legal experience. The length of judges' tenure is unlimited, but judges are subject to dismissal for cause by parliament. In the mid-1990s, the judicial system remained incomplete both in the filling of prescribed positions and in the establishment of judicial procedures and precedents. A Supreme Court was appointed, but its functioning was delayed in 1995 by parliament's refusal to approve Akayev's nominee as chief justice. Although the parliament of 1991–94 also mandated a national constitutional court (over the objections of Akayev), that body never has been established.

In general, the rule of law is not well established in the republic. The one area of the law that has flourished in Kyrgyzstan is libel law, which public figures have used widely to control the republic's press. By contrast, the observance of laws designed for the regulation of the economy is not uniform or consistent, even by government officials. The functioning of the State Arbitration Court, which has responsibility for financial and jurisdictional disputes within government agencies and between government agencies and private enterprises, has been extremely irregular and lacking in oversight by any other government institution.

### Local Government

The republic is divided into seven administrative regions: six provinces and the capital city of Bishkek. The so-called northern provinces are Naryn, Ysyk-Köl, Chu, and Talas, and the southern provinces are Osh and Jalal-Abad. Jalal-Abad was formed out of Osh Province in 1991, largely to disperse the political strength of the south that had become centered in Osh. Each province has a local legislature, but real power is wielded by the province governor (until 1996 called the *akim*), who is a presidential appointee. In some cases, the *akim* became a powerful spokesman for regional interests, running the district with considerable autonomy. Particularly notable in this regard was Jumagul Saadanbekov, the *akim* of Ysyk-Köl Province. The government reorganization of early 1996 widened the governors' responsibilities for tax collection, pensions, and a variety of other economic and social functions.

Akayev has had difficulty establishing control over the two southern provinces. Several southern politicians (the most important of whom was Sheraly Sydykov, scion of an old Osh family that enjoyed great prominence in the Soviet era) have taken the lead in national opposition against Akayev. Sydykov headed the parliamentary corruption commission in 1994, and he headed the influential banking and ethics committees of the parliament elected in 1995.

When the *akim* of Osh resigned to run for the new parliament, Akayev appointed as his replacement Janysh Rustambekov, an Akayev protégé who had been state secretary. Rustambekov, the first northerner to head this southern province and a highly controversial appointment, was considered to be a direct surrogate of Akayev in improving control over the south. Rustambekov, who has fired large numbers of local administrators, is opposed chiefly by Osh Province Council head Bekamat Osmonov, who is one of the most skilled and influential politicians in the south. Osmonov, who also was a deputy in the lower house of the new legislature, emerged as a powerful critic of Akayev and a possible presidential rival if Akayev could not prevent the next election.

## Political Parties

The period immediately preceding and following independence saw a proliferation of political groups of various sizes and platforms. Although President Akayev emerged from the strongest of those groups, in the early 1990s no organized party system developed either around Akayev or in opposition to him.

### *Communist Parties*

The Communist Party of Kyrgyzstan (CPK), which was the only legal political party during the Soviet years, was abolished in 1991 in the aftermath of the failed coup against the Gorbachev government of the Soviet Union. A successor, the Kyrgyzstan Communist Party, was allowed to register in September 1992. It elected two deputies to the lower house of parliament in 1995. In that party, significant oppositionists include past republic leader Absamat Masaliyev, a former first secretary of the CPK. The 1995 election also gave a deputy's mandate to T. Usubaliyev, who had been head of the CPK and leader of the republic between 1964 and 1982. Another party with many former communist officials is the Republican People's Party. Two other, smaller neocommunist parties are the Social Democrats of Kyrgyzstan, which gained three seats in the upper house and eight seats in the lower house of the 1995 parliament, and the People's Party of Kyrgyzstan, which holds three seats in the lower house.

### *Other Parties*

All of the other parties in existence in 1995 began as unsanctioned civic movements. The first is Ashar (Help), which was founded in 1989 as a movement to take over unused land for housing; Ashar took one seat in the upper house in the 1995 elections. A fluctuating number of parties and groups are joined under the umbrella of the Democratic Movement of Kyrgyzstan (DDK); the most influential is Erkin Kyrgyzstan (Freedom for Kyrgyzstan), which in late 1992 split into two parties, one retaining the name Erkin Kyrgyzstan, and the other called Ata-meken (Fatherland). In the 1995 elections, Erkin Kyrgyzstan took one seat and Ata-meken two seats in the upper house. In the spring of 1995, the head of Erkin Kyrgyzstan was indicted for embezzling funds from the university of which he is a rector; it is unclear whether or not this accusation was politically motivated.

Another democratically inclined party, Asaba (Banner) also took one seat in the upper house. Registration was denied to another group, the Freedom Party, because its platform includes the creation of an Uygur autonomous district extending into the Chinese Xinjiang Uygur Autonomous Region, which the Chinese government opposes. The Union of Germans took one seat in the lower house, and a Russian nationalist group, Concord, also took one seat.

For all their proliferation, parties have not yet played a large part in independent Kyrgyzstan. In the mid-1990s, early enthusiasm for the democratic parties faded as the republic's economy grew worse and party officials were implicated in the republic's proliferating political corruption. The communist successor parties, on the other hand, appeared to gain influence in this period. In the absence of elections, and with President Akayev belonging to no party, it is difficult to predict the future significance of any of these parties.

## The Media

For the first two years of independence, Kyrgyzstan's newspapers were a remarkable phenomenon, with real political significance and power. Save that Kyrgyzstan's newspapers had not yet developed a Western-style code of journalistic scrupulousness and restraint, it would have been possible to say that the press was beginning to become the fourth estate that the media represent in developed democracies. Through late 1993, Kyrgyzstan's newspapers enjoyed the greatest freedom of publication in any of the Central Asian nations, rivaling the freedom of the post-1991 Moscow press. Although a state secrecy committee had the power to require submission of materials in advance of publication, in fact the newspapers were able to discuss issues of public interest closely and dispassionately. During the gold scandals, for example, the newspapers played a crucial role in airing both opposition attacks on Akayev and his government, and the government's defense against those attacks.

Since 1993, however, the government has moved increasingly to impose control. In August 1993, formal censorship was briefly reimposed, but then a spirited outcry from the press brought a reversal of that move. More subtle methods of censorship were applied in January 1994, during the run-up to the public referendum on Akayev's performance. Although there are several independent or quasi-independent newspapers in the republic, all printing presses remain in government hands, which gives the state the option of simply refusing to print opposition newspapers.

In 1994 the Akayev government stepped up pressure on the local press, closing three newspapers entirely, including the popular Russian-language *Svobodnye gory*, the official organ of the parliament. Government officials also began to bring suits against newspapers as private individuals, claiming defamation and slander. One such case resulted in a costly judgement against the editor of *Delo No*, a tabloid-style scandal sheet that is perhaps the most widely read newspaper in the country. In the spring of 1995, Akayev used the same tactic against the editor of *Respublika*, long one of the most persistent and successful critics of the regime; the president succeeded in getting a judgement that forbids the editor from working for eighteen months.

Beginning in 1994, the Kyrgyz populace began to feel threatened by the government and other forces in the republic. The atmosphere has not been helped by a series of unexplained attacks on journalists, including one popular commentator, a persistent investigator of the gold scandals, who died after being struck on the head. Although the newsman's grave also was desecrated shortly after his burial, no government investigation was conducted. The government has shown reluctance to impose direct Soviet-style censorship, but Akayev warned in January 1995 that the press would be wise to begin practicing self-censorship and to print more positive news.

The economic conditions of journalism prevent any Kyrgyzstani newspaper from being totally free. None of the republic's papers has yet developed a sustaining readership, and because the economy is insufficiently developed to provide advertising revenue, all newspapers must depend on sponsors. For many papers, including *Slovo Kyrgyzstana*, which has the largest circulation, the sponsor is the government. Others such as *Asaba* have political sponsors, and at least one is sponsored by Turkish investors. Even the most independent of the papers, *Respublika*, has been forced to turn to commercial sponsors, which, according to rumor, include Seabeco-Kyrgyzstan, the scandal-tainted intermediary in the Kumtor gold deal.

The most important Russian-language newspapers are *Slovo Kyrgyzstana*, the official government paper (circulation about 15,000 in 1994); *Vechernii Bishkek*, a more domestic city paper (reaching 75,000 readers on Fridays); the tabloid scandal sheet *Delo No* (30,000 copies); *Asaba*, the organ of the party of the same name (20,000 copies); and *Respublika*, the most prominent surviving opposition paper (7,000 copies). The major Kyrgyz language newspapers are *Kyrgyz guusu* and *Kut Bilim*. A bilingual newspaper, *Erkin Too/Svobodnye gory*, has appeared, but, unlike its earlier namesake, it is not an opposition paper. One English-language paper, *Kyrgyzstan Chronicle*, mostly reproduces articles from foreign English-language sources.

The electronic media are unevenly developed in the republic, both because of the physical constraints imposed by the country's mountainous terrain and because of financial difficulties. Resources are concentrated in Bishkek, which is well supplied with television and with radio. Penetration of more remote areas, however, is incomplete.

The government retains ownership of all but one broadcast facility, giving it a strong voice in the development of independent programming. There is at least one independent radio company, called Piramida, and several independent television production companies. In June 1995, the government proposed reinstitution of formal state control over all broadcasting in the republic.

Financial problems have caused Kyrgyzstan to cut back on the number of hours of Russian television that it relays from Moscow, although the Russian government has shown an inclination to work with Kyrgyzstan to keep Russian-language programming on the air in the republic. In the south, most programming originates in Uzbekistan, a situation that tends to exacerbate the north-south split within Kyrgyzstan.

## Human Rights

In its early days, Kyrgyzstan demonstrated a strong commitment to observation of human rights, from which it has subsequently stepped back. Nevertheless, the republic remains generally more sensitive to human rights than are the states in its immediate environment.

The republic's constitution provides very strong guarantees of personal liberty, protection of privacy, freedom of assembly and expression, and other hallmarks of democratic societies. On several occasions, the government has violated or abrogated the constitution, raising the possibility of abuse of human rights.

In practice, however, the Akayev government has proven itself generally responsive on issues of human rights, at least in part because of the republic's dependence upon the approval of Western financial supporters. The present legal system, which remains based almost entirely upon Soviet-era practices, does permit pre-trial detention of up to one year (there is no bail), which in one or two celebrated cases has appeared abusive. However, international monitoring organizations have found no evidence of political arrests, detentions, disappearances, or extrajudicial punishments. There have been some unsubstantiated complaints by political activists of wiretapping and other illegal surveillance.

In a celebrated case in 1992, Uzbekistani security forces arrested two Uzbek delegates to a human rights conference held in Bishkek. Although this arrest was subsequently found to be in technical agreement with Kyrgyzstani law, the public manner in which the arrest was conducted demonstrated Kyrgyzstan's lack of resources to defend human rights activists.

## Foreign Relations

Kyrgyzstan's foreign policy has been controlled by two considerations—first, that the country is too small and too poor to be economically viable without considerable outside assistance, and second, that it lies in a volatile corner of the globe, vulnerable to a number of unpleasant possibilities. These two considerations have influenced substantially the international position taken by Kyrgyzstan, especially toward the developed nations and its immediate neighbors.

Akayev and his ministers have traveled the globe tirelessly since independence, seeking relations and partners. In the first four years of independence, Akayev visited the United States, Turkey, Switzerland, Japan, Singapore, and Israel. His emissaries have also been to Iran, Lebanon, and South Africa, and his prime minister made a trip through most of Europe. One consequence of these travels is that Kyrgyzstan is recognized by 120 nations and has diplomatic relations with sixty-one of them. The United States embassy opened in Bishkek in February 1992, and a Kyrgyzstani embassy was established in Washington later that year. Kyrgyzstan is a member of most major international bodies, including the UN, the Organization for Security and Cooperation in Europe (OSCE—see Glossary), the World Bank, the IMF, and the EBRD. It has also joined the Asian Development Bank, the Economic Cooperation Organization (ECO—see Glossary), and the Islamic Bank.

Akayev has stressed repeatedly that the principle behind his search for contacts is strict neutrality; Kyrgyzstan is a small, relatively resource-poor, remote nation more likely to seek help from the world community than to contribute to it. Especially in the first months of independence, Akayev stressed Kyrgyzstan's intellectual and political potential, hoping to attract the world community to take risks in an isolated experiment in democracy. Akayev referred to making his nation an Asian Switzerland, transformed by a combination of international finance and the light, clean industry, mostly electronic, that he expected to spring up from conversion of the Soviet-era defense industries. Largely because of Akayev's reputation and personality, Kyrgyzstan has become the largest per capita recipient of foreign aid in the CIS (see Foreign Investment, this ch.).

However, the decay of the domestic economy and increasing dissatisfaction among constituents have made the Akayev government distinctly less optimistic about the degree to which it can rely upon the distant world community. At the same time, political and social developments in the republic's immediate area have directed the republic's attention increasingly to foreign policy concerns much closer to home.

## Central Asian Neighbors

Kyrgyzstan is bordered by four nations, three of which—Kazakstan, Uzbekistan, and Tajikistan—are former Soviet republics. China's Xinjiang Uygur Autonomous Region, where a substantial separatist movement has been active, also adjoins the republic. Although Kazakstan and Uzbekistan have recognized their existing borders with Kyrgyzstan, as of 1996 Tajikistan had not done so. China recognizes the old Soviet Union border but is said to have objections to twelve specific points of its common border with Kyrgyzstan. The objections have been referred to a Chinese-CIS border committee for resolution.

Undoubtedly the most immediate concern is neighboring Uzbekistan, which, under the leadership of President Islam Karimov, is emerging as the strongest state in post-Soviet Central Asia. Although Uzbekistan faces serious economic problems of its own, it has a homogeneous and well-educated population of more than 20 million, a diversified and developed economy, and sufficient natural resources to allow the country to become self-sufficient in energy and a major exporter of gold, cotton, and natural gas (see The Economy, ch. 5).

Uzbekistan has the best organized and best disciplined security forces in all of Central Asia, as well as a relatively large and experienced army and air force. Uzbekistan dominates southern Kyrgyzstan both economically and politically, based on the large Uzbek population in that region of Kyrgyzstan and on economic and geographic conditions (see Ethnic Groups, this ch.). Much of Kyrgyzstan depends entirely on Uzbekistan for natural gas; on several occasions, Karimov has achieved political ends by shutting pipelines or by adjusting terms of delivery. In a number of television appearances broadcast in the Osh and Jalal-Abad provinces of Kyrgyzstan, Karimov has addressed Akayev with considerable condescension; Akayev, in turn, has been highly deferential to his much stronger neighbor. Although Uzbekistan has not shown overt expansionist tendencies, the Kyrgyz government is acutely aware of the implications of Karimov's assertions that he is responsible for the well-being of all Uzbeks, regardless of their nation of residence.

Although it presents no such expansionist threat, Kazakstan is as important to northern Kyrgyzstan as Uzbekistan is to the south. The virtual closure of Manas Airport at Bishkek makes Kazakstan's capital, Almaty, the principal point of entry to Kyrgyzstan. The northwestern city of Talas receives nearly all of its services through the city of Dzhambyl, across the border in Kazakstan. Although Kazakstan's president Nursultan Nazarbayev has cooperated in economic agreements, in May 1993 Kyrgyzstan's introduction of the som caused Nazarbayev to close his country's border with Kyrgyzstan to avoid a flood of worthless Kyrgyzstani rubles.

Kyrgyzstan's relations with Tajikistan have been tense. Refugees and antigovernment fighters in Tajikistan have crossed into Kyrgyzstan several times, even taking hostages. Kyrgyzstan attempted to assist in brokering an agreement between contesting Tajikistani forces in October 1992 but without success. Akayev later joined presidents Karimov and Nazarbayev in sending a joint intervention force to support Tajikistan's president Imomali Rahmonov against insurgents, but the Kyrgyzstani parliament delayed the mission of its small contingent for several months until late spring 1993. In mid-1995 Kyrgyzstani forces had the responsibility of sealing a small portion of the Tajikistan border near Panj from Tajikistani rebel forces.

The greater risk to Kyrgyzstan from Tajikistan is the general destabilization that the protracted civil war has brought to the region. In particular, the Khorugh-Osh road, the so-called "highway above the clouds," has become a major conduit of contraband of all sorts, including weapons and drugs (see Internal Security, this ch.). A meeting of the heads of the state security agencies of Tajikistan, Kyrgyzstan, Kazakstan, and Uzbekistan, held in Osh in the spring of 1995, also drew the conclusion that ethnic, social, and economic conditions in Osh were increasingly similar to those in Tajikistan in the late 1980s, thus recognizing the contagion of Tajikistan's instability.

Chinese-Kyrgyzstani relations are an area of substantial uncertainty for the government in Bishkek. China has become Kyrgyzstan's largest non-CIS trade partner, but China's influence is stronger in the north of Kyrgyzstan than in the south. This limitation could change if efforts to join the Karakorum Highway to Osh through Sary-Tash are successful. The free-trade zone in Naryn has attracted large numbers of Chinese businesspeople, who have come to dominate most of the republic's import and export of small goods. Most of this trade is in barter conducted by ethnic Kyrgyz or Kazaks who are Chinese citizens. The Kyrgyzstani government has expressed alarm over the numbers of Chinese who are moving into Naryn and other parts of Kyrgyzstan, but no preventive measures have been taken.

The Akayev government also must be solicitous of Chinese sensibilities on questions of nationalism because the Chinese do not want the independence of the Central Asian states to stimulate dreams of statehood among their own Turkic Muslim peoples. Although the Kyrgyz in China have been historically quiescent, China's Uygurs (of whom there is a small exile community in Kyrgyzstan) have been militant in their desire to attain independence. This is the major reason that Kyrgyzstan has refused to permit the formation of an Uygur party (see Political Parties, this ch.).

In the 1990s, trade with China has grown to such a volume that some officials in Kyrgyzstan fear that by the late 1990s Kyrgyzstan's economy will be entirely dominated by China. In some political quarters, the prospect of Chinese domination has stimulated nostalgia for the days of Moscow's control.

## Russia

In fact, whereas the other Central Asian republics have sometimes complained of Russian interference, Kyrgyzstan has more often wished for more attention and support from Moscow than it has been able to obtain. For all the financial support that the world community has offered, Kyrgyzstan remains economically dependent on Russia, both directly and through Kazakstan. In early 1995, Akayev attempted to sell Russian companies controlling shares in the republic's twenty-nine largest industrial plants, an offer that Russia refused.

Akayev has been equally enthusiastic about more direct forms of reintegration, such as the Euro-Asian Union that Nazarbayev proposed in June 1994. Because Kyrgyzstan presumably would receive much more from such a union than it would contribute, Akayev's enthusiasm has met with little response from Russia and the other, larger states that would be involved in such an arrangement. Akayev's invitation for Russian border guards to take charge of Kyrgyzstan's Chinese border, a major revision of his policy of neutrality, was another move toward reintegration (see Armed Forces, this ch.).

The Kyrgyzstani government also has felt compelled to request Russia's economic protection. The harsh reality of Kyrgyzstan's economic situation means that the nation is an inevitable international client state, at least for the foreseeable future. Despite concerted efforts to seek international "sponsors," Akayev has not received much more than a great deal of international good will. Even if the president had not lived seventeen years in Russia himself and even if his advisers, family, and friends were not all Soviet-era intellectuals with a high degree of familiarity with Russia, economic necessity probably would push Kyrgyzstan further toward Russia.

On his February 1994 visit to Moscow, Akayev signed several economic agreements. Having promised the republic a 75-billion-ruble line of credit (presumably for use in 1994) and some US$65 million in trade agreements, Russia also promised to extend to Kyrgyzstan most-favored-nation status for the purchase of oil and other fuels. For its part, Kyrgyzstan agreed to the creation of a Kyrgyzstani-Russian investment company, which would purchase idle defense-related factories in the republic to provide employment for the increasingly dissatisfied Russian population of Kyrgyzstan. In early 1995, prime ministers Jumagulov of Kyrgyzstan and Viktor Chernomyrdin of Russia signed a series of agreements establishing bilateral coordination of economic reform in the two states, further binding Kyrgyzstan to Russia. After lobbying hard for inclusion, Kyrgyzstan became a member of the customs union that Russia, Belarus, and Kazakstan established in February 1996.

For its part, Russia sees aid to Kyrgyzstan as a successful precedent in its new policy of gaining influence in its "near abroad," the states that once were Soviet republics. Russia does not want a massive in-migration of Russians from the new republics; some 2 million ethnic Russians moved back to Russia between 1992 and 1995, with at least that many again expected by the end of the century. Akayev, on the other hand, must find a way to stem the loss of his Russian population, which already has caused an enormous deficit of doctors, teachers, and engineers.

For these reasons, despite opposition from Kyrgyz nationalists and other independence-minded politicians, in 1995 Akayev granted the request of Russian president Boris N. Yeltsin to review the constitutional provision making Kyrgyz the sole official language. Early in 1996, Kyrgyzstan took legal steps toward making Russian the republic's second official language, subject to amendment of the constitution. That initiative coincided with the customs union signed with Russia, Kazakstan, and Belarus in February 1996. The long-term success of Akayev's search for reintegration is questionable because of Kyrgyzstan's minimal strategic importance and the potential cost to an outside country supporting the republic's shaky economy.

## National Security

Located in a region of low strategic importance and surrounded by nations with major concerns in other directions, Kyrgyzstan did not make developing its own armed forces a high priority after separation from the Soviet Union. The long-standing civil war in nearby Tajikistan, however, has forced reevaluation of that conservative position. Internal security has been a major concern because of rampant crime and a well-developed narcotics industry.

## Armed Forces

In the early 1990s, Kyrgyzstan began to build a small armed force based on the military doctrine that Russia will remain chief guarantor of Kyrgyzstan's national security interests. The only operational branch of the armed forces is the ground forces.

### Development of Military Policy

Kyrgyzstan made its first moves toward a national military force in September 1991, immediately after declaring independence, by drawing up plans to create a national guard. However, events overtook that plan, which was never realized. In the early months of independence, President Akayev was an avid supporter of a proposed "unified army" of the CIS, which would replace the former Soviet army. Those plans collapsed when Russia announced that it would not finance CIS troops. In April 1992, Kyrgyzstan formed a State Committee for Defense Affairs, and in June the republic took control of all troops on its soil (meaning remaining units of the former Soviet army). At that time, about 15,000 former Soviet soldiers of unknown ethnic identity remained in Kyrgyzstan.

Although the Kyrgyzstani government did not demand a new oath of service until after adoption of the Law on Military Service (the first draft of which in 1992 was copied so hastily from Soviet law that it included provisions for a navy), the majority of the officer corps (mostly Russian) refused to serve in a Kyrgyzstani army, and since that time many Russian officers have sought repatriation to Russia. A more informal outflow of draftees already had been underway before Kyrgyzstan's independence. According to one estimate, as many as 6,000 Russians deserted from duty in Kyrgyzstan, although that loss was partially offset by the return of almost 2,000 Kyrgyz who had been serving in the Soviet army outside their republic. According to reports, in 1993 between 3,000 and 4,000 non-Kyrgyz soldiers, mostly Russians, remained in the republic.

In the early days of independence, Kyrgyzstani authorities spoke of doing without an army entirely. That idea since has been replaced by plans to create a standing conscripted army

*Soldiers giving demonstration at Independence Day celebration,*
*August 31, Bishkek*
*Courtesy Hermine Dreyfuss*

of about 5,000 troops, with reserves of two to three times that number. The question of who would command these troops has been very troublesome. Russian officers continued leaving Kyrgyzstan through 1993 because of low pay and poor living conditions, and in 1994 Moscow was officially encouraging this exodus. To stem the out-migration, agreements signed in 1994 by Bishkek and Moscow obligate Kyrgyzstan to pay housing and relocation costs for Russian officers who agree to serve in the Kyrgyzstani army until 1999.

In 1994 Kyrgyzstan agreed to permit border troops of the Russian Army to assume the task of guarding Kyrgyzstan's border with China. This agreement followed Russia's complaints that continuing desertions by Kyrgyzstani border troops were leaving the former Soviet border—which Russia continues to argue is its proper border—essentially unguarded. Akayev has periodically pushed for even more Russian military presence in the republic, hinting broadly that if Russia is not interested in resuming control of the Soviet airbases in the republic, perhaps other powers, such as the United States or the North Atlantic Treaty Organization ( NATO—see Glossary), might be; however, the fact that Kyrgyzstan in early 1995 gave the last remnants of its Soviet-era air fleet to Uzbekistan in a debt swap suggests that neither Moscow nor Tashkent has taken such offers seriously.

It is not entirely clear what weapons Kyrgyzstan's army will possess. The republic lost twelve IL–39 jets in March 1992, when they were "repatriated" to Russia from a training field near the capital, and the 1995 swap with Uzbekistan lost an unknown number of MiG–21 fighters and L–39C close-support aircraft. Available information suggests strongly that Kyrgyzstan, as the least militarized of the Central Asian republics, is incapable of defending itself against a military threat from any quarter.

### Command Structure

Formally, the army is under the command of the president, in his role as commander in chief; the National Security Council is the chief agency of defense policy. Established in 1994, the National Security Council has seven members, not including the president, who is the chairman: the prime minister, the deputy prime minister, the state secretary, the minister of internal affairs, the minister of defense, the chairman of the State Committee for National Security (successor to the Kyrgyzstan branch of the Committee for State Security—KGB), and the commander of the National Guard. The president appoints and dismisses senior military officers. President Akayev also has followed the formulation of defense policy quite closely. The Ministry of Defense has operational command of military units; General Myrzakan Subanov has been minister of defense since the agency was founded in 1992. The Ministry of Defense and the National Security Council are advised by the Center for Analysis, a research institution established in 1992.

The chief of the General Staff, the second-ranking officer in the armed forces, is responsible for coordinating the National Security Council, the State Committee for National Security, the border troops, and civil defense. Since 1993 that position has been occupied by General Feliks Kulov, a Kyrgyz. The General Staff, modeled after the Russian structure, includes the commanders of the National Guard, the ground forces, the air and air defense forces, and the internal forces.

### Ground Forces

In 1996 the Kyrgyzstani ground forces included 7,000 troops, which comprise one motorized rifle division with armor and artillery capability. Sapper and signals regiments are attached, as is a mountain infantry brigade. Headquarters is at Bishkek. Plans called for the ground forces to be restructured in 1995 into a corps of two motorized rifle brigades and for an airborne battalion to be added. In 1994 about 30 percent of the officer corps was Russian; the commander was General Valentin Luk'yanov, a Ukrainian.

### Air and Air Defense Forces

Because of expense and military doctrine, Kyrgyzstan has not developed its air capability; a large number of the MiG–21 interceptors that it borrowed from Russia were returned in 1993, although a number of former Soviet air bases remain available. In 1996 about 100 decommissioned MiG–21s remained in Kyrgyzstan, along with ninety-six L–39 trainers and sixty-five helicopters.

The air defense forces have received aid from Russia, which has sent military advisory units to establish a defense system. Presently Kyrgyzstan has twenty-six SA–2 and SA–3 surface-to-air missiles in its air defense arsenal.

### Border Troops

In 1992 a Kyrgyzstani command took over the republic's directorate of the KGB's Central Asian Border Troops District, which had about 2,000 mostly Russian troops. In late 1992, alarmed by the possibility of penetration of the border from Tajikistan and China, Russia established a joint Kyrgyzstani-Russian Border Troop Command, under Russian command. However, that force has been plagued with desertions by Kyrgyz troops, about 200 of whom fled to China in 1993. Border troop bases are located at Isfara, Naryn, and Karakol.

### Training

Cadets and noncommissioned officers (NCOs) in the ground forces are trained at the Bishkek Military School, which played the same role in the Soviet era. Under a 1993 agreement, a small number of ground forces cadets study at Russian military schools, with the specific goal of bolstering the ethnic Kyrgyz officer corps. Small groups of Kyrgyz cadets also attend military schools in Uzbekistan and Turkey. Officers selected for higher commands attend a three-year course at Frunze Military Academy in Moscow and other Russian military academies.

For the air force, the main training site is the Bishkek Aviation School, once a major center for training foreign air cadets but reduced in 1992 to a small contingent of mostly Kyrgyz cadets. In 1992 Kyrgyzstan had five training regiments using 430 aircraft, but that number was depleted by the mid-1990s. A 1994 agreement calls for some Kyrgyz pilots to attend air force schools in Russia.

## Internal Security

In the early and mid-1990s, preservation of internal security against a variety of crimes, and especially against growing commerce in narcotics, became an extremely difficult task. White-collar crime and government corruption have added to the atmosphere of social disorder.

### Security Troops

In 1991 President Akayev abolished the Kyrgyzstan branch of the KGB and replaced it with the State Committee for National Security, whose role subsequently was prescribed in a 1992 law. In 1996 the armed force of the committee, the National Guard, was an elite force of 1,000 recruited from all national groups in Kyrgyzstan. Organized in two battalions, the National Guard has been commanded since its inception by a Kyrgyz general; the chief of the border troops also is under that commander. The National Guard has the prescribed function of protecting the president and government property and assisting in natural disasters; except under exceptional circumstances, its role does not include maintenance of domestic order.

### Police

The republic's police system is largely unchanged from the Soviet era. Still called "militia," the police are under the jurisdiction of the Ministry of Internal Affairs. A force estimated at 25,000 individuals, the militia is commanded by the Central Police Force in Bishkek. The republic's police have suffered the same large-scale resignations because of low pay and bad working conditions as have other former Soviet republics lacking resources to support internal security. In April 1995, the national power company shut off power to the Central Police Force headquarters for nonpayment of electric bills, leaving the capital without even emergency police service for five hours. The poor equipment of the police further hampers their ability to respond to crimes. Police personnel frequently have been implicated in crime. Nearly 700 police were caught in the commission of crimes in the two months after President Akayev replaced the entire administration of the Ministry of Internal Affairs in 1995.

## Crime

Kyrgyzstan's crime problem is generally regarded as out of control. In 1994 more than 40,000 crimes were reported, or more than one crime per 100 citizens, and a high percentage of those crimes were classified as serious.

Petty crime touches every sector of the economy. For example, although cellular telephone networks and satellite linkups have been established in Bishkek, telecommunications elsewhere have grown much worse because the theft and resale of cable has become common. Power outages are frequent for the same reason, and any sort of equipment with salvageable metal is said to be quickly stripped if left unattended.

Foreigners are not exempt from crime, as they were in the Soviet era. In 1994 some 185 crimes against foreigners were registered in Bishkek. Most of these crimes were apartment burglaries, although beatings and armed robberies also have been reported. In April 1995, a small bomb was left in front of a Belgian relief mission's door, and "Foreigners Out of Bishkek" was painted on the wall opposite.

President Akayev vowed to crack down on crime in the mid-1990s, proposing much stiffer penalties for common crimes, including life imprisonment for auto theft. One sign of his seriousness was the replacement in January 1995 of the entire senior staff of the Ministry of Internal Affairs. The new minister, the Kyrgyz Modolbek Moldashev, served in the Soviet KGB and lived most of his life outside the republic. When he took office, Moldashev brought in his own people from the State Committee for National Security and the Ministry of Defense. However, it is far from clear that Kyrgyzstan's security organizations are capable of cracking down on the drug-driven sector of the economy, and experts predict that if narcotics escape control, the spiral of criminal activities will continue to grow.

Government corruption and malfeasance also contribute to an atmosphere of lawlessness. In the mid-1990s, bribery, kick-backs, and influence peddling became increasingly common in government agencies. Law enforcement officials have received little cooperation from legislators in punishing their colleagues who are caught violating the law. In 1993 the Interregional Investigative Unit, established to combat bribery, found itself shut down after twenty successful investigations and replaced by an economic crimes investigation unit, some members of which began taking bribes themselves.

### Narcotics Control

Perhaps the most lucrative, and certainly the most problem-atic, of Kyrgyzstan's exports is narcotics, particularly opium and heroin. Government officials believe that the narcotics indus-try presents the greatest challenge to the internal security of Kyrgyzstan because of its capacity to destabilize the country.

In the Soviet era, the Kyrgyz Republic was a legal producer of opium, with about 2,000 hectares of land planted to poppies in 1974, the last year before world pressure forced such farms to be closed. At that point, an estimated 16 percent of the world's opium came from Kyrgyzstan. The country's climate is exceptionally well suited to cultivation of opium poppies and wild marijuana, producing unusually pure final products from both types of plant. Kyrgyzstan is said to produce even better poppies than does nearby Afghanistan, which has surpassed Burma as the world's leading supplier of heroin.

In 1992 Kyrgyzstan applied to the World Health Organiza-tion for permission to reinstitute the production of medicinal opium as a means of generating desperately needed revenue. The plan was to increase the planting in the northeastern Ysyk-Köl area to about 10,000 hectares and to open plantations in Talas and Naryn as well, yielding a projected annual profit of about US$200 million. Under pressure from the world commu-nity, the plan was dropped.

In 1992 republic narcotics police uncovered thirteen drug-refining laboratories and seized two tons of ready narcotics. The police reported that drug-related crime rose 222 percent from 1991 to 1992 and that 830 people had been arrested on drug-distribution charges. Another report indicated that 70 percent of the 44,000 crimes reported in the republic in 1992 had a connection to drugs in one way or another. At that time, the head of the country's narcotics police estimated that only about 20 percent of the narcotics traffic was being interdicted, mainly because resources are very inadequate. Government officials fear that this industry will continue to grow, especially in the absence of large-scale international assistance; in 1994 Russia ceased its cooperation with Kyrgyzstan in narcotics interdiction. An emerging distribution chain moves opium to Moscow, then to Poland, from where it is transferred to Europe and the United States.

Osh is said to have become a major new international point-of-purchase for opium and heroin, which is produced in all of the countries adjoining the Fergana Valley, including Kyrgyzstan. More than 300 kilograms of opium were seized in Osh Province in 1994, an amount estimated to be less than 10 percent of the total moving through Osh. At the end of 1994, the head of the National Security Committee characterized the narcotics trade as the republic's sole growth industry, which he warned was solidifying its grip on the republic's conventional economy.

### Court System

The court system remains essentially unchanged from the Soviet era. Nominally there are three levels in the court system: local courts, which handle petty crimes such as pickpocketing and vandalism; province-level courts, which handle crimes such as murder, grand larceny, and organized crime; and the Supreme Court, to which decisions of the lower courts can be appealed. However, there has been persistent conflict between Akayev and the legislature over the composition and authority of the Supreme Court, as well as over Akayev's choice of chief justice. As in the Soviet system, the office of the state procurator, chief civilian legal officer of the state, acts as both prosecuting attorney and chief investigator in each case.

The protections for individuals accused of crimes remain at the primitive level of Soviet law. According to law, the accused can be held for three days before a charge is made, and pretrial detention can last for as long as a year. There is no system of bail; the accused remains incarcerated until tried. Both the police and forces of the State Committee for National Security have the right to violate guarantees of privacy (of the home, telephone, mail, and banks), with the sanction of the state procurator. In theory search warrants and judicial orders for such things as wiretaps only are issued by authority of a judge; in practice this is not always done.

*Prisons*

Very little current information is known about Kyrgyzstan's prison system. In the Soviet era, at least twelve labor camps and three prisons operated in the republic, including at least one uranium mine-labor camp in which prisoners worked without protective gear. The total prison capacity and present population are not known, but it may be presumed that prisons in Kyrgyzstan are suffering the same overcrowding as are prisons elsewhere in the former Soviet Union. The 1995 purge of the Ministry of Internal Affairs included appointment of a new head of the prison system, a colonel who had been assistant minister of internal affairs prior to the shakeup.

## National Security Prospects

Although internal stability has not been a serious problem during the Akayev era, events in the mid-1990s threatened to make it so. By 1995 economic hardship, to which international experts did not predict a rapid end, combined with insufficient internal security forces and the opportunity for profits from organized narcotics activities to threaten the stability of Kyrgyzstan's society, especially in the major urban centers of Bishkek and Osh. The high crime rate also interfered with plans to attract Western tourist trade.

Meanwhile, as of 1995 external security came exclusively from Russia, a situation that Kyrgyzstan officially welcomed in the absence of domestic resources to build a credible military force for its very small and isolated nation. As in the economic field, however, policy makers were not sure how long Russia would view strong support of Kyrgyzstan's national security as an important element of Russian foreign policy. Although no major regional threat loomed in the mid-1990s, major policy questions remained unanswered.

\*     \*     \*

A useful reference for general historical background is *Central Asia: 120 Years of Russian Rule*, edited by Edward Allworth and revised in 1994. The Kyrgyzstan chapter of Martha Brill Olcott's *Central Asia's New States* is a concise description of the republic's status in the post-Soviet world. Several publications of the World Bank provide detailed information about social and economic developments in the 1990s. Among the most useful are those entitled *Kyrgyz Republic: Economic Report; Kyrgyz Republic: Agricultural Sector Review; Kyrgyz Republic: Energy Sector Review;* and *Kyrgyzstan: Social Protection in a Reforming Economy.* For general background on Kyrgyz society and customs, the government's *Discovery of Kyrghyzstan* is a valuable source. (For further information and complete citations, see Bibliography.)

# Chapter 3. Tajikistan

*Bronze vessel excavated at site of ancient city of Khujand*

## Country

**Formal Name:** Republic of Tajikistan.

**Short Form:** Tajikistan.

**Term for Citizens:** Tajikistani(s).

**Capital:** Dushanbe.

**Date of Independence:** September 9, 1991.

## Geography

**Size:** Approximately 143,100 square kilometers.

**Topography:** Mainly mountainous, with lower elevations in northwest, southwest, and Fergana Valley in far northern zone. Highest elevations in southeast, in Pamir-Alay system; numerous glaciers in mountains. Dense river network creates valleys through mountain chains. Lakes primarily in Pamir region to the east.

**Climate:** Mainly continental, with drastic changes according to elevation. Arid in subtropical southwest lowlands, which have highest temperatures; lowest temperatures at highest altitudes. Highest precipitation near Fedchenko Glacier, lowest in eastern Pamirs.

## Society

**Population:** By last Soviet census (1989), 5,092,603; no later reliable estimate available. Annual growth rate 3.0 percent in 1992; 1991 population density 38.2 persons per square kilometer.

**Ethnic Groups:** In 1989 census, Tajiks 62.3 percent, Uzbeks 23.5 percent, Russians 7.6 percent, Tatars 1.4 percent, and Kyrgyz 1.3 percent.

**Languages:** Official state language, Tajik, is spoken by an estimated 62 percent; Russian, widely used in government and business, a second language for most of urban non-Russian population.

**Religion:** Islam practiced by about 90 percent of population, mainly Sunni; remainder Russian Orthodox, with some other small Christian and Jewish groups.

**Education and Literacy:** Education compulsory through secondary school, but completion rate below 90 percent. Literacy estimated at 98 percent. In 1990s, facilities and materials extremely inadequate, and specialized secondary and higher education programs poorly developed.

**Health:** Generally low level of care in Soviet era continued or declined in 1990s. Number and quality of medical personnel, hospitals, and equipment undermined by low funding and civil war. Mortality and incidence of disease rose in 1990s because of pollution and shortage of medicines.

## Economy

**Gross National Product (GNP):** Estimated in 1993 at US$2.7 billion, or US$470 per capita. Average growth rate 1985–92 was –7.8 percent per year. Beginning 1992, economic growth in all sectors crippled by transformation from Soviet system and by effects of civil war.

**Agriculture:** Largest sector of economy, dominated by cotton, grain, vegetables; food production insufficient for domestic consumption. Nearly all agricultural labor unmechanized, and output declined sharply in mid-1990s. Commitment to cotton as primary crop continues in post-Soviet era, although production has decreased.

**Industry and Mining:** Advancement and diversification slow in 1990s after specialized roles in Soviet period emphasized aluminum processing and chemicals. Contributed about 30 percent of net material product (NMP—see Glossary) in 1991. Productivity of nearly all industries declined in mid-1990s. Several minerals, including gold, mined on a small scale.

**Energy:** Hydroelectric power only major source, providing 75 percent of electricity; must import petroleum fuels and coal, only minor exploitation of domestic deposits. Power imports from neighboring countries problematic in 1990s because of insufficient funds.

**Exports:** In 1995, worth about US$720 million. Principal items electric power, cotton, fertilizers, nonferrous metals (especially aluminum), silk, fruits, and vegetables. Postcommunist export markets outside Commonwealth of Independent States (CIS) very slow to form, and traditional barter ties remain strong; principal customers within CIS Russia, Kazakstan, Ukraine, and Uzbekistan; outside CIS Poland, Sweden, Afghanistan, Austria, Norway, and Hungary.

**Imports:** In 1995, worth about US$1.2 billion. Principal items fuels, grains, iron and steel, consumer goods, and finished industrial products. Principal suppliers in CIS Russia, Turkmenistan, Kazakstan, Uzbekistan, and Ukraine; outside CIS Poland, Austria, France, Britain, and Turkey. Total non-CIS imports in 1995 US$265 million.

**Balance of Payments:** Estimated 1994 budget deficit US$54.7 million.

**Exchange Rate:** Tajikistani ruble introduced in May 1995 after using Soviet ruble (withdrawn elsewhere in the CIS in late 1993) until January 1994, then joining Russian ruble zone and adopting new Russian rubles then in use. January 1996 value of Tajikistani ruble 284 per US$1.

**Inflation:** Consumer price index rose 416 percent 1993–94, 120 percent 1994–95; controlled in 1995 by antiinflationary government program.

**Fiscal Year:** Calendar year.

**Fiscal Policy:** Highly centralized government system, with little regional authority. Initial price decontrol in 1992 caused extensive hardship, led to retrenchment and resumption of strong government control of prices and wages. In 1993, major sources of national income value-added tax (30 percent), enterprise profits tax (26 percent), and excise tax (13 percent).

## Transportation and Telecommunications

**Highways:** In 1992, 32,750 kilometers of roads, of which 18,240 classified as main roads. One major highway connecting

Dushanbe in southwest with Khujand in northwest.

**Railroads:** Most important means of transportation, but do not link vital areas of northwest and southwest. In 1990 total track 891 kilometers, of which 410 industrial. Aging infrastructure depleting service reliability.

**Civil Aviation:** Airport at Dushanbe, only one with scheduled flights, in poor condition; cannot accommodate large international planes. Tajikistan International Airlines founded 1995 with Western aid.

**Inland Waterways:** None.

**Ports:** None.

**Pipelines:** Only short natural gas lines from Uzbekistan to Dushanbe and linking Uzbekistani points across Tajikistan's northwest extremity.

**Telecommunications:** In 1993, 259,600 telephones (one per twenty-two persons). Radio and television broadcasting is monopoly of the State Television and Radio Broadcasting Company. Thirteen AM and three FM stations offer programs in Tajik, Russian, and Uzbek. Television broadcasts from Dushanbe with relays from Iran, Russia, and Turkey. In 1992, 854,000 radios and 860,000 televisions in use.

# Government and Politics

**Government:** National government with nearly all administrative powers, centered in executive branch (president and Council of Ministers, appointed by president). Head of government is prime minister. Supreme Assembly, unicameral parliament, with 181 deputies elected to five-year terms (first election 1995). Divided into three provinces, one capital district (Dushanbe), and one autonomous province with disputed status. Judiciary with nominal independence but no actual power to enforce rule of law.

**Politics:** Essentially one-party system dominated by Communist Party of Tajikistan. In 1994 presidential election had only one nominal opposition candidate with similar platform. Several opposition parties formed around 1990 and influenced events in early years of independence, but all now operate from abroad. Substantial maneuvering for power among former communist elements within and outside current government.

**Foreign Relations:** Strong economic and military reliance on Russia and other CIS countries. Friction and distrust toward neighbors Uzbekistan and Kyrgyzstan. Postindependence cultivation of Afghanistan and Iran, the former complicated by Afghani role in Tajikistan civil war; limited relations with Western Europe and United States, despite policy of expanding contacts. Ongoing border dispute with China, 1996.

**International Agreements and Memberships:** United Nations (UN), Organization for Security and Cooperation in Europe (OSCE), World Bank, International Monetary Fund (IMF), CIS, and Economic Cooperation Organization (ECO).

## National Security

**Armed Forces:** Total forces 3,000 in 1996 (army only; no air force or navy). Officer corps dominated by Russians. Russian 201st Motorized Infantry Division, about 24,000 troops, contributes to CIS force, also including troops from Kazakstan, Kyrgyzstan, and Uzbekistan, and dominates overall national defense. Morale problems and local loyalties hinder conscription and organization of Tajikistani national force.

**Major Military Units:** Army includes two brigades of motorized infantry and one brigade of special forces. Heavily reliant on Russian equipment and arms supply. Border troops include 16,500 Russians, 12,500 Tajikistanis, 1995.

**Military Budget:** In 1995 estimated US$67 million.

**Internal Security:** Main agency Committee of National Security, based on Soviet-era Tajikistan Committee for State Security (KGB), with full cabinet status. Police authority divided between Committee for National Security and Ministry of Internal Affairs, which had 1,500 troops in 1993. Beginning 1992, internal security poor because of civil war, pervasive corruption.

Figure 10. *Tajikistan: Administrative Divisions and Transportation System, 1996*

TAJIKISTAN, LITERALLY THE "LAND OF THE TAJIKS," has ancient cultural roots. The people now known as the Tajiks are the Persian speakers of Central Asia, some of whose ancestors inhabited Central Asia (including present-day Afghanistan and western China) at the dawn of history. Despite the long heritage of its indigenous peoples, Tajikistan has existed as a state only since the Soviet Union decreed its existence in 1924. The creation of modern Tajikistan was part of the Soviet policy of giving the outward trappings of political representation to minority nationalities in Central Asia while simultaneously reorganizing or fragmenting communities and political entities.

Of the five Central Asian states that declared independence from the Soviet Union in 1991, Tajikistan is the smallest in area and the third largest in population. Landlocked and mountainous, the republic has some valuable natural resources, such as waterpower and minerals, but arable land is scarce, the industrial base is narrow, and the communications and transportation infrastructures are poorly developed.

As was the case in other republics of the Soviet Union, nearly seventy years of Soviet rule brought Tajikistan a combination of modernization and repression. Although barometers of modernization such as education, health care, and industrial development registered substantial improvements over low starting points in this era, the quality of the transformation in such areas was less impressive than the quantity, with reforms benefiting Russian-speaking city dwellers more than rural citizens who lacked fluency in Russian. For all the modernization that occurred under Soviet rule, the central government's policies limited Tajikistan to a role as a predominantly agricultural producer of raw materials for industries located elsewhere. Through the end of the Soviet era, Tajikistan had one of the lowest standards of living of the Soviet republics.

Independence came to Tajikistan with the dissolution of the Soviet Union in December 1991. The first few years after that were a time of great hardship. Some of the new republic's problems—including the breakdown of the old system of interdependent economic relationships upon which the Soviet republics had relied, and the stress of movement toward participation in the world market—were common among the Soviet successor states. The pain of economic decline was compounded in Tajikistan by a bloody and protracted civil conflict over whether the country would perpetuate a system of monopoly rule by a narrow elite like the one that ruled in the Soviet era, or establish a reformist, more democratic regime. The struggle peaked as an outright war in the second half of 1992, and smaller-scale conflict continued into the mid-1990s. The victors preserved a repressive system of rule, and the lingering effects of the conflict contributed to the further worsening of living conditions.

## Historical Background

Before the Soviet era, which began in Central Asia in the early 1920s, the area designated today as the Republic of Tajikistan underwent a series of population changes that brought with them political and cultural influences from the Turkic and Mongol peoples of the Eurasian steppe, China, Iran, Russia, and other contiguous regions. The Tajik people came fully under Russian rule, after a series of military campaigns that began in the 1860s, at the end of the nineteenth century.

### Ethnic Background

Iranian (see Glossary) peoples, including ancestors of the modern Tajiks, have inhabited Central Asia since at least the earliest recorded history of the region, which began some 2,500 years ago. Contemporary Tajiks are the descendants of ancient Eastern Iranian inhabitants of Central Asia, in particular the Soghdians and the Bactrians, and possibly other groups, with an admixture of Western Iranian Persians (see Glossary) and non-Iranian peoples. The ethnic contribution of various Turkic and Mongol peoples, who entered Central Asia at later times, has not been determined precisely. However, experts assume that some assimilation must have occurred in both directions.

The origin of the name *Tajik* has been embroiled in twentieth-century political disputes about whether Turkic or Iranian peoples were the original inhabitants of Central Asia. The explanation most favored by scholars is that the word evolved from the name of a pre-Islamic (before the seventh century A.D.) Arab tribe.

Until the twentieth century, people in the region used two types of distinction to identify themselves: way of life—either nomadic or sedentary—and place of residence. By the late nineteenth century, the Tajik and Uzbek peoples, who had lived in proximity for centuries and often used each other's languages, did not perceive themselves as two distinct nationalities. Consequently, such labels were imposed artificially when Central Asia was divided into five Soviet republics in the 1920s.

## Early History

Much, if not all, of what is today Tajikistan was part of ancient Persia's Achaemenid Empire (sixth to fourth centuries B.C.), which was subdued by Alexander the Great in the fourth century B.C. and then became part of the Greco-Bactrian kingdom, one of the successor states to Alexander's empire. The northern part of what is now Tajikistan was part of Soghdiana, a distinct region that intermittently existed as a combination of separate oasis states and sometimes was subject to other states. Two important cities in what is now northern Tajikistan, Khujand (formerly Leninobod; Russian spelling Leninabad) and Panjakent, as well as Bukhoro (Bukhara) and Samarqand (Samarkand) in contemporary Uzbekistan, were Soghdian in antiquity. As intermediaries on the Silk Route between China and markets to the west and south, the Soghdians imparted religions such as Buddhism, Nestorian Christianity, Zoroastrianism (see Glossary), and Manichaeism (see Glossary), as well as their own alphabet and other knowledge, to peoples along the trade routes.

Between the first and fourth centuries, the area that is now Tajikistan and adjoining territories were part of the Kushan realm, which had close cultural ties to India. The Kushans, whose exact identity is uncertain, played an important role in the expansion of Buddhism by spreading the faith to the Soghdians,who in turn brought it to China and the Turks.

By the first century A.D., the Han dynasty of China had developed commercial and diplomatic relations with the Soghdians and their neighbors, the Bactrians. Military operations also extended Chinese influence westward into the region. During the first centuries A.D., Chinese involvement in this region waxed and waned, decreasing sharply after the Islamic conquest but not disappearing completely. As late as the nineteenth century, China attempted to press its claim to the Pamir region of what is now southeastern Tajikistan. Since the breakup of the Soviet Union, China occasionally has revived its claim to part of this region.

## The Islamic Conquest

Islamic Arabs began the conquest of the region in earnest in the early eighth century. Conversion to Islam occurred by means of incentives, gradual acceptance, and force of arms. Islam spread most rapidly in cities and along the main river valleys. By the ninth century, it was the prevalent religion in the entire region. In the early centuries of Islamic domination, Central Asia continued in its role as a commercial crossroads, linking China, the steppes to the north, and the Islamic heartland.

## Persian Culture in Central Asia

The Persian influence on Central Asia, already prominent before the Islamic conquest, grew even stronger afterward. Under Iran's last pre-Islamic empire, the Sassanian, the Persian language and culture as well as the Zoroastrian religion spread among the peoples of Central Asia, including the ancestors of the modern Tajiks. In the wake of the Islamic conquest, Persian-speakers settled in Central Asia, where they played an active role in public affairs and furthered the spread of the Persian language and culture, their language displacing Eastern Iranian ones. By the twelfth century, Persian had also supplanted Arabic as the written language for most subjects.

## The Samanids

In the development of a modern Tajik national identity, the most important state in Central Asia after the Islamic conquest was the Persian-speaking Samanid principality (875–999), which came to rule most of what is now Tajikistan, as well as territory to the south and west. During their reign, the Samanids supported the revival of the written Persian language.

Early in the Samanid period, Bukhoro became well-known as a center of learning and culture throughout the eastern part of the Persian-speaking world. Samanid literary patronage played an important role in preserving the culture of pre-Islamic Iran. Late in the tenth century, the Samanid state came under increasing pressure from Turkic powers to the north and south. After the Qarakhanid Turks overthrew the Samanids in 999, no major Persian state ever again existed in Central Asia.

Beginning in the ninth century, Turkish penetration of the Persian cultural sphere increased in Central Asia. The influx of even greater numbers of Turkic peoples began in the eleventh century. The Turkic peoples who moved into southern Central

Asia, including what later became Tajikistan, were influenced to varying degrees by Persian culture. Over the generations, some converted Turks changed from pastoral nomadism to a sedentary way of life, which brought them into closer contact with the sedentary Persian-speakers. Cultural influences flowed in both directions as Turks and Persians intermarried.

During subsequent centuries, the lands that eventually became Tajikistan were part of Turkic or Mongol states. The Persian language remained in use in government, scholarship, and literature. Among the dynasties that ruled all or part of the future Tajikistan between the eleventh and fifteenth centuries were the Seljuk Turks, the Mongols, and the Timurids (Timur, or Tamerlane, and his heirs and their subjects). Repeated power struggles among claimants to these realms took their toll on Central Asia. The Mongol conquest in particular dealt a serious blow to sedentary life and destroyed several important cities in the region. Although they had come in conquest, the Timurids also patronized scholarship, the arts, and letters.

In the early sixteenth century, Uzbeks from the northwest conquered large sections of Central Asia, but the unified Uzbek state began to break apart soon after the conquest. By the early nineteenth century, the lands of the future Tajikistan were divided among three states: the Uzbek-ruled Bukhoro Khanate, the Ququn (Kokand) Khanate, centered on the Fergana Valley, and the kingdom of Afghanistan. These three principalities subsequently fought each other for control of key areas of the new territory. Although some regions were under the nominal control of Bukhoro, or Ququn, local rulers were virtually independent.

## The Russian Conquest

After several unsuccessful attempts in earlier times, the Russian conquest and settlement of Central Asia began in earnest in the second half of the nineteenth century. Spurred by various economic and geopolitical factors, increasing numbers of Russians moved into Central Asia in this period. Although some armed resistance occurred, Tajik society remained largely unchanged during this initial colonial period.

### The Occupation Process

By 1860 the Central Asian principalities were ripe for conquest by the much more powerful Russian Empire. Imperial policy makers believed that these principalities had to be subdued because of their armed opposition to Russian expansion into the Kazak steppe, which already was underway to the north of Tajikistan. Some proponents of Russian expansion saw it as a way to compensate for losses elsewhere and to pressure Britain, Russia's perennial nemesis in the region, by playing on British concerns about threats to its position in India. The Russian military supported campaigns in Central Asia as a means of advancing careers and building personal fortunes. The region assumed much greater economic importance in the second half of the nineteenth century because of its potential as a supplier of cotton.

An important step in the Russian conquest was the capture of Tashkent from the Quqon Khanate, part of which was annexed in 1866. The following year, Tashkent became the capital of the new Guberniya (Governorate General) of Turkestan, which included the districts of Khujand and Uroteppa (later part of Tajikistan). After a domestic uprising and Russian military occupation, Russia annexed the remainder of the Quqon Khanate in 1876.

The Bukhoro Khanate fought Russian invaders during the same period, losing the Samarqand area in 1868. Russia chose not to annex the rest of Bukhoro, fearing repercussions in the Muslim world and from Britain because Bukhoro was a bastion of Islam and a place of strategic significance to British India. Instead, the tsar's government made a treaty with Bukhoro, recognizing its existence but in effect subordinating it to Russia. Bukhoro actually gained territory by this agreement, when the Russian administration granted the amir of Bukhoro a district that included Dushanbe, now the capital of Tajikistan, in compensation for the territory that had been ceded to Russia.

In the 1880s, the principality of Shughnon-Rushon in the western Pamir Mountains became a new object of contention between Britain and Russia when Afghanistan and Russia disputed territory there. An 1895 treaty assigned the disputed territory to Bukhoro, and at the same time put the eastern Pamirs under Russian rule.

### Tajikistan under Russian Rule

Russian rule brought important changes in Central Asia, but many elements of the traditional way of life scarcely changed. In the part of what is now Tajikistan that was incorporated into the Guberniya of Turkestan, many ordinary inhabitants had limited contact with Russian officials or settlers before 1917.

Rural administration there resembled the system that governed peasants in the European part of the Russian Empire after the abolition of serfdom in 1861. Local administration in villages continued to follow long-established tradition, and prior to 1917 few Russians lived in the area of present-day Tajikistan. Russian authorities also left education in the region substantially the same between the 1870s and 1917.

An important event of the 1870s was Russia's initial expansion of cotton cultivation in the region, including the areas of the Fergana Valley and the Bukhoro Khanate that later became part of Tajikistan. The pattern of switching land from grain cultivation to cotton cultivation, which intensified during the Soviet period, was established at this time. The first cotton-processing plant was established in eastern Bukhoro during World War I.

Some elements of opposition to Russian hegemony appeared in the late nineteenth century. By 1900 a novel educational approach was being offered by reformers known as Jadidists (*jadid* is the Arabic word for "new.") The Jadidists, who received support from Tajiks, Tatars, and Uzbeks, were modernizers and nationalists who viewed Central Asia as a whole. Their position was that the religious and cultural greatness of Islamic civilization had been degraded in the Central Asia of their day. The Tatars and Central Asians who shared these views established Jadidist schools in several cities in the Guberniya of Turkestan. Although the Jadidists were not necessarily anti-Russian, tsarist officials in Turkestan found their kind of education even more threatening than traditional Islamic teaching. By World War I, several cities in present-day Tajikistan had underground Jadidist organizations.

Between 1869 and 1913, uprisings against the amir of Bukhoro erupted under local rulers in the eastern part of the khanate. The uprisings of 1910 and 1913 required Russian troops to restore order. A peasant revolt also occurred in eastern Bukhoro in 1886. The failed Russian revolution of 1905 resonated very little among the indigenous populations of Central Asia. In the Duma (legislature) that was established in St. Petersburg as a consequence of the events of 1905, the indigenous inhabitants of Turkestan were allotted only six representatives. Subsequent to the second Duma in 1907, Central Asians were denied all representation.

By 1916 discontent with the effects of Russian rule had grown substantially. Central Asians complained especially of discriminatory taxation and price gouging by Russian merchants. A flashpoint was Russia's revocation that year of Central Asians' traditional exemption from military service. In July 1916, the first violent reaction to the impending draft occurred when demonstrators attacked Russian soldiers in Khujand, in what would later be northern Tajikistan. Although clashes continued in various parts of Central Asia through the end of the year, Russian troops quickly brought the Khujand region back under control. The following year, the Russian Revolution ended tsarist rule in Central Asia.

In the early 1920s, the establishment of Soviet rule in Central Asia led to the creation of a new entity called Tajikistan as a republic within the Soviet Union. In contrast to the tsarist period, when most inhabitants of the future Tajikistan felt only limited Russian influence, the Soviet era saw a central authority exert itself in a way that was ideologically and culturally alien to the republic's inhabitants. The Tajik way of life experienced much change, even though social homogenization was never achieved.

## The Revolutionary Era

The indigenous inhabitants of the former Guberniya of Turkestan played no role in the overthrow of the Russian monarchy in March 1917 or in the seizure of power by the Russian Communist Party (Bolshevik) in November of that year. But the impact of those upheavals soon was felt in all parts of Central Asia. After the fall of the monarchy, Russia's Provisional Government abolished the office of governor-general of Turkestan and established in its place a nine-member Turkestan Committee, in which Russians had the majority and provided the leadership. The Provisional Government, which ruled Russia between March and November 1917, was unwilling to address the specific concerns of Central Asian reformers, including regional autonomy. Central Asians received no seats in Russia's short-lived Constituent Assembly. The events of 1917 finally alienated both conservatives and radicals from the revolution.

In 1917 the soviets (local revolutionary assemblies including soldiers and workers) that sprang up in Russian areas of Turkestan and Bukhoro were composed overwhelmingly of Russians. In November 1917, a regional congress of soviets in Tashkent declared a revolutionary regime and voted by a wide margin to continue the policies of the Provisional Government. Thus,

Central Asians again were denied political representation. Eventually, local communists established a figurehead soviet for Central Asians.

Having been denied access to the revolutionary organs of power, Central Asian reformers and conservatives formed their own organizations, as well as an umbrella group, the National Center. Although the groups cooperated on some issues of common interest, considerable animosity and occasional violence marked their relations. One group of Central Asian Muslims declared an autonomous state in southern Central Asia centered in the city of Quqon. At the beginning of 1919, the Tashkent Soviet declared the Quqon group counterrevolutionary and seized the city, killing at least 5,000 civilians.

Meanwhile, in 1918 the Tashkent Soviet had been defeated soundly in its effort to overthrow the amir of Bukhoro, who was seen by the communists and the Central Asian reformers alike as an obstacle to their respective programs. The attempted coup provoked a campaign of repression by the amir, and the defeat forced the Russian authorities in Tashkent to recognize a sovereign Bukhoran state in place of a Russian protectorate.

## Impact of the Civil War

An acute food shortage struck Turkestan in 1918–19, the result of the civil war, scarcities of grain caused by communist cotton-cultivation and price-setting policies, and the Tashkent Soviet's disinclination to provide famine relief to indigenous Central Asians. No authoritative estimate of famine deaths is available, but Central Asian nationalists put the number above 1 million.

In the fall of 1919, the collapse of the anti-Bolshevik White Army in western Siberia enabled General Mikhail Frunze to lead Red Army forces into Central Asia and gradually occupy the entire region. In 1920 the Red Army occupied Bukhoro and drove out the amir, declaring an independent people's republic but remaining as an occupation force. Turkestan, including the northern part of present-day Tajikistan, was officially incorporated into the Russian Soviet Federated Socialist Republic in 1921.

By 1921 the Russian communists had won the Russian Civil War and established the first Soviet republics in Azerbaijan, Armenia, Belorussia (present-day Belarus), Georgia, and Ukraine. At this point, the communists reduced the party's token Central Asian leadership to figurehead positions and expelled a large number of the Central Asian rank and file. In 1922 the Communist Party of Bukhoro was incorporated into the Russian Communist Party, which soon became the Communist Party of the Soviet Union (CPSU). Thereafter, most major government offices in Bukhoro were filled by appointees sent from Moscow, many of them Tatars, and many Central Asians were purged from the party and the government. In 1924 Bukhoro was converted from a people's republic to a Soviet socialist republic.

## The Basmachi

An indigenous resistance movement proved the last barrier to assimilation of Central Asia into the Soviet Union. In the 1920s, more than 20,000 people fought Soviet rule in Central Asia. The Russians applied a derogatory term, *Basmachi* (which originally meant brigand), to the groups. Although the resistance did not apply that term to itself, it nonetheless entered common usage. The several Basmachi groups had conflicting agendas and seldom coordinated their actions. After arising in the Fergana Valley, the movement became a rallying ground for opponents of Russian or Bolshevik rule from all parts of the region. Peasant unrest already existed in the area because of wartime hardships and the demands of the amir and the soviets. The Red Army's harsh treatment of local inhabitants in 1921 drove more people into the resistance camp. However, the Basmachi movement became more divided and more conservative as it gained numerically. It achieved some unity under the leadership of Enver Pasha, a Turkish adventurer with ambitions to lead the new secular government of Turkey, but Enver was killed in battle in early 1922.

Except for remote pockets of resistance, guerrilla fighting in Tajikistan ended by 1925. The defeat of the Basmachis caused as many as 200,000 people, including noncombatants, to flee eastern Bukhoro in the first half of the 1920s. A few thousand subsequently returned over the next several years.

The communists used a combination of military force and conciliation to defeat the Basmachis. The military approach ultimately favored the communist side, which was much better armed. The Red Army forces included Tatars and Central Asians, who enabled the invading force to appear at least partly indigenous. Conciliatory measures (grants of food, tax relief, the promise of land reform, the reversal of anti-Islamic policies launched during the Civil War, and the promise of an end to agricultural controls) prompted some Basmachis to reconcile themselves to the new order.

## Creation of Tajikistan

After establishing communist rule throughout formerly tsarist Central Asia in 1924, the Soviet government redrew internal political borders, eliminating the major units into which the region had been divided. The Soviet rationale was that this reorganization fulfilled local inhabitants' nationalist aspirations and would undercut support for the Basmachis. However, the new boundaries still left national groups fragmented, and nationalist aspirations in Central Asia did not prove as threatening as depicted in communist propaganda.

One of the new states created in Central Asia in 1924 was Uzbekistan, which had the status of a Soviet socialist republic. Tajikistan was created as an autonomous Soviet socialist republic within Uzbekistan. The new autonomous republic included what had been eastern Bukhoro and had a population of about 740,000, out of a total population of nearly 5 million in Uzbekistan as a whole. Its capital was established in Dushanbe, which had been a village of 3,000 in 1920. In 1929 Tajikistan was detached from Uzbekistan and given full status as a Soviet socialist republic. At that time, the territory that is now northern Tajikistan was added to the new republic. Even with the additional territory, Tajikistan remained the smallest Central Asian republic.

With the creation of a republic defined in national terms came the creation of institutions that, at least in form, were likewise national. The first Tajik-language newspaper in Soviet Tajikistan began publication in 1926. New educational institutions also began operation about the same time. The first state schools, available to both children and adults and designed to provide a basic education, opened in 1926. The central government also trained a small number of Tajiks for public office, either by putting them through courses offered by government departments or by sending them to schools in Uzbekistan.

From 1921 to 1927, during the New Economic Policy (NEP—see Glossary) Soviet agricultural policy promoted the expansion of cotton cultivation in Central Asia. By the end of the NEP, the extent of cotton cultivation had increased dramatically, but yield did not match prerevolutionary levels. At the same time, the cultivation of rice, a staple food of the region, declined considerably.

## Collectivization

The collectivization of agriculture was implemented on a limited scale in Tajikistan between 1927 and 1929, and much more aggressively between 1930 and 1934. The objective of Soviet agricultural policy was to expand the extent of cotton cultivation in Tajikistan as a whole, with particular emphasis on the southern part of the republic. The process included violence against peasants, substantial expansion of the irrigation network, and forcible resettlement of mountain people and people from Uzbekistan in the lowlands. Many peasants in Tajikistan fought forced collectivization, reviving the Basmachi movement in upland enclaves between 1930 and 1936. The interwar years also saw small-scale industrial development in the republic (see Industry, this ch.).

## The Purges

Like the CPSU branches elsewhere in the Soviet Union, the Communist Party of Tajikistan suffered waves of purges directed by the central government in Moscow between 1927 and 1934. Conditions particular to Tajikistan were used to provide additional justification for the crackdown. Many Tajik communists were highly critical of the ferocity with which the collectivization of agriculture was implemented, and central party authorities were dissatisfied with the local communists' advocacy of the republic's interests, including attempts to gain more autonomy and shield local intellectuals. About 70 percent of the party membership in Tajikistan—nearly 10,000 people at all levels of the organization—was expelled between 1933 and 1935. Between 1932 and 1937, the proportion of Tajiks in the republic's party membership dropped from 53 to 45 percent as the purges escalated. Many of those expelled from party and state offices were replaced by Russians sent in by the central government. Another round of purges took place in 1937 and 1938, during the Great Terror orchestrated by Joseph V. Stalin. Subsequently Russians dominated party positions at all levels, including the top position of first secretary. Whatever their nationality, party officials representing Tajikistan, unlike those from some other Soviet republics, had little influence in nationwide politics throughout the existence of the Soviet Union.

## The Postwar Period

The post-World War II era saw the expansion of irrigated agriculture, the further development of industry, and a rise in the level of education in Tajikistan. Like the rest of the Soviet Union, Tajikistan felt the effects of the party and government reorganization projects of Soviet leader Nikita S. Khrushchev (in office 1953–64). Especially in 1957 and 1958, Tajikistan's population and economy were manipulated as part of Khrushchev's overly ambitious Virgin Lands project, a campaign to forcibly increase the extent of arable land in the Soviet Union. Under Khrushchev and his successor, Leonid I. Brezhnev (in office 1964–82), Tajikistan's borders were periodically redrawn as districts and provinces were recombined, abolished, and restored, while small amounts of territory were acquired from or ceded to neighboring republics.

During the Soviet period, the only Tajikistani politician to become important outside his region was Bobojon Ghafurov (1908–77), a Tajik who became prominent as the Stalinist first secretary of the Communist Party of Tajikistan in the late 1940s. After Stalin's death in 1953, Ghafurov, a historian by training, established himself as a prominent Asia scholar and magazine editor, injecting notes of Tajik nationalism into some of his historical writings.

The fate of Ghafurov's successors illustrates important trends in the politics of Soviet Central Asia in the second half of the twentieth century. The next first secretary, Tursunbai Uljabayev (in office 1956–61), was ousted amid accusations that he had falsified reports to exaggerate the success of cotton production in the republic (charges also leveled in the 1980s against Uzbekistan's leadership); apparently the central government also objected to Uljabayev's preferential appointments of his cronies from Leninobod Province to party positions (see Russification and Resistance, ch. 5). Uljabaev's replacement as first secretary, Jabbor Rasulov, was a veteran of the prestigious agricultural bureaucracy of the republic. Like first secretaries in the other Central Asian republics, Rasulov benefited from Brezhnev's policy of "stability of cadres" and remained in office until Brezhnev's death in 1982.

Rasulov's successor, Rahmon Nabiyev, was a man of the Brezhnevite political school, who, like his predecessor, had spent much of his career in the agricultural bureaucracy. Nabiyev held office until ousted in 1985 as Soviet leader Mikhail S. Gorbachev (in office 1985–91) swept out the repub-

217

lic's old-guard party leaders. Nabiyev's 1991 installation as president of independent Tajikistan, by means of an old-guard coup and a rigged election, exacerbated the political tensions in the republic and was an important step toward the civil war that broke out in 1992.

All the post-Stalin party first secretaries came from Leninobod, in keeping with a broader phenomenon of Tajikistani politics from the postwar period to the collapse of the Soviet Union—the linkage between regional cliques, especially from Leninobod Province, and political power. Although certain cliques from Leninobod were dominant, they allowed allies from other provinces a lesser share of power. As the conflict in the early1990s showed, supporters of opposing camps could be found in all the country's provinces.

The forces of fragmentation in the Soviet Union eventually affected Tajikistan, whose government strongly supported continued unity. Bowing to Tajik nationalism, Tajikistan's Supreme Soviet adopted a declaration of sovereignty in August 1990, but in March 1991, the people of Tajikistan voted overwhelmingly for preservation of the union in a national referendum. That August the Moscow coup against the Gorbachev government brought mass demonstrations by opposition groups in Dushanbe, forcing the resignation of President Kahar Mahkamov. Nabiyev assumed the position of acting president. The following month, the Supreme Soviet proclaimed Tajikistan an independent state, following the examples of Uzbekistan and Kyrgyzstan. In November, Nabiyev was elected president of the new republic, and in December, representatives of Tajikistan signed the agreement forming the Commonwealth of Independent States (CIS—see Glossary) to succeed the Soviet Union.

Antigovernment demonstrations began in Dushanbe in March 1992. In April 1992, tensions mounted as progovernment groups opposing reform staged counterdemonstrations. By May, small armed clashes had occurred, causing Nabiyev to break off negotiations with the reformist demonstrators and go into hiding. After eight antigovernment demonstrators were killed in Dushanbe, the commander of the Russian garrison brokered a compromise agreement creating a coalition government in which one-third of the cabinet positions would go to members of the opposition. The collapse of that government heralded the outbreak of a civil war that plagued Tajikistan for the next four years (see Transition to Post-Soviet Government, this ch.).

## Physical Environment

Mountains cover 93 percent of Tajikistan's surface area. The two principal ranges, the Pamir and the Alay, give rise to many glacier-fed streams and rivers, which have been used to irrigate farmlands since ancient times. Central Asia's other major mountain range, the Tian Shan, skirts northern Tajikistan. Mountainous terrain separates Tajikistan's two population centers, which are in the lowlands of the southern and northern sections of the country. Especially in areas of intensive agricultural and industrial activity, the Soviet Union's natural resource utilization policies left independent Tajikistan with a legacy of environmental problems.

### Dimensions and Borders

With an area of 143,100 square kilometers, Tajikistan is about the same size as the state of Wisconsin. Its maximum east-to-west extent is 700 kilometers, and its maximum north-to-south extent is 350 kilometers. The country's highly irregular border is about 3,000 kilometers long, including 430 kilometers along the Chinese border to the east and 1,030 kilometers along the frontier with Afghanistan to the south. Most of the southern border with Afghanistan is set by the Amu Darya (*darya* is the Persian word for river) and its tributary the Panj River (Darya-ye Panj), which has headwaters in Afghanistan and Tajikistan. The other neighbors are the former Soviet republics of Uzbekistan (to the west and the north) and Kyrgyzstan (to the north).

### Topography and Drainage

The lower elevations of Tajikistan are divided into northern and southern regions by a complex of three mountain chains that constitute the westernmost extension of the massive Tian Shan system. Running essentially parallel from east to west, the chains are the Turkestan, Zarafshon, and Hisor (Gisar) mountains (see fig. 11). The last of these lies just north of the capital, Dushanbe, which is situated in west-central Tajikistan.

More than half of Tajikistan lies above an elevation of 3,000 meters. Even the lowlands, which are located in the Fergana Valley in the far north and in the southwest, are well above sea level. In the Turkestan range, highest of the western chains, the maximum elevation is 5,510 meters. The highest elevations of this range are in the southeast, near the border with Kyrgyzstan. That region is dominated by the peaks of the Pamir-Alay mountain system, including two of the three highest elevations in the former Soviet Union: Mount Lenin (7,134 meters) and Mount Communism (7,495 meters). Several other peaks in the region also exceed 7,000 meters. The mountains contain numerous glaciers, the largest of which, the Fedchenko, covers more than 700 square kilometers and is the largest glacier in the world outside the polar regions. Because Tajikistan lies in an active seismic belt, severe earthquakes are common.

The Fergana Valley, the most densely populated region in Central Asia, spreads across northern Tajikistan from Uzbekistan on the west to Kyrgyzstan on the east (see fig. 1). This long valley, which lies between two mountain ranges, reaches its lowest elevation of 320 meters at Khujand on the Syrdariya. Rivers bring rich soil deposits into the Fergana Valley from the surrounding mountains, creating a series of fertile oases that have long been prized for agriculture (see Agriculture, this ch.).

In Tajikistan's dense river network, the largest rivers are the Syrdariya and the Amu Darya; the largest tributaries are the Vakhsh and the Kofarnihon, which form valleys from northeast to southwest across western Tajikistan. The Amu Darya carries more water than any other river in Central Asia. The upper course of the Amu Darya, called the Panj River, is 921 kilometers long. The river's name changes at the confluence of the Panj, the Vakhsh, and the Kofarnihon rivers in far southwestern Tajikistan. The Vakhsh, called the Kyzyl-Suu upstream in Kyrgyzstan and the Surkhob in its middle course in north-central Tajikistan, is the second largest river in southern Tajikistan after the Amu-Panj system. In the Soviet era, the Vakhsh was dammed at several points for irrigation and electric power generation, most notably at Norak (Nurek), east of Dushanbe, where one of the world's highest dams forms the Norak Reservoir. Numerous factories also were built along the Vakhsh to draw upon its waters and potential for electric power generation.

The two most important rivers in northern Tajikistan are the Syrdariya and the Zarafshon. The former, the second longest river in Central Asia, stretches 195 kilometers (of its total length of 2,400 kilometers) across the Fergana Valley in far-northern Tajikistan. The Zarafshon River runs 316 kilometers (of a total length of 781 kilometers) through the center of Tajikistan. Tajikistan's rivers reach high-water levels twice a year: in the spring, fed by the rainy season and melting moun-

Figure 11. Tajikistan: Topography

KAZAKSTAN

KYRGYZSTAN

UZBEKISTAN

KYRGYZSTAN

UZBEKISTAN

CHINA

AFGHANISTAN

PAKISTAN

Syrdariya

Qayroqqum
Reservoir

Qarokul

Dushanbe

International boundary
National capital

I   Turkestan Range
II  Zarafshon Range
III Hisor Range
IV  Pamirs
V   Fedchenko Glacier

0   25  50  75  Kilometers

0   25   50   75  Miles

Boundary representation not
necessarily authoritative

tain snow, and in the summer, fed by melting glaciers. The summer freshets are the more useful for irrigation, especially in the Fergana Valley and the valleys of southeastern Tajikistan. Most of Tajikistan's lakes are of glacial origin and are located in the Pamir region. The largest, the Qarokul (Kara-Kul), is a salt lake devoid of life, lying at an elevation of 4,200 meters.

## Climate

In general, Tajikistan's climate is continental, subtropical, and semiarid, with some desert areas. The climate changes drastically according to elevation, however. The Fergana Valley and other lowlands are shielded by mountains from Arctic air masses, but temperatures in that region still drop below freezing for more than 100 days a year. In the subtropical southwestern lowlands, which have the highest average temperatures, the climate is arid, although some sections now are irrigated for farming. At Tajikistan's lower elevations, the average temperature range is 23° to 30° C in July and –1° to 3°C in January. In the eastern Pamirs, the average July temperature is 5° to 10°C, and the average January temperature is –15° to –20°C. The average annual precipitation for most of the republic ranges between 700 and 1,600 millimeters. The heaviest precipitation falls are at the Fedchenko Glacier, which averages 2,236 millimeters per year, and the lightest in the eastern Pamirs, which average less than 100 millimeters per year. Most precipitation occurs in the winter and spring.

## Environmental Problems

Most of Tajikistan's environmental problems are related to the agricultural policies imposed on the country during the Soviet period. By 1991 heavy use of mineral fertilizers and agricultural chemicals was a major cause of pollution in the republic. Among those chemicals were DDT, banned by international convention, and several defoliants and herbicides. In addition to the damage they have done to the air, land, and water, the chemicals have contaminated the cottonseeds whose oil is used widely for cooking. Cotton farmers and their families are at particular risk from the overuse of agricultural chemicals, both from direct physical contact in the field and from the use of the branches of cotton plants at home for fuel. All of these toxic sources are believed to contribute to a high incidence of maternal and child mortality and birth defects. In 1994 the infant mortality rate was 43.2 per 1,000 births, the second highest rate among former Soviet republics. The rate in 1990 had been 40.0 infant deaths per 1,000 births (see table 5, Appendix; Health Conditions, this ch.).

Cotton requires particularly intense irrigation (see Agriculture, this ch.). In Tajikistan's cotton-growing regions, farms were established in large, semiarid tracts and in tracts reclaimed from the desert, but cotton's growing season is summer, when the region receives virtually no rainfall. The 50 percent increase in cotton cultivation mandated by Soviet and post-Soviet agricultural planners between 1964 and 1994 consequently overtaxed the regional water supply. Poorly designed irrigation networks led to massive runoff, which increased soil salinity and carried toxic agricultural chemicals downstream to other fields, the Aral Sea, and populated areas of the region.

By the 1980s, nearly 90 percent of water use in Central Asia was for agriculture. Of that quantity, nearly 75 percent came from the Amu Darya and the Syrdariya, the chief tributaries of the Aral Sea on the Kazakstan-Uzbekistan border to the northwest of Tajikistan. As the desiccation of the Aral Sea came to international attention in the 1980s, water-use policy became a contentious issue between Soviet republics such as Tajikistan, where the main rivers rise, and those farther downstream, including Uzbekistan. By the end of the Soviet era, the central government had relinquished central control of water-use policy for Central Asia, but the republics had not agreed on an allocation policy.

Industry also causes pollution problems. A major offender is the production of nonferrous metals. One of Tajikistan's leading industrial sites, the aluminum plant at Regar (also known as Tursunzoda), west of Dushanbe near the border with Uzbekistan, generates large amounts of toxic waste gases that have been blamed for a sharp increase in the number of birth defects among people who live within range of its emissions.

In 1992 the Supreme Soviet of Tajikistan established a Ministry of Environmental Protection. However, the enforcement activity of the ministry was limited severely by the political upheavals that plagued Tajikistan in its first years of independence (see Transition to Post-Soviet Government, this ch.). The only registered private environmental group in Tajikistan in the early 1990s was a chapter of the Social-Ecological Alliance, the largest informal environmental association in the former Soviet Union. The Tajikistani branch's main functions have been to conduct environmental research and to organize protests against the Roghun Hydroelectric Plant project (see Energy, this ch.).

# Population

Tajikistan's population has been characterized as primarily rural, with a relatively high birth rate and substantial ethnic tensions. Substantial forced relocation has occurred, first as a result of various Soviet programs and then because of the civil war.

By the time Tajikistan became independent, its social structure reflected some of the changes that Soviet policy had consciously promoted, including urbanization, nearly universal adult literacy, and the increased employment of women outside the home. However, the changes were not as far-reaching as the central government had intended, nor did they take the exact form the government wanted. Tajikistan's cities grew, but the republic remained predominantly rural. More women had wage-paying jobs, but society still held traditional women's roles in higher regard. Tajikistan had an especially high birth rate and the highest rate of population increase of all the former Soviet republics.

## Population Characteristics

The 1970 census showed a population of 2,899,602. Overall, the rate of growth, which averaged 3.1 percent per year in the 1970s, rose to an annual average of 3.4 percent in the 1980s. According to the last Soviet census, taken in 1989, Tajikistan's population was 5,092,603. Since that time, no reliable estimate has been available; however, in the 1990s conditions in the country seem likely to preclude continuation of the rapid population increases of the 1970s and 1980s. The main factor in that change is the civil war and its repercussions: an estimated 50,000 dead, extensive shifting of populations within Tajikistan, heavy emigration, and a decreased birth rate caused by political turmoil and a plummeting standard of living. The birth rate was estimated at 3.0 percent in 1992.

Tajikistan's population is concentrated at the lower elevations; 90 percent of its inhabitants live in valleys, often in densely concentrated urban centers. In mid-1991, the overall population density for the republic was 38.2 persons per square kilometer, but density varied greatly among the provinces. In the northern Khujand Province, the density was 61.2; in the two southern provinces of Qurghonteppa and Kulob (which, at the time of the census and again after the civil war, merged into a single province, Khatlon), 71.5; in those districts not part of any province, including Dushanbe, 38.9; and in the eastern-most jurisdictions, the mountainous Gorno-Badakhshan Autonomous Province, whose borders encompass more than 40 percent of Tajikistan's territory, only 2.6.

The mountain areas, which never have been densely populated, lost many of their inhabitants beginning in the 1930s through a combination of voluntary migration in pursuit of better opportunities, forced relocations to the lowlands, and the destruction of villages for construction of Soviet-sponsored hydroelectric dams. This pattern reversed partially after 1992, as people fled to the mountains to escape the civil war.

According to the 1989 census, Tajikistan's population was overwhelmingly young and 50.3 percent female. People under age thirty made up 75 percent of the population; people under age fifteen were 47 percent of the total (see table 3, Appendix).

In the last two decades of the Soviet era, Tajikistan had the highest birth rate of any Soviet republic (see table 2, Appendix). Average family size in the republic, according to the 1989 census, was 6.1 people, the largest in the Soviet Union. The average Tajik woman gave birth to between seven and nine children. The average annual population growth rate for rural Tajikistan in the 1970s and 1980s was higher than the rate for urban areas.

The two main causes of Tajikistan's growth pattern were the high value placed by society on large families and the virtual absence of birth control, especially in rural areas, where the majority of the population lived. Women under the age of twenty gave birth to 5.1 percent of the babies born in Tajikistan in 1989, and a relatively high proportion of women continued to have children late into their child-bearing years. According to the 1989 census, 2 percent of all the babies born in Tajikistan were born to women between the ages of forty and forty-four; 81 percent of those babies had been preceded by at least six other children.

In the late 1980s, the Soviet government reacted to the high birth rate by encouraging family planning. The plan failed because of poor promotion of the pronatalist policy in the European republics of the union, inadequate birth control methods, and the Tajiks' traditional admiration for large families and opposition to birth control. In rural areas, the inade-

*Town of Kalay-Kum, across the Panj River from Afghanistan*
*Playing* bozkashi, *a traditional game played on horseback*
*Courtesy Stephane Herbert*

quacies of health care and the reluctance of women to undergo gynecological examinations contributed to the failure of family planning prior to independence.

## Urbanization

Statistically, Tajikistan is the least urban of all the former Soviet republics (see table 3, Appendix). By the 1980s, the republic had nineteen cities and forty-nine "urban-type settlements" (the term used for populated places developed as part of Soviet planning). At the time of the first Soviet census, in 1926, when Tajikistan still was an autonomous republic of Uzbekistan, only 10 percent of its inhabitants lived in cities. By the 1959 census, urbanization had risen to 33 percent. This growth reflected not only the development of Tajikistan in its own right but the resettlement of people from other parts of the Soviet Union to occupy government, party, and military positions. It also reflected an influx of political deportees. Most of the immigrants went to Tajikistan's two largest cities, Dushanbe and Leninobod. During the period before 1960, some populated places also were reclassified as urban or incorporated into an existing city's boundaries, thus creating an impression of even greater urbanization.

The growth of the urban population continued for most of the postwar era. Between the 1959 and 1979 censuses, Tajikistan's urban population more than doubled, while the rural population increased almost as rapidly. However, by the 1970s the rate of rural population growth had begun to outstrip that of urban areas. After reaching a peak of 35 percent in the 1979 census, the proportion of the urban population declined.

According to the 1989 census, although Tajikistan's urban population increased by 26 percent in the 1980s, the proportion of urban inhabitants in the total population declined to 32.5 percent during that period. By the start of 1991, the republic's five largest cities, Dushanbe, Khujand, Kulob, Qurghonteppa, and Uroteppa, accounted for 17 percent of the total population of the republic. Beginning with the 1979 census, emigration from cities exceeded immigration into them. In the 1980s, urban immigration also came predominantly from within Tajikistan rather than from other Soviet republics, as had been the case in earlier decades. As other ethnic groups emigrated from Tajikistan more rapidly beginning in the late Soviet period, the percentage of Tajiks in the cities rose. Nevertheless, Tajiks in Tajikistan were one of the Soviet nationalities least likely to move from villages to cities. Those who did so were usually single men reacting to the scarcity of employment in rural areas.

Tajikistan's largest city, Dushanbe (which was called Stalinabad from 1929 to 1961), was a Soviet-era development. Badly battered in the Russian Civil War of 1918–21, the village experienced a population drop from more than 3,000 in 1920 to 283 by 1924, and few buildings remained intact. Nevertheless, in 1924 Dushanbe was chosen as the capital of the new Tajikistan Autonomous Soviet Socialist Republic. Centrally planned development projects inaugurated in 1926, 1938, 1965, and 1983 established housing, government office buildings, cultural facilities, and sports and recreational facilities, as well as the municipal infrastructure. With the addition of about 100 factories, Dushanbe also became Tajikistan's industrial center. It is the headquarters of the republic's radio and television broadcasting facilities and film studio. Several institutions of higher education and scholarship are located there.

Soviet-era industrial development projects played a major role in the growth of cities on the sites of former villages. For example, Regar, which was established in 1952, is the center of Tajikistan's vital aluminum industry, as well as several factories dedicated to other activities. Norak and Yovon (Russian spelling Yavan—site of a large chemical plant), were developed as industrial centers near Dushanbe to play specific economic roles in the Soviet system.

## The Rural Majority

In the last decade of the Soviet era, the rural population of Tajikistan grew in both absolute and relative terms. By 1989 the rural population had risen to 3,437,498, or 68 percent of the total population, an increase of nearly 1 million people over the 1979 figure. By the 1980s, the republic had more than 3,000 inhabited villages, of which about one-quarter had 200 inhabitants or fewer. Observers have estimated that 75 to 89 percent of all Tajikistantis were villagers in 1990.

The rural standard of living is considerably below that of urban areas. Sanitation often is poor, and in many cases no safe source of drinking water is available. By the late 1980s, fewer than half of rural inhabitants and only 14 percent of collective farm residents had a piped-in water supply. In the same period, hundreds of villages lacked electricity, and some had no access to telephones or radio or television broadcasts (see Transportation and Telecommunications, this ch.). Many rural areas experienced shortages of doctors and teachers. The ratio of hospital beds to inhabitants is much lower in rural Tajikistan than in urban areas and far worse than the average for the former Soviet Union as a whole (see Health Care System, this ch.). Even large villages are unlikely to have libraries or other cultural facilities.

## Gender and Family Structure

The Soviet era saw the implementation of policies designed to transform the status of women. During the 1930s, the Soviet authorities launched a campaign for women's equality in Tajikistan, as they did elsewhere in Central Asia. Eventually major changes resulted from such programs, but initially they provoked intense public opposition. For example, women who appeared in public without the traditional all-enveloping veil were ostracized by society or even killed by relatives for supposedly shaming their families by what was considered unchaste behavior.

World War II brought an upsurge in women's employment outside the home. With the majority of men removed from their civilian jobs by the demands of war, women compensated for the labor shortage. Although the employment of indigenous women in industry continued to grow even after the war, they remained a small fraction of the industrial labor force after independence. In the early 1980s, women made up 51 percent of Tajikistan's population and 52 percent of the work force on collective farms, but only 38 percent of the industrial labor force, 16 percent of transportation workers, 14 percent of communications workers, and 28 percent of civil servants. (These statistics include women of Russian and other non-Central Asian nationalities.) In some rural parts of the republic, about half the women were not employed at all outside the home in the mid-1980s. In the late Soviet era, female underemployment was an important political issue in Tajikistan because it was linked to the Soviet propaganda campaign portraying Islam as a regressive influence on society.

The issue of female employment was more complicated than was indicated by Soviet propaganda, however. Many women remained in the home not only because of traditional attitudes about women's roles but also because many lacked vocational training and few child care facilities were available. By the end of the 1980s, Tajikistan's preschools could accommodate only

16.5 percent of the children of appropriate age overall and only 2.4 percent of the rural children. Despite all this, women provided the core of the work force in certain areas of agriculture, especially the production of cotton and some fruits and vegetables. Women were underrepresented in government and management positions relative to their proportion of the republic's population. The Communist Party of Tajikistan, the government (especially the higher offices), and economic management organizations were largely directed by men.

In the last decades of the twentieth century, Tajik social norms and even de facto government policy still often favored a traditionalist, restrictive attitude toward women that tolerated wife beating and the arbitrary dismissal of women from responsible positions. In the late Soviet period, Tajik girls still commonly married while under age despite official condemnation of this practice as a remnant of the "feudal" Central Asian mentality.

Tajik society never has been organized by tribal affiliation. The core of the traditional social structure of Tajiks and other sedentary peoples of Central Asia is usually the extended family, which is composed of an adult couple, their unmarried daughters, and their married sons and their wives and children. Such a group normally has joint ownership of the family homestead, land, crops, and livestock. The more prosperous a family, the more members it is likely to have. In the 1930s, some particularly wealthy Tajik families had fifty members or more. Although Islam permits polygamy, that practice has been illegal in Tajikistan for about seventy years; monogamy is the more typical form of spousal relationship because of the high bride-price traditionally required of suitors.

Traditional family ties remain strong. Tajikistan had one of the highest percentages of people living in families rather than singly in the Soviet Union. According to the 1989 census, 69 percent of the men aged sixteen or older and 67 percent of the women in that age group were married, 2 percent of the men and 10 percent of the women were widowers or widows, and 1.7 percent of the men and 4 percent of the women were divorced or separated. Only 7.5 percent of men over age forty and 0.4 percent of women over forty never had been married.

The strength of the family is sometimes misinterpreted as simply a consequence of Islam's influence on Tajik society. However, rural societies in general often emphasize the family as a social unit, and Islam does not forbid divorce. Grounds for

divorce in Tajikistan include childlessness, emotional estrange-
ment (in some cases the result of arranged marriages), a shortage of housing, drunkenness, and economic dissatisfaction.
The highest rate of divorce is in Dushanbe, which has not only
an acute housing shortage but a large number of inhabitants
belonging to non-Central Asian nationalities. Marriage across
nationality lines is relatively uncommon. Ethnically mixed marriages are almost twice as likely to occur in urban as in rural
areas.

## Emigration

After the Soviet census of 1989, a wave of emigration
occurred. In the absence of a more recent census, the scale of
that movement has not been determined reliably. It is known
that non-Central Asians, especially Russians, were a large component of the émigré group. According to one estimate, about
200,000 Tajikistani citizens had left by early 1992. Among the
causes of emigration in the late Soviet and early independence
eras were opposition to the 1989 law that made Tajik the official language of the republic, resentment of the growing
national assertiveness of Tajiks, dissatisfaction with the standard of living in the republic, fear of violence directed against
non-Central Asians (a fear based partly on the Dushanbe riots
of 1990 but intensified by rumor and the propaganda of communist hard-liners looking for support against a rising opposition), and, in 1992, the escalation of political violence into
outright civil war. Some of the people who left Tajikistan were
Germans and Jews who emigrated not just from the republic
but from the Soviet Union altogether.

According to the United Nations High Commissioner for
Refugees, 50,000 to 70,000 Tajiks fled from southern Tajikistan
to northern Afghanistan to escape the carnage of the civil war
that began in 1992. The total number of people who fled their
homes during the troubles of 1992 and 1993, either for other
parts of Tajikistan or for other countries, is estimated to be at
least 500,000. Most of these people probably returned to their
home districts in 1993 or 1994, with help from foreign governments and international aid organizations. The return entailed
hardships for many. Some were harmed or threatened by
armed bands from the victorious side in the civil war. For others the difficulty lay in the devastation of homes and the collapse of the economy in districts battered by the war.

Regardless of motive, the increased emigration in the late 1980s and early 1990s deprived the republic of needed skilled workers and professionals. The number of doctors and teachers declined, and industries lost trained workers who could not be replaced.

## Ethnic Groups

In creating the new Central Asian republics in the 1920s, the central political leadership arbitrarily defined national identities, which until that time had had little political importance. In the case of the Tajiks, this meant not only differentiating them from the Uzbeks, with whom they had much in common despite their different native languages, but also from fellow Persian-speakers outside the Soviet Union. Although the labels "Tajik" and "Uzbek" were not Soviet inventions, they had little meaning to many of the people to whom they were suddenly applied. This circumstance led to much confusion when people were required to identify themselves by one of these two national designations.

The Tajiks' language, which they traditionally had called Persian (Farsi), was relabeled Tajik. Major Persian-language writers were called Tajiks, even if they had not used that term to describe themselves and had not lived in Central Asia. Tajik, like the other Central Asian languages, underwent a two-stage alphabet reform by order of the Soviet regime. First, the Arabic alphabet was abandoned in 1929 in favor of the Latin. Then, in 1940 Moscow declared Cyrillic the official alphabet of the Tajik language.

Meanwhile, during the 1930s and 1940s Tajik culture was redefined and Sovietized to suit the political requirements of the central government of Soviet leader Joseph V. Stalin. In this period, the accusation of "bourgeois nationalism" could destroy a member of the intelligentsia or a political figure. In the renewed wave of Stalinist repression after World War II, Tajik intellectuals were purged for being nationalists, a loosely defined offense that could be applied to any form of opposition to central government policies.

By the time Tajikistan became an independent republic in 1991, its multiethnic population included an ethnic majority of Tajiks and an even larger religious majority of Muslims (see table 4, Appendix). Despite Soviet claims that ethnic and religious loyalties had diminished sharply and were bound for extinction, there were strong indications in the late 1980s and early 1990s that ethnic and religious identities remained essentially intact. Indeed, those factors began to exert greater influence as Soviet controls weakened and people sought alternative ideologies.

According to the latest census, taken in 1989, Tajikistan had a population of 5,092,603, of whom Tajiks constituted about 3.17 million, or 62.3 percent. The accuracy of subsequent population estimates suffers from the region's large-scale population movement. In 1989 about three-quarters of all Tajiks in the Soviet Union lived in Tajikistan. Of the remaining 1 million Tajiks, about 933,000 lived in neighboring Uzbekistan. Much smaller Tajik populations lived in Afghanistan and China. The other major nationalities living in Tajikistan were Uzbeks, 23.5 percent (1,197,841); Russians, 7.6 percent (388,481); Volga Tatars, 1.4 percent (72,228); and Kyrgyz, 1.3 percent (63,832). In order of size, the remaining 3.9 percent included populations of Ukrainians, Germans, Turkmen, Koreans, Jews (including those of European ancestry and "Bukhoran Jews," whose ancestors had lived in Central Asia for centuries), Belorussians, Crimean Tatars, and Armenians.

Although ethnically classified with the Tajiks in the Soviet era, several Eastern Iranian peoples who had not been assimilated over the centuries by their Persian- or Turkic-speaking neighbors preserved distinct identities. These groups were the Yaghnobs and seven Pamiri peoples. At the end of the Soviet era, the Dushanbe government allowed some leeway for education, broadcasting, and publication in the Pamiri languages. However, these limited reforms were more than outweighed by the repression that the victors in the civil war directed against the Pamiris in 1992 on the grounds that they tended to support political reform.

In the last decade of Soviet power, Tajiks became a larger proportion of the republic's total population. The 62.3 percent they constituted in the 1989 census was an increase from their 58.8 percent proportion in the 1979 census. This trend seemed likely to continue into the late 1990s, barring such countervailing factors as civil war and emigration, because Tajiks accounted for 70 percent of the republic's natural population increase in 1989.

For much of the Soviet era, the central government used inducements such as scholarships and cash bonuses, as well as outright reassignment, to increase the settlement of Russian workers in Tajikistan. In the 1920s and 1930s, the small number of Tajikistanis with industrial and professional skills prompted the central authorities to relocate individuals with special expertise to Tajikistan, and Moscow sent many other people as political prisoners. By 1940 roughly half of the republic's industrial work force belonged to nonindigenous nationalities; most of these people were Russian. The engineering profession had a particularly large proportion of Russians and other non-Central Asians. Non-Central Asians settled in Tajikistan during World War II as industries and their workers were shifted east of the Ural Mountains to prevent their capture by the German army. Additional Russians and other Europeans went to Tajikistan in this period as war refugees or political deportees. As a result, between 1926 and 1959 the proportion of Russians among Tajikistan's population grew from less than 1 percent to 13 percent. During the same period, the proportion of Tajiks dropped from 80 percent to about 50 percent. This figure fell especially fast during the agricultural collectivization of the 1930s.

Because of the prominence of Russians and other non-Tajiks in such urban activities as government and industry, Dushanbe, the capital, became a predominantly non-Tajik city. According to the 1989 census, Tajiks constituted 39.1 percent, Russians 32.4 percent, Uzbeks 10 percent, Tatars 4.1 percent, and Ukrainians 3.5 percent of Dushanbe's population of about 602,000. Although educated, urban Tajiks were likely to speak Russian well, few Russians living in Dushanbe spoke Tajik or felt a need to do so. This situation caused increasing resentment among Tajiks in the late 1980s and early 1990s.

By the end of the Soviet era, many educated Tajiks were criticizing what they perceived as the continued privileged position of Russians in society. Even after decades of improved education and indoctrination of younger generations of Tajiks, Russians and other nonindigenous peoples still occupied a disproportionate number of top positions in the republic's communist party (see Political Parties, this ch.). Tajiks also saw Russians perpetuating their dominance by hiring practices biased against Tajiks. By the end of the Soviet era, Tajiks often were a small minority in the administration of the republic's main industrial enterprises, including the chemical plants, the cotton textile industry, and large construction projects (see Labor, this ch.).

The preindependence government of Tajikistan made some provision for the distinctive needs of minority nationalities living within the republic's borders. It provided education, mass media, and cultural offerings in Russian (see Education; The Media, this ch.). In 1988 state radio began broadcasting in German, Kyrgyz, and Crimean Tatar. There were several Uzbek-language bookstores in the republic. Late in the Soviet era, Dushanbe had cultural centers for Uzbeks, Ukrainians, and members of other nationalities as well as restaurants that provided ethnic foods for Uzbeks, Tatars, Koreans, and Germans.

## Forces of Nationalism

Ethnic tensions increased in Tajikistan, as they did elsewhere in Central Asia, under the troubled conditions of the late Soviet era. Already in the late 1970s, some ethnic disturbances and anti-Soviet riots had occurred. One consequence of heightened resentment of Soviet power was violence directed at members of other nationalities, who were made scapegoats for their attackers' economic grievances (see Economic Conditions in the Early 1990s, this ch.). An example of this conflict was a clash between Tajiks and Kyrgyz over land and water claims in 1989. Antagonism between Uzbeks and Tajiks reached a new level during Tajikistan's civil war of 1992, when Uzbeks living in Tajikistan joined the faction attempting to restore a neo-Soviet regime to power (see Transition to Post-Soviet Government, this ch.).

In 1989 attacks on Meskhetians (one of the Muslim groups deported from Central Asia by Stalin) spilled over from Uzbekistan to Tajikistan when about 2,000 Meskhetians were evacuated from eastern Uzbekistan to a remote settlement in northern Tajikistan. A violent conflict between inhabitants of the area and the Meskhetians resulted in the intervention of security forces and removal of the Meskhetians entirely from Central Asia.

The late 1980s and early 1990s also saw open criticism by Tajiks of their treatment as a people by the central Soviet authorities and by their Turkic neighbors, especially the Uzbeks. A key issue was disparagement of the Tajik heritage in statements of Soviet nationalities policy, which labeled the Tajiks a "formerly backward" people that only began to progress under Russian and Soviet tutelage. Tajiks, who claimed a heritage of more than 2,000 years of Persian and Eastern Iranian civilization, also were indignant at the emphasis on Russian and Western civilization, at the expense of the Tajik heritage, in the history and literature curricula of Soviet-era schools in their republic. Soviet policy toward publication of literature and the two Soviet-mandated alphabet changes served to isolate Tajiks from their cultural heritage.

One of the important consequences of the growth of Tajik nationalism in the late Soviet era was the enactment in 1989 of a law declaring Tajik the state language (although the use of Russian, Uzbek, or other languages was still recognized under some circumstances). The law officially equated Tajik with Persian and called for a gradual reintroduction of the Arabic alphabet. By the early 1990s, however, the law's main impact was to alarm the republic's Russian speakers; although some Russian loanwords were dropped in favor of contemporary Iranian Persian terms, the use of the Arabic alphabet remained sharply limited.

Like the Russians, the Uzbeks were criticized for denying the Tajiks' distinctive ethnic identity and ancient roots in Central Asia. Tajik nationalists accused the authorities in Soviet Uzbekistan of practicing overt discrimination against the Tajik population by forcing Tajiks to register their nationality as Uzbek, undercounting the size of the Tajik minority in Uzbekistan, and failing to provide Tajiks there with adequate access to educational and cultural resources in Tajik. Tajik nationalists also complained that the central government and their Central Asian neighbors had exploited Tajikistan's raw materials and damaged its environment.

Although nationalism had an increased appeal in Tajikistan in the late Soviet and early independence periods, it was not a dominant political force there. No popular movement advocated secession from the Soviet Union before its dissolution at the end of 1991, although there was support for renegotiating the union treaty to obtain more favorable conditions for Tajikistan. In the late 1980s, supporters of the communist old guard played on nationalist feelings to enhance their own position, but after Tajikistan became independent, those individuals became increasingly antinationalist; identification with local patron-client networks continued to rival nationalism as a political force.

## Religion

Islam, the predominant religion of all of Central Asia, was brought to the region by the Arabs in the seventh century. Since that time, Islam has become an integral part of Tajik culture. Although Soviet efforts to secularize society were largely unsuccessful, the post-Soviet era has seen a marked increase in religious practice. The majority of Tajikistan's Muslims adhere to the Sunni (see Glossary) branch of Islam, and a smaller group belongs to the Shia (see Glossary) branch of that faith. Among other religions, the Russian Orthodox faith is the most widely practiced, although the Russian community shrank significantly in the early 1990s. Some other small Christian groups now enjoy relative freedom of worship. There also is a small Jewish community.

## Islam

The Sunni branch of Islam has a 1,200-year-old tradition among the sedentary population of Central Asia, including the Tajiks. A small minority group, the Pamiris, are members of a much smaller denomination of Shia Islam, Ismailism, which first won adherents in Central Asia in the early tenth century. Despite persecution, Ismailism has survived in the remote Pamir Mountains.

During the course of seven decades of political control, Soviet policy makers were unable to eradicate the Islamic tradition, despite repeated attempts to do so. The harshest of the Soviet anti-Islamic campaigns occurred from the late 1920s to the late 1930s as part of a unionwide drive against religion in general. In this period, many Muslim functionaries were killed, and religious instruction and observance were curtailed sharply. After the German invasion of the Soviet Union in 1941, official policy toward Islam moderated. One of the changes that ensued was the establishment in 1943 of an officially sanctioned Islamic hierarchy for Central Asia, the Muslim Board of Central Asia. Together with three similar organizations for other regions of the Soviet Union having large Muslim populations, this administration was controlled by the Kremlin, which required loyalty from religious officials. Although its administrative personnel and structure were inadequate to serve the needs of the Muslim inhabitants of the region, the administration made possible the legal existence of some Islamic institutions, as well as the activities of religious functionaries, a small number of mosques, and religious instruction at two seminaries in Uzbekistan.

In the early 1960s, the Khrushchev regime escalated anti-Islamic propaganda. Then, on several occasions in the 1970s and 1980s, the Kremlin leadership called for renewed efforts to combat religion, including Islam. Typically, such campaigns

*Morning ceremony of a Sufi
brotherhood group,
Naqshbandiya
Courtesy Stephane Herbert*

included conversion of mosques to secular use; attempts to reidentify traditional Islamic-linked customs with nationalism rather than religion; and propaganda linking Islam to backwardness, superstition, and bigotry. Official hostility toward Islam grew in 1979 with Soviet military involvement in nearby Afghanistan and the increasing assertiveness of Islamic revivalists in several countries. From that time through the early post-Soviet era, some officials in Moscow and in Tajikistan warned of an extremist Islamic menace, often on the basis of limited or distorted evidence. Despite all these efforts, Islam remained an important part of the identity of the Tajiks and other Muslim peoples of Tajikistan through the end of the Soviet era and the first years of independence.

Identification with Islam as an integral part of life is shared by urban and rural, old and young, and educated and uneducated Tajiks. The role that the faith plays in the lives of individuals varies considerably, however. For some Tajiks, Islam is more important as an intrinsic part of their cultural heritage than as a religion in the usual sense, and some Tajiks are not religious at all.

In any case, Tajiks have disproved the standard Soviet assertion that the urbanized industrial labor force and the educated population had little to do with a "remnant of a bygone era" such as Islam. A noteworthy development in the late Soviet and early independence eras was increased interest, especially among young people, in the substance of Islamic doctrine. In the post-Soviet era, Islam became an important element in the nationalist arguments of certain Tajik intellectuals.

Islam survived in Tajikistan in widely varied forms because of the strength of an indigenous folk Islam quite apart from the Soviet-sanctioned Islamic administration. Long before the Soviet era, rural Central Asians, including inhabitants of what became Tajikistan, had access to their own holy places. There were also small, local religious schools and individuals within their communities who were venerated for religious knowledge and piety. These elements sustained religion in the country-side, independent of outside events. Under Soviet regimes, Tajiks used the substantial remainder of this rural, popular Islam to continue at least some aspects of the teaching and practice of their faith after the activities of urban-based Islamic institutions were curtailed. Folk Islam also played an important role in the survival of Islam among the urban population. One form of this popular Islam is Sufism—often described as Islamic mysticism and practiced by individuals in a variety of ways. The most important form of Sufism in Tajikistan is the Naqshbandiyya, a Sufi order with followers as far away as India and Malaysia. Besides Sufism, other forms of popular Islam are associated with local cults and holy places or with individuals whose knowledge or personal qualities have made them influential.

By late 1989, the Gorbachev regime's increased tolerance of religion began to affect the practices of Islam and Russian Orthodoxy. Religious instruction increased. New mosques opened. Religious observance became more open, and participation increased. New Islamic spokesmen emerged in Tajikistan and elsewhere in Central Asia. The authority of the official, Tashkent-based Muslim Board of Central Asia crumbled in Tajikistan. Tajikistan acquired its own seminary in Dushanbe, ending its reliance on the administration's two seminaries in Uzbekistan.

By 1990 the Muslim Board's chief official in Dushanbe, the senior *qadi*, Hajji Akbar Turajonzoda (in office 1988–92), had become an independent public figure with a broad following. In the factional political battle that followed independence, Turajonzoda criticized the communist hard-liners and supported political reform and official recognition of the importance of Islam in Tajikistani society. At the same time, he repeatedly denied hard-liners' accusations that he sought the establishment of an Islamic government in Tajikistan. After the hard-liners' victory in the civil war at the end of 1992, Turajonzoda fled Dushanbe and was charged with treason.

Muslims in Tajikistan also organized politically in the early 1990s. In 1990, as citizens in many parts of the Soviet Union were forming their own civic organizations, Muslims from various parts of the union organized the Islamic Rebirth Party (IRP; see Political Parties, this ch.). By the early 1990s, the growth of mass political involvement among Central Asian Muslims led all political parties—including the Communist Party of Tajikistan—to take into account the Muslim heritage of the vast majority of Tajikistan's inhabitants.

Islam also played a key political role for the regime in power in the early 1990s. The communist old guard evoked domestic and international fears that fundamentalist Muslims would destabilize the Tajikistani government when that message was expedient in fortifying the hard-liners' position against opposition forces in the civil war. However, the Nabiyev regime also was willing to represent itself as an ally of Iran's Islamic republic while depicting the Tajik opposition as unfaithful Muslims.

## Other Religions

The vast majority of the non-Tajik population of Tajikistan is composed of peoples who were also historically Sunni Muslims (Uzbeks, Kyrgyz, Tatars, and Turkmen). The next largest religious community is presumably Russian Orthodox, the historical faith of many Ukrainians as well as Russians. A cathedral in Dushanbe, St. Nicholas, serves the Orthodox community. By the end of the Soviet era, Tajikistan also was home to small numbers of people belonging to other Christian denominations, including Roman Catholics (most of whom were German), Seventh-Day Adventists, and Baptists. There also was a small Armenian minority, most of whose members belonged historically to the Armenian Apostolic (Gregorian) Church. Other religious groups included small numbers of Jews and Bahais. The number of adherents to these minority religions probably decreased sharply in the 1990s because of the wave of emigration from Tajikistan in the early independence period.

## Culture and the Arts

As they did during the Soviet era, educated Tajiks define

their cultural heritage broadly, laying claim to the rich legacy of the supraethnic culture of Central Asia and other parts of the Islamic world from the eastern Mediterranean to India. Soviet rule institutionalized Western art forms, publishing, and mass media, some elements of which subsequently attracted spontaneous support in the republic. However, since the beginning of Soviet rule in the 1920s, the media and the arts always have been subject to political constraints.

## Literature

Despite long-standing Soviet efforts to differentiate between the Persian speakers of Central Asia and those elsewhere, Tajiks in Tajikistan describe all of the major literary works written in Persian until the twentieth century as Tajik, regardless of the ethnicity and native region of the author. In Soviet times, such claims were not merely a matter of chauvinism but a strategy to permit Tajiks some contact with a culture that was artificially divided by state borders. Nevertheless, very little Persian literature was published in Cyrillic transcription in the Soviet era.

Three writers dominated the first generation of Soviet Tajik literature. Sadriddin Aini (1878–1954), a Jadidist writer and educator who turned communist, began as a poet but wrote primarily prose in the Soviet era. His works include three major novels dealing with social issues in the region and memoirs that depict life in the Bukhoro Khanate. Aini became the first president of Tajikistan's Academy of Sciences.

Abu'l-Qasem Lahuti (1887–1957; in Tajik, Abdulqosim Lohuti) was an Iranian poet who emigrated to the Soviet Union for political reasons and eventually settled in Tajikistan. He wrote both lyric poetry and "socialist realist" verse. Another poet, Mirzo Tursunzoda (1911–77), collected Tajik oral literature, wrote poetry of his own about social change in Tajikistan, and turned out various works on popular political themes of the moment. Since the generation that included those three writers, Tajikistan has produced numerous poets, novelists, short story writers, and playwrights.

## Cultural Institutions

By the mid-1980s, more than 1,600 libraries were operating in Tajikistan. Of particular importance is the Firdavsi State Library, which houses a significant collection of Oriental manuscripts. In 1990 Tajikistan had twenty-seven museums, the fewest of any Soviet republic. Among the most notable are the

Behzed Museum of History, Regional Studies, and Art, and the Ethnographic Museum of the Academy of Sciences, both in Dushanbe. There are also significant museums of history and regional studies in several of the republic's other cities. The republic had fourteen theaters in 1990. Only the three Baltic republics, Kyrgyzstan, and Turkmenistan—all with smaller populations—had fewer. The republic's film studio, since 1958 called Tadzhikfil'm, opened in Dushanbe in 1930. By the mid-1980s, it was producing seven or eight feature films and thirty documentaries per year for cinemas and television.

The Soviet era saw the introduction of opera and ballet to Tajikistan, as well as the organization of Tajik-style song and dance troupes. Dushanbe's opera and ballet theater was the first large public building in the city; its construction began in 1939. Dushanbe also has theaters devoted to Tajik and Russian drama, as well as a drama school. There are theaters for music, musical comedy, and drama in several other Tajik cities as well.

Films are shown in theaters in Tajikistan's cities and in villages on an irregular basis. In the last decade of Soviet rule and in the early 1990s, video and audio cassettes became increasingly popular sources of entertainment, as well as a means of disseminating information outside government control. The political turmoil and economic problems of Tajikistan in the 1990s took a severe toll on the country's cultural life and on the elite that fostered it.

## Education

Soviet social policy created a modern education system in Tajikistan where nothing comparable had existed before. However, by the time the republic became independent the quality and availability of education had not reached the Soviet Union-wide average, still less the standards for Western industrial societies. After independence, the education system remained under the control of the national Ministry of Education with full state funding.

### Historical Development

By the 1920s, few Tajiks had received a formal education. According to the first Soviet census, in 1926 the literacy rate was 4 percent for Tajik men and 0.1 percent for Tajik women in the territory of present-day Tajikistan and in the Republic of Uzbekistan. During the late 1930s, the Soviet government began to expand the network of state-run schools. There was strong public opposition to this change, especially from Islamic leaders. As a result, some new state schools were burned and some teachers were killed.

Over the ensuing decades, however, the Soviet education system prevailed, although a uniform set of standards was not established in every instance. For the average Tajikistani citizen in the 1980s, the duration, if not necessarily the quality, of the education process was neither the greatest nor the least among Soviet republics. As elsewhere in the Soviet Union, the system was divided into schools for primary, middle (or secondary), and higher education. Middle schools were differentiated as either general or specialized. For the period between 1985 and 1990, an annual average of 86,800 students attended general-education middle schools and an average of 41,500 students attended specialized middle schools. In the academic year 1990–91, Tajikistan reported 68,800 students in institutions of higher education.

## Education in the 1980s and 1990s

Prior to 1991, the level of educational attainment in the adult Tajikistani population was below the average for Soviet republics. Of the population over age twenty-five in 1989, some 16 percent had only primary schooling, 21 percent had incomplete secondary schooling, and 55 percent had completed a secondary education. Those statistics placed Tajikistan ninth among the fifteen Soviet republics. Some 7.5 percent of inhabitants had graduated from an institution of higher education, placing Tajikistan last among Soviet republics in that category, and another 1.4 percent had acquired some higher education but not a degree.

In secondary education, 427 out of 1,000 Tajikistanis graduated from a nonspecialized middle school and another 211 out of 1,000 went through several grades of such schools without graduating. An additional 110 out of 1,000 had attended a specialized middle school. Despite the nominal emphasis placed by the Soviet system on science and mathematics, the quality of education in those subjects was rated as poor in the last decades of the Soviet period.

The languages of instruction in the state system were Tajik, Uzbek, Kyrgyz, and Russian. When Tajik became the state language in 1989, schools using Russian as the primary language of instruction began teaching Tajik as a second language from the first through the eleventh grades. After independence, school curricula included more Tajik language and literature study, including classical Persian literature. However, few textbooks were available in Tajik; by the end of the 1980s, only 10 to 25 percent of students attending Tajik-language schools had textbooks or other teaching materials in their own language.

By the late Soviet era, education in Tajikistan also suffered from infrastructure problems. School buildings were in poor repair. The construction industry, an area of particular weakness in the republic's economy, produced only a small fraction of the new school and preschool facilities it was assigned to complete each year. As a result, schools sometimes ran on triple shifts.

## Vocational Education

In the late Soviet era, the quality of technical training available in Tajikistan fell far below the standard for the Soviet Union as a whole. Graduates often were far less prepared for technical jobs than their counterparts elsewhere in the union. Many vocational schools were poorly equipped and lacked basic supplies. The general shortage of textbooks in Tajik also affected vocational courses. Although instruction was available in about 150 trades in 1990, that range fell far short of supplying the various types of expertise needed by the republic's economy. A large proportion of students in vocational secondary schools had poor skills in basic arithmetic and Russian. Although Tajikistan's population was nearly two-thirds rural, in 1990 only thirty-eight of eighty-five technical schools were located in the countryside, and fifteen of those were in serious disrepair. Many factories failed to provide students vocational training despite agreements to do so.

## Higher Education and Research

By the late 1980s, Tajikistan had twenty institutions of higher education. Despite the ample number of such institutions, the proportion of students receiving a higher education (115 per 10,000 inhabitants) was slightly below the average for the Soviet republics in the late 1980s. In scientific and technical fields, Tajikistan ranked near the bottom among Soviet republics in the proportion of residents receiving advanced degrees. During the Soviet era, Russian, rather than Tajik, was the preferred medium of instruction in several fields of higher education.

The first institution of higher education in Tajikistan was the State Pedagogical Institute in Dushanbe, which opened in 1931. Tajikistan State University opened in 1948. By the mid-1980s, about 14,000 students were enrolled in the university's thirteen departments. At that time, admission was highly competitive only for applicants seeking to study history, Oriental studies, Tajik philology, and economic planning. In 1994 the university had 864 faculty in fourteen departments and 6,196 full-time students.

The Tajikistan Polytechnic Institute opened in Dushanbe in 1956, then was reclassified as a university after independence. In 1994 it offered training in energy, construction, mechanical engineering, automobile repair, road building, and architecture. In 1996 preparations began to open a new university for the Pamiri peoples; it was to be located in Khorugh, the capital of Gorno-Badakhshan Autonomous Province.

# Health

Considering the virtual absence of modern health care in Tajikistan at the start of the Soviet era, the quality of medical services had improved markedly by the close of that era. Statistically, Tajikistan rated at or below the average for Soviet republics for most indicators of health conditions and health care delivery (see table 5, Appendix).

## Health Care System

After nearly seventy years of inclusion in the Soviet state, with its avowed aim of modernization, Tajikistan had a level of health care that was low both in absolute terms and by Soviet standards. State spending for health care and medical equipment in Tajikistan was a fraction of the average for the Soviet Union. Tajikistani regimes had long regarded social needs such as medical care as less important than economic development. Admission standards for the republic's best medical school, the Abu Ali ibn Sino Institute of Medicine in Dushanbe, were notoriously lax. In 1986, according to government statistics, Tajikistan had 325 hospitals with a total of 50,115 beds, 697 outpatient clinics, 1,313 paramedic and midwife facilities, and 567 maternity and pediatric clinics and hospitals. In 1994 the Ministry of Health reported 59,000 hospital beds. As in other parts of Central Asia, a large proportion of health care professionals in Tajikistan were members of nonindigenous nationali-

*Traditional herb doctor*
*preparing a potion in the*
*Pamir Mountains*
*Courtesy Stephane Herbert*

ties, especially Russians, Ukrainians, and Jews, many of whom emigrated after 1989. Within months of the February 1990 disturbances in Dushanbe, about 1,300 doctors and nurses emigrated from the republic.

In 1994 the republic had 13,000 doctors, one for every 447 inhabitants, by far the worst proportion among the Central Asian republics. The number of other health care workers, 80.3 per 1,000 inhabitants, was also far below the level for other republics. Rural Tajikistan suffered a particular deficiency of health care professionals. Dushanbe felt this scarcity less than the rest of the country.

In the late 1980s, the average number of hospital beds per 10,000 inhabitants in the Soviet Union was 130, but Tajikistan's proportion was 104.3 per 10,000. The figure was half that in rural areas. Dushanbe was estimated to have a 5,000-bed shortage, according to Soviet standards, in 1990. In the mid-1990s, there was a great backlog in the construction of new medical facilities. More than 80 percent of Tajikistan's health care facilities were evaluated as substandard, and most lacked running water and central heating. Only one drug treatment center existed in Dushanbe, with twenty to thirty beds, and there was no rehabilitation program (see Internal Security, this ch.).

Acquiring medicines is difficult or impossible for ordinary citizens. In some areas, one drug dispensary serves as many as

20,000 inhabitants, compared with the Soviet standard of one dispensary for every 8,000 people. According to one health organization, when the Soviet distribution system disappeared in 1992, Tajikistan, which had no modern pharmaceutical plants, lost access to 258 different kinds of drugs, including streptomycin and analgesics.

Since independence, steady reductions in the state health budget have further eroded the salaries of medical professionals and the availability of care. (In 1992 the Ministry of Health already had the smallest budget of the state ministries.) For that reason, health planners have considered privatization of the national health system an urgent priority. In the mid-1990s, however, little progress had been made toward that goal.

## Health Conditions

The life expectancy of a male born in Tajikistan in 1989 was 66.8 years, and of a female, 71.7 years. In 1989 this was the longest life span projection among the five Central Asian republics, but it was shorter than those of all the other Soviet republics except Moldavia. In Tajikistan, urban women had the longest life expectancy (72.9 years), and urban men had the shortest (65.2 years). According to the 1989 census, the most frequent causes of death in Tajikistan were infections and parasitic diseases, circulatory disorders, respiratory disorders, tumors, and accidents. Those causes accounted for 78 percent of the 33,395 deaths in that year. In the 1970s and the 1980s, Tajikistan's mortality rate rose from 8.5 to 9.8 per 100 male inhabitants and from 6.7 to 7.3 per 100 female inhabitants.

In the mid-1990s, the health of Tajikistan's citizens was threatened increasingly by the condition of the country's water supply, which conveyed disease-causing organisms as well as toxic chemicals from agricultural and industrial origins to the population. By the late Soviet era, cases of typhoid occurred thirteen times more frequently in Tajikistan than in the Soviet Union as a whole. The health of rural inhabitants was jeopardized by inadequate sanitation and improper storage of toxic substances, and by environmental pollution (see Environmental Problems, this ch.).

Maternal and infant mortality remained serious problems in Tajikistan in the 1990s. In 1988 Tajikistani women were 1.6 times more likely to die in childbirth than were women in the Soviet Union as a whole. By 1989, according to official statistics, forty of every 1,000 babies born in Tajikistan did not survive to the age of one year. In many parts of southern Tajikistan, the rate was more than sixty per thousand. (The rate of infant mortality was higher than indicated by official Soviet statistics, which were underreported in rural areas and often were adjusted downward.) Factors contributing to infant mortality include family poverty; inadequate nutrition for nursing mothers, babies, and schoolchildren (who receive inadequate meals in school); and a lack of safe drinking water. Experts believe that environmental pollution, especially that caused by the agricultural chemicals used in cotton production, plays a major role in the rising rates of maternal and child mortality, as well as in the relatively high incidence of birth defects.

Employment in heavy industry also poses health risks for women and their children. By the late 1980s, some 80 percent of low birth-weight babies were born to women employed in heavy industry at jobs posing the risk of physical injury. Most important of all was the poor quality of health care that mothers and infants received and the inadequacy of the maternal and child care facilities where care was delivered. By Soviet national standards, Tajikistan in the late 1980s lacked 8,000 beds in maternity facilities and 13,000 bed for infants. Problems related to infant and maternal health were more serious in rural areas than in the cities. Soviet studies linked infant death to poor preventive health care, a lack of proper medication, and a lack of professional medical care.

Narcotics use in Tajikistan is rated as a minor health problem; in 1995 there were an estimated 40,000 drug users in the country (see Internal Security, this ch.). Authorities discovered heroin traffic into the country in 1995. As of the end of 1995, Tajikistan had reported no cases of acquired immune deficiency syndrome (AIDS) to the World Health Organization, although the Ministry of Health reported that twenty-four AIDS diagnostic laboratories were in operation in 1993.

## The Economy

Tajikistan possesses many elements that will be needed to diversify its national economy after decades of specialization within the Soviet system. Significant deposits of gold, iron, lead, mercury, and tin exist, and some coal is present. Some regions have ample water for irrigation, and the country's rivers are a largely untapped source of hydroelectric power generation. The labor supply is sufficient, provided Tajikistan can retain qualified workers in critical fields. The civil war of 1992–

93, the collapse of the integrated Soviet economic system, and the lack of significant economic reform by the post-civil war government all have severely impeded economic performance, however.

Economic problems that had developed in Tajikistan during the Soviet era persisted into the first decade of independence. These included overreliance on production of cotton and raw materials in general, a high level of unemployment, and a low standard of living. Although the old Soviet economic system ceased to exist officially, several aspects of it survived after 1991. The transition to a market economy progressed slowly, and Russia and other former Soviet republics continued to play an important role in Tajikistan's economy. Yet Tajikistan also took the first steps toward developing economic relations with a wide assortment of other countries. Quite apart from the deliberate changes implemented by policy makers, the economy of Tajikistan was profoundly affected in the early stages of its independence by the political turmoil that accompanied the transition.

## Agriculture

In the early 1990s, Tajikistan remained primarily an agricultural state. In 1990 agriculture contributed 38 percent of the country's net material product (NMP—see Glossary). Despite development of an extensive irrigation network in the Soviet era, water supply problems combined with Tajikistan's mountainous topography to limit agriculture to 8 percent of the republic's land in 1990. Some 800,000 hectares were under cultivation in 1990, of which about 560,000 hectares were irrigated. The irrigated land was used mostly to grow cotton; potatoes, vegetables, and grains also were cultivated (see table 16, Appendix). In 1994 the republic produced about 490,000 tons of vegetables and about 254,000 tons of cereals. The dominance of cotton combined with the rapidly growing population to render Tajikistan unable to meet domestic consumption requirements for some basic foodstuffs, especially meat and dairy products, in the last years of the Soviet era, even though the republic produced a surplus of fruits, vegetables, and eggs. In the early 1990s, about 98 percent of agricultural labor remained almost entirely unmechanized.

Through the mid-1990s, agricultural output continued to decline precipitously as a consequence of the civil war and the awkward transition to a post-Soviet economy. By 1995 overall

*Head accountant of a cotton processing plant, Regar*
*Courtesy Stephane Herbert*

production was estimated at about half the 1990 level, and
shortages continued in urban areas. Besides the civil war, low
prices for agricultural products and a shortage of animal feed
contributed to the decline. Hardly any privatization of collective farms had occurred by the mid-1990s.

Cotton is by far the most important crop in Tajikistan's agrarian economy. In parts of the republic, 85 percent of the land
was planted to cotton by the late 1980s, a figure that even
republic officials described as excessive. At the same time, the
average cotton yield per hectare was about half that achieved in
the United States. Cotton production declined in the early
1990s. In 1993 Tajikistan produced about 754,000 tons, a drop
of 30 percent from the 1991 figure.

Although cotton is fundamental to Tajikistan's economy, the
republic's rewards for cotton production in the Soviet system
were disappointing. About 90 percent of the harvest was

shipped elsewhere for processing. Tajikistani factories produced thread from some of the cotton harvest, but, by the end of the Soviet era, more than 90 percent of the cotton thread that was spun went elsewhere to be turned into finished goods. In 1990 the two southern provinces of Qurghonteppa and Kulob produced roughly two-thirds of the republic's cotton, but they processed only 1 percent of the crop locally.

Despite widespread concern about overemphasis on cotton cultivation, the post-civil war government attempted to expand the production of the country's most important cash crop. For example, in 1995 it mandated an increase over the preceding year of 10,000 hectares in land assigned to cotton. However, the cotton output remained far below both the government quota and the production levels of the late Soviet era. Independent Tajikistan continued to send most of its cotton crop elsewhere—mainly to CIS countries—for processing.

## Industry

Industrial development in Tajikistan has proceeded slowly and inefficiently, both in the Soviet era and afterward. The civil war and ensuing political turmoil kept production levels low in the mid-1990s.

### *Historical Background*

Tajikistan's industrial development began in earnest in the late 1930s. The early emphasis was on processing cotton and manufacturing construction materials. World War II was a major stimulus to industrial expansion. The output of existing factories was increased to meet wartime demands, and some factories were moved to the republic from the European part of the Soviet Union to safeguard them from the advancing German army.

Skilled workers who relocated to Tajikistan from points west received preferential treatment, including substantially higher wages than those paid to Tajiks; this practice continued long after the war. Such migrants provided the bulk of the labor force in many of the republic's industries through the end of the Soviet era. Cotton textile mills and metallurgy, machine construction, the aluminum smelting plant, and the chemical industry all had disproportionately small percentages of Tajik workers, or none at all.

The Vakhsh River valley in southern Tajikistan became a center of extensive industrial development (see Topography and

Drainage, this ch.). The river was dammed at several points to provide water for agriculture and cheap hydroelectric power, which stimulated construction of factories in the area. Many of the plants in the valley process agricultural products or provide agricultural materials such as fertilizer. A large chemical plant also uses power from the Vakhsh.

### Industry in the 1990s

In the early 1990s, the configuration of industry continued to reflect the specialized roles assigned to Tajikistan within the Soviet system, hindering advancement of enterprises that utilized the republic's natural resources most effectively. The civil war also made industrial reorganization problematic.

In 1991 industry and construction contributed 43.5 percent of the country's NMP, of which industry's share was 30.6 percent—but those sectors employed only 20.4 percent of the work force. Tajikistan's only heavy manufacturing industries are aluminum and chemical production and a very small machinery and metalworking industry. The most important light industries are food processing and fabric and carpet weaving. After declining an estimated 40 percent between 1990 and 1993, industrial production dropped another 31 percent in 1994. Declines in the Dushanbe and Khujand regions exceeded that figure. The output of only five industrial products increased in 1994: high-voltage electrical equipment, textile equipment, winding machines, processed cereals, and salt. The most serious declines were in chemicals, engineering, metal processing, building materials, light industry, and food processing. According to government reports, production declines generally were greater in privately owned industries than in state enterprises.

Tajikistan's overall industrial production capacity was underutilized in the first half of the 1990s. The steadily rising cost of raw materials, fuel, and energy combined with the obsolescence of production equipment and the lack of qualified industrial workers to place Tajikistani industrial products, which never had been of especially high quality, at a great disadvantage in foreign markets.

### Aluminum

Tajikistan's major industrial enterprise is the aluminum processing plant at Regar in the western part of the republic. When the plant opened in 1975, it included the world's largest aluminum smelter, with a capacity of 500,000 tons per year. But difficulties arose in the early 1990s because of the civil war and unreliable raw material supply. Aluminum production and quality began to decline in 1992 because Azerbaijan and Russia cut the supply of semiprocessed alumina upon which the plant depended. By 1995 the plant's management was predicting a yearly output of 240,000 tons, still less than half the maximum capacity. The prolonged decline was caused by outmoded equipment, low world prices for aluminum, the emigration of much of the plant's skilled labor force, difficulties in obtaining raw materials, and continued disruption resulting from the civil war.

## Mining

In the Soviet period, several minerals, including antimony, mercury, molybdenum, and tungsten, were mined in Tajikistan; the Soviet system assigned Tajikistan to supply specific raw or partially processed goods to other parts of the Soviet Union. For example, nearly all of Tajikistan's gold went to Uzbekistan for processing. However, in the 1990s the presence in Tajikistan of a hitherto-secret uranium-mining and preliminary-processing operation became public for the first time. The operation, whose labor force included political prisoners and members of nationalities deported by Stalin from certain autonomous republics of the Russian Republic, may have accounted for almost one-third of total mining in the Soviet Union. According to official Tajikistani reports, the mines were exhausted by 1990.

## Energy

Tajikistan's domestic energy supply situation is dominated by hydroelectric power. The nation is an importer of petroleum-based fuels, of which only small domestic deposits are being exploited. Insufficient access to imported oil and natural gas, a persistent problem under the Soviet system, became more acute after 1991.

The Soviet central government, which determined energy policy for Tajikistan, saw the republic's rivers as prime locations for hydroelectric dams. However, Tajikistanis raised serious objections to the resettlement of villages, the potential for flooding if an earthquake damaged a dam, and the prospect of pollution from the factories that would be attracted by cheap electrical power. Although damming the rivers would increase

*Mining combine in central Tajikistan*
*Courtesy Stephane Herbert*

the supply of water for irrigation, the central government targeted much of the water for neighboring Uzbekistan and Turkmenistan rather than for domestic use. Resistance was especially strong in the case of the Roghun Dam on the Vakhsh River, initiated in 1976 as the largest dam of its kind in Central Asia. By 1992 some 75 percent of the country's electricity came from hydroelectric plants, and in the mid-1990s Russia provided aid for the construction of a new Roghun hydroelectric station.

Deposits of coal, petroleum, and natural gas are known to exist but by the mid-1990s had yet to be developed. In the Soviet era, the unreliability of fuel sources in other republics resulted in frequent power shortages. Fuel supply problems mounted during the transition to a post-Soviet economy, as oil-exporting former Soviet republics often chose not to abide by the delivery agreements upon which Tajikistan had depended.

Furthermore, beginning in 1993, independent Tajikistan's mounting economic problems left it unable to pay more than a small fraction of the cost of importing energy. Energy providers, especially Uzbekistan, responded with periodic interruptions of deliveries. Irregular delivery disrupted industrial production, crop harvests, and the flow of electricity to residential consumers.

## Labor

In 1991 some 1.95 million people were regularly employed outside the home in Tajikistan. However, about 2.4 million Tajikistanis were classified as being of working age. Of those who worked outside the home, 22 percent were employed in industry; 43 percent in agriculture; 18 percent in health care and social services; 6 percent in commerce, food services, state procurement, and "material-technical supply and sales"; 5 percent in transportation; 2 percent in the government bureaucracy; and 4 percent in miscellaneous services.

In the 1980s, light industry continued to employ the largest proportion of industrial workers, 38.6 percent. The processing of food and livestock feed employed an additional 11.7 percent. Machine building and metal-working employed 19.7 percent. Three of Tajikistan's main areas of heavy industrial development employed rather small proportions of the industrial work force: chemicals and petrochemicals, 7.4 percent; nonferrous metallurgy, 5.4 percent; and electric power, 2.4 percent.

One of the most serious economic problems in the late 1980s and early 1990s was unemployment. Unemployment and underemployment remained extensive after the civil war, and the republic's high birth rate led observers to predict that the number of unemployed people would continue to grow through 2000. Tajikistan's designation in the Soviet economy as primarily a producer of raw materials meant that until 1992 agriculture was expected to provide the bulk of employment opportunities for the population. However, the limited amount of arable land and the fast growth of the rural population made further absorption of labor impossible by the 1990s (see Agriculture, this ch.). Although Tajikistan had the resources to increase its production of consumer goods, Soviet economic planning did not develop as much light industry in the republic as the human and material resources could have supported. Two of Tajikistan's largest industrial complexes, which produced chemicals and aluminum, were capital-intensive and provided relatively few jobs.

Unemployment is a particular problem for the republic's young people. Roughly three-quarters of the graduates of general education middle schools (which most students attend) do not go on to further education (see Education, this ch.). Upon entering the job market with such basic qualifications, many cannot find employment. A disproportionate number of young Tajikistanis enter low-paying manual jobs; in 1989 about 40 percent of the agricultural labor force was below age thirty. By the end of the Soviet era, however, a growing number of Tajikistan's young people could not find employment even in agriculture. The paucity and low quality of schools at the vocational level and higher schools prevented those institutions from improving the employment prospects of large numbers of potential workers. In the 1980s, a Soviet campaign to shift labor into "labor deficit" regions in the European republics or in Siberia met with vocal opposition.

With skilled workers leaving the country in the mid-1990s, industrial and professional jobs, most notably in engineering, often go unfilled. Shortages have been especially acute in light industry, construction, health care, transportation, engineering, and education. The exodus of qualified workers intensified in the early 1990s. In 1992 and 1993, an estimated 123,000 specialists with higher education, mostly Russians, left Tajikistan.

## Standard of Living

Beginning in the late 1980s, the troubled state of the Soviet economy in general led to shortages of consumer necessities in Tajikistan, including flour, meat, sugar, and soap. In every year from 1986 through 1989, the value of per capita consumption of goods and services was substantially lower there than in any other Soviet republic. The government in Dushanbe began rationing food early in 1991, but Tajikistan's consumption of meat and dairy products already had been the lowest in the Soviet Union for the previous six years. In 1990 annual per capita meat consumption was twenty-six kilograms in Tajikistan, compared with sixty-seven kilograms for the Soviet Union as a whole. In the same year, annual per capita milk consumption was 161 kilograms in Tajikistan, compared with 358 kilograms for the Soviet Union as a whole.

The national consumer price index went up about 6,000 percent in 1993 alone (see table 10, Appendix). In 1994 breadlines began forming at Dushanbe's single bakery at five in the morning, and the demand often exceeded the supply. Meanwhile, most state stores stood empty as bazaars offered food at prohibitively high prices. Such conditions worsened in the mid-1990s. Although at times bread (whose price was still government subsidized), meat, rice, soap, and other commodities were rationed, basic necessities often were difficult to obtain. In 1995 a 150 percent increase in bread prices, meant as a step toward price decontrol, had the side effect of compounding the difficulty of maintaining an adequate diet. Fuel deliveries in Dushanbe were irregular, and city apartments were cold in the winter.

By the end of the Soviet era, the great majority of Tajikistan's citizens had extremely low incomes even by Soviet standards. Industrial wages ranked second lowest among the republics in 1990. The income of peasants on collective farms was the lowest among all republics; for those on state farms, it was the second to lowest. The situation did not improve in the first post-Soviet years. At the end of 1994, the average monthly wage was 25,000 rubles, or US$7.30, and wages often went unpaid for several months. The maximum weekly wage was set at US$19.30 by a government policy that automatically deposited any payment above that level in the recipient's bank savings account.

By the 1980s, housing had become a serious problem, especially in Dushanbe. The "Housing-93" project of that period promised to provide accommodations by 1993 to families that were on the waiting lists in 1988, but construction fell far behind. By 1990, some 150,000 families were waiting to get an apartment in the capital, a situation that contributed to the outbreak of riots there in February of that year. The housing shortage in the northern province of Leninobod was similarly acute.

## Economic Conditions in the Early 1990s

At the close of the Soviet phase of Tajikistan's history, the economy deteriorated rapidly, and the level of economic activity declined sharply in the early 1990s. In 1992 the gross domestic product (GDP—see Glossary) was approximately half of what it had been in 1990. In the first half of 1991, agricultural and industrial output dropped substantially, and construction, a chronic weak point of the economy, was especially sluggish. The state's revenues for the same period were half as large as its expenses. According to Soviet statistics, the generation of national income in Tajikistan had already declined 7.8 percent from 1988 to 1989 and 8.9 percent from 1989 to 1990. In 1990, the per capita generation of national income was the lowest by far among Soviet republics, and 17 percent below the 1985 level. These figures reflect not only Tajikistan's poverty but also the low prices that were assigned to agricultural products and raw materials, Tajikistan's main products, in the state-run economy. Although Tajikistan was primarily an agricultural republic, in 1989 it imported more agricultural products, including foodstuffs, than it exported.

Political turmoil and the civil war of 1992–93 did enormous damage to Tajikistan's economy. According to an official estimate, that damage extended to 80 percent of the republic's industries. The conflict spurred the departure of large numbers of Russians and Germans who had been key technical personnel in Tajikistan's industries (see Population, this ch.). After independence, the government was very slow to develop an institutional framework to promote movement toward a market economy. Through the mid-1990s, virtually no privatization of industry or agriculture occurred.

The scarcity of reliable statistics makes quantification of Tajikistan's economic situation difficult. In 1994 the total economic loss from the civil war was estimated at 15 trillion rubles (see Glossary for value of ruble)—about US$12 billion at the January 1, 1994, exchange rate. According to Western estimates, by 1994 production in industry had dropped 60 percent, in agriculture 33 percent, and in the transportation enterprises several hundred percent—all in comparison with 1990 levels. The GDP fell an estimated 28 percent in 1993, 12 percent in 1994, and 14 percent in 1995. Inflation soared at a rate of 1,157 percent in 1992; 2,195 percent in 1993; 341 percent in 1994; and 120 percent in 1995. The relatively lower rate in 1995 reflected the government's new anti-inflationary policies launched in the second half of the year.

## Transition to a Market Economy

In the last years of the Soviet system, Tajikistan followed the rest of the union in beginning a transition from the conventional Soviet centralized command system to a market economy. Early in 1991, the Dushanbe government legalized the leasing and privatization of state enterprises (excluding industries deemed critical for national security). However, the transition met firm resistance from individuals who still held positions that gave them access to economic power and technological know-how; political figures with ideological objections to market reforms also voiced opposition. Such influential people insisted that the previous system could be made efficient if Tajikistanis were urged to work harder. This view was made popular by the sharp price increases that followed price decontrol in the initial reform stage. Citizens' hardships, fear, and anger resulting from the initial economic shock greatly slowed the transition to a market economy. For instance, in the first year of independence, only four private farms were established.

The regime of Imomali Rahmonov, who came to power in December 1992, showed little interest in continuing the limited market reforms of 1991 and 1992. At the same time, the new regime declared its support for private enterprise on a small or moderate scale, expressing the hope that foreign investment would help revive the country's shattered economy. By the mid-1990s, about half of all small businesses, especially those in the service sector, were privately owned. In November 1995, the legislature approved a reform plan for the period 1995–2000, but the plan included no specific steps toward the general goals of privatization and the fostering of foreign and domestic investment.

In 1992 Tajikistan acquired its first commercial bank, the Tajikbankbusiness. Established primarily to invest in the republic's economy, the state-owned bank assumed the functions of the former Soviet State Bank (Gosbank); it also sought to develop links with the United States, Iran, China, Pakistan, Saudi Arabia, and Britain, among other countries. After the dissolution of the Soviet Union, Tajikistan continued to use the old Soviet ruble until Russia replaced that currency with the Russian ruble in 1994. At that time, Tajikistan joined the Russian ruble zone (see Glossary), a move that worked against Tajikistani interests. Russia did not send as many rubles as promised, and many of the new rubles that were sent quickly left Tajikistan as inhabitants bought commodities from other Soviet successor states, especially Uzbekistan and Russia. Thus handicapped, the cash economy often gave way to barter and promissory notes. As a result, the Dushanbe government decided to leave the ruble zone by introducing the Tajikistani ruble in 1995. At the time of its introduction, the new currency had an exchange rate of fifty per US$1, but its value slipped drastically through 1995, reaching 284 per US$1 in January 1996.

## Foreign Economic Relations

As the economic reforms of the Gorbachev regime relaxed restrictions on foreign business activity in the Soviet Union in the last years of the 1980s, Tajikistan began to make economic arrangements with foreign businesses. Despite some interest on the part of the Nabiyev regime in arranging joint ventures with foreign firms, only four such agreements were reached in 1991, and just six more were concluded by 1992. One of the joint-venture agreements of that period brought United States investment in the manufacture of fur and leather products in Tajikistan. Israeli businesses began irrigation projects in Tajikistan in 1992. A deal with two Austrian companies called for construction of a factory to produce prefabricated housing and other buildings to be financed by US$3.5 million raised from cotton export funds. A similar construction agreement was signed in 1992 with Czechoslovakia. In 1995 an Italian company began construction of a textile factory in Tajikistan. One of the most important foreign undertakings in the country was a joint venture with a Canadian firm, the Zarafshon Mining Project, to mine and process gold at three known sites in the Panjakent area of northwestern Tajikistan and to prospect in an area of 3,000 square kilometers for additional deposits. The agreement was concluded in 1994; production began in January 1996.

The post-civil war government has emphasized cultivation of economic relations with a variety of Western and Middle Eastern countries, China, and the other former Soviet republics (see table 17, Appendix). In 1991 an Afghan company opened shops in Dushanbe and the northern city of Uroteppa to sell clothing, textiles, fruits, and nuts that the company shipped into Tajikistan from Afghanistan and other countries. The company also planned to export textiles woven in Tajikistan. In 1992 fourteen people were sent from Tajikistan to Turkey to study banking procedures.

### Iran and Pakistan

In the early 1990s, Iran pursued economic cooperation as a means of expanding its regional influence by assuming part of the Soviet Union's role as the major customer for Tajikistani exports. The first foreign firm registered in Tajikistan was Iranian. In 1992 pacts were signed for cooperation in the spheres of banking and commerce, transportation, and tourism; a joint company, Tajiran, was established to handle bilateral trade. In October 1992, Iran declared its intention to buy 1 million tons of cotton and 400,000 tons of aluminum (a figure that exceeded Tajikistan's entire aluminum production for 1992).

The two countries continued to make economic cooperation agreements into the mid-1990s. Iran loaned Tajikistan US$10 million to be used to stimulate exports and imports while offering assistance in dealing with the costs of imported energy. In 1994, the two countries established a commission to promote bilateral economic and technical relations. In 1995 Iran agreed to pay for Tajikistan's importation of natural gas from Turkmenistan; Tajikistan then was to reimburse Iran in cotton rather than currency.

Pakistan extended US$20 million in credits to Tajikistan in 1994 for the purchase of Pakistani goods. However, the most ambitious parts of the cooperation plans between the two countries, the completion of the Roghun hydroelectric dam and the highway between the two countries, fell through; the reasons included Pakistan's own economic problems, political opposition in Tajikistan to allocating state funds on such a large scale to a foreign country, and the continued turmoil in Afghanistan and Tajikistan.

### The United States

In 1992 newly independent Tajikistan and the United States expressed an interest in developing trade relations. President Nabiyev made an urgent plea to a delegation from the United States Congress for development assistance, especially in the area of natural resource use. At about the same time, Tajikistan made a barter trade agreement with a United States company to exchange dried fruits from Tajikistan for bricks, greenhouse equipment, and consumer goods from the United States. In 1992 the United States offered Tajikistan credits to use for the purchase of food, and the United States Overseas Private Investment Corporation made an agreement to provide Tajikistan loans and other assistance to promote United States investment. In 1994 the United States established the Central Asian-American Enterprise Fund to provide loans and technical expertise that would promote the growth of the private sector in all the Central Asian states. Generally, however, the level of

United States involvement in Tajikistan has remained very low. The first significant undertaking in Tajikistan by a United States firm was a US$40 million textile mill established in 1995.

### Russia and the CIS

After Tajikistan achieved independence, it maintained extensive economic relations with other former Soviet republics individually and with the CIS. Relations with the CIS and the Russian Federation preserved some characteristics of Tajikistan's relationship with the Soviet central authorities. Until 1995 Tajikistan remained in the ruble zone rather than establishing its own national currency, as the other four Central Asian republics had done.

In the meantime, Russia retained the dominant position in the CIS and, hence, in commerce with Tajikistan that the Moscow government had enjoyed in the Soviet period. Russia and Tajikistan undertook to maintain their bilateral exchange of goods at existing levels as the republics made the transition to a market economy. In 1992 some 36 percent of Tajikistan's imports came from Russia, and 21 percent of its exports went to Russia; about 60 percent of total external trade was with CIS countries, and 45 percent of exports went to those countries. In 1992 a bilateral agreement called for Tajikistan to send Russia fruits and vegetables, vegetable oil, silk fabrics, and paint in return for automobiles, televisions, and other consumer and industrial goods.

Post-civil war Tajikistan was heavily dependent on Russia for fuel and other necessities. In 1993 Russia made another barter agreement, by which Tajikistan would send Russia agricultural products, machinery, and other goods in return for Russian oil. Despite the agreements, trade between the two countries encountered serious difficulties. In the 1990s, a sharp drop in independent Tajikistan's cotton production caused it to fall far short of the deliveries promised to Russia. This development impeded Tajikistan's ability to pay for vital fuel imports and disrupted Russia's textile industry. Nevertheless, private bilateral commercial activity expanded to some extent. By 1995 more than twenty Tajikistani businesses had made joint-venture agreements with Russian enterprises.

Membership in the ruble zone required Tajikistan to cede control over its money supply and interest rates to Russia and to comply with the regulations of Russia's central bank. After the civil war, Russia provided a majority of the funds for Tajikistan's budget and had considerable influence over budgetary policy. Russia also sent periodic infusions of cash to the Dushanbe government.

As the old interrepublic delivery system decayed at the end of the Soviet era, Tajikistan, like other republics, reduced sales of some commodities and consumer goods to other republics. At the same time, direct agreements were made with several republics to place commercial relations on a new footing. These pacts included statements of principle on economic cooperation and general promises to deliver products from one republic to the other and to set up joint ventures. In 1992 such agreements were made with Georgia, Armenia, and Belarus, and a separate trade agreement called for Turkmenistan to send Tajikistan natural gas and various other goods in exchange for aluminum, farm machinery, and consumer goods.

One of Tajikistan's most important trading partners among the Soviet successor states is Uzbekistan, the source of most of its natural gas since independence. In 1994 the two countries concluded a barter agreement, which the International Monetary Fund (IMF—see Glossary) subsequently criticized as disadvantageous to Tajikistan. According to the agreement, Uzbekistan was to send Tajikistan natural gas, fuel oil, and electricity. In return, Uzbekistan was to have mining rights to various metals in Tajikistan, which also would supply electricity to locations in southern Uzbekistan lacking generating capacity, as well as cotton, construction materials, various metals, and other goods. In 1995 Uzbekistan halted its natural gas deliveries several times, citing nonpayment by Tajikistan.

In the mid-1990s, the uncertain condition of Tajikistan's economy left the country in a weak position to conduct foreign trade. The balance of trade was consistently unfavorable; in 1994 imports exceeded exports by nearly US$116 million, and by 1995 Tajikistan's foreign debt exceeded US$731 million. Imports consisted mostly of food, energy, and medicines. The main exports were aluminum and cotton, with a large share of the production of both commodities earmarked for export. The income derived from cotton and aluminum sales went largely to pay for Tajikistan's energy imports, to repay foreign debts in general, and to cover government expenses.

## Transportation and Telecommunications

Topographical barriers between northern and southern

Tajikistan have prevented the effective transportation and communication linkage of the two regions (see Topography and Drainage, this ch.). The most important form of transportation has been the railroad; highways are few and of low quality (see fig. 10). Radio and television systems are limited and government controlled.

## Railroads

The north and the south are served by railway networks that link them to neighboring regions of Uzbekistan rather than to each other. Rail traffic between the two regions of Tajikistan must follow a 1,340-kilometer route through Uzbekistan. As is the case with other parts of the economic infrastructure in Central Asia, railway routes reflect the needs of the larger economic system of which Tajikistan was a part until 1991. The railway system in the north was established when that area was part of the Russian Empire's Guberniya of Turkestan. In that era, the railroad from Tashkent, the capital of Turkestan, extended into the agricultural and industrial centers in the Fergana Valley, which includes the far northern part of today's Tajikistan. The railroads in the south were built in the Soviet era, in part to facilitate the shipment of cotton grown in the southernmost parts of Central Asia, not just in Tajikistan, to other parts of the Soviet Union.

In the early 1990s, substandard equipment was the most serious problem of the Tajikistani railroad system. Levels of freight haulage and passenger service declined steadily as railroad cars sat idle, waiting for spare parts and repairs. By 1994 delivery of goods to the more remote regions of the country had become a hazardous and unpredictable operation.

## Roads

In 1992 Tajikistan had 32,750 kilometers of roads, of which 18,240 kilometers were classified as main roads. Unlike the railroads, the principal highway connects Dushanbe with the main northern city, Khujand, about 300 kilometers away. However, because the road crosses three chains of mountains, it is blocked by heavy snows, avalanches, and landslides for several months each year. Other main roads connect Dushanbe with Qurghonteppa and Kulob. In 1993 only about 1,500 private automobiles were in use.

## Air Travel

Tajikistan's principal airport is located in Dushanbe, the capital. By the mid-1990s, the facility's only runway, which was too short to accommodate large international planes, was in poor condition. In 1995 the European Bank for Reconstruction and Development (EBRD) gave Tajikistan a grant of US$4 million to repair and lengthen the runway.

Tajikistan made two attempts to start its own airline in the 1990s. Tajik Air, a private joint venture with a British company, lasted only a few months in the winter of 1993–94. That airline had only a single airplane, leased from United Airlines, with a crew of former employees of the defunct Pan American Airlines. The venture failed because of increasing debts and lack of support from the government. In 1995 Tajikistan entered into a joint venture with the Portuguese airline Transportes Aereos Portugueses (TAP) to provide two airplanes and personnel to a new national service, Tajikistan International Airlines; maintenance of the aircraft was to be performed by British Airways.

## Telecommunications

Television and radio broadcasting is the monopoly of the State Television and Radio Broadcasting Company of Tajikistan, which is controlled by the Ministry of Communications. In 1995 the radio broadcasting system included thirteen AM stations and three FM stations. Several frequencies offer relayed programming from Iran, Russia, and Turkey. Although radio broadcasting is primarily in Tajik, Russian and Uzbek programming also is offered. In 1988 broadcasting began in German, Kyrgyz, and Crimean Tatar as well. In February 1994, the state broadcasting company came under the direct control of head of state Imomali Rahmonov.

Television broadcasts first reached Tajikistan in 1959 from Uzbekistan. Subsequently, Tajikistan established its own broadcasting facilities in Dushanbe, under the direction of the government's Tajikistan Television Administration. Color broadcasts use the European SECAM system. Television programming is relayed from stations in Iran, Russia, and Turkey. In mountainous villages, television viewing is restricted by limited electrical supply and retransmission facilities.

In 1994 Tajikistan's telephone system remained quite limited. It included 259,600 main lines, an average of one line per twenty-two people—the lowest ratio among former Soviet republics.

## Government and Politics

In the first years of independence, politics in Tajikistan were overshadowed by a long struggle for political power among cliques that sought Soviet-style dominance of positions of power and privilege and a collection of opposition forces seeking to establish a new government whose form was defined only vaguely in public statements. The result was a civil war that began in the second half of 1992. A faction favoring a neo-Soviet system took control of the government in December 1992 after winning the civil war with help from Russian and Uzbekistani forces.

### Transition to Post-Soviet Government

In the late 1980s, problems in the Soviet system had already provoked open public dissatisfaction with the status quo in Tajikistan. In February 1990, demonstrations against government housing policy precipitated a violent clash in Dushanbe. Soviet army units sent to quell the riots inflicted casualties on demonstrators and bystanders alike. Using the riots as a pretext to repress political dissent, the regime imposed a state of emergency that lasted long after the riots had ended. In this period, criticism of the regime by opposition political leaders was censored from state radio and television broadcasts. The state brought criminal charges against the leaders of the popular front organization Rastokhez (Rebirth) for inciting the riots, although the Supreme Soviet later ruled that Rastokhez was not implicated. Students were expelled from institutions of higher education merely for attending nonviolent political meetings. The events of 1990 made the opposition even more critical of the communist old guard than it had been previously.

In the highly charged political atmosphere after the failure of the August 1991 coup attempt in Moscow, Tajikistan's Supreme Soviet voted for independence for the republic in September 1991. That vote was not intended to signal a break with the Soviet Union, however. It was rather a response to increasingly vociferous opposition demands and to similar declarations by Uzbekistan and Kyrgyzstan. Following the dissolution of the Soviet Union, a development in which Tajikistan played no role, the republic joined the CIS when that loose federation of former Soviet republics was established in December 1991.

The political opposition within Tajikistan was composed of a diverse group of individuals and organizations. The three major opposition parties were granted legal standing at various times in 1991. The highest-ranking Islamic figure in the republic, the chief *qadi*, Hajji Akbar Turajonzoda, sided openly with the opposition coalition beginning in late 1991. The opposition's ability to govern and the extent of its public support never were tested because it gained only brief, token representation in a 1992 coalition government that did not exercise effective authority over the entire country.

In the early independence period, the old guard sought to depict itself as the duly elected government of Tajikistan now facing a power grab by Islamic radicals who would bring to Tajikistan fundamentalist repression similar to that occurring in Iran and Afghanistan. Yet both claims were misleading. The elections for the republic's Supreme Soviet and president had been neither free nor truly representative of public opinion. The legislative election was held in February 1990 under the tight constraints of the state of emergency. In the presidential election of 1991, Nabiyev had faced only one opponent, filmmaker and former communist Davlat Khudonazarov, whose message had been stifled by communist control of the news media and the workplace. Despite Nabiyev's advantageous position, Khudonazarov received more than 30 percent of the vote.

In the first half of 1992, the opposition responded to increased repression by organizing ever larger proreform demonstrations. When Nabiyev assembled a national guard force, coalition supporters, who were concentrated in the southern Qurghonteppa Province and the eastern Pamir region, acquired arms and prepared for battle. Meanwhile, opponents of reform brought their own supporters to Dushanbe from nearby Kulob Province to stage counterdemonstrations in April of that year. Tensions mounted, and small-scale clashes occurred. In May 1992, after Nabiyev had broken off negotiations with the oppositionist demonstrators and had gone into hiding, the confrontation came to a head when opposition demonstrators were fired upon and eight were killed. At that point, the commander of the Russian garrison in Dushanbe brokered a compromise. The main result of the agreement was the formation of a coalition government in which one-third of the cabinet posts would go to members of the opposition.

For most of the rest of 1992, opponents of reform worked hard to overturn the coalition and block implementation of measures such as formation of a new legislature in which the opposition would have a voice. In the summer and fall of 1992, vicious battles resulted in many casualties among civilians and combatants. Qurghonteppa bore the brunt of attacks by antireformist irregular forces during that period. In August 1992, demonstrators in Dushanbe seized Nabiyev and forced him at gunpoint to resign. The speaker of the Supreme Soviet, Akbarsho Iskandarov—a Pamiri closely associated with Nabiyev—became acting president. Iskandarov advocated a negotiated resolution of the conflict, but he had little influence over either side.

The political and military battles for control continued through the fall of 1992. In November the Iskandarov coalition government resigned in the hope of reconciling the contending factions. Later that month, the Supreme Soviet, still dominated by hard-liners, met in emergency session in Khujand, an antireform stronghold, to select a new government favorable to their views. When the office of president was abolished, the speaker of parliament, Imomali Rahmonov, became de facto head of government. A thirty-eight-year-old former collective farm director, Rahmonov had little experience in government. The office of prime minister went to Abdumalik Abdullojanov, a veteran hard-line politician.

Once in possession of Dushanbe, the neo-Soviets stepped up repression. Three leading opposition figures, including Turajonzoda and the deputy prime minister in the coalition government, were charged with treason and forced into exile, and two other prominent opposition supporters were assassinated in December. There were mass arrests on nebulous charges and summary executions of individuals captured without formal arrest. Fighting on a smaller scale between the forces of the old guard and the opposition continued elsewhere in Tajikistan and across the border with Afghanistan into the mid-1990s.

The conflict in Tajikistan often was portrayed in Western news reports as occurring primarily among clans or regional cliques. Many different lines of affiliation shaped the configuration of forces in the conflict, however, and both sides were divided over substantive political issues. The old guard had never reconciled itself to the reforms of the Gorbachev era

(1985–91) or to the subsequent demise of the Soviet regime. Above all, the factions in this camp wanted to ensure for themselves a monopoly of the kinds of benefits enjoyed by the ruling elite under the Soviet system. The opposition coalition factions were divided over what form the new regime in Tajikistan ought to take: secular parliamentary democracy, nationalist reformism, or Islamicization. Proponents of the last option were themselves divided over the form and pace of change.

In April 1994, peace talks arranged by the United Nations (UN) began between the post-civil war government in Dushanbe and members of the exiled opposition. Between that time and early 1996, six major rounds of talks were held in several different cities. Several smaller-scale meetings also occurred directly between representatives of both sides or through Russian, UN, or other intermediaries. Observers at the main rounds of talks included representatives of Russia, other Central Asian states, Iran, Pakistan, the United States, the Conference on Security and Cooperation in Europe (CSCE— after 1994 the Organization for Security and Cooperation in Europe, OSCE—see Glossary), and the Organization of the Islamic Conference. In the first two years, these negotiations produced few positive results. The most significant result was a cease-fire agreement that took effect in October 1994. The initial agreement, scheduled to last only for a few weeks, was renewed repeatedly into 1996, albeit with numerous violations by both sides. As a result of the cease fire, the UN established an observer mission in Tajikistan, which had a staff of forty-three in early 1996.

## Government Structure

Independent Tajikistan's initial government conformed to the traditional Soviet formula of parliamentary-ministerial governance and complete obeisance to the regime in Moscow. The office of president of the republic was established in 1990, following the example set by the central government in Moscow. Until the establishment of the short-lived coalition government in 1992, virtually all government positions were held by communist party members. After December 1992, power was in the hands of factions opposed to reform. Former allies in that camp then contended among themselves for power.

### The 1994 Constitution

In 1994 Tajikistan adopted a new constitution that restored

the office of president, transformed the Soviet-era Supreme Soviet into the Supreme Assembly (Majlisi Oli), recognized civil liberties and property rights, and provided for a judiciary that was not fully independent. Like constitutions of the Soviet era, the document did not necessarily constrain the actual exercise of power. For example, the mechanism by which the constitution was formally adopted was a referendum held in November 1994. Balloting occurred simultaneously with the vote for president, even though that office could not legally exist until and unless the constitution was ratified.

### The Executive

The president was first chosen by legislative election in 1990. In the first direct presidential election, held in 1991, former communist party chief Rahmon Nabiyev won in a rigged vote. The office of president was abolished in November 1992, then reestablished de facto in 1994 in advance of the constitutional referendum that legally approved it. In the interim, the chairman of the Supreme Soviet, Imomali Rahmonov, was nominal chief of state. In the presidential election of November 1994, Rahmonov won a vote that was condemned by opposition parties and Western observers as fraudulent. Rahmonov's only opponent was the antireformist Abdumalik Abdullojanov, who had founded an opposition party after being forced to resign as Rahmonov's prime minister in 1993 under criticism for the country's poor economic situation.

The Council of Ministers is responsible for management of government activities in accordance with laws and decrees of the Supreme Assembly and decrees of the president. The president appoints the prime minister and the other council members, with the nominal approval of the Supreme Assembly. In 1996 the Council of Ministers included fifteen full ministers, plus six deputy prime ministers, the chairmen of five state committees, the presidential adviser on national economic affairs, the secretary of the National Security Council, and the chairman of the National Bank of Tajikistan.

### The Legislature

The republic's legislature, the Supreme Assembly, is elected directly for a term of five years. According to the 1994 constitution, any citizen at least twenty-five years of age is eligible for election. The unicameral, 230-seat Supreme Soviet elected in 1990 included 227 communists and three members from other parties. The constitution approved in November 1994 called for a unicameral, 181-seat parliament to replace the Supreme Soviet. In the first election under those guidelines, 161 deputies were chosen in February 1995 and nineteen of the remaining twenty in a second round one month later. (One constituency elected no deputy, and one elected deputy died shortly after the election.) In the 1995 parliamentary election, an estimated forty seats were uncontested, and many candidates reportedly were former Soviet regional and local officials. The sixty communist deputies who were elected gave Rahmonov solid support in the legislative branch because the majority of deputies had no declared party affiliation. Like the 1994 presidential election, the parliamentary election was not considered free or fair by international authorities.

### The Judiciary

The 1994 constitution prescribes an independent judiciary, including at the national level the Supreme Court, the Constitutional Court (theoretically, the final arbiter of the constitutionality of government laws and actions), the Supreme Economic Court, and the Military Court. The Gorno-Badakhshan Autonomous Province has a regional court, and subordinate courts exist at the regional, district, and municipal levels. Judges are appointed to five-year terms, but theoretically they are subordinate only to the constitution and are beyond interference from elected officials. However, the president retains the power to dismiss judges, and in practice Tajikistan still lacked an independent judiciary after the adoption of the 1994 constitution. In June 1993, the Supreme Court acted on behalf of the Rahmonov regime in banning all four opposition parties and all organizations connected with the 1992 coalition government. The ban was rationalized on the basis of an accusation of the parties' complicity in attempting a violent overthrow of the government.

As in the Soviet system, the Office of the Procurator General has authority for both investigation and adjudication of crimes within its broad constitutional mandate to ensure compliance with the laws of the republic. Elected to a five-year term, the procurator general of Tajikistan is the superior of similar officials in lower-level jurisdictions throughout the country.

### Local Government

Below the republic level, provinces, districts, and cities have their own elected assemblies. In those jurisdictions, the chief executive is the chairman of a council of people's deputies, whose members are elected to five-year terms. The chairman is appointed by the president of the republic. The Supreme Assembly may dissolve local councils if they fail to uphold the law. For most of the late Soviet and early independence periods, Tajikistan had four provinces: Leninobod in the north, Qurghonteppa and Kulob in the south, and the Gorno-Badakhshan Autonomous Province in the southeast. The precise status of that region is unclear because separatists have declared it an autonomous republic and even the government does not always call it a province (see fig. 10). Beginning in 1988, Qurghonteppa and Kulob were merged into a single province, called Khatlon. (The two parts were separated again between 1990 and 1992.) A large region stretching from the west-central border through Dushanbe to the north-central border is under direct federal control.

## Political Parties

As long as Tajikistan was a Soviet republic, political power resided in the Communist Party of Tajikistan, not in the state. Until 1991 the party was an integral part of the CPSU, subordinate to the central party leadership. In the years before independence, several opposition parties appeared with various agendas. Since the civil war, the opposition's official participation has been limited severely, although some parties remain active abroad.

### Communist Party of Tajikistan

During the 1920s, Tajik communist party membership increased substantially. But in the following decades, the percentage of Tajik membership in the Communist Party of Tajikistan rose and fell with the cycle of purges and revitalizations. Throughout the Soviet period, however, Russians retained dominant positions. For example, the top position of party first secretary was reserved for an individual of the titular ethnic group of the republic, but the powerful position of second secretary always belonged to a Russian or a member of another European nationality.

In the mid-1980s, the Communist Party of Tajikistan had nearly 123,000 members, of whom about two-thirds represented urban regions, with subordinate provincial, district, and municipal organizations in all jurisdictions. The Communist

Youth League (Komsomol), which provided most of the future party members, had more than 550,000 members in 1991. The end of the Soviet era witnessed a waning of interest in party membership, however, despite the privileges and opportunities the party could offer. By 1989 many districts were losing members much faster than new members could be recruited.

In August 1991, the failure of the coup by hard-liners in Moscow against President Gorbachev left the Communist Party of Tajikistan even less popular and more vulnerable than it had been before. However, although it was suspended in 1991, the party in Tajikistan was able to retain its property during its suspension. Just before sanctions were imposed, the party changed the adjective in its name from *communist* to *socialist*. In December 1991, the party reassumed its original name and began a vigorous campaign to recapture its earlier monopoly of power.

After the civil war, the communist party remained the country's largest party, although its membership was far smaller than it had been in the late Soviet era. In the early 1990s, the party rebuilt its organizational network, from the primary party organizations in the workplace to the countrywide leadership. Communist candidates did well in the legislative elections of 1995, although they did not win an outright majority.

### Opposition Parties

The end of the 1980s and the beginning of the 1990s saw the open establishment of opposition parties representing a variety of secular and religious views. In 1991 and 1992, these groups engaged in an increasingly bitter power struggle with those who wanted to preserve the old order in substance, if not in name. By the summer of 1992, the battle had escalated into an open civil war that would claim tens of thousands of lives.

A branch of the Islamic Rebirth Party (IRP) was established in Tajikistan in 1990 with an initial membership of about 10,000. The Tajikikistan IRP was established as an open organization, although it was rumored to have existed underground since the late 1970s. The IRP received legal recognition as a political party in the changed political climate that existed after the 1991 Moscow coup attempt. Despite its links to the party of the same name with branches throughout the Soviet Union, the Tajikistan IRP focused explicitly on republic-level politics and national identity rather than supranational issues. When the antireformists gained power in December 1992, they again banned the IRP. At that point, the party claimed 20,000 members, but no impartial figures were available for either the size of its membership or the extent of its public support. After the civil war, the party changed its name to the Movement for Islamic Revival.

Two other parties, the Democratic Party and Rastokhez (Rebirth), also were banned, with the result that no opposition party has had official sanction since early 1993. The Democratic Party, which has a secular, nationalist, and generally pro-Western agenda, was founded by intellectuals in 1990 and modeled on the contemporaneous parliamentary democratization movement in Moscow. In 1995 the party moved its headquarters from Tehran to Moscow. Although the government nominally lifted its ban on the Democratic Party in 1995, in practice the party remains powerless inside the republic. In early 1996, it joined several other parties in signing an agreement of reconciliation with the Dushanbe government.

Like the Democratic Party, Rastokhez was founded in 1990 with substantial support from the intellectual community; its visibility as an opposition popular front made Rastokhez a scapegoat for the February 1990 demonstrations and riots in Dushanbe (see Transition to Post-Soviet Government, this ch.). In 1992 Rastokhez, the Democratic Party, and another party, La"li Badakhshon, played an important role in the opposition movement that forced President Nabiyev to resign. The leadership of the much-weakened Rastokhez movement also made peace with the Dushanbe regime early in 1996.

La"li Badakhshon is a secularist, democratic group that was founded in 1991. The chief aim of the party, which represents mainly Pamiris, is greater autonomy for the Gorno-Badakhshan Autonomous Province. La"li Badakhshon joined with the other three opposition groups in the demonstrations of spring 1992.

Since the civil war, several new political parties have functioned legally in Tajikistan. Some are organized around interest groups such as businessmen, some around powerful individuals such as former prime minister Abdumalik Abdullojanov. All of these parties lack the means to influence the political process, however. For instance, the most important of them, Abdullojanov's Popular Unity Party, was prevented by the government from mounting an effective campaign in the legislative elections of February 1995.

## The Media

At the time of independence, Tajikistan had several long-established official newspapers that had been supported by the communist regime. These included newspapers circulated throughout the republic in Tajik, Russian, and Uzbek, as well as papers on the provincial, district, and city levels. Beginning in 1991, changes in newspapers' names reflected political changes in the republic. For example, the Tajik republican newspaper, long known as *Tojikistoni Soveti* (Soviet Tajikistan), became first *Tojikistoni Shuravi* (using the Persian word for "council" or "soviet") and then *Jumhuriyat* (Republic). The equivalent Russian-language newspaper went from *Kommunist Tadzhikistana* (Tajikistan Communist) to *Narodnaya gazeta* (People's Newspaper). Under the changing political conditions of the late-Soviet and early independence periods, new newspapers appeared, representing such groups as the journalists' union, the Persian-Tajik Language Foundation, cultural and religious groups, and opposition political parties. After antireformists returned to power at the end of 1992, however, the victors cracked down on the press.

In the Soviet era, Tajikistan's magazines included publications specializing in health, educational, rural, and women's issues, as well as communist party affairs. Several were intended especially for children. Literary magazines were published in both Russian and Tajik. The Academy of Sciences of Tajikistan published five scholarly journals. In the postindependence years, however, Tajikistan's poverty forced discontinuation of such items. In the early 1990s, Tajikistan had three main publishing houses. After the civil war, the combination of political repression and acute economic problems disrupted many publication activities. In this period, all of the country's major newspapers were funded fully or in part by the government, and their news coverage followed only the government's line. The only news agency, Khovar, was a government bureau. Tajikistan drew international criticism for the reported killing and jailing of journalists.

## Human Rights

Under the extension of emergency powers justified by the government in response to opposition in 1993 and 1994, numerous human rights violations were alleged on both sides of the civil war. A wave of executions and "disappearances" of opposition figures began after antireformist forces captured Dushanbe in December 1992. The People's Front of Tajikistan, a paramilitary group supported by the government, was responsible in many such cases. In 1993 and 1994, a number of journalists were arrested, and prisoners of conscience were tortured for alleged antigovernment activities. In 1994 some prisoners of conscience and political prisoners were released in prisoner exchanges with opposition forces. The death sentence, applicable by Tajikistani law to eighteen peacetime offenses, was officially applied in six cases in both 1993 and 1994, but only one person, a political prisoner, is known to have been executed in 1994. No state executions were reported in 1995.

Afghanistan-based oppositionist forces, who labeled themselves a government in exile, were accused by the Dushanbe government of killing a large number of civilians and some government soldiers near the Afghan border. These accusations had not been confirmed by impartial observers as of early 1996. Amnesty International appealed to both sides to desist, without apparent effect.

## Foreign Relations

Tajikistan had a ministry of foreign affairs for nearly forty years before it became an independent state at the end of 1991. As long as it was part of the Soviet Union, however, the republic had no power to conduct its own diplomacy. The central objective of newly independent Tajikistan's foreign policy was to maximize its opportunities by developing relations with as many states as possible. Particular diplomatic attention went to two groups of countries: the other former Soviet republics and Tajikistan's near neighbors, Iran and Afghanistan, which are inhabited by culturally related peoples. At the same time, Tajikistan pursued contacts with many other countries, including the United States, Turkey, and Pakistan. In 1995 Tajikistan opened its first embassy outside the former Soviet Union, in Turkey. The potential for political support and economic aid is at least as important in shaping Tajikistan's diplomacy as are ideological and cultural ties.

### Former Soviet Republics

Like the other Central Asian republics, Tajikistan joined the CIS, which was created in December 1991, three weeks before the Soviet Union collapsed officially. Shortly before opposition demonstrators forced President Rahmon Nabiyev to resign in August 1992, he asked several presidents of former Soviet republics, including President Boris N. Yeltsin of Russia, to help him stay in power. They refused this request. In the fall of 1992, the increasingly embattled coalition government that succeeded Nabiyev asked the other members of the CIS to intervene to end the civil war. However, such assistance was not provided.

Through the mid-1990s, Russia played a role in independent Tajikistan by its military presence there, in the form of the 201st Motorized Rifle Division and the Border Troops (see Russia's Role in the Early 1990s, this ch.). Russian personnel in Dushanbe acted as advisers to the post-civil war government. Russians also held important positions in the Dushanbe government itself, most notably the Ministry of Defense, which was led from 1992 to 1995 by Aleksandr Shishlyannikov. Yuriy Ponosov, who had a generation of experience as a CPSU official in Tajikistan before the breakup of the Soviet Union, became Tajikistan's first deputy prime minister in March 1996.

The protection of the Russian minority in strife-ridden Tajikistan is a stated foreign policy goal of the Russian government. Russia's concern was eased somewhat by the conclusion of a dual-citizenship agreement between the two countries in 1995. Russia also has justified its active involvement in the affairs of Tajikistan by citing the need to defend the Tajikistan-Afghanistan border—and thus, the CIS—from penetration by Islamic extremism and drug trafficking.

Independent Tajikistan has troubled relations with two neighboring former Soviet republics, Uzbekistan and Kyrgyzstan, a situation that began long before independence. In the 1980s, a dispute over two scarce resources in Central Asia, water and arable land, soured relations between Tajikistan and Kyrgyzstan. In June 1989, the situation burst into spontaneous, grassroots violence over competing claims to a small parcel of land. That conflict led to mutual recriminations that continued until a settlement was reached in 1993. Tensions were heightened in 1992 by Kyrgyzstan's fear that the Tajikistani civil war would spill over the border, which had never been defined by a bilateral treaty. Despite tense relations between the two republics, Kyrgyzstan attempted to negotiate an end to Tajikistan's civil war, and it sent medicine and other aid to its beleaguered neighbor. After the civil war, Kyrgyzstan sent a contingent of troops to Tajikistan as part of the joint CIS peacekeeping mission (see The Armed Forces, this ch.).

Tajikistan's relations with Uzbekistan present a contradictory picture. On the one hand, Tajik intellectuals, and at times the Dushanbe government, have criticized Uzbekistan for discrimination against its Tajik minority. In response, citing fears of Islamic radicalism in Tajikistan, Uzbekistan closed its Tajik-language schools in mid-1992. On the other hand, antireformists in both republics have maintained good relations based on the interest they shared in the defeat of reformers in Tajikistan in the early 1990s. Uzbekistan gave military support to the factions that won Tajikistan's civil war and closed its border with Tajikistan in the fall of 1992 to prevent opposition refugees from the civil war from fleeing to Uzbekistan.

After the civil war, Uzbekistan's attitude toward Tajikistan became increasingly ambivalent. One aspect of Uzbekistan's policy continued its earlier effort to prevent the opposition from taking power in Tajikistan; a 1993 cooperation treaty between the two countries, stipulating a role for Uzbekistan's air force in the defense of Tajikistan—which has no air force of its own—manifested that concern. However, the government in Tashkent was increasingly displeased that the dominant factions among the victors in Tajikistan's civil war were much less amenable to Uzbekistan's leadership than were the factions that had controlled Tajikistani politics before the war. By 1995 the Uzbekistani government was urging the government in Dushanbe to be more conciliatory toward the opposition in postwar peace talks.

The leaders of Kazakstan, Kyrgyzstan, Tajikistan, Turkmenistan, and Uzbekistan repeatedly extolled the value of regional economic and environmental cooperation in the early 1990s. In reality, however, only limited progress was made toward such cooperation. Oil and natural gas producers Kazakstan and Turkmenistan interrupted fuel deliveries to Tajikistan, in the hopes of improving the terms of the sales agreements that had prevailed under the Soviet system. With consumer goods generally in short supply, Tajikistan has taken measures to prevent citizens of the neighboring republics from purchasing such items from Tajikistani stockpiles. Tajikistan also is wary of regional water use plans that might increase the share of Uzbekistan and Turkmenistan in water emanating from Tajikistan.

## *Iran*

When Tajikistan declared independence, Iran was one of the first countries to extend diplomatic recognition, and the first to establish an embassy in Dushanbe. In 1992 Iran provided training for a group of Tajik diplomats from Tajikistan. After 1991 bilateral contacts in the mass media and in sports increased significantly, and Iran funded construction of several new mosques in Tajikistan. Some of Tajikistan's most important contacts with Iran in the early 1990s were cultural. For example, Tajikistan held an Iranian film festival, an exhibition of Iranian art, and two exhibits of Iranian publications. Dushanbe was the site of international conferences on Persian culture and the Tajik language. In the early 1990s, Iranian books and magazines became increasingly available in Tajikistan, and Dushanbe television carried programs from Iran. The main obstacle to such cultural contact is the fact that only a very small portion of the Tajikistani population can read the Arabic alphabet (see Ethnic Groups and Forces of Nationalism, this ch.).

Despite the obvious ideological differences between the Islamic revolutionary regime in Iran and the secular communist regime in newly independent Tajikistan, Nabiyev actively cultivated relations with Iran. When Nabiyev's position was threatened in 1992, his speeches repeatedly stressed both the cultural and the religious ties between the two countries. He subsequently made a direct request for aid from Iranian president Ali Akbar Hashemi Rafsanjani (see Transition to Post-Soviet Government, this ch.).

The leading figures of the Islamic revival movement in Tajikistan say emphatically that whatever eventual form of Islamic state they advocate for Tajikistan, Iran is not the model to be followed. Part of the reason for this position is that Iran is predominantly Shia Muslim while Tajikistan is mainly Sunni, a distinction with important implications for the organization of the religious leadership and its relationship with the state. An equally important reason is that the social structures of Tajikistan and Iran are considered too different for Iran's linkage of religious and political powers to be adopted in Tajikistan.

In the fall of 1992, Iran repeatedly offered to help mediate Tajikistan's civil war in cooperation with other Central Asian states. Although such offers produced no negotiations, Iran did send food and set up camps for refugees from Tajikistan. After the civil war, relations between Iran and the new government in Dushanbe included efforts to develop a modus vivendi as well as periodic recriminations. Iran worked with Russia in attempting to negotiate a peace agreement between the Dushanbe government and the opposition. In July 1995, Tajikistan opened an embassy in Tehran, one of its few outside the former Soviet Union.

### Afghanistan

Tajikistan's relations with Afghanistan, the country with which it shares its long southern border, have been affected not only by the cultural and ethnic links between inhabitants of the countries but also by the way the Soviet regime tried to use those links to ensure the survival of a communist government in Kabul after 1979. The Soviets put Tajiks from Tajikistan in positions of power in the Soviet-backed Afghan government and sent propaganda publications from Tajikistan to Afghanistan. Afghans were brought to Tajikistan for education and communist indoctrination, and Tajiks served in the Soviet military occupation of Afghanistan. In 1991 the political climate in Tajikistan allowed some citizens to criticize the war openly, although there was no reliable gauge of how widely this antiwar opinion was shared.

Into the early 1990s, the communist government in Dushanbe and the then-communist government in Kabul favored the development of economic relations and exchanges in the fields of education and publishing. During the civil war, the antireformist side alleged that its opponents relied heavily on the subversive actions of Afghan *mujahidin*. Most neutral observers dismissed the large-scale role of Afghans as a propaganda ploy.

Rugged terrain and poor border enforcement make the Tajikistan- Afghanistan border very permeable. Beginning in 1992, border crossings—for private smuggling, to escape the Tajikistani civil war, or to obtain weapons for one side or the other in that war—became increasingly numerous. By early 1993, the United Nations High Commissioner for Refugees estimated that 50,000 to 70,000 refugees had gone from southern Tajikistan to northern Afghanistan. By 1994 many of them had returned home, although the exact number is not available.

Relations between Tajikistan's post-civil war government and Afghanistan often were troubled through the first half of the 1990s. Tajikistan accused Afghanistan of complicity in cross-border attacks by exiled opposition members based in northern Afghanistan. In turn, Afghanistan accused Russian forces on the Tajikistan side of the border of killing Afghan civilians in reprisal attacks. The situation changed in late 1995 and early 1996, when Russia began to support President Burhanuddin Rabbani's faction in the ongoing Afghan civil war. Rabbani then tried to improve relations with the Dushanbe government and to mediate a settlement between it and the opposition.

### The United States

Although the United States was the second country to open an embassy in Dushanbe, that outpost was evacuated in October 1992, at the height of the civil war, and was not reopened until March 1993. Beginning in 1992, antireformists and the opposition both sought support from the United States. Thus, a trip by Secretary of State James Baker to Tajikistan in February 1992 antagonized members of the opposition, who saw the visit as granting tacit approval to Nabiyev's political repression. Relations with the opposition were improved somewhat a few months later, when a human rights delegation from the United States Congress met with several opposition leaders.

During the civil war, the United States provided emergency food supplies and medicines to Tajikistan, and independent Tajikistan continued the cooperative program on earthquake forecasting techniques that had begun with the United States during the Soviet era. By the mid-1990s, United States policy toward Tajikistan centered on support for peace negotiations and on encouraging Tajikistan to develop closer relations with the IMF and other financial organizations that could help in the rebuilding process.

### China

The main source of tension between China and Tajikistan is China's claim on part of Tajikistan's far eastern Gorno-Badakhshan region. Between 1992 and 1995, sixteen rounds of negotiations between China and a commission representing Russia, Tajikistan, Kazakstan, and Kyrgyzstan failed to produce a border agreement. An interim agreement, scheduled for signing in April 1996, stipulated that no attacks would be launched across the border in either direction and that both sides would provide ample notice of military exercises in the area. Despite their border dispute, China and the post-civil war government of Tajikistan share a hostility toward reformist political movements, especially those that could be stigmatized as Islamic fundamentalist. By the mid-1990s, this common ground had become the basis for a working relationship between the two governments.

### International Organizations

Tajikistan joined the UN in 1992. In the fall of that year, the Tajikistani coalition government requested UN aid in ending the civil war and supporting political democratization, but only a UN mission and a call for an end to hostilities resulted. Tajikistan joined the CSCE in February 1992. In 1993 and 1994, membership was obtained in the International Bank for Reconstruction and Development (IBRD), the World Bank (see Glossary), the IMF, and the Economic Cooperation Organization (see Glossary).

## National Security

In the years following independence, Tajikistan has made some efforts to establish independent national security institutions and forces. At the same time, in the mid-1990s a contingent of CIS troops remain in place under a Russian-dominated command. At least until resolution of its internal conflict, Tajikistan seems assured that more powerful countries will exert substantial influence on its national security affairs.

### Russia's Role in the Early 1990s

Before the dissolution of the Soviet Union at the end of 1991, Tajikistan had no army of its own. Administratively, the republic was part of the Soviet Union's Turkestan Military District, which was abolished in June 1992. By the end of the Soviet era, the old military system, which commonly (although not exclusively) assigned draftees from Tajikistan to noncombat units in the Soviet army, had begun to break down, and draft evasion became a common occurrence in Tajikistan. Reform plans for Tajikistan's conscription system were overtaken by the breakup of the union.

Following independence, the Nabiyev government made repeated efforts between December 1991 and June 1992 to organize a national guard. Those efforts met strong opposition from factions fearing that an antireformist president would use the guard as a tool of repression. When his national guard plans failed, Nabiyev turned to private armies of his political supporters to kill or intimidate political opponents. In 1992 additional armed bands were organized in Tajikistan, some associated with opposition political groups and others simply reflecting the breakdown of central authority in the country rather than loyalty to a political faction.

The main regular military force in Tajikistan at independence was the former Soviet 201st Motorized Rifle Division, headquartered in Dushanbe. This division, whose personnel are ethnically heterogeneous, came under jurisdiction of the Russian Federation in 1992 and remained under Russian command in early 1996. Officially neutral in the civil war, Russian and Uzbekistani forces, including armored vehicles of the 201st Division and armored vehicles, jets, and helicopters from Uzbekistan, provided significant assistance in antireformist assaults on the province of Qurghonteppa and on Dushanbe. The 201st Division failed to warn the inhabitants of Dushanbe that neo-Soviet forces had entered the city, nor did it interfere with the victors' wave of violence against opposition supporters in Dushanbe. In the ensuing months, the 201st Division was involved in some battles against opposition holdouts. Russian troops stationed in Tajikistan were a major source of weapons for various factions in the civil war. Combatants on both sides frequently were able to buy or confiscate Russian military hardware, including armored vehicles.

In January 1993, a Russian, Colonel (later Major General) Aleksandr Shishlyannikov, was appointed minister of defense of Tajikistan (a post he held until 1995, when he was replaced by Major General Sherali Khayrulloyev, a Tajik), and many positions in the Tajikistani high command were assumed by Russians in 1993. Meanwhile, in mid-1993 the joint CIS peacekeeping force was created. The force, which remained by far the largest armed presence in Tajikistan through 1995, included elements of the 201st Division, units of Russian border troops, and some Kazakstani, Kyrgyzstani, and Uzbekistani units. By 1995 the officially stated mission of the 201st Division in Tajikistan included artillery and rocket support for the border troops. Included in the division's weaponry in 1995 were 180 M–72 main battle tanks; 185 pieces of artillery, including sixty-five pieces of towed artillery; fifty self-propelled guns; fifteen rocket launchers; and fifty-five mortars.

Border security is a key part of Russia's continued military role in Tajikistan. In June 1992, the formerly Soviet border guards stationed in Tajikistan came under the direct authority

*"Kulabi" (Tajikistani communist forces, in black) and Russian soldiers
outside the parliament building, Dushanbe
Courtesy Stephane Herbert*

of Russia; in 1993 a reorganization put all Russian border
troops under the Russian Federal Border Service. By 1995 an
estimated 16,500 troops of that force were in Tajikistan, but
about 12,500 of the rank-and-file and noncommissioned officers were drawn from the inhabitants of Tajikistan.

## The Armed Forces

Tajikistan began assembling its own army in February 1993.
The initial units were drawn from Popular Front forces active
in the civil war. In the new army, those bands initially kept their
distinct identity and their old commanders. This proved to be
an impediment to the development of a cohesive military when
some units resisted subordination to any higher authority, and
casualties resulted from battles among units. Early in 1996, a
rebellion by the First Battalion of Tajikistan's army, based in the

Qurghonteppa area, brought about the replacement of the prime minister, a deputy prime minister, and the president's chief of staff to placate the rebel unit.

By the mid-1990s, Tajikistan's army numbered about 3,000 personnel. Russians, many of them veterans of the war in Afghanistan, made up almost three-quarters of the officer corps. The Russian Ministry of Defense continued to provide material assistance to Tajikistan's army. Through the mid-1990s, Tajikistan did not have an air force but relied instead on Russian air power; however, the Dushanbe government voiced the intention of purchasing some helicopters for military use and forming an air force squadron.

## Internal Security

Preservation of internal security was impossible during the civil war, whose concomitant disorder promoted the activities of numerous illegal groups. Because of Tajikistan's location, the international narcotics trade found these conditions especially inviting in the early and mid-1990s.

### Security Organizations

When Tajikistan was part of the Soviet Union, the republic's Committee for State Security (KGB) was an integral part of the Soviet-wide KGB. Neither the administration nor the majority of personnel were Tajik. When Tajikistan became independent, the organization was renamed the Committee of National Security and a Tajik, Alimjon Solehboyev, was put in charge. In 1995 the committee received full cabinet status as the Ministry of Security.

Police powers are divided between the forces of the Ministry of Internal Affairs and the Ministry of Security. The two most significant characteristics of the current system are the failure to observe the laws that are on the books in political cases and the penetration of the current regime by criminal elements.

### Narcotics

In the last years of the Soviet Union and in the Russian Federation of the mid-1990s, the issue of drug trafficking was embroiled in political rhetoric and public prejudices. The Yeltsin administration used the combined threats of narcotics and Islamic fundamentalism to justify Russian military involvement in Tajikistan, and the Rahmonov regime used accusations

*Preparing for an antinarcotics expedition supported by United States Drug Enforcement Administration*
*Courtesy Stephane Herbert*

of drug crimes to justify the repression of domestic political opponents.

Despite the presence of Russian border guards, the border between Afghanistan and Tajikistan has proved easily penetrable by narcotics smugglers, for whom the lack of stable law enforcement on both sides of the boundary provides great opportunities. For some Central Asians, the opium trade has assumed great economic importance in the difficult times of the post-Soviet era. An established transit line moves opium from Afghanistan and Pakistan to Khorugh in Tajikistan's Gorno-Badakhshan Autonomous Province, from which it moves to Dushanbe and then to Osh on the Kyrgyzstan-Uzbekistan border. The ultimate destination of much of the narcotics passing through Tajikistan is a burgeoning market in Moscow and other Russian cities, as well as some markets in Western

Europe and in other CIS nations. Besides Pakistan and Afghanistan, sources have been identified in Russia, Western Europe, Colombia, and Southeast Asia. A shipment of heroin was confiscated for the first time in 1995; previously, traffic apparently had been limited to opium and hashish.

An organized-crime network reportedly has developed around the Moscow narcotics market; Russian border guards, members of the CIS peacekeeping force, and senior Tajikistani government officials reportedly are involved in this activity. Besides corruption, enforcement has been hampered by antiquated Soviet-era laws and a lack of funding. In 1995 the number of drug arrests increased, but more than two-thirds were for cultivation; only twenty were for the sale of drugs. A national drug-control plan was under government consideration in early 1996. Regional drug-control cooperation broke down after independence. In 1995 the Tajikistani government planned to implement a new regional program, based in the UN Drug Control Program office in Tashkent, for drug interdiction along the Murghob-Osh-Andijon overland route. The Ministry of Internal Affairs, the customs authorities, the Ministry of Health, and the procurator general all have responsibilities in drug interdiction, but there are no formal lines of interagency cooperation.

### Criminal Justice and the Penal System

Independent Tajikistan's system of courts and police evolved from the institutional framework established in the Soviet era. The judiciary is not fully independent; the 1994 constitution gives the president the power to remove judges from office. In the wake of the victors' wave of violence against actual or potential supporters of the opposition at the end of the civil war, the post-civil war regime continued to ignore due process of law in dealing with opposition supporters. Numerous opposition figures were arrested and held without trial for prolonged periods; representatives of the International Committee of the Red Cross and Helsinki Watch were not permitted to see political prisoners. Extrajudicial killings, disappearances, warrantless searches, the probable planting of incriminating evidence, arrests for conduct that was not illegal, and physical abuse of prisoners were all part of the new regime's treatment of opposition supporters. The regime established its own secret prisons for those held on political charges.

In the new government installed at the end of the civil war, the minister of internal affairs, hence the national head of police, was Yaqub Salimov, who had no law enforcement experience and himself had led a criminal gang. Salimov was an associate of Sangak Safarov, a top antireformist military leader who also had an extensive criminal record. Salimov used his law enforcement position to shield his criminal confederates and to intimidate other members of the cabinet. In 1995 President Rahmonov finally maneuvered Salimov out of power by appointing him ambassador to Turkey. Salimov's successor as minister of internal affairs was Saidomir Zuhurov, a KGB veteran who had been minister of security in the post-civil war government.

Thus, in the mid-1990s Tajikistan's national security condition was tenuous from both domestic and international standpoints. Internally, the concept of uniform law enforcement for the protection of Tajikistani citizens had not taken hold, in spite of constitutional guarantees. Instead, the republic's law enforcement agencies were at the service of the political goals of those in power. Externally, Tajikistan remained almost completely reliant upon Russia and its Central Asian neighbors for military protection of its borders. By 1996 years of internationally sponsored negotiations had failed to bring about a satisfactory compromise between the government and the opposition, offering little hope that CIS troops could leave but providing the Rahmonov government a pretext for ongoing restraint of civil liberties.

*       *       *

Relatively little has been written in English about Tajikistan. An important study of the largely Persian civilization and political history of southern Central Asia in the early centuries of the Islamic era is Richard N. Frye's *Bukhara: The Medieval Achievement.* The first three chapters of *Turko-Persia in Historical Perspective,* edited by Robert L. Canfield, describe the interaction of Turkic- and Persian-speaking peoples in the region. The Russian scholar Vasilii V. Bartol'd wrote a seminal historical work that has been translated as *Turkestan Down to the Mongol Invasion.* Tajikistan's Persian-language literature is covered in the chapter "Modern Tajik Literature" in *Persian Literature,* edited by Ehsan Yarshater. Teresa Rakowska-Harmstone's *Russia and Nationalism in Central Asia* describes Tajikistani politics in the

Stalin and Khrushchev eras from the Russian viewpoint. Muriel Atkin's *The Subtlest Battle* and "Islam as Faith, Politics and Bogeyman in Tajikistan" (a chapter in *The Politics of Religion in Russia and the New States of Eurasia,* edited by Michael Bourdeaux) describe the role of Islam in Soviet and post-Soviet times. A description of events leading to the 1992 civil war is contained in Shahrbanou Tadjbakhsh's "The 'Tajik Spring' of 1992." Sergei Gretsky has covered aspects of the civil war in two articles, one appearing in *Critique* (Spring 1995) and the other in *Central Asia Monitor* (No. 1, 1994), and an assessment of Russian-Tajikistani relations in a chapter of *Regional Power Rivalries in the New Eurasia,* edited by Alvin Z. Rubinstein and Oles M. Smolansky. (For further information and complete citations, see Bibliography.)

# Chapter 4. Turkmenistan

*Ivory wine vessel excavated at site of Nisa, ancient city near Ashgabat*

# Country Profile

## Country

**Formal Name:** Republic of Turkmenistan.

**Short Form:** Turkmenistan.

**Term for Citizens:** Turkmenistani(s).

**Capital:** Ashgabat.

**Date of Independence:** October 27, 1991.

## Geography

**Size:** Approximately 488,100 square kilometers.

**Topography:** Center of country dominated by Turan Depression and Garagum Desert, flatlands of which occupy nearly 80 percent of country's area; Kopetdag Range along southwestern border reaches 2,912 meters; Balkan Mountains in far west and Kugitang Range in far east only other appreciable elevations.

**Climate:** Subtropical, desert, and severely continental, with little rainfall; winters mild and dry, most precipitation falling between January and May. Heaviest precipitation in Kopetdag Range.

## Society

**Population:** In 1991, population 3,808,900; 1989 annual growth rate 2.5 percent; 1991 population density 7.8 persons per square kilometer.

**Ethnic Groups:** In 1991, Turkmen 72 percent, Russians nearly 10 percent, Uzbeks 9 percent, and Kazaks 2 percent.

**Languages:** Turkmen, official national language, spoken by about 75 percent of population; Russian, replaced as official language in 1992 constitution, still much used in official communications despite campaigning to limit its influence; English given status behind Turkmen as second official language, 1993.

**Religion:** Approximately 87 percent Muslim (mainly Sunni), 11 percent Russian Orthodox; many who profess Islam are not active adherents.

**Education and Literacy:** In 1991, estimated 98 percent of those above age fifteen literate; education compulsory through eighth grade. Much of Soviet education system still in place; substantial modification in progress to raise quality of work force.

**Health:** Soviet system of free care for all citizens remains in place, but in early 1990s supply shortages and poor medical staff made care inadequate in many areas; infant mortality highest and life expectancy lowest in Central Asia.

## Economy

**Gross National Product (GNP):** 1994 estimate US$4.3 billion, or US$1,049 per capita. Real growth rate estimated at –24 percent, 1994.

**Agriculture:** Limited, gradual privatization of state-held arable land, with state control of marketing and inputs. Irrigation, a major expense in support of nearly all agricultural areas, hampered by inefficient delivery. Major crops cotton, grains, fodder crops, with wool, meat, and milk from raising of livestock, chiefly sheep.

**Industry and Mining:** Specialized for oil and gas industry and cotton products, post-Soviet diversification slow; some machine building, production of construction materials, carpet weaving, and food and wine processing. Fuel-related industries slowed in early 1990s by difficulties in fuel sales abroad. Wide variety of mineral deposits, especially sulfur, used in chemical industry.

**Energy:** Self-sufficient in natural gas and oil, with major untapped deposits expected to sustain supply in foreseeable future. Natural gas dominates domestic energy consumption and energy exports.

**Exports:** In 1995 worth about US$1.9 billion. Principal items natural gas, petroleum, cotton, chemicals, processed foods, and minerals. Postcommunist export market in Russia remains steady; markets with other former Soviet republics have declined. Post-1991 expansion of specific products, especially cotton, outside Commonwealth of Independent States (CIS), Western Europe, Mexico, Far East.

**Imports:** In 1995 worth about US$1.5 billion. Principal items food and beverages, textiles, and machinery. Principal import suppliers Russia, Ukraine, Kazakstan, Uzbekistan, Azerbaijan, and Germany.

**Balance of Payments:** In 1992, estimated as US$108 million deficit.

**Exchange Rate:** Manat introduced November 1993, replacing Russian ruble. One manat equals 100 tenge. Revaluation late 1995 from US$1=500 manat to US$1=2,100 manat, but wide variation of value in unofficial markets. Official rate January 1996, 200 manat per US$1.

**Inflation:** In 1995 estimated at more than 1,000 percent, about same rate as previous years. Increased entitlements and loose government lending policy caused repeated increases in early 1990s.

**Fiscal Year:** Calendar year.

**Fiscal Policy:** Highly centralized government policy, with no regional authority. Ministry of Economy and Finance has nominal control over public finance, but many extrabudgetary expenditures block effective control, incur deficits. Lack of experience hinders development of commercially oriented banking system.

## Transportation and Telecommunications

**Highways:** In 1990 about 23,000 kilometers of roads, of which 15,300 paved. One major highway connects eastern and western population centers.

**Railroads:** In 1993, about 2,120 kilometers of track in system inadequate to serve current needs. Major renovation and expansion in planning stage, including 1,000 kilometers of new track.

**Civil Aviation:** Seven airports, four with permanent-surface runways. Main international airport at Ashgabat. Turkmenistan Airlines offers connections to some European cities, Middle and Far East, and southern Asia.

**Inland Waterways:** None.

**Ports:** Main shipping facility at Turkmenbashy on Caspian Sea; three smaller Caspian ports, undergoing reconstruction 1995.

**Pipelines:** Critical part of economic infrastructure; in 1994, some 4,400 kilometers in operation, with plans for new natural gas lines westward to Bulgaria (4,000 kilometers) and eastward to China (6,700 kilometers) before 2000.

**Telecommunications:** In poorly developed telephone system, 28 percent of households with telephones, many villages lacking telephone service entirely, and much outdated equipment; modernization program began early 1990s. Two television broadcasting centers relaying satellite transmissions from Orbita and International Telecommunications Satellite Organization (Intelsat) to all cities and rural centers. All broadcasting controlled by State Committee for Television and Radio Broadcasting.

## Government and Politics

**Government:** Many Soviet-era officials still in place, 1996; constitution of 1992 stipulates democratic separation of powers, but presidency sole center of actual power under Saparmyrat Niyazov. Legislative branch, fifty-member Milli Mejlis, has same ratification functions as Soviet-era Supreme Soviet. Judiciary very weak—judges appointed by president; Supreme Court reviews constitutionality of legislation. Sixty-member National Council with advisory function, actually subsidiary to presidential power.

**Politics:** Constitution guarantees political freedom, but former Communist Party, now Democratic Party, dominates and retains same structure and propaganda machine as in Soviet era. Niyazov's cult of personality provides further domination. Small, weak opposition groups concentrate on single issues;

some groups outlawed.

**Foreign Relations:** Basic policy "positive neutrality"—noninterference and neutrality toward all countries and attempts to establish relations as widely as possible. Marketing and transport of natural gas and oil given priority in foreign economic deals. Remains independent of other Central Asian and CIS countries when possible, but maintains strong bilateral military and economic ties with Russia.

**International Agreements and Memberships:** Member of United Nations (UN), International Monetary Fund (IMF), World Bank, Economic Cooperation Organization (ECO), Organization for Security and Cooperation in Europe (OSCE), Islamic Development Bank, and CIS.

## National Security

**Armed Forces:** All personnel except officers conscripts. Turkmenistan army, includes about 11,000 Turkmen personnel (under joint Turkmen-Russian control); 12,000 Russian troops also present, 1995. Air force has 2,000 men, plus substantial Russian force remaining in country pending final distribution. Coastal defense force is included in multinational Caspian Flotilla. Border Guard, under joint Turkmen and Russian command, has 5,000 personnel, mainly on Afghan and Iranian borders.

**Major Military Units:** Army consists of one corps, including three motorized rifle divisions, one artillery brigade, one multiple rocket launcher regiment, one antitank regiment, three engineer regiments, one helicopter squadron, and signal, reconnaissance, and logistics support units. Air force includes four regiments, 175 combat aircraft; air defense force has two fighter regiments; air and air defense organization contingent on negotiations with Russia on disposition of former Soviet forces.

**Military Budget:** Estimated 1995, US$61 million.

**Internal Security:** Committee for National Security continues as main security force similar to Soviet-era Turkmenistan Committee for State Security (KGB). Ministry of Internal Affairs administers regular police, working closely with Committee for National Security in matters of national security. Criminal investigation under procurator's offices, not regular police, who have only routine functions. As in Soviet system, procurators investigate and prosecute crimes. Rule of law hampered by judiciary's subordinate position to executive branch and lack of independent judicial tradition.

Figure 12. Turkmenistan: Administrative Divisions and Transportation System, 1996

300

DURING MUCH OF ITS PAST, Turkmenistan has received little attention from the outside world. Apart from its role in establishing the Seljuk dynasty in the Middle East in the Middle Ages, for most of its history this territory was not a coherent nation but a geographically defined region of independent tribal groups and other political entities. Like other republics of the former Soviet Union, Turkmenistan has emerged on the world scene as a newly independent country in need of both national and international acceptance, security, and development.

Turkmenistan's authoritarian regime and regional social structure have produced the most politically and economically stable of the former Soviet republics. Although its leadership has gained a reputation abroad for repression of political opposition, it is perceived at home as promoting the social benefits, national traditions, and security of the Turkmen people. In addition, to ensure its national security and trade prospects, Turkmenistan has charted an independent course in establishing a military alliance with Russia and trade and security agreements with Iran and Central Asian countries. In terms of natural assets, Turkmenistan is a landlocked, desert country beneath whose surface lie substantial deposits of oil and the fifth largest reserves of natural gas in the world. Foreign investors, attracted by the republic's calm and receptive atmosphere, have sidestepped human rights issues on their way to establishing joint exploitation of Turkmenistan's rich energy resources.

## Historical Setting

Like the other Central Asian republics, Turkmenistan underwent the intrusion and rule of several foreign powers before falling under first Russian and then Soviet control in the modern era. Most notable were the Mongols and the Uzbek khanates, the latter of which dominated the indigenous Oghuz tribes until Russian incursions began in the late nineteenth century.

### Origins and Early History

Sedentary Oghuz tribes from Mongolia moved into present-day Central Asia around the eighth century. Within a few centuries, some of these tribes had become the ethnic basis of the Turkmen population.

### The Oghuz and the Turkmen

The origins of the Turkmen may be traced back to the Oghuz confederation of nomadic pastoral tribes of the early Middle Ages, which lived in present-day Mongolia and around Lake Baikal in present-day southern Siberia. Known as the Nine Oghuz, this confederation was composed of Turkic-speaking peoples who formed the basis of powerful steppe empires in Inner Asia. In the second half of the eighth century, components of the Nine Oghuz migrated through Jungaria into Central Asia, and Arabic sources located them under the term *Guzz* in the area of the middle and lower Syrdariya in the eighth century. By the tenth century, the Oghuz had expanded west and north of the Aral Sea and into the steppe of present-day Kazakstan, absorbing not only Iranians but also Turks from the Kipchak and Karluk ethnolinguistic groups. In the eleventh century, the renowned Muslim Turk scholar Mahmud al-Kashgari described the language of the Oghuz and Turkmen as distinct from that of other Turks and identified twenty-two Oghuz clans or sub-tribes, some of which appear in later Turkmen genealogies and legends as the core of the early Turkmen.

Oghuz expansion by means of military campaigns went at least as far as the Volga River and Ural Mountains, but the geographic limits of their dominance fluctuated in the steppe areas extending north and west from the Aral Sea. Accounts of Arab geographers and travelers portray the Oghuz ethnic group as lacking centralized authority and being governed by a number of "kings" and "chieftains." Because of their disparate nature as a polity and the vastness of their domains, Oghuz tribes rarely acted in concert. Hence, by the late tenth century, the bonds of their confederation began to loosen. At that time, a clan leader named Seljuk founded a dynasty and the empire that bore his name on the basis of those Oghuz elements that had migrated southward into present-day Turkmenistan and Iran. The Seljuk Empire was centered in Persia, from which Oghuz groups spread into Azerbaijan and Anatolia.

The name *Turkmen* first appears in written sources of the tenth century to distinguish those Oghuz groups who migrated south into the Seljuk domains and accepted Islam from those that had remained in the steppe. Gradually, the term took on the properties of an ethnonym and was used exclusively to designate Muslim Oghuz, especially those who migrated away from the Syrdariya Basin. By the thirteenth century, the term *Turkmen* supplanted the designation *Oghuz* altogether. The origin of the word *Turkmen* remains unclear. According to popular etymologies as old as the eleventh century, the word derives from *Turk* plus the Iranian element *manand*, and means "resembling a Turk." Modern scholars, on the other hand, have proposed that the element *man/men* acts as an intensifier and have translated the word as "pure Turk" or "most Turk-like of the Turks."

### The Seljuk Period

In the eleventh century, Seljuk domains stretched from the delta of the Amu Darya delta into Iran, Iraq, the Caucasus region, Syria, and Asia Minor. In 1055 Seljuk forces entered Baghdad, becoming masters of the Islamic heartlands and important patrons of Islamic institutions. The last powerful Seljuk ruler, Sultan Sanjar (d. 1157), witnessed the fragmentation and destruction of the empire because of attacks by Turkmen and other tribes.

Until these revolts, Turkmen tribesmen were an integral part of the Seljuk military forces. Turkmen migrated with their families and possessions on Seljuk campaigns into Azerbaijan and Anatolia, a process that began the Turkification of these areas. During this time, Turkmen also began to settle the area of present-day Turkmenistan. Prior to the Turkmen habitation, most of this desert had been uninhabited, while the more habitable areas along the Caspian Sea, Kopetdag Mountains, Amu Darya, and Murgap River (Murgap Deryasy) were populated predominantly by Iranians. The city-state of Merv was an especially large sedentary and agricultural area, important as both a regional economic-cultural center and a transit hub on the famous Silk Road.

## Formation of the Turkmen Nation

During the Mongol conquest of Central Asia in the thirteenth century, the Turkmen-Oghuz of the steppe were pushed from the Syrdariya farther into the Garagum (Russian spelling Kara Kum) Desert and along the Caspian Sea. Various components were nominally subject to the Mongol domains in eastern Europe, Central Asia, and Iran. Until the early sixteenth century, they were concentrated in four main regions: along the southeastern coast of the Caspian Sea, on the Mangyshlak Peninsula (on the northeastern Caspian coast), around the Balkan Mountains, and along the Uzboy River running across north-central Turkmenistan. Many scholars regard the fourteenth through the sixteenth centuries as the period of the reformulation of the Turkmen into the tribal groups that exist today. Beginning in the sixteenth century and continuing into the nineteenth century, large tribal conglomerates and individual groups migrated east and southeast.

Historical sources indicate the existence of a large tribal union often referred to as the Salor confederation in the Mangyshlak Peninsula and areas around the Balkan Mountains. The Salor were one of the few original Oghuz tribes to survive to modern times. In the late seventeenth century, the union dissolved and the three senior tribes moved eastward and later southward. The Yomud split into eastern and western groups, while the Teke moved into the Akhal region along the Kopetdag Mountains and gradually into the Murgap River basin. The Salor tribes migrated into the region near the Amu Darya delta in the oasis of Khorazm south of the Aral Sea, the middle course of the Amu Darya southeast of the Aral Sea, the Akhal oasis north of present-day Ashgabat and areas along the Kopetdag bordering Iran, and the Murgap River in present-day southeast Turkmenistan. Salor groups also live in Turkey, Afghanistan, Uzbekistan, and China.

Much of what we know about the Turkmen from the sixteenth to nineteenth centuries comes from Uzbek and Persian chronicles that record Turkmen raids and involvement in the political affairs of their sedentary neighbors. Beginning in the sixteenth century, most of the Turkmen tribes were divided among two Uzbek principalities: the Khanate (or amirate) of Khiva (centered along the lower Amu Darya in Khorazm) and the Khanate of Bukhoro (Bukhara). Uzbek khans and princes of both khanates customarily enlisted Turkmen military support in their intra- and inter-khanate struggles and in campaigns against the Persians. Consequently, many Turkmen tribes migrated closer to the urban centers of the khanates, which came to depend heavily upon the Turkmen for their military forces. The height of Turkmen influence in the affairs of their sedentary neighbors came in the eighteenth century, when on several occasions (1743, 1767–70), the Yomud invaded and controlled Khorazm. From 1855 to 1867, a series of Yomud rebellions again shook the area. These hostilities and the punitive raids by Uzbek rulers resulted in the wide dispersal of the eastern Yomud group.

## Incorporation into Russia

Russian attempts to encroach upon Turkmen territory began in earnest in the latter part of the nineteenth century. Of all the Central Asian peoples, the Turkmen put up the stiffest resistance against Russian expansion. In 1869 the Russian Empire established a foothold in present-day Turkmenistan with the foundation of the Caspian Sea port of Krasnovodsk (now Turkmenbashy). From there and other points, they marched on and subdued the Khiva Khanate in 1873. Because Turkmen tribes, most notably the Yomud, were in the military service of the Khivan khan, Russian forces undertook punitive raids against the Turkmen of Khorazm, in the process slaughtering hundreds and destroying their settlements. In 1881 the Russians under General Mikhail Skobelev besieged and captured Gokdepe, one of the last Turkmen strongholds, northwest of Ashgabat. With the Turkmen defeat (which is now marked by the Turkmen as a national day of mourning and a symbol of national pride), the annexation of what is present-day Turkmenistan met with only weak resistance. Later the same year, the Russians signed an agreement with the Persians and established what essentially remains the current border between Turkmenistan and Iran. In 1897 a similar agreement was signed between the Russians and Afghans.

Following annexation to Russia, the area was administered as the Trans-Caspian District by corrupt and malfeasant military officers and officials appointed by the Guberniya (Governorate General) of Turkestan (see fig. 3). In the 1880s, a railroad line was built from Krasnovodsk to Ashgabat and later extended to Tashkent. Urban areas began to develop along the railway. Although the Trans-Caspian region essentially was a colony of Russia, it remained a backwater, except for Russian concerns with British colonialist intentions in the region and with possible uprisings by the Turkmen.

## Soviet Turkmenistan

Because the Turkmen generally were indifferent to the advent of Soviet rule in 1917, little revolutionary activity occurred in the region in the years that followed. However, the years immediately preceding the revolution had been marked by sporadic Turkmen uprisings against Russian rule, most prominently the anti-tsarist revolt of 1916 that swept through the whole of Turkestan. Their armed resistance to Soviet rule was part of the larger Basmachi Rebellion throughout Central Asia from the 1920s into the early 1930s. Although Soviet sources describe this struggle as a minor chapter in the republic's history, it is clear that opposition was fierce and resulted in the death of large numbers of Turkmen.

In October 1924, when Central Asia was divided into distinct political entities, the Trans-Caspian District and Turkmen Oblast of the Turkestan Autonomous Soviet Socialist Republic became the Turkmen Soviet Socialist Republic. During the forced collectivization and other extreme socioeconomic changes of the first decades of Soviet rule, pastoral nomadism ceased to be an economic alternative in Turkmenistan, and by the late 1930s the majority of Turkmen had become sedentary. Efforts by the Soviet state to undermine the traditional Turkmen way of life resulted in significant changes in familial and political relationships, religious and cultural observances, and intellectual developments. Significant numbers of Russians and other Slavs, as well as groups from various nationalities mainly from the Caucasus, migrated to urban areas. Modest industrial capabilities were developed, and limited exploitation of Turkmenistan's natural resources was initiated.

## Sovereignty and Independence

Beginning in the 1930s, Moscow kept the republic under firm control. The nationalities policy of the Communist Party of the Soviet Union (CPSU) fostered the development of a Turkmen political elite and promoted Russification. Slavs, both in Moscow and Turkmenistan, closely supervised the national cadre of government officials and bureaucrats; generally, the Turkmen leadership staunchly supported Soviet policies. Moscow initiated nearly all political activity in the republic, and, except for a corruption scandal in the mid-1980s, Turkmenistan remained a quiet Soviet republic. Mikhail S. Gorbachev's policies of *glasnost* (see Glossary) and *perestroika* (see Glossary) did not have a significant impact on Turkmenistan. The republic found itself rather unprepared for the dissolution of the Soviet Union and the independence that followed in 1991.

When other constituent republics of the Soviet Union advanced claims to sovereignty in 1988 and 1989, Turkmenistan's leadership also began to criticize Moscow's economic and political policies as exploitative and detrimental to the well-being and pride of the Turkmen. By a unanimous vote of its Supreme Soviet, Turkmenistan declared its sovereignty in August 1990. After the August 1991 coup attempt against the Gorbachev regime in Moscow, Turkmenistan's communist leader Saparmyrat Niyazov called for a popular referendum on independence. The official result of the referendum was 94 percent in favor of independence. The republic's Supreme Soviet had little choice other than to declare Turkmenistan's independence from the Soviet Union and the establishment of the Republic of Turkmenistan on October 27, 1991.

## Physical Environment

Turkmenistan is the southernmost republic of the Commonwealth of Independent States (CIS—see Glossary), the loose federation created at the end of 1991 by most of the post-Soviet states. Its longest border is with the Caspian Sea (1,786 kilometers). The other borders are with Iran (to the south, 992 kilometers), Afghanistan (to the south, 744 kilometers), Uzbekistan (to the north and east, 1,621 kilometers) and Kazakstan (to the north, 379 kilometers). Turkmenistan is slightly larger than California in territory, occupying 488,100 square kilometers. That statistic ranks Turkmenistan fourth among the former Soviet republics. The country's greatest extent from west to east is 1,100 kilometers, and its greatest north-to-south distance is 650 kilometers (see fig. 12).

### Physical Features

Turkmenistan's average elevation is 100 to 220 meters above sea level, with its highest point being Mount Ayrybaba (3,137 meters) in the Kugitang Range of the Pamir-Alay chain in the far east, and its lowest point in the Transcaspian Depression (100 kilometers below sea level). Nearly 80 percent of the republic lies within the Turon Depression, which slopes from south to north and from east to west.

Turkmenistan's mountains include 600 kilometers of the northern reaches of the Kopetdag Range, which it shares with Iran. The Kopetdag Range is a region characterized by foothills, dry and sandy slopes, mountain plateaus, and steep ravines; Mount Shahshah (2,912 meters), southwest of Ashgabat, is the highest elevation of the range in Turkmenistan. The Kopetdag is undergoing tectonic transformation, meaning that the region is threatened by earthquakes such as the one that destroyed Ashgabat in 1948 and registered nine on the Richter Scale. The Krasnovodsk and Üstirt plateaus are the prominent topographical features of northwestern Turkmenistan.

A dominant feature of the republic's landscape is the Garagum Desert, which occupies about 350,000 square kilometers (see Environmental Issues, this ch.). Shifting winds create desert mountains that range from two to twenty meters in height and may be several kilometers in length. Chains of such structures are common, as are steep elevations and smooth, concrete-like clay deposits formed by the rapid evaporation of flood waters in the same area for a number of years. Large marshy salt flats, formed by capillary action in the soil, exist in many depressions, including the Kara Shor, which occupies 1,500 square kilometers in the northwest. The Sundukly Desert west of the Amu Darya is the southernmost extremity of the Qizilqum (Russian spelling Kyzyl Kum) Desert, most of which lies in Uzbekistan to the northeast.

## Climate

Turkmenistan has a subtropical desert climate that is severely continental. Summers are long (from May through September), hot, and dry, while winters generally are mild and dry, although occasionally cold and damp in the north. Most precipitation falls between January and May; precipitation is slight throughout the country, with annual averages ranging from 300 millimeters in the Kopetdag to eighty millimeters in the northwest. The capital, Ashgabat, close to the Iranian border in south-central Turkmenistan, averages 225 millimeters of rainfall annually. Average annual temperatures range from highs of 16.8°C in Ashgabat to lows of –5.5°C in Dashhowuz, on the Uzbek border in north-central Turkmenistan. The almost constant winds are northerly, northeasterly, or westerly.

## Hydrological Conditions

Almost 80 percent of the territory of Turkmenistan lacks a constant source of surface water flow. Its main rivers are located only in the southern and eastern peripheries; a few smaller rivers on the northern slopes of the Kopetdag are diverted entirely to irrigation. The most important river is the Amu Darya, which has a total length of 2,540 kilometers from its farthest tributary, making it the longest river in Central Asia. The Amu Darya flows across northeastern Turkmenistan, thence eastward to form the southern borders of Uzbekistan and Tajikistan. Damming and irrigation uses of the Amu Darya have had severe environmental effects on the Aral Sea, into which the river flows (see Environmental Issues, this ch.). The river's average annual flow is 1,940 cubic meters per second. Other major rivers are the Tejen (1,124 kilometers); the Murgap (852 kilometers); and the Atrek (660 kilometers).

## Environmental Issues

Since the collapse of the Soviet Union, environmental regulation is largely unchanged in Turkmenistan. The new government created the Ministry of Natural Resources Use and Environmental Protection in July 1992, with departments responsible for environmental protection, protection of flora and fauna, forestry, hydrometeorology, and administrative planning. Like other CIS republics, Turkmenistan has established an Environmental Fund based on revenues collected from environmental fines, but the fines generally are too low to accumulate significant revenue. Thanks to the former Soviet system of game preserves and the efforts of the Society for Nature Conservation and the Academy of Sciences, flora and fauna receive some protection in the republic; however, "hard-currency hunts" by wealthy Western and Arab businesspeople already are depleting animals on preserves.

### Desertification

According to estimates, as a result of desertification processes and pollution, biological productivity of the ecological systems in Turkmenistan has declined by 30 to 50 percent in recent decades. The Garagum and Qizilqum deserts are expanding at a rate surpassed on a planetary scale only by the desertification process in the Sahara and Sahel regions of Africa. Between 800,000 and 1,000,000 hectares of new desert now appears per year in Central Asia.

The most irreparable type of desertification is the salinization process that forms marshy salt flats. A major factor that contributes to these conditions is inefficient use of water because of weak regulation and failure to charge for water that is used. Efficiency in application of water to the fields is low, but the main problem is leakage in main and secondary canals, especially Turkmenistan's main canal, the Garagum Canal. Nearly half of the canal's water seeps out into lakes and salt swamps along its path. Excessive irrigation brings salts to the surface, forming salt marshes that dry into unusable clay flats. In 1989 Turkmenistan's Institute for Desert Studies claimed that the area of such flats had reached one million hectares.

The type of desertification caused by year-round pasturing of cattle has been termed the most devastating in Central Asia, with the gravest situations in Turkmenistan and the Kazak steppe along the eastern and northern coasts of the Caspian Sea. Wind erosion and desertification also are severe in settled areas along the Garagum Canal; planted windbreaks have died because of soil waterlogging and/or salinization. Other factors promoting desertification are the inadequacy of the collector-drainage system built in the 1950s and inappropriate application of chemicals.

## The Aral Sea

Turkmenistan both contributes to and suffers from the consequences of the desiccation of the Aral Sea. Because of excessive irrigation, Turkmen agriculture contributes to the steady drawdown of sea levels. In turn, the Aral Sea's desiccation, which had shrunk that body of water by an estimated 59,000 square kilometers by 1994, profoundly affects economic productivity and the health of the population of the republic. Besides the cost of ameliorating damaged areas and the loss of at least part of the initial investment in them, salinization and chemicalization of land have reduced agricultural productivity in Central Asia by an estimated 20 to 25 percent. Poor drinking water is the main health risk posed by such environmental degradation. In Dashhowuz Province, which has suffered the greatest ecological damage from the Aral Sea's desiccation, bacteria levels in drinking water exceeded ten times the sanitary level; 70 percent of the population has experienced illnesses, many with hepatitis, and infant mortality is high (see table 5, Appendix; Health Conditions, this ch.). Experts have warned that inhabitants will have to evacuate the province by the end of the century unless a comprehensive cleanup program is undertaken. Turkmenistan has announced plans to clean up some of the Aral Sea fallout with financial support from the World Bank (see Glossary).

## Chemical Pollution

The most productive cotton lands in Turkmenistan (the middle and lower Amu Darya and the Murgap oasis) receive as much as 250 kilograms of fertilizer per hectare, compared with the average application of thirty kilograms per hectare. Furthermore, most fertilizers are so poorly applied that experts have estimated that only 15 to 40 percent of the chemicals can be absorbed by cotton plants, while the remainder washes into the soil and subsequently into the groundwater. Cotton also uses far more pesticides and defoliants than other crops, and application of these chemicals often is mishandled by farmers. For example, local herdsmen, unaware of the danger of DDT, have reportedly mixed the pesticide with water and applied it to their faces to keep away mosquitoes. In the late 1980s, a drive began in Central Asia to reduce agrochemical usage. In Turkmenistan the campaign reduced fertilizer use 30 percent between 1988 and 1989. In the early 1990s, use of some pesticides and defoliants declined drastically because of the country's shortage of hard currency.

## Population

Turkmenistan's population is rather stable, with distribution between urban and rural areas and migration trends showing minor changes between censuses (see table 3, Appendix). The annual population growth rate, however, is rather high, and population density has increased significantly in the last forty years.

### Size and Distribution

In 1993 Turkmenistan had a population of 4,254,000 people, making it the fifth most sparsely populated former Soviet republic. Of that number, Turkmen comprised about 73 percent, Russians nearly 10 percent, Uzbeks 9 percent, Kazaks 2 percent, and other ethnic groups the remaining 5 percent (see table 4, Appendix). According to the last Soviet census (1989), the total Turkmen population in the Soviet Union was 2,728,965. Of this number, 2,536,606 lived in Turkmenistan and the remainder in the other republics. Outside of the CIS, approximately 1.6 million Turkmen live in Iran, Afghanistan, and China (see The Spoken Language, this ch.).

Population density increased in the republic from one person per square kilometer in 1957 to 9.2 persons per square kilometer in 1995. Density varies drastically between desert areas and oases, where it often exceeds 100 persons per square kilometer. Within Turkmenistan, the population is 50.6 percent female and 49.4 percent male. In 1995 the estimated annual growth rate was 2.0 percent, and the fertility rate was 3.7 births per woman (a decline of 1.5 births per woman since 1979) (see table 2, Appendix). The population was demographically quite young, with 40 percent aged fourteen or younger and only four percent aged over sixty-four.

## Migration Trends

In 1989 about 45 percent of the population was classified as urban, a drop of 3 percent since 1979. Prior to the arrival of Russians in the late nineteenth century, Turkmenistan had very few urban areas, and many of the large towns and cities that exist today were developed after the 1930s. Ashgabat, the capital and largest city in Turkmenistan, has a population of about 420,000. The second-largest city, Chärjew on the Amu Darya, has about 165,000 people. Other major cities are Turkmenbashy on the Caspian seacoast, Mary in the southeast, and Dashhowuz in the northeast. Because much of the Russian population only came to Turkmenistan in the Soviet period, separate Russian quarters or neighborhoods did not develop in Turkmenistan's cities as they did elsewhere in Central Asia. This fact, combined with a relatively small Slavic population, has led to integration of Turkmen and Slavs in neighborhoods and housing projects.

Apart from the outflow of small numbers of Russians immediately following Turkmenistan's independence, neither out-migration nor in-migration is a significant factor for Turkmenistan's population. In 1992 there were 19,035 emigrants from Turkmenistan to the Russian Federation and 7,069 immigrants to Turkmenistan.

# Society

Fundamental social institutions generally remained unchanged by the presence of Marxist dogma for over seventy years, although the presence of large numbers of Russians changed the distribution of the classes and the cultural loyalties of the intelligentsia. With some weakening in urban areas in the twentieth century, kinship and tribal affiliation retain a strong influence over the structure of Turkmen society.

## National Traditions

Today's Turkmen have fully embraced the concepts of national unity and a strong national consciousness, which had been elusive through most of their history. The Turkmen have begun to reassess their history and culture, as well as the effects of Soviet rule. Some of the more notable changes since independence have been a shift from open hostility to cautious official sanctioning of Islam, the declaration of Turkmen as the state language, and the state's promotion of national and religious customs and holidays. For example, the vernal equinox, known as Novruz ("New Year's Day"), is now celebrated officially country-wide.

Interest and pride in national traditions were demonstrated openly prior to independence, particularly following the introduction of *glasnost'* by Soviet President Mikhail S. Gorbachev in 1985. Since independence, the government has played a less restrictive and at times actively supportive role in the promotion of national traditions. For example, in a move to replace the Soviet version of Turkmen history with one more in harmony with both traditional and current values, President Niyazov formed a state commission to write the "true history of sunny Turkmenistan."

The Soviet period dampened but did not suppress the expression of prominent Turkmen cultural traditions. Turkmen carpets continue to receive praise and special attention from Western enthusiasts. The high sheepskin hats worn by men, as well as distinctive fabrics and jewelry, also are age-old trademarks of Turkmen material culture. The Ahal-Teke breed of horse, world-renowned for its beauty and swiftness, is particular to the Turkmen. Aside from a rich musical heritage, the Turkmen continue to value oral literature, including such epic tales as *Korkut Ata* and *Gurogly.*

Increased national awareness is reflected in modifications of the school curriculum as well. Among new courses of instruction is a class on *edep,* or proper social behavior and moral conduct according to traditional Turkmen and Islamic values. Officially sanctioned efforts also have been made to contact members of the Turkmen population living outside of Turkmenistan, and several international Turkmen organizations have been established.

## Social Structure

Although it is not a basis for political groupings, the rather vague phenomenon of tribal identity is a complex social phenomenon that retains important influence at the end of the twentieth century. The Soviet era added an element of cohesion to a previously loose and unassertive set of social loyalties among Turkmen.

### Social Classes

Turkmen society recognizes a class structure, ideologically based on Marxist doctrine, composed of intelligentsia, workers, and peasants. In practical terms, the intelligentsia and peasantry consist of Turkmen, while the worker class is the domain of Russians. Power and some wealth are associated with the Western-oriented intelligentsia, who hold the key positions in government, industry, and education. Most intelligentsia are educated in Russian language schools, often complete higher educational institutions in Russia, speak Russian as their language of choice, and are concentrated in urban centers, especially in Ashgabat.

Although many members of the intelligentsia favor cultural revival, more support restricting nationalist manifestations and the role of Islam in society. Many who are atheists and have identified with Soviet ideals harbor anxieties that distance from traditional values and especially from the Turkmen language will limit their career potential in the post-Soviet era.

### Kinship

Before the Soviet period, the Turkmen were organized into a segmentary system of territorial groups that Western scholars loosely designate as tribes. These groupings featured little sharp social stratification within or strong unity among them. Tribal structure always has been complex, and the Turkmen-language terminology used to designate lineage affiliation sometimes is confusing. Generally, the largest groupings, which may be equivalent to what Western scholarship labels "tribes," are called *khalk, il,* or *taipa* in Turkmen. Smaller lineage groups are equivalent to Western terms like "clans," "sub-tribes," or "branches." The smallest affiliations are equivalent to subclans or lineages in Western terminology.

In the past, Turkmen tribes remained relatively isolated and politically independent from one another. All tribes possessed specific distinguishing features. Their dialects differed greatly, and in terms of material culture each large tribe had a unique carpet pattern, clothing, headgear, and brand of identification.

Although Soviet nationality policy was somewhat successful in diluting tribal consciousness, tribal identity remains a factor in present-day social relations. Except in such urban areas as

*Street scene in Turkmenbashy, formerly Krasnovodsk*
*Courtesy A. James Firth, United States Department of Agriculture*

Chärjew and Ashgabat, virtually all Turkmen have a knowledge of their parents' and consequently their own tribal affiliation. A Turkmen's tribal affiliation still is a reliable indicator of his or her birthplace, for example. Lineage still may play a role in the arranging of marriages in rural areas. In Soviet Turkmenistan, the membership of collective and state farms often was formed according to clan and tribal affiliation. Although kinship undoubtedly retains significance in contemporary Turkmen society, attempts to use tribal affiliation as the determining factor in such realms as current politics usually are not instructive.

Until the Soviet period, the Turkmen lacked paramount leaders and political unity. The Turkmen rarely allied to campaign against sedentary neighbors, nor did they form a unified front against the Russian conquest. Unlike other Central Asian peoples, the Turkmen recognized no charismatic bloodline. Leaders were elected according to consensus, and their authority was based on conduct. Raids and other military pursuits could be organized by almost any male, but the power he exercised lasted only as long as the undertaking. Turkmen tribal structure did include a leader or chief (*beg*), but these positions, too, were mostly honorary and advisory, based on kinship ties and perceived wisdom. Real power was located among the community's older members, whose advice and consent usually were required prior to any significant endeavor.

Although women rarely assumed prominent political rank and power, there were instances of influential female leaders in the nineteenth century.

## The Family

Prior to Soviet rule, the extended family was the basic and most important social and economic unit among the Turkmen. Grouped according to clan, small bands of Turkmen families lived as nomads in their traditional regions and consolidated only in time of war or celebration. In most cases, the families were entirely self-sufficient, subsisting on their livestock and at times on modest agricultural production. For some groups, raiding sedentary populations, especially the Iranians to the south, was an important economic activity.

Although Soviet power brought about fundamental changes in the Turkmen family structure, many traditional aspects remain. Families continue to be close-knit and often raise more than five children. Although no longer nomadic, families in rural areas still are grouped according to clan or tribe, and it is the rule rather than the exception for the inhabitants of a village to be of one lineage. Here, also, it is common for sons to remain with their parents after marriage and to live in an extended one-story clay structure with a courtyard and an agricultural plot. In both rural and urban areas, respect for elders is great. Whereas homes for the elderly do exist in Turkmenistan, Turkmen are conspicuously absent from them; it is almost unheard of for a Turkmen to commit his or her parent to such an institution because grandparents are considered integral family members and sources of wisdom and spirituality.

The marriage celebration, together with other life-cycle events, possesses great importance in Turkmen society. In rural areas especially, marriages are often arranged by special matchmakers (*sawcholar*). Aside from finding the right match in terms of social status, education, and other qualities, the matchmakers invariably must find couples of the same clan and locale. Most couples have known each other beforehand and freely consent to the marriage arrangement. Divorce among Turkmen is relatively rare. One important custom still practiced in Turkmenistan is the brideprice (*kalong*). Depending on region and a family's wealth, the bride's family may demand huge sums of money from the groom in return for the bride's hand in marriage.

The role of women in Turkmen society has never conformed to Western stereotypes about "Muslim women." Although a division of labor has existed and women usually were not visible actors in political affairs outside the home, Turkmen women never wore the veil or practiced strict seclusion. They generally possessed a host of highly specialized skills and crafts, especially those connected with the household and its maintenance. During the Soviet period, women assumed responsibility for the observance of some Muslim rites to protect their husbands' careers. Many women entered the work force out of economic necessity, a factor that disrupted some traditional family practices and increased the incidence of divorce. At the same time, educated urban women entered professional services and careers.

## The Spoken Language

Turkmen belongs to the family of Turkic languages spoken in Eastern Europe (Tatar, Bashkir, Chuvash), the Caucasus (Azeri, Kumik), Siberia (Yakut, Tuva, Khakas), China (Uygur, Kazak), Central Asia (Kazak, Kyrgyz, Uzbek), and the Near East (Turkish, Azeri). Its closest relatives are the languages of the Turks in northeastern Iran and the Khorazm Province of south central Uzbekistan (Khorasani), Azerbaijan (Azeri), and Turkey (Turkish), all of which belong to the Oghuz group of this language family.

In 1989 some 2,537,000 speakers of Turkmen lived in Turkmenistan, with 121,578 in Uzbekistan (the vast majority in the Khorazm region on Turkmenistan's north central border), 39,739 in the Russian Federation (including 12,000 in the Stavropol' region along Russia's southwestern border), 20,487 in Tajikistan, and 3,846 in Kazakstan. A high degree of language loyalty was reflected in the fact that some 99.4 percent of Turkmen in the republic claimed Turkmen as their native language in the 1989 census. At the same time, 28 percent claimed Russian as their second language—a figure that remained constant between the 1979 and 1989 censuses. More than half of the second category were part of the urban population. Only 3 percent of Russians in the republic spoke Turkmen.

The total number of Turkmen speakers in Europe and Asia has been estimated at between 4 and 4.8 million. These figures include the 2,517,000 Turkmen in the republic, 185,000 Turkmen in other Central Asian states and Russia, an estimated 700,000 Turkmen in Afghanistan, and 850,000 Turkmen in

Iran who speak a closely related but distinct language called Khorasanli.

## The Written Language

Beginning in the eighteenth century, Turkmen poets and chroniclers used the classical Chaghatai language, which was written in Arabic script and reflected only occasional Turkmen linguistic features. Famous poets who wrote in this language include Mammetveli Kemine (1770–1840), Mollanepes (1810–62), and the most honored literary figure, Magtymguly (1733?–90?), whose legacy helped mold Turkmen national consciousness. In the years 1913–17, periodicals were published in Chaghatai. Two reforms of this script undertaken in 1922 and 1925 were designed to reflect features of the spoken Turkmen language. From 1928 to 1940, early Soviet Turkmen literature was written in a Latin alphabet that accurately reflected most of its features. Since 1940, standard Turkmen has been written in the Cyrillic script.

In the mid-1990s, language policy in independent Turkmenistan has been marked by a determination to establish Turkmen as the official language and to remove the heritage of the Russian-dominated past. The 1992 constitution proclaims Turkmen the "official language of inter-ethnic communication." In 1993 English was moved ahead of Russian as the "second state language," although in practical terms Russian remains a key language in government and other spheres. That same year, President Niyazov issued a decree on the replacement of the Cyrillic-based alphabet with a Latin-based script that would become the "state script" by 1996. Some publications and signs already appear in this Latin script, but its full implementation will not occur until after the year 2000. The new alphabet has several unique letters that distinguish it from those of Turkey's Latin alphabet and the newly adopted Latin scripts of other republics whose dominant language is Turkic.

Other steps were taken to erase the Russian linguistic overlay in the republic. A resolution was adopted in May 1992 to change geographic names and administrative terms from Russian to Turkmen. As a result, the names of many streets, institutions, collective farms, and buildings have been renamed for Turkmen heroes and cultural phenomena, and the terminology for all governmental positions and jurisdictions has been changed from Russian to Turkmen.

# Religion

Traditionally, the Turkmen of Turkmenistan, like their kin in Uzbekistan, Afghanistan, and Iran, are Sunni Muslims (see Glossary). Shia Muslims (see Glossary), the other main branch of Islam, are not numerous in Turkmenistan, and the Shia religious practices of the Azerbaijani and Kurdish (see Glossary) minorities are not politicized. Although the great majority of Turkmen readily identify themselves as Muslims and acknowledge Islam as an integral part of their cultural heritage, many are non-believers and support a revival of the religion's status only as an element of national revival. They do not attend mosque services or demonstrate their adherence publicly, except through participation in officially sanctioned national traditions associated with Islam on a popular level, including life-cycle events such as weddings, burials, and pilgrimages.

## History and Structure

Islam came to the Turkmen primarily through the activities of Sufi (see Glossary) shaykhs rather than through the mosque and the "high" written tradition of sedentary culture. These shaykhs were holy men critical in the process of reconciling Islamic beliefs with pre-Islamic belief systems; they often were adopted as "patron saints" of particular clans or tribal groups, thereby becoming their "founders." Reformulation of communal identity around such figures accounts for one of the highly localized developments of Islamic practice in Turkmenistan.

Integrated within the Turkmen tribal structure is the "holy" tribe called *övlat.* Ethnographers consider the *övlat,* of which six are active, as a revitalized form of the ancestor cult injected with Sufism. According to their genealogies, each tribe descends from the Prophet Muhammad through one of the Four Caliphs. Because of their belief in the sacred origin and spiritual powers of the *övlat* representatives, Turkmen accord these tribes a special, holy status. In the eighteenth and nineteenth centuries, the *övlat* tribes became dispersed in small, compact groups in Turkmenistan. They attended and conferred blessings on all important communal and life-cycle events, and also acted as mediators between clans and tribes. The institution of the *övlat* retains some authority today. Many of the Turkmen who are revered for their spiritual powers trace their lineage to an *övlat,* and it is not uncommon, especially in rural areas, for such individuals to be present at life-cycle and other communal celebrations.

In the Soviet era, all religious beliefs were attacked by the communist authorities as superstition and "vestiges of the past." Most religious schooling and religious observance were banned, and the vast majority of mosques were closed. An official Muslim Board of Central Asia with a headquarters in Tashkent was established during World War II to supervise Islam in Central Asia. For the most part, the Muslim Board functioned as an instrument of propaganda whose activities did little to enhance the Muslim cause. Atheist indoctrination stifled religious development and contributed to the isolation of the Turkmen from the international Muslim community. Some religious customs, such as Muslim burial and male circumcision, continued to be practiced throughout the Soviet period, but most religious belief, knowledge, and customs were preserved only in rural areas in "folk form" as a kind of unofficial Islam not sanctioned by the state-run Spiritual Directorate.

## Religion after Independence

The current government oversees official Islam through a structure inherited from the Soviet period. Turkmenistan's Muslim Religious Board, together with that of Uzbekistan, constitutes the Muslim Religious Board of Mavarannahr. The Mavarannahr board is based in Tashkent and exerts considerable influence in appointments of religious leaders in Turkmenistan. The governing body of Islamic judges (Kaziat) is registered with the Turkmenistan Ministry of Justice, and a council of religious affairs under the Cabinet of Ministers monitors the activities of clergy. Individuals who wish to become members of the official clergy must attend official religious institutions; a few, however, may prove their qualifications simply by taking an examination.

Since 1990, efforts have been made to regain some of the cultural heritage lost under Soviet rule. President Niyazov has ordered that basic Islamic principles be taught in public schools. More religious institutions, including religious schools and mosques, have appeared, many with the support of Saudi Arabia, Kuwait, and Turkey. Religious classes are held in both the schools and the mosques, with instruction in Arabic language, the Koran (Quran) and the hadith, and the history of Islam.

Turkmenistan's government stresses its secular nature and its support of freedom of religious belief, as embodied in the 1991 Law on Freedom of Conscience and on Religious Organizations in the Turkmen Soviet Socialist Republic and institutionalized in the 1992 constitution. That document guarantees the separation of church and state; it also removes any legal basis for Islam to play a role in political life by prohibiting proselytizing, the dissemination of "unofficial" religious literature, discrimination based on religion, and the formation of religious political parties. In addition, the government reserves the right to appoint and dismiss anyone who teaches religious matters or who is a member of the clergy. Since independence, the Islamic leadership in Turkmenistan has been more assertive, but in large part it still responds to government control. The official governing body of religious judges gave its official support to President Niyazov in the June 1992 elections.

On the other hand, some Muslim leaders are opposed to the secular concept of government and especially to a government controlled by former communists (see Centers of Political Power, this ch.). Some official leaders and teachers working outside the official structure have vowed to increase the population's knowledge of Islam, increase Islam's role in society, and broaden adherence to its tenets. Alarmed that such activism may aggravate tensions between Sunnis and Shiites and especially alienate Orthodox Slavs, the government has drawn up plans to elevate the council of religious affairs to ministry status in an effort to regulate religious activities more tightly.

## Education

According to Soviet government statistics, literacy in Turkmenistan was nearly universal in 1991. Experts considered the overall level of education to be comparable to the average for the Soviet republics. According to the 1989 census, 65.1 percent of the population aged fifteen and older had completed secondary school, compared with 45.6 percent in 1979. In the same period, the percentage of citizens who had completed a higher education rose from 6.4 percent to 8.3 percent.

Education is free of charge, although introduction of fees is being considered by selected institutions. Formal schooling begins with kindergarten (*bagcha*) and primary school (*mekdep*). School attendance is compulsory through the eighth grade. At this point, students are tested and directed into technical, continuing, and discontinuing tracks. Some students graduate to the workforce after completing the tenth grade, while others leave in the ninth grade to enter a trade or technical school.

## Education System

Although the education system in Turkmenistan retains the centralized structural framework of the Soviet system, significant modifications are underway, partly as a response to national redefinition, but mainly as a result of the government's attempts to produce a highly skilled work force to promote Turkmenistan's participation in international commercial activities. Reforms also include cultural goals such as the writing of a new history of Turkmenistan, the training of multilingual cadres able to function in Turkmen, English, and Russian, and the implementation of alphabet reform in schools.

Turkmenistan's educational establishment is funded and administered by the state. The Ministry of Education is responsible for secondary education and oversees about 1,800 schools offering some or all of the secondary grades. Of that number, 43.5 percent are operated on one shift and 56.5 percent on two shifts (primarily in cities). Secondary schools have 66,192 teachers who serve 831,000 students. Thirty-six secondary schools specialize in topics relevant to their ministerial affiliation. The primary and secondary systems are being restructured according to Western models, including shorter curricula, more vocational training, and human resource development.

## Curriculum

The curriculum followed by schools is standardized, allowing little variation among the country's school districts. The prescribed humanities curriculum for the ninth and tenth grades places the heaviest emphasis on native language and literature, history, physics, mathematics, Turkmen or Russian language, chemistry, foreign language, world cultures, and physical education. A few elective subjects are available.

Although teaching continues to enjoy respect as a vocation, Turkmenistan's school system suffers from a shortage of qualified teachers. Many obstacles confront a teacher: heavy teaching loads and long hours, including Saturdays and double shifts; wholly inadequate textbooks and instructional materials; serious shortages of paper, supplies, and equipment; low salaries; and, at times, even failure to be paid. An estimated 13 percent of schools have such serious structural defects in their physical plants that they are too dangerous to use for classes.

Instruction in 77 percent of primary and general schools is in Turkmen, although the 16 percent of schools that use Russian as their primary language generally are regarded as providing a better education. Some schools also instruct in the languages of the nation's Uzbek and Kazak minorities. Especially since the adoption of Turkmen as the "state language" and English as the "second state language," the study of these two languages has gained importance in the curriculum, and adults feel pressure to learn Turkmen in special courses offered at schools or at their workplaces.

## Higher Education

After completing secondary school, students may continue their education at one of the dozens of specialized institutes or at Turkmenistan State University in Ashgabat. Admittance into higher education institutions often is extremely competitive, and personal connections and bribes may play a role in gaining entry and later advancement. Prospective students must pass a lengthy, pressure-packed entrance examination. Like all the other tests and evaluations in the educational system, this examination consists of both written and oral parts.

Completion of a course of study in higher institutions may take up to five years. Attempts are being made to decrease the number of years one must study so that young women may finish their higher education by their twentieth or twenty-first birthday, by which time they are expected to be married. Graduate study is an option for outstanding students at the university or in one of the Academy of Science's many research institutes.

The recently formed Council of Higher Education supervises Turkmenistan State University, the republic's eight institutes, and its two pedagogical institutes; these institutes are located in Ashgabat, with the exception of a pedagogical institute in Chärjew. These higher education institutions served 41,700 students in 1991, of which 8,000 were enrolled in the state university. Some institutes that train professionals for specific sectors of the national economy fall under the aegis of the relevant ministries. An education committee also functions under the president of the republic.

# Health

As under the Soviet system, health care continues to be universally available to all citizens without charge. The health care system that Turkmenistan inherited from the Soviet regime is fraught with deficiencies, however. On the whole, physicians are poorly trained, modern medical technologies are almost unheard of, and many basic medicines are in short supply. Although health care is available to most urban residents, the system is financially bankrupt, and treatment is often primitive. Only recently have some medical professionals been allowed to offer private medical care, and the state maintains a near monopoly of health care.

## Structure of Health Care

Health and welfare institutions are administered by the ministries of health, culture, education, and social welfare. Various coordination committees also operate under the aegis of presidential advisers. Between 1989 and 1992, health care as a share of the state budget declined from 11.2 to 6.9 percent, leaving inadequate local budgets to bear the brunt of expenditures. The comparison of health care statistics before and after 1991 is somewhat misleading, however, because the statistics do not account for changes in health budgeting at the end of the communist era.

In 1989 the republic had about 13,000 doctors and 298 hospitals, totaling more than 40,000 beds (111 per 10,000 persons). Some industrial enterprises had separate clinics for their workers. The number of doctors reached 13,800 or (36.2 per 10,000 persons) in 1991; at that time, medical personnel numbered 40,600, or 106.9 per 10,000. Until the early 1990s, all health personnel were government employees.

## Health Care Conditions

Despite the nominally universal availability of free health care, in the rural areas medical care often is deplorable by Western standards. In both rural and urban areas, undertrained physicians and staff, underequipped facilities, shortages of medicines and supplies, and chronic sanitation problems contribute to the system's inadequacy. For example, one study found that because 70 percent of the obstetricians and gynecologists in Dashhowuz Province lacked adequate surgical training, half of their patients died. A factor in the high

*Army conscripts unloading
food and medicine donated
by United States,
Ashgabat airport
Courtesy A. James Firth,
United States Department
of Agriculture*

mortality rate is the provision of piped-in water to only 15 percent of maternity clinics in the republic. Because of the disruption of trade at the end of the Soviet period, pharmaceuticals must be obtained with hard currency, making them even more scarce than before. Of particular concern are shortages of oral rehydration salts for children, syringes and needles, and vaccines, which previously had been imported from Russia and Finland. According to experts, current conditions of conventional medical care may prompt many Turkmen to turn once again to "traditional" medicine. Healers employing herbs and prayer are common, and in some rural areas this type of treatment may be the only medical attention that is available.

## Health Conditions

According to health statistics, life expectancy in Turkmenistan (62.9 for males, 69.7 for females) is the lowest in the CIS. The relatively high rate of natural population growth (2.0 percent per year), is based on a birth rate of 29.9 per 1,000 persons and a death rate of 7.3 per 1,000 persons. In 1992 cardiovascular disease was the most common cause of death, followed by cancer, respiratory disease, and accidents (see table 5, Appendix). Poor diet, polluted drinking water, and industrial wastes and pesticides cause or exacerbate many medical problems, which are especially acute in the northeastern areas of the country near the Amu Darya and Aral Sea. Women in their child-bearing years and children appear to be in the poorest health and the most susceptible to disease and sickness. Of CIS countries, in 1991 Turkmenistan ranked first in infant mortality rate, with forty-seven deaths per 1,000 live births, and very high on maternal death rate, with fifty-five deaths per 100,000 births. Some specialists attribute high infant mortality to factors of diet and health care while others relate it to poor hygienic practices and lack of family planning.

## Welfare

Under the conditions of independence in the early 1990s, the standard of living in Turkmenistan did not drop as dramatically as it did in other former Soviet republics. Thus, the relatively small population of the nation of Turkmenistan did not require extensive state investment for the basic requirements of survival as the nation attempted the transition to a market economy.

### Living Standards

Although living standards have not declined as sharply in Turkmenistan as in many other former Soviet republics, they have dropped in absolute terms for most citizens since 1991. Availability of food and consumer goods also has declined at the same time that prices have generally risen. The difference between living conditions and standards in the city and the village is immense. Aside from material differences such as the prevalence of paved streets, electricity, plumbing, and natural gas in the cities, there are also many disparities in terms of culture and way of life. Thanks to the rebirth of national culture, however, the village has assumed a more prominent role in society as a valuable repository of Turkmen language and traditional culture.

#### *Wages*

Most families in Turkmenistan derive the bulk of their income from state employment of some sort. As they were under the Soviet system, wage differences among various types of employment are relatively small. Industry, construction, transportation, and science have offered the highest wages; health, education, and services, the lowest. Since 1990 direct employment in government administration has offered relatively high wages. Agricultural workers, especially those on collective farms, earn very low salaries, and the standard of living in rural areas is far below that in Turkmen cities, contributing to a widening cultural difference between the two segments of the population.

In 1990 nearly half the population earned wages below the official poverty line, which was 100 rubles per month at that time (for value of the ruble—see Glossary). Only 3.4 percent of the population received more than 300 rubles per month in 1990. In the three years after the onset of inflation in 1991, real wages dropped by 47.6 percent, meaning a decline in the standard of living for most citizens (see Labor, this ch.).

### Prices

Prices of all commodities rose sharply in 1991 when the Soviet Union removed the pervasive state controls that had limited inflation in the 1980s. Retail prices rose by an average of 90 percent in 1991, and then they rose by more than 800 percent when the new national government freed most prices completely in 1992. The average rate for the first nine months of 1994 was 605 percent. As world market prices rise and currency fluctuations affect prices and purchasing power, consumer price increases continue to outstrip rises in per capita incomes. In 1989 the average worker spent about two-thirds of his or her salary on food, fuel, clothing, and durable goods, but that ratio increased sharply in the years that followed. As prices rose, the supply of almost all food and many consumer goods was curtailed. The introduction of the manat (see Glossary) as the national currency in November 1993 likely worsened the already deteriorating consumer purchasing power. The prices of forty basic commodities immediately rose 900 percent, and wages were raised only 200 percent to compensate.

### Housing

In 1989 the state owned more than 70 percent of urban housing and about 10 percent of rural housing. The remainder of urban housing was owned privately or by housing cooperatives. The average citizen had 11.2 square meters of housing space in urban areas, 10.5 square meters in rural areas. In 1989 some 31 percent of housing (urban and rural areas combined) had running water, 27 percent had central heating, and 20 percent had a sewer line.

In 1991 nearly all families had television sets, refrigerators, and sewing machines, and 84 percent had washing machines. Only 26 percent owned cars, however, and the quality of durable goods was quite low by Western standards.

## Government Welfare Programs

In 1992, President Niyazov announced "Ten Years of Prosperity," a government program that provides virtually free natural gas, electricity, and drinking water to all households in the republic; increases minimum wages and other social payments, confirms food subsidies and price liberalizations, and aims at giving families their own house, car, and telephone. In 1993 two-thirds of the state budgetary expenditures went toward such "social needs," and half of that amount for the subsidization of food prices. Social programs also accounted for 60 percent of the 1995 budget.

The pension system has two main types of expenditures: retirement and disability payments and children's payments. Employees pay 1 percent of their wages to their pension fund, and the employer's share totals 80.5 percent of the total payroll contribution. In industries, the payroll contribution is 37 percent of the total pension fund; in agricultural enterprises, it is 26 percent. Because pension fund expenditures always exceed their receipts at this ratio of contribution, additional funds are allotted from the state budget. The normal retirement age is sixty for men and fifty-five for women, but the age is five or ten years less for occupations classified as hazardous. In the early 1990s, the number of pensioners grew at a rate of 17,000 per year; in 1993 some 404,000 individuals were in this category.

In December 1994, President Niyazov issued an edict setting the minimum wage at 1,000 manat per month and the minimum old-age pension at up to 1,000 manat per month. Pensions set at 60 percent of wages will be given to men retiring at the age of sixty and women at the age of fifty-five if they have worked for twenty-five and twenty years, respectively. In 1995 pensions for invalids and war veterans were set at 3,000 manat per month. Pensions are indexed to increases in minimum wages and are funded by payroll taxes. Allowances are granted to households with children under age sixteen. Payments depend on the age of the children and the economic and marital status of their parents. In 1993 such payments ranged from 110 rubles to 270 rubles per month. That year payments were made for about 1.75 million children. Funding is from the general budget for children age six and older and from the pension fund for those younger than six.

## The Economy

Turkmenistan's economy is predominantly agricultural. Agriculture accounts for almost half of the gross domestic product (GDP—see Glossary) and more than two-fifths of total employment, whereas industry accounts for about one-fifth of GDP and slightly more than one-tenth of total employment. In 1988 the per capita net material product (NMP—see Glossary) output was 61 percent of the Soviet average, fourth lowest of the Soviet republics. In 1991, 17.2 percent of the work force was engaged in private-sector occupations such as farming, individual endeavors, and employment on agreement; 0.7 percent worked in rented enterprises, and the rest worked for state enterprises, social organizations, and collective farms.

Macroeconomic indicators of the performance of Turkmenistan's national economy have differed widely in the late Soviet and early independence years, making precise assessment difficult. According to one source, the per capita GDP was US$2,509 in 1992, placing it higher than Tajikistan and Uzbekistan, but lower than Kazakstan and much lower than some of the other former Soviet republics. Another source lists a 17 percent increase in industrial output between 1991 and 1992. On the other hand, several sources agree that the NMP aggregate figure for 1992 was a 15 percent decline from the previous year (see table 6, Appendix). One source claims that GDP in Turkmenistan increased by 8.5 percent in 1993, while another regards as suspect the statistical methods applied to the data on which this figure is based.

### Natural Resources

Turkmenistan has substantial reserves of oil and gas, and geologists have estimated that 99.5 percent of its territory is conducive to prospecting. The republic also has deposits of sulfur, hydrocarbons, iodine, celestine, potassium salt, magnesium salt, sodium chloride, bentonite clays, limestone, gypsum, brown coal, cement, basalt, and dolomite. Its soils, which have been formed under conditions of continental climate, are mostly desert sands, with a variety of other types such as desert loess, meadow clays, and "irrigated" soils, in some regions.

Under those conditions, large-scale agriculture must be supported by irrigation in nearly all areas.

## Agriculture

Turkmenistan inherited the system of state and collective farms from the Soviet Union, with its command structure of production quotas, fixed procurement prices, and soft budget constraints. The state still controls marketing and distribution of agricultural produce through the Ministry of Trade in urban areas and the Cooperative Alliance in rural locales; the Ministry of Agriculture's Commercial Center has a monopoly on cotton exports. Turkmenistan is highly dependent upon external sources for its agricultural inputs, the price of which has escalated more that those for agricultural products since independence.

### Structure of the Agriculture Sector

Instead of restructuring the agricultural economy, the government's "New Countryside" policy envisions only limited privatization of agricultural enterprises and expansion of grain production to reduce dependence on imports. The development of transportation is critical to agricultural reform in Turkmenistan.

In 1991 field and orchard crops accounted for 70.4 percent of the value of agricultural sales prices (computed in 1983 prices), while livestock raising accounted for the remaining 29.6 percent (see table 18, Appendix). Almost half the cultivated land was under cotton, and 45 percent of the land under grains and fodder crops. Livestock raising centered on sheep, especially for the production of Karakul wool. Whereas production of meat and milk rose substantially in the 1986–91 period (increases of 14,000 and 110,000 tons, respectively), actual production in 1991 of 100,000 tons of meat and 458,000 tons of milk represented a decrease from 1990. Production of meat in 1992 declined 21 percent from that of 1991. Fishing, bee-keeping, and silk-rendering occupy small areas of the agricultural sector.

### Irrigation

Under the prevailing climatic conditions, irrigation is a necessary input for agriculture and has been developed extensively throughout Turkmenistan. Irrigation management is divided between the Ministry of Irrigation, which is responsible for

*Selling furs at market
outside Ashgabat
Courtesy Barry Peterson*

operation and maintenance along the Garagum Canal and for interrepublic water management, and the Irrigation Institute, which designs, evaluates, and builds new projects. State farms and collective farms are responsible for operation and maintenance on their own farms, but they have no other autonomy. Because only 55 percent of the water delivered to the fields actually reaches the crops, an average of twelve cubic meters of water is expended annually per hectare of cotton.

As a result of the construction of irrigation structures, and especially of the Garagum Canal, the hydrological balance of the republic has changed, with more water in the canals and adjacent areas and less in the rivers and the Aral Sea. The largest of the republic's eleven reservoirs are the Sary Yazy on the Murgap River, which occupies forty-six square kilometers of surface and has a capacity of 239 million cubic meters, and the Hawuz Khan on the Garagum Canal, which occupies ninety square kilometers of surface and has a capacity of 460 million cubic meters.

In 1983 Turkmenistan had an irrigated area of 1,054,000 hectares. Its most developed systems are along the middle and lower course of the Amu Darya and in the Murgap Basin. The Garagum Canal, which flows 1,100 kilometers with a capacity of 500 cubic meters per second, accounts for almost all irrigation in Ahal and Balkan provinces along the northern reaches of the Kopetdag Range. The canal also supplies additional water to the Murgap oasis in southeastern Turkmenistan. The main canal was built in sections between 1959 and 1976, initially providing irrigation for about 500,000 hectares. Plans call for construction to continue until the canal reaches a length of 1,435 kilometers and a carrying capacity of 1,000 cubic meters per second, enabling it to irrigate 1,000,000 hectares.

### Cotton

At a rate of 300 kilograms per citizen, Turkmenistan produces more cotton per capita than any other country in the world. Among the Soviet republics, Turkmenistan was second only to Uzbekistan in cotton production. In 1983 Turkmenistan contributed 12.7 percent of the cotton produced in the Soviet Union. Four of the republic's five provinces are considered to be "cotton provinces": Ahal, Mary, Chärjew, and Dashhowuz. Convinced that cotton is its most marketable product, the post-Soviet government is committed to maintaining previous levels of cotton production and area under cultivation.

In accordance with the Soviet policy of delegating the Central Asian republics as the nation's cotton belt, the area under cotton climbed rapidly from 150,400 hectares in 1940 to 222,000 hectares in 1960, 508,000 hectares in 1980, and 602,000 hectares in 1991. Because independence brought fuel and spare-parts shortages, the cotton harvest declined in the first half of the 1990s, however.

Industrial inputs for cotton production such as harvesters, sowing machines, mechanized irrigation equipment, fertilizer, pesticides, and defoliants have become less available to cotton farms in Turkmenistan because the other former Soviet republics, which were the chief suppliers of such items, raised their prices sharply in the first years of independence.

For most Turkmen farmers, cotton is the most important source of income, although cotton's potential contribution to the republic's economy was not approached in the Soviet period. Experts predict that by the year 2000, Turkmenistan will process one-third of its raw cotton output in textile mills located within the republic, substantially raising the rate achieved in the Soviet and early post-Soviet periods. In 1993, the state's procurement prices were raised significantly for high-grade raw seeded cotton. State planners envision selling 70 percent of the crop to customers outside the CIS.

### Other Crops

Since independence, Turkmenistan's agricultural policy has emphasized grain production in order to increase self-sufficiency in the face of a sharp decline in trade among the former Soviet republics. A 50 percent increase in the grain harvest in 1992 was followed by a rise of 70 percent in 1993, despite unfavorable climatic conditions. Production of vegetables declined in 1992 to 13 percent below the 1991 level, whereas that of potatoes rose by 24 percent. High-quality melons are grown in the lower and middle reaches of the Amu Darya and in the Tejen and Murgap oases. In addition to these crops, subtropical fruits and nuts, especially pomegranates, almonds, figs, and olives, are grown in the Ertek and Sumbar valleys.

## Industry

Turkmenistan possesses a formidable resource base for industry, although that base was not utilized to build diversified industry in the Soviet period. In the post-Soviet period, extraction and processing of natural gas and oil remain the country's most important industrial activities.

### Structure of Industry

Turkmenistan did not inherit a substantial industrial base from the Soviet Union. Beginning in the 1970s, Moscow made major investments only in the oil and gas production and cotton-processing sectors. As a result, industry is highly specialized and potentially vulnerable to external shocks. Well-developed cotton ginning, natural gas, and cottonseed oil dominate at the expense of other sectors, such as the petrochemical and chemical industries, cotton textile production, food processing, and labor-intensive assemblage, in which Turkmenistan has a comparative advantage (see table 19, Appendix).

The shocks of independence slowed industrial production in the early 1990s. In the first half of 1994, macroeconomic fluctuations caused by the introduction of the manat as the national currency and limitations placed on gas exports caused aggregate industrial production to fall to 68.3 percent compared with the same period in 1993 (see Fiscal and Monetary Conditions, this ch.). The price index for industrial producers was 858 percent, indicating runaway inflation in this sector.

## Gas and Oil

Turkmenistan ranks fourth in the world to Russia, the United States, and Canada in natural gas and oil extraction. The Turkmenistan Natural Gas Company (Turkmengaz), under the auspices of the Ministry of Oil and Gas, controls gas extraction in the republic. Gas production is the youngest and most dynamic and promising sector of the national economy. Turkmenistan's gas reserves are estimated at 8.1–8.7 trillion cubic meters and its prospecting potential at 10.5. trillion cubic meters. The Ministry of Oil and Gas oversees exploration of new deposits. Sites under exploration are located in Mary Province, in western and northern Turkmenistan, on the right bank of the Amu Darya, and offshore in the Caspian Sea.

In 1958 Turkmenistan produced only 800,000 cubic meters of natural gas. With the discovery of large deposits of natural gas at Achak, Qizilqum, Mary, and Shatlik, production grew to 1.265 billion cubic meters by 1966, and since then the yield has grown dramatically. In 1992 gas production accounted for about 60 percent of GDP. As a result of a dispute with Ukraine over payments for gas deliveries, in 1992 gas production fell by 20 billion cubic meters to around 60 billion cubic meters. In the first eight months of 1994, transportation restrictions forced Turkmenistan to cut gas production to 26.6 billion cubic meters, only 57 percent of the production for the same period in 1993. An additional factor in this reduction was the failure of CIS partners, to whom Russia distributes Turkmenistan's gas, to pay their bills.

Most of Turkmenistan's oil is extracted from fields at Koturdepe, Nebitdag, and Chekelen near the Caspian Sea, which have a combined estimated reserve of 700 million tons. The oil extraction industry started with the exploitation of the fields in Chekelen in 1909 and Nebitdag in the 1930s, then production leaped ahead with the discovery of the Kumdag field in 1948 and the Koturdepe field in 1959. All the oil produced in Turkmenistan is refined in Turkmenbashy.

Oil production reached peaks of 14,430,000 tons in 1970 and 15,725,000 tons in 1974, compared with 5,400,000 tons in 1991. Since the years of peak production, general neglect of the oil industry in favor of the gas industry has led to equipment depreciation, lack of well repairs, and exhaustion of deposits for which platforms have been drilled.

## Other Industries

Besides petrochemical processing at the Turkmenbashy and Chärjew refineries, the chemicals industry is underdeveloped in comparison with the potential provided by the republic's mineral and fuel resources. The industry has specialized in fertilizer for cotton at the Chärjew superphosphate plant and such chemicals as sulfur, iodine, ammonia, mirabilite, salt, and various sulfates at the Turkmenbashy facility.

Because of the ready availability of natural gas, Turkmenistan is a net exporter of electrical power to Central Asian republics and southern neighbors. The most important generating installations are the Hindukush Hydroelectric Station, which has a rated capacity of 350 megawatts, and the Mary Thermoelectric Power Station, which has a rated capacity of 1,370 megawatts. In 1992 electrical power production totaled 14.9 billion kilowatt-hours.

Turkmenistan's machine building capability has not developed significantly since the conversion of agricultural repair installations for that purpose in Ashgabat and Mary in the late 1960s. Goods produced at these plants include dough kneading and confectionery mixing machines, ventilators, centrifugal oil pumps, gas stove pieces, cables, and lighting equipment.

Construction has grown as a result of a shift in state investment toward housing, education, and joint enterprises. Since 1989, construction has accounted for around 10 percent of the GDP. Building materials produced in the republic include lime, cement, brick and wall stone, ferro-concrete structures, asbestos-concrete pipes, silicate concrete, lime, brick, slate, and glass.

Most food processing consists of rendering cottonseed oil and such related products as soap and grease from cotton plants. Because of the distance between plants and farms and an inadequate transportation infrastructure, only 8 percent of the fruits and vegetables grown in the republic are processed. Other processing capabilities include winemaking, brewing, baking, meat packing and processing, and production of table salt.

Turkmenistan's carpets are famous for their density, which reaches 240,000 knots per square meter in some traditional weaves. The Turkmenistan Carpet Production Association supervises ten carpet factories, but home looms account for a substantial share of production. Other traditional crafts include the fashioning of national clothing such as wool caps and robes, galvanized dishes, and jewelry in forms that state enterprises do not produce or supply. In the mid-1990s, other light industries provided secondary processing of cotton, wool, and silk for yarn, some finished textiles, and wadding.

## Labor

The labor force comprised 1,923,000 people in 1991–92, of whom 1,571,000 (almost 46 percent of the population) were employed in the national economy. Over half of this number worked in state enterprises—a number that is expected to decline in general and to vary radically from sector to sector during the transitional phases of privatization.

In 1990, 37 percent of the workforce was in agricultural and 15 percent in industrial employment; however, one-fourth of industrial employment was in industries related to agriculture. Between 1970 and 1990, the percentage of the workforce employed in industry decreased slightly from 23.4 to 20.0 percent. The share of the agricultural sector within the workforce rose slightly in this period from 38.4 to 41.1 percent. In transportation and communications, the percentages were 7.0 and 6.3, respectively, while in the sectors of health, education, social services, arts and sciences, they rose from 16.5 to 18.6 percent. The state apparatus maintained a share ranging from 2.9 percent of the labor force in 1970 to 2.5 in 1989.

In 1989, some 62.5 percent of all workers were employed at state enterprises, 22.3 percent on collective farms, 1.1 percent in cooperatives (up from 0 in 1986), 0.1 percent in individual labor (a constant percentage since 1970), and 14.1 percent in private plots (up from 8.5 percent in 1970, largely at the expense of the collective farm percentage).

Figures from 1989 for the distribution of the populace according to source of sustenance show that of the entire population of Turkmenistan, 40.6 percent worked in the national economy, 1.9 percent held stipends, 10.9 percent were pensioners and others receiving state welfare, 46.5 percent were dependents and those employed only on individual supplemental endeavors, and 0.1 percent had other unspecified means of subsistence.

The percentage of women within the total work force of Turkmenistan was 41.7 in 1989, reflecting a near constant since 1970 (39.5). The percentage of women within the total number of specialists in the work force who have completed middle and upper special education rose from 44.0 in 1970 to 49.4 in

*Carpet bazaar outside Ashgabat*
*Courtesy Barry Peterson*

1989. Workers under thirty years of age who have completed a secondary general education accounted for 66.4 percent of Turkmenistan's work force in 1989; those with middle specialized education, 16.0 percent; those with an incomplete higher education, 1.6 percent; and those with a complete higher education, 8.7 percent.

The national minimum wage is a critical component of the macro-level "price-wage feedback" in inflationary processes; this wage is established by presidential decree. The basic wage structure is set by a cross-classification of occupations and physical exertion levels, which determines relative minimum wages for various sectors. After a negotiating process, minimum wages can be set above the national minimum in profitable sectors. Wages in agriculture and industry were similar until 1991, when agricultural wages declined relative to average wage.

337

Plans call for the Ministry of Labor to be replaced by a State Corporation for Specialist Training, with the bulk of the ministry's nontraining functions to shift to the Ministry of Economy, Finance, and Banking. Those functions include oversight of unemployment, salary administration and minimum wage determination, and labor protection. There is no independent labor union movement in Turkmenistan. Trade union leaders are appointed by the president, meaning that no true collective bargaining can occur.

Labor productivity is one of the major concerns of economic planners in Turkmenistan. According to Soviet statistics, for industrial enterprises this indicator grew at a rate of 6.3 percent per year in the period 1971–5; then it declined drastically to 0.1 percent per year in 1976–80 before reaching 3.2 percent in 1989. Similar changes occurred in agricultural labor productivity in the 1970s and the 1980s, moving from 2.6 percent growth in 1971–75 to negative 1.4 percent in 1976–80 and then to 4.0 percent in 1989.

## Economic Structure

Although Turkmenistan's economic situation has deteriorated somewhat since 1990, the overall standard of living has not dropped as dramatically as it has in other former Soviet republics (see table 10, Appendix). Economic reforms have been modest, and the majority of businesses remain state-owned. Thanks to government subsidies, basic food products continue to be relatively affordable despite inflation. One of the most important modifications in economic policy took effect in early 1993 when President Niyazov decreed that natural gas, water, and electricity would be supplied virtually free of charge to all homes in Turkmenistan for an indefinite period. Gasoline and other fuels also remain cheap, relative to neighboring republics. Such economic stability has been possible because Turkmenistan has a comparatively small population and it is rich in important resources such as natural gas and oil.

The main blueprint for Turkmenistan's development is the Ten Years of Prosperity program, which was announced in December 1992. It calls for a ten-year transition to a market economy, with a first phase that maintains the Soviet system of planned management accompanied by extensive social protection programs. The program envisages development of Turkmenistan's natural resources and restructuring of industry to provide import substitution.

## Privatization

One of the most important reforms of Turkmenistan's economic plan is privatization. Article 9 of the 1992 constitution guarantees citizens the right to own capital, land, and other material or intellectual property, but no law has stipulated the source from which land could be acquired. No fund of land available for private purchase has been established. A law on land ownership allows every citizen the right to own and bequeath to heirs plots smaller than fifty hectares, so long as they are continuously cultivated, and to obtain a long-term lease on up to 500 hectares. Such land may not be bought or sold, however. In 1993 only about 100 peasant farms were privately run, and they were leased rather than owned. Nevertheless, after the government announced the 1993 law allowing fifty-hectare plots, it soon received more than 5,000 applications.

In February 1993, a State Committee on Land Reform was established, with a goal of privatizing 10 to 15 percent of all agricultural land. Beginning in May 1993, the state began leasing land on the condition that 35 percent of the state procurement for cotton be surrendered, with no monetary compensation, as payment of rent. Estimates of the irrigated land since leased or under private ownership range from 3 to 12 percent. The state also intends to privatize all unprofitable agricultural enterprises.

The privatization process is managed by the Department of State Property and Privatization, which is part of the Ministry of Economy, Finance, and Banking. Short-term plans call for continued state control of the gas, oil, railway, communications, and energy industries and agriculture—sectors that combine to account for 80 percent of the economy. Laws on leasing, joint-stock companies, and entrepreneurship were adopted in the early 1990s. A general privatization law passed in 1992 describes the gradual denationalization of state property through a variety of methods.

In 1992 only 2,600 small enterprises—mostly individual ventures such as trading outlets and home-worker operations—were privately owned. Through the end of 1993, only a few small trade and service enterprises had moved to private ownership, mostly sold to foreign buyers. Plans called for conversion of large manufacturing firms into joint-stock enterprises by the end of 1994, and private ownership of all trade and service-sector enterprises with fewer than 500 employees by the end of 1995. However, the state would maintain a "controlling interest" in businesses that become joint stock companies and would retain control over profitable larger concerns.

A second important component of Turkmenistan's economic development plan is marketization. To promote this process, a decree was issued in March 1993 for the formation of a joint-stock bank, the granting of additional credits to the Agroindustrial Bank for the development of entrepreneurship, and the establishment of seven free economic zones. Agricultural entrepreneurs are to be granted special profits tax and land payment exemptions. Within free economic zones, companies with more than 30 percent foreign ownership are to receive special exemptions from profit tax and rental payments.

## Fiscal and Monetary Conditions

In the first half of the 1990s, Turkmenistan slowly established independent fiscal and monetary institutions and policies to replace the centralized Soviet system upon which the republic had relied prior to independence. These innovations have included a separate national currency, an independent national bank, and mechanisms to control budgetary deficits.

### Banking System

Until Turkmenistan became independent, its banks essentially functioned as accounting branches of the Soviet State Bank. Especially after introducing its own currency in November 1993, Turkmenistan experienced a need to develop a true banking system. The current structure, defined by the 1993 State Banking Law, includes a central bank (called by the Russian term Gosbank) that is responsible for the conduct of monetary policy and supervision of the banking system, a state-run savings bank (called by the Russian term Sberbank) and an external trade bank (called by the Russian term Vneshekonombank), and commercial banks such as the Turkmenistan International Bank for Reconstruction and Development. The latter institution is designed specifically to attract investments and promote exports in the gas and oil industries.

Turkmenistan's banks are expected to operate under a fractional reserve system that allows commercial banks to set interest rates based upon the increase or decline of their reserves in the state bank, giving them an incentive to allocate credit more easily or stringently as the market allows. However, in reality the republic's Ministry of Economy, Finance, and Banking determines the levels of bank access to central bank credit.

The central bank favors credits to lower-level banks for supporting privatization, developing market infrastructures, expanding exports, and strengthening the banking structure. Generally, foreign companies are encouraged to seek external sources for financing projects in the republic. Banking policies include loans at significantly lower interest rates for agriculture than those granted to industrial enterprises. Goods purchased from state administrations can be paid for by checks that will be debited to accounts in the commercial banks.

### Currency

Turkmenistan introduced its own currency, the manat, in November 1993, beginning at an exchange rate of two manat to one United States dollar and one manat to 500 rubles (for value of the manat—see Glossary). Manat banknotes are printed in denominations of 1, 5, 10, 20, 50, 100, and 500, and tenge coins (100 tenge to 1 manat) are minted in denominations of 1, 5, 10, 20, and 50.

Procedures were devised to prevent a run on the currency and to stabilize the economy as much as possible during the introduction of the manat, including the closing of currency stores, posting of new prices that were to remain stable until an exchange rate had been reached, limiting the conversion of rubles to manat to a one-time 30,000 rubles exchange, and giving everybody sixty manat gratis. However, people began to produce false passports to get the free manat and to exceed the 30,000-ruble exchange limit. The state did not have enough stocks of the new currency to satisfy those who had "overcome their suspicions of the banking system."

Following the inauspicious introduction of the manat, Turkmenistan's government has not tried to artificially support official exchange rates, which have varied significantly from those in illegal money markets. By May 1994, the official rate was 60 manat to US$1, while in black markets it was 80–85 manat to US$1. In January 1996, the official rate was 200 manat per US$1.

### Fiscal Policy

Turkmenistan was the only CIS country to have a balanced budget in 1992. Under the Interrepublican Memorandum of Understanding of October 1991, Turkmenistan's share of the

Soviet Union's remaining international debt was fixed at 0.7 percent, or about US$420 million. An agreement with Russia in July 1992 erased this debt entirely when Turkmenistan renounced claims to former Soviet assets. This agreement virtually eliminated all of Turkmenistan's hard-currency debt.

In 1993 increases in the minimum wage and social safety net strained fiscal discipline, but the government introduced a "sub-soil" tax on oil and gas exploration by Turkmengaz and other companies, as well as a value-added tax (VAT—see Glossary) of 20 percent and a profits tax of 30–45 percent to increase government revenues for its social programs. Despite this strategy, the 1993 deficit was estimated at 10 percent of GDP, far more than the 2–3 percent projected by the government.

By the mid-1990s, increased entitlements such as free utilities had combined with careless monetary management to reduce investment and raise deficit spending and inflation. Until other gas pipelines are opened up to paying customers, experts predicted that Turkmenistan's hard currency reserves (estimated at US$500 million in 1993) would not remain at a high enough level to cover the government's undisciplined approach to budgeting.

## Foreign Trade

In the early 1990s, Turkmenistan's foreign trade remained completely under the control of the central government. During that period, the most important trading partners remained the former republics of the Soviet Union, with which the great majority of trade had been conducted during the Soviet era. Natural gas is the most profitable item available for foreign sale.

### Trade Structure

In controlling Turkmenistan's trade sector, the main goal of government policy is to maintain and expand foreign markets for gas, fuel products, electricity, and cotton. Just prior to independence, trade with other Soviet republics accounted for 93 percent of Turkmenistan's exports and 81 percent of its imports. In the mid-1990s, the country's main trading partners (as they were in 1990) were Russia, Kazakstan, and Uzbekistan in the CIS and Germany and countries in Eastern Europe outside the CIS (see table 20, Appendix). In 1990 nearly 27 percent of exports were mineral products, 6 percent were chemical industry products, 46 percent were some form of cotton fiber, and 17 percent were processed food products.

In 1991 the largest components of Turkmenistan's imports were food (17 percent of the total), chemical products (6 percent), light industry products including textiles (22 percent), and machinery (30 percent). Among Western countries, Turkmenistan imported the most goods from Finland, France, and Italy in 1992.

In 1990, the overall trade deficit was US$500 million, which declined to $US300 million in 1991. In 1991 the trade deficit constituted some 13.9 percent of the net material product (NMP—see Glossary). In 1992 the deficit with Russia, Turkmenistan's main trading partner, was about US$38 million. That year the value of exports to Russia was 52.7 percent of the value of imports from Russia, the highest percentage among Russia's CIS trading partners. However, because it exports fuel, in the mid-1990s Turkmenistan maintained a positive trade balance at world prices with the CIS as a whole, making it the only republic besides Russia to do so.

In 1993 Turkmenistan's main CIS import partners were (in order of import volume) Russia, Azerbaijan, Uzbekistan, Ukraine, and Tajikistan. The main CIS customers were (in order of export volume) Ukraine, Russia, Uzbekistan, Kazakstan, and Georgia. In 1992 Turkmenistan had bilateral trade surpluses with Ukraine, Tajikistan, Uzbekistan, and Georgia.

Russia continues to trade with Turkmenistan in much the same way as in the Soviet era, although by 1992 trade with the other republics was curtailed by difficulties in collecting payments and other factors. Central Asian republics traditionally traded more with Russia than with each other; the conditions of the 1990s promote even less regional trade because several of the republics specialize in similar products. For example, cotton and gas are the chief export products of both Turkmenistan and Uzbekistan.

Because of its specialization in cotton and natural gas, Turkmenistan imports a large percentage of the food it consumes. In 1991 the republic imported 65 percent of its grain consumption, 45 percent of its milk and dairy products, 70 percent of its potatoes, and 100 percent of its sugar—a profile typical of the Central Asian republics. In 1991 the trade deficit was 684 million rubles in food goods, compared with a deficit of 1.25 billion rubles in non-food goods.

Turkmenistan's cotton exports follow the pattern of other Central Asian republics. Governments of these countries have raised the price of cotton for trade with their Central Asian neighbors nearly to world market levels while discounting their cotton on the world market because of its relatively poor quality and less reliable delivery. Since 1991, Central Asian countries have more than doubled their exports of cotton to countries outside the CIS, accounting for 70 percent of West European cotton imports. Exports to the Far East and Mexico also have increased. In 1992 Turkmenistan cut its cotton export prices by 30 percent to stimulate sales. In response, the National Cotton Council of America refused to make subsidized shipments of cotton to Russia, where around 350 textile mills were threatened with closure because of insufficient imports, unless Central Asian republics reversed their aggressive stance in the world cotton market.

Natural gas, Turkmenistan's main export for foreign currency, accounted for an estimated 70 percent of its exports in 1993. Planners expected per capita earnings from sales of gas in 1993 to approach US$1,300, but Azerbaijan and Georgia failed to make payments. Turkmenistan, like Russia, has introduced a policy of cutting off gas supplies in response to such situations. In the case of Azerbaijan and Georgia, supply was curtailed until the bills were paid. In the mid-1990s, the practice of shutting off delivery was a thorny issue between Turkmenistan and Ukraine, which owns the main pipeline to Europe but has failed to pay for gas deliveries on many occasions (see Transportation and Telecommunications, this ch.).

CIS agreements on tariffs and customs have been worked out, but in reality a "legal vacuum" exists with regard to interrepublic economic ties. Technically, CIS members are not allowed to discriminate against one another in trade, but trade wars began to break out immediately upon independence. As a result, most republics have made a series of bilateral accords. A month before the major CIS agreement was worked out in 1992, Turkmenistan signed a customs union agreement with Russia and the other Central Asian republics. Later, it renegotiated its terms with Russia.

In a move toward trade liberalization in early 1993, Turkmenistan abolished import duties on around 600 goods, including all CIS goods. Imports from former Soviet republics outside the ruble zone (see Glossary) were prohibited. Tariffs for goods exported for hard currency have remained in place to increase government revenue and prevent capital flight; thus, for natural gas the tariff is 80 percent; for oil, 20 percent; and for chemicals, 15 percent. The state can fix the volume, price, and tariff of any export leaving Turkmenistan.

Beginning in November 1993, Turkmenistan stopped the Soviet-era practice of accepting goods in exchange for natural gas, restricting payments to hard currency, precious metals, and precious stones. However, this policy may not be successful because Russia buys gas from Turkmenistan and then redistributes it to CIS customers rather than to Europe. Under these conditions, some customers may turn to Uzbekistan, which sells its gas directly and at a much lower price. Turkmenistan found it necessary to negotiate barter agreements with certain nonpaying customers such as Azerbaijan and Georgia. Until the end of 1994, Kazakstan was the only CIS customer to pay in cash.

In 1993 gas constituted 66.2 percent of Turkmenistan's exports to non-CIS countries, cotton 26.1 percent, and other goods 7.7 percent. Turkmenistan barters large quantities of cotton for textile-processing equipment from Italy, Argentina, and Turkey. Almost half of cotton exports (more than 20 percent of total exports) have been diverted to non-CIS customers since 1992. An increase in barter trade with China and Iran partially offsets the collapse of interrepublic supply. In 1994 Iran bought 20,000 tons of cotton fiber, a volume expected to increase by five times in 1995. Turkmenistan also will sell surplus electrical power via Iran.

Despite payment problems, Turkmenistan's export position has improved substantially since independence. Its consolidated current account surplus rose from US$447 million to US$927 million between 1991 and 1992, so that the increase in gas and cotton exports has offset the increase in imports. By mid-1994, the United States Export-Import Bank extended US$75.7 million to insure Turkmenistan's trade deals, and the United States Department of Agriculture offered US$5 million in grain credits. Turkey's export-import bank extended a credit line worth $US90 million to Turkmenistan to help cover the growing volume of trade between these two countries. Japan's Eximbank allocated $5 million in trade credits for machinery.

### Investments from Abroad

In November 1991, Turkmenistan officially opened its system to foreign economic activity by ratifying the laws "On

Enterprises in Turkmenistan" and "On Entrepreneur Activity in Turkmenistan." Subsequent laws on foreign investment have covered protection against nationalization, tax breaks on reinvestment of hard currency obtained for profits, property ownership, and intellectual property rights protection to attract foreign investment, and the important 1993 decree allowing domestic enterprises to form joint ventures with foreign oil companies. The Ten Years of Prosperity plan envisages "free economic zones, joint enterprises, and a broadening of entrepreneurship."

Foreign investors have been attracted by the republic's calm and receptive atmosphere. In 1993 parts of the country took on the appearance of a huge construction site, with twenty-six foreign joint ventures operating there. Turkish joint ventures alone were building sixty factories for the processing of agricultural produce. Despite official discouragement of economic activity on the grounds of human rights violations in Turkmenistan, United States business people have been attracted by the republic's stable conditions, and they have invested in a number of significant projects. In the early 1990s, United States companies paid particular attention to the oil and gas industry, establishing investment agreements with the consultative aid of former United States secretaries of state Alexander Haig and James Baker.

### Economic Agreements Abroad

In the formative phase following independence, Turkmenistan concluded several key agreements with trade partners. In December 1991, President Niyazov became the first Central Asian leader to secure cooperation agreements with Turkey on trade, rail and air links, communications, education, and culture. Turkmenistan also secured Turkey's agreement on a gas pipeline routed through its territory and assistance in the trading of petroleum, electricity, and cotton. Also in 1991, Turkmenistan established terms with Russia on cotton-for-oil trades, as well as for other industrial goods such as automobiles. In 1992 agreements with Iran established Iranian aid to Turkmenistan's gas and oil industry and its livestock raising, grain, sugar beet, and fruit sectors, in return for aid to Iran's cotton sector. At the same time, Iran pledged support for Turkmenistan's pipeline project through Iran to Turkey.

Since its initial agreement, Turkmenistan has pursued its trade relationship with Iran with great vigor. Agreements focus on the pipeline project that will bring gas from Turkmenistan to Europe via Iran and Turkey, transportation projects such as the Tejen-Saragt-Mashhad railroad link, whose construction was undertaken in 1993, and development of the oil and gas industries, including the establishment of a joint venture in Turkmenistan for the transport of petroleum products and construction of a plant to produce motor oil. Cooperation in mining and other fields also has been discussed.

At the beginning of 1992, Turkmenistan, Iran, Azerbaijan, Russia and Kazakstan formed the Caspian States Cooperation Organization to reach regional agreements on fishing, shipping, environmental protection, and cooperation among the member nations' oil and gas operations. Iran also has sought to gain support for a project, discontinued in 1979, that would replenish the sturgeon population of the Caspian Sea.

The participation of foreign companies in the development of Turkmenistan's oil industry is expected to triple extraction by the year 2000. In February 1993, the United States firm Vivtex designed a competition among oil companies to win contracts in Turkmenistan. The "winners" for three of the seven blocks put up for bid were Larmag Energy of the Netherlands, Noble Drilling of the United States, Eastpac of the United Arab Emirates, and the Bridas firm of Argentina. Just for holding the competition, Turkmenistan received an initial non-returnable "bonus" payment of US$65 million. The total investment of competition winners was to amount to US$160 million over the course of three years. Turkmenistan would receive between 71 and 75 percent of the profits from these joint enterprises.

In the mid-1990s, Turkmenistan has sought to establish a natural gas pipeline that would pass through Afghanistan, Pakistan, and China to reach Japan, as well as an interim rail line for liquefied gas through China until the pipeline is finished. President Niyazov visited Beijing in November 1992 for talks on the pipeline, at the same time securing credits of 45 million Chinese yuan to be repaid after two years. Niyazov then held talks with representatives of the Japanese firm Mitsubishi and the Chinese Ministry of Oil in December 1992. A delegation of Japanese experts visited Ashgabat in February 1993 to discuss prospects for aid. Declaring Turkmenistan the "most solvent" of the Central Asian republics, the delegation signed agreements for the development of oil deposits in the Caspian shelf, communications, and water desalinization.

In the mid-1990s, the International Monetary Fund (IMF—see Glossary) denied assistance to Turkmenistan on the grounds that Turkmenistan has not taken the required human rights steps for economic cooperation. However, in March 1993, the United States conferred most-favored-nation trading status on Turkmenistan.

## Transportation and Telecommunications

The current government has an aggressive program aimed at developing a transport infrastructure both within the republic and to the outside world (see Foreign Trade; Foreign Policy, this ch.). The highest priorities of this program are railroads and interstate gas pipelines. The capabilities of the various components of Turkmenistan's transport system to carry freight are indicated by the following percentages: railroads 37.4 percent, highways 56.1, pipelines 4.4, and internal waterways 2.0. In the early 1990s, air transport accounted for only 0.02 percent of total freight.

### Railroads

Turkmenistan inherited from the Soviet Union 2,120 kilometers of railways, all 1,000-millimeter gauge, a length insufficient to serve even the current economy of the republic. In addition, it received 13,000 highly depreciated railway cars, outdated signaling and communications systems, and deteriorating depots. The Ashgabat line of the Central Asian Railway has been especially neglected and poorly administered. In 1993 the State Railway Administration assumed responsibility for the railroad system, and moved immediately to join the International Union of Railroads. Membership in this organization will alleviate the problem of standardization created by Turkmenistan's wider Soviet-gauge rails and rolling stock, which do not match the specifications of non-CIS neighbors.

The primary railroad line in Turkmenistan is the Turkmenbashy-Ashgabat-Chärjew Line, which links Turkmenistan with Uzbekistan and European countries. It was built in the 1880s as a military line to facilitate Russian maneuvers in the "Great Game" played with the British Empire over dominance of Central Asia. Other major lines are the Mary-Gushgy Line and the Bukhoro-Kerki-Termez Line (via the Chärjew Line), both of which provide transport to the Afghani border,

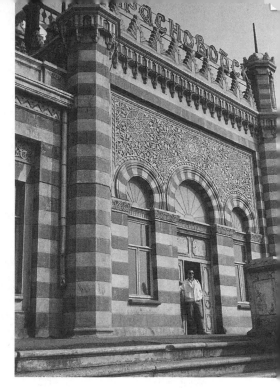

*Train station entrance,*
*Turkmenbashy*
*Courtesy A. James Firth,*
*United States*
*Department*
*of Agriculture*

while smaller branch lines such as the Nebitdag-Vyshka railroad are used to transport oil, workers, and supplies.

Plans call for building 1,000 kilometers of new rail lines, improving signaling and communications, reconstructing depots, and computerizing operations. One priority in railroad development is the construction or expansion of branch lines and links with Turkey via Iran; in the mid-1990s, new lines were underway at Saragt, Kerki, Kernay, Kulisol, Gyzylgaya, and Gyzyletrek, some of which will be combined and linked to the West Kazakstan Line along the Caspian Sea. Efforts also are being made to overhaul and acquire rolling stock.

### Roads

An upgraded highway system is especially important in the mountains and deserts of the republic, where only camels provide an alternate means of transport. In 1926, the republic had 5,716 kilometers of roads, 3,310 kilometers of which were "camel paths" and the rest "somewhat passable" for wheeled transport. By 1975, 9,000 kilometers of roads existed, 6,000 kilometers of which were paved. By 1990 this number had increased dramatically to 23,000 kilometers, of which 15,300 were paved; concomitant increases in freight and passenger traffic strain the system, however.

Eastern Turkmenistan is connected with western Turkmenistan by the Turkmenbashy-Ashgabat-Chärjew highway. Other important highways are the Chärjew-Dashhowuz (520 kilometers), the Chärjew-Kerki (225 kilometers), and the Mary-Gushgy. Stable motor vehicle routes to Iran have been established, and border-crossing procedures have been simplified and regularized.

## Pipelines

The interstate pipeline system retained its value at the time of independence and is a priority of the republic's economic development plans. The government has pursued international projects to build gas pipelines through Iran to Turkey, through Afghanistan to Pakistan, and through Afghanistan, Pakistan, and China to Japan.

Despite Russia's opposition and United States pressure not to do so, in August 1994, President Niyazov signed an agreement with Iran to begin the Turkmenistan-Iran-Turkey-Europe gas pipeline. The pipeline will extend 4,000 kilometers through Iran, Turkey, and Bulgaria, with an initial capacity of 15 billion cubic meters annually, later to be expanded to 28 billion cubic meters. The project will cost US$8 billion, of which Iran will finance US$3.5 billion, and construction will begin in 1998.

After a Japanese delegation held talks in Ashgabat in 1992, the Mitsubishi corporation developed plans to build a 6,700-kilometer gas pipeline through Uzbekistan, Kazakstan, and China to the Yellow Sea coast opposite Japan, where a natural gas liquefaction plant will be built to convert the gas prior to shipment. The plan calls for constructing a pipeline with a capacity of 30 billion cubic meters annually at a cost of US$12 billion. Turkmenistan, Kazakstan, and Uzbekistan also have petitioned the Russian Federation to help them build a new 725-kilometer gas pipeline through Russia and Ukraine for exporting natural gas to Ukraine and Europe.

Of the two main existing lines, the Shatlik-Khiva line running south-north from near Saragt to Khiva connects with a pipeline from the Uzbekistan gas field near Bukhoro. Intersecting this line is the Mary-Ashgabat line running east-west from near Mary to Ashgabat. The other main line is the Central Asia-Center line running north from Okarem to Nebitdag, northwest to the Garabogaz Gulf on the Caspian Sea, and connecting with the main line to Europe through Ukraine.

## Airlines

Turkmenistan has seven airports, of which four have permanent-surface runways between 1,200 and 2,500 meters in length. The main international airport in Ashgabat includes a new terminal complex constructed by companies from Turkey, the United States, the United Kingdom, and Germany. Plans call for using Boeing aircraft alongside the current stock of Aeroflot aircraft belonging to Turkmenistan Air Lines. Current routes provide service to China, India, Pakistan, Iran, the United Arab Emirates, Saudi Arabia, Turkey, Slovakia, and Italy. The two other international facilities, located at Chärjew and Dashhowuz, serve mostly flights within Central Asia. Local airports also exist at Mary, Nebitdag, and other locales. The national administration of Turkmenistan Civil Aviation has been admitted as a member of the International Commercial Aviation Organization. Membership enables Turkmenistan Airlines to have its routes entered into all major airline computer terminals and scheduling references and thus to issue international airline tickets.

## Merchant Marine

Turkmenistan has a main Caspian Sea port at Turkmenbashy and a shipping line running from that port to Astrakhan in the Russian Federation on the north shore of the Caspian. However, the majority of freight is shipped from Turkmenbashy to Baku on the western shore of the Caspian. Other ports are Alaja, Okarem, and Chekelen, all of which were slated for reconstruction in the mid-1990s. In 1993 Turkmenistan bought two ships from Slovakia to use for export from the port at Sukhumi in Georgia. They are currently stationed at Novorossiysk on the Black Sea coast.

## Telecommunications

Turkmenistan's Ministry of Communications is the sole supplier of telecommunications services in Turkmenistan; the ministry also operates the postal and special delivery services and the delivery of press publications. Because of very low state-fixed rates, the ministry's budget is inadequate to perform all these services adequately.

There are two television broadcasting centers, the Orbita satellite station in Ashgabat and a second one in Nebitdag. The State Committee for Television and Radio Broadcasting is responsible for both. Through Orbita and Intelsat satellite transmissions, broadcasts reach all cities and rural centers. Broadcasting centers are linked by landline or microwave to other CIS states and Iran. Since 1992, the republic has received daily transmissions from Turkey.

Turkmenistan experiences many problems concerning communications technology. The telephone network is poorly developed. Only 28 percent of households have a telephone, and 550 villages lacked telephone service entirely in 1994. More than one-third of all subscribers use telephone exchanges that are thirty to forty years old and highly depreciated. Between 1986 and 1991, the number of telephones per 1,000 outlet accesses increased from 61 to 75, which represents 140 for urban and 22 for rural citizens. In 1994 there were eight main telephone lines per 100 inhabitants.

The Turkish government, working through the private Netas company of Turkey, began upgrading Turkmenistan's phone system in the early 1990s. The first electronic exchange was installed in Ashgabat. Implementation of the Intelsat IBS earth station, which will provide international circuit capacity via Ankara, is expected to improve the operation of local, long-distance, and international networks in the republic. Two telex networks provide telex and telegraph services. Only twenty international subscribers are linked via Moscow, and a few other specialized networks exist.

## Government and Politics

The post-Soviet government of the Republic of Turkmenistan retains many of the characteristics and the personnel of the communist regime of Soviet Turkmenistan. The government has received substantial international criticism as an authoritarian regime centering on the dominant power position of President Saparmyrat Niyazov. Nevertheless, the 1992 constitution does characterize Turkmenistan as a democracy with separation of powers among the executive, legislative, and judicial branches.

### Centers of Political Power

In 1994 members of the former Communist Party of Turkmenistan continued to fill the majority of government and civic leadership posts, and much of the ideologically justified Soviet-era political structure remained intact. Besides serving as head of the Democratic Party (as the reconstituted Communist Party of Turkmenistan is called) and chairman of the advisory People's Council and the Cabinet of Ministers, Niyazov also appoints the procurator general and other officers of the courts. In criticizing Turkmenistan's political leadership, experts have cited the single-party system, strict censorship, repression of political dissent, and the "cult of personality" that has formed around President Niyazov. Niyazov's name has been given to streets, schools, communal farms, and numerous other places; his portrait and sayings receive prominent public display; the country's mass media give him extensive exposure that always characterizes him in a positive light; and a law "Against Insulting the Dignity and Honor of the President" is in force.

At the same time, Western and Russian criticism generally has revealed misunderstandings and stereotypes of the political and social dynamics of the region that dilute the authority of such evaluations. Beneath the surface of the presidential image, political life in Turkmenistan is influenced by a combination of regional, professional, and tribal factors. Regional ties appear to be the strongest of these factors; they are evident in the opposing power bases of Ashgabat, center of the government, and Mary, which is the center of a mafia organization that controls the narcotics market and illegal trade in a number of commodities. Although both areas are settled primarily by Turkmen of the Teke tribe, factions in Ashgabat still express resentment and distrust of those in Mary for failing to aid the fortress of Gokdepe against the 1881 assault that led to Russian control of the Turkmen khanates (see Incorporation into Russia, this ch.).

Political behavior also is shaped by the technocratic elites, who were trained in Moscow and who can rely on support from most of the educated professionals in Ashgabat and other urban areas. Most of the elites within the national government originate from and are supported by the intelligentsia, which also is the source of the few opposition groups in the republic.

Tribal and other kinship ties rooted in genealogies play a much smaller role than presumed by analysts who view Turkmen society as "tribal" and therefore not at a sophisticated political level. Nonetheless, clan ties often are reflected in patterns of appointments and networks of power. Regional and clan ties have been identified as the bases for political infighting in the republic. For example, in the early 1990s power bases pitted the Mary district chieftain Gurban Orazov against the Ashgabat millionaire and minister of agriculture Payzgeldi Meredov, and the Teke clan's hold on power through Niyazov conflicted with the Yomud clan's hold on the oil and gas industry through minister Nazar Soyunov. In July 1994, Niyazov removed both Meredov and Soyunov from office on the basis of evidence that the two ministers had misappropriated funds obtained from the sale of state-owned resources. To correct such problems, a Ministry of Foreign Economic Relations was formed to handle exports and imports, and a Control and Revision Commission was established to review contracts with foreign firms.

According to a law passed in December 1992, all permanent residents of Turkmenistan are accorded citizenship unless they renounce that right in writing. Non-residents may become citizens if they can demonstrate that they have resided in Turkmenistan for the past seven years and that they have some knowledge of the Turkmen language. Dual citizenship with certain other former Soviet republics is permitted. The CIS summit held in Ashgabat in December 1993 resulted in an accord on dual citizenship between the Russian Federation and Turkmenistan, allowing Turkmenistan's 400,000 ethnic Russians to achieve that status.

In May 1992, Turkmenistan became the first newly independent republic in Central Asia to ratify a constitution. According to the constitution and to literature printed by the government, Turkmenistan is a democratic, secular, constitutional republic based on law and headed by a president. It is also termed a "presidential republic," one that is "based on the principles of the separation of powers—legislative, executive, and judicial—which operate independently, checking and balancing one another."

## Government Structure

The government of Turkmenistan is divided into three branches—the executive branch headed by the president, the legislative branch consisting of the National Assembly (Milli Majlis), and the judicial branch embodied in the Supreme Court. A People's Council nominally has the ultimate power to oversee the three branches. A Council of Elders exists as an advisory body to the government, everyday affairs of which are conducted by a Cabinet of Ministers appointed by the president.

### President

The office of president (*türkmenbashi*, "Leader of the Turkmen") was established in conjunction with the ratification of the 1992 constitution. The president functions as head of state and government and as commander in chief of the armed forces, serving for an elected term of five years. Presidential powers include the right to issue edicts having the force of law, to appoint and remove state prosecutors and judges, and to discontinue the National Assembly if it has passed two no-confidence votes on the sitting government (Cabinet) within an eighteen-month period. The government is administered by the Cabinet of Ministers, who are appointed by the president with National Assembly approval.

Niyazov, who was president of the Turkmen Soviet Socialist Republic at the time of independence, is a Turkmen of the Teke tribe who was born in 1940. Trained as an engineer, Niyazov rose through the ranks of the Communist Party of Turkmenistan, reaching the top of the party hierarchy as first secretary in 1985. During his tenure, Niyazov remained aloof from *glasnost* and *perestroika*, the reforms of CPSU First Secretary Mikhail S. Gorbachev, even terming Gorbachev's program "pseudo-reform." When Moscow hard-liners attempted to unseat Gorbachev in the coup of August 1991, Niyazov refrained from condemning the conspiracy until after its failure was certain. After his appointment as president of the Turkmen Soviet Socialist Republic in October 1990, Niyazov ran as an uncontested candidate in the republic's first presidential election in June 1991, winning over 99 percent of the vote. From that position, he presided over the declaration of independence in October 1991. The 1992 constitution of the independent Republic of Turkmenistan called for a new presidential election, which Niyazov won in June 1992. In January 1994, a referendum extended his presidency from a five-year term to a ten-year term that would end in the year 2002; of the 99 percent of the electorate that voted, officially only 212 voted against the extension.

### Legislative Branch

The 1992 constitution provides for a legislative body called the National Assembly, a body that retains the structure and procedures of the Soviet-era Supreme Soviet. The body's fifty members are elected directly to five-year terms, and they are prohibited from holding other offices during their tenure. The

National Assembly is charged with the enactment of criminal legislation and approving amendments to the constitution. It also ratifies legislative bills introduced by the president, the Cabinet of Ministers, and individual members of the National Assembly.

### Supreme Court

Established by the 1992 constitution, the Supreme Court comprises twenty-two judges appointed by the president to five-year terms. Of the three branches of government, the judiciary has the fewest powers; its prescribed functions are limited to review of laws for constitutionality and decisions concerning the judicial codex or Supreme Law.

### National Council

The 1992 constitution also established the National Council (Halk Maslahati) to serve as "the highest representative organ of popular power." Intended to unite the three branches of government, it comprises the president of Turkmenistan; the deputies of the National Assembly; members of the Supreme Court, the Cabinet of Ministers, and the Supreme Economic Court; sixty people's representatives elected from the districts specifically to the National Council; and officials from scientific and cultural organizations. Members of the National Council serve for five years without compensation. This body meets at the request of the president or the National Assembly, or when mandated by a one-third vote of its members. Functions of the National Council include advising the president, recommending domestic and foreign policy, amending the constitution and other laws, ratifying treaties, and declaring war and peace. In theory, its powers supersede those of the president, the National Assembly, and the Supreme Court. However, the council has been described as a kind of "super-congress of prominent people" that rubber-stamps decisions made by the other national bodies, in most cases the executive.

### Council of Elders

In addition, the constitution created the Council of Elders, which is designed to embody the Turkmen tradition of reliance on the advice of senior members of society in matters of importance. According to the constitution, the president is bound to consult with this body prior to making decisions on both domestic and foreign affairs. The Council of Elders also is assigned the task of selecting presidential candidates. Its chairman is the president of Turkmenistan.

## Political Parties

Although the constitution guarantees the right to form political parties, in fact the former Communist Party of Turkmenistan has retained the political control exercised by its predecessor. Opposition parties and other politically active groups have remained small and without broad support.

### Democratic Party of Turkmenistan

At the twenty-fifth congress of the Communist Party of Turkmenistan held in December 1991, the party was renamed the Democratic Party of Turkmenistan, and Niyazov was confirmed as its chairman. According to its new program, the Democratic Party serves as a "mother party" that dominates political activity and yet promotes the activity of a loyal political opposition. Following a proposal of Niyazov, a party called the Peasant Justice Party, composed of regional secretaries of the Democratic Party, was registered in 1992 as an opposition party.

The Democratic Party of Turkmenistan essentially retains the apparatus of the former communist party. Party propaganda aims at explaining the need for preserving stability, civil peace, and interethnic accord. Party publications boast that its primary organizations operate in every enterprise, organization, and institution, and that its membership includes over 165,000, whereas critics claim that most citizens hardly are aware of the party's existence.

### Opposition Parties

The 1992 constitution establishes rights concerning freedom of religion, the separation of church and state, freedom of movement, privacy, and ownership of private property. Both the constitution and the 1991 Law on Public Organizations guarantee the right to create political parties and other public associations that operate within the framework of the constitution and its laws. Such activity is restricted by prohibitions of parties that "encroach on the health and morals of the people" and on the formation of ethnic or religious parties. This provision has been used by the government to ban several groups.

In the mid-1990s, Niyazov described opposition groups as lacking both popular support and political programs offering constructive alternatives to existing policy. He has cited these qualities in disqualifying groups from eligibility to register as opposition parties. Insofar as such groups have the potential to promote ethnic or other tensions in society, they may be viewed as illegal, hence subject to being banned under the constitution.

Given such an environment, opposition activity in Turkmenistan has been quite restrained. A small opposition group called Unity (Agzybirlik), originally registered in 1989, consists of intellectuals who describe the party program as oriented toward forming a multiparty democratic system on the Turkish model. Unity has devoted itself to issues connected with national sovereignty and the replacement of the communist political legacy. After being banned in January 1990, members of Unity founded a second group called the Party for Democratic Development, which focused on reforms and political issues. That party's increasing criticism of authoritarianism in the postindependence government led to its being banned in 1991. The original Unity group and its offspring party jointly publish a newspaper in Moscow called *Daynach* (Support), distribution of which is prohibited in Turkmenistan. In 1991 these two opposition groups joined with others in a coalition called Conference (Gengesh), aimed at effecting democratic reforms in the republic.

## Human Rights

President Niyazov has stated his support for the democratic ideal of a multiparty system and of protection of human rights, with the caveat that such rights protect stability, order, and social harmony. While acknowledging that his cult of personality resembles that of Soviet dictator Joseph V. Stalin, Niyazov claims that a strong leader is needed to guide the republic through its transition from communism to a democratic form of government.

Although the Niyazov government has received consistent criticism from foreign governments and international organizations such as Helsinki Watch for its restrictive policies toward opposition groups, in general the government has not taken extreme steps against its political opposition. In 1993 no political prisoners, political executions, or instances of torture or other inhumane treatment were reported. The government has made conscious efforts to protect equal rights and opportunities for groups of citizens it considers benign. Such measures have been applied especially in safeguarding the security of Russian residents, who receive special attention because they offer a considerable body of technical and professional expertise.

Nevertheless, government control of the media has been quite effective in suppressing domestic criticism of the Niyazov regime. In addition, members of opposition groups suffer harassment in the form of dismissal from jobs, evictions, unwarranted detentions, and denial of travel papers. Their rights to privacy are violated through telephone tapping, electronic eavesdropping, reading of mail, and surveillance. United States officials have protested human rights violations by refusing to sign aid agreements with Turkmenistan and by advising against economic aid and cooperation.

## Foreign Policy

Turkmenistan has declared "positive neutrality" and "open doors" to be the two major components of its foreign policy. Positive neutrality is defined as gaining international recognition of the republic's independence, agreeing upon mutual non-interference in internal affairs, and maintaining neutrality in external conflicts. The open- doors policy has been adopted to encourage foreign investment and export trade, especially through the development of a transport infrastructure. Turkmenistan gained membership in the United Nations (UN) in early 1992.

### Background

Pervasive historical and geopolitical factors shape Turkmenistan's foreign policy. With the removal of the protective Soviet "umbrella," the foreign policy tasks facing independent Turkmenistan are the establishment of independent national security and economic systems, while coping with the long legacy of existence in the empires of tsarist Russia and the Soviet Union. As of 1996, all of Turkmenistan's gas pipelines went north into the Russian Federation or other CIS states, thus subordinating sectors of its economic development to that of relatively poor countries. Because Turkmenistan lacks a strong military, independence depends on establishing military pacts with Russia and on developing balanced diplomatic and economic ties with Russia and neighboring countries (see Role of Russia and CIS, this ch.).

Turkmenistan's geographical location close to conflict-riven Afghanistan and Tajikistan also requires a guarded posture toward the irredentist and Islamic forces at play in those countries. Concern over border security was heightened by an incident in October 1993 when two Afghan jets bombed Turkmen territory, despite recent talks with Afghan officials aimed at ensuring equality and non-interference.

Turkmenistan's status as an Islamic state also affects Turkmenistan's relations with Iran and Saudi Arabia. Although in need of the foreign aid and developmental opportunities offered by these countries, Turkmenistan's government also endeavors to blunt any perceived threats to its secular status that arise from Muslim activists. The Turkic identity of the bulk of its population thus far has not proven to be a significant factor in foreign affairs because Turkmenistan must compete with other Central Asian Turkic republics for markets and for closer socioeconomic ties with Turkey.

An important historical factor in current policy is that prior to independence the Soviet government conducted Turkmenistan's foreign affairs. The only involvement of republic officials in international relations was in the form of ceremonial contacts aimed at showcasing Soviet nationality policy by presenting Turkmenistan as a developmental model for Third World countries.

## Foreign Relations Issues

Since independence, Turkmenistan has taken major initiatives by making national security and economic development agreements. Security agreements have focused on military cooperation with Russia and on border security with Iran and Afghanistan. In the economic area, President Niyazov has concentrated on developing gas and oil exports and the pipeline transport infrastructure, especially in cooperation with Iran, Turkey, and Pakistan.

A recent transportation dispute underscored the urgency of Turkmenistan's finding a new pipeline route by which to send its natural gas to Europe through Iran and Turkey. From February through September 1992, Turkmenistan was engaged in a gas-transport price war with Ukraine that provoked the latter to withhold food shipments. In addition, Ukraine refused to transship 500 tons of Turkmenistan's cotton to Turkey, prompting an ambitious program to build Turkmenistan's railroad links with its southern neighbors.

## The United States

Initial concern over human rights policy delayed United States recognition of Turkmenistan's independence until after February 1992, when alarms over Iran's ventures in Central Asia brought a reevaluation of United States policy. Relations declined in September 1993 when the United States cut trade credits to Turkmenistan to protest the arrest of four human rights activists. Generally, such human rights violations have not impeded relations between the two countries, however. Alexander Haig, former United States secretary of state, acting as consultant to President Niyazov, played a leading role in negotiating most-favored-nation trading status for Turkmenistan in 1993.

## Western Europe

President Niyazov has visited European countries and received European delegations to promote foreign investments, diplomatic ties, and applications for membership in international aid organizations. During talks with officials of the North Atlantic Treaty Organization (NATO—see Glossary) in 1993, Niyazov stated that Turkmenistan would welcome NATO assistance in the creation of its national armed forces. In April 1994, French President François Mitterrand visited Ashgabat, where he signed agreements on investments, cultural exchange, and tariffs. At that time, France also allocated US$35 million in trade credits for the construction of a presidential palace. In November 1994, Niyazov toured Austria, Romania, and Slovakia to attract oil and gas investments.

## Asian Neighbors

After the Russian Federation, Turkmenistan has established its closest relations with Iran, especially on issues of joint concern within the Economic Cooperation Organization (ECO—see Glossary), but also on issues of border security, transport cooperation, cultural exchange, and business ventures. In 1993 the two countries signed a joint statement emphasizing territorial sovereignty and non-interference in Tajikistan. At the same time, Turkmenistan's diplomats conveyed concern over the controversial agreement between Iran and Russia to build a nuclear power plant near the Caspian Sea and the Turkmenistan border.

In January 1994, Niyazov made an official visit to Tehran, and the two countries held a second round of talks in Ashgabat in June to create an intergovernmental center for consultation and coordination on socioeconomic questions. According to bilateral agreements, Iranian specialists will aid in renovating the Turkmenbashy Oil Refinery and the Mary Cotton Processing Plant, building the Turkmenistan-Iran-Europe Gas Pipeline, and constructing the Ashgabat-Tehran, Mary- Mashhad-Turkmenbashy, and Gudurol-Gorgan highways. In January 1996, Niyazov signed agreements with Iran linking the two countries' electric power networks, a joint dam on the Hari River, and cooperation in oil, gas, and agriculture. A joint statement expressed concern about Azerbaijan's exploitation of Caspian Sea resources, although Turkmenistan generally has sided with Azerbaijan and Kazakstan, and against Iran and Russia, on resource rights in the Caspian.

Contrary to initial expectations that Turkey would play a "big brother" role in Turkmenistan's social and cultural development following independence, Turkmenistan charts its own course in such matters. An example is the adoption of a Latin script that owes little if anything to that used for Turkish. However, Turkey has played a prominent role in the development of Turkmenistan's economic potential. Turkish firms are constructing US$1 billion worth of enterprises, stores, and hotels in Turkmenistan. The Turkish Development and Cooperation Agency manages a slate of projects in agriculture, civil aviation, education, health care, minerals extraction, reconstruction of infrastructure, initiation of small enterprises, and construction of a complex of mosques and religious schools. Turkish high schools and universities are hosting more than 2,000 Turkmenistani students, and, in 1994, Turkey began daily four-hour television broadcasts to the republic.

Because of continuing fragmentation of political power in neighboring Afghanistan and concern that civil strife in that country could threaten the security of its borders, Turkmenistan's government pursued direct agreements with the northern Afghan leader General Abdul Rashid Dostum, an ethnic Uzbek. With the support of Uzbekistan's Karimov regime, Dostum had carved out an Uzbek domain controlling 600 of the 850 kilometers along the Afghan-Turkmen border. In July 1993, President Niyazov discussed border security with officials from northern Afghanistan, resulting in the establishment of consulates in the Afghan cities of Mazari Sharif and Herat.

Talks in 1994 focused on building a railroad link and supplying electricity to Herat. A direct telephone communications line was completed connecting Ashgabat and Mary with Herat.

Besides initiatives taken under the aegis of the ECO, Turkmenistan signed a cooperation agreement with Pakistan in late 1991 and obtained a promise of US$10 million in credit and goods from Pakistan in 1992. The two countries signed memoranda in 1995 for the construction of a gas pipeline from Turkmenistan through Afghanistan to Pakistan. The Bridas company of Argentina was engaged to do a feasibility study for the pipeline.

## CIS Relations

Turkmenistan has been hesitant to sign economic agreements within the CIS framework. Niyazov has criticized the weakness of CIS mechanisms and proposed a new CIS structure that would be exclusively consultative in nature. As an example of its approach, Turkmenistan declined to attend the Surgut Conference with Russia and Kazakstan (1994), whose goal was to stabilize falling gas and oil output, stating that the domestic gas industry was sufficiently stable without CIS investment funds. At that time, Russian Federation deputy prime minister Aleksandr Shokhin declared that Turkmenistan must decide whether it is with the CIS countries or not. Despite such friction, Turkmenistan has maintained close bilateral economic and military ties with Russia.

Regional cooperation among Central Asian republics has not been as profound as anticipated upon the dissolution of the Soviet Union. In 1993 the other four Central Asian republics accounted for about one-fifth of Turkmenistan's imports and exports. Turkmenistan has followed its own path in all areas of post-Soviet reform, preferring bilateral to regional agreements in the economic sphere; for example, it has agreed to supply Kazakstan with electricity in return for grain. The decisions of all five republics to switch to Latin-based alphabets will not necessarily have the expected result of improving cultural ties because the romanization of distinct sounds in the respective languages will be far from uniform. Fragmentation is evident also in the introduction by all five nations of separate national currencies.

## Caspian Sea Issues

An important goal of Turkmenistan's foreign policy is working in international groups to solve a range of issues involving the Caspian Sea. That body of water, which affords Turkmenistan a 500-kilometer coastline with numerous natural resources, including oil and fish, is threatened by extreme levels of pollution, as well as fluctuating water levels. In August 1993, Turkmenistani delegates attended a meeting in Moscow to discuss the status of international claims to jurisdiction over the Caspian Sea and its resources. Treaties between the Soviet Union and Iran dating from 1921 and 1940 gave each country free navigation and fishing rights within ten miles (sixteen kilometers) of the entire Caspian coastline, putting other coastal nations at a disadvantage. A second issue is the cartel formed by Turkmenistan, Kazakstan, Russia, Azerbaijan, and Iran to control sales of Caspian caviar on the world market as a means of preventing individual Caspian Sea states from selling too much to obtain hard currency. Thus far, however, the cartel lacks an enforcement mechanism. Turkmenistan is a member of the Caspian Sea Forum, which includes all the nations bordering the sea. Until 1995 that organization had not taken concrete action to limit pollution by oil extraction and shipping activities of the member countries, however. In late 1994, Turkmenistan joined Kazakstan, Azerbaijan, and Russia in forming the Caspian Border Patrol force for joint border security (see Military Doctrine, this ch.). In 1995 and 1996, friction increased among the Caspian states as Iran and Russia exerted pressure for the sea's resources to be divided equally among the group, a formula that would pervent the other three countries from taking advantage of their proximity to rich offshore oil deposits.

## National Security

During the Soviet era, military planners regarded Turkmenistan as a crucial border region because of its proximity to Iran and other strategic areas such as the Persian Gulf and Afghanistan. Consequently, a large number of Soviet army troops were stationed in the republic, which was virtually closed to foreigners. Since independence and the formation of a national armed force, Turkmenistan has maintained a posture of neutrality and isolationism, while at the same time pursuing a bilateral military alliance with the Russian Federation. Russia continues to regard Turkmenistan as a key element in its sphere of military interests. For that reason, Russia has secured agreements for stationing border guards and air defense forces in Turkmenistan. Russia also supports the building of the national armed forces by providing training for officers and sharing force maintenance costs.

## Strategic Considerations

The 1992 constitution provides that the republic shall maintain armed forces to defend state sovereignty and that military service for males is a universal obligation that prevails over other constitutional obligations. Turkmenistan's government is adamant about the need to develop and maintain strong, well-trained, and well-equipped armed forces to defend the country's independence. At the same time, it has stated that it will maintain a posture of "positive neutrality" in regard to national security.

Under the agreement for shared command, the presidents of Turkmenistan and the Russian Federation act as joint commanders in chief. By agreement, troops under joint command cannot act without the consent of both ministries of defense. In Turkmenistan the chief military policy-making body, the Supreme Defense Committee, consists of the president, the ministers of defense and internal affairs, the chairman of the Supreme Court, the procurator general, and the leaders of the five provinces. Prior to the creation of the Turkmenistan Ministry of Defense in January 1992, the republic's military establishment fell under the command of the Turkestan Military District of the Soviet armed forces.

Turkmenistan's dependence on the Russian Federation for security against aggressive neighbors, at least until the republic's armed forces become a viable deterrent, creates tension with the foreign policy goal of remaining as independent as possible from Russia. These conflicting national security considerations explain the Niyazov government's implementation of a bilateral military alliance with Russia while at the same time refusing to commit itself to substantial participation in regional military agreements that possibly would alienate Iran.

## Military Doctrine

President Niyazov has acknowledged Russia's legitimate military interests in the region, stating that his country's security interests can be better served through cooperation with Russia than through participation in multinational military organizations. Membership in the latter contradicts its foreign policy of noninterference, as well as its military doctrine that the principal function of Turkmenistan's army is to protect the country from external aggression. Another military doctrine holds that local wars, border conflicts, and military buildups in adjacent countries are the main source of danger to Turkmenistan. Although Turkmenistan has no disputed borders, its doctrine is based on concerns about the civil conflicts in Tajikistan and the instability in northern Afghanistan, especially after the collapse of its pro-Soviet regime in 1989, as well as on traditional tensions with Iran. On the other hand, Turkmenistan's leadership completely discounts the fear that Islamic fundamentalism would spread from Iran into the republic, a prospect of low probability considering that Iranian fundamentalists adhere to the Shia branch of Islam, while the state-controlled Islam of Turkmenistan belongs to the Sunni branch. Traditional animosity between Turkmen and Iranians is also a reason for reaching this conclusion (see Religion, this ch.).

## Role of Russia and the CIS

The Treaty on Joint Measures signed by Russia and Turkmenistan in July 1992 provided for the Russian Federation to act as guarantor of Turkmenistan's security and made former Soviet army units in the republic the basis of the new national armed forces. The treaty stipulated that, apart from border troops and air force and air defense units remaining under Russian control, the entire armed forces would be under joint command, which would gradually devolve to exclusive command by Turkmenistan over a period of ten years. For a transitional period of five years, Russia would provide logistical support and pay Turkmenistan for the right to maintain special installations, while Turkmenistan would bear the costs of housing, utilities, and administration.

More recent agreements between the two countries have strengthened their military alliance. In August 1992, accord was reached on the deployment of Russian border troops in the republic for a five-year period, with an option to renew for another five years. In September 1993, Turkmenistan agreed to assume all costs of maintaining forces on its soil following a five-year period of shared financing. This agreement granted Russia the right to maintain air force and air defense systems with limited control by Turkmenistan. It addressed the continuing majority of Russians in the command structure by permitting Russian citizens to perform military duty in Turkmenistan and by making allowance for the training of

Turkmenistani officers in Russian military schools. At the CIS summit held in Ashgabat in December 1993, the military alliance between the two countries was affirmed, and provisions were made for the participation of 2,000 Russian officers in Turkmenistan in the development of the national armed forces.

Despite the Russian Federation's deep involvement in Turkmenistan's military and pressures to do so, the republic has not joined the CIS collective security agreement. However, regional conflicts have led Turkmenistan to deviate from its posture of avoiding multinational commitments. The republic joined Uzbekistan and Tajikistan in drawing up a draft agreement on joint border defense along the Amu Darya. In addition, Turkmenistan has indicated willingness to cooperate in limited ways in a CIS-sponsored Central Asian Zone that would integrate military units of Uzbekistan, Tajikistan, part of Kyrgyzstan, and possibly Turkmenistan, and provide joint response in cases of aggression by a southern neighbor against any member. In May 1994, Turkmenistan became the first Central Asian member nation of the Partnership for Peace, the NATO initiative offering limited participation in the Western military alliance in return for participation in some NATO exercises. As a result, Turkmenistan has pursued the possibly of training its officers with the military cadre of NATO member nations. The Russian monopoly on military training was broken by a 1994 agreement by which Pakistan would train Turkmenistani air force cadets.

When the Ministry of Defense was formed, most ethnic Turkmen appointees were former communist party and government officials, illustrating the lack of Turkmen senior officers. The first minister of defense, Lieutenant General Danatar Kopekov, had been chairman of the Turkmenistan State Security Committee. In 1994 the chief of staff and first deputy minister of defense was Major General Annamurat Soltanov, a career officer who had served in Cuba and Afghanistan; another deputy minister of defense, Major General Begdzhan Niyazov, had been a law enforcement administrator prior to his appointment. Russian commanders included Major General Viktor Zavarzin, chief of staff and first deputy commander of the Separate Combined-Arms Army of Turkmenistan, and commander of the Separate Combined-Arms Army of Turkmenistan and deputy minister of defense Lieutenant General Nikolay Kormil'tsev. Russian Major General Vladislav Shunevich served together with Turkmen Major General Akmurad Kabulov as joint commanders of the border troops in the Turkmen Border Guard.

## Force Structure

Of the 108,000 uniformed soldiers and officers and 300 units of the former Soviet armed forces that were in Turkmenistan in April 1992, nearly 50,000 personnel and thirty units were withdrawn or disbanded within the following year. By 1993 the republic's armed forces comprised around 34,000 active-duty personnel attached primarily to the army and air force. At that point, the reduced force operated 200 military units while seventy remained under Russian control. Turned over to Turkmenistan's command were one army corps directorate, two combined arms units stationed at Gushgy and Gyzylarbat, several air defense and air force aviation units, technical support and logistical units, and virtually all the armaments and other military property. The armed forces are divided into four branches: the army, air force, and border guards. The government has announced plans to establish a naval force on the Caspian Sea.

### Army

The army, which had been reduced to about 11,000 personnel by 1996, is organized into one corps headquarters, three motorized rifle divisions, one artillery brigade, one multiple rocket launcher regiment, one antitank regiment, one engineer brigade, and one independent helicopter squadron. There are also signal, reconnaissance, and logistics support units. The three motorized rifle divisions are based at Ashgabat, Gushgy, and Gyzylarbat. The army's inventory includes about 530 M–72 main battle tanks, 338 armored infantry fighting vehicles, 543 armored personnel carriers, 345 pieces of towed artillery, sixteen self-propelled guns, 114 multiple rocket launchers, sixty-three mortars, fifty-four antitank guns, and fifty air defense guns.

### Air Force

Turkmenistan's air force has four regiments with 2,000 men and 171 fighter and bomber aircraft, of which sixty-five are Su–17s. The main air force base is at Gyzylarbat. In 1994 the organization of the air force remained contingent on further negotiation on disposition and control of former Soviet units.

*Army conscripts pose inside
a transport aircraft,
Ashgabat.
Courtesy A. James Firth,
United States Department
of Agriculture*

Pending such negotiation, the Ministry of Defense of the Russian Federation maintained one air force and one air defense group in Turkmenistan. In the meantime, air force readiness was hampered by the resignation of most Russian pilots in the early 1990s and a shortage of trained Turkmen pilots.

### Border Guards

About 5,000 personnel serve in the Turkmenistan Border Guard, which is commanded jointly by Turkmenistan and Russia. The Border Guard Command was established in 1992 to replace the Soviet-era Central Asian Border Troops District of the Committee for State Security (KGB) of the Soviet Union. The border guards patrol the wild, mountainous Afghan and Iranian frontiers, which total 1,750 kilometers and are rated the most sensitive borders of the country. The guards have small arms and some armored personnel carriers; experts evaluate them as an effective border force.

### Matériel Supply

In the mid-1990s, Turkmenistan lacked adequate matériel and technical support for its armed forces. However, a protocol with the Russian Arms Company (Rosvooruzheniye) provided for delivery of much-needed arms to Turkmenistan's military in 1995–96 in return for natural gas. Under this agreement,

Turkmenistan was to supply 6 billion cubic meters of gas annually to the Russian Natural Gas Company (Gazprom) for sale to
industries that will fill arms orders for Turkmenistan. Rosvooruzheniye also was to transfer 30 percent of this revenue to
hard-currency accounts in Turkmenistan.

### Recruitment and Training

The 1992 constitution provides for universal conscription of
males for service in the national armed forces. The period of
regular service is eighteen months for army draftees and one
year for those with higher education. Draft deferments from
active military duty are granted only to individuals involved in
seasonal animal herding. A presidential decree of July 1992
allowed two-year alternative service at a state enterprise for
conscripts in certain categories, but this decree was nullifed in
December 1994.

Conditions of service seriously deteriorated in the years
immediately following independence. Large numbers of Turkmen were absent without leave from units outside and within
Turkmenistan, hazing and fighting on ethnic and regional
grounds were common among conscripts, instances of insubor-
dination and failure to comply with orders increased, and relations between the Russian officer corps and Turkmen troops
were strained to the breaking point. In recent years, discipline
has been strengthened somewhat by improved working conditions, amnesty for some cases of absence without leave, the
removal of political organs from the armed services, and
increased opportunities for service within Turkmenistan. In
addition, legislation has improved pensions given to career
personnel in the Ministry of Defense, the Committee for
National Security, the Border Guard, and the Interior Troops
of the Ministry of Internal Affairs, when men reach the age of
fifty-five and women the age of fifty.

All of the personnel except officers in the armed forces are
conscripts, more than 90 percent of whom are Turkmen. By
contrast, about 95 percent of the officer corps is made up of
Slavs. After many Russian officers had left Turkmenistan under
the negative conditions of the early 1990s, others were prevented from leaving by a September 1993 agreement giving
Russian citizens the option of fulfilling their military obligation
in Turkmenistan, swearing allegiance to either state, or transferring to any region of Russia after five years of service in
Turkmenistan.

Turkmenistani officers are trained in military educational establishments of the Russian Federation's Ministry of Defense, while Russian officers in Turkmenistan train draftee sergeants and specialists. Some limited training is provided in the military faculty established at Turkmenistan State University. Turkmenistan has sent about 300 of its officers to training schools in Turkey, but it declined an offer from Pakistan's general staff to provide officer training in Pakistani war colleges.

## Internal Security Forces

The criminal justice system of Turkmenistan is deeply rooted in Soviet institutions and practices. Its Committee for National Security, headed by chairman Saparmurad Seidov, retains essentially the same functions, operations, and personnel of the Soviet-era KGB. As it did in the Soviet period, the Ministry of Internal Affairs continues to direct the operations of police departments and to work closely with the Committee for National Security on matters of national security.

The national police force, estimated to include 25,000 personnel, is under the jurisdiction of the Ministry of Internal Affairs. The force is located in cities and settlements throughout the country, with garrisons in Ashgabat, Gyzylarbat, and Dashhowuz. Police departments do not have an investigative function in Turkmenistan; that role is filled by the procurator's offices in Ashgabat and other cities (see Criminal Justice, this ch.). The police role is confined to routine maintenance of public order and to certain administrative tasks such as controlling the internal passport regime, issuing visas for foreign travel, and registering foreign guests.

At the national level, the primary security concerns are prevention of trafficking in drugs and other illegal commodities, and combatting organized and international crime. In December 1994, Turkmenistan's Committee for National Security and the Russian Federation's Foreign Intelligence Service (a successor agency to the KGB) signed a five-year agreement for cooperation in state security and mutual protection of the political, economic, and technological interests of the two states.

## Criminal Justice

The 1992 constitution declares that Turkmenistan is a state based on the rule of law, and that the constitution is the supreme law of the land. As one of the three branches of government, the judiciary is charged with upholding the constitution and the Supreme Law, as the national codex of civil and criminal law is called. The Ministry of Justice oversees the judicial system, while the Office of the Procurator General is responsible for ensuring that investigative agencies and court proceedings are in compliance with the constitution and the Supreme Law. The president appoints the republic's procurator general and the procurators in each province, and the procurator general appoints those for the smallest political jurisdictions, the districts and the cities.

The court system is divided into three levels. At the highest level, the Supreme Court consists of twenty-two members, including a president and associate judges, and is divided into civil, criminal, and military chambers. The Supreme Court hears only cases of national importance; it does not function as an appeals court. At the next level, appellate courts function as courts of appeal in the six provinces and the city of Ashgabat. Sixty-one trial courts operate in the districts and in some cities, with jurisdiction over civil, criminal, and administrative matters. In courts at this level, a panel of judges presides in civil and criminal suits, and typically one judge decides administrative cases. Outside this structure, military courts decide cases involving military discipline and crimes committed by and against military personnel. Also, the Supreme Economic Court performs the same function as the state arbitration court of the Soviet period, arbitrating disputes between enterprises and state agencies. The constitution stipulates that all judges at all levels are appointed by the president to terms of five years, and they may be reappointed indefinitely. Enjoying immunity from criminal and civil liability for their judicial actions, judges can be removed only for cause.

In 1996, thirteen crimes were punishable by death, but few executions were known to have been carried out. Prison riots in 1996 revealed that prison administration is corrupt and that conditions are overcrowded and squalid.

Observers of several trends in the administration of justice in this court system have concluded that rudimentary elements of legal culture are absent in the implementation of legal proceedings in Turkmenistan. First, the judiciary is subservient to the Ministry of Justice, and it is especially deferential to the wishes of the president. Second, because the Office of the Procurator General fills the roles of grand jury, criminal investigator, and public prosecutor, it dominates the judicial process, especially criminal proceedings. Third, disregard for due process occurs frequently when higher officials apply pressure to judges concerned about reappointment, a practice known as "telephone justice." Fourth, the legal system disregards the role of lawyers in civil and criminal proceedings, and the Ministry of Justice has not permitted an organized bar. Finally, the republic's citizenry remains largely ignorant of the procedures and issues involved in the nation's legal system.

The condition of the legal system and international doubts about human rights in Turkmenistan are indicators that this potentially prosperous former Soviet republic is far from Western-style democracy, despite the stability its government has achieved and the eagerness with which Western investors have approached it. Future years will determine whether this is a transitional stage of independent democracy, whether liberation from the Soviet empire has produced a permanently authoritarian nation, or whether the independent stance of the mid-1990s will yield to closer ties and more economic and military reliance on the Russian Federation.

\*      \*      \*

The social structure of the Turkmen people is studied in *The Yomut Turkmen* by William Irons. Traditional religious practices are described in an article by Vladimir Basilov, "Popular Islam in Central Asia and Kazakhstan," which appeared in the *Journal of the Institute of Muslim Minority Affairs* in 1987. Murray Feshbach and Alfred Friendly, Jr. describe environmental and health conditions in *Ecocide in the USSR.* Detailed current information on the economy is provided in country studies by the International Monetary Fund (1994), the World Bank (1994), and the Economist Intelligence Unit. Summaries of postindependence political events are supplied by Bess Brown in a series of articles in 1992 and 1993 issues of *RFE/RL Research Report.* Concise accounts and statistics on Turkmenistan's current national security position are found in *Jane's Sentinel Regional Security Assessment: Commonwealth of Independent States,* and further statistics are available in annual issues of *The Military Balance.* (For further information and complete citations, see Bibliography.)

# Chapter 5. Uzbekistan

*Painted design pattern in Khorazm style at nineteenth-century Pahlavan-Mahmud Mausoleum, Khiva*

# Country Profile

## Country

**Formal Name:** Republic of Uzbekistan.

**Short Form:** Uzbekistan.

**Term for Citizens:** Uzbekistani(s).

**Capital:** Tashkent.

**Date of Independence:** August 31, 1991.

## Geography

**Size:** Approximately 447,000 square kilometers.

**Topography:** About 80 percent flat, desert; mountain ranges dominate far southeast and far northeast and traverse middle of eastern provinces, east to west. Fergana Valley in northeast most fertile region. Few lakes and rivers; shrinking Aral Sea, shared with Kazakstan, in northwest. Most of country seismically active.

**Climate:** Continental; hot summers, cool winters. Annual rainfall very sparse in most regions, irrigation needed for crops.

## Society

**Population:** Approximately 23 million, 1994; growth rate in 1995, 2.5 percent per year; 1993 population density 48.5 persons per square kilometer.

**Ethnic Groups:** In 1995, Uzbek 71 percent, Russian 8 percent, Tajik 5 percent, Kazak 4 percent, Tatar 2 percent, and Karakalpak 2 percent.

**Language:** Uzbek designated preferred language, required for citizenship, but Russian in wide official and commercial use, 1995. In 1994, Uzbek first language of 74 percent, Russian of 14 percent, and Tajik of 4 percent.

**Religion:** Muslim (mostly Sunni) 88 percent, Russian Orthodox 9 percent, about 93,000 Jews. Islam practiced in individualized forms; little political Islam although post-Soviet religious practice greatly increased.

**Education and Literacy:** Literacy 97 percent, 1989. Program to restructure Soviet-era system hampered by low budget, poor condition of infrastructure, and loss of teachers. Attendance compulsory through grade nine. In 1993, 86 percent of population ages six to sixteen in regular or vocational school. Fifty-three institutions of higher learning active, 1993.

**Health:** Universal free health care; some private practices and health insurance introduced, early 1990s. Shortages of medicine, equipment, and trained personnel. Health crises, epidemics caused by high pollution levels, especially in Aral Sea region. Infant mortality increased very fast beginning in 1970s.

## Economy

**Gross National Product (GNP):** In 1993, US$31 billion, or US$1,346 per capita. In 1994 growth rate –4 percent. Cautious reform avoided major post-Soviet declines of other Central Asian states; strong resource base promises prosperity given systemic reform.

**Agriculture:** Cotton remains primary crop, requiring heavy irrigation; entire system geared for its production. Failure to expand grain culture has led to heavy food imports. Other crops wheat, oats, corn, barley, rice, fodder crops, fruits, and vegetables.

**Industry and Mining:** Slow diversification, early 1990s, from Soviet-era specialization in cotton-related and mineral-processing operations. Heavy industry, centered in northeast, mainly petroleum and mineral processing, machinery, ferrous metallurgy, chemicals, and electric power. Light industry dominated by fabric and food processing. Gold, copper, zinc, lead, tungsten, uranium, molybdenum, and fluorospar mined.

**Energy:** Large untapped natural gas reserves, small coal and oil production; two newly tapped oil fields have high potential. Coal mainly in northeastern industrial region. Hydroelectric power system well-developed on three major rivers; thermoelectric stations burn natural gas or coal.

**Exports:** Worth US$3.0 billion in 1994. As in Soviet period, dominated by minerals, cotton, cotton-related machinery, textiles, and fertilizers. Chief customers remain in Commonwealth of Independent States (CIS): Russia, Kazakstan, Ukraine, Turkmenistan, and Kyrgyzstan. Export licensing liberalized 1994, but market expansion slow.

**Imports:** Worth US$2.5 billion in 1994. Mostly non-textile consumer goods, grain and other foods, machinery, and ferrous metals; chief suppliers Russia, Ukraine, Kazakstan, Turkmenistan, Belarus, and Kyrgyzstan. Import licensing discontinued, quotas reduced, 1994.

**Balance of Payments:** In 1992, US$107 million deficit.

**Exchange Rate:** Provisional currency unit, som, introduced November 1993, made permanent July 1994. In 1996, rate thirty-five som per US$1. Stabilized and convertibility liberalized 1995; full convertibility promised 1996.

**Inflation:** Hyperinflation (1,100 percent) 1993, 270 percent 1994 after second-half slide of som's value. Government control remains on prices of basic commodities and fuels, but prices of other items rose very fast after decontrol, 1992 and 1993.

**Fiscal Year:** Calendar year.

**Fiscal Policy:** Tax system reformed with addition of value-added and profits tax, beginning 1992; main revenues of 1993 state budget from value-added tax, corporate income tax, cotton marketing, and individual income tax; 1993 state budget deficit 200 million rubles, 12 percent of revenue.

## Transportation and Telecommunications

**Highways:** About 67,000 kilometers paved. Three major roads connect Tashkent and Termiz, Samarqand and Chärjew, and Tashkent and Quqon, respectively. Fergana Ring serves industries of the northeast. Highways carry about 25 percent of freight traffic.

**Railroads:** About 3,500 kilometers of track, much needing repair, carry about 75 percent of freight traffic. Main line

Transcaspian Railroad connecting Tashkent with Amu Darya.

**Civil Aviation:** Nine airports, of which four accommodate international flights. Largest airport, at Tashkent, a hub linking Central Asia with Western Europe and United States.

**Inland Waterways:** Steamship travel on Amu Darya reduced because of low water levels.

**Ports:** None.

**Pipelines:** In 1992, 325 kilometers of oil pipeline, 2,470 kilometers of natural gas pipeline.

**Telecommunications:** Telephone service available to 7 percent of population in 1994. Much outmoded equipment remains in service; system expansion slow. Satellite television broadcasts in some regions. Radio and television controlled by Ministry of Communications.

## Government and Politics

**Government:** Constitution, adopted 1992, provides for strong presidency, with power to appoint government and dissolve legislature. In practice, authoritarian state with all power in executive and suppression of dissent. Referendum, 1995, extended term of President Islam Karimov to 2000. Local government with little autonomy; judiciary ineffective.

**Politics:** Successor to Communist Party, People's Democratic Party, dominates legislature and government; other major legal party, Fatherland Progress Party, has no opposition role; opposition parties weak, fragmented, many excluded by government and their leaders exiled or jailed.

**Foreign Relations:** To avoid domination by Russia, wide relations sought, early 1990s. Major goal cooperation among Central Asian states, which fear domination by Uzbekistan. Free-trade zone with Kazakstan, Kyrgyzstan and cooperation on Aral Sea matters are major steps. Economic and military dependence on CIS, especially Russia, continues. Renewed economic ties with Iran, Turkey, possible major role in Economic Cooperation Organization. Major aid programs from United States, Western Europe, mid-1990s.

**International Agreements and Memberships:** United Nations

(UN), World Bank, International Monetary Fund (IMF), Economic Cooperation Organization (ECO), Organization for Security and Cooperation in Europe (OSCE), North Atlantic Cooperation Council, CIS, and North Atlantic Treaty Organization (NATO) Partnership for Peace.

## National Security

**Armed Forces:** Best-equipped of Central Asian forces. Ground forces have 20,400 troops, air force and air defense forces have estimated 4,000 troops, border troops about 1,000, National Guard about 700.

**Major Military Units:** One ground force corps, divided into three motorized rifle brigades, one tank regiment, one airborne brigade, one engineer brigade, and support units for aviation, logistics, and communications.

**Military Budget:** 1995 estimate, US$315 million.

**Internal Security:** National Security Service continues intelligence function of Soviet-era Committee for State Security (KGB), with estimated 8,000 troops. Major crime problem narcotics sales and transport, inadequately addressed in early 1990s. Regular police force has about 25,000 troops. Political corruption and bribery widespread, including state procurator and courts.

## Republic and Provinces

| | |
|---|---|
| I | Autonomous Republic of Karakalpakstan |
| II | Khorazm |
| III | Nawoiy |
| IV | Bukhoro |
| V | Samarqand |
| VI | Qashqadaryo |
| VII | Jizzakh |
| VIII | Surkhondaryo |
| IX | Sirdaryo |
| X | Toshkent |
| XI | Namangan |
| XII | Andijon |
| XIII | Farghona |

*Figure 13. Uzbekistan: Administrative Divisions, 1996*

BEFORE THE COLLAPSE of the Soviet Union, Uzbekistan was the third largest Soviet republic by population and the fourth largest in territory. Because it has a population that is more than 40 percent of the combined population of the five Central Asian states of the former Soviet Union, and because it has rich natural resources, many experts believe that Uzbekistan is likely to emerge as the dominant new state in Central Asia. But Uzbekistan's history also has given rise to serious problems: deeply rooted ethnic tensions; serious economic, political, and environmental challenges; and an uncertain security and foreign policy environment. Like its neighbors in Central Asia, Uzbekistan emerged suddenly from more than sixty years within a highly structured, and in many ways protective, political and economic system. In the years following that emergence, survival has depended on the development of new international relationships as well as on solutions to the dilemmas of the Soviet era. By 1996 Uzbekistan showed signs of progress in both directions.

## Historical Background

Uzbekistan, the most populous and arguably the most powerful state in Central Asia, has a long and magnificent history. Located between two rivers—the Amu Darya to the north and the Syrdariya to the south—the region that is modern Uzbekistan has been one of the cradles of world civilization. Some of the world's oldest sedentary populations and several of its most ancient cities are located here. Beginning at the height of the Roman Empire, the region was a crossroads on the transcontinental trade routes between China and the West. Subject to constant invasion and to in-migration of nomads from the great grasslands to the north, Uzbekistan became a region of legendary conquests where various peoples with different traditions have consistently had to live together.

### Early History

The first people known to have occupied Central Asia were Iranian nomads who arrived from the northern grasslands of what is now Uzbekistan sometime in the first millennium B.C. These nomads, who spoke Iranian (see Glossary) dialects, settled in Central Asia and began to build an extensive irrigation system along the rivers of the region. At this time, cities such as Bukhoro (Bukhara) and Samarqand (Samarkand) began to appear as centers of government and culture. By the fifth century B.C., the Bactrian, Soghdian, and Tokharian states dominated the region. As China began to develop its silk trade with the West, Iranian cities took advantage of this commerce by becoming centers of trade. Using an extensive network of cities and settlements in the province of Mawarannahr (a name given the region after the Arab conquest) in Uzbekistan and farther east in what is today China's Xinjiang Uygur Autonomous Region, the Soghdian intermediaries became the wealthiest of these Iranian merchants. Because of this trade on what became known as the Silk Route, Bukhoro and Samarqand eventually became extremely wealthy cities, and at times Mawarannahr was one of the most influential and powerful Persian (see Glossary) provinces of antiquity.

The wealth of Mawarannahr was a constant magnet for invasions from the northern steppes and from China. Numerous intraregional wars were fought between Soghdian states and the other states in Mawarannahr, and the Persians and the Chinese were in perpetual conflict over the region. Alexander the Great conquered the region in 328 B.C., bringing it briefly under the control of his Macedonian Empire.

In the same centuries, however, the region also was an important center of intellectual life and religion. Until the first centuries after Christ, the dominant religion in the region was Zoroastrianism (see Glossary), but Buddhism, Manichaeism (see Glossary), and Christianity also attracted large numbers of followers.

## The Early Islamic Period

The conquest of Central Asia by Islamic Arabs, which was completed in the eighth century A.D., brought to the region a new religion and culture that continue to be dominant. The Arabs first invaded Mawarannahr in the middle of the seventh century through sporadic raids during their conquest of Persia. Available sources on the Arab conquest suggest that the Soghdians and other Iranian peoples of Central Asia were unable to defend their land against the Arabs because of internal divisions and the lack of strong indigenous leadership. The Arabs, on the other hand, were led by a brilliant general, Qutaybah ibn Muslim, and they also were highly motivated by the desire to spread their new faith (the official beginning of which was in A.D. 622). Because of these factors, the population of Mawarannahr was easily conquered. The new religion brought by the Arabs spread gradually in the region. The native cultures, which in some respects already were being displaced by Persian influences before the Arabs arrived, were displaced farther in the ensuing centuries. Nevertheless, the destiny of Central Asia as an Islamic region was firmly established by the Arab victory over the Chinese armies in 750 in a battle at the Talas River.

Under Arab rule, Central Asia retained much of its Iranian character, remaining an important center of culture and trade for centuries after the Arab conquest. However, until the tenth century the language of government, literature, and commerce was Arabic. Mawarannahr continued to be an important political player in regional affairs, as it had been under various Persian dynasties. In fact, the Abbasid Caliphate, which ruled the Arab world for five centuries beginning in 750, was established thanks in great part to assistance from Central Asian supporters in their struggle against the then-ruling Umayyad Caliphate.

During the height of the Abbasid Caliphate in the eighth and the ninth centuries, Central Asia and Mawarannahr experienced a truly golden age. Bukhoro became one of the leading centers of learning, culture, and art in the Muslim world, its magnificence rivaling contemporaneous cultural centers such as Baghdad, Cairo, and Cordoba. Some of the greatest historians, scientists, and geographers in the history of Islamic culture were natives of the region.

As the Abbasid Caliphate began to weaken and local Islamic Iranian states emerged as the rulers of Iran and Central Asia, the Persian language began to regain its preeminent role in the region as the language of literature and government. The rulers of the eastern section of Iran and of Mawarannahr were Persians. Under the Samanids and the Buyids, the rich culture of Mawarannahr continued to flourish.

## The Turkification of Mawarannahr

In the ninth century, the continued influx of nomads from the northern steppes brought a new group of people into Central Asia. These people were the Turks who lived in the great grasslands stretching from Mongolia to the Caspian Sea. Introduced mainly as slave soldiers to the Samanid Dynasty, these

Turks served in the armies of all the states of the region, including the Abbasid army. In the late tenth century, as the Samanids began to lose control of Mawarannahr and northeastern Iran, some of these soldiers came to positions of power in the government of the region, and eventually they established their own states. With the emergence of a Turkic ruling group in the region, other Turkic tribes began to migrate to Mawarannahr.

The first of the Turkic states in the region was the Ghaznavid Empire, established in the last years of the tenth century. The Ghaznavid state, which ruled lands south of the Amu Darya, was able to conquer large areas of Iran, Afghanistan, and northern India during the reign of Sultan Mahmud. The dominance of Ghazna was curtailed, however, when large-scale Turkic migrations brought in two new groups of Turks who undermined the Ghaznavids. In the east, these Turks were led by the Qarakhanids, who conquered the Samanids. Then the Seljuk family led Turks into the western part of the region, conquering the Ghaznavid territory of Khorazm (also spelled Khorezm and Khwarazm).

Attracted by the wealth of Central Asia as were earlier groups, the Seljuks dominated a wide area from Asia Minor to the western sections of Mawarannahr, in Afghanistan, Iran, and Iraq in the eleventh century. The Seljuk Empire then split into states ruled by various local Turkic and Iranian rulers. The culture and intellectual life of the region continued unaffected by such political changes, however. Turkic tribes from the north continued to migrate into the region during this period.

In the late twelfth century, a Turkic leader of Khorazm, which is the region south of the Aral Sea, united Khorazm, Mawarannahr, and Iran under his rule. Under the rule of the Khorazm shah Kutbeddin Muhammad and his son, Muhammad II, Mawarannahr continued to be prosperous and rich. However, a new incursion of nomads from the north soon changed this situation. This time the invader was Chinggis (Genghis) Khan with his Mongol armies.

## The Mongol Period

The Mongol invasion of Central Asia is one of the turning points in the history of the region. That event left imprints that were still discernible in the early twentieth century. The Mongols had such a lasting impact because they established the tradition that the legitimate ruler of any Central Asian state could only be a blood descendant of Chinggis Khan.

The Mongol conquest of Central Asia, which took place from 1219 to 1225, led to a wholesale change in the population of Mawarannahr. The conquest quickened the process of Turkification in the region because, although the armies of Chinggis Khan were led by Mongols, they were made up mostly of Turkic tribes that had been incorporated into the Mongol armies as the tribes were encountered in the Mongols' southward sweep. As these armies settled in Mawarannahr, they intermixed with the local populations, increasingly making the Iranians a minority. Another effect of the Mongol conquest was the large-scale damage the warriors inflicted on cities such as Bukhoro and on regions such as Khorazm. As the leading province of a wealthy state, Khorazm was treated especially severely. The irrigation networks in the region suffered extensive damage that was not repaired for several generations.

## The Rule of Timur

Following the death of Chinggis Khan in 1227, his empire was divided among his three sons. Despite the potential for serious fragmentation, Mongol law maintained orderly succession for several more generations, and control of most of Mawarannahr stayed in the hands of direct descendants of Chaghatai, the second son of Chinggis. Orderly succession, prosperity, and internal peace prevailed in the Chaghatai lands, and the Mongol Empire as a whole remained strong and united.

In the early fourteenth century, however, as the empire began to break up into its constituent parts, the Chaghatai territory also was disrupted as the princes of various tribal groups competed for influence. One tribal chieftain, Timur (Tamerlane), emerged from these struggles in the 1380s as the dominant force in Mawarannahr. Although he was not a descendant of Chinggis, Timur became the de facto ruler of Mawarannahr and proceeded to conquer all of western Central Asia, Iran, Asia Minor, and the southern steppe region north of the Aral Sea. He also invaded Russia before dying during an invasion of China in 1405.

Timur initiated the last flowering of Mawarannahr by gathering in his capital, Samarqand, numerous artisans and scholars from the lands he had conquered. By supporting such people, Timur imbued his empire with a very rich culture. During

Timur's reign and the reigns of his immediate descendants, a wide range of religious and palatial construction projects were undertaken in Samarqand and other population centers. Timur also patronized scientists and artists; his grandson Ulugh Beg was one of the world's first great astronomers. It was during the Timurid dynasty that Turkish, in the form of the Chaghatai dialect, became a literary language in its own right in Mawarannahr—although the Timurids also patronized writing in Persian. Until then only Persian had been used in the region. The greatest Chaghataid writer, Ali Shir Nava'i, was active in the city of Herat, now in northwestern Afghanistan, in the second half of the fifteenth century.

The Timurid state quickly broke into two halves after the death of Timur. The chronic internal fighting of the Timurids attracted the attention of the Uzbek nomadic tribes living to the north of the Aral Sea. In 1501 the Uzbeks began a wholesale invasion of Mawarannahr.

## The Uzbek Period

By 1510 the Uzbeks had completed their conquest of Central Asia, including the territory of the present-day Uzbekistan. Of the states they established, the most powerful, the Khanate of Bukhoro, centered on the city of Bukhoro. The khanate controlled Mawarannahr, especially the region of Tashkent, the Fergana Valley in the east, and northern Afghanistan. A second Uzbek state was established in the oasis of Khorazm at the mouth of the Amu Darya. The Khanate of Bukhoro was initially led by the energetic Shaybanid Dynasty. The Shaybanids competed against Iran, which was led by the Safavid Dynasty, for the rich far-eastern territory of present-day Iran. The struggle with Iran also had a religious aspect because the Uzbeks were Sunni (see Glossary) Muslims, and Iran was Shia (see Glossary).

Near the end of the sixteenth century, the Uzbek states of Bukhoro and Khorazm began to weaken because of their endless wars against each other and the Persians and because of strong competition for the throne among the khans in power and their heirs. At the beginning of the seventeenth century, the Shaybanid Dynasty was replaced by the Janid Dynasty.

Another factor contributing to the weakness of the Uzbek khanates in this period was the general decline of trade moving through the region. This change had begun in the previous century when ocean trade routes were established from Europe to India and China, circumventing the Silk Route. As

*Bazaar outside Bibi Khanym Mosque, built by Timur, Samarqand*
*Courtesy Hermine Dreyfuss*

European-dominated ocean transport expanded and some trading centers were destroyed, cities such as Bukhoro, Merv, and Samarqand in the Khanate of Bukhoro and Khiva and Urganch (Urgench) in Khorazm began to steadily decline.

The Uzbeks' struggle with Iran also led to the cultural isolation of Central Asia from the rest of the Islamic world. In addition to these problems, the struggle with the nomads from the northern steppe continued. In the seventeenth and eighteenth centuries, Kazak nomads and Mongols continually raided the Uzbek khanates, causing widespread damage and disruption. In the beginning of the eighteenth century, the Khanate of Bukhoro lost the fertile Fergana region, and a new Uzbek khanate was formed in Quqon.

### Arrival of the Russians

The following period was one of weakness and disruption,

with continuous invasions from Iran and from the north. In this period, a new group, the Russians, began to appear on the Central Asian scene. As Russian merchants began to expand into the grasslands of present-day Kazakstan, they built strong trade relations with their counterparts in Tashkent and, to some extent, in Khiva. For the Russians, this trade was not rich enough to replace the former transcontinental trade, but it made the Russians aware of the potential of Central Asia. Russian attention also was drawn by the sale of increasingly large numbers of Russian slaves to the Central Asians by Kazak and Turkmen tribes. Russians kidnapped by nomads in the border regions and Russian sailors shipwrecked on the shores of the Caspian Sea usually ended up in the slave markets of Bukhoro or Khiva. Beginning in the eighteenth century, this situation evoked increasing Russian hostility toward the Central Asian khanates.

Meanwhile, in the late eighteenth and early nineteenth centuries new dynasties led the khanates to a period of recovery. Those dynasties were the Qongrats in Khiva, the Manghits in Bukhoro, and the Mins in Quqon. These new dynasties established centralized states with standing armies and new irrigation works. But their rise coincided with the ascendance of Russian power in the Kazak steppes and the establishment of a British position in Afghanistan. By the early nineteenth century, the region was caught between these two powerful European competitors, each of which tried to add Central Asia to its empire in what came to be known as the Great Game. The Central Asians, who did not realize the dangerous position they were in, continued to waste their strength in wars among themselves and in pointless campaigns of conquest.

## The Russian Conquest

In the nineteenth century, Russian interest in the area increased greatly, sparked by nominal concern over British designs on Central Asia; by anger over the situation of Russian citizens held as slaves; and by the desire to control the trade in the region and to establish a secure source of cotton for Russia. When the United States Civil War prevented cotton delivery from Russia's primary supplier, the southern United States, Central Asian cotton assumed much greater importance for Russia.

As soon as the Russian conquest of the Caucasus was completed in the late 1850s, therefore, the Russian Ministry of War

*Registan, an architectural monument of the fifteenth–seventeenth
centuries, Samarqand
Courtesy Tom Skipper*

began to send military forces against the Central Asian khanates. Three major population centers of the khanates—Tashkent, Bukhoro, and Samarqand—were captured in 1865, 1867,
and 1868, respectively. In 1868 the Khanate of Bukhoro signed
a treaty with Russia making Bukhoro a Russian protectorate.
Khiva became a Russian protectorate in 1873, and the Quqon
Khanate finally was incorporated into the Russian Empire, also
as a protectorate, in 1876.

By 1876 the entire territory comprising present-day Uzbekistan either had fallen under direct Russian rule or had become
a protectorate of Russia. The treaties establishing the protectorates over Bukhoro and Khiva gave Russia control of the foreign relations of these states and gave Russian merchants
important concessions in foreign trade; the khanates retained

control of their own internal affairs. Tashkent and Ququn fell directly under a Russian governor general.

During the first few decades of Russian rule, the daily life of the Central Asians did not change greatly. The Russians substantially increased cotton production, but otherwise they interfered little with the indigenous people. Some Russian settlements were built next to the established cities of Tashkent and Samarqand, but the Russians did not mix with the indigenous populations. The era of Russian rule did produce important social and economic changes for some Uzbeks as a new middle class developed and some peasants were affected by the increased emphasis on cotton cultivation.

In the last decade of the nineteenth century, conditions began to change as new Russian railroads brought greater numbers of Russians into the area. In the 1890s, several revolts, which were put down easily, led to increased Russian vigilance in the region. The Russians increasingly intruded in the internal affairs of the khanates. The only avenue for Uzbek resistance to Russian rule became the Pan-Turkish movement, also known as Jadidism, which had arisen in the 1860s among intellectuals who sought to preserve indigenous Islamic Central Asian culture from Russian encroachment. By 1900 Jadidism had developed into the region's first major movement of political resistance. Until the Bolshevik Revolution (see Glossary) of 1917, the modern, secular ideas of Jadidism faced resistance from both the Russians and the Uzbek khans, who had differing reasons to fear the movement.

Prior to the events of 1917, Russian rule had brought some industrial development in sectors directly connected with cotton. Although railroads and cotton-ginning machinery advanced, the Central Asian textile industry was slow to develop because the cotton crop was shipped to Russia for processing. As the tsarist government expanded the cultivation of cotton dramatically, it changed the balance between cotton and food production, creating some problems in food supply—although in the prerevolutionary period Central Asia remained largely self-sufficient in food. This situation was to change during the Soviet period when the Moscow government began a ruthless drive for national self-sufficiency in cotton. This policy converted almost the entire agricultural economy of Uzbekistan to cotton production, bringing a series of consequences whose negative impact still is felt today in Uzbekistan and other republics.

## Entering the Twentieth Century

By the turn of the twentieth century, the Russian Empire was in complete control of Central Asia. The territory of Uzbekistan was divided into three political groupings: the khanates of Bukhoro and Khiva and the Guberniya (Governorate General) of Turkestan, the last of which was under direct control of the Ministry of War of Russia (see fig. 3). The final decade of the twentieth century finds the three regions united under the independent and sovereign Republic of Uzbekistan. The intervening decades were a period of revolution, oppression, massive disruptions, and colonial rule.

After 1900 the khanates continued to enjoy a certain degree of autonomy in their internal affairs. However, they ultimately were subservient to the Russian governor general in Tashkent, who ruled the region in the name of Tsar Nicholas II. The Russian Empire exercised direct control over large tracts of territory in Central Asia, allowing the khanates to rule a large portion of their ancient lands for themselves. In this period, large numbers of Russians, attracted by the climate and the available land, immigrated into Central Asia. After 1900, increased contact with Russian civilization began to have an impact on the lives of Central Asians in the larger population centers where the Russians settled.

## The Jadidists and Basmachis

Russian influence was especially strong among certain young intellectuals who were the sons of the rich merchant classes. Educated in the local Muslim schools, in Russian universities, or in Istanbul, these men, who came to be known as the Jadidists, tried to learn from Russia and from modernizing movements in Istanbul and among the Tatars, and to use this knowledge to regain their country's independence. The Jadidists believed that their society, and even their religion, must be reformed and modernized for this goal to be achieved. In 1905 the unexpected victory of a new Asiatic power in the Russo-Japanese War and the eruption of revolution in Russia raised the hopes of reform factions that Russian rule could be overturned, and a modernization program initiated, in Central Asia. The democratic reforms that Russia promised in the wake of the revolution gradually faded, however, as the tsarist government restored authoritarian rule in the decade that followed 1905. Renewed tsarist repression and the reactionary politics of the rulers of Bukhoro and Khiva forced the reformers underground or into exile. Nevertheless, some of the future leaders of Soviet Uzbekistan, including Abdur Rauf Fitrat and others, gained valuable revolutionary experience and were able to expand their ideological influence in this period.

In the summer of 1916, a number of settlements in eastern Uzbekistan were the sites of violent demonstrations against a new Russian decree canceling the Central Asians' immunity to conscription for duty in World War I. Reprisals of increasing violence ensued, and the struggle spread from Uzbekistan into Kyrgyz and Kazak territory. There, Russian confiscation of grazing land already had created animosity not present in the Uzbek population, which was concerned mainly with preserving its rights.

The next opportunity for the Jadidists presented itself in 1917 with the outbreak of the February and October revolutions in Russia. In February the revolutionary events in Russia's capital, Petrograd (St. Petersburg), were quickly repeated in Tashkent, where the tsarist administration of the governor general was overthrown. In its place, a dual system was established, combining a provisional government with direct Soviet power and completely excluding the native Muslim population from power. Indigenous leaders, including some of the Jadidists, attempted to set up an autonomous government in the city of Quqon in the Fergana Valley, but this attempt was quickly crushed. Following the suppression of autonomy in Quqon, Jadidists and other loosely connected factions began what was called the Basmachi revolt against Soviet rule, which by 1922 had survived the civil war and was asserting greater power over most of Central Asia. For more than a decade, Basmachi guerrilla fighters (that name was a derogatory Slavic term that the fighters did not apply to themselves) fiercely resisted the establishment of Soviet rule in parts of Central Asia.

However, the majority of Jadidists, including leaders such as Fitrat and Faizulla Khojayev, cast their lot with the communists. In 1920 Khojayev, who became first secretary of the Communist Party of Uzbekistan, assisted communist forces in the capture of Bukhoro and Khiva. After the amir of Bukhoro had joined the Basmachi movement, Khojayev became president of the newly established Soviet Bukhoran People's Republic. A People's Republic of Khorazm also was set up in what had been Khiva.

The Basmachi revolt eventually was crushed as the civil war in Russia ended and the communists drew away large portions of the Central Asian population with promises of local political autonomy and the potential economic autonomy of Soviet leader Vladimir I. Lenin's New Economic Policy (NEP—see Glossary). Under these circumstances, large numbers of Central Asians joined the communist party, many gaining high positions in the government of the Uzbek Soviet Socialist Republic (Uzbek SSR), the administrative unit established in 1924 to include present-day Uzbekistan and Tajikistan. The indigenous leaders cooperated closely with the communist government in enforcing policies designed to alter the traditional society of the region: the emancipation of women, the redistribution of land, and mass literacy campaigns.

## The Stalinist Period

In 1929 the Tajik and Uzbek Soviet socialist republics were separated. As Uzbek communist party chief, Khojayev enforced the policies of the Soviet government during the collectivization of agriculture in the late 1920s and early 1930s and, at the same time, tried to increase the participation of Uzbeks in the government and the party. Soviet leader Joseph V. Stalin suspected the motives of all reformist national leaders in the non-Russian republics of the Soviet Union. By the late 1930s, Khojayev and the entire group that came into high positions in the Uzbek Republic had been arrested and executed during the Stalinist purges.

Following the purge of the nationalists, the government and party ranks in Uzbekistan were filled with people loyal to the Moscow government. Economic policy emphasized the supply of cotton to the rest of the Soviet Union, to the exclusion of diversified agriculture. During World War II, many industrial plants from European Russia were evacuated to Uzbekistan and other parts of Central Asia. With the factories came a new wave of Russian and other European workers. Because native Uzbeks were mostly occupied in the country's agricultural regions, the urban concentration of immigrants increasingly Russified Tashkent and other large cities. During the war years, in addition to the Russians who moved to Uzbekistan, other nationalities such as Crimean Tatars, Chechens, and Koreans were exiled to the republic because Moscow saw them as subversive elements in European Russia.

## Russification and Resistance

Following the death of Stalin in 1953, the relative relaxation of totalitarian control initiated by First Secretary Nikita S. Khrushchev (in office 1953–64) brought the rehabilitation of some of the Uzbek nationalists who had been purged. More Uzbeks began to join the Communist Party of Uzbekistan and to assume positions in the government. However, those Uzbeks who participated in the regime did so on Russian terms. Russian was the language of state, and Russification was the prerequisite for obtaining a position in the government or the party. Those who did not or could not abandon their Uzbek lifestyles and identities were excluded from leading roles in official Uzbek society. Because of these conditions, Uzbekistan gained a reputation as one of the most politically conservative republics in the Soviet Union.

As Uzbeks were beginning to gain leading positions in society, they also were establishing or reviving unofficial networks based on regional and clan loyalties. These networks provided their members support and often profitable connections between them and the state and the party. An extreme example of this phenomenon occurred under the leadership of Sharaf Rashidov, who was first secretary of the Communist Party of Uzbekistan from 1959 to 1982. During his tenure, Rashidov brought numerous relatives and associates from his native region into government and party leadership positions. The individuals who thus became "connected" treated their positions as personal fiefdoms to enrich themselves.

In this way, Rashidov was able to initiate efforts to make Uzbekistan less subservient to Moscow. As became apparent after his death, Rashidov's strategy had been to remain a loyal ally of Leonid I. Brezhnev, leader of the Soviet Union from 1964 to 1982, by bribing high officials of the central government. With this advantage, the Uzbek government was allowed to merely feign compliance with Moscow's demands for increasingly higher cotton quotas.

## The 1980s

During the decade following the death of Rashidov, Moscow attempted to regain the central control over Uzbekistan that had weakened in the previous decade. In 1986 it was announced that almost the entire party and government leadership of the republic had conspired in falsifying cotton production figures. Eventually, Rashidov himself was also implicated (posthumously) together with Yuriy Churbanov, Brezhnev's son-in-law. A massive purge of the Uzbek leadership was carried out, and corruption trials were conducted by prosecutors brought in from Moscow. In the Soviet Union, Uzbekistan became synonymous with corruption. The Uzbeks themselves felt that the central government had singled them out unfairly; in the 1980s, this resentment led to a strengthening of Uzbek nationalism. Moscow's policies in Uzbekistan, such as the strong emphasis on cotton and attempts to uproot Islamic tradition, then came under increasing criticism in Tashkent.

In 1989 ethnic animosities came to a head in the Fergana Valley, where local Meskhetian Turks were assaulted by Uzbeks, and in the Kyrgyz city of Osh, where Uzbek and Kyrgyz youth clashed. Moscow's response to this violence was a reduction of the purges and the appointment of Islam Karimov as first secretary of the Communist Party of Uzbekistan. The appointment of Karimov, who was not a member of the local party elite, signified that Moscow wanted to lessen tensions by appointing an outsider who had not been involved in the purges.

Resentment among Uzbeks continued to smolder, however, in the liberalized atmosphere of Soviet leader Mikhail S. Gorbachev's policies of *perestroika* (see Glossary) and *glasnost* (see Glossary). With the emergence of new opportunities to express dissent, Uzbeks expressed their grievances over the cotton scandal, the purges, and other long-unspoken resentments. These included the environmental situation in the republic, recently exposed as a catastrophe as a result of the long emphasis on heavy industry and a relentless pursuit of cotton (see Environmental Problems, this ch.). Other grievances included discrimination and persecution experienced by Uzbek recruits in the Soviet army and the lack of investment in industrial development in the republic to provide jobs for the ever-increasing population.

By the late 1980s, some dissenting intellectuals had formed political organizations to express their grievances. The most important of these, Birlik (Unity), initially advocated the diversification of agriculture, a program to salvage the desiccated Aral Sea, and the declaration of the Uzbek language as the state language of the republic. Those issues were chosen partly because they were real concerns and partly because they were a safe way of expressing broader disaffection with the Uzbek government. In their public debate with Birlik, the government and party never lost the upper hand. As became especially clear after the accession of Karimov as party chief, most Uzbeks, especially those outside the cities, still supported the communist party and the government. Birlik's intellectual leaders never were able to make their appeal to a broad segment of the population (see Opposition Parties, this ch.).

## Independence

The attempted coup against the Gorbachev government by disaffected hard-liners in Moscow, which occurred in August 1991, was a catalyst for independence movements throughout the Soviet Union. Despite Uzbekistan's initial hesitancy to oppose the coup, the Supreme Soviet of Uzbekistan declared the republic independent on August 31, 1991. In December 1991, an independence referendum was passed with 98.2 percent of the popular vote. The same month, a parliament was elected and Karimov was chosen the new nation's first president.

Although Uzbekistan had not sought independence, when events brought them to that point, Karimov and his government moved quickly to adapt themselves to the new realities. They realized that under the Commonwealth of Independent States (CIS—see Glossary), the loose federation proposed to replace the Soviet Union, no central government would provide the subsidies to which Uzbek governments had become accustomed for the previous seventy years. Old economic ties would have to be reexamined and new markets and economic mechanisms established. Although Uzbekistan as defined by the Soviets had never had independent foreign relations, diplomatic relations would have to be established with foreign countries quickly. Investment and foreign credits would have to be attracted, a formidable challenge in light of Western restrictions on financial aid to nations restricting expression of political dissent. For example, the suppression of internal dissent in 1992 and 1993 had an unexpectedly chilling effect on foreign investment. Uzbekistan's image in the West alternated in the ensuing years between an attractive, stable experimental zone for investment and a post-Soviet dictatorship whose human rights record made financial aid inadvisable. Such alternation exerted strong influence on the political and economic fortunes of the new republic in its first five years (see International Financial Relations, this ch.).

## Physical Environment

With an area of 447,000 square kilometers (approximately the size of France), Uzbekistan stretches 1,425 kilometers from west to east and 930 kilometers from north to south. Bordering Turkmenistan to the southwest, Kazakstan to the north, and Tajikistan and Kyrgyzstan to the south and east, Uzbekistan is not only one of the larger Central Asian states but also the only Central Asian state to border all of the other four. Uzbekistan also shares a short border with Afghanistan to the south (see fig. 1).

### Topography and Drainage

The physical environment of Uzbekistan is diverse, ranging from the flat, desert topography that comprises almost 80 percent of the country's territory to mountain peaks in the east reaching about 4,500 meters above sea level. The southeastern portion of Uzbekistan is characterized by the foothills of the Tian Shan mountains, which rise higher in neighboring Kyrgyzstan and Tajikistan and form a natural border between Central Asia and China. The vast Qizilqum (Turkic for "red sand"—Russian spelling Kyzyl Kum) Desert, shared with southern Kazakstan, dominates the northern lowland portion of Uzbekistan (see fig. 2). The most fertile part of Uzbekistan, the Fergana Valley, is an area of about 21,440 square kilometers directly east of the Qizilqum and surrounded by mountain ranges to the north, south, and east. The western end of the valley is defined by the course of the Syrdariya, which runs across the northeastern sector of Uzbekistan from southern Kazakstan into the Qizilqum. Although the Fergana Valley receives just 100 to 300 millimeters of rainfall per year, only small patches of desert remain in the center and along ridges on the periphery of the valley.

Water resources, which are unevenly distributed, are in short supply in most of Uzbekistan. The vast plains that occupy two-thirds of Uzbekistan's territory have little water, and there are few lakes. The two largest rivers feeding Uzbekistan are the Amu Darya and the Syrdariya, which originate in the mountains of Tajikistan and Kyrgyzstan, respectively. These rivers form the two main river basins of Central Asia; they are used primarily for irrigation, and several artificial canals have been built to expand the supply of arable land in the Fergana Valley and elsewhere.

Another important feature of Uzbekistan's physical environment is the significant seismic activity that dominates much of the country. Indeed, much of Uzbekistan's capital city, Tashkent, was destroyed in a major earthquake in 1966, and other earthquakes have caused significant damage before and since the Tashkent disaster. The mountain areas are especially prone to earthquakes.

## Climate

Uzbekistan's climate is classified as continental, with hot summers and cool winters. Summer temperatures often surpass 40°C; winter temperatures average about –23°C, but may fall as low as –40°C. Most of the country also is quite arid, with average annual rainfall amounting to between 100 and 200 millimeters and occurring mostly in winter and spring. Between July and September, little precipitation falls, essentially stopping the growth of vegetation during that period.

## Environmental Problems

Despite Uzbekistan's rich and varied natural environment, decades of environmental neglect in the Soviet Union have combined with skewed economic policies in the Soviet south to make Uzbekistan one of the gravest of the CIS's many environmental crises. The heavy use of agrochemicals, diversion of huge amounts of irrigation water from the two rivers that feed the region, and the chronic lack of water treatment plants are among the factors that have caused health and environmental problems on an enormous scale.

Environmental devastation in Uzbekistan is best exemplified by the catastrophe of the Aral Sea. Because of diversion of the Amu Darya and Syrdariya for cotton cultivation and other purposes, what once was the world's fourth largest inland sea has shrunk in the past thirty years to only about one-third of its 1960 volume and less than half its 1960 geographical size. The desiccation and salinization of the lake have caused extensive storms of salt and dust from the sea's dried bottom, wreaking havoc on the region's agriculture and ecosystems and on the population's health. Desertification has led to the large-scale loss of plant and animal life, loss of arable land, changed climatic conditions, depleted yields on the cultivated land that remains, and destruction of historical and cultural monuments. Every year, many tons of salts reportedly are carried as far as 800 kilometers away. Regional experts assert that salt and

dust storms from the Aral Sea have raised the level of particulate matter in the earth's atmosphere by more than 5 percent, seriously affecting global climate change.

The Aral Sea disaster is only the most visible indicator of environmental decay, however. The Soviet approach to environmental management brought decades of poor water management and lack of water or sewage treatment facilities; inordinately heavy use of pesticides, herbicides, defoliants, and fertilizers in the fields; and construction of industrial enterprises without regard to human or environmental impact. Those policies present enormous environmental challenges throughout Uzbekistan.

### Water Pollution

Large-scale use of chemicals for cotton cultivation, inefficient irrigation systems, and poor drainage systems are examples of the conditions that led to a high filtration of salinized and contaminated water back into the soil. Post-Soviet policies have become even more dangerous; in the early 1990s, the average application of chemical fertilizers and insecticides throughout the Central Asian republics was twenty to twenty-five kilograms per hectare, compared with the former average of three kilograms per hectare for the entire Soviet Union. As a result, the supply of fresh water has received further contaminants. Industrial pollutants also have damaged Uzbekistan's water. In the Amu Darya, concentrations of phenol and oil products have been measured at far above acceptable health standards. In 1989 the minister of health of the Turkmen SSR described the Amu Darya as a sewage ditch for industrial and agricultural waste substances. Experts who monitored the river in 1995 reported even further deterioration.

In the early 1990s, about 60 percent of pollution control funding went to water-related projects, but only about half of cities and about one-quarter of villages have sewers. Communal water systems do not meet health standards; much of the population lacks drinking water systems and must drink water straight from contaminated irrigation ditches, canals, or the Amu Darya itself.

According to one report, virtually all the large underground fresh-water supplies in Uzbekistan are polluted by industrial and chemical wastes. An official in Uzbekistan's Ministry of Environment estimated that about half of the country's population lives in regions where the water is severely polluted. The government estimated in 1995 that only 230 of the country's 8,000 industrial enterprises were following pollution control standards.

### Air Pollution

Poor water management and heavy use of agricultural chemicals also have polluted the air. Salt and dust storms and the spraying of pesticides and defoliants for the cotton crop have led to severe degradation of air quality in rural areas.

In urban areas, factories and auto emissions are a growing threat to air quality. Fewer than half of factory smokestacks in Uzbekistan are equipped with filtration devices, and none has the capacity to filter gaseous emissions. In addition, a high percentage of existing filters are defective or out of operation. Air pollution data for Tashkent, Farghona, and Olmaliq show all three cities exceeding recommended levels of nitrous dioxide and particulates. High levels of heavy metals such as lead, nickel, zinc, copper, mercury, and manganese have been found in Uzbekistan's atmosphere, mainly from the burning of fossil fuels, waste materials, and ferrous and nonferrous metallurgy. Especially high concentrations of heavy metals have been reported in Toshkent Province and in the southern part of Uzbekistan near the Olmaliq Metallurgy Combine. In the mid-1990s, Uzbekistan's industrial production, about 60 percent of the total for the Central Asian nations excluding Kazakstan, also yielded about 60 percent of the total volume of Central Asia's emissions of harmful substances into the atmosphere. Because automobiles are relatively scarce, automotive exhaust is a problem only in Tashkent and Farghona.

### Government Environmental Policy

The government of Uzbekistan has acknowledged the extent of the country's environmental problems, and it has made an oral commitment to address them. But the governmental structures to deal with these problems remain confused and ill defined. Old agencies and organizations have been expanded to address these questions, and new ones have been created, resulting in a bureaucratic web of agencies with no generally understood commitment to attack environmental problems directly. Various nongovernmental and grassroots environmental organizations also have begun to form, some closely tied to the current government and others assuming an opposition stance. For example, environmental issues were prominent points in the original platform of Birlik, the first major opposition movement to emerge in Uzbekistan (see The 1980s, this ch.). By the mid-1990s, such issues had become a key concern of all opposition groups and a cause of growing concern among the population as a whole.

In the first half of the 1990s, many plans were proposed to limit or discourage economic practices that damage the environment. Despite discussion of programs to require payments for resources (especially water) and to collect fines from heavy polluters, however, little has been accomplished. The obstacles are a lack of law enforcement in these areas, inconsistent government economic and environmental planning, corruption, and the overwhelming concentration of power in the hands of a president who shows little tolerance of grassroots activity (see Postindependence Changes, this ch.).

International donors and Western assistance agencies have devised programs to transfer technology and know-how to address these problems (see International Financial Relations, this ch.). But the country's environmental problems are predominantly the result of abuse and mismanagement of natural resources promoted by political and economic priorities. Until the political will emerges to regard environmental and health problems as a threat not only to the government in power but also to the very survival of Uzbekistan, the increasingly grave environmental threat will not be addressed effectively.

# Population

The population of Uzbekistan, estimated in 1994 at about 23 million, is the largest of the Central Asian republics, comprising more than 40 percent of their total population. Growing at a rapid rate, the population is split by ethnic and regional differences. The Russian component of the population shrank steadily in the years after independence.

## Size and Distribution

Relative to the former Soviet Union as a whole, Uzbekistan is still largely rural: roughly 60 percent of Uzbekistan's population lives in rural areas (see Table 3, Appendix). The capital city is Tashkent, whose 1990 population was estimated at about 2.1 million people. Other major cities are Samarqand (population 366,000), Namangan (308,000), Andijon (293,000), Bukhoro (224,000), Farghona (200,000), and Quqon (182,000).

The population of Uzbekistan is exceedingly young. In the early 1990s, about half the population was under nineteen years of age. Experts expected this demographic trend to continue for some time because Uzbekistan's population growth rate has been quite high for the past century: on the eve of the collapse of the Soviet Union, only Tajikistan had a higher growth rate among the Soviet republics. Between 1897 and 1991, the population of the region that is now Uzbekistan more than quintupled, while the population of the entire territory of the former Soviet Union had not quite doubled. In 1991 the natural rate of population increase (the birth rate minus the death rate) in Uzbekistan was 28.3 per 1,000—more than four times that of the Soviet Union as a whole, and an increase from ten years earlier (see table 2, Appendix).

*Typical neighborhood in old section of Tashkent*

These characteristics are especially pronounced in the Autonomous Republic of Karakalpakstan (the Uzbek form for which is Qoroqalpoghiston Respublikasi), Uzbekistan's westernmost region. In 1936, as part of Stalin's nationality policy, the Karakalpaks (a Turkic Muslim group whose name literally means "black hat") were given their own territory in western Uzbekistan, which was declared an autonomous Soviet socialist republic to define its ethnic differences while maintaining it within the republic of Uzbekistan. In 1992 Karakalpakstan received republic status within independent Uzbekistan. Since that time, the central government in Tashkent has maintained pressure and tight economic ties that have kept the republic from exerting full independence.

Today, the population of Karakalpakstan is about 1.3 million people who live on a territory of roughly 168,000 square kilometers. Located in the fertile lower reaches of the Amu Darya where the river empties into the Aral Sea, Karakalpakstan has a long history of irrigation agriculture. Currently, however, the shrinking of the Aral Sea has made Karakalpakstan one of the poorest and most environmentally devastated parts of Uzbekistan, if not the entire former Soviet Union (see Environmental Problems, this ch.).

Because the population of that region is much younger than the national average (according to the 1989 census, nearly three-quarters of the population was younger than twenty-nine years), the rate of population growth is quite high. In 1991 the rate of natural growth in Karakalpakstan was reportedly more than thirty births per 1,000 and slightly higher in the republic's rural areas. Karakalpakstan is also more rural than Uzbekistan as a whole, with some of its administrative regions (*rayony*; sing., *rayon*) having only villages and no urban centers—an unusual situation in a former Soviet republic.

The growth of Uzbekistan's population was in some part due to in-migration from other parts of the former Soviet Union. Several waves of Russian and Slavic in-migrants arrived at various times in response to the industrialization of Uzbekistan in the early part of the Soviet period, following the evacuations of European Russia during World War II, and in the late 1960s to help reconstruct Tashkent after the 1966 earthquake. At various other times, non-Uzbeks arrived simply to take advantage of opportunities they perceived in Central Asia. Recently, however, Uzbekistan has begun to witness a net emigration of its European population. This is especially true of Russians, who have faced increased discrimination and uncertainty since 1991 and seek a more secure environment in Russia. Because most of Uzbekistan's population growth has been attributable to high rates of natural increase, the emigration of Europeans is expected to have little impact on the overall size and demographic structure of Uzbekistan's population. Demographers project that the population, currently growing at about 2.5 percent per year, will increase by 500,000 to 600,000 annually between the mid-1990s and the year 2010. Thus, by the year 2005 at least 30 million people will live in Uzbekistan.

High growth rates are expected to give rise to increasingly sharp population pressures that will exceed those experienced by most other former Soviet republics. Indeed, five of the eight most densely populated provinces of the former Soviet Union—Andijon, Farghona, Tashkent, Namangan, and Khorazm—are located in Uzbekistan, and populations continue to grow rapidly in all five. In 1993 the average population density of Uzbekistan was about 48.5 inhabitants per square kilometer, compared with a ratio of fewer than six inhabitants per square kilometer in neighboring Kazakstan. The distribution of arable land in 1989 was estimated at only 0.15 hectares per person. In the early 1990s, Uzbekistan's population growth had an increasingly negative impact on the environment, on the economy, and on the potential for increased ethnic tension.

## Ethnic Composition

Population pressures have exacerbated ethnic tensions. In 1995 about 71 percent of Uzbekistan's population was Uzbek. The chief minority groups were Russians (slightly more than 8 percent), Tajiks (officially almost 5 percent, but believed to be much higher), Kazaks (about 4 percent), Tatars (about 2.5 percent), and Karakalpaks (slightly more than 2 percent) (see table 4, Appendix). In the mid-1990s, Uzbekistan was becoming increasingly homogeneous, as the outflow of Russians and other minorities continues to increase and as Uzbeks return from other parts of the former Soviet Union. According to unofficial data, between 1985 and 1991 the number of nonindigenous individuals in Uzbekistan declined from 2.4 to 1.6 million.

The increase in the indigenous population and the emigration of Europeans have increased the self-confidence and often the self-assertiveness of indigenous Uzbeks, as well as the sense of vulnerability among the Russians in Uzbekistan. The Russian population, as former "colonizers," was reluctant to learn the local language or to adapt to local control in the post-Soviet era. In early 1992, public opinion surveys suggested that most Russians in Uzbekistan felt more insecure and fearful than they had before Uzbek independence.

The irony of this ethnic situation is that many of these Central Asian ethnic groups in Uzbekistan were artificially created and delineated by Soviet fiat in the first place. Before the Bolshevik Revolution, there was little sense of an Uzbek nationhood as such; instead, life was organized around the tribe or clan (see Entering the Twentieth Century, this ch.). Until the twentieth century, the population of what is today Uzbekistan was ruled by the various khans who had conquered the region in the sixteenth century.

But Soviet rule, and the creation of the Uzbek Soviet Socialist Republic in October 1924, ultimately created and solidified a new kind of Uzbek identity. At the same time, the Soviet policy of cutting across existing ethnic and linguistic lines in the region to create Uzbekistan and the other new republics also sowed tension and strife among the Central Asian groups that inhabited the region. In particular, the territory of Uzbekistan was drawn to include the two main Tajik cultural centers, Bukhoro and Samarqand, as well as parts of the Fergana Valley to which other ethnic groups could lay claim. This readjustment of ethnic politics caused animosity and territorial claims among Uzbeks, Tajiks, Kyrgyz, and others through much of the Soviet era, but conflicts grew especially sharp after the collapse of central Soviet rule.

The stresses of the Soviet period were present among Uzbekistan's ethnic groups in economic, political, and social spheres. An outbreak of violence in the Fergana Valley between Uzbeks and Meskhetian Turks in June 1989 claimed about 100 lives. That conflict was followed by similar outbreaks of violence in other parts of the Fergana Valley and elsewhere. The civil conflict in neighboring Tajikistan, which also involves ethnic hostilities, has been perceived in Uzbekistan (and presented by the Uzbekistani government) as an external threat that could provoke further ethnic conflict within Uzbekistan (see Impact of the Civil War, ch. 3). Thousands of Uzbeks living in Tajikistan have fled the civil war there and migrated back to Uzbekistan, for example, just as tens of thousands of Russians and other Slavs have left Uzbekistan for northern Kazakstan or Russia. Crimean Tatars, deported to Uzbekistan at the end of World War II, are migrating out of Uzbekistan to return to the Crimea.

Two ethnic schisms may play an important role in the future of Uzbekistan. The first is the potential interaction of the remaining Russians with the Uzbek majority. Historically, this relationship has been based on fear, colonial dominance, and a vast difference in values and norms between the two populations. The second schism is among the Central Asians themselves. The results of a 1993 public opinion survey suggest that even at a personal level, the various Central Asian and Muslim communities often display as much wariness and animosity toward each other as they do toward the Russians in their midst. When asked, for example, whom they would not like to have as a son- or daughter-in-law, the proportion of Uzbek respondents naming Kyrgyz and Kazaks as undesirable was about the same as the proportion that named Russians. (About

10 percent of the Uzbeks said they would like to have a Russian son- or daughter-in-law.) And the same patterns were evident when respondents were asked about preferred nationalities among their neighbors and colleagues at work. Reports described an official Uzbekistani government policy of discrimination against the Tajik minority.

## Other Social Affiliations

Other social factors also define the identities and loyalties of individuals in Uzbekistan and influence their behavior. Often regional and clan identities play an important role that supersedes specifically ethnic identification. In the struggle for political control or access to economic resources, for example, regional alliances often prevail over ethnic identities. A United States expert has identified five regions—the Tashkent region, the Fergana Valley, Samarqand and Bukhoro, the northwest territories, and the southern region—that have played the role of a power base for individuals who rose to the position of first secretary of the Communist Party of Uzbekistan. Often clan-based, these regional allegiances remain important in both the politics and the social structure of post-Soviet Uzbekistan.

## Language and Literature

As with ethnic patterns and boundaries of post-Soviet Uzbekistan, the dominant native language, Uzbek, is in many ways a creation of the Soviet state. Indeed, until the beginning of the Soviet period, the languages spoken among the native population presented a colorful and diverse mosaic. Under Soviet rule, officially at least, this mosaic was replaced by Uzbek, which almost overnight became the official language of the Turkic population of the republic. But Russian, which at the same time was declared the "international language" of Uzbekistan, was favored above even Uzbek in official usage. Many Russian words made their way into Uzbek because Russian was the language of higher education, government, and economic activity throughout the Soviet era. In the 1980s, Uzbeks began a strong effort to eliminate the recent Russian borrowings from the language. The Latin alphabet was introduced to begin a gradual process of replacing the Cyrillic alphabet. But in the mid-1990s Russian still was widely used in official and economic circles.

## Linguistic Background

Uzbek is a Turkic language of the Qarluq family, closely related to Uyghur and Kazak. Although numerous local dialects and variations of the language are in use, the Tashkent dialect is the basis of the official written language. The dialects spoken in the northern and western parts of Uzbekistan have strong Turkmen elements because historically many Turkmen lived in close proximity to the Uzbeks in those regions. The dialects in the Fergana Valley near Kyrgyzstan show some Kyrgyz influence. Especially in the written dialect, Uzbek also has a strong Persian vocabulary element that stems from the historical influence of Iranian culture throughout the region (see Early History, this ch.).

Uzbek has a relatively short history as a language distinct from other Turkic dialects. Until the establishment of the Soviet republic's boundaries in the 1920s, Uzbek was not considered a language belonging to a distinct nationality. It was simply a Turkic dialect spoken by a certain segment of the Turkic population of Central Asia, a segment that also included the ruling tribal dynasties of the various states. The regional dialects spoken in Uzbekistan today reflect the fact that the Turkic population of Southern Central Asia has always been a mixture of various Turkic tribal groups (see Ethnic Groups, ch. 1; Social Structure, ch. 2; Population, ch. 5). When the present-day borders among the republics were established in 1929, all native peoples living in Uzbekistan (including Tajiks) were registered as Uzbeks regardless of their previous ethnic identity.

Until 1924 the written Turkic language of the region had been Chaghatai, a language that had a long and brilliant history as a vehicle of literature and culture after its development in the Timurid state of Herat in the late fifteenth century. Chaghatai also was the common written language of the entire region of Central Asia from the Persian border to Eastern Turkestan, which was located in today's China. The language was written in the Arabic script and had strong Persian elements in its grammar and vocabulary. Experts identify the Herat writer Ali Shir Nava'i as having played the foremost role in making Chaghatai a dominant literary language.

In modern Uzbekistan, Chaghatai is called Old Uzbek; its origin in Herat, which was an enemy state of the Uzbeks, is ignored or unknown. Use of the language was continued by the Uzbek khanates that conquered the Timurid states. Some early Uzbek rulers, such as Mukhammad Shaybani Khan, used

Chaghatai to produce excellent poetry and prose. The seventeenth-century Khivan ruler Abulgazi Bahadur Khan wrote important historical works in Chaghatai. However, all of those writers also produced considerable literature in Persian. Chaghatai continued in use well into the twentieth century as the literary language of Central Asia. Early twentieth-century writers such as Fitrat wrote in Chaghatai.

In the late nineteenth century and early twentieth century, Chaghatai was influenced by the efforts of reformers of the Jadidist movement, who wanted to Turkify and unite all of the written languages used in the Turkic world into one written language (see The Russian Conquest, this ch.). These efforts were begun by the Crimean Tatar Ismail Gaspirali (Gasprinskiy in Russian), who advocated this cause in his newspaper *Terjuman* (Translator). Gaspirali called on all the Turkic peoples (including the Ottoman Turks, the Crimean and Kazan Tatars, and the Central Asians) to rid their languages of Arabic, Persian, and other foreign elements and to standardize their orthography and lexicon. Because of this effort, by the early 1920s the Turkic languages of Central Asia had lost some of the Persian influence.

## Influences in the Soviet Period

Unfortunately for the reformers and their efforts to reform the language, following the national delimitation the Soviet government began a deliberate policy of separating the Turkic languages from each other. Each nationality was given a separate literary language. Often new languages had to be invented where no such languages had existed before. This was the case for Uzbek, which was declared to be a continuation of Chaghatai and a descendant of all of the ancient Turkic languages spoken in the region. In the initial stage of reform, in 1928–30, the Arabic alphabet was abandoned in favor of the Latin alphabet. Then in 1940, Cyrillic was made the official alphabet with the rationale that sharing the Arabic alphabet with Turkey might lead to common literature and hence a resumption of the Turkish threat to Russian control in the region.

Because of this artificial reform process, the ancient literature of the region became inaccessible to all but specialists. Instead, the use of Russian and Russian borrowings into Uzbek was strongly encouraged, and the study of Russian became compulsory in all schools. The emphasis on the study of Rus-

sian varied at various times in the Soviet period. At the height
of Stalinism (1930s and 1940s), and in the Brezhnev period
(1964–82), the study of Russian was strongly encouraged.
Increasingly, Russian became the language of higher education
and advancement in society, especially after Stalin orchestrated
the Great Purge of 1937–38, which uprooted much indigenous
culture in the non-Slavic Soviet republics. The language of the
military was Russian as well. Those Uzbeks who did not study in
higher education establishments and had no desire to work for
the state did not make a great effort to study Russian. As a
result, such people found their social mobility stifled, and
males who served in the armed forces suffered discrimination
and persecution because they could not communicate with
their superiors. This communication problem was one of the
reasons for disproportionate numbers of Uzbeks and other
Central Asians in the noncombat construction battalions of the
Soviet army.

## Language in the 1990s

The official linguistic policy of the Karimov government has
been that Uzbek is the language of the state, and Russian is the
second language. Residents of Uzbekistan are required to study
Uzbek to be eligible for citizenship. Following similar decisions
in Azerbaijan and Turkmenistan, in September 1993 Uzbekistan announced plans to switch its alphabet from Cyrillic,
which by that time had been in use for more than fifty years, to
a script based on a modified Latin alphabet similar to that used
in Turkey. According to plans, the transition will be complete
by the year 2000. The primary reason for the short deadline is
the urgent need to communicate with the outside world using
a more universally understood alphabet. The move also has the
political significance of signaling Uzbekistan's desire to break
away from its past reliance on Russia and to limit the influence
of Muslim states such as Saudi Arabia and Iran, which use the
Arabic alphabet. A major project is under way to eradicate Russian words from the language and replace these words with
"pure" Turkic words that have been borrowed from what is
believed to be the ancient Turkic language of Inner Asia. At
the same time, Uzbekistan's linguistic policies also are moving
toward the West. In the early 1990s, the study of English has
become increasingly common, and many policy makers express
the hope that English will replace Russian as the language of
international communication in Uzbekistan.

## Literature

Uzbekistan's literature suffered great damage during the Stalinist purges of the 1930s; during that period, nearly every talented writer in the republic was purged and executed as an enemy of the people. Prior to the purges, Uzbekistan had a generation of writers who produced a rich and diverse literature, with some using Western genres to deal with important issues of the time. With the death of that generation, Uzbek literature entered a period of decline in which the surviving writers were forced to mouth the party line and write according to the formulas of socialist realism. Uzbek writers were able to break out of this straitjacket only in the early 1980s. In the period of *perestroika* and *glasnost,* a group of Uzbek writers led the way in establishing the Birlik movement, which countered some of the disastrous policies of the Soviet government in Uzbekistan. Beginning in the 1980s, the works of these writers criticized the central government and other establishment groups for the ills of society.

A critical issue for these writers was the preservation and purification of the Uzbek language. To reach that goal, they minimized the use of Russian lexicon in their works, and they advocated the declaration of Uzbek as the state language of Uzbekistan. These efforts were rewarded in 1992, when the new national constitution declared the Uzbek language to be the state language of the newly independent state. At the same time, however, some of these writers found themselves at odds with the Karimov regime because of their open criticism of post-Soviet policies.

## Religion

Islam is by far the dominant religious faith in Uzbekistan. In the early 1990s, many of the Russians remaining in the republic (about 8 percent of the population) were Orthodox Christians. An estimated 93,000 Jews also were present. Despite its predominance, Islam is far from monolithic, however. Many versions of the faith have been practiced in Uzbekistan. The conflict of Islamic tradition with various agendas of reform or secularization throughout the twentieth century has left the outside world with a confused notion of Islamic practices in Central Asia. In Uzbekistan the end of Soviet power did not bring an upsurge of a fundamentalist version of Islam, as many had predicted, but rather a gradual reacquaintance with the precepts of the faith.

## Islam in the Soviet Era

Soviet authorities did not prohibit the practice of Islam as much as they sought to coopt and utilize religion to placate a population that often was unaware of the tenets of its faith. After its introduction in the seventh century, Islam in many ways formed the basis of life in Uzbekistan. The Soviet government encouraged continuation of the role played by Islam in secular society. During the Soviet era, Uzbekistan had sixty-five registered mosques and as many as 3,000 active mullahs and other Muslim clerics. For almost forty years, the Muslim Board of Central Asia, the official, Soviet-approved governing agency of the Muslim faith in the region, was based in Tashkent. The grand mufti who headed the board met with hundreds of foreign delegations each year in his official capacity, and the board published a journal on Islamic issues, *Muslims of the Soviet East.*

However, the Muslims working or participating in any of these organizations were carefully screened for political reliability. Furthermore, as the Uzbekistani government ostensibly was promoting Islam with the one hand, it was working hard to eradicate it with the other. The government sponsored official antireligious campaigns and severe crackdowns on any hint of an Islamic movement or network outside of the control of the state.

Moscow's efforts to eradicate and coopt Islam not only sharpened differences between Muslims and others. They also greatly distorted the understanding of Islam among Uzbekistan's population and created competing Islamic ideologies among the Central Asians themselves.

## The Issue of Fundamentalism

In light of the role that Islam has played throughout Uzbekistan's history, many observers expected that Islamic fundamentalism would gain a strong hold after independence brought the end of the Soviet Union's official atheism. The expectation was that an Islamic country long denied freedom of religious practice would undergo a very rapid increase in the expression of its dominant faith. President Karimov has justified authoritarian controls over the populations of his and other Central Asian countries by the threat of upheavals and instability

*Wedding party at the Summer Palace, a traditional stopping place, Bukhoro*
*Courtesy Hermine Dreyfuss*

caused by growing Islamic political movements, and other Central Asian leaders also have cited this danger.

In the early 1990s, however, Uzbekistan did not witness a surge of Islamic fundamentalism as much as a search to recapture a history and culture with which few Uzbeks were familiar. To be sure, Uzbekistan is witnessing a vast increase in religious teaching and interest in Islam. Since 1991, hundreds of mosques and religious schools have been built or restored and reopened. And some of the Islamic groups and parties that have emerged might give leaders pause.

## Mainstream Islam in the 1990s

For the most part, however, in the first years of independence Uzbekistan is seeing a resurgence of a more secular

Islam, and even that movement is in its very early stages. According to a public opinion survey conducted in 1994, interest in Islam is growing rapidly, but personal understanding of Islam by Uzbeks remains limited or distorted. For example, about half of ethnic Uzbek respondents professed belief in Islam when asked to identify their religious faith. Among that number, however, knowledge or practice of the main precepts of Islam was weak. Despite a reported spread of Islam among Uzbekistan's younger population, the survey suggested that Islamic belief is still weakest among the younger generations. Few respondents showed interest in a form of Islam that would participate actively in political issues. Thus, the first years of post-Soviet religious freedom seem to have fostered a form of Islam related to the Uzbek population more in traditional and cultural terms than in religious ones, weakening Karimov's claims that a growing widespread fundamentalism poses a threat to Uzbekistan's survival. Available information suggests that Islam itself would probably not be the root cause of a conflict as much as it would be a vehicle for expressing other grievances that are far more immediate causes of dissension and despair. Experts do not minimize the importance of Islam, however. The practice of the Islamic faith is growing in Uzbekistan, and the politicization of Islam could become a real threat in the future.

## Education

In developing a national education system to replace the centralized education prescriptions of Moscow, Uzbekistan has encountered severe budgeting shortfalls. The education law of 1992 began the process of theoretical reform, but the physical base has deteriorated, and curriculum revision has been slow.

### Education System

Education is supervised by two national agencies, the Ministry of People's Education (for primary, secondary, and vocational education) and the Ministry of Higher Education (for postsecondary education). In 1993 Uzbekistan had 9,834 preschool centers, most of which were run by state enterprises for the children of their employees. An estimated 35 percent of children ages one to six attend such schools, but few rural areas have access to preschools. In the early 1990s, enterprises began closing schools or transferring them to direct administration of the Ministry of People's Education. A modest government construction program adds about 50,000 new places annually—a rate that falls far short of demand. Although experts rate most of Uzbekistan's preschools as being in poor condition, the government regards them as contributing vitally to the nutrition and education of children, especially when both parents work, a situation that became increasingly frequent in the 1990s.

In 1993 enrollment in regular and vocational schools, which covered grades one through eleven (ages six through sixteen), was 4.9 million of the estimated 5.7 million children in that age-group. Because of funding shortages, in 1993 the period of compulsory education was shortened from eleven to nine years. The infrastructure problem of schools is most serious at the primary and secondary levels; the government categorizes 50 percent of school buildings as unsuitable, and repair budgets are inadequate. Construction of new schools has been delayed because the boards of capital construction of the two education ministries do not have direct control over contractor pricing or construction practices at local levels. School nutritional levels often are below state standards; an estimated 50 percent of students do not receive a hot meal. In 1992 about 5,300 of Uzbekistan's 8,500 schools had double shifts; because most of these schools were rural, this situation affected only 25 percent of students, however.

In 1993 an estimated 220,000 students were in vocational training programs, with about 100,000 students graduating annually from 440 schools. Working in close cooperation with local employers, the schools choose from 260 trades to offer instruction conforming with industrial needs. In the post-Soviet era, vocational curricula were modified to accommodate an upsurge in light industry. Experts agree that, as the national economy diversifies and expands, the vocational program must expand its coverage of key industries and streamline its organization, which suffered disorientation in its transition from the rigid Soviet system.

In 1992 some 321,700 students were enrolled in institutions of higher learning; of those, about 43 percent were in evening or correspondence courses. The enrollment represented about 19 percent of the seventeen to twenty age-group, a decrease from the more than 23 percent reported in 1990. In 1992 enrollment declined because an entrance examination was used for the first time, Russian emigration continued, and the economy's demand for college graduates fell. Experts predicted that the government would restrict admittance levels until its policies succeed in expanding the economy. Fifty-three institutions of higher learning, many with productive research programs, were active in 1993. Higher education is hindered, however, by a shortage of laboratories, libraries, computers and data banks, and publishing facilities to disseminate research findings.

The state higher education system includes three universities, located at Nukus, Samarqand, and Tashkent. Tashkent State University, which has 19,300 students and 1,480 teachers, is the largest university in Central Asia; it has sixteen full departments, including three devoted to philology and one to Asian studies. Some twenty research institutes offer courses in specialized areas of medicine, veterinary science, and industry and technology. Another thirty institutes of higher learning offer postsecondary studies in medicine, agriculture, teaching, engineering, industrial technology, music, theater, economics, law, pharmacy, and political science; seventeen of the latter category are located in Tashkent.

## Curriculum

In the early 1990s, the greatest controversy in curriculum policy was which language should be used for teaching in state schools. In 1992 Uzbek and the other Central Asian languages were made the official languages of instruction, meaning that Uzbek schools might use any of five Central Asian languages or Russian as their primary language. Uzbek and Russian language courses are taught in all schools. After independence, a new emphasis was placed on courses in Uzbek history and culture and on increasing the short supply of textbooks in Uzbek in many fields. For a time, the Karimov regime closed Samarqand University, which taught in Tajik, as part of a broader crackdown on the country's Tajik minority.

The expansion of curricula, including the addition of courses in French, Arabic, and English, has placed new stress on a limited supply of teachers and materials. In the mid-1990s, a major curriculum reform was underway to support the post-Soviet economic and social transformation. Among the changes identified by Western experts are a more commercial approach to the mathematics curriculum, more emphasis in economics courses on the relationship of capital to labor, more emphasis in social science courses on individual responsibility for the environment, and the addition of entirely new subjects such as business management. Because such changes involve new materials and a new pedagogical approach by staff, the reform period is estimated at ten to fifteen years.

### Instruction

In the early 1990s, the thirty-six technical schools and six teacher colleges produced about 20,000 new teachers annually for the primary and secondary levels, and another 20,000 for higher education. In 1993 the ratio of staff to students was 1 to 12 in preschool institutions, 1 to 11.5 in primary and secondary schools, 1 to 12 in vocational schools, and 1 to 6.8 in institutions of higher education. The range of these ratios indicates that Uzbekistan prepares too many teachers for the needs of the existing student population, but experts do not consider the existing staff adequately trained to deal with upcoming curriculum changes and with the need to teach in Uzbek.

Experts have noted that the teacher training program must be reduced to concentrate government funds on a few high-quality research and training centers. Such a shift would free resources for material support, salaries, and administrative and supervisory personnel, all in short supply in the mid-1990s. Currently, teachers for preschool and grades one through four are trained at technical schools; those for grades five through eleven must train at the university level. The technical school program is five years beginning after grade nine, and the university program is four years beginning after grade eleven. Both programs combine pedagogical and general courses.

In the early 1990s, the government made significant improvements in teacher salaries and benefits. Many top teachers were lost to other sectors, however, because salaries still were not competitive with those elsewhere in the economy. In higher education, salaries were competitive with those in other occupations in Uzbekistan but not with those on the international teaching market.

## Health

As Uzbekistan struggled to revise its Soviet-era health care system, the physical condition of its population was exacerbated by severe environmental conditions that were inherited from the Soviet period and were not addressed effectively in the first years of independence. Key health indicators showed a correlation between the high level of air and water pollution and health problems (see table 5, Appendix).

## Health Care System

In the mid-1990s, Uzbekistan continued a health care system in which all hospitals and clinics were state owned and all medical personnel were government employees. Although health care ostensibly was free of change, this rarely was the case in practice. In the early 1990s, some private medical practices have supplemented state facilities to a small extent. In 1993 Uzbekistan undertook a program of privatization that began with the introduction of health insurance and continued with the gradual privatization of health care facilities, which is optimistically projected at about three years. Under the new program, the government would require private health facility owners to maintain the same standards as state facilities and to offer minimum free health care for the indigent. In the first few years of the program, however, only pharmacies and small clinics were privatized. Plans for 1995 called for privatizing twenty-four dental clinics and twelve prenatal clinics. In 1995 no plan provided for government divestiture of medium-sized health care facilities.

The government disburses its funds through the national Ministry of Health, through the health agencies of local and province governments, and through specialized facilities serving ministries and state enterprises. Treatment in the last two categories is generally better than in general state facilities because staff salaries and work conditions are better. As in the Soviet system, special facilities exist for top political, cultural, and scientific dignitaries. In 1994 some US$79 million, or 11.1 percent of the annual budget, was allocated for health care. Of that amount, about 60 percent went to state hospitals, 30 percent to outpatient clinics, and less than 6 percent to medical research.

Despite marked growth throughout the Soviet era, the public health care system in Uzbekistan is not equipped to deal with the special problems of a population long exposed to high levels of pollutants or with other health problems. Although the numbers of hospitals and doctors grew dramatically under Soviet rule—from almost no doctors in 1917 to 35.5 doctors per 10,000 population and to 1,388 hospitals and clinics per 10,000 population in 1991—the increasing incidence of serious disease raises questions about the effectiveness of care by these doctors and their facilities.

In 1993 a total of 16.8 million patients were treated, of whom 4.8 million were treated in hospitals and about 275,000 in out-patient clinics—meaning that the vast majority of patients received treatment only at home. Experts predicted that this trend would continue until the level of care in government facilities improved substantially.

Among the serious problems plaguing health care delivery are the extremely short supply of vaccines and medicines in hospitals; the generally poor quality of medical training; and corruption in the medical profession, which exacerbates the negative impact of changes in the system for the average patient and diverts treatment to favored private patients. According to a 1995 private study, the state system provided less than 20 percent of needed medicine and less than 40 percent of needed medical care, and budget constraints limited salaries for medical professionals. In 1990 the percentage of children receiving vaccines for diphtheria, pertussis, measles, and polio averaged between 80 and 90 percent. That statistic fell sharply in the first years of independence; for example, in 1993 fewer than half the needed doses of measles vaccine were adminis-tered.

The Ministry of Health has recognized that Uzbekistan has a serious narcotics addiction problem; illicit drug use reportedly stabilized between 1994 and 1996. The seven substance abuse rehabilitation clinics treat both alcoholism and narcotics abuse. The Ministry of Health has identified the following as its priorities, should expansion of services become possible: improvement of maternal and infant health care, prevention of the spread of infectious disease, and improvement of environ-mental conditions leading to health problems. In 1995 Uzbeki-stan was receiving aid from the United States Agency for International Development (AID), the United Nations Chil-dren's Fund (UNICEF), and the World Health Organization (WHO) for improving infant and maternal health care and for storage and distribution of vaccines.

## Health Conditions

According to experts, the most immediate impact of the environmental situation in Uzbekistan is on the health condi-tion of the population (see Environmental Problems, this ch.). Although it is difficult to establish a direct cause and effect between environmental problems and their apparent consequences, the cumulative impact of these environmental problems in Uzbekistan appears to have been devastating. Frequently cited in Uzbekistan's press are increasing occurrences of typhoid, paratyphoid, and hepatitis from contaminated drinking water; rising rates of intestinal disease and cancers; and increased frequency of anemia, dystrophy, cholera, dysentery, and a host of other illnesses. One Russian specialist includes among the ailments "lag in physical development," especially among children. According to this observer, sixty-nine of every 100 adults in the Aral Sea region are deemed to be "incurably ill." In 1990 life expectancy for males in all of Uzbekistan was sixty-four years, and for females, seventy years. The average life span in some villages near the Aral Sea in Karakalpakstan, however, is estimated at thirty-eight years.

In the early 1990s, only an estimated 30 percent of women in Uzbekistan practiced contraception of any kind. The most frequently used method was the intrauterine device, distribution of which began in a government program introduced in 1991. In 1991 the average fertility rate was 4.1 children per woman, but about 200,000 of the women in the childbearing age range have ten or more children.

Infant mortality increased by as much as 49 percent between 1970 and 1986 to an average of 46.2 deaths per 1,000 live births. In 1990 the average rate of mortality before age one for the entire country was sixty-five deaths per 1,000 live births. In the mid-1990s, official data estimated the level of infant mortality in parts of Karakalpakstan at 110 per 1,000 live births; unofficial estimates put the level at twice that figure. In 1992 the national maternal mortality rate was 65.3 per 100,000 live births, with considerably higher rates in some regions.

According to the WHO, Uzbekistan reported one case of acquired immune deficiency syndrome (AIDS) in 1992, one in 1993, and none in 1994. No treatment centers or AIDS research projects are known to exist in Uzbekistan.

## The Economy

Chief among the causes of dissension and despair in Uzbekistan is the country's economic situation. According to United Nations (UN) figures, in 1994 Uzbekistan was one of the poorest of the developed countries in the world, with the average monthly wage less than US$50. But vast natural resources suggest the potential for Uzbekistan to become one of the most prosperous countries in Central Asia, provided the necessary reforms can be made to unleash that potential. At the end of the Soviet era, Uzbekistan was rated as one of the least industrialized Soviet republics. Government reform, with the theoretical goal of achieving a market economy, moved cautiously and unevenly in the directions of industrialization and market reform in the early 1990s. By the mid-1990s, signs indicated a more serious reform effort (see table 6, Appendix).

## Mineral Resources

One of Uzbekistan's most abundant and strategic resources is gold. Before 1992, Uzbekistan accounted for about one-third of Soviet gold production, at a time when the Soviet Union ranked third in world gold production. The Muruntau Gold Mine, about 400 kilometers northwest of Tashkent in the Qizilqum Desert, is estimated to be the largest gold mine in the world, and other gold reserves are located in the Chadaq area of the Fergana Valley, on the southern slopes of the Qurama Mountains. In 1992, a reported 80 tons of gold were mined in Uzbekistan, making it the eighth largest producer of gold in the world. Fluorospar, the most important source of fluorine, is mined at Tuytepa between Olmaliq and Tashkent. In the region of Olmaliq, southeast of Tashkent, are deposits of copper, zinc, lead, tungsten, and molybdenum that are used in the well-developed metallurgical processing industries centered in northeastern Uzbekistan. Uranium is mined and processed on the slopes of the Chatkal and Qurama ranges that surround the Fergana Valley.

## Energy

Uzbekistan is also rich in energy resources, although it was a net importer of fuels and primary energy throughout the Soviet period. The republic was the third largest producer of natural gas in the former Soviet Union behind Russia and Turkmenistan, producing more than 10 percent of the union's natural gas in the 1980s. In 1992 Uzbekistan produced 42.8 billion cubic meters of natural gas; although this output was used mostly within the republic in the Soviet period, pipelines to Tajikistan, Kazakstan, and Russia exported increasing amounts of natural gas to those countries in the early 1990s. Gas reserves are estimated at more than 1 trillion cubic meters. Deposits are concentrated mainly in Qashqadaryo Province in

425

the southeast and near Bukhoro in the south-central region. Bukhoro gas is used to fuel local thermoelectric power plants. The biggest gas deposit, Boyangora-Gadzhak, was discovered in southeastern Surkhondaryo Province in the 1970s.

Uzbekistan also has small coal reserves, located mainly near Angren, east of Tashkent. In 1990 the total coal yield was 6 million tons. Oil production has likewise been small; Uzbekistan has relied on Russia and Kazakstan for most of its supply. Oil production was 3.3 million tons in 1992. But the discovery in 1994 of the Mingbulak oil field in the far northeastern province of Namangan may ultimately dwarf Uzbekistan's other energy resources. Experts have speculated that Mingbulak may prove to be one of the world's most productive oil fields. Located in the central basin of the Fergana Valley, the deposits could produce hundreds of millions of dollars worth of oil in the late 1990s. Qoqdumalaq in western Uzbekistan also has rich oil and natural gas deposits, reportedly containing hundreds of millions of tons of oil.

The coal deposits on the Angren River east of Tashkent and the natural gas deposits near Bukhoro are prime fuels for Uzbekistan's thermoelectric power plants. The well-developed hydroelectric power generating system utilizes the Syrdariya, Naryn, and Chirchiq rivers, all of which arise to the east in the mountains of Kyrgyzstan. Agreements with Kyrgyzstan and Tajikistan, through which the Syrdariya also flows, ensure a continued water flow for Uzbek power plants.

## Agriculture

Uzbekistan has the advantages of a warm climate, a long growing season, and plentiful sources of water for irrigation. In the Soviet period, those conditions offered high and reliable yields of crops with specialized requirements. Soviet agricultural policy applied Uzbekistan's favorable conditions mainly to cotton cultivation. As Uzbekistan became a net exporter of cotton and a narrow range of other agricultural products, however, it required large-scale imports of grain and other foods that were not grown in sufficient quantities in domestic fields.

### Organization of Agriculture

In the last decades of Soviet rule, the private agricultural sector produced about 25 percent of total farm output almost exclusively on the small private plots of collective and state farmers and nonagricultural households (the maximum private landholding was one-half hectare). In the early 1990s, Uzbekistan's agriculture still was dominated by collective and state farms, of which 2,108 were in operation in 1991. Because of this domination, average farm size was more than 24,000 hectares, and the average number of workers per farm was more than 1,100 in 1990. More than 99 percent of the value of agricultural production comes from irrigated land (see table 21, Appendix).

### Economic Structure of Agriculture

Uzbekistan's economy depends heavily on agricultural production. As late as 1992, roughly 40 percent of its net material product (NMP—see Glossary) was in agriculture, although only about 10 percent of the country's land area was cultivated. Cotton accounts for 40 percent of the gross value of agricultural production. But with such a small percentage of land available for farming, the single-minded development of irrigated agriculture, without regard to consumption of water or other natural resources, has had adverse effects such as heavy salinization, erosion, and waterlogging of agricultural soils, which inevitably have limited the land's productivity. According to the Ministry of Land Reclamation and Water Resources, for example, after expansion of agricultural land under irrigation at a rate of more than 2 percent per year between 1965 and 1986, conditions attributed to poor water management had caused more than 3.4 million hectares to be taken out of production in the Aral Sea Basin alone. According to other reports, about 44 percent of the irrigated land in Uzbekistan today is strongly salinated. The regions of Uzbekistan most seriously affected by salinization are the provinces of Syrdariya, Bukhoro, Khorazm, and Jizzakh and the Karakalpakstan Republic (see fig. 13). Throughout the 1980s, agricultural investments rose steadily, but net losses rose at an even faster rate.

### Cotton

Uzbekistan's main agricultural resource has long been its "white gold," the vast amounts of cotton growing on its territory. Uzbekistan always was the chief cotton-growing region of the Soviet Union, accounting for 61 percent of total Soviet production; in the mid-1990s it ranks as the fourth largest producer of cotton in the world and the world's third largest cotton exporter. In 1991 Uzbekistan's cotton yield was more than 4.6 million tons, of which more than 80 percent was classified in the top two quality grades. In 1987 roughly 40 percent of the workforce and more than half of all irrigated land in Uzbekistan—more than 2 million hectares—were devoted to cotton.

### Other Crops

In light of increasing water shortages in Central Asia and the end of the Soviet distribution system that guaranteed food imports, government leaders have proposed reducing cotton cultivation in favor of grain and other food plants to feed an increasingly impoverished population. In fact, between 1987 and 1991 land planted to cotton decreased by 16 percent, mainly in favor of grains and fruits and vegetables. But Uzbekistan's short-term needs for hard currency make dramatic declines in cotton cultivation unrealistic. Likewise, Uzbekistan's entire existing agricultural infrastructure—irrigation systems, configuration of fields, allocation and type of farm machinery, and other characteristics—is geared toward cotton production; shifting to other crops would require a massive overhaul of the agricultural system and a risk that policy makers have not wished to take in the early years of independence. Under these circumstances, continued commitment to cotton is seen as a good base for longer-term development and diversification.

In 1991 Uzbekistan's main agricultural products, aside from cotton, were grains (primarily wheat, oats, corn, barley, and rice), fodder crops, and fruits and vegetables (primarily potatoes, tomatoes, grapes, and apples). That year 41 percent of cultivated land was devoted to cotton, 32 percent to grains, 11 percent to fruits, 4 percent to vegetables, and 12 percent to other crops. In the early 1990s, Uzbekistan produced the largest volume of fruits and vegetables among the nations of the former Soviet Union. Because Uzbekistan's yield per hectare of noncotton crops is consistently below that for other countries with similar growing conditions, experts believe that productivity can be improved significantly.

## Industry

Uzbekistan's industrial sector accounted for 33 percent of its NMP in 1991. Despite some efforts to diversify its industrial base, industry remains dominated by raw materials extraction and processing, most of which is connected with cotton pro-

*Woman harvesting cotton,*
*Zarafshon River Valley*
*Courtesy Hermine Dreyfuss*

duction and minerals (see table 22, Appendix). As illustrated especially by the domestic oil industry, in the Soviet era industrial production generally lagged behind consumption, making Uzbekistan a net importer of many industrial products. Under the difficult economic conditions caused by the collapse of the Soviet Union's system of allocations and interdependence of republics, this situation has worsened. In 1993 total manufacturing had decreased by 1 percent from its 1990 level, and mining output had decreased by more than 8 percent (see table 6, Appendix).

### Heavy Industry

The Tashkent region, in the northeastern "peninsula" adjacent to the Fergana Valley, accounts for about one-third of the industrial output of Uzbekistan, with agricultural machinery the most important product. The city is the nucleus of an industrial region that was established near mineral and hydroelectric resources stretching across northeastern Uzbekistan from the Syrdariya in the west to the easternmost point of the nation. Electricity for the industries of the region comes from small hydroelectric stations along the Chirchiq River and from a gas-fired local power station.

Uzbekistan's most productive heavy industries have been extraction of natural gas and oil; oil refining; mining and mineral processing; machine building, especially equipment for cotton cultivation and the textile industry; coal mining; and the ferrous metallurgy, chemical, and electrical power industries. The chemical manufacturing industry focuses primarily on the production of fertilizer.

Two oil refineries in Uzbekistan, located at Farghona and Amtiari, have a combined capacity of 173,000 barrels per day. Other centers of the processing industries include Angren (for coal), Bekobod (steel), Olmaliq (copper, zinc, and molybdenum), Zarafshon (gold), and Yangiobod (uranium). The Uzbek fertilizer industry was established at Chirchiq, northeast of Tashkent, near Samarqand, and at several sites in the Fergana Basin. Uzbekistan is the largest producer of machinery for all phases of cotton cultivation and processing, as well as for irrigation, in the former Soviet Union. The machine building industry is centered at Tashkent, Chirchiq, Samarqand, and Andijon in the east, and at Nukus in Karakalpakstan.

### Light Industry

The predominant light industries are primary processing of cotton, wool, and silk into fabric for export, and food processing. In 1989 light industry accounted for 27.1 percent of industrial production; that category was completely dominated by two sectors, textiles (18.2 percent) and agricultural food processing (8.9 percent). The nature of the Uzbek textile industry in the mid-1990s reflects the Soviet allotment to Uzbekistan of primary textile processing rather than production of finished products. Food processing has diversified to some degree; the industry specializes in production of dried apricots, raisins, and peaches. Other products are cottonseed oil for cooking, wine, and tobacco.

## Labor Force

The swelling of the working-age population has led to high rates of unemployment and underemployment (see Population, this ch.). At the same time, despite relatively high average levels of education in the population, the shortage of skilled personnel in Uzbekistan is also a major constraint to future development (see Education, this ch.). Russians and other nonindigenous workers traditionally were concentrated in the heavy industrial sectors, including mining and heavy manufacturing. With the independence of Uzbekistan and the outbreak of violence in several parts of Central Asia, many of these skilled personnel left the country in the early 1990s. In 1990 as many as 90 percent of personnel in Uzbekistan's electric power stations were Russians. Because Russian emigration caused a shortage of skilled technicians, by 1994 half of the power generating units of the Syrdariya Hydroelectric Power Station had been shut down, and the newly constructed Novoangrenskiy Thermoelectric Power Station could not go on line because there was nobody to operate it. In the mid-1990s, training programs were preparing skilled indigenous cadres in these and other industrial sectors, but the shortfall has had a strong impact.

## Postcommunist Economic Reform

With the collapse of the Soviet Union, Uzbekistan faced serious economic challenges: the breakdown of central planning from Moscow and the end of a reliable, if limited, system of interrepublican trade and payments mechanisms; production inefficiencies; the prevalence of monopolies; declining productivity; and loss of the significant subsidies and payments that had come from Moscow. All these changes signaled that fundamental reform would be necessary if the economy of Uzbekistan were to continue to be viable.

Traditionally a raw materials supplier for the rest of the Soviet Union, Uzbekistan saw its economy hard hit by the breakdown of the highly integrated Soviet economy. Factories in Uzbekistan could not get the raw materials they needed to diversify the national economy, and the end of subsidies from Moscow was exacerbated by concurrent declines in world prices for Uzbekistan's two major export commodities, gold and cotton.

## Structural and Legal Reform

From the time of independence, Uzbekistan's political leaders have made verbal commitments to developing a market-based economy, but they have proceeded cautiously in that direction. The first few years were characterized mainly by false starts that left little fundamental change. The initial stages of reform, instituted in 1992, were partial price liberalization, unification of foreign-exchange markets, new taxes, removal of import tariffs, and privatization of small shops and residential housing. Laws passed in 1992 provided for property and land ownership, banking, and privatization. Modernization of the tax system began in 1992; the first steps were a value-added tax

(VAT—see Glossary) and a profits tax designed to replace income from the tax structure of the Soviet period.

In its first effort at price liberalization in 1992 and 1993, the government maintained some control on all prices and full control on the prices of basic consumer goods and energy. A wide range of legislation set new conditions for property and land ownership, banking, and privatization—fundamental conditions for establishing a market economy—but in general these provisions were limited, and they often were not enforced. International financial institutions initially were encouraged to believe that structural adjustments would be made in the national economy to accommodate international investment, but later such promises were rescinded. In 1994 the government maintained control of levels of production, investment, and trade, just as Moscow had done in the Soviet era. Several agencies, most notably the State Committee for Forecasting and Statistics, the State Association for Contracts and Trade, the Ministry of Foreign Economic Relations, and the Ministry of Finance, inherited responsibility for planning, finance, procurement, and distribution from the Soviet central state system. Economic policy making remains based on a national economic plan that sets production and consumption targets. State-owned enterprises remain in virtually all sectors of the economy. In 1994 no laws had established standards for bankruptcy, collateral, or contracts. But by 1995 Uzbekistan had made some significant movement toward reform, which experts interpreted as a possible harbinger of wider-ranging changes in the second half of the decade.

### Privatization

Privatization of the large state industrial and agricultural enterprises, which dominated the economy in the Soviet era, proceeded very slowly in the early 1990s. The initial stage of privatization, which began in September 1992, targeted the housing, retail trade and services, and light industry sectors to promote the supply of consumer goods.

Beginning with the 1991 Law on Privatization, a number of laws and decrees have provided the policy framework for further privatization. A state privatization agency, established in 1992, set a goal of moving 10 to 15 percent of state economic assets into private hands by the end of 1993. Movement in that direction was slow in 1992, however, with only about 350 small shops being privatized. In the same period, housing was priva-

*Central outdoor market, Samarqand*
*Courtesy Tom Skipper*

tized at a somewhat faster pace by outright transfers or low-cost sales of state housing properties. By 1994 about 20,000 firms in small industry, trade, and services had been transferred from state ownership to the ownership of managers and employees of the firms. Nearly all such transfers were through the issuance of joint-stock shares or by direct sale.

Agricultural privatization, which began in 1990, has moved faster. Since the state began distributing free parcels of land that could be inherited but not sold, the number of peasant farms has risen dramatically (cotton-growing lands were excluded from this process). Between January 1991 and April 1993, the number of private farms rose from 1,358 to 5,800, promising a significant new contribution from private farms to Uzbekistan's overall agricultural output (see Agriculture, this ch.). Another government program, initiated in 1993, transfers unprofitable state farms to cooperative ownership. A law permitting the transfer of privately owned land was planned for 1995.

In the mid-1990s, the role of the state was gradually reduced in the productive sectors, except for energy, public utilities, and gold. The government's privatization program for 1994–95 emphasized the sale of large and medium-sized state-owned construction, manufacturing, and transportation enterprises. A set of guidelines for large-scale privatization, which went into effect in March 1994, contained several contradictory provisions that required clarification, and privatization also was slowed by the need to change the monopoly structure of state-owned enterprises before sale.

In mid-1995, the government reported that 69 percent of enterprises (46,900 of 67,700) had been privatized. Most firms in that category are relatively small, however, and all heavy industry remained in state ownership at that stage. Although the government has promised accelerated privatization of larger firms, experts did not expect the slow pace to improve in the late 1990s.

### Currency Reform

According to some experts, a turning point came in late 1993 after Uzbekistan and Kazakstan were expelled from the ruble zone (see Glossary), in which Uzbekistan had remained with vague plans to adopt an independent national currency at some time in the future. Following the example of Kyrgyzstan, which already had created its own currency the previous May, in November 1993 Uzbekistan issued an interim som coupon. The permanent currency unit, the som, went into effect in the summer of 1994 (for value of the som—see Glossary). The introduction of the som was followed by an improving domestic economic situation, including some progress toward economic stabilization and structural reform. Beginning in late 1994, the national economy achieved substantial price liberalization, a reduction in subsidies, elimination of state orders on most commodities, and some freeing of state controls in the agricultural sector. In 1994 the som was one of the weaker new currencies in Central Asia; it lost two-thirds of its value in the second half of 1994. By the end of the year, however, inflation had leveled off, and the free-market exchange rate of the som stabilized by January 1995. In July 1995, the government announced plans to make the som fully convertible by the end of the year. At the beginning of 1996, the som's value was thirty-six to US$1.

## Banking and Finance

Uzbekistan began a movement toward a two-tier banking system under the old Soviet regime. The new structure, which was ratified by the Banking Law of 1991, has a government-owned Central Bank wielding control over a range of joint-stock sectoral banks specializing in agricultural or industrial enterprise, the Savings Bank (Sberbank), and some twenty commercial banks. The Central Bank is charged with establishing national monetary policy, issuing currency, and operating the national payment system. In performing these operations, the Central Bank manipulates as much as 70 percent of deposits in the more than 1,800 branches of the Savings Bank (all of which are state owned) for its own reserve requirements. A National Bank for Foreign Economic Affairs, established in 1991 as a joint-stock commercial bank, conducts international financial exchanges on behalf of the government. The national bank holds Uzbekistan's foreign currency reserves; in 1993 it was converted from its initial status to a state bank.

In the mid-1990s, the banking structure in Uzbekistan was limited to only a handful of primarily state-owned banks, and, compared with Western banking systems, the commercial banking system was still in its infancy. But the establishment in the spring of 1995 of Uzbekistan's first Western-style banking operation—a joint venture between Mees Pierson of the Netherlands and other international and Uzbekistani partners—suggests that this sector, too, may have prospects for change. The Uzbekistan International Bank that would result from the new joint venture is intended primarily to finance trade and industrial projects. The bank is to be based in Tashkent, with 50 percent of ownership shares in Western hands. If successful, this and other similar ventures may reward policy makers' cautious approach to reform by establishing an infrastructure from which economic growth can begin.

## International Financial Relations

Foreign trade traditionally has provided Uzbekistan with supplies of needed foodstuffs, including grain, and industrial raw materials, whereas Uzbekistan exported primarily nonferrous metals and cotton. On the eve of independence, Uzbekistan was a net importer, with roughly 22 percent of total domestic consumption composed of imports, and with exports accounting for 18 percent of production.

### Trade Reform in the 1990s

Before the breakup of the Soviet Union, foreign trade was heavily dependent on the Russian Republic. In the 1980s, more than 80 percent of Uzbekistan's foreign trade was within the Soviet Union, with Russia accounting for half of imports and almost 60 percent of exports. The other Central Asian republics accounted for another quarter of Uzbekistan's total foreign trade. Even interrepublican trade was directed through Moscow and organized in the interests of centralized planning goals.

In the early 1990s, the Soviet-era pattern of exported and imported products remained approximately the same: nearly all ferrous metals and machinery, except that relating to the cotton industry, plus about 40 percent of consumer goods and processed foods, were imported. A significant aspect of the trade balance was that a single item, grain, accounted for 45 percent of imports in the early 1990s, as the republic imported about 75 percent of the grain it consumed. Traditionally strong exports are basic metals, cotton-related machinery, textiles, agricultural and aviation equipment, fertilizers, and cotton.

In 1993 about 80 percent of foreign trade, with both former Soviet and other partners, was on the basis of bilateral agreements (see table 23, Appendix). In the early 1990s, such agreements were heavily regulated by quotas, licenses, and distribution controls. In 1993 and 1994, however, the list of commodities requiring export licenses was cut in half, import licensing virtually ended, and the use of fixed quotas was cut by two-thirds. Plans called for adoption of a unified system of licenses and quotas in 1995. Private barter agreements with partners in the former Soviet Union became illegal in 1993; they were replaced by agreements based on international prices. In 1994 the government eliminated its tax on foreign-currency earnings.

In 1993 Uzbekistan's current accounts foreign trade deficit rose to 9.4 percent of gross domestic product (GDP—see Glossary), increasing from 3.1 percent in 1992; at that point, the deficit was financed mainly through transactions backed by the country's gold supply and by bilateral trade credits—measures not sustainable over the long term. Since independence, Uzbekistan has made aggressive efforts to expand foreign trade and to diversify its trading partners (see Foreign Relations, this ch.). Expansion of trade relations beyond the contiguous states of the former Soviet Union has been hindered, however, by Uzbekistan's landlocked position and the complexity of moving goods overland through several countries to reach customers (see Transportation, this ch.).

### Foreign Investment

Although limited, the foreign investment law adopted in mid-1991 was a first step in promoting foreign contacts. Foreign investment, which moved quite cautiously in the early 1990s, expanded significantly in 1994 and 1995. By 1995 a variety of United States and foreign companies were investing in Uzbekistan. The United States Stan Cornelius Enterprises, for example, helped cap an oil well blowout at the Mingbulak oil field in March 1992, and the company has subsequently established a joint venture with the Uzbekistan State Oil Company (Uzbekneft) to develop the oil field and explore and develop other oil reserves in the country. The directors of the joint venture expect the Mingbulak Field to remain productive for twelve to twenty years. Likewise, the Colorado-based Newmont Mining Company has established a joint venture valued at roughly US$75 million with the Nawoiy Mining and Metallurgical Combine and the State Committee for Geology and Mineral Resources of Uzbekistan to produce gold at the Muruntau mine. A production rate of eleven tons per year was envisioned at the time the project was financed by a consortium of fifteen British banks.

The United States firm Bateman Engineering also is working in the gold sector, and various South Korean, Japanese, Turkish, German, British, and other companies are investing in a wide range of industrial and extraction operations including oil, sugar, cotton and woolen cloth production, tourism, production of automobiles, trucks, and aircraft, and production of medical equipment and ballpoint pens.

There are some significant barriers to investment. Uzbekistan's landlocked location makes commerce more difficult for potential investors. And, despite new legislation concerning such areas as tax holidays, repatriation of profits, and tax incentives, the investment climate for foreign companies remains problematic. The Karimov regime is relatively stable, but highly bureaucratic and centralized control, lack of infrastructure, and corruption remain major structural impediments that have prevented many joint ventures from getting off the ground. Small and medium-sized foreign firms are discouraged by persistent corruption among the lower-level officials with whom they must deal; larger companies such as Newmont Mining are able to deal directly with top-level politicians. Enterprise taxation rates vary widely, but the rate for joint ventures with more than 30 percent foreign backing is 10 percent. Five-year tax exemptions are granted to such firms in specific areas. All firms must pay a 40 percent social insurance tax to fund the state's welfare and unemployment programs.

## Transportation and Telecommunications

Uzbekistan inherited Soviet-era methodology and systems in both its transportation and telecommunications networks. That legacy has meant a gradual process of reorientating lines whose configuration was determined by Uzbekistan's need for a primary connection with the Russian Republic of the Soviet Union.

### Transportation

The Soviet legacy included a relatively solid transportation and communications infrastructure in Uzbekistan, at least relative to other less developed countries. The landlocked position of the country determines Uzbekistan's transportation needs, especially as commercial ties are sought with more distant partners in the post-Soviet era. On the eve of independence in 1991, Uzbekistan could boast an extensive railway and road network that connected all parts of the country. Rail transport is the major means of freight transport within Uzbekistan, but the country has an extensive road network as well. On the eve of independence, Uzbekistan had close to 3,500 kilometers of rail lines and nearly 80,000 kilometers of roads. Most cities and urban settlements in Uzbekistan also provided local transportation networks. In 1991, some seventy-three of 123 urban settlements offered their citizens internal bus transport, and more than 100 offered transport on trolley lines. Although the structure of national transportation is regarded as adequate, much transportation equipment and application technology is of 1950s and 1960s vintage (see fig. 14).

#### *Railroads*

In 1990 railroads carried about 75 percent of Uzbekistan's

Figure 14. Uzbekistan: Transportation System, 1996

freight, excluding materials carried by pipeline. In 1993 the rail system included about 3,500 kilometers of track, of which 270 kilometers were electrified. More than 600 mainline engines served the system. However, an estimated 1,000 kilometers of track require rehabilitation, and 40 percent of the locomotive fleet has exceeded its service life.

Because the main line connecting Uzbekistan with the Black Sea crosses the Turkmenistan border twice, the withdrawal of the latter country from the Central Asia rail system in 1992 cut that line (which also must pass through Kazakstan and Russia) into several parts. The segments now are alternately controlled by the Turkmenistani or the Uzbekistani national railroad authorities. The Transcaspian Railroad between the Amu Darya in the southwest and Tashkent in the northeast is the main transportation route within Uzbekistan, connecting Bukhoro and Samarqand in the south with the capital city in the northeast. The Transcaspian line also has two major spurs to other parts of the country. One spur runs southeast from Kagan, near Bukhoro, through Qarshi to Termiz, reaching the southeastern oases of the Qashqadaryo and Surkhondaryo valleys. The second spur branches from the main Samarqand-Tashkent line east of Jizzakh, passing northward to serve the Fergana Valley cities of Angren, Andijon, Farghona, and Namangan.

In the Fergana Valley, a number of short spurs reach the local mining centers of that region. The Kazalinsk line goes northwest from Tashkent, across Kazakstan and into Russia; its main role is moving cotton to the Russian mills. Especially for natural gas, a pipeline network also is well developed, linking Uzbekistan to the neighboring Central Asian countries and to the central regions of the former European Soviet Union and the Urals. The share of the railroads in passenger transportation is much more modest than that in freight transportation; in 1990 less than one-third of passenger kilometers was traveled on the rails.

### Roads

The road network in Uzbekistan includes approximately 67,000 kilometers of surfaced roads and an additional 11,000 kilometers of unsurfaced roads. At a density of about six kilometers per 1,000 inhabitants, the network is about twice as dense as the average for the entire Soviet Union in 1991 and about the same density as the current average for East European countries. (Density by territory is about half that of Eastern Europe.)

The highway system carries about one-fourth of freight traffic and about two-thirds of all passenger traffic (of which the bulk is accounted for by bus lines.) The three major stretches of highway are the Great Uzbek Highway, which links Tashkent and Termiz in the far southeast; the Zarafshon Highway between Samarqand and Chärjew in northeastern Turkmenistan; and the connector road between Tashkent and Ququon. The Samarqand-Chärjew route connects with a road that roughly parallels the northwestward course of the Syrdariya along the Uzbekistan-Turkmenistan border, passing through Urganch and Nukus before ending at Muynoq, just south of the Aral Sea. The Fergana Ring connects industries and major settlements in the Fergana Valley.

### Air Travel

In 1993 Uzbekistan had nine civilian airports, of which four were large enough to land international passenger jets. Tashkent's Yuzhnyy Airport, the largest in the country, now serves as a major air link for the other former republics of the Soviet Union with South Asia and Southeast Asia, as well as a major hub linking Central Asia with Western Europe and the United States. The addition of Tashkent to the flight routes of Germany's national airline, Lufthansa, greatly increased this role, and Uzbekistan's own airline, Uzbekistan Airways, flies from Tashkent and Samarqand to major cities in Western Europe and the Middle East. In 1994 its fleet included about 400 former Soviet aircraft, including the Yakovlev 40, Antonov 24, Tupolev 154, Ilyushin 62, 76, and 86, and two French Airbus A310–200s.

### Transportation Policy

Because of the country's long political isolation from its historical trading partners to the south, Uzbekistan's transportation infrastructure, aside from air transport, is largely designed to tie the region to Russia. The only rail outlets are northward. Uzbekistan's nearest rail-connected ports are in St. Petersburg, 3,500 kilometers to the northwest; the Black Sea ports, 3,000 kilometers to the west; and Vladivostok and the main Chinese ports, 5,000 kilometers to the northeast and east, respectively. Moscow is 3,500 kilometers away. Such distances add significantly to export prices. For example, the transportation of one ton of cotton sold in Western Europe adds as much as US$175 to the selling price. Land routes to potential customers rely on the stability and the transport system reliability of the several countries through which Uzbekistani goods must pass. Because of these conditions, transportation planners have emphasized the availability of alternative routes and modes, relying mainly on roads and railroads. To improve versatility, in 1993 the national airline signed intergovernmental treaties with China, the United Kingdom, Germany, India, Israel, Pakistan, and Turkey.

Connections with the Iranian rail system and with the Pakistani highway system are in the long-term planning stage. Under discussion is a series of rail links that would connect Central Asia's rail network with those of the region's southern neighbors. Rail and road links planned with China through Kyrgyzstan and Kazakstan also will expand Uzbekistan's reach and help to gradually reverse the influence of Soviet-era commercial patterns on the configuration of Uzbekistan's transportation network.

## Telecommunications

The Soviet-era telecommunications system was centralized, with Moscow acting as the hub for routing international communications. Investment in this system was generally low throughout the Soviet era, leaving the republics with low-quality equipment and service that have deteriorated further in the first years of independence. In the early 1990s, the installation of new lines dropped significantly in Uzbekistan. Recognizing the vital role of telecommunications in any modernization process, the government has sought international investment in updating its systems.

### Structure

Beginning in 1992, the Ministry of Communications has had responsibility for all modes of telecommunications, plus postal service and all print and broadcast media. Its purview also extends to construction and some manufacturing operations. Its Uzbekistan Telecommunications Administration (Uzbektelecom) includes fourteen enterprises, one in each of the country's thirteen regions plus one in Tashkent. Some twenty-six other communications enterprises are controlled directly. A planning enterprise is in charge of reconfiguring the transmission facilities designed by Soviet authorities for broadcast across the entire Soviet Union. Many of the Soviet system's technical operations, such as frequency control and international connections, were centered in Moscow, meaning that Uzbekistani broadcast personnel have had to absorb all those functions without the expertise to manage all the technical aspects of an independent national broadcast system. Long-term plans call for decreased involvement by the ministry and decentralization, with the operation gradually turned over to private enterprises.

### Service System

In 1994 Uzbekistan's telephone system served about 1.46 million customers, or about 7 percent of the population. Of that number, 1.12 million were in urban areas and 340,000 were rural customers; 1.08 million were residential customers and 380,000 were businesses. The official waiting list for telephone installation included 360,000 individuals, not counting an estimated 1 million who had not registered but required service. Average waiting time was three to five years. Of the 1.86 million lines existing in 1994, nearly all were manufactured in the former Soviet Union or in Eastern Europe. An estimated 20 percent of urban lines used switching equipment that no longer was in production, and about half of those lines were at least twenty years old. Because of these conditions, lack of spare parts is an increasing source of customer dissatisfaction and faulty service. Installation efficiency dropped significantly in the early 1990s. For example, in Tashkent in 1987 some 42,500 new telephones were installed; in 1992 only 9,000 new telephones were installed, although requests increased to 50,000 that year. In the mid-1990s, the Ministry of Communications lacked the technology to install digital telephone technology. Tashkent is the hub for international telephone connections. In 1993 nearly 90 percent of international calls passed through that city (only about 0.03 percent of total calls made in Uzbekistan were international).

In 1993 the Ministry of Communications purchased an Intelsat A satellite earth station and made agreements with several Western firms to establish thirty stations of international television broadcast programming from Japan, Southeast Asia, the United States (in cooperation with American Telephone and Telegraph), Western Europe (through Germany), and Pakistan. The satellite broadcasts were available, however, only in targeted locations such as large hotels and government offices.

*Central post office, telephone, and telegraph office, Tashkent*

In 1995 a Turkish satellite began relaying communications to Azerbaijan and all the Central Asian states. In 1994 negotiations among ten regional countries discussed installation of an 11,000-kilometer fiber-optic link between Europe and Asia, which would terminate in Tashkent and provide access to all the Central Asian states.

## Government and Politics

The movement toward economic reform in Uzbekistan has not been matched by movement toward democratic reform. The government of Uzbekistan has instead tightened its grip since independence, cracking down increasingly on opposition groups, curbing basic human rights, and making little attempt to develop democratic political norms and practices. Although the names have changed, the institutions of government remain similar to those that existed before the breakup of the

445

Soviet Union. The government has justified its restraint of personal liberty and freedom of speech by emphasizing the need for stability and a gradual approach to change during the transitional period, citing the conflict and chaos in the other former republics (most convincingly, neighboring Tajikistan). This approach has found credence among a large share of Uzbekistan's population, although such a position may not be sustainable in the long run.

## Postindependence Changes

Despite the trappings of institutional change, the first years of independence saw more resistance than acceptance of the institutional changes required for democratic reform to take hold. Whatever initial movement toward democracy existed in Uzbekistan in the early days of independence seems to have been overcome by the inertia of the remaining Soviet-style strong centralized leadership.

In the Soviet era, Uzbekistan organized its government and its local communist party in conformity with the structure prescribed for all the republics. The Communist Party of the Soviet Union (CPSU) occupied the central position in ruling the country. The party provided both the guidance and the personnel for the government structure. The system was strictly bureaucratic: every level of government and every governmental body found its mirror image in the party. The tool used by the CPSU to control the bureaucracy was the system of *nomenklatura*, a list of sensitive jobs in the government and other important organizations that could be filled only with party approval. The *nomenklatura* defined the Soviet elite, and the people on the list invariably were members of the CPSU.

Following the failure of the coup against the Gorbachev government in Moscow in August 1991, Uzbekistan's Supreme Soviet declared the independence of the republic, henceforth to be known as the Republic of Uzbekistan. At the same time, the Communist Party of Uzbekistan voted to cut its ties with the CPSU; three months later, it changed its name to the People's Democratic Party of Uzbekistan (PDPU), but the party leadership, under President Islam Karimov, remained in place. Independence brought a series of institutional changes, but the substance of governance in Uzbekistan changed much less dramatically.

On December 21, 1991, together with the leaders of ten other Soviet republics, Karimov agreed to dissolve the Soviet

Union and form the Commonwealth of Independent States (CIS—see Glossary), of which Uzbekistan became a charter member according to the Alma-Ata Declaration. Shortly thereafter, Karimov was elected president of independent Uzbekistan in the new country's first contested election. Karimov drew 86 percent of the vote against opposition candidate Mohammed Salikh, whose showing experts praised in view of charges that the election had been rigged. The major opposition party, Birlik, had been refused registration as an official party in time for the election.

In 1992 the PDPU retained the dominant position in the executive and legislative branches of government that the Communist Party of Uzbekistan had enjoyed. All true opposition groups were repressed and physically discouraged. Birlik, the original opposition party formed by intellectuals in 1989, was banned for allegedly subversive activities, establishing the Karimov regime's dominant rationalization for increased authoritarianism: Islamic fundamentalism threatened to overthrow the secular state and establish an Islamic regime similar to that in Iran. The constitution ratified in December 1992 reaffirmed that Uzbekistan is a secular state. Although the constitution prescribed a new form of legislature, the PDPU-dominated Supreme Soviet remained in office for nearly two years until the first parliamentary election, which took place in December 1994 and January 1995.

In 1993 Karimov's concern about the spread of Islamic fundamentalism spurred Uzbekistan's participation in the multinational CIS peacekeeping force sent to quell the civil war in nearby Tajikistan—a force that remained in place three years later because of continuing hostilities. Meanwhile, in 1993 and 1994 continued repression by the Karimov regime brought strong criticism from international human rights organizations. In March 1995, Karimov took another step in the same direction by securing a 99 percent majority in a referendum on extending his term as president from the prescribed next election in 1997 to 2000. In early 1995, Karimov announced a new policy of toleration for opposition parties and coalitions, apparently in response to the need to improve Uzbekistan's international commercial position. A few new parties were registered in 1995, although the degree of their opposition to the government was doubtful, and some imprisonments of opposition political figures continued.

The parliamentary election, the first held under the new constitution's guarantee of universal suffrage to all citizens eighteen years of age or older, excluded all parties except the PDPU and the progovernment Progress of the Fatherland Party, despite earlier promises that all parties would be free to participate. The new, 250-seat parliament, called the Oly Majlis or Supreme Soviet, included only sixty-nine candidates running for the PDPU, but an estimated 120 more deputies were PDPU members technically nominated to represent local councils rather than the PDPU. The result was that Karimov's solid majority continued after the new parliament went into office.

## The Constitution

From the beginning of his presidency, Karimov remained committed in words to instituting democratic reforms. A new constitution was adopted by the legislature in December 1992. Officially it creates a separation of powers among a strong presidency, the Oly Majlis, and a judiciary. In practice, however, these changes have been largely cosmetic. Uzbekistan remains among the most authoritarian states in Central Asia. Although the language of the new constitution includes many democratic features, it can be superseded by executive decrees and legislation, and often constitutional law simply is ignored.

The president, who is directly elected to a five-year term that can be repeated once, is the head of state and is granted supreme executive power by the constitution. As commander in chief of the armed forces, the president also may declare a state of emergency or of war. The president is empowered to appoint the prime minister and full cabinet of ministers and the judges of the three national courts, subject to the approval of the Oly Majlis, and to appoint all members of lower courts. The president also has the power to dissolve the parliament, in effect negating the Oly Majlis's veto power over presidential nominations in a power struggle situation.

Deputies to the unicameral Oly Majlis, the highest legislative body, are elected to five-year terms. The body may be dismissed by the president with the concurrence of the Constitutional Court; because that court is subject to presidential appointment, the dismissal clause weights the balance of power heavily toward the executive branch. The Oly Majlis enacts legislation, which may be initiated by the president, within the parliament, by the high courts, by the procurator general (highest law enforcement official in the country), or by the government of the Autonomous Province of Karakalpakstan. Besides legislation, international treaties, presidential decrees, and states of emergency also must be ratified by the Oly Majlis.

The national judiciary includes the Supreme Court, the Constitutional Court, and the High Economic Court. Lower court systems exist at the regional, district, and town levels. Judges at all levels are appointed by the president and approved by the Oly Majlis. Nominally independent of the other branches of government, the courts remain under complete control of the executive branch. As in the system of the Soviet era, the procurator general and his regional and local equivalents are both the state's chief prosecuting officials and the chief investigators of criminal cases, a configuration that limits the pretrial rights of defendants.

## Local Government

The country is divided into twelve provinces (*wiloyatlar;* sing., *wiloyat*), one autonomous republic (the Karakalpakstan Republic), 156 regions, and 123 cities. In Uzbekistan's system of strong central government, local government has little independence. The chief executive of each province and of Tashkent is the *hakim,* who is appointed by the president. Although these appointments must be confirmed by local legislative bodies that are elected by popular vote, the power of the president is dominant. The Autonomous Republic of Karakalpakstan also officially elects its own legislature; the chairman of the legislature serves as the republic's head of state and as a deputy chairman of the national parliament. But in the autonomous republic, too, government officials are generally powerless against Tashkent. Indeed, Karakalpak officials often are not included even in meetings of heads of state to discuss the fate of the Aral Sea, which is located within Karakalpakstan.

## Opposition Parties

Through the early 1990s, the government's stated goal of creating a multiparty democracy in Uzbekistan went unrealized. When independence was gained, the Communist Party of Uzbekistan was officially banned, but its successor, the PDPU, assumed the personnel, structure, and political domination of its predecessor. Since forcing out a small number of deputies from opposition parties, PDP members have complete control of the Supreme Soviet, and most members of other government bodies also are PDP members. The only other legal party in Uzbekistan, the Progress of the Fatherland Party, was created by a key adviser to President Karimov, ostensibly to give the country a semblance of a multiparty system; but it differs little in substance from the PDP.

Of the several legitimate opposition parties that emerged in Uzbekistan before the collapse of the Soviet Union, none has been able to meet the official registration requirements that the government created to maintain control and exclude them from the public arena. The first opposition party, Birlik, was created in 1989, primarily by intellectuals and writers under the leadership of the writer Abdurakhim Pulatov (see The 1980s, this ch.). The movement attempted to draw attention to problems ranging from environmental and social concerns to economic challenges, and to participate in their solution. The main weakness of Birlik was that it never was able to present a united front to the government. Soon after the party's establishment, a group of Birlik leaders left to set up a political party, Erk (Freedom), under the leadership of Mohammed Salikh. The Uzbek government was able to exploit the disunity of the opposition and eventually to undermine their position. Following the establishment of independent Uzbekistan, the Karimov regime was able to suppress both Birlik and Erk. Both parties were banned officially; Erk was reinstated in 1994.

Other parties include the Movement for Democratic Reforms, the Islamic Rebirth Party (banned by the government in 1992), the Humaneness and Charity group, and the Uzbekistan Movement. A former prime minister (1990–91) and vice president (1991) of Uzbekistan, Shukrullo Mirsaidov, created a new party, Adolat (Justice) in December 1994. Like Birlik and Erk, the new party calls for liberal economic reforms, political pluralism, and a secular society, but experts describe its opposition to the government as quite moderate. Nevertheless, Adolat has not been able to operate freely.

In 1995 opposition parties continued to be divided among themselves, further diluting their potential effectiveness, and many of the leaders have been either imprisoned or exiled. In mid-1995, Mohammed Salikh was in Germany; Abdurakhim Pulatov was in exile in Turkey; and his brother Abdumannob Pulatov, also active in the opposition and a victim of brutal government oppression, took refuge in the United States.

### The Media

Despite the fact that the constitution explicitly bans censor-

*Library and reception rooms of Uzbekistan Supreme Soviet, Tashkent*

ship, press censorship is routine. In 1992 twelve daily newspapers, with a total circulation of 452,000, were published. In 1993 the government required all periodicals to register, and the applications of all independent titles were denied. In early 1996, no independent press had emerged, and all forms of information dissemination were monitored closely. The largest daily newspapers were *Khalk Suzi* (People's World), the organ of the Oly Majlis; *Narodnoye Slovo*, a Russian-language government daily; *Pravda Vostoka*, an organ of the Oly Majlis and the cabinet, in Russian; and *Uzbekiston Adabiyoti va San'ati* (Uzbekistan Literature and Art), the organ of the Union of Writers of Uzbekistan. The only news agency was the government-controlled Uzbekistan Telegraph Agency (UzTAG).

## Human Rights

Despite extensive constitutional protections, the Karimov

government has actively suppressed the rights of political movements, continues to ban unsanctioned public meetings and demonstrations, and continues to arrest opposition figures on fabricated charges. The atmosphere of repression reduces constructive opposition and freedom of expression, and continues to distort the political process, even when institutional changes have been made. In the mid-1990s, legislation established significant rights for independent trade unions, separate from the government, and enhanced individual rights; but enforcement is uneven, and the role of the state security services remains central (see Internal Security, this ch.).

Amnesty International, the Human Rights Watch, and the United States Department of State consistently have identified the human rights record of Uzbekistan as among the worst in the former Soviet Union. With the exception of sporadic liberalization, all opposition movements and independent media are essentially banned in Uzbekistan. The early 1990s were characterized by arrests and beatings of opposition figures on fabricated charges. For example, one prominent Uzbek, Ibrahim Bureyev, was arrested in 1994 after announcing plans to form a new opposition party. After reportedly being freed just before the March referendum, Bureyev shortly thereafter was arrested again on a charge of possessing illegal firearms and drugs. In April 1995, fewer than two weeks after the referendum extending President Karimov's term, six dissidents were sentenced to prison for distributing the party newspaper of Erk and inciting the overthrow of Karimov. Members of opposition groups have been harassed by Uzbekistan's secret police as far away as Moscow.

## Foreign Relations

Uzbekistan's location, bordering the volatile Middle East, as well as its rich natural resources and commercial potential, thrust it into the international arena almost immediately upon gaining independence. During the early 1990s, wariness of renewed Russian control led Uzbekistan increasingly to seek ties with other countries. Indeed, little over a year after independence, Uzbekistan had been recognized by 120 countries and had opened or planned to open thirty-nine foreign embassies. Experts believed that in this situation Uzbekistan would turn first to neighboring countries such as Iran and Turkey. Although the cultural kinship and proximity of those countries has encouraged closer relations, Uzbekistan also has shown eagerness to work with a range of partners to create a complex web of interrelationships that includes its immediate Central Asian neighbors, Russia and other nations of the CIS, and the immediate Middle Eastern world, with the goal of becoming an integral part of the international community on its own terms.

## Central Asian States

Chief among Uzbekistan's foreign policy challenges is establishing relations with the other Central Asian states, which at the beginning of the 1990s still were simply neighboring administrative units in the same country. The ties that emerged between Uzbekistan and the other Central Asian states in the first years of independence are a combination of competition and cooperation.

Because they have similar economic structures defined by a focus on raw material extraction and cotton and by the need to divide scarce resources such as water among them, the inherent competition among them contains the potential for enormous strife. This condition was emphasized, for example, in May 1993, when Uzbekistan halted the flow of natural gas to Kyrgyzstan in response to that country's introduction of a new currency.

The potential for strife is exacerbated by the perception of the other Central Asian states that Uzbekistan seeks to play a dominant role in the region. As the only Central Asian state bordering on all the others, Uzbekistan is well placed geographically to become the dominant power in the region. And Uzbekistan has done little to contradict the notion that it has historically based claims on the other Central Asian states: as the historical center of the Quqon and Bukhoro khanates, for example, Uzbekistan believes that it can claim parts of Kyrgyzstan, Turkmenistan, and Kazakstan. Uzbekistan's large and relatively homogeneous population provides it a distinct advantage in exerting control over other republics. Uzbeks also constitute a significant percentage of the populations of the other Central Asian states. For example, roughly one-fourth of Tajikistan's population is Uzbek, and large numbers of Uzbeks populate southern Kyrgyzstan and southern Kazakstan. And Uzbekistan's active role in aiding the communist government of Imomali Rahmonov to defeat its opposition in the long-standing civil war in Tajikistan has demonstrated that it is well prepared to use its own armed forces—which are the best armed in Central Asia—to promote its own strategic interests (see The Armed Forces, this ch.). The government of Uzbekistan already has declared its right to intervene to protect Uzbeks living outside its borders.

At the same time, however, economic and political exigencies have also required close cooperation between Uzbekistan and the other Central Asian states. The near collapse of their respective economies and the need to reduce their economic dependence on Russia have also encouraged ties among the Central Asian republics, including Uzbekistan. Isolated from Moscow in some ways and manipulated by Moscow in others, Uzbekistan has found it especially advantageous to enhance relations with Kazakstan and Kyrgyzstan. In January 1994, following their formal departure from the ruble zone in November 1993, Kazakstan and Uzbekistan agreed to create their own economic zone to allow for free circulation of goods, services, and capital within the two republics and to coordinate policies on credit and finance, budgets, taxes, customs duties, and currency until the year 2000. Although many other former republics had made similar statements of intent, this marked the first firm economic agreement between two former republics within the CIS.

Since its signing, this agreement has expanded its coverage for the two charter nations and by the addition of a third signatory, Kyrgyzstan. In April 1994, the agreement was extended among all three former republics to abolish all customs controls; and in July 1994, the leaders of the three states met in Almaty to agree to a program of greater economic integration in what they have identified as their "Unified Economic Space." This agreement produced the first steps toward a modicum of institutional change, such as the creation of a Central Asian Bank and an interstate council to formalize bilateral ties. It also marked a commitment for further expansion of direct ties.

Renewed cooperation between Uzbekistan and the other Central Asian states also has been evidenced in areas such as joint efforts to address the Aral Sea problem. For some time even before the breakup of the Soviet Union, conferences and declarations by leaders in Central Asia had called for more cooperation among the five Central Asian republics to resolve the problem of the Aral Sea and regional use of water resources. In December 1992, with World Bank (see Glossary) support, President Karimov took the lead in proposing the creation of a strong, unified interstate organization to resolve the problems of the Aral Sea. The heads of state of all of the Central Asian republics have met several times to coordinate activities, and all members pledged roughly 1 percent of their respective GDPs toward an Aral Sea fund. Although compliance has varied, this type of constructive and unified approach to a mutual problem remained theoretical in the early 1990s.

## Russia and the CIS

Equally unclear is the long-term direction of Uzbekistan's relations with Russia. Having had independence thrust upon them by events in Moscow in 1991, the new Central Asian states, Uzbekistan among them, pressed to become "founding members" of the CIS on December 21, 1991. It was clear that none of the countries in that group could soon disentangle the complex of economic and military links that connected them with the Slavic members of the new CIS, and especially with Russia. In Uzbekistan's case, this limitation was characterized mainly by the significant Russian population in Uzbekistan (at that time, nearly 2 million people in a population of 22 million), by certain common interests in the region, and by the close entanglement of the Uzbek economy with the Russian, with the former more dependent on the latter.

Since achieving independence, Uzbekistan's foreign policy toward Russia has fluctuated widely between cooperation and public condemnation of Russia for exacerbating Uzbekistan's internal problems. Serious irritants in the relationship have been Russia's demand that Uzbekistan deposit a large portion of its gold reserves in the Russian Central Bank in order to remain in the ruble zone (which became a primary rationale for Uzbekistan's introduction of its own national currency in 1993) and Russia's strong pressure to provide Russians in Uzbekistan with dual citizenship. In 1994 and 1995, a trend within Russia toward reasserting more control over the regions that Russian foreign policy makers characterize as the "near abroad," boosted by the seeming dominance of conservative forces in this area in Moscow, has only compounded Uzbekistan's wariness of relations with Russia.

In its period of post-Soviet transformation, Uzbekistan also has found it advantageous to preserve existing links with Russia and the other former Soviet republics. For that pragmatic reason, since the beginning of 1994 Uzbekistan has made particular efforts to improve relations with the other CIS countries. Between 1993 and early 1996, regional cooperation was most visible in Tajikistan, where Uzbekistani troops fought alongside

Russian troops, largely because of the two countries' shared emphasis on Islamic fundamentalism as an ostensible threat to Central Asia and to Russia's southern border. And 1994 and 1995 saw increased efforts to widen economic ties with Russia and the other CIS states. Economic and trade treaties have been signed with Russia, Ukraine, Moldova, Azerbaijan, Kyrgyzstan, and Kazakstan, and collective security and/or military agreements have been signed with Russia, Armenia, and other Central Asian states. Largely because of its important role in Uzbekistan's national security, Russia has retained the role of preferred partner in nonmilitary treaties as well (see External Security Conditions, this ch.).

## The Middle East and Pakistan

Because of Uzbekistan's long historical and cultural ties to the Persian, Turkish, and Arab worlds, its immediate neighbors to the south—Iran, Pakistan, and Turkey—were the natural direction for expanded foreign relations. Although cultural relations with formerly dominant Iran and Turkey ended with the Soviet Revolution in 1917, Uzbekistan's relations with its southern neighbors increased dramatically after independence. Iran and Turkey have been especially active in pursuing economic projects and social, cultural, and diplomatic initiatives in Uzbekistan. Turkey was the first country to recognize Uzbekistan and among the first to open an embassy in Tashkent. The Turks made early commitments for expansion of trade and cooperation, including the promise to fund 2,000 scholarships for Uzbek students to study in Turkey. Uzbekistan also has been the recipient of most of the US$700 million in credits that Turkey has given the new Central Asian states.

Although initially apprehensive about the spread of an Iranian-style Islamic fundamentalist movement in Central Asia, Uzbekistan also has found mutual economic interests with Iran, and the two have pursued overland links and other joint ventures. Relations with Pakistan have followed suit, with particular commercial interest in hydroelectric power, gas pipelines, and other projects. And a meeting of the heads of state of Pakistan, Iran, and Turkey in Turkmenistan in early 1995 underscored the continuing interest of those countries in the Central Asian region as a whole.

One forum that has emerged as a potentially important structure for cooperation among these countries has been the Economic Cooperation Organization (ECO—see Glossary), a

loose regional economic organization to foster trade and cooperation among its members in the Middle East and South Asia.
Although during its almost two decades of existence ECO has
achieved little concrete economic cooperation, in November
1992 the inclusion of the five new Central Asian states, Afghanistan, and Azerbaijan brought significant efforts to reinvigorate
the organization. At a meeting in Quetta, Pakistan, in February
1993, an ambitious plan was announced to create a new
regional economic bloc among ECO's members by the year
2000. The plan calls for expanding ties in all economic sectors,
in training, and in tourism; setting up an effective transportation infrastructure; and ultimately abolishing restrictions limiting the free flow of people and commodities. Energy trade also
is to be expanded through the laying of oil and gas pipelines
and power transmission lines throughout the region. Given
ECO's past performance, however, in 1996 the potential for ful-
fillment of such plans was quite unclear.

Trade and cooperation agreements have also been signed
with Saudi Arabia, Jordan, and other Middle Eastern states.
The pragmatic rather than religious background of such
endeavors is underscored by Uzbekistan's rapidly expanding
ties with Israel, a nation that shares none of the history and culture of Uzbekistan. Following a visit of Israeli Foreign Minister
Shimon Peres to Uzbekistan in July 1994, Israel and Uzbekistan
signed agreements expanding commercial relations, protecting foreign investments and the development of business ties,
aviation links, and tourism. In the early 1990s, Israel's long participation in Uzbekistani irrigation projects has been supplemented by aid projects in health care, industry, and the two
countries' common battle against radical Islamic groups.

## China

China also has sought to develop relations with Central Asia.
This was highlighted in May 1994, by the visit of the Chinese
premier, Li Peng, to Tashkent. Since 1991 China has become
the second largest trading partner in Central Asia after Russia.
During Li Peng's visit, Uzbekistan and China signed four agreements designed to increase trade, including the granting of a
Chinese loan to Uzbekistan, the establishment of air freight
transport between the two countries, and the Chinese purchase
of Uzbekistani cotton and metals. The two countries also
agreed to settle all territorial disputes through negotiation, and
they found common territory in their desire to reform their

457

economies without relinquishing strict political control. At the same time, however, policy makers in Uzbekistan also view China as one of Uzbekistan's chief potential threats, requiring the same kind of balanced approach as that adopted toward Russia. Indeed, despite the large volume of trade between China and Central Asia, China is lowest on the list of desired trading partners and international donors among Uzbekistan's population. In a 1993 survey, only about 3 percent of respondents believed that China is a desirable source of foreign financial assistance.

## Western Europe and Japan

In the first four years of independence, the West occupied an increasing place in Uzbekistan's foreign policy. As relations with its immediate neighbors have been expanding, pragmatic geopolitical and economic considerations have come to dominate ethnic and religious identities as motivations for policy decisions. This approach has increased the interest of the Uzbekistani government in expanding ties with the West and with Japan.

In the early 1990s, Uzbekistan became a member of the United Nations, the World Bank, the International Monetary Fund (IMF—see Glossary), the Organization for Security and Cooperation in Europe (OSCE, formerly the Conference on Security and Cooperation in Europe, CSCE—see Glossary), the North Atlantic Cooperation Council, and a number of other international organizations. In that context, Uzbekistan is the beneficiary of several aid projects of varying magnitudes. The World Bank has designed missions and projects totaling hundreds of millions of dollars for such programs as the Cotton Sub-Sector Development Program to improve farm productivity, income, and international cotton marketing conditions and a program to address the problems of the Aral Sea. In April 1995, the World Bank allocated US$160 million in credit to Uzbekistan. In February 1995, the IMF approved a loan to support the Uzbekistani government's macroeconomic stabilization and systemic reform program. The first installment of the loan, roughly US$75 million, will be funded over a ten-year period; the second installment is to follow six months later, provided the government's macroeconomic stabilization program is being implemented. The European Bank for Reconstruction and Development (EBRD) likewise approved several million dollars for projects in Uzbekistan. These signs of

*World Bank offices, Tashkent*
*Courtesy K.S. Sangam Iyer*

greater involvement by the international community in Uzbekistan are largely stimulated by the political stability that the government has been able to maintain and in disregard of the human rights record, but many investors still are cautious.

## The United States

The United States recognized Uzbekistan as an independent state in December 1991; diplomatic relations were established in February 1992, following a visit by Secretary of State James Baker to the republic, and the United States opened an embassy in Tashkent the following month. During 1992, a variety of United States aid programs were launched. Operation Provide Hope delivered an estimated US$6 million of food and medical supplies for emergency relief of civilians affected by the Tajik civil war; the Peace Corps sent its first group of about

459

fifty volunteers to Uzbekistan; an agreement with the Overseas Private Investment Corporation (OPIC) began encouraging United States private investment in Uzbekistan by providing direct loans and loan guarantees and helping to match projects with potential investors; and humanitarian and technical assistance began to move to a wide range of recipients. In 1993 the United States granted Uzbekistan most-favored-nation trade status, which went into force in January 1994. In March 1994, a bilateral assistance agreement and an open lands agreement were signed. In 1995 a variety of investment and other treaties were under discussion, and several United States non-governmental organizations were initiating joint projects throughout Uzbekistan.

In the first two years of Uzbekistan's independence, the United States provided roughly US$17 million in humanitarian assistance andUS$13 million in technical assistance. For a time, continued human rights violations in Uzbekistan led to significant restrictions in the bilateral relationship, and Uzbekistan received significantly less United States assistance than many of the other former Soviet republics. Because Uzbekistan was slow to adopt fundamental economic reforms, nonhumanitarian United States assistance was largely restricted to programs that support the building of democratic institutions and market reform. By the end of 1995, however, United States-Uzbekistan relations were improving, and significantly more bilateral economic activity was expected in 1996.

## National Security

As it declared independence, Uzbekistan found itself in a much better national security position than did many other Soviet republics. In 1992 Uzbekistan took over much of the command structure and armaments of the Turkestan Military District, which was headquartered in Tashkent as the defense organization of the region of Central Asia under the Soviet system. With the abolition of that district the same year and a subsequent reduction and localization of military forces, Uzbekistan quickly built its own military establishment, which featured a gradually decreasing Slavic contingent in its officer corps. That inheritance from the Soviet era has enabled post-Soviet Uzbekistan to assume a role as an important military player in Central Asia and as the successor to Russia as the chief security force in the region. Following independence, Uzbekistan accepted all of the relevant arms control obligations that had been assumed by the former Soviet Union, and it has acceded to the Nuclear Nonproliferation Treaty as a nonnuclear state.

## External Security Conditions

Although its forces are small by international standards, Uzbekistan is rated as the strongest military power among the five Central Asian nations. In 1992 the Karimov regime sent military forces to Tajikistan to support forces of the old-guard communist Tajik government struggling to regain political power and oust the coalition government that had replaced them. Karimov's policy toward Tajikistan was to use military force in maintaining a similarly authoritarian regime to the immediate east. Although Tajikistan's civil war has had occasional destabilizing effects in parts of Uzbekistan, paramilitary Tajikistani oppositionist forces have not been strong enough to confront Uzbekistan's regular army. In the early 1990s, small-scale fighting occurred periodically between Tajikistani and Uzbekistani forces in the Fergana Valley.

In the mid-1990s, no military threat to Uzbekistan existed. An area of territorial contention is the Osh region at the far eastern end of the Fergana Valley where Kyrgyz and Uzbeks clashed violently in 1990 (see Recent History, ch. 2). The Uzbeks have used the minority Uzbek population in Osh as a reason to demand autonomous status for the Osh region; the Kyrgyz fear that such a change would lead to incorporating the region into Uzbekistan. The primary role of the Uzbekistan Armed Forces is believed to be maintaining internal security. This is possible because Uzbekistan remains protected by Russia under most conditions of external threat.

As defined in the 1992 Law on Defense, Uzbekistan's military doctrine is strictly defensive, with no territorial ambitions against any other state. Although its policy on the presence of CIS or Russian weapons has not been stated clearly, Uzbekistan's overall military doctrine does not permit strategic weapons in the inventory of the Uzbekistani armed forces. Battlefield chemical weapons, believed to have been in the republic during the Soviet period, allegedly have been returned to the Russian Federation. In 1994 Uzbekistan, like most of the other former Soviet republics, became a member of the Partnership for Peace program of the North Atlantic Treaty Organization (NATO—see Glossary), providing the basis for some joint military exercises with Western forces.

## Background of Military Development

One week after independence was declared in August 1991, Uzbekistan established a Ministry for Defense Affairs. The first minister of defense was charged with negotiating with the Soviet Union the future disposition of Soviet military units in Uzbekistan. In enforcing its independent status in military matters, a primary consideration was abolishing the Soviet Union's recruitment of Uzbekistani citizens for service in other parts of the union and abroad. For this purpose, a Department of Military Mobilization was established. In early 1992, when international interest in a joint CIS force waned, the Ministry for Defense Affairs of Uzbekistan took over the Tashkent headquarters of the former Soviet Turkestan Military District. The ministry also assumed jurisdiction over the approximately 60,000 Soviet military troops in Uzbekistan, with the exception of those remaining under the designation "strategic forces of the Joint CIS Command." In the same period, the Supreme Soviet approved laws establishing national defense procedures, conditions for military service, social and legal welfare of service personnel, and the legal status of CIS strategic forces.

A presidential decree in March 1992 declared the number of former Soviet troops in Uzbekistan to exceed strategic requirements and the financial resources of Uzbekistan. With the subsequent abolition of the Turkestan Military District, Uzbekistan established a Ministry of Defense, replacing the Ministry for Defense Affairs. The CIS Tashkent Agreement of May 15, 1992, distributed former Soviet troops and equipment among the former republics in which they were stationed. Among the units that Uzbekistan inherited by that agreement were a fighter-bomber regiment at Chirchiq, an engineer brigade, and an airborne brigade at Farghona.

For the first two years, the command structure of the new force was dominated by the Russians and other Slav officers who had been in command in 1992. In 1992 some 85 percent of officers and ten of fifteen generals were Slavs. In the first year, Karimov appointed Uzbeks to the positions of assistant minister of defense and chief of staff, and a Russian veteran of the Afghan War to the position of commander of the Rapid Reaction Forces. Lieutenant General Rustam Akhmedov, an Uzbek, has been minister of defense since the establishment of the ministry. In 1993 Uzbekistan nationalized the three former Soviet military schools in Tashkent.

## The Armed Forces

The president of Uzbekistan is the commander in chief of the armed forces, and he has authority to appoint and dismiss all senior commanders. The minister of defense and the chief of staff have operational and administrative control. Since early 1992, President Karimov has exercised his supreme authority in making appointments and in the application of military power. The staff structure of the armed forces retains the configuration of the Turkestan Military District. The structure includes an Operational and Mobilization Organization Directorate and departments of intelligence, signals, transport, CIS affairs, aviation, air defense, and missile troops and artillery. In 1996 total military strength was estimated at about 25,000. The armed forces are divided into four main components: ground defense forces, air force, air defense, and national guard.

### Army

The ground defense forces, largest of the four branches, numbered 20,400 troops in 1996, of which about 30 percent were professional soldiers serving by contract and the remainder were conscripts. The forces are divided into an army corps of three motorized rifle brigades, one tank regiment, one engineer brigade, one artillery brigade, two artillery regiments, one airborne brigade, and aviation, logistics, and communications support units. The ground forces' primary mission is to conduct rapid-reaction operations in cooperation with other branches. Combined headquarters are at Tashkent; the headquarters of the 360th Motor Rifle Division is at Termiz, and that of the Airmobile Division is at Farghona. (Although the force structure provides for no division-level units, they are designated as such for the purpose of assigning headquarters.)

In 1996 Uzbekistan's active arsenal of conventional military equipment included 179 main battle tanks; 383 armored personnel carriers and infantry vehicles; 323 artillery pieces; forty-five surface-to-air missiles; and fifteen antitank guns.

### Air Force and Air Defense

A treaty signed in March 1994 by Russia and Uzbekistan defines the terms of Russian assistance in training, allocation of air fields, communications, and information on air space and air defense installations. In 1995 almost all personnel in Uzbekistan's air force were ethnic Russians. The Chirchiq

Fighter Bomber Regiment, taken over in the initial phase of nationalization of former Soviet installations, has since been scaled down by eliminating older aircraft, with the goal of reaching a force of 100 fixed-wing aircraft and thirty-two armed helicopters. According to the Soviet structure still in place, separate air and air defense forces operate in support of ground forces; air force doctrine conforms with Soviet doctrine. Some thirteen air bases are active.

In 1994 Uzbekistan's inventory of aircraft was still in the process of reduction to meet treaty requirements. At that stage, the air force was reported to have two types of interceptor jet, twenty of the outmoded MiG–21 and thirty of the more sophisticated MiG–29. For close air support, forty MiG–27s (foundation of the Chirchiq regiment) and ten Su–17Ms were operational. Twenty An–2 light transport planes, six An–12BP transports, and ten An–26 transports made up the air force's transport fleet. Training aircraft included twenty L–39C advanced trainers and an unknown number of Yak–52 basic trainers. Six Mi–8P/T transport helicopters were available. The air defense system consisted of twenty operational Nudelman 9K31 low-altitude surface-to-air missiles, which in 1994 were controlled by two Russian air defense regiments deployed along the Afghan border.

### National Guard

The National Guard was created immediately after independence (August 1991) as an internal security force under the direct command of the president, to replace the Soviet Internal Troops that had provided internal security until that time. Although plans called for a force of 1,000 troops including a ceremonial guard company, a special purpose detachment, and a motorized rifle regiment, reports indicate that only one battalion of the motorized rifle regiment had been formed in 1994. The National Guard forces in Tashkent, thought to number about 700, moved under the jurisdiction of the Ministry of Internal Security in 1994.

### Border Guards

The Uzbekistan Border Troop Command was established in March 1992, on the basis of the former Soviet Central Asian Border Troops District. In 1994 the Frontier Guard, as it is also called, came under the control of the Ministry of Internal Security. The force, comprising about 1,000 troops in 1996, is under the command of a deputy chairman of the National Security Committee, which formerly was the Uzbekistan Committee for State Security (KGB). The Frontier Guard works closely with the Russian Border Troops Command under the terms of a 1992 agreement that provides for Russian training of all Uzbekistani border troops and joint control of the Afghan border.

### Military Training

Three major Soviet-built training facilities are the foundation of the military training program. The General Weapons Command Academy in Tashkent trains noncommissioned officers (NCOs); the Military Driving Academy in Samarqand is a transport school; and the Chirchiq Tank School trains armor units. In 1993 all three schools were stripped of the Soviet-style honorific names they bore during the Soviet period. Plans call for expansion of the three schools. Bilateral agreements with Russia and Turkey also provide for training of Uzbekistani troops in those countries. For aircraft training, Uzbekistan retains some Aero L–39C Albatross turbofan trainers and piston-engine Yak–52 basic trainers that had been used by the Soviet-era air force reserves.

## Internal Security

Uzbekistan defines its most important security concerns not only in terms of the potential for military conflict, but also in terms of domestic threats. Primary among those threats are the destabilizing effects of trafficking in narcotics and weapons into and across Uzbekistani territory. Although the government has recognized the dangers of such activities to society, enforcement often is stymied by corruption in law enforcement agencies.

### Narcotics

With an estimated 2,000 to 3,000 hectares of domestic opium poppy grown annually, Uzbekistan's society long has been exposed to the availability of domestic narcotics as well as to the influx of drugs across the border from Afghanistan (often by way of Tajikistan). Since independence, border security with Afghanistan and among the former Soviet Central Asian republics has become more lax, intensifying the external source problem. Uzbekistan is centrally located in its region, and the transportation systems through Tashkent make that city an attractive hub for narcotics movement from the Central Asian fields to destinations in Western Europe and elsewhere in the CIS.

In 1992 and 1993, shipments of thirteen and fourteen tons of hashish were intercepted in Uzbekistan on their way to the Netherlands. Increasingly in the 1990s, drug sales have been linked to arms sales and the funding of armed groups in neighboring Afghanistan and Tajikistan. Drug-related crime has risen significantly in Uzbekistan during this period. Uzbekistani authorities have identified syndicates from Georgia, Azerbaijan, and other countries active in the Tashkent drug trade.

Domestic drug use has risen sharply in the 1990s as well. In 1994 the Ministry of Health listed 12,000 registered addicts, estimating that the actual number of addicts was likely about 44,000. Opium poppy cultivation is concentrated in Samarqand and along the border with Tajikistan, mainly confined to small plots and raised for domestic consumption. Cannabis, which grows wild, is also increasingly in use. In 1995 government authorities recognized domestic narcotics processing as a problem for the first time when they seized several kilograms of locally made heroin.

To deal with this threat, three agencies—the National Security Service, the Ministry of Internal Affairs, and the State Customs Committee—share jurisdiction, although in practice their respective roles often are ill-defined. The international community has sought to provide technical and other assistance to Uzbekistan in this matter. In 1995 Uzbekistan established a National Commission on Drug Control to improve coordination and public awareness. A new criminal code includes tougher penalties for drug-related crimes, including a possible death penalty for drug dealers. The government's eradication program, which targeted only small areas of cultivation in the early 1990s, expanded significantly in 1995, and drug-related arrests more than doubled over 1994. In 1992 the United States government, recognizing Central Asia as a potential route for large-scale narcotics transport, began urging all five Central Asian nations to make drug control a priority of national policy. The United States has channeled most of its narcotics aid to Central Asia through the UN Drug Control Program, whose programs for drug-control intelligence centers and canine narcotics detection squads were being adopted in Uzbekistan in 1996. In 1995 Uzbekistan signed a bilateral counternarcotics cooperation agreement with Turkey and acceded to the 1988 UN Convention Against Illicit Traffic in Narcotic Drugs and Psychotropic Substances.

### Law Enforcement and Crime

The Uzbekistani police force is estimated to number about 25,000 individuals trained according to Soviet standards. The United States Department of Justice has begun a program to train the force in Western techniques. Interaction also has been expanded with the National Security Service, the chief intelligence agency, which still is mainly staffed by former KGB personnel. About 8,000 paramilitary troops are believed available to the National Security Service.

But these efforts are expected to have little impact on the widespread and deeply entrenched organized crime and corruption throughout Uzbekistan, especially in the law enforcement community itself. According to experts, the government corruption scandals that attracted international attention in the 1980s were symptomatic of a high degree of corruption endemic in the system. In a society of tremendous economic shortage and tight political control from the top down, the government and criminal world become intertwined. Citizens routinely have been required to pay bribes for all common services. More than two-thirds of respondents in a recent survey of Uzbekistan's citizens stated that bribes are absolutely necessary to receive services that nominally are available to all. These bribes often involve enormous sums of money: in 1993 admission to a prestigious institution of higher learning, while technically free, commonly cost nearly 1 million Russian rubles, or more than twice the average annual salary in Uzbekistan in 1993.

Narcotics and weapons trafficking are only an extension of this system, widely viewed as sustained and supported by law enforcement and government officials themselves. In the same survey, a majority of Uzbekistanis stated that bribery occurs routinely in the police department, in the courts, and in the office of the state procurator, the chief prosecutor in the national judicial system. About 25 percent of police surveyed agreed that other officers were involved in the sale of drugs or taking bribes.

The condition of the internal security system is an indicator that progress remains to be made in Uzbekistan's journey out of Soviet-style governance. In the first five years of independence, efforts to establish profitable relations with the rest of the world (and especially the West) have been hindered by a preoccupation with maintaining the political status quo. However, by the mid-1990s Uzbekistan began to take advantage of its considerable assets. Uzbekistan does not suffer from poor natural resources or hostile neighboring countries; its mineral resources are bountiful, and Russia continues to watch over its former provinces in Central Asia. According to government rhetoric, market reforms and expanding international trade will make the nation prosperous—beginning in 1995, an improved human rights record and more favorable investment conditions supplemented the country's political stability in attracting foreign trade and fostering at least the beginning of democratic institutions.

\*       \*       \*

For historical background on Uzbekistan, three books are especially useful: Elizabeth E. Bacon's *Central Asians under Russian Rule*, Edward Allworth's *Central Asia: 120 Years of Russian Rule*, and Vasilii V. Bartol'd's *Turkestan Down to the Mongol Invasion*. James Critchlow's *Nationalism in Uzbekistan* provides useful background on the development of nationalism among the elites of Uzbekistan during the Soviet period, and William Fierman's *Soviet Central Asia: The Failed Transformation* covers social issues and the development of Islam. For information on environmental issues in Uzbekistan, Murray Feshbach and Alfred Friendly, Jr.'s *Ecocide in the USSR* and Philip R. Pryde's *Environmental Resources and Constraints in the Former Soviet Republics* are useful sources.

For a discussion of economic issues, the World Bank country studies and the weekly *Business Eastern Europe*, published by the Economist Intelligence Unit, provide the most current information. Nancy Lubin's *Labour and Nationality in Soviet Central Asia* provides a detailed description of the background to the development of corruption and organized crime. The quarterly journal *Central Asian Monitor* and the daily reports of the Open Media Research Institute (OMRI) provide the most current information regarding events in Central Asia. (For further information and complete citations, see Bibliography.)

# Appendix

## Table 1. *Metric Conversion Coefficients and Factors*

| When you know | Multiply by | To find |
|---|---|---|
| Millimeters.......................... | 0.04 | inches |
| Centimeters........................ | 0.39 | inches |
| Meters............................. | 3.3 | feet |
| Kilometers ......................... | 0.62 | miles |
| Hectares........................... | 2.47 | acres |
| Square kilometers ................... | 0.39 | square miles |
| Cubic meters ....................... | 35.3 | cubic feet |
| Liters ............................. | 0.26 | gallons |
| Kilograms.......................... | 2.2 | pounds |
| Metric tons........................ | 0.98 | long tons |
| ................................. | 1.1 | short tons |
| ................................. | 2,204.0 | pounds |
| Degrees Celsius (Centigrade)........... | 1.8 and add 32 | degrees Fahrenheit |

Table 2. *Central Asia: Demographic Indicators, 1989–93*

| Indicator | Kazakstan[1] | Kyrgyzstan[2] | Tajikistan[3] | Turkmenistan[4] | Uzbekistan[5] |
|---|---|---|---|---|---|
| Live births | 316,369 | 128,352 | 186,504 | 124,992 | 711,000 |
| Birth rate[6] | 18.7 | 28.6 | 32.5 | 34.9 | 33.3 |
| Deaths | 156,253 | 32,163 | 49,326 | 27,609 | 139,900 |
| Death rate[6] | 9.2 | 7.2 | 8.6 | 7.7 | 6.5 |
| Life expectancy, male | 63.8 | 64.6 | 66.8 | 61.8 | 66.0 |
| Life expectancy, female | 73.0 | 72.7 | 71.7 | 68.4 | 72.1 |
| Marriages | 146,161 | 40,818 | 53,946 | 34,890 | 235,900 |
| Marriage rate[6] | 8.6 | 9.1 | 0.9 | 9.8 | 11.0 |
| Divorces | 45,516 | 8,043 | 5,293 | 4,940 | 29,953 |
| Divorce rate[6] | 2.7 | 1.8 | 0.9 | 1.4 | 1.5 |

[1] All figures 1993 except life expectancy (1990).
[2] All figures 1992 except life expectancy (1991).
[3] All figures 1993 except life expectancy (1989).
[4] All figures 1989.
[5] All figures 1992 except life expectancy (1989).
[6] Per 1,000 population.

Source: Based on information from United Nations, Department for Economic and Social Information and Policy Analysis, *Demographic Yearbook 1994*, New York, 1996, 140–43.

*Table 3. Central Asia: Population Distribution, 1989–92[1] (in thousands)*

| Population Group | Kazakstan[2] | Kyrgyzstan[3] | Tajikistan[4] | Turkmenistan[4] | Uzbekistan[4] |
|---|---|---|---|---|---|
| Urban male. . . . . . . . . . . . . . . . . . | 4,577 | 800 | 813 | 783 | 3,937 |
| Urban female . . . . . . . . . . . . . . . . | 5,029 | 881 | 842 | 808 | 4,104 |
| Urban total . . . . . . . . . . . . . . . . . | 9,606 | 1,681 | 1,655 | 1,591 | 8,041 |
| Urban percentage. . . . . . . . . . . . . | 57.6 | 37.9 | 32.5 | 43.9 | 40.6 |
| Rural male. . . . . . . . . . . . . . . . . . | 3,539 | 1,383 | 1,717 | 952 | 5,847 |
| Rural female . . . . . . . . . . . . . . . . | 3,576 | 1,388 | 1,720 | 980 | 5,922 |
| Rural total. . . . . . . . . . . . . . . . . . | 7,115 | 2,771 | 3,437 | 1,932 | 11,769 |
| Total male. . . . . . . . . . . . . . . . . . | 8,116 | 2,183 | 2,530 | 1,735 | 9,784 |
| Total female . . . . . . . . . . . . . . . . | 8,605 | 2,269 | 2,562 | 1,788 | 10,026 |
| 14 and younger. . . . . . . . . . . . . . . | 5,248 | 1,673 | 2,187 | n.a.[5] | 8,083 |
| 15 to 39 . . . . . . . . . . . . . . . . . . . | 6,851 | 1,794 | 1,996 | 1,453 | 8,029 |
| 50 to 64 . . . . . . . . . . . . . . . . . . . | 3,623 | 756 | 717 | 510 | 2,894 |
| 65 and older . . . . . . . . . . . . . . . . | 999 | 228 | 192 | 132 | 804 |

[1] Figures do not add to totals because of rounding and because of small numbers of unidentified age in census.
[2] 1991 figures.
[3] 1992 figures.
[4] 1989 figures.
[5] n.a.—not available.

Source: Based on information from United Nations, Department for Economic and Social Information and Policy Analysis, *Demographic Yearbook 1994*, New York, 1996, 240–45.

*Table 4.  Central Asia: Ethnic Composition, Selected Years, 1989–94*
(in percentages)

| Country and Ethnic Group | 1989 | 1991 | 1993 | 1994 |
|---|---|---|---|---|
| Kazakstan | | | | |
| Kazak...................... | 39.7 | 41.9 | 43.2 | 44.3 |
| Russian .................... | 37.8 | 37.0 | 36.5 | 35.8 |
| Ukrainian ................. | 5.4 | 5.2 | 5.2 | 5.1 |
| German.................... | 5.8 | 4.7 | 4.1 | 3.6 |
| Uzbek ..................... | 2.0 | 2.1 | 2.2 | 2.2 |
| Tatar ...................... | 2.0 | 2.0 | 2.0 | 2.0 |
| Kyrgyzstan | | | | |
| Kyrgyz ..................... | 52.4 | n.a.[1] | 56.5 | n.a. |
| Russian .................... | 21.5 | n.a. | 18.8 | n.a. |
| Uzbek ..................... | 12.9 | n.a. | 12.9 | n.a. |
| Ukrainian ................. | 2.5 | n.a. | 2.1 | n.a. |
| German.................... | 2.4 | n.a. | 1.0 | n.a. |
| Tajikistan | | | | |
| Tajik ...................... | 62.3 | 63.8 | n.a. | n.a. |
| Uzbek ..................... | 23.5 | 24.0 | n.a. | n.a. |
| Russian .................... | 7.6 | 6.5 | n.a. | n.a. |
| Tatar ...................... | 1.4 | 1.4 | n.a. | n.a. |
| Turkmenistan | | | | |
| Turkmen.................. | 72.0 | n.a. | 73.3 | n.a. |
| Russian .................... | 9.8 | n.a. | 9.5 | n.a. |
| Uzbek ..................... | 9.0 | n.a. | 9.0 | n.a. |
| Kazak...................... | 2.0 | n.a. | 2.5 | n.a. |
| Uzbekistan | | | | |
| Uzbek ..................... | 71.4 | 73.0 | n.a. | n.a. |
| Russian .................... | 8.3 | 7.7 | n.a. | n.a. |
| Tajik ...................... | 4.7 | 4.8 | n.a. | n.a. |
| Kazak...................... | 4.1 | n.a. | n.a. | n.a. |
| Tatar ...................... | 2.4 | 2.3 | n.a. | n.a. |

[1] n.a.—not available.

Source: Based on information from *The Europa World Year Book 1994*, 2, London, 1994, 1679; *The Europa World Year Book 1995*, 2, London, 1995, 1679, 1735, 1823, 2950, 3070, 3363; United States, Central Intelligence Agency, *The World Factbook 1994*, Washington, 1994, 210, 222, 385, 403, 420; and *1995 Britannica Book of the Year*, Chicago, 1995, 726, 746.

*Table 5. Central Asia: Incidence of Selected Diseases and Mortality, 1989–91*

|  | Kazakstan | Kyrgyzstan | Tajikistan | Turkmenistan | Uzbekistan |
|---|---|---|---|---|---|
| Viral hepatitis[1] ... | 465.6 | 710.8 | 918.3 | 735.1 | 1,074.5 |
| Cancer[2] ........ | 289.9 | 219.0 | 163.1 | 203.0 | 169.2 |
| Tuberculosis[2].... | 65.8 | 53.3 | 44.4 | 63.6 | 46.1 |
| Maternal mortality[3] .... | 53.1 | 42.7 | 38.9 | 55.2 | 42.8 |
| Infant mortality[4] .... | 27.1 | 29.6 | 40.0 | 46.6 | 35.8 |

[1] Per 100,000 population in 1989.
[2] Per 100,000 population in 1990.
[3] Deaths per 100,000 live births in 1991.
[4] Deaths per 1,000 live births in 1989.

Source: Based on information from Christopher M. Davis, "Health Care Crisis: The Former Soviet Union," *RFE/RL Research Report* [Munich], 2, No. 40, October 8, 1993, 36.

*Table 6. Central Asia: Percentage Change in Major Economic Indicators, 1992–93 and 1993–94*

| Country | GDP[1] | | Industrial Output | | Agricultural Output | |
|---|---|---|---|---|---|---|
|  | 1992–93 | 1993–94 | 1992–93 | 1993–94 | 1992–93 | 1993–94 |
| Kazakstan ......... | −12 | −26 | −17 | −28 | −3 | −23 |
| Kyrgyzstan ........ | −13 | −25 | −24 | −25 | −8 | −17 |
| Tajikistan ......... | −21 | −12 | −20 | −31 | −4 | −26 |
| Turkmenistan ..... | 8 | −24 | 6 | −24 | 9 | −2 |
| Uzbekistan ........ | −3 | −4 | −4 | 1 | 0 | 13 |

[1] GDP—gross domestic product.

Source: Based on information from United States, Central Intelligence Agency, *Handbook of International Economic Statistics 1995*, Washington, 1995, 52.

*Table 7. Kazakstan: Production of Principal Agricultural Crops,*
*1992–94*
(in thousands of tons)

| Crop | 1992 | 1993 | 1994 |
|------|------|------|------|
| Wheat............................. | 18,285 | 11,585 | 9,052 |
| Barley.............................. | 8,511 | 7,149 | 5,497 |
| Potatoes........................... | 2,570 | 2,295 | 1,950 |
| Oats .............................. | 727 | 802 | 822 |
| Tomatoes.......................... | 380 | 320 | 300 |
| Rice .............................. | 467 | 403 | 283 |
| Rye............................... | 524 | 835 | 264 |
| Watermelons....................... | 250 | 202 | 250 |
| Corn.............................. | 370 | 355 | 233 |
| Sugar beets ....................... | 1,276 | 925 | 169 |
| Millet ............................ | 447 | 233 | 130 |

Source: Based on information from *The Europa World Year Book 1996*, 2, London, 1996, 1811.

*Table 8. Kazakstan: Production of Principal Industrial Products,*
*1991–93*
(in thousands of tons unless otherwise indicated)

| Product | 1991 | 1992 | 1993 |
|---------|------|------|------|
| Coke....................................... | 3,711 | 3,404 | 3,300 |
| Cotton yarn ................................ | 40 | 37 | 39 |
| Crude steel ............................... | 6,754 | 6,337 | n.a.[1] |
| Electric power (in millions of kilowatt-hours) ...... | 87,379 | 86,128 | 79,174 |
| Fabric (in thousands of square meters) ........... | 325,461 | 248,708 | n.a. |
| Footwear (in thousands of pairs)................ | 36,464 | 35,410 | n.a. |
| Margarine .................................. | 71 | 48 | n.a. |
| Pig iron ................................... | 5,226 | 4,952 | 4,666 |
| Rubber tires (in thousands)..................... | 2,633 | 3,029 | 2,899 |
| Sulfuric acid ............................... | 3,151 | 2,815 | 2,349 |

[1] n.a.—not available.

Source: Based on information from *The Europa World Year Book 1996*, 2, London, 1996, 1811.

### Table 9.  Kazakstan: Structure of Employment, 1990–92 (in thousands of workers)

| Sector | 1990 | 1991 | 1992 |
|---|---|---|---|
| Agriculture, forestry, and fishing . . . . . . . . . . . . . . . | 1,686 | 1,715 | 1,762 |
| Mining and quarrying. . . . . . . . . . . . . . . . . . . . . . . | 235 | 251 | 257 |
| Manufacturing. . . . . . . . . . . . . . . . . . . . . . . . . . . . | 1,247 | 1,218 | 1,160 |
| Construction . . . . . . . . . . . . . . . . . . . . . . . . . . . . | 833 | 690 | 681 |
| Trade, restaurants, and hotels . . . . . . . . . . . . . . . . | 470 | 461 | 437 |
| Transport and communications. . . . . . . . . . . . . . . . | 704 | 700 | 665 |
| Community, social, and personal services . . . . . . . . . | 1,867 | 1,901 | 1,906 |
| Utilities. . . . . . . . . . . . . . . . . . . . . . . . . . . . . . . . . | 66 | 73 | 83 |
| Other activities. . . . . . . . . . . . . . . . . . . . . . . . . . . . | 690 | 736 | 662 |
| TOTAL. . . . . . . . . . . . . . . . . . . . . . . . . . . . . . . . . . | 7,798 | 7,745 | 7,613 |

Source: Based on information from *The Europa World Year Book, 1995*, 2, London, 1995,
1736.

### Table 10.  Central Asia: Cost of Living, 1990–93

| Country and Category | 1990 | 1991 | 1992 | 1993 |
|---|---|---|---|---|
| Kazakstan[1] | | | | |
|     Food . . . . . . . . . . . . . . . . . . . . . | n.a.[2] | 4.7 | 100 | 2,297 |
|     Clothing . . . . . . . . . . . . . . . . . | n.a. | 4.7 | 100 | 1,606 |
|     Rent. . . . . . . . . . . . . . . . . . . . . . | n.a. | n.a. | 100 | 16,258 |
|     Average for all items. . . . . . . . . . | n.a. | 3.3 | 100 | 2,265 |
| Kyrgyzstan (all items)[3] . . . . . . . . . | 100 | 185.0 | 954.0 | n.a. |
| Tajikistan[4] | | | | |
|     Food . . . . . . . . . . . . . . . . . . . . . | 101.8 | 194.4 | 1,450.5 | n.a. |
|     Alcoholic beverages . . . . . . . . . . | 100.6 | 163.4 | 1,152.1 | n.a. |
|     Average for all items. . . . . . . . . . | 104.0 | 193.0 | 1,153.9 | n.a. |
| Turkmenistan (all items)[4]. . . . . . . . | 104.2 | 202.5 | 592.9 | n.a. |
| Uzbekistan (all items)[3] . . . . . . . . . . | 100 | 205.0 | 627.7 | 951.1 |

[1] Base year 1992=100.
[2] n.a.—not available.
[3] Base year 1990=100.
[4] Base year 1989=100.

Source: Based on information from *The Europa World Year Book 1995*, 2, London, 1995,
1737, 1825, 2952, 3071, 3364.

Table 11.   *Kazakstan: Foreign Trade with Selected Countries, 1992–94*

|  | 1992 | 1993 | 1994 |
|---|---|---|---|
| Imports |  |  |  |
| Former Soviet Union[1] |  |  |  |
| Armenia............................. | 0.1 | 0.1 | 0.0 |
| Azerbaijan ........................... | 1.1 | 0.6 | 0.8 |
| Belarus.............................. | 4.6 | 3.0 | 1.9 |
| Estonia.............................. | 0.1 | 0.3 | 0.0 |
| Georgia ............................. | 0.3 | 0.4 | 0.1 |
| Kyrgyzstan .......................... | 3.2 | 1.3 | 0.9 |
| Latvia............................... | 0.1 | 0.5 | 0.2 |
| Lithuania............................ | 0.3 | 0.7 | 0.1 |
| Moldova............................. | 0.2 | 0.8 | 0.1 |
| Russia............................... | 72.4 | 70.9 | 89.3 |
| Tajikistan ........................... | 0.9 | 0.5 | 0.2 |
| Turkmenistan ........................ | 2.5 | 4.7 | 0.1 |
| Ukraine ............................. | 10.5 | 7.3 | 3.6 |
| Uzbekistan........................... | 3.7 | 9.0 | 2.6 |
| Exports |  |  |  |
| Former Soviet Union[1] |  |  |  |
| Armenia............................. | 0.1 | 0.0 | 0.0 |
| Azerbaijan ........................... | 1.7 | 3.2 | 2.0 |
| Belarus.............................. | 2.7 | 5.0 | 2.6 |
| Estonia.............................. | 0.1 | 0.0 | 0.1 |
| Georgia ............................. | 0.1 | 0.2 | 0.0 |
| Kyrgyzstan .......................... | 2.5 | 2.3 | 2.2 |
| Latvia............................... | 0.3 | 0.2 | 1.2 |
| Lithuania............................ | 0.6 | 0.5 | 1.3 |
| Moldova............................. | 0.3 | 0.4 | 0.1 |
| Russia............................... | 71.0 | 69.7 | 78.7 |
| Tajikistan ........................... | 1.2 | 1.4 | 0.6 |
| Turkmenistan ........................ | 3.3 | 2.1 | 0.7 |
| Ukraine ............................. | 9.7 | 8.1 | 5.2 |
| Uzbekistan........................... | 6.5 | 6.9 | 5.3 |
| Imports |  |  |  |
| Other countries[2] |  |  |  |
| Austria .............................. | 30 | 21 | 16 |
| China................................ | 213 | 80 | 46 |
| Czech Republic[3] ...................... | 4 | 48 | n.a.[4] |
| Finland.............................. | 25 | 5 | 4 |
| France .............................. | 7 | 9 | 21 |
| Germany ............................ | 19 | 76 | 125 |
| Hungary............................. | 27 | 23 | 14 |

*Table 11. (Continued) Kazakstan: Foreign Trade with Selected Countries, 1992–94*

|  | 1992 | 1993 | 1994 |
|---|---|---|---|
| Italy................................... | 30 | 21 | 37 |
| Switzerland............................ | 15 | 18 | 40 |
| Turkey ............................... | 5 | 15 | 17 |
| United Kingdom ....................... | 23 | 19 | 17 |
| United States ......................... | 6 | 38 | 42 |
| Exports |  |  |  |
| Other Countries[2] |  |  |  |
| Australia.............................. | 835 | 940 | 809 |
| Austria ............................... | 1 | 21 | 30 |
| Belgium .............................. | 11 | 13 | 16 |
| Bulgaria .............................. | 18 | 22 | 9 |
| China ................................ | 237 | 172 | 85 |
| Czech Republic[3] ...................... | 80 | 19 | 14 |
| Finland............................... | 43 | 9 | 1 |
| France................................ | 19 | 7 | 5 |
| Germany.............................. | 123 | 131 | 65 |
| Hungary.............................. | 21 | 37 | 12 |
| Italy.................................. | 40 | 84 | 24 |
| Japan................................. | 49 | 37 | 31 |
| Korea, Democratic People's Republic of...... | 18 | 22 | 3 |
| Korea, Republic of...................... | 12 | 46 | 22 |
| Netherlands........................... | 52 | 49 | 42 |
| Poland ............................... | 49 | 37 | 13 |
| Slovakia[3]............................. | 80 | 30 | 11 |
| Sweden............................... | 150 | 91 | 5 |
| Switzerland............................ | 104 | 175 | 345 |
| Turkey ............................... | 16 | 56 | 40 |
| United Kingdom ....................... | 26 | 97 | 87 |
| United States ......................... | 101 | 145 | 121 |

[1] Percentage of total trade with former Soviet republics.
[2] In millions of United States dollars.
[3] 1992 amounts for Czechoslovakia; 1993 and 1994 amounts divided between Czech Republic and Slovakia.
[4] n.a.—not available.

Source: Based on information from World Bank, *Statistical Handbook 1995: States of the Former USSR*, Washington, 1995, 152–54.

*Table 12. Central Asia: Military Budgets and Personnel, 1992–95*
(budgets in millions of United States dollars)

| Country | 1992 | 1993 | 1994 | 1995 |
|---|---|---|---|---|
| Kazakstan | | | | |
|   Budget ................... | 1,600 | 707 | 450 | 297 |
|   Personnel ................. | 68,000[1] | 44,000 | 40,000 | 40,000 |
| Kyrgyzstan | | | | |
|   Budget ................... | 47 | 51 | 57 | 13 |
|   Personnel ................. | 8,000[1] | 12,000 | 12,000 | 12,000 |
| Tajikistan | | | | |
|   Budget ................... | 107 | 110 | 115 | 67 |
|   Personnel ................. | 6,000[1] | 3,000 | 3,000 | 3,000 |
| Turkmenistan | | | | |
|   Budget ................... | 114 | 143 | 153 | 61 |
|   Personnel ................. | 34,000[1] | 28,000[1] | 28,000[1] | 11,000[1] |
| Uzbekistan | | | | |
|   Budget ................... | 420 | 390 | 375 | 315 |
|   Personnel ................. | 15,000[1] | 40,000 | 39,000 | 25,000 |

[1] Under joint control with Russian Federation.

Source: Based on information from *The Military Balance, 1993–1994*, London, 1993,
140, 144–45; *The Military Balance, 1994–1995*, London, 1994, 156–57, 162–63;
*The Military Balance, 1995–1996*, London, 1995, 160–61, 165–67; and *The
Worldwide Directory of Defense Authorities 1996*, 2, Bethesda, 1996.

*Table 13. Kyrgyzstan: Production of Principal Agricultural Crops, 1992–94*
(in thousands of tons)

| Crop | 1992 | 1993 | 1994 |
|------|------|------|------|
| Wheat.................................... | 634 | 863 | 611 |
| Barley................................... | 582 | 539 | 300 |
| Potatoes ................................ | 362 | 291 | 288 |
| Tomatoes ............................... | 201 | 150 | 160 |
| Corn.................................... | 281 | 184 | 120 |
| Sugar beets.............................. | 135 | 207 | 110 |
| Apples.................................. | 75 | 69 | 65 |
| Tobacco, leaf ........................... | 56 | 60 | 58 |
| Cotton seed ............................. | 34 | 38 | 40 |
| Cabbage................................. | 61 | 32 | 35 |
| Grapes ................................. | 31 | 30 | 28 |

Source: Based on information from *The Europa World Year Book 1996*, 2, London, 1996, 1900.

*Table 14. Kyrgyzstan: Production of Principal Industrial Products, 1991–94*

| Product | 1991 | 1992 | 1993 | 1994 |
|---------|------|------|------|------|
| Carpets (in thousands of square meters) ............... | 1,661 | 1,701 | 1,609 | 1,083 |
| Cement (in thousands of tons) ..... | 1,320 | 1,095 | 672 | 426 |
| Electric power (in millions of kilowatt-hours) ............... | 14,170 | 11,890 | 11,200 | 12,900 |
| Fabric (in thousands of square meters) .................... | 142,778 | 123,781 | 89,138 | 62,144 |
| Footwear (in thousands of pairs) ....................... | 9,504 | 5,343 | 3,528 | 1,631 |
| Trucks....................... | 23,600 | 14,800 | 5,000 | 200 |
| Washing machines............... | 209,400 | 94,000 | 76,800 | 17,100 |

Source: Based on information from *The Europa World Year Book 1995*, 2, London, 1995, 1824; and *The Europa World Yearbook 1996*, 2, London, 1996, 1900.

*Table 15.  Kyrgyzstan: Foreign Trade with Selected Countries, 1992–94*

|  | 1992 | 1993 | 1994 |
|---|---|---|---|
| Imports |  |  |  |
| Former Soviet Union[1] |  |  |  |
| Armenia.............................. | 0.1 | 0.1 | 0.0 |
| Azerbaijan ........................... | 0.5 | 0.6 | 0.3 |
| Belarus.............................. | 1.5 | 0.9 | 1.2 |
| Estonia.............................. | 0.0 | n.a.[2] | n.a. |
| Georgia ............................. | 0.4 | 0.2 | 0.1 |
| Kazakstan............................ | 23.3 | 28.9 | 28.0 |
| Latvia ............................... | 0.2 | n.a. | n.a. |
| Lithuania............................ | 0.3 | n.a. | n.a. |
| Moldova............................. | 0.5 | 0.1 | 0.0 |
| Russia............................... | 49.0 | 47.1 | 33.4 |
| Tajikistan ........................... | 0.7 | 0.4 | 0.5 |
| Turkmenistan ........................ | 6.1 | 2.1 | 4.8 |
| Ukraine ............................. | 8.1 | 2.0 | 1.4 |
| Uzbekistan........................... | 9.1 | 17.3 | 30.2 |
| Exports |  |  |  |
| Former Soviet Union[1] |  |  |  |
| Armenia.............................. | 0.2 | 0.0 | 0.0 |
| Azerbaijan ........................... | 0.9 | 1.4 | 0.7 |
| Belarus.............................. | 3.0 | 2.0 | 1.7 |
| Estonia.............................. | 0.2 | n.a. | n.a. |
| Georgia ............................. | 0.4 | 0.1 | 0.1 |
| Kazakstan............................ | 22.4 | 29.0 | 42.9 |
| Latvia ............................... | 0.3 | n.a. | n.a. |
| Lithuania............................ | 1.5 | n.a. | n.a. |
| Moldova............................. | 0.6 | 0.4 | 0.2 |
| Russia............................... | 39.1 | 45.8 | 26.0 |
| Tajikistan ........................... | 1.4 | 2.5 | 1.4 |
| Turkmenistan ........................ | 2.4 | 3.5 | 3.4 |
| Ukraine ............................. | 17.3 | 5.7 | 4.0 |
| Uzbekistan........................... | 10.4 | 9.6 | 19.6 |
| Imports |  |  |  |
| Other countries[3] |  |  |  |
| Belgium ............................. | n.a. | 4.8 | n.a. |
| China................................ | 16.3 | 18.6 | 11.0 |
| Czech Republic[4] ..................... | 3.3 | 5.4 | 0.0 |
| France .............................. | 6.3 | 3.0 | 1.8 |
| Germany ............................ | n.a. | 3.0 | 6.8 |
| Hungary............................. | 3.7 | n.a. | n.a. |
| Italy ................................ | 1.8 | 0.7 | 0.9 |

*Table 15.  (Continued)  Kyrgyzstan: Foreign Trade with Selected Countries, 1992–94*

|  | 1992 | 1993 | 1994 |
|---|---|---|---|
| Japan. | 0.2 | 0.1 | 2.7 |
| Korea, Republic of. | 0.7 | 0.2 | 4.0 |
| Netherlands | n.a. | 0.1 | 1.8 |
| Poland | 0.2 | 8.8 | 15.0 |
| Slovakia[4]. | 3.3 | 2.7 | 1.0 |
| Sweden | 0.0 | 0.1 | 2.6 |
| Switzerland. | n.a. | 0.3 | 2.5 |
| Turkey | 3.4 | 4.5 | 2.0 |
| Exports |  |  |  |
| Other countries[3] |  |  |  |
| Austria | 1.0 | 3.1 | 0.2 |
| China | 28.0 | 59.1 | 56.1 |
| France. | 6.8 | 0.0 | 2.2 |
| Italy. | 0.5 | 0.4 | 1.8 |
| Japan. | 2.7 | 0.0 | 0.0 |
| Korea, Democratic People's Republic of. | 3.4 | 0.2 | 0.6 |
| Poland | 0.3 | 2.6 | 3.9 |
| Sweden | 1.5 | 1.1 | n.a. |
| Turkey | 1.8 | 1.1 | 2.4 |
| United Kingdom | 11.6 | 30.0 | 29.5 |

[1] Percentage of total trade with former Soviet republics.
[2] n.a.—not available.
[3] In millions of United States dollars.
[4] 1992 amounts for Czechoslovakia; 1993 and 1994 amounts divided between Czech Republic and Slovakia.

Source: Based on information from World Bank, *Statistical Handbook 1995: States of the Former USSR*, Washington, 1995, 288-90.

*Table 16.  Tajikistan: Production of Principal Agricultural Crops,
1992–94*
(in thousands of tons)

| Crop | 1992 | 1993 | 1994 |
|---|---|---|---|
| Vegetables | 679 | 552 | 490 |
| Cottonseed | 415 | 382 | 401 |
| Wheat | 170 | 175 | 165 |
| Fruits and berries | 181 | 135 | 140 |
| Cotton lint | 126 | 150 | 135 |
| Watermelons | 136 | 107 | 105 |
| Grapes | 100 | 88 | 85 |
| Barley | 42 | 32 | 34 |
| Corn | 32 | 34 | 23 |

Source: Based on information from *The Europa World Year Book 1996*, 2, London, 1996,
3077.

*Table 17.  Tajikistan: Foreign Trade with Selected Countries,  1992–
94*

| | 1992 | 1993 | 1994 |
|---|---|---|---|
| Imports | | | |
| Former Soviet Union[1] | | | |
| Armenia | 0.2 | 0.0 | 0.1 |
| Azerbaijan | 1.1 | 0.5 | 0.1 |
| Belarus | 2.8 | 3.4 | 0.5 |
| Estonia | 0.3 | 0.1 | 0.3 |
| Georgia | 0.2 | 0.2 | 0.2 |
| Kazakstan | 12.2 | 32.9 | 13.2 |
| Kyrgyzstan | 2.0 | 1.1 | 0.4 |
| Latvia | 0.6 | 0.5 | 0.4 |
| Lithuania | 0.7 | 2.2 | 5.5 |
| Moldova | 0.3 | 0.2 | 0.0 |
| Russia | 46.7 | 42.1 | 24.4 |
| Turkmenistan | 14.5 | 13.1 | 15.9 |
| Ukraine | 7.3 | 2.2 | 5.5 |
| Uzbekistan | 11.0 | 32.9 | 33.5 |
| Exports | | | |
| Former Soviet Union[1] | | | |
| Armenia | 0.4 | 0.0 | 0.0 |

*Table 17. (Continued) Tajikistan: Foreign Trade with Selected Countries, 1992–94*

| | 1992 | 1993 | 1994 |
|---|---|---|---|
| Azerbaijan | 3.9 | 0.9 | 0.1 |
| Belarus | 4.1 | 5.6 | 2.8 |
| Estonia | 0.5 | 0.1 | 0.5 |
| Georgia | 0.1 | 0.0 | 0.0 |
| Kazakstan | 14.7 | 13.7 | 9.2 |
| Kyrgyzstan | 2.3 | 3.5 | 1.8 |
| Latvia | 0.8 | 6.1 | 3.1 |
| Lithuania | 0.2 | 3.8 | 12.4 |
| Moldova | 0.4 | 2.8 | 1.3 |
| Russia | 47.5 | 52.6 | 42.0 |
| Turkmenistan | 4.3 | 2.9 | 1.6 |
| Ukraine | 11.7 | 4.2 | 4.6 |
| Uzbekistan | 8.9 | 17.0 | 20.6 |
| Imports | | | |
| Other countries[2] | | | |
| Austria | n.a.[3] | 13 | 10 |
| Belgium | n.a. | 28 | 23 |
| France | n.a. | 43 | 2 |
| Italy | n.a. | 11 | 1 |
| Netherlands | n.a. | 165 | 16 |
| Sweden | n.a. | 34 | 2 |
| Switzerland | n.a. | 4 | 98 |
| Turkey | n.a. | 5 | 17 |
| United Kingdom | n.a. | 6 | 68 |
| United States | n.a. | 33 | 32 |
| Exports | | | |
| Other countries[2] | | | |
| Austria | n.a. | 12 | 17 |
| Belgium | n.a. | 19 | 30 |
| Finland | n.a. | 10 | 18 |
| Germany | n.a. | 1 | 13 |
| Japan | n.a. | 22 | 11 |
| Netherlands | n.a. | 143 | 148 |
| Sweden | n.a. | 19 | 1 |
| Switzerland | n.a. | 1 | 45 |
| United Kingdom | n.a. | 2 | 30 |
| United States | n.a. | 24 | 27 |

[1] Percentage of total trade with former Soviet republics.
[2] In millions of United States dollars.
[3] n.a.—not available.

Source: Based on information from World Bank, *Statistical Handbook 1995: States of the Former USSR*, Washington, 1995, 471–73.

Table 18.  *Turkmenistan: Production of Principal Agricultural Crops,*
*1992–94*
(in thousands of tons)

| Crop | 1992 | 1993 | 1994 |
|---|---|---|---|
| Wheat.................................... | 368 | 502 | 1,063 |
| Cottonseed ............................ | 822 | 721 | 830 |
| Cotton lint............................. | 390 | 402 | 403 |
| Corn.................................... | 147 | 202 | 252 |
| Melons and squash ....................... | 180 | 248 | 250 |
| Tomatoes................................ | 133 | 150 | 200 |
| Rice ................................... | 64 | 88 | 149 |
| Grapes.................................. | 91 | 79 | 147 |
| Barley.................................. | 124 | 197 | 108 |
| Onions.................................. | 71 | 98 | 100 |

Source: Based on information from *The Europa World Year Book 1996*, 2, London, 1996,
3201.

Table 19.  *Turkmenistan: Production of Principal Industrial Products,*
*1990–92*
(in thousands of tons unless otherwise indicated)

| Product | 1990 | 1991 | 1992 |
|---|---|---|---|
| Carpets and rugs (in thousands of square meters) ..... | 1,288 | 1,384 | 1,070 |
| Cement ......................................... | 1,085 | 904 | 1,051 |
| Cotton yarn..................................... | 416 | 420 | 437 |
| Diesel oil ....................................... | 1,573 | 2,236 | 1,942 |
| Electric power (in millions of kilowatt-hours) ......... | 16,637 | 14,915 | 13,136 |
| Gasoline........................................ | 773 | 814 | 1,031 |
| Heavy fuel oil................................... | 1,218 | 1,991 | 1,667 |
| Kerosene ....................................... | 110 | 98 | 327 |
| Vegetable oil ................................... | 105 | 104 | 85 |

Source: Based on information from *The Europa World Year Book 1995*, 2, London, 1995,
3071.

*Table 20. Turkmenistan: Trade with Republics of the Former Soviet Union, 1990–92*
(in percentages of total trade with former Soviet republics)

|  | 1990 | 1991 | 1992 |
|---|---|---|---|
| Imports |  |  |  |
| Armenia | n.a.[1] | n.a. | 0.4 |
| Azerbaijan | n.a. | n.a. | 8.5 |
| Belarus | 3.6 | 3.6 | 4.1 |
| Estonia | 2.9 | 2.9 | n.a. |
| Georgia | n.a. | n.a. | n.a. |
| Kazakstan | 4.0 | 4.0 | 11.8 |
| Kyrgyzstan | n.a. | n.a. | 1.4 |
| Latvia | n.a. | n.a. | n.a. |
| Lithuania | n.a. | n.a. | n.a. |
| Moldova | n.a. | n.a. | 0.0 |
| Russia | 41.8 | 41.8 | 35.1 |
| Tajikistan | n.a. | n.a. | 4.3 |
| Ukraine | 15.6 | 15.6 | 4.6 |
| Uzbekistan | 5.7 | 5.7 | 8.1 |
| Exports |  |  |  |
| Armenia | n.a. | 2.3 | 1.6 |
| Azerbaijan | n.a. | 3.9 | 4.3 |
| Belarus | 2.1 | 1.9 | 0.6 |
| Estonia | 2.3 | 2.4 | 0.5 |
| Georgia | n.a. | 6.7 | 7.5 |
| Kazakstan | 2.6 | 8.1 | 12.8 |
| Kyrgyzstan | n.a. | 3.1 | 0.5 |
| Latvia | n.a. | n.a. | 0.7 |
| Lithuania | n.a. | n.a. | 0.2 |
| Moldova | n.a. | 5.8 | 1.0 |
| Russia | 49.8 | 21.0 | 10.0 |
| Tajikistan | n.a. | 6.5 | 1.2 |
| Ukraine | 7.4 | 17.5 | 49.4 |
| Uzbekistan | 27.8 | 17.0 | 9.7 |

[1] n.a.—not available.

Source: Based on information from World Bank, *Statistical Handbook 1995: States of the Former USSR*, Washington, 1995, 503.

### Table 21. *Uzbekistan: Production of Principal Agricultural Crops, 1992–94*
### (in thousands of tons)

| Crop | 1992 | 1993 | 1994 |
|------|------|------|------|
| Vegetables[1] | 4,244 | 3,500 | 3,737 |
| Cottonseed | 2,452 | 2,537 | 2,380 |
| Wheat | 964 | 876 | 1,200 |
| Potatoes | 365 | 463 | 562 |
| Fruit | 701 | 520 | 555 |
| Rice | 539 | 545 | 544 |
| Grapes | 439 | 480 | 450 |
| Barley | 361 | 292 | 340 |
| Corn | 367 | 404 | 200 |

[1] Includes melons and squash.

Source: Based on information from *The Europa World Year Book 1996*, 2, London, 1996, 3501.

### Table 22. *Uzbekistan: Production of Principal Industrial Products, 1991–93*
### (in thousands of tons unless otherwise indicated)

| Product | 1991 | 1992 | 1993 |
|---------|------|------|------|
| Cement | 6,191 | 5,935 | 5,277 |
| Cotton fabric | 392 | 482 | 370 |
| Electric power (in millions of kilowatt-hours) | 54,164 | 50,911 | 49,272 |
| Footwear (in thousands of pairs) | 45,400 | 39,200 | 39,500 |
| Insecticides | 35 | 28 | 32 |
| Mineral fertilizers | 1,660 | 1,361 | 1,273 |
| Paper | 20 | 16 | 13 |
| Plastics | 142 | 115 | 53 |
| Refrigerators and freezers (in thousands of units) | 212 | 84 | 77 |
| Tractors (in thousands of units) | 21 | 17 | 8 |

Source: Based on information from *The Europa World Year Book 1996*, 2, London, 1996, 3501.

*Table 23.   Uzbekistan: Foreign Trade with Selected Countries, 1992–94*

|  | 1992 | 1993 | 1994 |
|---|---|---|---|
| **Imports** | | | |
| Former Soviet Union[1] | | | |
| Armenia............................... | 0.1 | 0.2 | 0.1 |
| Azerbaijan ............................ | 0.4 | 0.0 | 0.0 |
| Belarus................................ | 5.8 | 2.1 | 0.7 |
| Estonia................................ | 0.1 | 0.1 | 0.0 |
| Georgia............................... | 0.3 | 0.1 | 0.0 |
| Kazakstan............................. | 12.2 | 17.2 | 11.0 |
| Kyrgyzstan ........................... | 3.4 | 1.5 | 1.6 |
| Latvia................................. | 0.2 | 0.5 | 0.4 |
| Lithuania............................. | 0.5 | 0.3 | 1.1 |
| Moldova.............................. | 0.3 | 0.1 | 0.1 |
| Russia................................. | 52.9 | 58.9 | 55.0 |
| Tajikistan ............................ | 33.2 | 1.3 | 18.9 |
| Turkmenistan......................... | 7.0 | 11.3 | 6.0 |
| Ukraine .............................. | 13.6 | 6.5 | 5.1 |
| **Exports** | | | |
| Former Soviet Union[1] | | | |
| Armenia............................... | 0.2 | 0.2 | 0.1 |
| Azerbaijan ............................ | 0.9 | 0.0 | 0.0 |
| Belarus................................ | 3.5 | 3.1 | 1.9 |
| Estonia................................ | 0.9 | 0.1 | 0.0 |
| Georgia............................... | 0.3 | 0.1 | 0.0 |
| Kazakstan............................. | 11.2 | 16.9 | 17.3 |
| Kyrgyzstan ........................... | 3.7 | 2.8 | 3.7 |
| Latvia................................. | 0.6 | 0.1 | 0.4 |
| Lithuania............................. | 1.4 | 0.8 | 0.7 |
| Moldova.............................. | 2.0 | 0.2 | 0.1 |
| Russia................................. | 53.1 | 55.5 | 42.8 |
| Tajikistan ............................ | 3.0 | 6.0 | 19.0 |
| Turkmenistan......................... | 5.3 | 6.6 | 5.0 |
| **Imports** | | | |
| Other countries[2] | | | |
| Australia.............................. | 5 | 19 | 24 |
| Austria ............................... | 15 | 11 | 27 |
| Belgium .............................. | 31 | 13 | 15 |
| China................................. | 67 | 35 | 88 |
| Former Czechoslovakia[3].................. | 17 | 5 | 16 |
| France................................ | 5 | 14 | 11 |
| Germany.............................. | 28 | 56 | 164 |
| Hungary.............................. | 12 | 21 | 61 |

*Table 23.   (Continued)   Uzbekistan: Foreign Trade with Selected Countries, 1992–94*

|  | 1992 | 1993 | 1994 |
|---|---|---|---|
| Italy | 8 | 27 | 24 |
| Korea, Republic of | 1 | 9 | 26 |
| Netherlands | 2 | 102 | 52 |
| Poland | 15 | 44 | 17 |
| Sweden | 7 | 20 | 12 |
| Switzerland | 196 | 226 | 321 |
| Turkey | 35 | 229 | 68 |
| United Kingdom | 14 | 10 | 18 |
| United States | 21 | 32 | 95 |
| Exports | | | |
| Other countries[2] | | | |
| Australia | 4 | 16 | n.a.[4] |
| Austria | 29 | 12 | 42 |
| Belgium | 112 | 46 | 8 |
| China | 40 | 137 | 77 |
| France | 39 | 12 | 1 |
| Germany | 94 | 20 | 32 |
| Hungary | 52 | 30 | 2 |
| Italy | 11 | 17 | 26 |
| Korea, Republic of | 3 | 55 | 41 |
| Netherlands | 20 | 38 | 153 |
| Switzerland | 16 | 72 | 224 |
| Turkey | 77 | 41 | 42 |
| United Kingdom | 117 | 134 | 175 |
| United States | 38 | 44 | 21 |

[1] Percentage of total trade with former Soviet republics.
[2] In millions of United States dollars.
[3] For 1993 and 1994, figures of Czech Republic and Slovakia are combined.
[4] n.a.—not available.

Source: Based on information from World Bank, *Statistical Handbook 1995: States of the Former USSR, Washington,* 1995, 578–80.

# Bibliography

## Chapter 1

Adshead, Samuel Adrian M. *Central Asia in World History.* New York: St. Martin's Press, 1993.

Akiner, Shirin. *Islamic Peoples of the Soviet Union: An Historical and Statistical Handbook.* New York: Kegan Paul International, 1986.

Akiner, Shirin, ed. *Economic and Political Trends in Central Asia.* New York: Routledge & Kegan Paul, 1992.

Allworth, Edward, ed. *Central Asia: 120 Years of Russian Rule.* Durham: Duke University Press, 1989.

Allworth, Edward, ed. *Muslim Communities Reemerge: Historical Perspectives.* Durham: Duke University Press, 1994.

Bachmann, Berta. *Memories of Kazakhstan: A Report on the Life Experiences of a German Woman in Russia.* Lincoln, Nebraska: American History Society, 1983.

Bacon, Elizabeth E. *Central Asians under Russian Rule: A Study in Culture Change.* Ithaca: Cornell University Press, 1980.

Banuazizi, Ali, and Myron Weiner, eds. *The New Geopolitics of Central Asia and Its Borderlands.* Bloomington: Indiana University Press, 1994.

*Bilan du Monde: l'Année économique et sociale 1995.* Ed., Jacques-François Simon. Paris: Le Monde, 1996.

Blank, Stephen. "Energy, Economics, and Security in Central Asia: Russia and Its Rivals," *Central Asian Survey,* 14, No. 3, 1995, 373–406.

Bradley, Catherine. *Kazakhstan.* Brookfield, Connecticut: Millbrook Press, 1992.

Brezhnev, Leonid. *Virgin Lands: Two Years in Kazakhstan, 1954–55.* Tarrytown, New York: Elsevier Science, 1982.

Broxup, Marie. "Islam in Central Asia since Gorbachev," *Asian Affairs* [London], 18, October 1987, 283–93.

Carrère D'Encausse, Hélène. *Islam and the Russian Empire: Reform and Revolution in Central Asia.* Berkeley: University of California Press, 1989.

"Central Asia," *Current History,* 93, April 1994, 145–86.

Dave, Bhavna. "Kazakhstan Staggers under Its Nuclear Burden," *Transition*, November 17, 1995, 12–13.

Dave, Bhavna. "A New Parliament Consolidates Presidential Authority," *Transition*, March 22, 1996, 33-37.

Davis, Christopher M. "Health Care Crisis: The Former Soviet Union," *RFE/RL Research Report* [Munich], 2, No. 40, October 8, 1993, 35–43.

Dawisha, Karen, and Bruce Parrott. *Russia and the New States of Eurasia: The Politics of Upheaval.* Port Chester, New York: Cambridge University Press, 1994.

Deweese, Devin. *Islamization and Native Religion in the Golden Horde.* University Park: Pennsylvania State University Press, 1994.

Diuk, Nadia, and Adrian Karatnycky. *The Hidden Nations: The People Challenge the Soviet Union.* Fairfield, New Jersey: William Morrow, 1990.

Dorian, James P. "The Kazakh Oil Industry: A Potential Critical Role in Central Asia," *Energy Policy*, 22, August 1994, 685–98.

Eickelman, Dale F., ed. *Russia's Muslim Frontiers: New Directions in Cross-Cultural Analysis.* Bloomington: Indiana University Press, 1993.

*The Europa World Year Book 1993*, 2. London: Europa, 1993.

*The Europa World Year Book 1994*, 2. London: Europa, 1994.

*The Europa World Year Book 1995*, 2. London: Europa, 1995.

*The Europa World Year Book 1996*, 2. London: Europa, 1996.

Evans, John L. *Russia and the Khanates of Central Asia to 1865.* New York: Associated Faculty Press, 1982.

Ferdinand, Peter. *The New States of Central Asia and Their Neighbours.* New York: Council on Foreign Relations Press, 1994.

Fierman, William, ed. *Soviet Central Asia: The Failed Transformation.* Boulder, Colorado: Westview Press, 1991.

Forsythe, Rosemarie. "The Politics of Oil in the Caucasus and Central Asia," *Adelphi Papers*, 300, May 1996, whole issue.

Fuller, Graham. *Central Asia: The New Geopolitics.* Santa Monica, California: Rand, 1992.

Fuller, Graham. "Central Asia: The Quest for Identity," *Current History*, 93, April 1994, 145–49.

Fuller, Graham. "The Emergence of Central Asia," *Foreign Policy*, Spring 1990, 49–67.

Ghorban, Narsi. "The Role of the Multinational Oil Companies in the Development of Oil and Gas Resources in Central Asia and the Caucasus," *Iranian Journal of International Affairs*, 5, Spring 1993, 1–15.

Gross, Jo-Ann, ed. *Muslims in Central Asia: Expressions of Identity and Change.* Durham: Duke University Press, 1992.

Haghayeghi, Mehrdad. *Islam and Politics in Central Asia.* New York: St. Martin's Press, 1995.

Janabel, Jiger. "When National Ambition Conflicts with Reality: Studies on Kazakhstan's Ethnic Relations," *Central Asian Survey*, 15, No. 1, March 1996, 5–22.

Malik, Hafeez, ed. *Central Asia: Its Strategic Importance and Future Prospects.* New York: St. Martin's Press, 1994.

Mandelbaum, Michael, ed. *Central Asia and the World: Kazakhstan, Uzbekistan, Tajikistan, Kyrgyzstan, and Turkmenistan.* New York: Council on Foreign Relations Press, 1994.

Mesbahi, Mohiaddin, ed. *Central Asia and the Caucasus after the Soviet Union: Domestic and International Dynamics.* Gainesville: University Press of Florida, 1994.

*The Military Balance 1992–1993.* London: International Institute for Strategic Studies, 1992.

*The Military Balance 1993–1994.* London: International Institute for Strategic Studies, 1993.

*The Military Balance 1994–1995.* London: International Institute for Strategic Studies, 1994.

*The Military Balance 1995–1996.* London: International Institute for Strategic Studies, 1995.

*1995 Britannica Book of the Year.* Chicago: 1995.

Olcott, Martha Brill. "Central Asia's Islamic Awakening," *Current History*, 93, April 1994, 150–54.

Olcott, Martha Brill. *Central Asia's New States: Independence, Foreign Policy, and Regional Security.* Washington: United States Institute of Peace Press, 1996.

Olcott, Martha Brill. *The Kazakhs.* 2d ed. Studies of Nationalities in the USSR. Stanford, California: Hoover Institution Press, 1995.

Paksoy, H.B., ed. *Central Asia Reader: The Rediscovery of History.* Armonk, New York: M.E. Sharpe, 1994.

PlanEcon. *Review and Outlook for the Former Soviet Republics.* Washington: 1995.

Pomfret, Richard. *The Economies of Central Asia.* Princeton: Princeton University Press, 1995.

Potter, William C. "The 'Sapphire' File: Lessons for International Nonproliferation Cooperation," *Transition*, 1, November 17, 1995, 14–19.

Ro'i, Yaacov, ed. *Muslim Eurasia: Conflicting Legacies.* London: Frank Cass, 1995.

Rumer, Boris Z. *Soviet Central Asia: "A Tragic Experiment."* Boston: Unwin Hyman, 1989.

Rywkin, Michael. *Moscow's Muslim Challenge: Soviet Central Asia.* Armonk, New York: M.E. Sharpe, 1990.

*The Statesman's Year-Book 1992–1993.* Ed., Brian Hunter. New York: St. Martin's Press, 1992.

*The Statesman's Year-Book 1993–1994.* Ed., Brian Hunter. New York: St. Martin's Press, 1993.

*The Statesman's Year-Book 1994–1995.* Ed., Brian Hunter. New York: St. Martin's Press, 1994.

*The Statesman's Year-Book 1995–1996.* Ed., Brian Hunter. New York: St. Martin's Press, 1995.

Undeland, Charles, and Nicholas Platt. *The Central Asian Republics: Fragments of Empire, Magnets of Wealth.* New York: Asia Society, 1994.

United Nations. Department for Economic and Social Information and Policy Analysis. *Demographic Yearbook 1993.* New York: 1995.

United States. Central Intelligence Agency. *Handbook of International Economic Statistics 1995.* Washington: GPO, 1995.

United States. Central Intelligence Agency. *Kazakhstan: An Economic Profile.* Springfield, Virginia: National Technical Information Service, 1993.

United States. Central Intelligence Agency. *The World Factbook 1994.* Washington: GPO, 1994.

United States. Central Intelligence Agency. *The World Factbook 1995.* Washington: GPO, 1995.

United States. Department of State. Bureau of International Narcotics Matters. *International Narcotics Strategy Report March 1996.* Washington: GPO, 1996.

WEFA Group. *Eurasia Economic Outlook, February 1996.* Eddystone, Pennsylvania: 1996.

Wixman, Ronald. *Peoples of the USSR: An Ethnographic Handbook.* Armonk, New York: M.E. Sharpe, 1984.

World Bank. *Kazakhstan: Agricultural Sector Review.* Washington: 1994.

World Bank. *Kazakhstan: The Transition to a Market Economy.* Washington: 1993.

World Bank. *Statistical Handbook 1995: States of the Former USSR.* Washington: 1995.

*World Radio TV Handbook 1996.* Ed., Andrew G. Sennitt. Amsterdam: Billboard, 1996.

*Worldwide Directory of Defense Authorities 1996,* 1. Ed., Kenneth Gause. Bethesda, Maryland: Worldwide Government Directories, 1996.

(Various issues of the following publications also were used in the preparation of this chapter: *Christian Science Monitor;* Foreign Broadcast Information Service, *Daily Report: Central Eurasia;* Foreign Broadcast Information Service, *FBIS Report: Environment and World Health* (before August 1995, *FBIS Report: Environment*); *Keesing's Record of World Events* [Cambridge]; Jamestown Foundation, *Monitor* and *Prism; New York Times; Transition;* and *Washington Post.*)

## Chapter 2

Adshead, Samuel Adrian M. *Central Asia in World History.* New York: St. Martin's Press, 1993.

Akchurin, Marat. "Soviet Muslims: Seeking Reform, Not Revolution," *World and I,* 6, October 1991, 86–93.

Akiner, Shirin. *Islamic Peoples of the Soviet Union: An Historical and Statistical Handbook.* New York: Routledge, 1986.

Akiner, Shirin, ed. *Central Asia: 130 Years of Russian Dominance, an Historical Overview.* Durham: Duke University Press, 1994.

Akiner, Shirin, ed. *Economic and Political Trends in Central Asia.* New York: Routledge & Kegan Paul, 1992.

Allworth, Edward, ed. *Central Asia: 120 Years of Russian Rule.* Durham: Duke University Press, 1989.

Alptekin, Erkin. "Chinese Policy in Eastern Turkestan," *Institute of Muslim Minority Affairs Journal,* 13, January 1992, 185–95.

Andreyev, Nikolai. "Central Asia: From Marx to Mohammed," *New Times International* [Moscow], No. 39, 1992, 19–22.

Andreyev, Nikolai. "What Future for Uzbekistan, Kirgizia, Turk-menia?" *Current Digest of the Post-Soviet Press*, 44, July 22, 1992, 8–11.

Aziz, Sartaj. "The Rediscovery of Central Asia," *Economics Review* [Karachi], 23, June 1992, 15–17.

Baldick, Julian. *Imaginary Muslims: The Uwaysi Sufis of Central Asia.* Irvington: New York University Press, 1994.

Banuazizi, Ali, and Myron Weiner, eds. *The New Geopolitics of Central Asia and Its Borderlands.* Bloomington: Indiana University Press, 1994.

Baumann, Robert F. *Russian-Soviet Unconventional Wars in the Caucasus, Central Asia, and Afghanistan.* Fort Leavenworth, Kansas: Combat Studies Institute, 1993.

Bourdeaux, Michael, ed. *The Politics of Religion in Russia and the New States of Eurasia.* Armonk, New York: M.E. Sharpe, 1995.

Brown, Bess. "Central Asia: The First Year of Unexpected State-hood," *RFE/RL Research Report* [Munich], 2, No. 1, January 1, 1993, 25–36.

Brown, Bess. "Three Central Asian States Form Economic Union," *RFE/RL Research Report* [Munich], 3, No. 11, April 1, 1994, 33–35.

"Central Asia: Five-State Commonwealth Set Up," *Current Digest of the Post-Soviet Press*, 45, February 3, 1993, 1–8.

"Central Asia: Patterns of Change, Past, Present, and Future," *Harvard International Report*, 15, Spring 1993, 6–12.

Clark, Susan L. *Security in Russia and Eurasia: The New National Militaries and Emerging Defense Policies.* Boulder, Colorado: Westview Press, 1995.

Davis, Christopher M. "Health Care Crisis: The Former Soviet Union," *RFE/RL Research Report* [Munich], 2, No. 40, October 8, 1993, 35–43.

Dawisha, A.I., and Karen Dawisha, eds. *The Foreign Policy Interests of Russia and the New States of Eurasia.* Armonk, New York: M.E. Sharpe, 1995.

Dawisha, Karen, and Bruce Parrott. *Russia and the New States of Eurasia: The Politics of Upheaval.* Port Chester, New York: Cambridge University Press, 1994.

Deweese, Devin. *Islamization and Native Religion in the Golden Horde.* University Park: Pennsylvania State University Press, 1994.

Dienes, Leslie. "Economic Geographic Relations in the Post-Soviet Republics," *Post-Soviet Geography*, 34, October 1993, 497–529.

Diller, Daniel C., ed. *Russia and the Independent States.* Washington: Congressional Quarterly, 1993.

Doolotaliyev, S. "Some Issues in the Development of the Sary-Dzhaz Mining Industrial Center, Kirghiz SSR," *Sovetskaya Geografiya*, 30, May 1989, 371–4.

Eickelman, Dale F., ed. *Russia's Muslim Frontiers: New Directions in Cross-Cultural Analysis.* Bloomington: Indiana University Press, 1993.

Elebayeva, Aynur B. "The Osh Incident: Problems for Research," *Post-Soviet Geography*, 33, February 1992, 78–86.

*The Europa World Year Book 1994*, 2. London: Europa, 1994.

*The Europa World Year Book 1995*, 2. London: Europa, 1995.

*The Europa World Year Book 1996*, 2. London: Europa, 1996.

Evans, John L. *Russia and the Khanates of Central Asia to 1865.* New York: Associated Faculty Press, 1982.

Ferdinand, Peter. *The New States of Central Asia and Their Neighbors.* New York: Council on Foreign Relations Press, 1994.

Fierman, William, ed. *Soviet Central Asia: The Failed Transformation.* Boulder, Colorado: Westview Press, 1991.

Fuller, Graham. *Central Asia: The New Geopolitics.* Santa Monica, California: Rand, 1992.

Furtado, Charles F., and Henry R. Huttenback, eds. "The Ex-Soviet Nationalities Without Gorbachev," *Nationalities Papers*, 20, Fall 1992, 1–124.

Gleason, Gregory. "The Political Economy of Dependency under Socialism: The Asian Republics in the USSR," *Studies in Comparative Communism*, 24, December 1991, 335–53.

Goron, Leonard, and Alex Pravda, eds. *Who's Who in Russia and the New States.* London: I.B. Tauris, 1993.

Gross, Jo-Ann, ed. *Muslims in Central Asia: Expressions of Identity and Change.* Durham: Duke University Press, 1992.

Haghayeghi, Mehrdad. *Islam and Politics in Central Asia.* New York: St. Martin's Press, 1995.

Henze, Paul B. *Whither Turkestan?* Santa Monica, California: Rand, 1992.

Hostler, Charles Warren. *The Turks of Central Asia.* Westport, Connecticut: Praeger, 1993.

Kaiser, Robert J. *The Geography of Nationalism in Russia and the USSR.* Princeton: Princeton University Press, 1994.

Karasik, Theodore. *Azerbaijan, Central Asia, and Future Persian Gulf Security.* Santa Monica, California: Rand, 1993.

Kedzie, Christopher R. *Stumbling Blocks and Stepping Stones: The Crossing from Soviet Domination to Self Rule in the Republics of Central Asia.* Santa Monica, California: Rand, 1994.

Landau, Jacob M. *Pan-Turkism: From Irredentism to Cooperation.* Bloomington: Indiana University Press, 1995.

Lipski, Andrei. "The Community of Central Asia: Inside or Outside the CIS?" *International Affairs* [Moscow], October 1993, 51–5.

Maier, Frith. *Trekking in Russia and Central Asia: A Traveler's Guide.* Seattle: Mountaineers Books, 1994.

Malik, Hafeez, ed. *Central Asia: Its Strategic Importance and Future Prospects.* New York: St. Martin's Press, 1994.

Mandelbaum, Michael, ed. *Central Asia and the World: Kazakhstan, Uzbekistan, Tajikistan, Kyrgyzstan, and Turkmenistan.* New York: Council on Foreign Relations Press, 1994.

Manz, Beatrice F., ed. *Central Asia in Historical Perspective.* Boulder, Colorado: Westview Press, 1994.

Martin, Keith. "Environment: Central Asia's Forgotten Tragedy," *RFE/RL Research Report* [Munich], 3, No. 29, July 29, 1994, 35–48.

Mesbahi, Mohiaddin, ed. *Central Asia and the Caucasus after the Soviet Union: Domestic and International Dynamics.* Gainesville: University Press of Florida, 1994.

Migranyan, Andranik. "Russia and the Near Abroad," *Current Digest of the Post-Soviet Press,* 47, March 9, 1994, 1–4 and March 16, 1994, 6–11.

*The Military Balance 1993–1994.* London: International Institute for Strategic Studies, 1993.

*The Military Balance 1994–1995.* London: International Institute for Strategic Studies, 1994.

*The Military Balance 1995–1996.* London: International Institute for Strategic Studies, 1995.

Naumkin, Vitaly. *State, Religion, and Society in Central Asia: A Post-Soviet Critique.* London: Ithaca Press, 1993.

Olcott, Martha Brill. *Central Asia's New States: Independence, Foreign Policy, and Regional Security.* Washington: United States Institute of Peace Press, 1996.

Paksoy, G.B., ed. *Central Asia Reader: The Rediscovery of History.* Armonk, New York: M.E. Sharpe, 1994.

Pilkington, John. "Kyrgyzstan: A Tale of Two Journeys," *Geographical Magazine,* 65, April 1993, 8–12.

Pipes, Daniel. "The Politics of the 'Rip Van Winkel' States: The Southern Tier States of the Ex-Soviet Union Have Moved the Borders of the Middle East North," *Middle East Insight,* 10, November–December 1993, 30–40.

PlanEcon. *Review and Outlook for the Former Soviet Republics.* Washington: 1995.

Pryde, Ian. "Kyrgyzstan: Secularism vs. Islam," *World Today,* 48, November 1992, 208–11.

Pryde, Ian. "Kyrgyzstan: The Trials of Independence," *Journal of Democracy,* 5, January 1994, 109–20.

Rashid, Ahmed. *The Resurgence of Central Asia: Islam or Nationalism?* Karachi: Oxford University Press, 1994.

Ro'i, Yaacov, ed. *Muslim Eurasia: Conflicting Legacies.* London: Frank Cass, 1995.

Rotor, Igor. "Kyrgyzstan: Capitalist Experiment in Central Asia," *Current Digest of the Post-Soviet Press,* 44, April 8, 1992, 4–5.

Rumer, Boris Z. *Soviet Central Asia: "A Tragic Experiment."* Winchester, Massachusetts: Unwin Hyman, 1990.

Shlapentokh, Vladimir, Munir Sendich, and Emil Payin, eds. *The New Russian Diaspora: Russian Minorities in the Former Soviet Republics.* Armonk, New York: M.E. Sharpe, 1994.

Shome, Parthasarathi, and Julio Escolano. "The State of Tax Policy in the Central Asian and Transcaucasian Newly Independent States," *Bulletin of International Fiscal Documentation,* 48, April 1994, 159–66.

Shukurov, E., ed. *Discovery of Kyrghyzstan.* Bishkek: International Foundation "A Discovery of Kyrghyzstan," 1993.

Sparks, John. *Realms of the Russian Bear: A Natural History of Russia and the Central Asian Republics.* Waltham, Massachusetts: Little Brown, 1992.

Starr, S. Frederick, ed. *The Legacy of History in Russia and the New States of Eurasia.* Armonk, New York: M.E. Sharpe, 1994.

*The Statesman's Year-Book 1993-1994.* Ed., Brian Hunter. New York: St. Martin's Press, 1993.

*The Statesman's Year-Book 1994–1995.* Ed., Brian Hunter. New York: St. Martin's Press, 1994.

*The Statesman's Year-Book 1995–1996.* Ed., Brian Hunter. New York: St. Martin's Press, 1995.

Szporluk, Roman, ed. *National Identity and Ethnicity in Russia and the New States of Eurasia.* Armonk, New York: M.E. Sharpe, 1994.

Thomas, Paul. *The Central Asian States: Tajikistan, Uzbekistan, Kyrgyzstan, Turkmenistan.* Brookfield, Connecticut: Millbrook Press, 1992.

United Nations. Department for Economic and Social Information and Policy Analysis. *Demographic Yearbook 1994.* New York: 1996.

United States. Central Intelligence Agency. *Handbook of International Economic Statistics 1995.* Washington: GPO, 1995.

United States. Central Intelligence Agency. *The World Factbook 1994.* Washington: GPO, 1994.

United States. Department of State. Bureau of International Narcotics Matters. *International Narcotics Strategy Report March 1996.* Washington: GPO, 1996.

WEFA Group. *Eurasia Economic Outlook February 1996.* Eddystone, Pennsylvania: 1996.

Wixman, Ronald. *Peoples of the USSR: An Ethnographic Handbook.* Armonk, New York: M.E. Sharpe, 1984.

World Bank. *Kyrgyzstan: Social Protection in a Reforming Economy.* Washington: 1993.

World Bank. *Kyrgyzstan: The Transition to a Market Economy.* Washington: 1993.

World Bank. *Kyrgyz Republic: Agricultural Sector Review.* Washington: 1995.

World Bank. *Kyrgyz Republic: Economic Report.* Washington: 1994.

World Bank. *Kyrgyz Republic: Energy Sector Review.* Washington: 1995.

World Bank. *Kyrgyz Republic: National Environmental Action Plan.* Washington: 1995.

World Bank. *Kyrgyz Republic: Poverty Assessment and Strategy.* Washington: 1995.

World Bank. *Statistical Handbook 1995: States of the Former USSR.* Washington: 1995.

*World Radio TV Handbook 1996.* Ed., Andrew G. Sennitt. Amsterdam: Billboard, 1996.

*Worldwide Directory of Defense Authorities, 1996,* 1. Ed., Kenneth Gause. Bethesda, Maryland: Worldwide Government Directories, 1996.

(Various issues of the following periodicals also were used in the preparation of this chapter: *Christian Science Monitor;* Foreign Broadcast Information Service, *Daily Report: Central Eurasia;* Jamestown Foundation, *Monitor* and *Prism; Keesing's Record of World Events* [Cambridge]; *New York Times; Transition;* and *Washington Post.*)

# Chapter 3

Akademiya nauk SSSR. Institut etnografii. *Sotsial'no-kul'turnyy oblik sovetskikh natsiy* (The Social-Cultural Aspect of the Soviet Nations). Moscow: Nauka, 1986.

Akademiya nauk Tadzhikskoy SSR. *Istoriya tadzhikskogo naroda* (A History of the Tajik People), 3. Moscow: Nauka, 1965.

Akademiya nauk Tadzhikskoy SSR. *Tadzhikistan: priroda i resursy* (Tajikistan: Nature and Resources). Dushanbe: Donish, 1982.

Akademiya nauk Tadzhikskoy SSR. *Tadzhikskaya Sovetskaya Sotsialisticheskaya Respublika* (The Tajik Soviet Socialist Republic). Ed., M.S. Asimov. Dushanbe: 1974.

Allworth, Edward, ed. *Central Asia: A Century of Russian Rule.* New York: Columbia University Press, 1967.

Allworth, Edward, ed. *The Nationality Question in Soviet Central Asia.* New York: Praeger, 1973.

Amnesty International. *Tadzhikistan.* London: 1993.

Andreyev, M.S. "Po etnografii tadzhikov: Nekotoryye svedeniya" (On the Ethnography of the Tajiks: Some Information). Pages 151–77 in *Tadzhikistan.* Tashkent: Obshchestvo dlya izucheniya Tadzhikistana i iranskikh narodnostey za yego predelami, 1925.

Atkin, Muriel. "Islamic Assertiveness and the Waning of the Old Soviet Order," *Nationalities Papers,* 20, No. 1, Spring 1992, 55–72.

Atkin, Muriel. "Religious, National, and Other Identities in Central Asia." Pages 46–72 in Jo Ann Gross, ed., *Muslims in Central Asia.* Durham: Duke University Press, 1992.

Atkin, Muriel. *The Subtlest Battle: Islam in Soviet Tajikistan.* Philadelphia: Foreign Policy Research Institute, 1989.

Atkin, Muriel. "The Survival of Islam in Soviet Tajikistan," *Middle East Journal,* 43, No. 4, Autumn 1989, 605–18.

Atkin, Muriel. "Tajikistan: Ancient Heritage, New Politics." Pages 361–83 in Ian Bremmer and Ray Taras, eds., *Nation and Politics in the Soviet Successor States.* Cambridge: Cambridge University Press, 1993.

Bacon, Elizabeth. *Central Asians under Russian Rule.* Ithaca: Cornell University Press, 1980.

Bartol'd, Vasilii Vladimirovich. *Histoire des Turcs d'Asie centrale.* Trans., M. Donskis. Philadelphia: Porcupine Press, 1977.

Bartol'd, Vasilii Vladimirovich. *Turkestan Down to the Mongol Invasion.* London: Lazac, 1968.

Becker, Seymour. "National Consciousness and the Politics of the Bukharan People's Counciliar Republic." Pages 159–67 in Edward Allworth, ed., *The Nationality Question in Soviet Central Asia.* New York: Praeger, 1973.

Becker, Seymour. *Russia's Protectorates in Central Asia: Bukhara and Khiva, 1865–1924.* Cambridge: Harvard University Press, 1968.

Bourdeaux, Michael, ed. *The Politics of Religion in Russia and the New States of Eurasia.* Armonk, New York: M.E. Sharpe, 1995.

Bremmer, Ian, and Ray Taras, eds. *Nation and Politics in the Soviet Successor States.* Cambridge: Cambridge University Press, 1993.

Canfield, Robert L., ed. *Turko-Persia in Historical Perspective.* Cambridge: Cambridge University Press, 1991.

Carrère d'Encausse, Hélène. *Réforme et révolution chez les Musulmans de l'Empire russe.* Paris: Librarie Armand Colin, 1966.

Corbin, Henry. "Nasir-i Khusrau and Iranian Isma'ilism." Pages 520–42 in Richard N. Frye, ed., *The Cambridge History of Iran,* 4. Cambridge: Cambridge University Press, 1975.

Davis, Christopher M. "Health Care Crisis: The Former Soviet Union," *RFE/RL Research Report* [Munich], 2, No. 40, October 8, 1993, 35–43.

Drobizheva, L.M. "Kul'tura i mezhnatsional'yye otnosheniya v SSSR" (Culture and Inter-national Relations in the USSR), *Voprosy istorii* [Moscow], 1979, No. 11, 3–15.

Dzharylgasimova, R.Sh., and L.S. Tolstova, eds. *Etnicheskiye protsessy u natsional'nykh grupp Sredney Azii i Kazakhstana* (Ethnic Processes in the National Groups of Central Asia and Kazakstan). Moscow: Nauka, 1980.

Entsiklopediyai sovetii Tojik (Soviet Tajik Encyclopedia). Dushanbe: Sarredaktsiyai ilmii entsiklopediyai sovetii Tojik, 1978–1987.

*The Europa World Year Book 1994*, 2. London: Europa, 1994.

*The Europa World Year Book 1995*, 2. London: Europa, 1995.

*The Europa World Year Book 1996*, 2. London: Europa, 1996.

Fedorova, T.I. *Goroda Tadzhikistana i problemy rosta i razvitiya* (Cities of Tajikistan and Problems of Growth and Development). Dushanbe: Irfon, 1981.

Feshbach, Murray, and Alfred Friendly, Jr. *Ecocide in the USSR: Health and Nature under Siege.* New York: Basic Books, 1992.

*The FirstBook* [sic] *of Demographics for the Republics of the Former Soviet Union, 1951–1990.* Shady Side, Maryland: New World Demographics, 1992.

Freidin, Gregory. "Coup II," *The New Republic*, 205, No. 16, October 14, 1991, 16–18.

Frye, Richard N. *Bukhara: The Medieval Achievement.* Norman: University of Oklahoma Press, 1965.

Frye, Richard N. "The Samanids." Pages 136–61 in Richard N. Frye, *The Cambridge History of Iran.* Cambridge: Cambridge University Press, 1975.

Frye, Richard N., ed. *The Cambridge History of Iran.* Cambridge: Cambridge University Press, 1975.

Gleason, Gregory. "The Struggle for Control over Water in Central Asia: Republican Sovereignty and Collective Action." *RFE/RL Report on the USSR* [Munich], 3, No. 25, June 21, 1991, 11–19.

Gretsky, Sergei. "Civil War in Tajikistan and Its International Repercussions," *Critique*, Spring 1995, 3–24.

Gretsky, Sergei. "Qadi Akbar Turajonzoda," *Central Asia Monitor*, 1994, No. 1, 16–24.

Gretsky, Sergei. "Russia and Tajikistan." Pages 231–51 in A.Z. Rubinstein and O.M. Smolansky, eds. *Regional Power Rivalries* in the New Eurasia: Russia, Turkey, and Iran. Armonk, New York: M.E. Sharpe, 1995.

Grousset, Rene. *The Empire of the Steppes*. Trans., N. Walford. New Brunswick: Rutgers University Press, 1970.

Hambly, Gavin, ed. *Central Asia*. New York: Delacorte Press, 1969.

Helsinki Watch. *Conflict in the Soviet Union*. New York: Human Rights Watch, 1991.

Hitchins, Keith. "Modern Tajik Literature." Pages 454–75 in E. Yarshater, ed., *Persian Literature*. Albany: Bibliotheca Persica, 1988.

Hooson, David. *The Soviet Union: People and Regions*. Belmont, California: Wadsworth, 1966.

*Istoriya kul'turnogo stroitel'stva v Tadzhikistane, 1917–1977 gg* (The History of Cultural Construction in Tajikistan, 1917–1977, 2.) Dushanbe: Donish, 1983.

Karasik, Theodore, ed. *USSR Facts and Figures Annual 1992*. Gulf Breeze, Florida: Academic International Press, 1992.

Kojaoglu, T. "The Existence of a Bukharan Nationality in the Recent Past." Pages 151–8 in Edward Allworth, ed., *The Nationality Question in Soviet Central Asia*. New York: Praeger, 1973.

"Konflikt na granitse Kirgizii i Tadzhikistana" (Conflict on the Border of Kyrgyzia and Tajikistan), *Turkestan* [Ashgabat], 1990, No. 1, 5.

Korsunskiy, L. "Podzemnyy atomnyy gulag deystvuyet" (An Underground Atomic Gulag Is in Operation). *Stolitsa* [Moscow] 1992, No. 35, 22–6.

Krader, Lawrence. *Peoples of Central Asia*. Uralic and Altaic Series, No. 26. Bloomington: Indiana University Press, 1963.

*The Military Balance 1993–1994*. London: International Institute for Strategic Studies, 1993.

*The Military Balance 1994-1995*. London: International Institute for Strategic Studies, 1994.

*The Military Balance 1995–1996*. London: International Institute for Strategic Studies, 1995.

Monogarova, L.F. "Evolyutsiya natsional'nogo samosoznaniya pripamirskikh narodnostey" (The Evolution of National Self-Awareness of the Pamiri Peoples). Pages 125–35 in

*Etnicheskiye protsessy u natsional'nykh grupp Sredney Azii i Kazakhstana.* Moscow: Nauka, 1980.

Nahaylo, Bohdan, and Viktor Swoboda. *Soviet Disunion.* New York: The Free Press, 1990.

"Natsional'nyy vopros i mezhnatsional'nyye otnosheniya v SSSR: Istoriya i sovremennost'" (The National Question and Inter-national Relations in the USSR: History and the Present). *Voprosy istorii,* 1989, No. 5, 3–97.

*1995 Britannica Book of the Year.* Chicago: 1995.

Olcott, Martha Brill. "The Basmachi or Freemen's Revolt in Turkestan 1918–1924," *Soviet Studies,* 33, No. 3, July 1981, 352–69.

Park, A.G. *Bolshevism in Turkestan, 1917–1927.* New York: Columbia University Press, 1957.

Pierce, Richard A. *Russian Central Asia, 1867–1917.* Berkeley: University of California Press, 1960.

Rakowska–Harmstone, Teresa. *Russia and Nationalism in Central Asia: The Case of Tadzhikistan.* Baltimore: Johns Hopkins Press, 1970.

Rubinstein, Alvin Z., and Oles M. Smolansky, eds. *Regional Power Rivalries in the New Eurasia: Russia, Turkey, and Iran.* Armonk, New York: M.E. Sharpe, 1995.

Rubin, Barry M. "The Fragmentation of Tajikistan," *Survival,* 35, No. 4, Winter 1993–1994, 71–91.

Rumer, Boris Z. *Soviet Central Asia: "A Tragic Experiment."* Boston: Unwin Hyman, 1989.

"Russia: World Drugs Capital?" *The Economist Foreign Report,* April 27, 1995, 3–4.

Sharipov, I. *Zakonomernosti formirovaniya sotsialisticheskikh obshchestvennykh otnosheniy v Tadzhikistane* (The Regularity of the Formation of Socialist Social Relations in Tajikistan). Dushanbe: Donish, 1983.

Shukurov, Maksud Rakhmatullayevich. *Kul'turnaya zhizn' Tadzhikistana* (The Cultural Life of Tajikistan). Dushanbe: Irfon, 1980.

Simon, Gerhard. *Nationalism and Policy Toward the Nationalities in the Soviet Union.* Trans., K. Forster and O. Forster. Boulder, Colorado: Westview Press, 1991.

Smirnov, Yu. "Strannyy Islam" (Strange Islam), *Pamir,* No. 2, 1988, 104–25.

Soviet Union. Central Statistical Administration. *Chislennost' i sostav naseleniy SSSR* (Size and Composition of the Populations of the USSR). Moscow: Finansy i statistika, 1984.

Soviet Union. State Committee on Statistics. *Chislennost' naseleniya soyuznykh respublik po gorodskim poseleniyam i rayonam* (Size of the Population of the Union Republics by Urban Settlement and District). Moscow: Informatsionno-izdatel'skiy tsentr Goskomstata SSSR, 1991.

Soviet Union. State Committee on Statistics. *Demograficheskiy yezhegodnik SSSR 1990* (Demographic Yearbook of the USSR 1990). Moscow: Finansy i statistika, 1990.

Soviet Union. State Committee on Statistics. *Soyuznyye respubliki: Osnovnyye ekonomicheskiye i sotsial'nyye pokazateli* (The Union Republics: Basic Economic and Social Indicators). Moscow: Informatsionno-izdatel'skiy tsentr Goskomstata SSSR, 1991.

*The Statesman's Year-Book 1994–1995.* Ed., Brian Hunter. New York: St. Martin's Press, 1994.

*The Statesman's Year-Book 1995–1996.* Ed., Brian Hunter. New York: St. Martin's Press, 1995.

Symon, L. "Tadzhikistan: A Developing Country in the Soviet Union," *Asian Affairs,* 61, pt. 3, October 1974, 249–56.

Tadjbakhsh, Shahrbanou. "Causes and Consequences of the Civil War," *Central Asia Monitor,* 1993, No. 1, 10–14.

Tadjbakhsh, Shahrbanou. "The 'Tajik Spring' of 1992," *Central Asia Monitor,* No. 2, 1993, 21–9.

*Tadzhikistan.* Tashkent: Obshchestvo dlya izucheniya Tadzhikistana i iranskikh narodnostey za yego predelami, 1925.

Tajik SSR. Supreme Soviet. Presidium. "Soobshcheniye komissii Prezidiuma Verkhovnogo Soveta Tadzhikskoy SSR po proverke sobytiy 12–14 fevralya 1990 g. v Dushanbe" (Report of the Commission of the Presidium of the Supreme Soviet of the Tajik SSR on Examining the Events of February 12–14, 1990, in Dushanbe), *Sogdiana* [Dushanbe],1990. No. 3, entire issue.

United Nations. Department for Economic and Social Information and Policy Analysis. *Demographic Yearbook 1993.* New York: 1995.

United States. Central Intelligence Agency. *The World Factbook 1994.* Washington: GPO, 1994.

United States. Congress. Commission on Security and Cooperation in Europe. *Report on the Helsinki Commission Visit to Armenia, Azerbaijan, Tajikistan, Uzbekistan, Kazakhstan, and Ukraine.* Washington: GPO, 1992.

United States. Congress. 103d, 2d Session. House of Representatives. Foreign Affairs Subcommittee on Europe and the Middle East. Prepared testimony of Holly Burkhalter of Human Rights Watch/Helsinki, Sept. 22, 1994. Washington: GPO, 1994.

United States. Congress. 103d, 2d Session. House of Representatives. Subcommittee on International Security, International Operations, and Human Rights. Testimony from Pamela B. Cohen, National President, and Micah H. Naftalin, National Director of the Union of Councils, April 26, 1994. Washington: GPO, 1994.

United States. Department of State. Bureau of International Narcotics Matters. *International Narcotics Strategy Report March 1996.* Washington: GPO, 1996.

Veselovskiy, Vladimir Glebovich, et al. *Arkhitektura sovetskogo Tadzhikistana* (The Architecture of Soviet Tajikistan). Moscow: Stroyizdat, 1987.

Vinnikov, Ya. R. "Natsional'nyye i etnograficheskiye gruppy Sredney Azii po dannym etnicheskoy statistiki" (The National and Ethnographic Groups of Central Asia According to Ethnic Statistical Data). Pages 11–42 in R. Sh. Dzharylgasimova and L.S. Tolstova, eds., *Etnicheskiye protsessy u natsional'nykh grupp Sredney Azii i Kazakhstana.* Moscow: Nauka, 1980.

Wheeler, Geoffrey. *The Modern History of Soviet Central Asia.* New York: Praeger, 1964.

World Bank. *Statistical Handbook 1995: States of the Former USSR.* Washington: 1995.

*World Radio TV Handbook 1996.* Ed., Andrew G. Sennitt. Amsterdam: Billboard: 1996.

*Worldwide Directory of Defense Authorities*, 2. Ed., Kenneth Gause. Bethesda, Maryland: Worldwide Government Directories, 1996.

Wright, R. "Report from Turkestan," *New Yorker*, April 6, 1992, 53–75.

Yarshater, Ehsan, ed. *Persian Literature.* Albany: Bibliotheca Persica, 1988.

(Various issues of the following periodicals also were used in the preparation of this chapter: *Central Asia Monitor; Christian Science Monitor; Current Digest of the Post-Soviet Press; Daily Telegraph;* Foreign Broadcast Information Service, *Daily Report: Central Asia; Financial Times* [London]; *Guardian* [London]; *Izvestiya* [Moscow]; *Jane's Intelligence Review* [Coulsdon, United Kingdom]; *Literaturnaya gazeta* [Moscow]; *Los Angeles Times; Manchester Guardian Weekly* [London]; *Le Monde* [Paris]; *Moscow News* [Moscow]; *New York Times; Nezavisimaya gazeta* [Moscow]; *Pravda* [Moscow]; *RFE/RL Daily Report* [Munich]; *RFE/RL Research Report* [Munich]; *Times* [London]; *Tojikistoni Shuravi* [Dushanbe]; *Tojikistoni Soveti* [Dushanbe]; *Transition;* and *Washington Post.*)

## Chapter 4

Ahmed, Akbar, and David Hart, eds. *Islam in Tribal Societies.* London: Routledge and Kegan Paul, 1984.

Allworth, Edward, ed. *Central Asia: 120 Years of Russian Rule.* Durham: Duke University Press, 1989.

Anderson, John. "Authoritarian Political Development in Central Asia: The Case of Turkmenistan," *Central Asian Survey* [Abingdon, United Kingdom], 14, No. 4, 1995, 509–28.

Bacon, Elizabeth. *Central Asians under Russian Rule: A Study in Culture Change.* Ithaca: Cornell University Press, 1980.

Bartol'd, Vasilii Vladimirovich. "A History of the Turkman People (An Outline)." Pages 73–170 in *Four Studies on the History of Central Asia* III. Trans., V. and T. Minorsky. Leiden: E.J. Brill, 1962.

Barylski, Robert V. "The Caucasus, Central Asia, and the Near-Abroad Syndrome," *Central Asia Monitor,* No. 4, 1993, 31.

Basilov, Vladimir Nikolayevich. "Honor Groups in Traditional Turkmenian Society." Pages 220–43 in Akbar Ahmed and David Hart, eds., *Islam in Tribal Societies.* London: Routledge and Kegan Paul, 1984.

Basilov, Vladimir Nikolayevich. "Popular Islam in Central Asia and Kazakhstan," *Journal of the Institute of Muslim Minority*

*Affairs,* 8, No. 1, 1987, 7–17.

Batalden, Stephen K., and Sandra L. Batalden. *The Newly Independent States of Eurasia: Handbook of Former Soviet Republics.* Phoenix: Oryx, 1993.

Becker, Seymour. *Russia's Protectorates in Central Asia: Bukhara and Khiva, 1865–1924.* Cambridge: Harvard University Press, 1968.

Bennigsen, Alexandre. *Mystics and Commissars: Sufism in the Soviet Union.* London: Hurst, 1985.

Bennigsen, Alexandre, and S. Enders Wimbush. *Muslims of the Soviet Empire.* Bloomington: Indiana University Press, 1986.

Berdi Murat, Aman. "Turkmenistan and the Turkmen." Pages 262–82 in Zev Katz, ed., *Handbook of Major Soviet Nationalities.* New York: Free Press, 1975.

Bregel, Yuriy. "The Peoples of Southern Turkmenistan and Khorasan in the 17th and 18th Centuries," *Central Asian Review,* 8, No. 3, 1960, 264–72.

Bregel, Yuriy. "Nomadic and Sedentary Elements among the Turkmens," *Central Asiatic Journal,* 25, Nos. 1–2, 1981, 5–37.

Canfield, Robert, ed. *Turco-Persia in Historical Perspective.* New York: Cambridge University Press, 1991.

Chalidze, F. "Aral Sea Crisis: A Legacy of Soviet Rule," *Central Asia Monitor,* 1992, No. 1, 30–34.

Clark, Susan L. "The Central Asian States: Defining Security Priorities and Developing Military Forces." Pages 177–206 in Michael Mandelbaum, ed., *Central Asia and the World: Kazakhstan, Uzbekistan, Tajikistan, Kyrgyzstan, and Turkmenistan.* New York: Council on Foreign Relations Press, 1994.

Commonwealth of Independent States. Statistical Committee. *Strany-chleny Sodruzhestva nezavisimykh gosudarstv: Statisticheskiy yezhegodnik* (The Member Nations of the Commonwealth of Independent States: A Statistical Yearbook). Moscow: Finansovyy inzhiniring, 1992.

Davis, Christopher M. "Health Care Crisis: The Former Soviet Union," *RFE/RL Research Report* [Munich], 2, No. 40, October 8, 1993, 35–43.

Demidov, Sergey Mikhaylovich. *Istoriya religioznykh verovaniy narodov Turkmenistana* (A History of the Religious Faiths of Turkmenistan). Ashgabat: Ylym, 1990.

Durdyyev, Marat, and Shukhrat Kadyrov. *Turkmeny mira* (Turkmen of the World). Ashgabat: Kharp, 1991.

Dzhikiyev, Ata. *Ocherki proiskhozhdeniya i formirovaniya turkmenskogo naroda v epokhu srednovekov'ya* (Essays on the Origin and Formation of the Turkmen People in the Middle Ages). Ashgabat: Ylym, 1991.

Economist Intelligence Unit. *Country Report: Georgia, Armenia, Azerbaijan, Central Asian Republics.* London: 1994.

Ellis, C.H. *The Transcaspian Episode, 1918–1919.* London: Hutchinson, 1963.

*Encyclopedia Iranica,* 5. Costa Mesa, California: Mazda, 1990.

*The Europa World Year Book 1993,* 2. London: Europa, 1993.

*The Europa World Year Book 1994,* 2. London: Europa, 1994.

*The Europa World Year Book 1995,* 2. London: Europa, 1995.

*The Europa World Year Book 1996,* 2. London: Europa, 1996.

Farmayan, Hafez. "Turkoman Identity and Presence in Iran," *Iran,* 4, Summer 1981, 45–63.

Feldman, Walter. "Interpreting the Poetry of Makhtumquli." Pages 167-89 in Jo-Ann Gross, ed., *Muslims in Central Asia: Expressions of Identity and Change.* Durham: Duke University Press, 1992.

Feshbach, Murray, and Alfred Friendly, Jr. *Ecocide in the USSR: Health and Nature under Siege.* New York: Basic Books, 1992.

Friedman, L. "Ethnic and National Composition of Population in Newly Independent Countries of the Middle East and Caucasus," *Central Asia Today,* 1993, No. 1, 56–60.

Geldiyev, B., S.P. Tokarev, and T. Sakhatliyev. *Razvitiye promyshlennosti Turkmenistana za 50 let* (The Development of Industry in Turkmenistan over 50 Years). Ashgabat: Turkmenistan, 1974.

Gleason, Gregory. "Central Asia: Land Reform and the Ethnic Factor," *RFE/RL Research Report* [Munich], 2, No. 3, 1993, 28–33.

Gleason, Gregory. *An Introduction to the History of the Turkic Peoples.* Wicsbadcn: Otto Harrasowitz, 1992.

Goetz, Roland, and Uwe Halbach. *Informationen über eine unbekannte Republik, I–II.* Berichte des Bundesinstituts für ostwissenschaftliche und internationale Studien. Cologne: 1995.

Howard, G. "The Caspian Oil and Gas Oasis: Turkmenistan," *Russian Oil and Gas Guide,* 3, No. 1, 1994, 54–58.

International Monetary Fund. *Economic Review: Turkmenistan.* Washington: 1992.

International Monetary Fund. *Turkmenistan.* Washington: 1994.

Irons, William. "The Turkmen of Iran: A Brief Research Report," *Iranian Studies,* 2, Winter 1969, 27–38.

Irons, William. *The Yomut Turkmen: A Study of Social Organization among a Central Asian Turkic-Speaking Population.* Ann Arbor: University of Michigan Press, 1975.

*Istoriya Turkmenskoy SSR* (History of the Turkmen SSR). Ashgabat: Akademiya nauk Turkmenskoy SSR, 1957.

*Jane's Sentinel Regional Security Assessment: Commonwealth of Independent States.* Ed., Paul Beaver. Coulsdon, United Kingdom: Jane's Information Group, 1994.

Kaiser, Robert J. *The Geography of Nationalism in Russia and the USSR.* Princeton: Princeton University Press, 1994.

Katz, Zev, ed. *Handbook of Major Soviet Nationalities.* New York: Free Press, 1975.

Keller, S. "Islam in Soviet Central Asia, 1917–1930: Soviet Policy and the Struggle for Control," *Central Asian Survey* [Abingdon, United Kingdom], 11, No. 1, 1992, 25–50.

Khrushchev, Anatoliy Timofeyevich, and O.D. Chuvilkin. "Resursy gaza gosudarstv Tsentral'noy Azii: Ekonomiko-geograficheskiye aspekty" (Gas Resources of the States of Central Asia: Economic-Geographic Aspects), *Vestnik Moskovskogo universiteta: Geografiya* [Moscow], 1994, No. 4, 51-57.

Kirpichenko, V. "Khozyaystvennyye svyazi stran-chlenov SNG" (Economic Relations of CIS Member States). *Ekonomist* [Moscow], 1993, No. 4, 53–62.

Krader, Lawrence. *Peoples of Central Asia.* Uralic and Altaic Series, No. 26. Bloomington: Indiana University, 1963.

Maksudov, Sergey. "On Infant Mortality in Turkmenistan," *Central Asia Monitor,* 1992, No. 1, 26–30.

Mandelbaum, Michael, ed. *Central Asia and the World: Kazakhstan, Uzbekistan, Tajikistan, Kyrgyzstan, and Turkmenistan.* New York: Council on Foreign Relations Press, 1994.

Mesbahi, Mohiaddin, ed. *Central Asia and the Caucasus after the Soviet Union: Domestic and International Dynamics.* Gainesville: University Press of Florida, 1994.

Micklin, Phillip P. *The Water Management Crisis in Soviet Central Asia.* The Carl Beck Papers in Russian and East European

Studies, No. 905. Pittsburgh: University of Pittsburgh Press, 1992.

*The Military Balance 1993–1994.* London: International Institute for Strategic Studies, 1993.

*The Military Balance 1994–1995.* London: International Institute for Strategic Studies, 1994.

*The Military Balance 1995–1996.* London: International Institute for Strategic Studies, 1995.

*Narody mira: Etnograficheskiye ocherki* (Peoples of the World: Ethnographic Sketches). Moscow: Nauka, 1963.

Nichol, James, and Leah Titerence. "Turkmenistan: Basic Facts," *CRS Report for Congress.* Washington: Library of Congress, Congressional Research Services, March 16, 1993.

*1995 Britannica Book of the Year.* Chicago: 1995.

Nissman, David B. "Iran and Soviet Islam: The Azerbaijan and Turkmen SSRs," *Central Asia Survey* [Abingdon, United Kingdom], 2, No. 4, 1983, 45–60.

PlanEcon. *Review and Outlook for the Former Soviet Republics.* Washington: 1995.

Plyshevskiy, B. "Ekonomicheskoye polozheniye gosudarstv SNG" (The Economic Situation of the CIS States), *Ekonomist* [Moscow], 1993, No. 4, 63–75.

Polyakov, Sergey Petrovich. *Etnicheskaya istoriya severo-zapadnoy Turkmenii v sredniye veka* (The Ethnic History of Northwest Turkmenia in the Middle Ages). Ashgabat: 1973.

Rashid, Ahmed. *The Resurgence of Central Asia: Islam or Nationalism?* Atlantic Highlands, New Jersey: Zed Books, 1994.

Saray, Mehmet. *The Turkmens in the Age of Imperialism: A Study of the Turkmen People and Their Incorporation into the Russian Empire.* Ankara: Turkish Historical Society, 1989.

Simon, Gerhard. *Nationalism and Policy Toward the Nationalities in the Soviet Union.* Trans., K. Forster and O. Forster. Boulder, Colorado: Westview Press, 1991.

Sizov, Andrey Yevgen'yevich. "Ekonomika Rossii i drugikh stran SNG v nachale 90-kh godov" (The Economy of Russia and the Other Countries of the CIS at the Beginning of the 1990s). *Mirovaya ekonomika i mezhdunarodnyye otnosheniya* [Moscow], 1993, No. 7, 20–29.

*The Statesman's Year-Book 1995–1996.* Ed., Brian Hunter. New York: St. Martin's Press, 1995.

Subtelny, E. "The Cult of Holy Places: Religious Practices among Soviet Muslims," *Middle East Journal,* 43, No. 4, 1989, 593–604.

*Turkmenenforschung* (Research on the Turkmen), 1–15. Hamburg and Berlin: Reinhold Schletzer Verlag, 1979–93.

Tyson, David, and Larry Clark. *Turkmen: Language Competencies for Peace Corps Volunteers in Turkmenistan.* Washington: GPO, 1994.

United Nations. Department for Economic and Social Information and Policy Analysis. *Demographic Yearbook 1993.* New York: 1995.

United States. Agency for International Development. Center for Health Information. *USAID Health Profile: Turkmenistan.* Arlington, Virginia: USAID, 1992.

United States. Bureau of International Narcotics Matters. *International Narcotics Strategy Report March 1996.* Washington: GPO, 1996.

United States. Central Intelligence Agency. *Handbook of International Economic Statistics 1992.* Washington: GPO, 1992.

United States. Central Intelligence Agency. *Handbook of International Economic Statistics 1995.* Washington: GPO, 1995.

United States. Central Intelligence Agency. *Piecing Together Central Asia: A Look at Key Leaders.* Washington: GPO, 1993.

United States. Central Intelligence Agency. *Turkmenistan: An Economic Profile.* Springfield, Virginia: National Technical Information Service, 1993.

United States. Central Intelligence Agency. *The World Factbook 1994.* Washington: GPO, 1994.

United States. Central Intelligence Agency. *The World Factbook 1995.* Washington: GPO, 1995.

United States. Congress. Commission on Security and Cooperation in Europe. *Human Rights and Democratization in the Newly Independent States of the Former Soviet Union.* Washington: GPO, 1993.

United States. Department of Agriculture. Economic Research Service. *Former USSR: Agriculture and Trade Report 1991.* Washington: GPO, 1992.

United States. Department of Agriculture. Economic Research Service. *Former USSR: Agriculture and Trade Report 1992.* Washington: GPO, 1993.

United States. Department of Commerce. Business Information Service for the Newly Independent States. *Commercial Overview of Turkmenistan.* Washington: 1993.

United States. Department of State. *Country Reports on Human Rights Practices for 1993.* (Report submitted to United States Congress, 103d, 2d Session, House of Representatives, Committee on Foreign Affairs, and Senate, Committee on Foreign Relations.) Washington: GPO, 1994.

WEFA Group. *Eurasia Economic Outlook, February 1996.* Eddystone, Pennsylvania: 1996.

Wheeler, Geoffrey. *The Modern History of Soviet Central Asia.* New York: Praeger, 1964.

Wolfson, Zeev. "Central Asian Environment: A Dead End," *Environmental Policy Review,* 4, No. 1, January 1990, 29–46.

World Bank. *Statistical Handbook 1995: States of the Former USSR.* Washington: 1995.

World Bank. *Turkmenistan.* World Bank Country Study. Washington: 1994.

*World Radio TV Handbook 1996.* Ed., Andrew G. Sennitt. Amsterdam: Billboard, 1996.

Yekayev, Orazpolat. *Turkmenistan i turkmeny v kontse XV-pervoy polovine XVI v* (Turkmenistan and the Turkmen at the End of the Fifteenth-First Half of the Sixteenth Centuries). Ashgabat: Ylym, 1981.

(Various issues of the following periodicals also were used in the preparation of this chapter: Foreign Broadcast Information Service, *Daily Report: Central Eurasia;* Jamestown Foundation, *Monitor; RFE/RL Research Report* [Munich]; *Transition;* and *Washington Post.*)

# Chapter 5

Abduvakhitov, Abdujabar. "Independent Uzbekistan: A Muslim Community in Development." Pages 293–306 in Michael Bourdeaux, ed., *The Politics of Religion in Russia and the New States of Eurasia.* Armonk, New York: M.E. Sharpe, 1995.

Akbarzadeh, Shahram. "Nation Building in Uzbekistan," *Central Asian Survey* [Abingdon, United Kingdom], 15, March 1996, 23–32.

Alikhanov, B. B., and S. S. Tursunov, *Ekonomicheskiye problemy okhrany okruzhayushchey sredy v usloviyakh Uzbekistana* (Economic Problems of Environmental Protection in the Conditions of Uzbekistan). Tashkent: State Committee on Hydrology, 1990.

Allworth, Edward, ed. *Central Asia: 120 Years of Russian Rule.* Durham: Duke University Press, 1989.

Azv'yalova, L.V., O.A. Agafonova, and L.A. Semakina. *Zagryazneniye atmosfery Sredney Azii tyazhelymi metallami* (Atmospheric Pollution by Heavy Metals in Central Asia). Tashkent: State Committee on Hydrology, 1991.

Bacon, Elizabeth E. *Central Asians under Russian Rule.* Ithaca: Cornell University Press, 1980.

Banuazizi, Ali, and Myron Weiner, eds. *The New Geopolitics of Central Asia and Its Borderlands.* Bloomington: Indiana University Press, 1994.

Bartol'd, Vasilii Vladimirovich. *Turkestan Down to the Mongol Invasion.* London: Luzac, 1968.

Bohr, Annette. "Health Catastrophe in Karakalpakstan," *Report on the USSR* [Munich], 1, July 21, 1989, 37–38.

Bourdeaux, Michael, ed. *The Politics of Religion in Russia and the New States of Eurasia.* Armonk, New York: M.E. Sharpe, 1995.

Brown, Bess. "National Security and Military Issues in Central Asia." Pages 234–52 in Bruce Parrott, ed., *State Building and Military Power in Russia and the New States of Eurasia.* Armonk, New York: M.E. Sharpe, 1995.

Brown, Bess. "Three Central Asian States Form Economic Union," *RFE/RL Research Report* [Munich], 3, No. 13, April 1, 1994, 33–35.

Carlisle, Donald S. "Power and Politics in Soviet Uzbekistan: From Stalin to Gorbachev." Pages 93–130 in William Fierman, *Soviet Central Asia: The Failed Transformation.* Boulder, Colorado: Westview Press, 1991.

Colton, Timothy J., and Robert C. Tucker, eds. *Patterns in Post-Soviet Leadership.* Boulder, Colorado: Westview Press, 1995.

Critchlow, James. *Nationalism in Uzbekistan.* Boulder, Colorado: Westview Press, 1991.

Dannreuther, Roland. *Creating New States in Central Asia.* Adelphi Paper No. 288. London: Brassey's for International Institute for Strategic Studies, 1994.

Davis, Christopher M. "Health Care Crisis: The Former Soviet Union," *RFE/RL Research Report* [Munich], 2, No. 40, October 8, 1993, 35–43.

Drobizheva, Leokadia, et al., eds. *Ethics Conflict in the Post-Soviet World: Case Studies and Analysis.* Armonk, New York: M. E. Sharpe, 1996.

Economist Intelligence Unit. *Country Report: Kazakhstan, Kyrgyz Republic, Tajikistan, Turkmenistan, Uzbekistan* [London], No. 1, 1996.

*The Europa World Year Book 1993*, 2. London: Europa, 1993.

*The Europa World Year Book 1994*, 2. London: Europa, 1994.

*The Europa World Year Book 1995*, 2. London: Europa, 1995.

*The Europa World Year Book 1996*, 2. London: Europa, 1996.

Fane, Daria. "Ethnicity and Regionalism in Uzbekistan: Maintaining Stability Through Authoritarian Control." Pages 271-302 in Leokadia Drobizheva, et al., eds. *Ethnic Conflict in the Post- Soviet World: Case Studies and Analysis.* Armonk, New York: M.E. Sharpe, 1996.

Ferdinand, Peter, ed. *The New States of Central Asia and Their Neighbors.* New York: Council on Foreign Relations Press, 1994.

Feshbach, Murray, and Alfred Friendly, Jr. *Ecocide in the USSR: Health and Nature under Siege.* New York: Basic Books, 1992.

Fierman, William. "Independence and the Declining Priority of Language Law Implementation in Uzbekistan." Pages 205–30 in Yaacov Ro'i, ed., *Muslim Eurasia: Conflicting Legacies.* London: Frank Cass, 1995.

Fierman, William, ed. *Soviet Central Asia: The Failed Transformation.* Boulder, Colorado: Westview Press, 1991.

Hale, Henry. "Islam, State-building, and Uzbekistan Foreign Policy," Pages 136–72 in Ali Banuazizi and Myron Weiner, eds., *The New Geopolitics of Central Asia and Its Borderlands.* Bloomington: Indiana University Press, 1994.

Henley, John S., and George B. Assaf. "Re-Integrating the Central Asian Republics into the World Economy," *Intereconomics*, 30, September–October 1995, 235–45.

Horton, Scott, and Tatiana Geller. "Investing in Uzbekistan's Natural Resources Sector," *Central Asia Monitor*, 1996, No. 1, 25–35.

Horton, Scott, and Tatiana Geller. "Secured Transactions in Uzbekistan," *Central Asia Monitor,* 1996, No. 2, 21–7.

Institute for National Strategic Studies. *Strategic Assessment 1995: U.S. Security Challenges in Transition.* Washington: GPO, 1995.

Karpat, Kemal. "The Foreign Policy of the Central Asian States, Turkey, and Iran," *OSCE Bulletin,* 3, No. 1, Winter 1994–95, 17–30.

Konyukhov, V.G. *Ekologicheskaya obstanovka v Uzbekistanskoy SSR i mery po yeye uluchsheniyu* (The Ecological Situation in the Uzbek SSR and Measures to Improve It). Tashkent: State Committee on Environmental Protection, 1990.

Lawyers' Committee for Human Rights. Freedom of Association Project. *Karimov's Way: Freedom of Association and Assembly in Uzbekistan.* Briefing Paper No. 1. New York: 1994.

Lubin, Nancy. *Central Asians Take Stock.* Washington: United States Institute of Peace Press, 1995.

Lubin, Nancy. "Islam and Ethnic Identity in Central Asia: A View from Below." Pages 53–70 in Yaacov Ro'i, ed., *Muslim Eurasia: Conflicting Legacies.* London: Frank Cass, 1995.

Lubin, Nancy. *Labour and Nationality in Soviet Central Asia: An Uneasy Compromise.* Princeton: Princeton University Press, 1985.

Lubin, Nancy. "Leadership in Uzbekistan and Kazakhstan: The Views of the Led." Pages 217–34 in Timothy J. Colton and Robert C. Tucker, eds., *Patterns in Post-Soviet Leadership.* Boulder, Colorado: Westview Press, 1995.

Lubin, Nancy. "Uzbekistan." Pages 289–306 in Philip R. Pryde, ed., *Environmental Resources and Constraints in the Former Soviet Republics.* Boulder, Colorado: Westview Press, 1995.

Lubin, Nancy. "Uzbekistan: The Challenges Ahead," *Middle East Journal,* 43, No. 4, Autumn 1989, 619–34.

Micklin, Philip. "The Aral Sea Crisis: Introduction to the Special Issue," *Post-Soviet Geography,* 33, No. 5, May 1992, 269–82.

Nichol, James. "Central Asia's New States: Political Developments and Implications for U.S. Interests," *CRS Issue Brief,* July 31, 1996.

Nichol, James. "Uzbekistan: Basic Facts," *CRS Report for Congress,* May 28, 1996.

*1995 Britannica Book of the Year.* Chicago: 1995.

Olcott, Martha Brill. *Central Asia's New States: Independence, Foreign Policy, and Regional Security.* Washington: United States Institute of Peace Press, 1996.

Olcott, Martha Brill. "The Myth of 'Tsentral'naia Aziia'," *Orbis,* 38, No. 3, Summer 1995, 549–66.

Polat, Abdumannob. "Uzbekistan: Does the Government Want a Dialogue with the Opposition," *Caspian Crossroads,* Winter 1995, 26–28.

Posner, Michael. *Human Rights and Legal Issues in Uzbekistan.* New York: Lawyers' Committee for Human Rights, 1993.

Pryde, Philip R., ed. *Environmental Resources and Constraints in the Former Soviet Republics.* Boulder, Colorado: Westview Press, 1995.

Ro'i, Yaacov, ed. *Muslim Eurasia: Conflicting Legacies.* London: Frank Cass, 1995.

Rubinstein, Alvin Z. "The Geopolitical Pull on Russia," *Orbis,* 38, No. 3, Summer 1995, 567–84.

Rumer, Boris Z. *Soviet Central Asia: A "Tragic Experiment."* Boston: Unwin Hyman, 1989.

Sagers, Matthew J. "News Notes," *Post-Soviet Geography,* 33, No. 3, 1992, 190.

Staar, S. Frederick. "Making Eurasia Stable," *Foreign Affairs,* 75, January–February 1996, 80–92.

*The Statesman's Year-Book 1993–1994.* Ed., Brian Hunter. New York: St. Martin's Press, 1993.

*The Statesman's Year-Book 1994–1995.* Ed., Brian Hunter. New York: St. Martin's Press, 1994.

*The Statesman's Year-Book 1995–1996.* Ed., Brian Hunter. New York: St. Martin's Press, 1995.

United Nations. Department for Economic and Social Information and Policy Analysis. *Demographic Yearbook 1993.* New York, 1995.

United States. Central Intelligence Agency. *Handbook of International Economic Statistics 1995.* Washington: GPO, 1995.

United States. Central Intelligence Agency. *The World Factbook 1994.* Washington: GPO, 1994.

United States. Central Intelligence Agency. *Uzbekistan: An Economic Profile.* Springfield, Virginia: National Technical Information Service, 1993.

United States. Department of State. Bureau of International Narcotics Matters. *International Narcotics Strategy Report March 1996.* Washington: GPO, 1996.

"Uzbekistan," *Central Asia Monitor,* 1996, No. 3, entire issue.

Uzbekistan. State Committee on Projections and Statistics. *Chislennost', sostav i dvizheniye naseleniya Respubliki Uzbekistan* (The Size, Composition, and Movement of the Population of the Republic of Uzbekistan). Tashkent: 1992.

Uzbekistan. State Committee on Projections and Statistics. *Okhrana zdorov'ya v respublike Uzbekistana* (Health Protection in the Republic of Uzbekistan). Tashkent: 1991.

Vaisman, Demian. "Regionalism and Clan Loyalty in the Political Life of Uzbekistan." Pages 105–22 in Yaacov Ro'i, ed., *Muslim Eurasia: Conflicting Legacies.* London: Frank Cass, 1995.

World Bank. *Statistical Handbook 1995: States of the Former USSR.* Washington: 1995.

World Bank. *Uzbekistan: An Agenda for Economic Reform.* Washington: 1993.

*World Radio TV Handbook 1996.* Ed., Andrew G. Sennitt. Amsterdam: Billboard, 1996.

(Various issues of the following periodicals also were used in the preparation of this chapter: *Central Asian Monitor; Christian Science Monitor;* Foreign Broadcast Information Service, *Daily Report: Central Eurasia;* Jamestown Foundation, *Monitor* and *Prism; New York Times; Transition;* and *Washington Post.*)

# Glossary

Bolshevik Revolution—Coup organized by Vladimir I. Lenin and carried out by the Bolshevik radical group of the Russian Social Democratic Labor Party to overthrow the Provisional Government of Russia in November 1917. Also known as the October Revolution.

Commonwealth of Independent States (CIS)—Official designation of the former republics of the Soviet Union that remained loosely federated in economic and security matters after the Soviet Union disbanded as a unified state in 1991. Members in 1996 were Armenia, Azerbaijan, Belarus, Georgia, Kazakstan, Kyrgyzstan, Moldova, Russia, Tajikistan, Turkmenistan, Ukraine, and Uzbekistan.

Conventional Forces in Europe (CFE) Treaty—An agreement signed in 1990 by members of the Warsaw Pact and the North Atlantic Treaty Organization (NATO—*q.v.*) to establish parity in conventional weapons between the two organizations from the Atlantic to the Urals. Included a strict system of inspections and information exchange. In 1995 Russia requested exemptions for forces stationed in the Caucasus region, and substantial changes were negotiated by the thirty signatory nations in 1997.

Economic Cooperation Organization (ECO)—Established in 1985, an economic union of Islamic countries to promote regional cooperation in trade, transportation, communications, culture, and overall economic development. Members in 1996 were Afghanistan, Azerbaijan, Iran, Kazakstan, Kyrgyzstan, Pakistan, Tajikistan, Turkey, the "Turkish Republic of Northern Cyprus," Turkmenistan, and Uzbekistan.

*glasnost*—Russian term, literally meaning "public voicing." Applied in the Soviet Union beginning in 1987 to official permission for public discussion of issues and public access to information, initially intended as a means for the regime of Mikhail S. Gorbachev to publicize the need for political and economic reform.

gross domestic product (GDP)—The total value of goods and services produced exclusively within a nation's domestic economy, in contrast to the gross national product (GNP—*q.v.*). Normally computed over one-year periods.

gross national product (GNP)—The total value of goods and services produced within a country's borders and the income received from abroad by residents, minus payments remitted abroad by nonresidents. Normally computed over one-year periods.

hard currency—National currencies that are freely convertible and traded on international currency markets.

International Monetary Fund (IMF)—Established with the World Bank (*q.v.*) in 1945, a specialized agency affiliated with the United Nations and responsible for stabilizing international exchange rates and payments. Its main function is to provide loans to its members (including industrialized and developing countries) when they experience balance of payments difficulties. These loans frequently have conditions that require substantial internal economic adjustments by the recipients, most of which are developing countries.

Iranian—Linguistically, a subgroup of the Indo-Iranian branch of Indo-European languages, which in modern times includes Persian (*q.v.*)—the most widely used—Pushtu, Kurdish (*q.v.*) dialects, and Ossetic. In the Middle Iranian stage of the group's development (third century B.C. to tenth century A.D.), the chief languages were Parthian, Pahlavi (middle Persian), and Soghdian.

Kurdish—Term referring to a mainly Muslim people speaking an Indo-European language similar to Persian. Kurds constitute significant minorities in Iran, Iraq, and Turkey, with smaller groups in Armenia and Syria. Despite international proposals in response to minority persecution, never united in a single state.

manat—Beginning in 1993, national currency of Turkmenistan. Inflation rapid in 1994 and 1995. In January 1996, official rate 200 per US$1.

Manichaeism—A dualistic religious movement founded in Persia, third century A.D., incorporating elements of Christianity and Iranian and Indian religions.

net material product (NMP)—In countries having centrally planned economics, the official measure of the value of goods and services produced within the country. Roughly equivalent to the gross national product (*q.v.*), NMP is based on constant prices and does not account for depreciation.

New Economic Policy (Novaya ekonomicheskaya politika—

NEP)—Instituted in 1921 by Vladimir I. Lenin, program allowing peasants in the Soviet Union to sell produce on an open market and small enterprises to be privately owned and operated. Officially ended in 1929 with enforcement of national central planning of all economic activities.

North Atlantic Treaty Organization (NATO)—During the postwar period until the dissolution of the Soviet Union in 1991, the primary collective defense agreement of the Western powers against the military presence of the Warsaw Pact nations in Europe. Founded in 1949. Its military and administrative structure remained intact after 1991, but early in 1994 the Partnership for Peace offered partial membership to all former Warsaw Pact nations and former republics of the Soviet Union.

Organization for Security and Cooperation in Europe (OSCE)—Beginning in 1995, the name of the former Conference on Security and Cooperation in Europe (CSCE). Established in 1972 as an international forum for negotiation, the organization consisted of fifty-three member nations in 1996, including all European countries. The Charter of Paris (1990) changed the CSCE from an ad hoc forum to an organization with permanent institutions. In 1992 the CSCE took on new roles in conflict mediation, including crises in the former Yugoslavia, the Caucasus region, and Nagorno-Karabakh. Beginning in 1994, Russia advocated CSCE/OSCE as the chief European peacekeeping agency in preference to possible NATO expansion.

*perestroika*—Russian term meaning "restructuring." Applied in the late 1980s to an official Soviet program of revitalization of the Communist Party of the Soviet Union (CPSU), the economy, and the society by adjusting economic, social, and political mechanisms in the central planning system. Identified with the tenure of Mikhail S. Gorbachev as leader of the Soviet Union.

Persian—As a language, a member of the Iranian subgroup in the Indo-European language family. The official language of modern Iran and spoken widely in Afghanistan. Middle Persian (Pahlavi) was used between the third century B.C. and the ninth century A.D. and was the official language of the Sassanid Empire that ruled parts of Central Asia from the third century to the sixth century A.D. Modern Persian is called Farsi by native speakers.

ruble—Currency of the Soviet Union; then, beginning in 1992, of Russia. In February 1997, the exchange rate was 5,670 rubles to US$1.

ruble zone—Currency exchange arrangement by which former republics of the Soviet Union continued using the ruble as their national currency, forcing dependence on Russian currency valuations and economic developments elsewhere in the Commonwealth of Independent States (*q.v.*). In 1993 all Central Asian republics except Tajikistan established national currencies independent of the ruble.

Shia—The smaller of the two great divisions of Islam, supporting the claims of Ali to leadership of the Muslim community, in opposition to the Sunni (*q.v.*) view of succession to Muslim leadership—the issue causing the central schism within Islam.

som—Beginning in 1993, currency of Kyrgyzstan and Uzbekistan. In 1996 average exchange rate of Uzbekistani som was thirty-five to US$1; of Kyrgyzstani som, eleven to US$1.

Sunni—The larger of the two fundamental divisions of Islam, opposed to the Shia (*q.v.*) on the issue of succession to Muslim leadership.

Tajikistani ruble—Beginning in 1995, currency of Tajikistan. In January 1996, exchange rate 284 rubles per US$1.

tenge—Beginning in 1993, currency of Kazakstan. In January 1996, exchange rate sixty-four tenge to US$1.

value-added tax (VAT)—A tax applied to the additional value created at a given stage of production and calculated as a percentage of the difference between the product value at that stage and the cost of all materials and services purchased or introduced as inputs.

World Bank—Informal name for a group of four affiliated international institutions: the International Bank for Reconstruction and Development (IBRD); the International Development Association (IDA); the International Finance Corporation (IFC); and the Multilateral Investment Guaranty Agency (MIGA). The four institutions are owned by the governments of the countries that subscribe their capital for credit and investment in developing countries; each institution has a specialized agenda for aiding economic growth in target countries. To participate in the World Bank group, member states first must belong to the International Monetary Fund (IMF—*q.v.*).

World Trade Organization (WTO)—Established 1995 as successor to the General Agreement on Tariffs and Trade (GATT), aimed at liberalizing and securing international trade. Formed in the Uruguay Round of trade negotiations, the WTO had 115 member nations in 1996, and fifteen others applied WTO rules to their trade policies. Administered by a general council, trade dispute negotiation panel, and secretariat.

Zoroastrianism—Religion founded in the sixth century B.C. by the Iranian prophet Zoroaster. With monotheistic and dualistic aspects, it influenced subsequently founded religions, including Christianity and Islam. Now practiced most widely by Persian immigrants in India.

# Index

communist parties, local, xxxv
Communist Party of Bukhoro, 214
Communist Party of Kazakstan, 78; first
  secretaries of, 16; outlawed, 20, 78;
  purges of, 17; reinstated, 78
Communist Party of Kyrgyzia (CPK),
  113, 118
Communist Party of Kyrgyzstan, 174
Communist Party of Tajikistan, 273–74;
  membership in, 273, 274; purges in,
  216, 273; Russians in, 216, 235, 273;
  suspended, 274; Tajiks in, 216
Communist Party of the Soviet Union
  (CPSU), 115, 214, 446; nationalities
  policy of, 306
Communist Party of Turkmenistan:
  former members in government, 352
Communist Party of Uzbekistan, 446,
  449; membership in, 397, 398
Communist Youth League (Komsomol),
  273–74
Concord Party (Kyrgyzstan), 175
Conference (Gengesh) coalition (Turkmenistan), 358
Conference on Security and Cooperation in Europe (CSCE): Kazakstan in,
  83; in Tajikistan peace talks, 270
conscription, military, 15, 283
Constitutional Council (Kazakstan), 95
Constitutional Court (Kazakstan), 74,
  94; dissolved, xliv, 94–95
Constitutional Court (Tajikistan), 272
Constitutional Court (Uzbekistan), 449
constitution of Kazakstan, xliv, 71–72;
  adopted, 72; Council of Ministers
  under, 11, 72; distribution of power in,
  xliv, 11; drafted, 72; languages under,
  72; legislature under, 72; media under,
  81; political parties under, 11–12, 31;
  president under, 72; prime minister
  under, 11, 72; religion under, 31;
  rights under, 72, 94; women under, 28
constitution of Kyrgyzstan, 117–18, 169–
  70; adopted, 117; draft of, 117; executive under, 169–70; human rights
  under, 178; judiciary under, 170; language under, 117, 118; parliament
  under, 169; president under, 118;
  property under, 118; religion under,
  117, 118, 137
constitution of Tajikistan, 270–71;
  adopted, 271; executive under, liii,

271; human rights under, liii, 271;
  judiciary under, 271, 288; legislature
  under, liii, 271–72; president under,
  271; property rights under, 271
constitution of Turkmenistan: criminal
  justice under, 371; political parties
  under, 357; rights under, 339, 357;
  separation of powers under, 352
constitution of Uzbekistan, 448–49;
  human rights under, lx; judiciary
  under, 448; legislature under, 448;
  president under, 448; religion under,
  447; separation of powers under, 448
construction: of dams, 124, 226; decline
  in Tajikistan, 258–59; employment in,
  57, 326; of housing, 43, 112; investment in Kyrgyzstan, 159-60; of irrigation, 386; of mosques in Kazakstan, 86;
  as percentage of Turkmenistan's gross
  domestic product, 335; as percentage
  of Tajikistan's net material product,
  253; of pipelines, xliii, xliv; privatization in Uzbekistan, 434; of railroads,
  305; of roads, 112; of schools in
  Uzbekistan, 419
consumer goods: durable, 328; imports
  of, 63, 85, 436; in Kazakstan, 85; in
  Kyrgyzstan, 154; prices of, 432; production of, xlvii, 154; shortages of,
  xxxii, 257, 279, 326, 327; in Tajikistan,
  256, 257; in Turkmenistan, 326, 327;
  in Uzbekistan, 432, 436
consumer price index: in Tajikistan, 258
Contagious Disease Association (Kazakstan), 40
Control and Revision Commission
  (Turkmenistan), 354
Cooperative Alliance (Turkmenistan),
  330
Coordination Council for Combating
  AIDS (Kazakstan), 40
corruption, xli; in Akayev family, 169; in
  commerce, xlvii; in government, xlvii,
  96, 116, 117, 159, 164, 169, 188, 190,
  288, 438; in Kyrgyzstan, xlvii, 116, 117,
  118, 159, 164, 169, 175, 188, 190; in
  police force, 95, 465; in politics, 175;
  in prisons, 95, 372; in Tajikistan, 288;
  in Turkmenistan, 372; in Uzbekistan,
  398–99, 405
Cossacks, 14, 79
cotton, xxxii; area planted to, 332;

availability of, 324; availability of medications, 324, 325; funding for, 324; problems in, 324; structure of, 324

health care (Uzbekistan), 421–23; aid for, 457; budget for, 422; for children, 423; insurance for, 422; number of patients, 423; privatization of, 422; problems in, 423

health care professionals: emigration of, 143, 247; in Kazakstan, 38, 57; in Kyrgyzstan, 142; number of, 38, 230, 247, 324, 422; salaries of, 38, 63, 142–43; strikes by, 38; in Tajikistan, 230, 246–47, 256; training of, 324; in Turkmenistan, 324, 336

health conditions: in Kazakstan, 40–42; in Kyrgyzstan, 144–45; in Turkmenistan, 324–26

health facilities: geographic distribution of, 142; in Kazakstan, 38; in Kyrgyzstan, 142; number of, 38, 142, 230, 422; privatization of, 422; quality of, 247; in Tajikistan, 230, 246; in Turkmenistan, 324

Helsinki Watch, 288, 358

High Economic Court (Uzbekistan), 449

Hindukush Hydroelectric Station (Turkmenistan), 335

Hisor (Gisor) Mountains, 219

holidays: in Kazakstan, 31; in Kyrgyzstan, 138; in Turkmenistan, 313

Horde of Alash. *See* Alash Orda

hordes *(see also under individual hordes)*, 13–14

House of National Representatives (Kyrgyzstan), 172

housing: construction, 43, 112; investment in, 160; in Kazakstan, 34, 42–43, 58; in Kyrgyzstan, 112, 133, 160; privatization of, 42, 58; in rural areas, 327; shortages, 42–43, 232, 258; space, 327; in Tajikistan, 232, 258; traditional, 34; in Turkmenistan, 327–28; in urban areas, 327; utilities in, 327

Housing-93 project (Tajikistan), 258

Humaneness and Charity group (Uzbekistan), 450

human rights: abuses, 276–77, 288, 348, 359, 445, 460; guarantees of, 72; in Kazakstan, 82–83; in Kyrgyzstan, 178; in Tajikistan, liii, 276–77, 288; in Turkmenistan, 358–59, 445, 447; in Uzbeki-

stan, 445–46, 451–52, 460

Human Rights Watch, 452

Huns, 110

Hydrometeorological Administration (Gidromet) (Kyrgyzstan), 125

hyperinflation, 62, 161, 333

IBRD. *See* International Bank for Reconstruction and Development

Ichkilik clan, 133

IMF. *See* International Monetary Fund

imports: of agricultural products, 259; of chemicals, 343; of coal, 255–56; of consumer goods, 63; cost of, 160–61; of energy, 264; from Finland, 343; of food, 264, 343, 426, 435; from France, 343; of gas, 56, 155, 156, 254, 255–56; from Italy, 343; by Kazakstan, 56, 63, 65; by Kyrgyzstan, 155, 160; of machinery, 343; of medicine, 264; of oil, 56, 155, 254, 255–56; from Russia, 56, 160–61, 343; by Tajikistan, 255–56, 259; of textiles, 343; by Turkmenistan, lv, 342, 343; by Uzbekistan, 429, 435–36

income distribution: in Kyrgyzstan, 153

independence: of Kazakstan, 11, 20; of Kyrgyzstan, 109, 114, 115; of Tajikistan, 218, 267; of Turkmenistan, 306–7; of Uzbekistan, 400, 446

India: trade routes through, 443

Industrial and Construction Bank (Promstroybank) (Kyrgyzstan), 159

industrial development: in Kazakstan, 44; in Kyrgyzstan, 155; under Soviet Union, 44, 229; in Tajikistan, 205, 229, 252–53; in Uzbekistan, 457

industrial infrastructure: in Kazakstan, 12; Soviet legacy, xlii, xlvi

industrial production: declines in, 154–55, 259; increases in, 329; in Kazakstan, 47–48, 58; in Kyrgyzstan, xlvii, 154–55; in Tajikistan, 253, 258, 259; in Turkmenistan, 329, 333

industry *(see also under individual industries)*: conversion of, xlvi; debt in, 48; employment in, 57, 230, 256, 326, 336; energy consumption by, 55, 429; ethnic distribution in, 252; foreign investment in, lix, 64; geographic distribution of, 47; inputs for, xxxii; in

stan, 430, 437

theaters: in Tajikistan, 243

Tian Shan mountain range, 21, 119, 219, 401

Tibet: trade with, 110

Timur (Tamerlane), 209; invasions by, 389; rule by, 389–90

Timurids, 209

Tobol (Tobyl) River, 21

Tobyl River. *See* Tobol River

*Tojikistoni Shuravi* (newspaper), 276

*Tojikistoni Soveti* (newspaper), 276

Tokharian state, 386

Toktogol Reservoir (Kyrgyzstan), 156; created, 124

topography: elevations, 21, 119, 219, 307; of Kazakstan, xxxi, 21; of Kyrgyzstan, xxxi, 119–20; of Tajikistan, xxxi, 219–23; of Turkmenistan, xxxi, 307; of Uzbekistan, 401–2

Torghay coal field (Kazakstan), 44, 55

tourism: in Kyrgyzstan, 192; in Tajikistan, 262; in Uzbekistan, 437

trade (*see also* exports; imports), xxxix; with Argentina, 345; with Armenia, lv; with Asia, 344; attempts to open, 436–37; with Azerbaijan, 343, 345; barter, lv, 65, 156, 163, 164, 181, 262, 263, 264, 345, 363, 369, 436; bilateral agreements for, 436; with China, xlix, 84, 163, 181, 182, 385, 386, 345; with Commonwealth of Independent States, 65, 263; credits, 64; decline in, 164; deficit, 65, 155, 164, 264, 343, 435–36; diversification of, 65, 437; employment in, 57; with former Soviet republics, 342; with Georgia, 343, 345; with Germany, 342; with Iran, 345; with Italy, 345; by Kazakstan, xliii, 48, 64–65, 84–85, 163, 164, 342, 343, 363; by Kyrgyzstan, xxxix, xlvii, xlix, 65, 110, 155, 160, 163–65, 456; with Mexico, 344; as percentage of gross domestic product, 164; as percentage of net material product, 343; reform, 436–37; routes, xl, 385; with Russia, xxxii, xxxix, xliii, liv, 48, 65, 110, 163, 342, 392; with Soviet Union, 436; by Tajikistan, xxxix, l, 255–56, 259, 261, 262, 263, 343; tariff agreements in, 344–45; total, 163–64; with Turkey, liv, lv, 345; by Turkmenistan, xxxix, liv, lv, 255–56,

259, 301, 330, 342–48, 359, 363; with Ukraine, lv, 343; with United States, 262; by Uzbekistan, xxxix, lviii, lix, lx–lxi, 65, 163, 164, 264, 342, 343, 385, 392, 436–37, 442–43

Transcaspian Depression, 307

Trans-Caspian District, 305, 306

Transcaspian Railroad, 441

Transoxania, 13

transportation (Kazakstan), xliv, 66–70; air, 70; airports, xlix, 70; construction, 86; development of, 66; employment in, 57, 148, 256; freight, 66; infrastructure, 69; passenger, 66; public, 66; railroads, 66, 69; roads, 66–69; by water, 70

transportation (Kyrgyzstan), 109, 165–67, 181; air, 167; freight, 166, 167; infrastructure, 165–66; international integration of, 165; passenger, 166, 167; public, 166; railroad, 166–67; roads, 166

transportation (Tajikistan), 264–66; air, 266; barriers to, 264–65; decline in, 259; employment in, 230; infrastructure, 205; international partnerships in, 262; railroads, 265; roads, 265

transportation (Turkmenistan), 348–51; and agriculture, 330; air, 348; employment in, 326, 336; infrastructure, 348, 359; railroads, xl, liv, 348; roads, 348, 362; state control of, liv; waterways, 348

transportation (Uzbekistan), 438–43; air, 442; for exports, 442–43; freight, 438–41, 442, 443; infrastructure, 442; passenger, 438, 441, 442; policy, 442–43; privatization in, 434; railroads, 438–41, 443; roads, 438, 441–42, 443; Soviet legacy in, 438

Transportes Aereos Portugueses, 266

Treaty on Joint Measures (1992), 366

tribes (*see also* clans): geographic distribution of, 304; holy *(övlat)*, 319–20; identification with, 313, 314–15; in Kazakstan, 12–13; in Kyrgyzstan, 110; migrations of, 304; nomadic, 12, 110; in politics, 353–54; religions of, 136–37; under Russian Empire, 12; under Soviet system, 12; in Turkmenistan, liv, 304, 313, 314, 353–54

Turajonzoda, Hajji Akbar, 240–41, 268;

# Contributors

**Muriel Atkin** is professor of history at George Washington University.

**Larry V. Clark** is professor of Central Eurasian studies at Indiana University.

**Glenn E. Curtis** is senior research analyst for Central Eurasia and Central Europe in the Federal Research Division, Library of Congress.

**Nancy Lubin** is president of JNA Associates, Inc., a consulting firm specializing in Central Asian studies.

**Martha Brill Olcott** is professor of political science at Colgate University and senior associate of the Carnegie Endowment for International Peace.

**Michael Thurman** is a Ph.D. candidate in Central Eurasian Studies at Indiana University.

**David Tyson** is a Ph.D. candidate in Central Eurasian Studies at Indiana University.

# Published Country Studies

## (Area Handbook Series)

| | | | | |
|---|---|---|---|---|
| 550–65 | Afghanistan | 550–36 | Dominican Republic and Haiti |
| 550–98 | Albania | | |
| 550–44 | Algeria | 550–52 | Ecuador |
| 550–59 | Angola | 550–43 | Egypt |
| 550–73 | Argentina | 550–150 | El Salvador |
| 550–111 | Armenia, Azerbaijan, and Georgia | 550-113 | Estonia, Latvia, and Lithuania |
| 550–169 | Australia | 550–28 | Ethiopia |
| 550–176 | Austria | 550–167 | Finland |
| 550–175 | Bangladesh | 550–173 | Germany |
| 550–112 | Belarus and Moldova | 550–153 | Ghana |
| 550–170 | Belgium | 550–87 | Greece |
| 550–66 | Bolivia | 550–78 | Guatemala |
| 550–20 | Brazil | 550–174 | Guinea |
| 550–168 | Bulgaria | 550–82 | Guyana and Belize |
| 550–61 | Burma | 550–151 | Honduras |
| 550–50 | Cambodia | 550–165 | Hungary |
| 550–166 | Cameroon | 550–21 | India |
| 550–159 | Chad | 550–154 | Indian Ocean |
| 550–77 | Chile | 550–39 | Indonesia |
| 550–60 | China | 550–68 | Iran |
| 550–26 | Colombia | 550–31 | Iraq |
| 550–33 | Commonwealth Caribbean, Islands of the | 550–25 | Israel |
| | | 550–182 | Italy |
| 550–91 | Congo | 550–30 | Japan |
| 550–90 | Costa Rica | 550–34 | Jordan |
| 550–69 | Côte d'Ivoire (Ivory Coast) | 550–114 | Kazakstan, Kyrgyzstan, Tajikistan, Turkmenistan, and Uzbekistan |
| 550–152 | Cuba | | |
| 550–22 | Cyprus | 550–56 | Kenya |
| 550–158 | Czechoslovakia | 550–81 | Korea, North |

| 550–41 | Korea, South | 550–37 | Rwanda and Burundi |
| 550–58 | Laos | 550–51 | Saudi Arabia |
| 550–24 | Lebanon | 550–70 | Senegal |
| 550–38 | Liberia | 550–180 | Sierra Leone |
| 550–85 | Libya | 550–184 | Singapore |
| | | | |
| 550–172 | Malawi | 550–86 | Somalia |
| 550–45 | Malaysia | 550–93 | South Africa |
| 550–161 | Mauritania | 550–95 | Soviet Union |
| 550–79 | Mexico | 550–179 | Spain |
| 550–76 | Mongolia | 550–96 | Sri Lanka |
| | | | |
| 550–49 | Morocco | 550–27 | Sudan |
| 550–64 | Mozambique | 550–47 | Syria |
| 550–35 | Nepal and Bhutan | 550–62 | Tanzania |
| 550–88 | Nicaragua | 550–53 | Thailand |
| 550–157 | Nigeria | 550–89 | Tunisia |
| | | | |
| 550–94 | Oceania | 550–80 | Turkey |
| 550–48 | Pakistan | 550–74 | Uganda |
| 550–46 | Panama | 550–97 | Uruguay |
| 550–156 | Paraguay | 550–71 | Venezuela |
| 550–185 | Persian Gulf States | 550–32 | Vietnam |
| | | | |
| 550–42 | Peru | 550–183 | Yemens, The |
| 550–72 | Philippines | 550–99 | Yugoslavia |
| 550–162 | Poland | 550–67 | Zaire |
| 550–181 | Portugal | 550–75 | Zambia |
| 550–160 | Romania | 550–171 | Zimbabwe |